This book is dedicated to Michael Firestone, my husband and protector of my Spirit
— Carol Albert

For my parents, Alberta and Adam Dickie, who always encouraged me to do my best
and provided me the opportunity to do so
— John Dickie

For Rachel and Zev, my children and inspirations
— David Lyman

Contents

Chapter 5   The Landlord's Obligation to Repair

Chapter 6   Other Rights and Obligations

Chapter 7   Procedures Under the RTA

Chapter 8   Tenant Applications

Chapter 9   Terminating Tenancies: Fault Grounds

Chapter 10   Terminating the Tenancy Agreement: No-Fault Grounds

Chapter 11   Processing Applications Under the RTA

Chapter 12   Negotiations, Mediation, and Hearings

Chapter 13   The Order and Beyond

Chapter 14 Parting with Possession by the Tenant

Chapter 15 Additional Grounds for Termination

Chapter 16 Increasing the Rent

Chapter 17 Increasing the Rent by Application

Chapter 18   Increasing the Rent by Agreement

Chapter 19   Rent Reductions and Rebates

Chapter 20   Offences Under the RTA

Chapter 21   Conclusion

Appendixes

Glossary

References

Index

Preface to the Third Edition

This work is referred to as the third edition of *Working with the Residential Tenancies Act*, but you will search in vain for a first edition with the same title. The first edition, by Carol Albert and John Dickie, was published as *Working with the Tenant Protection Act*, because that was the title of the Ontario statute on residential tenancies when the first edition was published in 2000. The acknowledgments and preface to the first edition, by Carol Albert and John Dickie, appear on page xiii, and they hold as true today as they did in 2000.

Carol Albert practised residential tenancy law for 16 years, but she has not practised in this area of law since her appointment as a Master of the Ontario Superior Court in 1998. As noted in the acknowledgments to the first edition, Carol asked John to assist with the work due to that appointment. We wish to thank Carol for starting John down the path of co-authoring this work and for her work on the first edition, which is the foundation on which the second and third editions have been built. When the occasion arose to revise the first edition to reflect the changes brought about by the new *Residential Tenancies Act*, Carol graciously allowed John to build on the work with his law partner David Lyman.

Together John and David practise residential tenancies law in Ottawa. We wish to thank our staff, former and present, for all their assistance provided to us while *Working with the Residential Tenancies Act* was being prepared.

Any errors in this work, including the appendixes, are the responsibility of the two current authors alone.

John Dickie
David Lyman

Preface to the First Edition

Life is an adventure in continuous learning. I would like to acknowledge and say "thank you" to the many teachers who have participated in my adventure. First, throughout 16 years in the private practice of law my clients have been my most provocative teachers. In particular, Ricky and Annette must be singled out for their enthusiasm and dedication to the rental housing industry. Second, my former partners and associates at Gardiner, Roberts are acknowledged for their support and encouragement of my work in this field. In particular, I acknowledge Robert Doumani for introducing me to this area of practice when I joined the law firm in 1983. Robert Maxwell was always ready to challenge me with new, creative approaches to problem solving in this complex area of law. Third, I acknowledge with gratitude the willingness of two leading experts in the field of rent control to share information—John Andrade and Heather Waese. Last, but certainly not least, I acknowledge my partner in this work, John Dickie, for stepping up to the plate upon my appointment to the bench and assisting me in completing this text. John has brought with him his vast knowledge and experience in this area and the work has reached the publisher's desk as a direct result of John's tireless energy. Thank you, John.

Carol Albert

I wish to thank my colleague David Debenham; my summer student, Andrew Grayson; my legal assistant, Lana Craig; and my family, for all the help they provided to me while this book was being prepared.

I also wish to thank my many clients and associates who allowed me the opportunity to learn this area of law. They include the tenants and tenant associates I worked with from 1981 to 1990. They also include the landlords and landlord groups I have worked with since 1987. I wish especially to thank Arnon Development Corporation and Levinson-Viner Ltd. (now Commvesco/Levinson-Viner Group) who invited me to make the transition from working for tenants to working for landlords. In particular, for all I learned from and with them, my thanks go to Gilad Vered, Joe Viner, Jacie Levinson, Susan Viner-Vered, and Tony Mancini.

Finally, I wish to thank Carol Albert for inviting me to join her in writing this book.

John Dickie

Overview

BACKGROUND: HOW DID WE GET HERE?

Rent control began in Ontario in 1975. Since then, we have had seven different rent control systems.[1] Generally, a change in the provincial governing party has triggered a change in rent control and residential tenancy laws.

Most tenants who continue to live in a particular rental unit are protected by rent control. Most landlords must restrict rent increases to the statutory **guideline** or to an ordered amount no more than once a year. As well, virtually all landlords must give proper notice to take any rent increase. However, "vacancy decontrol" permits the setting of a new market rent when a tenant leaves and a new tenant rents the premises (mobile home parks and land lease communities are excepted).

Before June 17, 1998, federally appointed judges heard landlord and tenant cases such as eviction and disrepair claims. Since that date, all disputes involving residential rental premises have been heard by a specialized tribunal or board, whose members are appointed by the provincial government. The members of the board may or may not be legally trained and are appointed for fixed terms (usually three years). This systemic change resulted from a 1996 decision of the Supreme Court of Canada.[2]

From 1998 until 2006, under the *Tenant Protection Act, 1997* (TPA), the board was called the Ontario Rental Housing Tribunal. Most people referred to it in short as "the tribunal" or the "ORHT." Under the *Residential Tenancies Act, 2006* (RTA), the tribunal was renamed the Landlord and Tenant Board ("the board" or the

guideline
a percentage fixed each year by which a landlord can increase the rent without the board's approval

---

1   Rent control in Ontario has been governed by the following legislation: the *Residential Premises Rent Review Act*, in effect from 1975 to December 1979; the *Residential Tenancies Act*, in effect from December 1979 to December 1986; the *Residential Rent Regulation Act*, in effect from January 1987 to August 1990 or August 1992, with specific retroactive application to July 1, 1985; the *Residential Rent Regulation Amendment Act*, in effect from August 1990 to August 1992, the *Rent Control Act*, in effect from August 1992 to June 1998; the *Tenant Protection Act, 1997*, in effect from June 17, 1998 until January 30, 2007, and now the *Residential Tenancies Act, 2006*. Prior to the introduction of the *Tenant Protection Act*, residential landlord–tenant matters (evictions and other relationship matters) had been governed by part IV of the *Landlord and Tenant Act* since the early 1970s.

2   *Reference re: Act to Amend the Residential Tenancies Act (NS)* (1996), 131 DLR (4th) 609 (SCC), where the Supreme Court found that because residential tenancy disputes were not exclusively within the jurisdiction of federally appointed judges at the time of Confederation, it is not necessary for decisions in these matters to be made by judges at that level.

"LTB"). The board deals with virtually all residential landlord–tenant and rent disputes in Ontario.

WHAT DOES THE RTA REGULATE?

The RTA governs virtually all aspects of all residential tenancies in Ontario, including the relationship between landlords and residential tenants, the amount of rent permitted to be charged, and permissible rent increases.

Relationship issues include

- the creation of a tenancy;
- the **tenancy agreement**;
- the right to remain in occupation following the termination date of a tenancy unless grounds for eviction exist;
- **eviction** proceedings;
- rights on terminations for repairs or renovations;
- **assignments** and **sublets of tenancies**;
- entry;
- changing locks;
- maintenance, repair, vital service, and cleanliness obligations;
- remedies for harassment by a landlord;
- selecting tenants;
- eviction proceedings, including grounds and procedures; and
- special rules for care home rental units, mobile home sites, and land lease sites.

Rent-related issues include

- application of the RTA;
- lawful rent determination;
- lawful rent increases;
- impact on rents when services are added or removed;
- rent decreases for certain property tax decreases;
- rent-discounting rules; and
- notice requirements.

WHOM DOES THE RTA REGULATE?

In general, the RTA applies to landlords and tenants of all residential rental units in Ontario. This includes landlords and tenants of all types of rental housing from units in high-rise apartment buildings to single-family homes. Most of the rules are the same for rentals in those widely different building types.

However, there are special rules for certain types of rental units, such as care homes, mobile home parks, and land lease communities. There are partial exemptions for specific types of rental units, such as government housing where rent is

tenancy agreement
an agreement in which a property or part of a property is rented by a landlord to a tenant

eviction
removal of a tenant from a rented property, not by the tenant's choice

assignment of a tenancy
a tenant turning over the rights and obligations of a tenancy to a different tenant

sublet of a tenancy
a tenant turning over the rights and obligations of a tenancy to a different tenant for a limited period of time

geared to income. There are also certain exemptions from the rent-setting restrictions for new construction and for some new rentals.

Chapter 3 examines in detail who is regulated by the RTA.

WHO DOES THE REGULATION?

The Landlord and Tenant Board is the decision-making body created by the RTA. Through its members, the board makes decisions in applications filed under the RTA. Members are appointed by the provincial government for a fixed term (generally three years). Members are often reappointed for a second three-year term, although it is uncommon for members to be reappointed for a third term. Across Ontario, there is one board chair, several vice-chairs, and about twenty-five regular members of the board, who are known as adjudicators. The board has administrative staff located in Toronto and in various offices across Ontario. Each office has a manager, and there are managers for the various regions, such as the North, the East, the South-West, Toronto South, Toronto North, and so on.

The board has **exclusive jurisdiction** over virtually all disputes that might arise between a landlord and a residential tenant. However, the board does not have jurisdiction over issues related to tenancies that are exempt from the RTA (see Chapter 3 for more detail). Nor does the board have jurisidiction to deal with a landlord application that was filed after the tenant moved out. If a landlord wants to pursue a claim against a former tenant, he or she must proceed before the Small Claims Court. Finally, the board does not have jurisdiction over claims of more than $25,000.

exclusive jurisdiction
being the only legal body that can rule on a particular matter

Usually a single adjudicator hears an application. However, the RTA gives the board the power to sit as a panel of more than one member. It might exercise this power if an application raises a significant issue that will affect many cases.

APPLICATIONS CONCERNING THE LANDLORD–TENANT RELATIONSHIP

The RTA governs all applications that deal with the rights and obligations that arise in the relationship between residential landlords and tenants. These include a tenant's obligations to pay rent and behave in a manner appropriate to the rental community, and a landlord's obligations to maintain the premises properly and provide the tenant with the facilities to which the tenant is entitled.

Applications to the board may be made by landlords or tenants. The types of applications that a landlord might make under the RTA about the landlord–tenant relationship include applications for

- termination because of non-payment of rent;
- termination because of inappropriate behaviour;
- termination to perform major repairs or renovations;
- termination because the tenant failed to leave after giving notice or agreeing to do so;
- termination because the tenant failed to meet the terms of a settlement or order;

arrears
payments that are past due

- an order to collect **arrears** of rent or compensation for damage;
- an order requiring the tenant to provide a key to a lock that the tenant changed without permission; and
- a remedy for an unauthorized assignment or sublet.

The types of applications that a tenant might make under the RTA about the landlord–tenant relationship include applications for

abatement
reduction in a rent because
of deficiencies in a rental unit
or building

vital services
fuel oil, electricity, gas, hot
water, cold water, and heat
between Sept 1 and June 15

- a rent **abatement** for inadequate maintenance;
- a rent rebate on the grounds that the landlord failed to apply or pay interest on the last month's rent deposit, or for the proceeds of disposition upon the sale of a tenant's property;
- a remedy because the landlord harassed the tenant, withheld a **vital service**, entered the tenant's unit illegally, changed the locks without supplying a key, or interfered with the tenant's quiet enjoyment of the premises;
- a remedy because the landlord gave a notice of termination in bad faith; and
- an order authorizing an assignment or sublet.

APPLICATIONS CONCERNING THE AMOUNT OF RENT

The RTA governs the amount of rent and other charges that a landlord is permitted to require or that can be agreed upon by the parties. Accordingly, where disputes arise or where a landlord wants to apply for an **above-guideline rent increase**, the board will hear and determine the case.

**above-guideline
rent increase**
a rent increase greater than
the guideline

Applications to the board concerning the rent and charges may be made by landlords or tenants. The types of applications about the rent that a landlord might make under the RTA include applications

- about whether the RTA applies and
- for an above-guideline rent increase.

The types of applications about the rent that a tenant might make under the RTA include applications for

services and facilities
things provided with a rental
unit such as parking,
appliances, common-area
cleaning, lockers, laundry
facilities, heating, and
air conditioning

- a rent rebate because the landlord charged an illegal rent or charge;
- a rent reduction because the landlord removed or reduced a **service or facility**;
- a rent reduction because of a decrease in municipal taxes; and
- a rent reduction because the landlord failed to comply with the terms of an agreement for an above-guideline rent increase.

KEY TERMS

abatement

above-guideline rent increase

arrears

assignment of a tenancy

eviction

exclusive jurisdiction

guideline

services and facilities

sublet of a tenancy

tenancy agreement

vital services

REVIEW QUESTIONS

1. What Act or Acts apply to rent disputes today?

2. Name two Acts that applied to rent disputes in the past.

3. What Act or Acts apply to maintenance disputes today?

4. Name two Acts that applied to maintenance disputes in the past.

5. Are the basic rules the same, or different, for rentals in large apartment buildings and rentals of single-family homes?

6. If a landlord of a large apartment building wants to evict a tenant, what tribunal or court does the landlord apply to?

7. Name three applications a landlord might want to make.

8. Name three applications a tenant might want to make.

Legal Framework

2

The current system is governed by the *Residential Tenancies Act, 2006* (RTA),[1] the regulations to that Act,[2] the rules of practice,[3] the guidelines,[4] the case law, and relevant texts. This chapter will describe these different sources of the law and how they relate to each other.

You need to check with the Landlord and Tenant Board ("the board"), established by the RTA to administer the RTA on a regular basis to check for updates and additions to the regulations, the rules of practice, and the guidelines, because that material is always subject to change. Those updates are posted on the board's website at www.ltb.gov.on.ca.

THE RESIDENTIAL TENANCIES ACT, 2006

The RTA sets out the laws that govern residential tenancies in Ontario. Like other Acts, the RTA is enacted by the Ontario legislature and can be amended only by a further Act of the legislature. Like most Acts, the RTA is divided into parts, known by roman numerals. Each part is divided into sections. The sections are known by Arabic numerals, and numbered consecutively through the entire Act. The short way to refer to a particular section is to say, for example, "section 7" or to write "s. 7," which is said as "section 7." Sections 7 to 14 can be referred to in writing as ss. 7–14, which is said as "sections 7 to 14." In turn, sections are sometimes divided into subsections identified by an Arabic numeral within parentheses, such as ss. 91(2), which is said as "subsection 91, two" or "section 91, subsection two." Subsections are sometimes divided into paragraphs, identified by a letter, such as para. 91(2)(a).

---

1 An Act is passed by the provincial legislature and then as a formality given royal assent by the lieutenant governor on behalf of the Queen. Acts often come into force at a date later than royal assent so that the necessary regulations and forms can be prepared. The RTA was given royal assent on June 22, 2006 but came into force on January 31, 2007.

2 Regulations are made by the provincial Cabinet and are signed by the lieutenant governor. Regulations are said as being made by the lieutenant governor in council.

3 Rules of practice and procedure are issued by the Landlord and Tenant Board. They deal with procedural matters.

4 Guidelines are also issued by the board. They suggest appropriate interpretations of sections of the Act and regulations. A board member will usually follow a guideline, but is not required to follow a guideline.

Part I of the RTA (ss. 1 to 9) includes definitions that assist the reader in under-standing how the defined words are used in the RTA. When working with any particular section of the RTA, you must always refer to the definitions. For example, if you are considering whether to make an application that concerns a service or facility provided with respect to a rental unit, it is important to review the defin-itions of the words "rental unit" and "services and facilities" found in s. 2 of the RTA. Part I also includes various sections that establish circumstances in which the RTA applies and circumstances that are exempt from the operation of the RTA as a whole or from parts of the RTA.

According to s. 3 of the RTA, where a tenancy agreement is in conflict with the RTA, the RTA overrides the agreement. However, there are a limited number of areas in which the RTA states that parties can agree to terms other than those set out in the RTA.

In part II (ss. 10 to 19), the RTA addresses tenancy agreements, identifying some of the rights and obligations of landlords and tenants. These include what infor-mation a landlord may use to select prospective tenants (s. 10), a requirement that a landlord provide a tenant certain information with or in the tenancy agreement (ss. 11 and 12), a rule about when a tenancy agreement starts (s. 13), rules that say that certain terms are void (ss. 14 and 15), and certain rules that automatically apply to a tenancy agreement whether or not it addresses those rules (ss. 16 to 19).

In parts III and IV (ss. 20 to 36), the RTA sets out responsibilities of landlords and tenants. These include landlord responsibilities regarding the making of re-pairs, steps to be taken on changing locks, entry into the rental unit, and ensuring that tenants are not harassed or unduly bothered in their enjoyment of the rental unit. They also include tenant responsibilities with regard to cleanliness, repairs, locks, and ensuring that landlords are not harassed by tenants.

Part V of the RTA (ss. 37 to 94) governs the termination of tenancies and creates **security of tenure**. A residential tenancy may be terminated only for one of the reasons set out in the RTA. The procedure for terminating a tenancy is set out in the Act and must be followed meticulously. Even a small error can prove fatal to an application. These grounds and procedures are discussed in greater detail in Chapters 9, 10, and 11.

Part VI of the RTA (ss. 95 to 104) sets out the rules for assigning or subletting a rental unit. In most cases, a tenant must obtain the consent of the landlord before assigning or subletting a lease. In the case of a request for sublet, the landlord cannot arbitrarily or unreasonably withhold consent. In the case of a request for assignment, a landlord can refuse to consent, but if the landlord refuses consent, the tenant can terminate the tenancy. Assignment and subletting a lease are dis-cussed in greater detail in Chapter 14.

Part VII of the RTA (ss. 105 to 136) sets out the law concerning the amount of rent a landlord is allowed to charge new tenants and continuing tenants. This in-cludes the procedure that must be followed and the timing that must be observed for rent increases. The limited circumstances in which the parties may contract out of the restrictions on rent increases are also set out in part VII. Many of those rules about the amount of rent that a landlord can charge do not apply to newly constructed buildings or newly rented buildings (s. 6). Many of the rules about the amount of rent that a landlord can charge also do not apply to many tenancies in

security of tenure
the right of a residential tenant in Ontario to keep the tenancy unless the landlord has a specific reason to end the tenancy, as set out in the *Residential Tenancies Act*

Table 2.1   Legislative Framework: Residential Tenancies Act, 2006

Act	*Residential Tenancies Act, 2006*, SO 2006, c. 17, in force January 31, 2007. See Appendix A.
Regulations under the RTA	O. Reg. 516/06, O. Reg. 517/06. See Appendix B.
Regulations under the Human Rights Code	O. Reg. 290/98: business practices permissible to landlords in selecting prospective tenants. See Appendix H.
Rules of Practice	See Appendix C.
Guidelines	See Appendix D.

social housing (s. 7). In those tenancies, tenants often pay a **rent geared to income**, sometimes referred to as RGI. RGI tenants are also not governed by the usual rules regarding rent increases (s. 8).

Parts IX and X (ss. 139 to 167) set out rules for two special types of residential tenancies: **care homes** (part IX) and mobile home parks and land lease communities (part X). When taking any steps related to these special types of units, you must check whether, and in what way, the rules differ from those applicable to ordinary rental units.

For example, if you are asked to bring an application about the price charged for personal hygiene services provided at a care home rental unit, you must look under the definition section of the RTA and under part IX for provisions that deal with care homes. The regulations also play an important role in implementing the rules for care homes.

Parts XI through XIX deal with the board, its procedures, and various other matters. Sections 233 to 236 make certain actions provincial offences. Section 241 allows the Ontario Cabinet to make regulations that implement the provisions of the RTA.

The RTA is the most important legal document governing residential tenancies.

THE REGULATIONS

The regulations rank next in importance to the RTA itself. In other words, if there is a conflict between the RTA and a regulation, the RTA prevails; however, if there is a conflict between a regulation and anything else (such as a rule, a guideline, or a decision of the board), the regulation prevails. Regulations are enacted by the Ontario Cabinet but need not be approved by the entire legislature. Accordingly, the process for enacting, amending, or repealing a regulation is more streamlined than the process for amending the RTA itself.

The power to make regulations is conferred by s. 241 of the RTA. If the power to make a regulation is not given by the RTA, then the regulation is open to challenge as having been made without proper authority. For that reason, if you are faced with a problem that relies on a provision in a regulation, and the power to make that regulation is not found in the RTA, then it is possible that the regulation cannot be enforced.

social housing
housing provided by a city or provincial housing authority, or other agencies such as non-profit housing corporations, primarily to those with low incomes

rent geared to income
a rent determined on the basis of the tenant's income, which in Ontario social housing is usually 30 percent of the tenant's income

care home
building for people to receive care services such as health care or assistance with daily living

The following example illustrates how a regulation is made for the purpose of implementing the RTA. Section 241(1)22 provides that the lieutenant governor in council (the Ontario Cabinet) may make regulations "prescribing services, facilities, privileges, accommodations and things for the purposes of paragraph 2 of subsection 123(1)." That paragraph provides that a landlord may increase the rent charged to a tenant for a rental unit as prescribed at any time if the landlord and the tenant agree that the landlord will add the prescribed service. Read together, those two paragraphs gave the lieutenant governor in council the power to pass s. 16 of O. Reg. 516/06, which lists 12 services and facilities for which the parties may agree to a rent increase and prescribes how the increase is to be calculated.

RULES OF PRACTICE

The rules of practice are made by the Landlord and Tenant Board. The board's power to make rules is set out in the RTA in s. 176. This section requires the formation of a rules and guidelines committee, which in turn is required to adopt rules of practice and procedure under the authority of s. 176 of the RTA and s. 25.1 of the *Statutory Powers Procedure Act*.

Statutory Powers Procedure Act
the Ontario statute that sets out the basic procedural rules for all tribunals

The rules set out a code of procedures that must be followed in each proceeding that comes before the board for determination. The rules address such issues as serving documents, filing disputes, extending and shortening time limits, amending applications, conducting mediations, making settlements, and paying money into and out of the board. In addition, the rules deal with issues of protocol, such as communications with the board and public access to the files and to the hearing. The rules are set out in Appendix C. Regular updates of the rules are available from board offices. Failure to follow the rules can result in the board's refusing to hear your application or your defence to an application brought against you or the person you represent. You must also know and understand the rules so that you are able to assess the strength or weakness of the position you propose to take in any particular application or proceeding.

The rules of practice are made by the board itself; and so, amendments, additions, and deletions can be made by the board as the need arises. A thorough knowledge of the up-to-date rules of practice is critical. Remember, though, that in the hierarchy of documents, the rules are below the RTA and the regulations. This means that if there is a conflict between a rule and a regulation, or between a rule and the RTA, then the regulation or the RTA governs.

INTERPRETATION GUIDELINES

The board also publishes non-binding interpretation guidelines, which are one further layer in the legislative framework. The power to adopt these guidelines is found in s. 176(3) of the RTA. The guidelines are helpful because they assist you in understanding the circumstances in which certain relief is likely to be granted. However, the **discretion** exercised by an independent decision-maker (the adjudicator) must not be fettered by a guideline that purports to tell the decision-maker how to decide. Accordingly, while the guidelines suggest how the RTA and regulations may be interpreted, an adjudicator who does not agree with an interpretation

discretion
independent decision-making power

in a guideline need not apply the guideline. General administrative law requires that adjudicators be fair and hear the parties' arguments with an open mind. The difficulty lies in determining what is fair and proper in each situation. Most adjudicators follow most of the rules almost all of the time.

The guidelines under the RTA cover such matters as **adjourning** and **rescheduling hearings**, costs awards, what constitutes harassment, abandonment of a unit, and various issues involved in evictions for non-payment of rent or behavioural problems. See Appendix D for the guidelines. In the hierarchy of the legislative framework, the guidelines are at the bottom.

There is sometimes room to challenge a guideline on the basis that it is in conflict with the RTA or the regulations, and therefore should not be applied. In that case, you may want to argue that the board member should not apply the interpretation guideline.

CASE LAW

In administering the RTA, the board makes decisions about specific cases. A number of decisions are published by the board and available on the board website at www.ltb.gov.on.ca. Board decisions are also reported in online legal search services such as CanLII (www.canlii.org/en/on/onltb), Quicklaw, and WestLaw Canada. The decisions chosen for publication are decisions that are thought to be useful in clarifying what is meant by various sections of the Act, and in dealing with certain situations. These are called precedent cases, although any previous decision can be used as a precedent if the facts are similar to the facts in the current case. A decision of one board member does not bind any other board member to decide the same way, but board members will usually decide in the same way as a matter has been previously decided. You should expect a board member to follow a precedent unless you or another representative makes a good argument that the original decision is incorrect or should not be followed. Decisions that do not bind a board or court to decide in the same way are called "persuasive" rather than "binding."

Parties sometimes ask the board to review a decision. Review decisions also do not bind any other board member to decide the same way. However, they are more persuasive than ordinary decisions of the board. You should expect a board member to decide in the same way as a matter has been previously decided on a review hearing unless you or another representative makes a very good argument that the review decision is incorrect or should not be followed.

Because many sections of the RTA are the same as sections of the *Tenant Protection Act* (TPA), you can use decisions of the Ontario Rental Housing Tribunal (the "tribunal") under the TPA to interpret the equivalent sections of the RTA. Decisions of the tribunal should be almost as persuasive as decisions of the current board if the section in question is identical. Some of the interpretation of the RTA in the rest of this text is based on decisions under the TPA. If the section in question has been changed, then you must decide or argue whether the change affects the decision.

Appendix F sets out a table of concordance so that you can determine which sections of the TPA may be identical or equivalent to sections of the RTA. By using the table of concordance you can search online for precedent cases under the TPA

adjournment
postponement, usually of a hearing, and usually at the time that the hearing was to begin or after it has begun

rescheduling
postponement, usually of a hearing, before the hearing was scheduled to begin

hearing
a formal meeting at which a decision-maker hears evidence and argument in order to make a decision

using the correct section number. The Emond Montgomery website for this book (www.emp.ca/wrta) sets out a table of differences so that you can determine whether the sections are identical, and if not, what changes were made. This table is useful in determining the law as it relates to tricky questions and in your preparation to argue such issues before the board.

Many sections of the RTA originated in the *Landlord and Tenant Act* (LTA)—the Act that applied before the TPA was enacted. Applications under the LTA were decided by the courts of first instance. At different times that court was the county or district court or the Ontario Court (General Division). Decisions of those courts under the LTA are also relevant, persuasive precedents to interpret and apply the RTA.

Divisional Court
a branch of the Superior Court of Justice of Ontario in which judges hear appeals and applications for judicial review, including appeals of final orders from the Landlord and Tenant Board, Small Claims Court, and other administrative tribunals

Parties sometimes appeal decisions of the board to the **Divisional Court**. Decisions of the Divisional Court do bind the board. If an appeal to the Divisional Court was decided in a way that hurts your client, the only way to argue that the board should not decide a current case in the same way is to find a conflicting decision of the Divisional Court, or to distinguish the unhelpful precedent case from your case. Cases are distinguished by showing that, although the facts of the precedent case may seem to be similar to the facts of your case, there is some legally relevant difference that should alter the result.

On rare occasions, a party will appeal a decision of the Divisional Court to the **Ontario Court of Appeal**. Decisions of the Court of Appeal bind the Divisional Court and the board. If an appeal to the Court of Appeal was decided in a way that hurts your client, the only way to argue that the board should not decide a current case in the same way is to find a conflicting decision of the Court of Appeal (which would be rare) or to distinguish the precedent case from your case.

Ontario Court of Appeal
Ontario's highest court, which considers appeals from decisions of the Superior Court of Justice and the Ontario Court of Justice, including the Divisional Court

Occasionally, decisions of the Supreme Court of Canada, the courts of other provinces, or the courts of other common-law jurisdictions (such as the United Kingdom, Australia, New Zealand, and the United States) are relevant. UK court cases established many of the rules that are now found in the RTA. When using cases from other jurisdictions, you need to consider whether the legislation of the other jurisdiction is the same as the RTA in all relevant respects, and whether the issue under the RTA is the same as the issue in the other case.

Sometimes different precedent cases have reached different results. In arguing which case the board should follow, the issues are: how close is the applicable legislation to Ontario's RTA, and what "authority" does the other court have? As you would expect, the highest authority is the Supreme Court of Canada, followed by the Ontario Court of Appeal and the Ontario Divisional Court, in that order. The decisions of those courts are binding on the board, regardless of what other courts have decided. After the Ontario appellate courts, the next best authority is the board itself, or the Ontario courts of first instance that decided cases under previous landlord–tenant legislation. Along with those cases, you should look to the appellate courts of other provinces. After those sources of authority, you should look to the courts of other common-law jurisdictions beginning with the highest UK courts (i.e., the House of Lords or the Court of Appeal), the Supreme Court of Australia, and then other courts of England, Australia, and New Zealand, or courts of the United States.

Taken together, the decisions of the board, the tribunal, and the courts of Ontario (and the rest of the common-law world) make up what is called the case law. The case law has different argumentative weight depending on the situation. An un-contradicted decision of the Ontario Court of Appeal or the Ontario Divisional Court, which cannot be distinguished, on the RTA or on the same section with identical wording in a previous Act should determine the law that applies under the RTA. However, cases are often similar in some ways but different in other ways, and often the words in successor Acts have been changed. These similarities and differences allow you the opportunity to argue your interpretation of current sections of the RTA.

RELEVANT TEXTS

Another source of law for the RTA and other areas of law are the relevant texts. In making decisions, courts and tribunals will take into account what authors have written about the interpretation of the RTA and its predecessor legislation. Text-books often assemble the case law on issues, and the authors provide their views on the correct resolution of points where the case law conflicts. Authors also comment on new sections of the legislation, saying what they think the correct inter-pretation is before the board has addressed certain issues. In those cases what is written in the texts is the authority on the particular point. The very text you are reading can be used as an authority in this way. It is not as powerful as some other texts, though, because we have deliberately avoided providing detailed citations of case law in order to make the material easier to read.

For many years, the main text on landlord–tenant law in Ontario was a looseleaf service by Williams and Rhodes[5] that covered both commercial and residential tenancies, and was not limited to Ontario. In 1970, Donald Lamont, QC, published his book entitled *Residential Tenancies*,[6] which covered the law under the Ontario *Landlord and Tenant Act*. Mr. Lamont continued to update his text through six edi-tions. The 6th edition covered the *Tenant Protection Act*, and was published in 2000. Then Mr. Lamont and his publisher turned to Richard A. Feldman to update and expand their text, issuing the 7th edition under the names of both Mr. Lamont and Mr. Feldman. Richard Feldman was an adjudicator on the Ontario Rental Housing Tribunal (as the LTB was then known) from 1998 to 2004. He served as a full-time member of that tribunal for six years, training and mentoring new adjudicators and issuing over 9,000 orders. A thick volume entitled *Residential Tenancies*, by Richard Feldman, is now the pre-eminent text on the RTA. In 2009, the 9th edition was published.[7]

In 1999, Joe Hoffer published his *Practical Guide to the Tenant Protection Act*.[8] Like the text you are reading, Hoffer's text provides few citations, but does comment on how sections of the Act should be interpreted, particularly regarding practical

---

5   F.W. Rhodes and E.K. Williams, *Canadian Law of Landlord and Tenant*, 6th ed. (Toronto: Carswell, 1988).

6   D.H.L. Lamont, *Residential Tenancies*, 7th ed. (Toronto: Thomson Canada, 2004).

7   Richard A. Feldman, *Residential Tenancies*, 9th ed. (Toronto: Carswell, 2009).

8   J. Hoffer, *Practical Guide to the Tenant Protection Act* (Aurora, ON: Canada Law Book, 1999).

issues that landlords face in the day-to-day business of operating a rental building. In 1998, Jack Fleming published a detailed book entitled *Residential Tenancies in Ontario*,[9] also covering the *Tenant Protection Act*. Written from the tenant's point of view, the Fleming text covers in more detail many of the issues covered in this text and provides the citations for the case law in great detail. The second edition is due to be published this year. Mr. Fleming is also the author of *Ontario Landlord and Tenant Law Practice*.[10]

You can also refer to *Ontario Residential Tenancies Law* by Robert Doumani and Carol Albert,[11] now edited by Joy Overtveld. This is a looseleaf service that reports the case law on each section of the Act as it develops and provides commentary. The *Annotated Ontario Landlord and Tenant Statutes* is edited by Mavis Butkus and published annually.[12] Ms. Butkus provides the latest regulations, rules, and guidelines, as well as case law on each section of the Act.

CONCLUSION

In summary, the RTA and its regulations are a complete code that governs residential tenancies in Ontario. They are implemented and clarified through the rules of practice, and interpreted in some respects through the guidelines. All of that statute law is interpreted with the aid of the case law and the relevant texts.

KEY TERMS

adjournment	rent geared to income
care home	rescheduling
discretion	security of tenure
Divisional Court	social housing
hearing	*Statutory Powers Procedure Act*
Ontario Court of Appeal	

---

9   J. Fleming, *Residential Tenancies in Ontario* (Markham, ON: Butterworths Canada, 1998).

10   J. Fleming, *Ontario Landlord and Tenant Law Practice* (Markham, ON: LexisNexis Canada, 2010).

11   Carol Albert was the co-author of the first edition of the text, which was called *Working with the Tenant Protection Act*. C. Albert, R. Doumani, and J. Overtveld, ed., *Ontario Residential Tenancies Law* (Toronto: Thomson Professional Publishing Canada, 2004).

12   M. Butkus, ed., Annotated *Ontario Landlord and Tenant Statutes*, 2011 ed. (Toronto: Carswell, looseleaf).

REVIEW QUESTIONS

1. What is "security of tenure"?

2. a. What Act (or Acts) governs residential tenancies today?

   b. When did that Act or those Acts come into force?

3. a. What are three other types of law that affect residential tenancies and proceedings about residential tenancies?

   b. Which source of law is the most important after the Act itself?

4. What is case law?

Does the RTA Apply?

When dealing with a situation that looks like a landlord–tenant dispute, the first question you must ask is whether the *Residential Tenancies Act, 2006* (RTA) applies. Generally, the RTA governs all rental housing in Ontario. However, there are a number of exemptions and exceptions. For example, the restrictions on setting and increasing rent do not apply to new rental housing, but the rules governing the relationship of landlord and tenant do apply. Furthermore, certain categories of rental units, such as care home units and sites in mobile home parks and land lease communities, have special rules. If you are dealing with a matter that involves a care home, a mobile home park, or a land lease community, you must review the law as it applies to these special types of rental units.

If it is not clear whether the RTA applies to the property you are dealing with, you can make an application to the Landlord and Tenant Board ("the board") under s. 9 for a determination of whether the RTA applies. An application can also be used to determine whether particular sections of the RTA apply to properties or units within properties.

EXEMPTIONS FROM THE ACT

The RTA applies to all residential rental units in Ontario unless there is a specific exemption for the unit (s. 3(1)). Landlords and tenants cannot make a valid agreement that to which the RTA does not apply (s. 3(1)). (However, landlords and tenants can make their own agreements about some of the issues that are governed by the RTA. These matters will be dealt with as they arise in later chapters.)

Exemptions from the RTA can arise because a particular use of a property does not fall within the definitions of rented residential premises or because the RTA lists a specific exemption. Exemptions can be "full exemptions" to which no rule in the RTA applies. These are generally listed in s. 5. Exemptions can also be "partial exemptions," in which case some, but not all, of the rules in the RTA apply. The partial exemptions are listed in ss. 6, 7, and 8.

FULL EXEMPTIONS

Provided that certain conditions are met, the RTA does not apply to the following types of uses: commercial uses, rentals to employees, rentals at institutions, "tenants" who are really owners, educational institutions, and situations of close contact. The government can exempt other classes of accommodation (s. 5(n)).

Commercial Uses

A use of a property that is solely commercial is not subject to any part of the RTA. Some examples of commercial uses are stores, offices, restaurants, barber shops, and hair salons. The RTA does not apply to commercial uses because s. 3(1) states that the Act applies to "rental units in residential complexes" and the definition of a rental unit is "any living accommodation used or intended for use as *residential* premises [emphasis added]."

The situation is somewhat uncertain where a unit is intended for use as residential premises but is in fact used as commercial premises. In our opinion, the tenancy for the commercial use would usually not be subject to the RTA. However, each case is determined on its own particular facts, which must be examined carefully before concluding whether the use is residential or commercial and whether the RTA applies. Of course, if the unit were later re-rented as residential premises, it would be subject to the RTA.

The RTA provides certain specific exemptions for mixed commercial-and-living situations. The following paragraphs in s. 5 of the RTA describe the units that are exempt for that reason.

> (a) living accommodation intended to be provided to the travelling or vacationing public or occupied for a seasonal or temporary period in a hotel, motel or motor hotel, resort, lodge, tourist camp, cottage or cabin establishment, inn, campground, trailer park, tourist home, bed and breakfast vacation establishment or vacation home; ...
>
> (h) living accommodation located in a building or project used in whole or in part for non-residential purposes if the occupancy of the living accommodation is conditional upon the occupant continuing to be an employee of or perform services related to a business or enterprise carried out in the building or project; ...
>
> (j) premises occupied for business or agricultural purposes with living accommodation attached if the occupancy for both purposes is under a single lease and the same person occupies the premises and the living accommodation.

Employee Exemptions

Rental units provided solely during the course of employment are exempt from the RTA. These units are described in s. 5 as follows:

> (b) living accommodation whose occupancy is conditional upon the occupant continuing to be employed on a farm, whether or not the accommodation is located on that farm; ...
>
> (h) living accommodation located in a building or project used in whole or in part for non-residential purposes if the occupancy of the living accommodation is conditional upon the occupant continuing to be an employee of or perform services related to a business or enterprise carried out in the building or project.

There are special rules, but no full exemption, for units occupied by superintendents. Unless otherwise agreed, a superintendent's tenancy terminates on the date on which the employment of the tenant as superintendent is terminated (s. 93). This applies whether the termination is proper or wrongful under employment law. The former superintendent is required to vacate the rental unit within one week after the termination of the tenancy (s. 93(2)). The landlord may not charge or receive rent or compensation for that one-week period (s. 93(3)). The landlord may apply to the board for an order for eviction if the former superintendent does not vacate the rental unit within the one-week period (s. 94).

Institutional Exemptions

There is a full exemption from the RTA under s. 5 for the following living accommodation occupied for an institutional purpose:

(d) living accommodation occupied by a person for penal or correctional purposes;

(e) living accommodation that is subject to the *Public Hospitals Act*, the *Private Hospitals Act*, the *Long-Term Care Homes Act, 2007*, the *Ministry of Correctional Services Act* or the *Child and Family Services Act*;

(f) short-term living accommodation provided as emergency shelter; ...

(k) living accommodation occupied by a person for the purpose of receiving rehabilitative or therapeutic services agreed upon by the person and the provider of the living accommodation, where,

(i) the parties have agreed that,

(A) the period of occupancy will be of a specified duration, or

(B) the occupancy will terminate when the objectives of the services have been met or will not be met, and

(ii) the living accommodation is intended to be provided for no more than a one-year period;

(l) living accommodation in a care home occupied by a person for the purpose of receiving short-term respite care.

Because other legislation governs such facilities as hospitals and prisons, RTA protection is not necessary. Other exempt facilities—for example, emergency shelters, short-term respite care facilities, and rehabilitation care facilities—are temporary in nature.

Owner-Like Occupation

Under the RTA, "rent" is defined as consideration paid by a tenant to a landlord for the right to occupy a rental unit and for services and facilities. The definition of "tenant" excludes a person who has the right to occupy a rental unit by virtue of being

- a **co-owner** of the residential complex in which the rental unit is located or
- a **shareholder** of a **corporation** that owns the residential complex.

In this situation, a multi-unit property has been bought by several people, and together they have agreed on a division of the living space. Such a situation can happen when a building is not suitable for registration as a **condominium**, but is still attractive for owner occupation. A developer may renovate the building and in effect sell individual units to people who intend to occupy the units. However, as a matter of law, all the owners own the whole building and each owner has the

co-owner
someone who owns property in common or jointly with one or more other persons

shareholder
someone who holds shares in a corporation

corporation
a legal entity distinct from its shareholders or members, with liability separate from its shareholders or members, vested with the capacity of continuous succession

condominium
a type of ownership of individual units, generally in a multi-unit development or project

right to occupy a specific individual unit as if that owner were a tenant of all the owners, including themselves. The exemption in the RTA recognizes the underlying or "real" situation. If there is a conflict among the owners, the conflict must be resolved under the agreement among them—whether in or out of the courts—and not at the board.

There is a full exemption for living accommodation provided by a non-profit housing cooperative to tenants in member units (s. 5(c)). However, members of **non-profit housing co-operatives** are given a number of rights similar to the rights of tenants by ss. 171.7 to 171.25 of the *Co-operative Corporations Act*. Eviction applications are made to the Ontario Court (General Division).

In addition, the holders of estates for life, who are sometimes referred to as "tenants for life" under "life leases," are not subject to the RTA. (A life lease is a form of rental housing usually aimed at seniors where the term tends to be long—for example, 50 years or as long as the tenant lives—and the tenant typically pays an entrance fee for the rental unit along with a monthly charge for maintenance and other expenses.) In this situation, a life tenant is, in effect, an owner of a residential unit, rather than a tenant. The exemption was established in the 1998 case of *Peterson v. Charboneau*.[1] If you are faced with a life lease situation, you should compare the facts of your case with the facts in the *Peterson* case to assess whether the reasoning in that case applies.

Some Educational Institutions

There is a full exemption from the RTA (s. 5(g)) for living accommodation provided by an educational institution to its students or staff where

> (i) the living accommodation is provided primarily to persons under the age of majority, or all major questions related to the living accommodation are decided after consultation with a council or association representing the residents, and
>
> (ii) the living accommodation does not have its own self-contained bathroom and kitchen facilities or is not intended for year-round occupancy by full-time students or staff and members of their households.

Where there is a council or association representing the residents, and there has not been consultation with the council or association respecting a rent increase, limits on rent increases do apply (s. 7(6)).

Situations of Close Contact

Under s. 5(i), there is a full exemption for

> (i) living accommodation whose occupant or occupants are required to share a bathroom or kitchen facility with the owner, the owner's spouse, child or parent or the spouse's child or parent, and where the owner, spouse, child or parent lives in the building in which the living accommodation is located.

non-profit housing co-operative
non-profit housing community where the residents are members of a co-op corporation, which typically owns the whole property, and are actively involved in the running of the community

---

1 *Peterson v. Charboneau* (January 13, 1998), file no. 97-DV-12 (Ont. Div. Ct.) [unreported].

This exemption exists so that security of tenure does not prevent an eviction when the owner lives in close contact with the occupant of a room or other rental unit.

To evict a tenant in a situation of close contact, the owner should give the tenant a letter telling the tenant to move out of the premises by a certain date and time. To avoid a claim for damages, the date should be a reasonable one. For a serious fault by the tenant, such as theft, the time period can be short—24 hours after discovery of the fault, for example. For less serious faults, including failure to pay the rent, the time should be at least a few days or a week. If the problem is a clash of personalities, the safest time period is the length of the rental period (that is, a week if rent is paid weekly or a month if rent is paid monthly). However, less time than a month can be given. Any extra rent must be returned, subject to deductions for amounts needed to pay for damages to the property.

If the tenant does not leave in response to the letter, the owner can ask for police assistance in evicting the tenant because, at the end of the notice period, the tenant becomes a trespasser. In some areas, the police act in this situation only if the owner has a lawyer's letter addressed to them indicating why they should act and why the RTA does not apply.

In law, the tenant has no right to remain in the room after the date specified in the owner's notice, even if the notice period is too short. However, if the notice period is too short, or if the eviction was contrary to the agreement or implied agreement between the owner and the tenant, the tenant may have a claim against the landlord for breach of contract. In that case, the Small Claims Court could award damages for any out-of-pocket expenses that the owner's breach of contract has caused. These expenses may consist of the cost of staying in a hotel for a few nights while finding another room or the cost of renting a car to move the tenant's belongings. Unlike a tenant who is subject to the RTA, the tenant who is not covered by the RTA has no right to remain in the accommodation while the parties' rights are sorted out.

In cases when the RTA does not apply (which are mostly those cases of close contact), the *Innkeepers Act* governs the ability of a "landlord" to hold the tenant's personal belongings. If the landlord holds the property wrongfully, the tenant can apply to a provincial judge (in the Ontario Court of Justice—Provincial Division) for an order to recover personal belongings.

PARTIAL EXEMPTIONS

New Construction or New Rentals

An ordinary apartment or ordinary house rented as living accommodation normally falls within the RTA. A major exemption from the limits on rent increases applies to a rental unit if, according to s. 6(2):

- it has not been occupied for any purpose before June 17, 1998;
- no part of it has been previously rented since July 29, 1975; or
- it is in a building no part of which has been occupied for residential purposes before November 1, 1991.

Landlords of rental units that meet any one of these tests can increase the rent without legal limit on the amount. There is usually a practical limit if the landlord wants to keep the tenant or to obtain a tenant for the unit. The landlord must give 90 days written notice of the increase and take the increase no sooner than 12 months after the previous increase (s. 6(2)). If you are dealing with such a rental unit, check the list of provisions that do not apply as listed in s. 6(2) of the RTA. Also note that increases in these circumstances use a Form N2 notice, rather than the normal notice, which is Form N1.

Partial Institutional Exemptions

Numerous sections of the RTA do not apply to accommodation that is subject to the *Homes for Special Care Act*, or the *Developmental Services Act* (s. 6(1)). These exemptions include rules related to rent as well as those related to demolition and conversion of rental units.

Numerous sections of the RTA do not apply to a building owned, operated, or administered by a religious institution for a charitable use on a non-profit basis (ss. 7(1)6 and 7(2)(b)). One example might be a hospice operated by a religious institution, where the occupants contribute part of the cost and the balance is dependent on charitable donations. These exemptions include rules relating to rent, rules relating to demolition and conversion, and rights to assign or sublet a rental unit.

Public Housing

public housing
rental housing provided by a government body, usually at reduced rent to people with low income

rent geared to income
the calculation of rent based on the tenant's income, typically 30 percent of the tenant's income

Numerous sections of the RTA do not apply to **public housing** (s. 7(1)1).

Numerous sections of the RTA do not apply to tenants whose **rent is geared to income** (ss. 7(2)(a), 7(3), 8(1), and 8(2)). Among the inapplicable rules are the rules limiting rent increases and the rule requiring 12 months between rent increases (s. 7(2)(a)). The entire RTA applies to rental units where a landlord who is not the government or a government agency receives the rent from the tenants, even though the rent is subsidized by the government (s. 7(4)).

Numerous sections of the RTA do not apply to non-profit housing developed under a prescribed federal or provincial program or in non-member units of a housing co-operative (ss. 7(1)2 and 3).

Other Educational Institutions (Partial Exemption)

A rental unit provided by an educational institution to a student or staff member that is not exempt from the RTA under s. 5(g) has a partial exemption from the RTA (s. 7(1)5). However, part of the partial exemption is lost if there is a council or association representing the residents and the institution has not consulted with the council or association respecting the rent increase (s. 7(6)).

Under ss. 37(5), (6), and (7), post-secondary institutions (and landlords who make certain agreements with them) are exempt from the rule that an agreement to terminate is void if it is made at the time that a tenancy agreement is made.

KEY TERMS

co-owner

condominium

corporation

non-profit housing co-operative

public housing

rent geared to income

shareholder

REVIEW QUESTIONS

1. Which of these tenancies are covered (at least in part) by the RTA, and which are completely exempt from the RTA?

   a. a detached house (if rented)

   b. a social housing unit

   c. a trailer in a mobile home park

   d. a room in a halfway house

   e. a room in a house that has one bathroom, where a niece pays her aunt rent to live in the house

   f. a room above a restaurant rented to the tenant on the condition that the tenant work at the restaurant

   g. a condominium unit built and rented in 1980

   h. an apartment in an apartment building built in 1995

   i. a condominium unit in a building built in 2005.

2. Which of the units in question 1 are subject to rent control, and which are exempt from rent control?

The Tenancy Agreement

4

PURPOSE OF THE TENANCY AGREEMENT

The main purpose of the tenancy agreement is to establish and define the relationship between the landlord and the tenant. The agreement can be in writing or by spoken words, or it can be implied by actions. The *Residential Tenancies Act, 2006* (RTA) imposes many terms on tenancy agreements and restricts the ability of the parties to agree to other terms. Nevertheless, the contents of the tenancy agreement are important in many respects.

For tenants, the purpose of renting is to obtain living accommodation without the cost and the long-term commitment of home ownership. For landlords, the purpose of renting is to obtain money in exchange for the use of their property. While not entirely in conflict, these different goals tend to put landlords and tenants on opposite sides on a number of issues. The RTA balances the interests of landlords against those of tenants and, in some cases, the interests of some tenants against those of other tenants.

The tenancy agreement is essential in determining whether the RTA applies to a particular relationship. As was explained in Chapter 3, there are numerous "grey areas" where a rental has a living-accommodation component and another component. To determine whether the RTA applies to a particular relationship, you need to consider the provisions of the tenancy agreement, the provisions of the RTA, and the actual facts of a particular situation.

BASIC ELEMENTS OF A TENANCY AGREEMENT

The basic elements addressed in a tenancy agreement are the following: the premises being rented, the use of the premises, the amount to be paid, the starting date, and the ending date.

The premises being rented can be a house or an apartment. Most apartments are in apartment buildings that were built as apartment buildings. Such apartment buildings are called "purpose-built" rental buildings. Other apartments are in converted buildings—that is, buildings that were built for a different purpose (for example, as a large, single-family home), but converted to apartments. The premises being rented can also be a room or rooms with a shared bathroom and with or without kitchen facilities. In the agreement, it is usually clear what living accommodation is being rented, but there can easily be disputes about the other facilities included in the tenancy agreement. For example, is the exclusive or shared

tandem parking space
a parking space immediately in front of or behind another parking space

use of a garden or yard included? Is a parking space or a **tandem parking space** included? What about storage? What about the use of laundry facilities?

If the RTA applies, the premises will be primarily used for living accommodation; however, the exact nature of the agreed use will often determine whether the RTA applies.

The amount of rent to be paid is usually clear. However, under the RTA some landlords use marketing and/or prompt payment discounts. These discounts are further explained in Appendix G.

The start date of the tenancy is usually clear. However, tenants are sometimes allowed to move in or to move their belongings in before the date when the rent becomes payable. In some situations, it matters when the tenant was first entitled to occupy the rental unit. Under s. 13(2) of the RTA, that is the date the tenancy agreement takes effect.

The date on which the tenancy ends is often specified in the tenancy agreement. However, the RTA provides that a tenancy is deemed to be renewed on certain terms if the landlord and tenant have not terminated it by notice or renewed it by agreement (s. 38). This means that a landlord cannot insist that a tenant adhere to a termination date unless the landlord has a reason to terminate the tenancy that is specified in the RTA. In that provision the RTA has favoured the tenant's interest in having a secure home over the landlord's interest in being able to control to whom and for how long the property is rented.

RESPONSIBILITY FOR UTILITIES

The tenancy agreement sets out who is responsible for paying and arranging for the **utilities**.

utilities
heat, hydro, and water supplied to the rental unit

Historically, in most high-rise apartment leases, all utilities were included in the rent (that is, the landlord was responsible for paying and arranging for the utilities). However today, there are many high-rise apartment leases where the tenant is responsible for some or all of the utilities.

In the case of most walk-up apartment building leases, the landlord tends to include the heat and water in the rent, but the tenant is responsible for paying for the electricity (or, as it is often called, the "hydro"). In some cases the tenants open their own accounts with the municipal electricity authority to service the rental unit. In those cases the landlord should check with the electricity authority to ensure that the tenant has opened their own account.

In the case of townhouses, the landlord usually pays for the supply of water, but the tenant is responsible for heat and hydro for the unit. In the case of detached houses, most leases provide that the tenant is responsible for all utilities. Other arrangements can be made in the tenancy agreement, but it can be helpful to know what the most common arrangement is for each type of unit.

Under the RTA, the landlord may change the tenancy agreement to require the tenant to pay for the electricity in some cases and subject to various conditions, including a reduction in the rent. O. Reg. 394/10 sets out the situations and conditions in which the landlord may require the tenant to assume responsibility for paying for the electricity (either in whole or in part).

Under O. Reg. 394/10, a number of rules apply in the situation where the unit is separately metered, no matter how long the unit has been separately metered. If the prospective tenant is to pay for the electricity, the landlord must give the prospective tenant

- electricity consumption information for the previous 12 months, or the period in which the unit has been separately metered, whichever is less (if the information is available to the landlord);
- the best information available about the date of manufacture and the energy efficiency of the refrigerator;
- a refrigerator manufactured on or after January 1, 1994; or
- if the refrigerator is being replaced, a replacement refrigerator manufactured on or after December 31, 2002.

When the RTA was enacted in 2006, it included s. 138, which dealt with apportioning utility costs in buildings with six or fewer units. However, that section was not brought into force with the rest of the Act. An amended s. 138 was brought into force on January 1, 2011. Sections 13 to 18 of O. Reg. 394/10 provide rules under which landlords of such buildings can apportion utility costs among tenants, based on billings from meters for the whole building. These rules apply to any utility—namely, electricity, water, and heat. Existing arrangements for utility apportionment are **grandfathered**. For any new apportionment of utility costs on or after the in-force date, the following rules apply:

- the same apportionment method must be used for all tenants;
- the apportionment can be an equal amount to each unit *or* an amount based on the area of each unit;
- the charge to be apportioned can include the utility costs for the common areas related to the rental units;
- 30 days' notice must be given to the tenant before the landlord begins to charge the tenant a portion of the cost of the utility;
- the corresponding rent reduction must be stated in the notice; and
- the notice must describe the method of apportioning and how the rent reduction is calculated.

grandfathered
a situation or action is said to be grandfathered when it is allowed to continue even though a new rule or set of rules would prohibit it, or would impose new conditions on the person doing it

As well, if the landlord charges any tenant a portion of the cost of electricity, all refrigerators in the building must be manufactured on or after January 1, 1994, and if any refrigerator is replaced, the replacement refrigerator must be manufactured on or after December 31, 2002. For apportionment arrangements in place on October 13, 2010, a landlord has two years to comply with the two rules regarding refrigerators.

If a landlord fails to comply with the rules set out in O. Reg.394/10, a tenant may file an application (T7) with the Landlord and Tenant Board ("the board") seeking compensation or other relief. Tenant applications are explained in more detail in Chapter 8.

Under s. 19 of O. Reg. 394/10, most social housing units are exempt from the rent reduction requirements of the separate metering and apportionment rules described above.

TYPES OF TENANCY AGREEMENTS

A tenancy agreement can be written or oral, or it can be implied by actions. A formal written tenancy agreement is often called a lease, although the term "lease" is sometimes applied to other tenancy agreements. Leases or true tenancy agreements can be contrasted to "licences," as will be explained below.

Written Tenancy Agreements

Professional landlords usually use an application-to-lease form as well as a lease. After deciding they want to rent the unit, a tenant completes an application form that sets out the address of the unit, the rent, and the proposed starting and ending dates for the tenancy. The application form usually requires the prospective tenant to list previous landlords and to give employment references. The landlord checks the references and then notifies the tenants that their application is rejected or accepted. If the application is accepted, there is a tenancy agreement between the landlord and the tenants. The application form usually requires the tenant to sign the landlord's lease. In the rare case when the lease is not signed, the parties can enforce the agreement that arose when the landlord notified the tenant of accepting the application. Unless it is the landlord's fault that the lease was not signed, the landlord can probably rely on the terms in the lease because the tenant was obliged under the agreement to sign it.

Leases vary considerably in formality and clarity. Large landlords usually use a long, detailed document that covers virtually every situation that could arise. Naturally, these leases are written to protect the landlord, just as car-rental contracts protect the car-rental company. The RTA overrides any term in a tenancy agreement that conflicts with the RTA (s. 3(1)). It might appear that a lease no longer matters because the RTA can override it; however, there are some situations in which the terms of the lease do matter. For example, a lease may specify rights of entry in addition to those the RTA provides (see Chapter 6).

Landlords sometimes obtain leases from the publishers of legal forms, such as Dye & Durham, or from industry groups, such as landlord associations or real estate boards. These leases are usually designed to protect landlords, not tenants. Like landlords' own leases, these leases are usually consistent with the Ontario legislation and relatively up to date.

Landlords and tenants sometimes use forms from self-help publications or computerized leases sold as part of business software products. These forms are often difficult to work with because they are often inconsistent with the Ontario legislation or out of date.

Oral Tenancy Agreements

Some small landlords make oral tenancy agreements with their tenants, although this is uncommon among large landlords. Oral tenancy agreements often come back to haunt the parties when a dispute arises over when the tenancy is to end. This issue is often complicated if the landlord has accepted a series of postdated cheques. For example, if the tenants want to stay, they could argue that the cheques reflect an agreement for a term until the cheques run out. If the tenants want to leave, they could argue that the cheques were provided for convenience and do not represent an agreement for a term until the cheques run out. Similar arguments may be made by the landlord. At the least, parties who make an oral tenancy agreement should confirm the most important elements of the agreement in a letter as soon as possible. If the letter is signed by both parties, a written tenancy agreement exists.

Implied Tenancy Agreements

Implied tenancy agreements can arise in numerous ways, most commonly through an unauthorized assignment. Take, for example, the situation of a tenant, George, who has a friend, John, move in with him. Unless John's presence creates an overcrowding situation, the landlord has no effective remedy even though the landlord did not agree to rent to John, and John may have poor references from previous landlords. Assume that John signs and gives the landlord a rent cheque and that the landlord cashes the cheque without comment. If this goes on for some months with George's approval, then arguably there is an implied tenancy agreement between the landlord and John, or perhaps between the landlord and George and John together. The landlord can avoid this situation by checking the name on the rent cheque, but many landlords do not do this regularly.

Licences

The RTA includes **licences** within tenancy agreements by the definition in s. 2. The RTA also includes rooms in boarding or lodging houses as rental units by the definition in s. 2 of "rental unit." Before 1987, the law distinguished between tenancies—in which the tenant had exclusive possession of the rental unit—and licences—in which the rooming-house operator retained control over what happened in the room and the occupant did not have exclusive possession. Now these rooms are clearly subject to the RTA unless the roomer is required to share a bathroom or kitchen with the owner or a member of the owner's immediate family, and the owner or family member lives in the building. If the rent is charged and collected on a weekly basis, a landlord or tenant may terminate the tenancy on 28 days notice, rather than the usual 60 days notice, but roomers are deemed to be tenants. They have all the rights of other tenants, including the right not to be evicted for a reason other than a reason set out in the RTA.

licence
an agreement for the use of a property in which the owner does not give the user the full rights that a tenant would have

INFORMATION THAT A LANDLORD MUST PROVIDE TO TENANTS

Whether or not a tenancy agreement is in writing, a landlord is required to provide to the tenant general information explaining the rights and responsibilities of landlords and tenants, the role of the Landlord and Tenant Board ("the board"), and how to contact the board (s. 11(1)). The form providing that information is available on the board's website. Most landlords will attach the form with the information to the lease.

Written tenancy agreements are required to set out the landlord's legal name and address for service (that is, the address at which a tenant can give the landlord any notices) (s. 12(1)). The owner of a property is a landlord. If the owner employs a property manager who decides on whether to rent to tenants and whether to evict tenants, that property manager is also a landlord under the RTA. In that case, the lease should set out the property manager's name and address. If the lease does not set out the landlord's name and address, the tenant's obligation to pay rent is suspended until the landlord gives the tenant written notice of its name and address (s. 12(4)). When starting to act for a landlord, you should check whether your client's leases include a legal name and address. If they do not, you should bring s. 12 to your client's attention and recommend that your client comply with it.

After making an oral tenancy agreement, the landlord is required to give the tenant a written notice setting out the landlord's legal name and address for service (s. 12(3)). Until the landlord gives that notice, the tenant is not obliged to pay the rent (s. 12(4)). However, once the notice is given, the rent is due for the period before the notice was given (s. 12(5)).

The purpose of s. 12 of the RTA is to ensure that tenants have a means of contacting their landlord.

RULES RELATED TO LANDLORDS SELECTING TENANTS

There are no restrictions in the RTA respecting a landlord's right to accept or reject prospective tenants. However, there are restrictions under the Ontario *Human Rights Code*. The prohibited grounds of discrimination are race, ancestry, place of origin, colour, ethnic origin, citizenship, religion, sex (that is, whether a person is male or female, now more commonly termed gender), sexual orientation (that is, whether a person is gay, lesbian, straight, or bisexual), age, marital status, family status, pregnancy, handicap, or receipt of public assistance (*Human Rights Code*, s. 2(1)).

In general, a landlord can refuse to rent for reasons not listed in the *Human Rights Code*. For example, a landlord can refuse to rent to smokers or to paralegals.

Landlords cannot refuse to rent to people because they are receiving public assistance. In addition, landlords cannot set a fixed rule about the maximum proportion of a person's income that can go to paying the rent. For example, a landlord cannot say, "I will rent only to people who can pay the rent to me with less than 30 percent of their income" (or less than 40 percent, or any fixed percentage). The landlord can take prospective tenants' income into account along with credit checks, their credit history (past history of paying their rent and other obligations), their credit references, and whether they can provide a co-signer or guarantor. In fact, many tenants on social assistance or receiving Old Age Security pension pay more than 30 or 40 percent of their income as rent. Some pay over 50 percent.

While landlords cannot refuse to rent to people on the basis of their gender, there is an exception to the prohibition on discrimination because of gender where all the residential accommodation in a building, other than that of the owner or the owner's family, is restricted to persons who are of the same gender.

The board will not rule on complaints against landlords by people whose rental applications were refused. If a prospective tenant believes that the landlord has unlawfully discriminated against them by refusing to rent to them, the tenant can make a complaint to the Human Rights Tribunal of Ontario.

No Pet Provisions

Landlords can refuse to rent to a prospective tenant because they own a pet. However, once the landlord and tenant enter into the tenancy agreement, any prohibition in the tenancy agreement against having a pet is void (s. 14). In other words, a landlord can ask a tenant to promise not to bring in a pet, but if the tenant breaks the promise, the landlord cannot rely on that provision of the tenancy agreement to claim any relief. The landlord cannot claim damages for the mere breach of the agreement in Small Claims Court nor can the landlord evict the tenant solely for breaking the agreement or for having a pet.

If a pet causes damage to the property, is inherently dangerous (for example, a poisonous snake), causes serious interference with the reasonable enjoyment of other tenants (for example, messes up the lawn and the owner doesn't clean up the excrement), or causes the landlord or another tenant in the building to suffer a serious allergic reaction, the landlord may bring an application to evict the tenant (ss. 62, 64, 65, 66, and 76). In some cases the board may allow the tenant time to remove the pet, and only failing to do so will result in the tenant being evicted.

Where the rental unit is in a condominium, there may be a condominium rule or bylaw against having pets in the building. In that case, the condominium board could bring an application to the Ontario Superior Court to force the tenant to remove the pet. Generally, the tenant would be responsible for the condominium board's legal costs in bringing that application. In that respect, condominium owners have greater rights than landlords or tenants of units that are not condominiums.

KEY TERMS

grandfathered	tandem parking space
licence	utilities

REVIEW QUESTIONS

1. What basic elements are addressed in most tenancy agreements?

2. Can a landlord charge a tenant an amount for the electricity they consume based on a separate meter?

3. When does a landlord have to provide a refrigerator manufactured after December 31, 2002?

4. In what circumstances can a landlord charge a tenant an amount for water based on water consumption in the whole rental building?

5. Does a tenancy agreement have to be in writing?

6. Name the three types of tenancy agreements.

7. Is it legal for a landlord to refuse to rent to any of the following?

    a. paralegals

    b. smokers

    c. non-Christians

    d. Christians

    e. recipients of social assistance

    f. same-sex couples

    g. people with children

The Landlord's Obligation to Repair

5

Under the *Residential Tenancies Act, 2006* (RTA), a landlord is responsible for the maintenance and repair of a rental unit and the common areas of a residential complex. There are three separate and distinct obligations:

1. to provide and maintain the unit and complex in a good state of repair;
2. to provide and maintain the unit and complex fit for habitation; and
3. to comply with health, safety, housing, and maintenance standards (s. 20(1)).

These obligations apply even if the tenant was aware of a state of non-repair or of a contravention of a health, safety, housing, or maintenance standard before entering into the tenancy agreement (s. 20(2)).

"A GOOD STATE OF REPAIR"

According to the case law, the requirement to keep the unit and complex in "a good state of repair" does not mean that the premises must be kept in or restored to new condition. If a new item must be provided in order to repair an old item, then that must be done. However, if work done renders the conditions in good repair, then that is sufficient. For example, it may be necessary to replace only certain boards on a porch, or to replace only certain supports or parts of a banister on a railing. On a stove, it may be necessary to replace only certain heating elements. In a refrigerator, it may be necessary to replace only a compressor or a shelf. If the apartment was rented with an old refrigerator, then it is sufficient to replace an old refrigerator with a used refrigerator. If an apartment was rented 12 or 15 years ago with a new refrigerator, it is sufficient to replace the now used refrigerator with a used refrigerator. (As a practical matter, it is more difficult to obtain good used refrigerators than good used stoves. Therefore, a landlord may find it more cost-effective to replace a broken refrigerator with a new refrigerator.)

All the amenities that the tenant rents are covered by the repair obligation. This applies whether or not all the amenities are listed in the tenancy agreement.

However, a distinction must be drawn between non-repair and the removal of a service or facility. If a landlord closes a swimming pool or a laundry room, that action would be dealt with under the sections of the RTA covering the discontinuance of services and facilities (see Chapter 19).

There is a grey area if, for example, a unit has an air conditioner in it when the unit is rented, but the air conditioner is broken. Generally, a landlord and a tenant cannot contract out of the RTA. However, it is clear that the landlord and the tenant can specify the services and facilities that are included in the tenancy agreement. Therefore, in our opinion, if the tenancy agreement provides that air conditioning is not a service or facility included in the rent, the landlord would not be obliged to repair a broken air conditioning unit that was present in the unit. (As a practical matter, it would be much better for the landlord to remove the broken air conditioner before showing the rental unit to prospective tenants.)

Generally, the requirement to provide the unit and the complex in a good state of repair does not oblige the landlord to improve the complex. According to the case law, the quality of the repair that is required is what a reasonable tenant would consider satisfactory, even if a particular tenant finds the repair unsatisfactory because of the tenant's high standards.

FITNESS FOR HABITATION

The second part of the landlord's repair obligation is to keep the premises fit for habitation. The standard of fitness for habitation requires the landlord to keep the rental unit and the complex in such a condition that it is both physically and mentally healthy for a reasonable tenant to live there. The standard is not breached only when the tenant cannot live there without taking extreme measures. The landlord's obligation is to maintain heat; to provide drinkable cold water and hot water suitable for washing dishes, clothes, and persons, with a reasonable amount of water pressure for most of the time; and to provide adequate ventilation, serviceable plumbing facilities, secure windows and doors, and adequate light.

In addition, if other tenants are rendering the premises unsafe, the landlord must take reasonable measures to make them safe again. For example, if tenants are selling illegal weapons in the complex, the landlord must take all reasonable steps to stop that behaviour reasonably promptly. There is a general principle of law that a person is not responsible for the illegal act of a third person. However, the landlord is obliged to take any steps that are reasonably required to eliminate the negative effects of illegal acts by other tenants and by outsiders on the landlord's tenants.

HEALTH, SAFETY, HOUSING, AND MAINTENANCE STANDARDS

The RTA makes a landlord responsible for complying with health, safety, housing, and maintenance standards.

The standards referred to are primarily municipal property standards, as well as any standards set by the health department of the city or municipality in which you are working. Maintenance standards are prescribed under the RTA in O. Reg 517/06, but they do not apply if the municipality has maintenance standards applicable to both the interior and exterior of properties (s. 224(1)(b) and O. Reg. 517/06, s. 4). That is the case in all of Ontario's larger municipalities. If you are dealing with a case in a municipality that does not have property standards, then the standards set for maintenance under the RTA will apply (s. 224(1)). Breach of those standards constitutes a breach of s. 20 of the RTA. If the municipality has property standards but they do not apply to the inside of dwelling units, then the standards set under the RTA for the inside of dwelling units will apply (O. Reg. 517/06, s. 4).

ENERGY CONSERVATION STANDARDS

The RTA imposes an additional standard for landlords where their tenants are responsible for paying for the utilities. Those provisions are set out in ss. 137 and 138 of the RTA, and in regulation O. Reg. 394/10.

If a landlord receives a heat, hydro, and/or water bill for the rental complex and divides the cost among tenants, the landlord is obliged to ensure that the unit satisfies the prescribed utility conservation rules. This includes ensuring that all appliances provided by the landlord meet the prescribed requirements (s. 138(5)). The rules also require the landlord to provide prospective tenants with information about the recent electricity consumption in the unit.

A similar requirement exists for electricity conservation if a **smart meter** is installed (s. 137(7)).

O. Reg. 394/10 also provides rules for obtaining consent for the transfer of the responsibility to pay for electricity to the tenant from the landlord.

smart meter
a meter that tracks how much electricity is being used and relays to the hydro provider the time of day in which that electricity is being used

REPAIR OBLIGATIONS AT TENANT TURNOVER

When a tenant vacates a rental unit, a landlord will usually inspect the unit to determine whether the outgoing tenant has caused any damage, and then repair the damage and any deficiencies in the unit before renting it to a new tenant. If there is time between tenants, the landlord has a duty to inspect the unit to ensure that it is delivered to the new tenant in compliance with the landlord's maintenance and repair obligations. The landlord is entitled to rent the unit to a new tenant before the repairs are done, and then do the repairs before the new tenant moves in.

It is an excellent idea for a landlord to complete an in-unit inspection report when the tenant moves in, so that the landlord has evidence that the unit was delivered in compliance with the landlord's maintenance obligation. Ideally, this inspection is done with the tenant. Landlords often use a form that lists the various aspects of the unit, room by room, including hardwood floors, carpets, walls, ceilings, appliances, and plumbing fixtures. Usually there are columns on the form to be marked off regarding whether items are in excellent, good, fair, or inadequate condition.

A practical problem arises for a landlord when the tenant who is leaving moves out on the last day of the month, and the new tenant moves in either a few hours after the tenant leaves or on the next day. Small landlords may not have enough time to do all the repairs that they would usually do themselves. Large landlords may not have enough staff to do all of the repairs that may be required. Arguably, some repairs should be conducted before the departing tenant moves out; however, many repairs, particularly those of a cosmetic nature, are best done after the departing tenant has moved out. As a practical matter, therefore, the Landlord and Tenant Board ("the board") will not award tenants a remedy for minor or cosmetic non-repairs that last only for a few days at the beginning of the tenancy, as long as landlords can show that they or their staff were working diligently to complete all the necessary repairs in the units being turned over. This applies especially at heavy turnover dates—that is, May 1, June 1, July 1, and September 1.

The cleaning of a rental unit between tenants can also be an issue. When a unit is vacant for some time, the landlord will usually clean it in order to make it more attractive to a new tenant. However, when there is no time between the move out and the move in, the condition of the unit will depend on the cleanliness of the tenant who moved out. New tenants may well want to clean the unit themselves in order to get on with moving in their furniture and dishes. In that case, the board would be reluctant to provide a tenant with a remedy even if the unit was not particularly clean. However, the board would be sympathetic if the unit was absolutely filthy and the landlord did nothing at all to clean it. The landlord would be expected to do at least some level of cleaning so that the unit is more or less ready to be moved into. In some cases, a landlord will attempt to charge the cost of cleaning the unit to the tenant who has moved out. Unless the unit was equally dirty when the tenant moved in, the landlord would be entitled to charge the outgoing tenant for any cleaning required if the tenant failed to maintain the "ordinary cleanliness" of the unit (s. 33).

INSPECTION VERSUS REQUESTS FOR REPAIRS

Once a tenant has moved in, it is generally considered that the landlord does not have a duty to inspect the rental unit on an annual or biannual basis to determine whether there are any items that require repair. Usually, tenants do not like landlords inspecting their units in a detailed manner. Like homeowners, tenants may leave certain things unrepaired until a convenient time arises to repair them or to have them repaired. For example, the proper repair of damage to a wall would require tenants to remove all of their wall hangings and move their furniture away from the wall so that the landlord can repair and repaint the whole wall. Tenants may find this an inconvenience either at any time or at a particular time in their lives. Therefore, it is generally sufficient for a landlord to have a system in place under which the landlord responds to requests for repairs.

The landlord's response time must be reasonable. What time is reasonable depends on the nature of the repair required and on all the circumstances. The relevant circumstances include

- what impact the repair problem has on the tenant;
- what is required to fix the problem;
- how much time is required to obtain replacement parts;
- whether the landlord needs to call in an outside contractor;
- whether the repair request is made on a weekday or on a Saturday, Sunday, or holiday; and
- whether other more serious repair problems are occupying the landlord or the repair personnel.

For example, suppose a tenant reported a leaking tap on December 23, 2011. Other priorities and staff holidays could prevent it from being looked after through the holiday season. Suppose there was a power outage throughout the city. A landlord who had other priorities concerning the building could reasonably put off the tap repair until the landlord dealt with more important matters. However, the tap leak should be repaired as soon as the more important matters are dealt with.

Landlords can require that the tenant do the repair if the repair is required because of the wilful or negligent conduct of the tenant. In other words, if the tenant breaks something, the tenant is responsible for repairing it. There are sometimes cases of uncertainty because an item is broken during the tenant's use of it, but the tenant argues that the cause was wear and tear. In an arguable case, the landlord is usually better off doing the repair.

Under some conditions, a landlord may have a duty to inspect. For example, if systems in a building are reaching the end of their normal useful life, the landlord may need to inspect those items to determine whether they require replacement. An example of this is water pipes. Depending on the quality of the pipes, they may last up to 40 or 50 years. However, if on inspection it is apparent that the pipes will fail earlier than that, then the landlord must pay proper attention to the issue. Also, if pipes burst in some apartments within a building, then the landlord may have an obligation to inspect all of the pipes to determine whether they require replacement. The same applies to electrical wiring, heating, roofing, foundations, basement drainage systems, and hallway ventilating and air conditioning equipment. In apartment buildings there are many systems that the landlord needs to care for properly, and this includes preventive maintenance and inspections.

EXTENT OF LANDLORD'S LIABILITY

There is some uncertainty in the case law about the exact nature of the landlord's liability under the maintenance and repair provision of the RTA.

It is clear that the landlord cannot avoid the obligation to repair when the need for repair has arisen through normal wear and tear. If an item in an apartment is not in a good state of repair, it must be repaired by the landlord unless it was damaged by the present tenant. If undue damage is caused by the wilful or negligent conduct of the present tenant (or other persons permitted in the complex by the tenant), the tenant is responsible for repairing it (s. 34).

It is also clear that, regarding repairs, the landlord's obligation is absolute. Apart from damage caused by a specific tenant and apart from the discontinuance of services or facilities (discussed in Chapter 19), the landlord has an obligation to each tenant to repair anything that is broken in the tenant's unit or in the common areas. Even when damage is caused by a specific tenant, the landlord must still ensure that the item is repaired to meet their responsibility under property standards bylaws and under their obligations under s. 20 of the RTA; therefore, the landlord may end up doing the repair and charging back the cost of the repair to the specific tenant.

The area of uncertainty is the landlord's responsibility for damage to a tenant's belongings or for personal injury that results from a repair problem. The case law suggests that the landlord has certain duties to inspect (discussed above), and thus the landlord's obligation is high; but the landlord is not subject to absolute liability and is not responsible for making good any damage that a tenant suffers through problems that develop at the landlord's property. Put another way, the landlord is not an insurer for the tenant. For this reason, landlords often recommend that their tenants carry insurance. Insurance companies routinely pay damage claims to tenants without exercising their right to claim against the landlord in the tenant's name for the damage.

Until a problem manifests itself, a landlord is probably not liable for damage to a tenant's belongings or for personal injury. However, after a problem has occurred once or twice, the landlord probably has a duty to investigate the cause of the problem and to eliminate the problem. If the landlord fails to act properly, the landlord may well be liable for damage to a tenant's belongings or for personal injury damages.

SUCCESSOR LANDLORDS

abatement of rent
reduction in rent because of
deficiencies in a rental unit
or building, or other
breaches by the landlord

If a landlord buys a property and the property was in a state of disrepair, the purchasing landlord (the "successor landlord") is responsible for **abatements of rent** to which tenants are entitled because of this lack of repair. Purchasing landlords find this requirement harsh because they do not feel responsible for existing disrepair. However, when taking over a property, the purchaser becomes responsible for the property's condition. If purchasing landlords are sensible, they will have taken into account the condition of the property when negotiating the property's purchase price. In extreme situations, the purchasing landlord will need to make an adjustment in his or her calculations, or an outright adjustment in the closing of the transaction, to account for deficiencies in the property.

In our opinion, the purchasing landlord would not be responsible for paying the tenant any abatement or reduction of rent for the period prior to taking over the property. Tenant advocates sometimes take the opposite position. In practice, this situation is difficult for the purchasing landlord, because tenants may simply withhold the abatement or reduction from their rent and take the position that the purchasing landlord has to sort out the claim with the vendor. The purchasing landlord should make the date at which he or she took over the property clear to the board. It is usually not helpful to show how horrible the conditions were when the new landlord took over the property, because the new landlord is responsible for those conditions until they are appropriately rectified.

RECOMMENDED TENANT ACTION

If a landlord fails to fulfill repair obligations, the tenant should make a request in writing for the landlord to do so.

In some cases it is appropriate for the tenant to give the landlord a letter stating that if the landlord has not done the repair by a certain date, the tenant will do it and deduct the repair cost from the rent. A broken refrigerator, for example, should be repaired quickly or the tenant's use of the kitchen will be seriously hindered. This haste would also apply when an entire stove is inoperable. However, if one element of a stove is inoperable, the repair request does not require immediate attention. In this case, a tenant might give a landlord a time limit, but it should be a reasonable time limit of perhaps two weeks. Some landlords do not take kindly to being given this kind of ultimatum by their tenants. Therefore, tenants should resort to stating a date only if they are of the view that the situation has deteriorated into an adversarial one.

If the letter approach does not obtain the desired action, a tenant has two effect-ive recourses. First, the tenant can make a complaint to the municipal property standards office.[1] In many cities it is best to call between 8 a.m. and 9 a.m. because that is when the office is sorting which property standards officer (PSO) will deal with which calls. The PSO will arrange a time to inspect the problem in the next few days. Once the PSO is satisfied that there is a repair problem, the officer can do one of three things:

1. notify the landlord informally,
2. issue a notice of violation, or
3. issue a work order.

In most cities, the PSO will notify the landlord informally if the landlord has usually cooperated with informal notices in the past. The PSO will issue a notice of violation if the officer believes that the landlord needs a "wake-up call," or if there are a number of significant problems. The PSO will issue an actual work order if the landlord has not cooperated in the past or if the city's policy calls for it. The landlord can appeal the work order to a committee of the city. In the case of a prov-incial work order under s. 225 of the RTA, the landlord can appeal the order to the board under s. 226.

A tenant's second recourse is to apply to the board under ss. 29(1) and 30(1). The tenant or former tenant may apply for an order determining that the landlord breached the obligations outlined under s. 20(1). The application must be made within one year after the day the alleged conduct giving rise to the application oc-curred (s. 29(2)). The process for tenant applications is discussed in Chapter 8.

NECESSITY OF THE REPAIR

Tenants are sometimes deprived of the use of some of their amenities while the landlord carries out necessary repairs. For example, because of water and salt in-filtration, balconies or parking garages may need to be closed for repairs.

For a number of years the law was unclear regarding whether tenants were en-titled to rent abatements for necessary repairs. Consider a balcony that is closed for two months because it is undergoing necessary repairs. Tenant representatives argued that, because apartments with balconies rent for say $20 or $30 more than apartments without balconies, tenants should be entitled to abatements of at least $20 or $30 if they do not have access to their balconies. Landlord representatives argued that it is unfair for landlords to reduce their revenue stream while they are spending large sums of money to do necessary repairs. Moreover, landlord repre-sentatives argued that it cannot be that *doing* a specific repair is a breach of the landlord's responsibility (serious interference with a tenant's reasonable enjoy-ment) but at the same time *not doing* the repair is also a breach (of the obligation to repair).

---

[1] Where there is no municipal property standards bylaw, a tenant can make a complaint to the enforcement office of the Ministry of Municipal Affairs and Housing. The enforcement office will investigate whether the landlord is in compliance with the maintenance standards set out in O. Reg. 517/06.

A regulation was introduced in October 2002 under the *Tenant Protection Act, 1997* that resolved this issue (O. Reg. 286/02). That provision has largely been incorporated into s. 8 of O. Reg. 516/06. That section sets out standards and criteria to be applied by the board when determining whether a landlord, superintendent, or agent of a landlord has substantially interfered with the reasonable enjoyment of a rental unit or complex in carrying out maintenance, repairs, or capital improvements to the unit. The regulation also sets out criteria to be applied in determining whether to order an abatement of rent when such interference has been found.

Maintenance, repairs, or capital improvements are not considered substantial interference with the tenant unless the carrying out of the work constituted an interference with the tenant's use and enjoyment of the complex that was unreasonable in the circumstances. Furthermore, even if the interference was unreasonable in the circumstances, the board is, generally, not to order an abatement of rent if the landlord gave advance notice to the tenant; the notice was accurate, comprehensive, and given in a timely manner; the necessary building permits were obtained; the work was carried out at reasonable times; the duration of the work was reasonable; and the landlord took reasonable steps to minimize any interference resulting from noise associated with the work. To be "eligible" for that treatment, the work must fall into one of the following categories:

1. necessary to protect or restore the physical integrity of the complex;
2. necessary to maintain maintenance, health, or safety standards required by law;
3. necessary to maintain the provision of a plumbing, heating, mechanical, electrical, ventilation, or air conditioning system;
4. provides access for persons with disabilities;
5. promotes energy or water conservation; or
6. maintains or improves the security of the complex.

Where the board finds there was substantial interference and an abatement is not prohibited, as outlined above, the board shall consider the following when determining whether it is appropriate to order an abatement of rent and the amount of the abatement:

1. the nature, duration, and degree of interference with the tenant's reasonable enjoyment caused by the carrying out of the work;
2. whether the tenant is responsible for any undue delay in the carrying out of the work;
3. the steps taken by the landlord during the work to minimize interference with the tenant's reasonable enjoyment;
4. whether the tenant has taken advantage of any service provided by the landlord or arrangement made by the landlord that would minimize interference with the tenant's reasonable enjoyment;
5. whether a failure to carry out the work could reasonably be expected to result in any of the following within a reasonable period of time:

a. interference with the tenant's reasonable enjoyment of the rental unit or the residential complex;

b. a reduction or discontinuation of a service or facility;

c. damage or additional damage to the rental unit, the residential complex, or anything in the unit or complex;

d. risk to any person's health or personal safety; or

e. a breach of s. 20(1) of the Act by the landlord.

An abatement award is limited to 25 percent of the monthly rent for a rental unit unless

1. a larger abatement is warranted in the circumstances because the substantial interference with the tenant's reasonable enjoyment far exceeded the level that would normally be expected and

2. an adjudicator is satisfied that

   a. the work is not eligible work;

   b. the work was carried out at unreasonable times or at a time that is not permitted under any applicable noise-control bylaw;

   c. the work was carried out in a manner that contravened a condition or requirement of a building permit;

   d. the work was carried out over a period of time far in excess of the amount of time that normally would be required, after taking into consideration any exceptional circumstances beyond the control of the landlord; or

   e. the landlord refused to take reasonable steps during the work to minimize interference with the tenant's reasonable enjoyment of the rental unit or residential complex.

An abatement award cannot exceed 100 percent of the monthly rent for each month or part of a month during which an adjudicator determines that the work substantially interfered with the tenant's reasonable enjoyment of the rental unit or residential complex.

KEY TERMS

abatement of rent
smart meter

REVIEW QUESTIONS

1. What are the three obligations of repair, and how do they differ?

2. How long does a landlord have to do a repair?

3. If a former tenant caused damage in the unit, does the landlord need to fix it for a new tenant?

4. If the current tenant causes damage in the unit, does the landlord need to fix it?

5. Is a tenant entitled to a rent abatement while the landlord is in the process of doing a major repair, and if so, under what circumstances?

6. Should a landlord do regular inspections of the state of repair of a rental unit? If so, how often?

Other Rights and Obligations

6

ILLEGAL RENT AND CHARGES (BY LANDLORD OR TENANT)

If a landlord charges more rent than allowed under the *Residential Tenancies Act, 2006* (RTA), a tenant or former tenant can apply for an order to force the landlord to pay back the rent (s. 135). The application is also available for any illegal charges that the landlord has made, including charges associated with the rental application or illegal payments, such as a requirement that the tenant pay for goods or services in order to rent the unit (ss. 134(1) and 135). It is illegal for a landlord to require a tenant to pay for painting a unit or to buy furniture, for example. A prospective tenant may apply for a repayment order even if the person never becomes a tenant (s. 135(2)). The application must be made within one year of the date of the illegal charge (s. 135(4)). These issues will be addressed in more detail in Chapter 18.

Tenants are also prohibited from requiring other tenants of the unit to pay illegal charges (s. 134(2)). Tenants may want to levy charges when they are subletting their rental unit or bringing in a roommate. They are prohibited from charging more for their unit than the rent they have to pay or from renting rooms for a total of more than they have to pay (s. 134(3)(a)). Tenants are prohibited from charging bonuses or key money for subletting or assigning their rental units (s. 134(3)(b)). Tenants or prospective sublet tenants of a tenant may apply for an order requiring the tenant who took their money to repay any such charges (s. 135(3)). The application must be made within one year of the date of the illegal charge (s. 135(4)).

INTERFERENCE WITH QUIET ENJOYMENT (BY LANDLORD)

Besides failing to maintain a rental unit, other conduct that the landlord may not engage in includes

- withholding a reasonable supply of any vital service (s. 21);
- interfering with the reasonable enjoyment of the rental unit or residential complex (s. 22);
- harassing, obstructing, coercing, threatening, or interfering with the tenant (s. 23);
- altering the locking system on a door of the unit or the complex without giving replacement keys (s. 24); and
- illegally entering the rental unit (s. 25).

Under s. 29, a tenant can apply to the Landlord and Tenant Board ("the board") for an order that the landlord or a superintendent or agent has committed one of the prohibited acts listed above. Such an application is referred to as a "tenant's rights application," and is made using Form T2. Under s. 31, the board may

1. order that the landlord, superintendent, or agent may not engage in any further activities listed above against any of the tenants in the residential complex;

2. order that the landlord, superintendent, or agent reimburse the tenant for any reasonable costs the tenant has incurred or will incur as a result of the improper action;

3. order an abatement of rent;

4. order that the landlord pay to the board an administrative fine not exceeding the greater of $10,000 or the monetary jurisdiction of the Small Claims Court (which is now $25,000);

5. order that the tenancy be terminated; or

6. make any other order that it considers appropriate.

Administrative fines are described in more detail in Chapter 20.

For an order to be appropriate, it must be related in a reasonable way to the rental unit, or the residential complex, and to the landlord's prohibited behaviour, or the prohibited behaviour of the superintendent or agent. For example, the board would have no jurisdiction to order the landlord or superintendent to get a haircut or to dress differently.

See Appendix D for Guideline 6, which the board has issued to provide guidance about various matters that frequently arise in such applications, including:

- properly naming respondents;
- abatement orders, and the factors that should be considered when deciding the amount of an abatement;
- orders prohibiting actions against tenants;
- orders terminating tenancies; and
- compensation for future rent and moving expenses.

ENTRY

Privacy and Entry Rights

The RTA sets out the conditions under which a landlord is allowed to enter a rental unit. A landlord is prohibited from entering a rental unit except in accordance with the RTA. Section 25 provides that "a landlord may enter a rental unit only in accordance with section 26 or 27." The RTA ensures that tenants have privacy but at the same time allows a landlord entry in order to manage the property properly.

The RTA sets out a landlord's rights to enter in a clear manner and gives a landlord such rights even if they are not provided for in the tenancy agreement.

The RTA deals with different circumstances in different ways. In some circumstances the landlord may enter a rental unit at any time without any notice. In other circumstances, the landlord may enter between 8 a.m. and 8 p.m. if the landlord informs or attempts to inform the tenant of the intention to enter. In still other circumstances, the landlord may enter the rental unit only between 8 a.m. and 8 p.m., and only if the landlord has given a written notice to the tenant at least 24 hours before the time of entry.

Emergencies

The landlord may enter the rental unit at any time without any notice in cases of emergency or if the tenant consents to the entry at the time of entry (s. 26(1)). An "emergency" is not defined in the RTA; therefore, it would be given its ordinary dictionary meaning and further construed according to the rights and obligations of the parties under the RTA. For example, a burst pipe in a tenant's unit would be an emergency. This situation may come to the landlord's attention because the tenant in whose unit the pipe has burst calls the landlord, or, more commonly, because a tenant in the unit below calls the landlord to report a flood. In that situation, the landlord may enter immediately and without notice in order to avoid further damage to the building and to the property of tenants. As another example, a landlord who observes an open window under weather conditions sufficiently cold to freeze pipes would have the right to enter to close the window to avoid damage to the property and to the property of tenants.

There are other situations that might not appear to be emergencies, but would be treated as emergencies under the RTA. Most older buildings do not have pressure-compensating faucets in the bathroom and kitchen. This is one important reason that landlords usually prohibit tenants from operating clothes washers and dishwashers in their apartments. Operating such appliances on older faucets can cause "water switching," where hot water comes out of the cold water tap or out of the single tap when the tap is turned on for cold water. Therefore, when water switching occurs in one unit, it appears that a landlord has the right to enter other units without notice in order to seek the source of the problem and prevent possible personal injury to tenants.

In all of the circumstances discussed above, landlords should exercise courtesy by knocking on the door loudly and announcing their presence on entering the apartment. Particular care should be taken if, upon entering the apartment, it appears that a tenant is in the bathroom, because the tenant may have difficulty hearing the landlord and may be frightened or embarrassed by a surprise contact.

Tenant's Consent

A landlord may enter a rental unit at any time without notice if the tenant consents to the entry at the time of entry. This situation often arises if the tenant has requested a repair and the landlord is on site or has a repair person on site for another job. Entry with consent can also occur when the landlord goes to the tenant's unit to discuss something with the tenant, and the tenant invites the landlord in to sit down to have the discussion. A landlord who wants to enter a rental unit for any reason is perfectly at liberty to ring the bell or knock on the tenant's door and ask for permission to enter. As a practical matter, landlords should observe the normal hours during which the tenant can be expected to be awake and available.

When a landlord is selling a small property, the landlord will often want to show the property to numerous prospective buyers. This may annoy the resident tenants. Tenants will not usually see any benefit from the purchase, and they may in fact end up being evicted by the purchaser so that the purchaser can occupy the unit. Thus, tenants are sometimes reluctant to permit the landlord entry to show the unit to prospective buyers. The landlord has a right to enter with 24 hours written notice, as described below. However, it is usually more convenient if the landlord (or the real estate agent) and the tenant can work out times at which the property may be shown. Occasionally, tenants are unreasonable in this regard, and then it is for the real estate agent and the landlord to determine whether it is easier to give the 24 hours written notice or to comply with the tenant's terms for consent to entry.

Some landlords are required to clean the rental unit under the tenancy agreement. That requirement occurs most often in rooming houses. To carry out cleaning obligations, landlords may enter the rental unit without notice during the times specified in the tenancy agreement, or, if no times are specified, between the hours of 8 a.m. and 8 p.m. (s. 26(2)).

Showings to Prospective Tenants

A landlord may enter a rental unit without written notice in order to show the unit to a prospective tenant under three conditions. First, the landlord and the tenant must have agreed to terminate the tenancy, or one of them must have given notice of termination to the other. Second, the entry must take place between 8 a.m. and 8 p.m. Third, the landlord, before entering, must inform the tenant of the intention to enter, specifying the time, or make a reasonable effort to inform the tenant (s. 26(3)). The RTA does not define a "reasonable effort," and what is considered reasonable will depend on the circumstances. A reasonable effort to notify the tenant presumably includes making a telephone call to both the tenant's residence and the tenant's workplace (if the landlord knows that number). If the landlord knows only one number, the landlord should try twice to reach the tenant at that number. If the tenant provides the landlord with a different telephone number, such as that of a neighbour or a relative for the purpose of notifying the tenant, the landlord should try to contact the tenant at that number. Sending the tenant an email can also be considered a reasonable effort if it is clear that the tenant checks his or her email frequently. If the landlord has no telephone number for the tenant and no email address, a reasonable effort may include the landlord's going to the unit to post a note on the door of the unit or to slide a note under the door, telling the tenant when the landlord will return with the prospective tenant.

Entry with Written Notice

A landlord may enter a rental unit after giving written notice to the tenant at least 24 hours before the time of entry, provided that one or more of the following purposes listed in s. 27(1) apply:

1. to carry out a repair or replacement or do work in the rental unit;

2. to allow a potential mortgagee or insurer of the residential complex to view the rental unit;

3. to allow an engineer, architect, or similar professional to inspect the unit for the purpose of converting the property to a condominium;

4. to inspect the rental unit to determine whether it requires repair; or

5. for any other reasonable reason for entry specified in the tenancy agreement.

In addition, landlords or their real estate agents may enter a rental unit after giving 24 hours written notice to allow a potential purchaser to view the rental unit (s. 27(2)).

The written notice must specify the reason for entry, the day of entry, and the time of entry between 8 a.m. and 8 p.m.

Landlords often ask how exact they have to be in giving the time of entry. In our opinion, that depends on how exact the landlords are able to be in specifying the time of entry. If the landlord has made an appointment with a potential purchaser or insurer, the landlord may well be able to specify the time as a two-hour period—for example, between 10 a.m. and noon. If the landlord has arranged for a repair person to attend at the rental unit to make a repair, the landlord cannot usually be that exact. Electricians, plumbers, and other repair or delivery people typically tell owners that they will be at the property sometime in the morning or sometime in the afternoon. If told that the repair person will be at the unit sometime in the morning, for a repair that is expected to take two hours, the landlord might want to specify the time of entry as between 8 a.m. and 3 p.m. Note that this period extends into the first half of the afternoon to allow entry if the repair person is later, or the repair time takes longer than expected.

Note also that the reference to a potential mortgagee or insurer includes an agent of the potential mortgagee or insurer, including a valuer who is being asked to give an opinion of the property value to the potential mortgagee or insurer. Provincial property assessors or valuers acting on behalf of the owner are not included in the list. It would be ideal if rights to enter for these persons were specified in the tenancy agreement. Alternatively, in our opinion, they can be taken into the unit with the landlord to determine whether the unit requires repair (which is one of their main concerns).

Tenant's Remedies

Landlords should remember to instruct their superintendents and real estate agents to comply with the RTA requirements. A tenant or former tenant can apply to the board for an order determining that the landlord's superintendent or agent has illegally entered the rental unit (s. 29(1)6). If the board determines that the landlord's superintendent or agent has entered the unit illegally, the board may order an abatement of rent or assess an administrative fine, or it may order that the tenancy be terminated or make an order that the board considers appropriate (s. 31(1)).

Illegal entry is also an offence under s. 234(a) of the RTA. On conviction, an individual is liable to a fine of not more than $25,000, and a corporation is liable to a fine of not more than $100,000. See Chapter 20 for further details regarding administrative fines and provincial offences.

If the illegal entry or other prohibited behaviour was so bad that the tenant was driven to leave the rental unit as a result, the board can also order the landlord to compensate the tenant for any moving expenses and for any increased rent that the tenant has incurred, or will incur, for a one-year period after the tenant has left the rental unit.

REVIEW QUESTIONS

1. Is it possible for a tenant to charge another tenant illegal rent, and if so, how?

2. If a tenant applies to the board because a superintendent has entered a unit without proper notice, what is that application called?

3. What is the Guideline the board has issued that deals with violation of tenants' rights by landlords?

4. Under what circumstances can a landlord enter a tenant's unit without written notice?

5.   a. Under what circumstances can a landlord enter a unit with written notice?

    b. How long does the notice period need to be?

    c. Is there any special way in which the written notice can be served?

6. Is a tenant entitled to be consulted about the time of day that a repair will be done?

7. How exact does a landlord have to be about the time of entry given in a written notice?

Procedures Under the RTA

7

SERVING DOCUMENTS (GIVING NOTICES)

In legal terms, giving a notice to another party is usually referred to as serving the notice on that party. The topic of giving notices or other documents is called "service"; however, in everyday language we will refer to "giving notices."

There are similarities in the ways landlords and tenants are required to give each other notices. However, because there are also differences, it is clearer to look specifically at what each party must do. We will start with notices from the landlord to the tenant.

When a landlord must give a notice or a document to a tenant under the *Residential Tenancies Act, 2006* (RTA), the landlord may do it themselves or have the notice given to the tenant by an employee or by some other person, such as a **process server**. The ways of giving notices are set out in s. 191 of the RTA and in Rule 5 of the Landlord and Tenant Board ("the board") Rules of Practice.

According to s. 191, a landlord may give notice by

- handing it to the tenant;[1]
- handing it to an apparently adult person in the rental unit;
- leaving it in the mailbox where mail is ordinarily delivered to the tenant;
- if there is no mailbox, leaving it at the place where mail is ordinarily delivered to the tenant;
- sending it by mail to the last-known address where the tenant resides or carries on business; or
- any other means allowed in the rules as amended from time to time.

The additional methods of service set out in board Rule 5 are:

- sending the document by courier to the tenant;
- sending the document by fax if there is a fax machine where the tenant lives or carries on business;
- placing the document under the door or through a mail slot in the door of a tenant who occupies a rental unit; or

process server
a person whose job is to deliver court documents and other important notices

---

1 This is called "personal service" even when someone other than the landlord does it.

- if the document is an application or was created after the application was filed,

  - by hand delivery, mail, courier, or fax to the representative of the tenant, or

  - by any other means permitted by the board in writing under Rule 5.2.

Except for notices of entry, the rules do not allow posting a notice on the tenant's door as a means of service. However, a landlord may sometimes want to post a notice on the tenant's door as well as using another means of service to try to prove to the board that the notice would have definitely come to the attention of the tenant. The landlord may give a **notice of entry** by posting it on the tenant's door.

notice of entry
notice that the landlord
intends to enter the
rental unit

A notice sent by mail is deemed to have been given on the fifth day after mailing (s. 191(3)). That time delay also applies to Express Post, even though Express Post is advertised as being a courier-like service (Rule 5.4). When counting days, generally include Saturdays, Sundays, and holidays. However, a document sent by courier is deemed to be received on the next day that is not a Saturday, Sunday or holiday (Rule 5.3). A document sent by fax is deemed to be delivered on the date imprinted on the fax (Rule 5.5).

In the case of multiple tenants, the notice should list all of the tenants by name, but it is usually sufficient for the landlord to serve one copy of the notice of termination on all the tenants. Separate notices must be given if the notice is served by mail or courier and the last-known addresses of the tenants are different. This also applies where the notice is being served by fax and the fax numbers of the tenants are different.

The provision for the board to permit another means of service is to cover the situation where a person is difficult to serve under the regular means, perhaps because they have left the community and the landlord has no address for them. To obtain the board's permission (or "direction") to serve by another means, you must explain to the board in writing why you are having trouble serving the notice. If satisfied that the difficulty exists, the board may permit service by serving a relative of the tenant (or the landlord) or by advertising in a local newspaper or in a newspaper in the community where you believe the tenant (or the landlord) has gone. Because it is possible to serve notice by mail to a last-known address, applying to the board for direction about service is rare.

When a tenant must give a notice to a landlord, the tenant may do it him or herself or have the notice given to the landlord by some other person, such as a process server. The ways of giving notice are set out in s. 191 of the RTA and in board Rule 5.

According to s. 191, a tenant may give notice by

- handing it to the landlord (which is known as personal service);

- handing it to one of the landlord's employees who exercises authority in the residential complex to which the notice relates;

- leaving it in the mailbox where mail is ordinarily delivered to the landlord;

- if there is no mailbox, leaving it at the place where mail is ordinarily delivered to the landlord;

- sending it by mail to the last-known address where the landlord resides or carries on business; or
- any other means allowed in the rules as amended from time to time.

The additional methods of service set out in Rule 5 are:

- sending the document by courier to the landlord;
- sending the document by fax if there is a fax machine where the landlord carries on business or lives; or
- if the document is an application or was created after the application was filed,
  - by hand delivery, mail, courier or fax to the representative of the landlord, or
  - by any other means permitted by the board in writing under Rule 5.2.

Section 191(2) of the RTA allows for validating service effected by a means other than those listed above, provided that the contents of the notice actually came to the attention of the person for whom it was intended within the required time period.

COMPUTING TIME: COUNTING DAYS

Time must be computed in accordance with the rules (s. 193). When computing the time between two events, count the day the second event occurs, but do not count the day the first event occurs (Rule 4.1). When counting days, include Saturdays, Sundays, and holidays, which are referred to in the Rules as non-business days (Rule 4.2). For example, you serve Juanita with a notice of termination for non-payment of rent by sending it by regular mail on June 1. The notice is deemed to have been served five days after the notice was put in the mail. In this case, the notice is deemed to have been served on Juanita on June 6. This applies whether or not June 6 is a business day.

If there is a time limit for filing a document in an application to the board that expires on a Saturday, Sunday, or holiday, then the document can be filed on the next day that is not a Saturday, Sunday, or holiday (Rule 4.3). For example, imagine Scott had until June 11 to file a request for review but June 11 is a Saturday and June 12 is a Sunday. Scott would therefore have until June 13 to file the request. However, if possible, it is desirable to file the request by the previous Friday, because it is possible that the board or the opposing party might miscount the days.

IMPORTANT NOTICE PERIODS

Under the RTA, many actions are taken by a landlord that require notice to a tenant, or by a tenant that require notice to a landlord. These notices must almost always be in writing, and they often must be given in a form approved by the board. The board can extend or shorten some, but not all, of the time limits. The following are examples of some of the more common and important time limits.

In general, a landlord must give a written notice 24 hours before entering a rental unit (ss. 25 and 27(1)).

To terminate a tenancy, a tenant must generally give the landlord 60 days written notice before the end of a tenancy or a period of a tenancy (ss. 43, 44, and 47). However, the notice is 28 days for a daily or weekly tenancy (s. 44(1)).

To terminate a tenancy at the end of its term, a landlord must generally give the tenant written notice 60 days before the end of a tenancy or a period of a tenancy (ss. 43, 44, 48, and 58). However, the notice is 28 days for a daily or weekly tenancy (s. 44(1)).

To terminate a tenancy before the end of its term, a landlord must generally give the tenant written notice either 10, 14, or 20 days before the termination date (ss. 43 and 59 to 68).

If a landlord gives written notice of termination and the tenant does not vacate the rental unit, the landlord generally has 30 days to apply for an order terminating the tenancy; otherwise, the notice of termination is void (s. 46). (This does not apply to a notice of termination for non-payment of rent (s. 46(2)).)

Once a landlord applies for termination of a tenancy, the board gives the landlord a notice of application. The landlord then must give the tenant the application and the notice of hearing at least 10 days before the hearing date.[2] Therefore, if those documents are being delivered by mail, they must be mailed at least 15 days before the hearing date. These time limits can be shortened. However, you cannot rely on receiving an abridgement of time (that is, a shortening of the time limit). Failure to comply with the time limits for service of an application can delay an application or termination significantly. The same issues apply to a tenant application against a landlord.

To raise a rent, a landlord must give written notice in the approved form at least 90 days before the intended increase date.

The rules about extending or shortening time limits are set out in the next section.

EXTENSIONS AND ABRIDGEMENTS OF TIME

To represent landlords or tenants properly, you should be aware of the following:

- There are time limits covering many of the steps that your clients will want you to take.
- Some of these time limits can be extended or shortened.
- Some of these time limits cannot be extended or shortened.

A number of important time limits were addressed in the preceding section. This section addresses why some of those time limits cannot be extended, why other time limits can be extended, and how and when extensions are obtained.

The law on extending and shortening time limits is found in s. 190, s. 56 of O. Reg. 516/06, and board Rule 15. Section 190(1) of the RTA provides that the

---

2   Some applications that deal with serious and time-sensitive matters such as an illegal act, impaired safety, and the eviction of a superintendent after his or her employment has ended, are only required to be served at least 5 days before the hearing.

board may extend the time limit for applying for an above-guideline rent increase or for applying to review a provincial work order. Such a work order is made if a municipality lacks a property standards bylaw, if a current tenant makes a written complaint, and if an inspector finds that the minimum standards prescribed under s. 224(1) have not been met.

Section 190(2) of the RTA provides that the board "may extend or shorten the time requirements with respect to any matter in its proceedings, other than the prescribed time requirements." These prescribed time requirements that cannot be shortened are set out in s. 56 of the regulation and include all time requirements related to notice requirements for terminating tenancies.

Shortening a time limit is sometimes called "abridging" a time limit.

When deciding whether to extend or shorten time limits, the adjudicator making the decision considers the following:

- the length of the delay,
- the reason for the delay,
- whether a party will be prejudiced by granting the request,
- whether a party will be prejudiced by not granting the request,
- whether the prejudice can be remedied,
- whether the request is made in good faith, and
- any other relevant factors.

To obtain an extension of time, the key factors are good faith and prejudice.

The opposite of **good faith** is **bad faith**. An example of bad faith is missing a time limit in order to put the other party at a disadvantage. A party or representative who has missed a time limit for this reason will have great difficulty obtaining an extension or abridgement of time.

good faith
honestly, for the stated purpose, not meaning to obtain an unfair advantage

bad faith
for improper purposes, in order to obtain an unfair advantage

More commonly, a time limit is missed in good faith. Often the need for an extension or abridgement of time arises because of an error, such as not knowing of a particular time limit or overlooking a deadline. Deadlines can be missed because of illness, staff turnover, lack of cooperation from other people, or excessive workload.

Provided that the good faith test is met, the most important issue is prejudice to the parties. By **prejudice**, the law means a party's inability or reduced ability to deal with a claim or event because of a delay. The legal concept of prejudice does not include the fact that there will be one result if the extension or abridgement is granted and a different result if the extension or abridgement is denied.

prejudice
inability or reduced ability to deal with a situation because of an act or omission

In general, parties or their representatives should make a request for an extension of time in writing, promptly after becoming aware of the need for the request. In the written request, a party should set out the reason that the extension is needed (i.e., why the time limit was missed).

Where the need for an extension of time is the result of an innocent mistake, you can ask the opposing party or representative to consent to the requested extension. As a representative of the opposing party, you should advise your client that the extension is likely to be granted by the board, and that consenting is the reasonable thing to do. If your client agrees to consent, you should do so. You might want agreement from the party asking for the extension concerning the scheduled date for the hearing or the identification of issues in the dispute.

On receiving a request for an extension or abridgement of time, the adjudicator dealing with the request can seek submissions from the other party, or the other party may make submissions without waiting for the adjudicator to call for them. This is especially important if there is prejudice to the other party. For example, suppose the tenant did not appear at the eviction hearing and is requesting an extension of time for a review of the order because the tenant claims to have just learned of the order. The landlord may have rented the apartment to a third party in reliance on the order, or the tenant may have used delaying tactics before. In the first situation, the landlord (and the third party) would be prejudiced if the time extension was granted. In the second situation, the request for an extension of time may not be made in good faith. Both of these examples are reasons for the board to deny the request for an extension of time.

FILING DOCUMENTS AT THE LANDLORD AND TENANT BOARD

The board provides services and receives documents through two different types of offices—namely, regional offices and ServiceOntario centres. At the time of writing, there are three regional offices in Toronto and one each in Mississauga, Hamilton, London, Ottawa, and Sudbury. Those are the major urban areas where most landlord and tenant disputes take place. The regional offices process the files and organize the hearings for the surrounding area. For example, the Toronto East office serves the Regional Municipality of Durham as well as Scarborough. Regional offices have customer service representatives available during regular business hours. Customer service representatives can provide people with information about the board and the law.[3]

There are also 67 ServiceOntario centres located across Ontario, servicing major municipalities smaller than London, many towns in the South, and many places in the North. For an up-to-date list of the ServiceOntario centres see the section entitled office locations on the website of the board at www.ltb.gov.on.ca. Unlike regional offices, the ServiceOntario centres do not have staff of the board working behind the counters. They cannot provide information about the law, but they can accept documents. You can file applications and supporting documents in person at any of the ServiceOntario centres (Rule 6.1). If you want to file documents by mail or fax, you must send them to the appropriate regional office for the rental unit involved (Rules 6.2 and 6.3).

Landlords and tenants often need to give documents to the board. In most cases the first document the board receives from a party is an application. That is called

---

3   The board is careful to state that its staff do not provide legal advice. You cannot rely on what a board staff person tells you if an issue is disputed before a board adjudicator. (Relying on such information may be an explanation of why you took a particular step in a proceeding, but that reason will not in itself validate what you have done.)

filing an application. When a party files an application and pays the relevant application fee at a regional office, the board will almost always issue a notice of hearing. If a party is filing just one application at a board office (or sometimes two applications), the board staff person will usually prepare the notice of hearing while the party waits so that he or she can take it away with them. If a party files multiple applications, the board will prepare the notices of hearing and make them available the next business day (or sometimes two days later).

Parties are able to submit applications by fax or by mail. You should mail or fax the document to the regional office for the rental unit involved. Fees to file by fax are paid through a credit card. Otherwise cash or a certified cheque or money order may be used. Parties do not usually file applications by mail because that would delay the receipt of the application. If the board has not issued a single application while the party waits, the board will sometimes fax it to the applicant to save them making a trip to the board office to pick it up. Except for emergency situations, the notice of hearing for an application filed at a ServiceOntario centre will usually be mailed to the applicant. You should check what the board will do when you leave an application with a regional office or a ServiceOntario centre.

SERVING APPLICATIONS

As of December 2010, the RTA requires that the applicant serve the notice of hearing and application on the respondent (i.e., give a copy of the notice of hearing and the application to the respondent). The board will generally send the respondent a letter telling them in general terms that an application has been made against them for a particular rental unit. However, in November 2010 the government introduced legislation that will, if enacted, change the law so that the obligation to serve notices of hearing and application will fall on the board. Your instructor may be able to verify what the current law is. That should be clear from the information the board provides with the applicant's copy of the notice of hearing. If those instructions say to serve the notice of hearing and application (that is, to give it to the respondent), then you will still need to do that. Otherwise, the instructions may say that the board is responsible for service.

CERTIFICATES OF SERVICE

Whenever a person serves a notice or document under the RTA, it is advisable or necessary for that person to record having served the notice or document. If you expect the notice or document to be used in an application before the board, you should have the person who served the notice complete a certificate of service immediately. The certificate of service form is available from the board's website. You should be careful when filling it out. When they first complete the certificate of service, landlords can easily mix up which name goes where. Another possible error is that a landlord may want to sign the certificate him or herself even though a superintendent or other employee actually gave the notice to the tenant. You should insist that the person who actually served the notice sign it. Note that in the case of service by courier, it is the person who gave the notice and instructions to the courier who should sign. Likewise, in the case of service by mail, the person who placed the notice in the mail should sign. The same person should also put the notice in its envelope and put the envelope in the mail. (Alternatively, the person who prepares the notice can leave the envelope unsealed so that the person who will mail it can see the notice before sealing and mailing the envelope.

Process servers may provide you with an affidavit of service rather than a certificate of service. The difference is that an affidavit is sworn before a person who is qualified to take oaths, whereas a certificate is stated to be true by the act of the person signing it. The board will accept an affidavit of service instead of a certificate of service provided that the affidavit states that service was effected by one of the methods available under the RTA.

For many landlord applications, the landlord or landlord's agent needs to file a previous notice given to the tenant (or sometimes two previous notices). In filing the application, you or the landlord need to file a certificate of service of that previous notice or those previous notices, as well as copies of the notices themselves. That is the main reason why it is wise to have the certificate prepared and signed immediately after the notice has been given to the tenant. Certificates of service and notices that are filed with an application are usually filed in person (and you should keep a copy for the landlord's file). Later in the application process, certificates of service are usually filed by sending them by fax to the appropriate regional office of the board. The top corner of the certificate has a place to show the file number. The file number must be shown, but a fax cover sheet is not needed.

FRENCH LANGUAGE SERVICES

Parties are entitled to services from the board in French in those parts of the province designated under the *French Languages Services Act*. The designated areas include most of Eastern and Northern Ontario (including Ottawa and Sudbury), as well as the cities of Toronto, Mississauga, Brampton, Hamilton, London, and Windsor, and other pockets of French settlement such as Penetanguishene. At the time of writing, the schedule of designated areas can be found at http://www.e-laws.gov .on.ca/html/statutes/english/elaws_statutes_90f32_e.htm. Rule 7 sets out the details of the provision of French language services.

CONCLUSION

You should review the rules about service and time limits in this chapter carefully after you are familiar with the time limits for notices of termination and for applications, which will be addressed in later chapters.

KEY TERMS

bad faith	prejudice
good faith	process server
notice of entry	

REVIEW QUESTIONS

1. What is personal service (of a document)?

2. Besides personal service, name three ways a landlord can give a notice to a tenant under the RTA.

3. Name three ways, other than personal service, that a tenant can give a notice to a landlord under the RTA.

4. What period of notice does a tenant usually have to give a landlord to end a tenancy?

5. For what tenancies is the notice of termination shorter than the usual period?

6. How much notice does a landlord have to give in order to increase a tenant's rent?

7. What is meant by abridging time?

8. What are some examples of missing a time limit in good faith?

9. Give an example of why a person might miss a time limit in bad faith.

DISCUSSION ISSUES

1. Can a landlord give an N4 notice of termination as an email attachment?

2. The landlord is going to serve an N5 notice of termination but is worried that the tenant will deny receiving it. What should the landlord do?

Tenant Applications

There are seven types of tenant applications that are listed below along with their forms. The tenant applications are:

- request for maintenance (Form T6);
- complaint regarding tenant rights (Form T2);
- request for a rent rebate (Form T1);
- allegation that the landlord gave notice of termination in bad faith (Form T5)—discussed in Chapter 10 in the section on terminations for personal or family use;
- request for a rent reduction as a result of the discontinuance of a service or facility or a reduction in municipal taxes (Form T3)—discussed in Chapter 19; and
- complaints regarding a landlord who has failed to comply with an agreement to increase rent above the guideline (Form T4)—discussed in Chapter 18.
- allegations that a landlord failed to follow the proper rules when requiring the tenant to become responsible to pay for the electricity or other utilities (Form T7)—discussed in Chapter 4.

As of February 2011, the Landlord and Tenant Board ("the board") fees for filing a T6, T1, T3, and T4 are $45. There is no fee for filing a T2 or T5. However, the tenant should ensure that he or she files the right form for their claim, and not file using a T2 or T5 form merely as a means of saving the $45 fee.

To succeed in a tenant application, it is crucial for tenants to present persuasive evidence. Rather than simply relying on their own evidence to establish that the landlord has failed to meet its obligations, a tenant is much more likely to succeed by presenting evidence from third parties, as well as documentary evidence.

BREACH OF MAINTENANCE OBLIGATIONS

If the tenant believes that the landlord has failed to properly maintain the rental unit or residential complex, he or she can file an application (T6) with the board seeking compensation or other relief.

The remedies that the board may order are set out in s. 30(1) of the RTA. The board may

1. terminate the tenancy;
2. order an abatement of the rent;
3. authorize the repair that has been or is to be made, and order its costs to be paid by the landlord to the tenant;

4. order the landlord to do specified repairs or replacements or other work within a specified time;

5. order the landlord to pay the reasonable costs that the tenant has incurred or will incur as a result of the landlord's breach, including paying to repair or replacing the tenant's property that was damaged as a result of the landlord's breach;

6. prohibit the landlord from giving a rent increase to the tenant, or to future tenants of the rental unit, until specified repairs have been completed; or

7. make any other order that the board considers appropriate.

When determining the remedy, the board considers whether the tenant or former tenant advised the landlord of the alleged breaches of the repair obligation before applying to the board (s. 30(2)). If the tenant did not advise the landlord of a needed repair, the board is entitled not to award any abatement until the time that the need for the repair was brought to the landlord's attention. That stipulation may not apply if the landlord had a duty to inspect the premises and should have found the need for the repair. The tenant's lack of notice to the landlord also helps the board decide whether it is fair to terminate the tenancy, or whether it is fair to allow the tenant to make the repair and have the landlord reimburse the tenant for the costs that the tenant has paid or will pay. However, it is still important to determine the extent to which the disrepair negatively affected the tenant.

If the tenant has done a repair without giving the landlord the opportunity to do it, the board will probably carefully scrutinize the amount of the cost claimed for the repair. In particular, this scrutiny will apply to any labour component of the repair. The labour component is the part of the cost of the repair that small landlords might avoid by doing the repair themselves, or that large landlords might not incur personally because the repair may have been done by employees of the landlord.

LANDLORD DEFENCES

The most effective landlord defence to a tenant repair claim is to show that the disrepair has been caused by the tenant and not by normal wear and tear. An in-unit inspection report can be very useful evidence in such a case A tenant will have difficulty disproving what the move-in inspection report shows, especially if the tenant has signed the report.

The landlord may also take the position that the defect claimed does not render the premises in a bad state of repair, unfit for habitation, or in violation of a standard. This defence can succeed only against a tenant who is being unreasonable about the level of repair that is required. An example of the use of this defence would be a situation in which the landlord has made a drywall repair and then has painted only that section of the repaired wall in a colour matching the rest of the wall. Housing standards may not require that the whole wall be painted, and the standard of good state of repair would not require that either, so long as the match of the paint is good.

In the case of actual disrepair, landlords may want to show that they responded as quickly as they could and that they were delayed in doing the repair because of the need to order parts or the lack of available trades to perform the work. This defence has its limits. It will do landlords little good to say that they could not do the repair themselves because they were ill, out of the city, or tied up at their regular job. In any of these cases, it is the landlord's obligation to have the repair done by someone else if they cannot do it themselves. It will also be of little use for large landlords to allege that they could perform a repair within a reasonable period of time because they had too many other repairs to do. Their obligation is to hire more staff to meet the demand for repairs or to bring in trades to meet any particular surge in the need for repairs. An exception exists, however, if the demand surge is clearly only an occasional and sporadic one. For example, many units turn over on May 1, June 1, July 1, and September 1. A landlord, therefore, cannot be expected to increase staffing year-round in order to meet the unusual demand for repairs or cleaning that lasts for four periods of five days out of the entire year.

The remedy of termination of the tenancy applies mostly in cases where the apartment has been found to be unfit for habitation. A reasonable tenant would move out of a rental unit that is unfit for habitation, and it may be unreasonable for the landlord to expect the tenant who has moved out to go through the inconvenience of moving back in after the repairs are made.

PRACTICAL CONCERNS

Tenants who undertake their own repairs run the risk of not being reimbursed for them. To minimize that risk, the tenant should give the landlord written notice of a deadline by which to make the repair. The tenant should undertake a repair only when the repair is too serious to wait for an application to the board, or the repair must be made in order to minimize other damages. For example, this would be the case for repairs to a refrigerator or freezer where the tenant may be keeping food in a cooler with ice or in a friend's refrigerator or freezer until the repairs are done. In addition, tenants should generally have the repair done by a professional so that they have an invoice for the work. Where the repair is more than merely a service call, tenants should try to get two repair quotes to show that they have been reasonable in minimizing the cost of the repair.

The board can order the landlord to do specific repairs. In that case, it is appropriate for the tenant to seek to have the application adjourned so that it can be brought back if the repairs are not done by a specified date. In dealing with such a request by the tenant, the landlord should be sure to obtain sufficient time to do the work, which may turn out to be more complicated than was first anticipated. This applies particularly to water penetration or roof problems, where the problem may be much greater than appears at first glance. In addition, such problems may occur only under certain seasonal or unique conditions, and may be difficult to diagnose. In that situation, landlords should show that they have made efforts to repair the problem and should ask the board to let them continue to do so until repairs are complete. If the board makes an order for a repair and the first repair attempt does not work, the landlord will appear to be in breach of the order. It is better to avoid an order from the board, and it is important to have the evidence of a roofer, an engineer, or a qualified consultant regarding the difficulty of being precise about the repairs that may be required in a particular situation.

ABATEMENTS

A tenant's most common remedy for disrepair is an order for an abatement of rent. The usual test to determine the proper amount of the abatement is that it is "the difference between the fair value of the premises if they had been as they were supposed to be and the fair value of the premises as they were." The board will often determine the abatement as a percentage of the rent.

In applying for an abatement of rent, tenants should emphasize the inconvenience that they have suffered and the disruption in their normal lifestyle as a result of the disrepair. In opposing an abatement of rent, the landlord should list the total package of services that the tenant was to receive and show that the tenant has still received most of them.

For example, if a roof leak renders completely useless the second bedroom in a two-bedroom apartment, then as the tenant's representative, you would note that a two-bedroom apartment typically rents for significantly more than a one-bedroom apartment. For example, Central Mortgage and Housing Corporation (CMHC) reports average rents for apartments by size. Table 8.1 shows the average rents for one- and two-bedroom apartments in various Ontario cities for October 2009 and 2010. Similar figures are available from the CMHC website for each year for most Ontario cities.

Suppose there are two tenants and Tenant A normally sleeps in the first bedroom and Tenant B normally sleeps in the second bedroom. If Tenant A uses the apartment during the day, as the tenant's representative you would lead evidence that the second bedroom is by far the most important area of the apartment to Tenant B because it is the only area where Tenant B enjoys privacy. If the leak led Tenant B to sleep in the living room, leaving clothes and personal effects there during the day, thenTenant B will have suffered loss of privacy. Furthermore, Tenant A will have suffered the loss of the main living space—the shared living room.

On the other hand, as the landlord's representative, you would point out that the apartment is to be heated and lighted, and the apartment remains heated and lighted; that the tenants are to have the use of a fridge, stove, and hot and cold running water, and the tenants still have all of these things; that the tenants are to have the use of a bathroom with hot and cold running water, light, mirrors, and plumbing fixtures, and the tenants still have all of these things; that the tenant are entitled to a living space consisting of six areas (living room, kitchen, dining area, bathroom, and two bedrooms), and the tenants have been deprived of only one-sixth of the area. Because the tenants retain the other amenities, the tenants have lost perhaps only one-tenth of the total package, so the abatement should be only one-tenth of the total rent. This approach works especially well if only part of a room is rendered unusable by the leak. Indeed, one may undertake a square-footage analysis to show that the apartment has, say, 800 square feet and only 10 square feet of it were rendered unusable. On that analysis, the entitlement to an abatement would be 1.25 percent of the rent (10 ÷ 800). Even where a tenant has been deprived of the living room and kitchen, if the tenant is still occupying the unit and still using two bedrooms and a bathroom, the appropriate abatement may be only 40, 50, or 60 percent of the rent, depending on the size of the areas given up and still in use by the tenant.

Table 8.1 Average Rents for One- and Two-Bedroom Apartments

	One-bedroom		Two-bedroom	
	Apr. 2009	Apr. 2010	Apr. 2009	Apr. 2010
Toronto	$930	$943	$1,093	$1,134
Ottawa	$817	$873	$995	$1,061
London	$682	$688	$849	$862
Thunder Bay	$600	$620	$730	$759
Windsor	$630	$622	$748	$736

DAMAGES

Under the *Landlord and Tenant Act* and the *Tenant Protection Act*, the courts and the tribunal used to allow damages for damage to tenants' belongings under their power to make "any other order that it considers appropriate." The courts and the tribunal would sometimes allow compensation to tenants for buying meals out if their kitchen was unusable, or for some nights in a hotel or motel if the rental unit was completely unusable. In the 1970s and 1980s there was some debate in the case law about whether these awards were valid and appropriate.

The courts considered the different forms of damages, which include general damages, special damages, punitive damages, exemplary damages, and aggravated damages (though the last two or three damages may be the same). Damages are an award of money to compensate a person for a loss he or she has suffered. General damages are awarded either for loss of income, for inconvenience, or for future losses (which at this point can only be estimated). Special damages are damages awarded for specific out-of-pocket expenses. Punitive, exemplary, or aggravated damages are awarded to punish the opposing party because the party has deliberately done something wrong.

The RTA provides a specific power to the board to order the landlord to pay the tenant for

1. the reasonable costs that the tenant has incurred or will incur in repairing or, when repairing is not reasonable, replacing belongings ("property") of the tenant that was damaged, destroyed, or disposed of as a result of the landlord's breach; and

2. other reasonable out-of-pocket expenses that the tenant has incurred or will incur as a result of the landlord's breach.

The board, like the tribunal and court before it, still has the power to make any other order it considers appropriate. In the unusual case of *Mejia v. Cargini*, the landlord had arranged for some people to beat up his tenant, in front of the tenant's children, in an effort to drive the tenant from the rental unit. The Divisional Court held that the board had jurisdiction to award general damages flowing from the landlord's interference with reasonable enjoyment, and awarded the tenant damages in the amount of $4,000. In determining whether an award of repair costs or out-of-pocket expenses is appropriate, remember that the landlord is not an insurer for the tenant, and that in the absence of a causal link between the landlord's breach of obligation and the damage to the tenant's belongings or the expenses, the landlord is not liable to pay the tenant for damage to the belongings or for the expenses. The landlord may be obliged to address a problem in the rental unit and to abate the rent for the part of the total package of space and amenities that the tenant did not receive. However, the landlord should only be required to pay for repairs to the tenant's belongings or for expenses if the landlord breached an obligation to prevent the damage to the rental unit that led to the damage to the tenant's belongings or the expenses.

TENANT RIGHTS

If the landlord has illegally entered the rental unit, interfered with the tenant's reasonable enjoyment of the unit, or has harassed the tenant, a tenant can file a T2 application with the board.

The remedies that the board can order are set out in s. 31(1) of the RTA. The board can

1. order that the landlord, superintendent, or agent may not engage in any further activities listed above against any of the tenants in the residential complex;

2. order that the landlord, superintendent, or agent reimburse the tenant for any reasonable costs the tenant has incurred or will incur as a result of the improper action;

3. order an abatement of rent;

4. order that the landlord pay to the board an administrative fine not exceeding $25,000 (because that is now the monetary jurisdiction of the Small Claims Court);

5. order that the tenancy be terminated; or

6. make any other order that it considers appropriate.

If the landlord's actions forced the tenant to vacate the unit, s. 31(2) permits the board to order the landlord to pay as compensation all or a portion of any increased rent the tenant will pay for up to a one-year period after they left the unit, and any reasonable out-of-pocket moving or storage costs.

LANDLORD DEFENCES

The most effective landlord defence to a tenant harassment or illegal entry claim is to show that the alleged activities did not take place.

Faced with a claim of harassment, the landlord may also want to show that the alleged events were not egregious, repetitive, or expected to bother most people. Harassment is seen as engaging in a course of conduct that ought to reasonably be known to be unwelcome. Typically, multiple events must be shown to establish harassment, but with particularly serious actions, a single act could suffice. Although tenants sometimes make claims about such actions, it is usually not harassment to seek to collect the rent or to tell the tenant that they need to change their behaviour to stop bothering other tenants. Such communications can be harassment if they are done too aggressively, too late at night, or at other times the landlord knows the tenant should not be expected to deal with such communications. Communicating with the tenant about such issues in a professional manner should not be considered to be harassment.

Sometimes tenants bring an application about tenant rights because they are not satisfied that the landlord has taken sufficient action to address a complaint about another tenant's behaviour. A landlord can avoid liability if they show that they took all reasonable steps to address the complaining tenant's claim. For instance, if a tenant brings a T2 claim because a neighbour has been keeping them up at night by playing loud music, if the landlord shows that he or she investigated all complaints and is taking all reasonable steps to make the offending neighbour stop, the board ought not award any remedy to the tenant. One technique is for the landlord to seek to have the complaining tenant's application heard at the same time as the landlord's application against the tenant who is alleged to be making too much noise. That way the board can decide which of the tenants is being unreasonable.

APPLICATION FOR A RENT REBATE

A tenant, former tenant, or prospective tenant can apply to the board if they believe the landlord has charged unlawful rent, collected an illegal charge, retained a rent deposit of more than one month, failed to pay annual interest on the rent deposit, of failed to refund the rent deposit when required (s. 135). The only remedy available for these matters is the repayment of the money unlawfully charged or collected. Unlike the remedies available for the other tenant applications, the board cannot issue any further remedies for losses suffered as a result of these matters.

Because the applicant is the tenant, rather than the landlord, the tenant must bring evidence to prove that the landlord did not properly follow the RTA. Such evidence would often be leases, notices of rent increases, and cancelled cheques. At the hearing, the tenant should ensure they have at least three copies of all documents that they want to rely on—one for the landlord to look at, one for the board, and one for the tenant to use at the hearing and to keep. If there are more than just two documents, it is best to assemble them, number the pages, and attach a table of contents listing the documents to the front. Then the adjudicator, the landlord, and the tenant can easily keep the pieces of paper straight.

The defences available to the landlord would be to show that the payment was not collected, or was not improper. In some cases the landlord can show that the payment in question was made too long before the application for the tenant to claim it back. Generally, a tenant needs to apply within one year of any wrongful payment (s. 135(4)).

REVIEW QUESTIONS

1. What are the different types of tenant applications?

2. What is the difference between a T2 and a T6 application?

3. Can a tenant file more than one tenant application at a time?

4. What options does a tenant have if the landlord refuses to do a repair in a timely manner?

5. What can the board order against a landlord who does not do one or more necessary repairs?

6. What evidence should a tenant gather if they were to pursue a tenant application alleging that the superintendent was harassing them?

7. What steps should a landlord take if they are served with a tenant application alleging that the superintendent is harassing a tenant?

DISCUSSION ISSUES

When Walter was looking for an apartment, he found one that had a very small kitchen with a stove that didn't work and a refrigerator that was constantly breaking down and in need of replacement. Walter told the landlord that he didn't mind if the appliances stayed as is because he doesn't cook and doesn't keep much food in his home. Because the landlord didn't pay for new appliances he agreed to rent the unit for $25 less than advertised. A few months into the tenancy, Walter's girlfriend moved in and insisted that there be a working stove and fridge. Can Walter file an application? If so, what remedies can he get?

Terminating Tenancies: Fault Grounds

9

This chapter deals with the grounds on which landlords can terminate tenancies before the end of the term and the notices that landlords must give in order to do so. As you will see below, a landlord needs a specific reason to terminate a tenancy, which must be one of the grounds listed in the *Residential Tenancies Act, 2006* (RTA). In order to terminate a tenancy before the end of the term, the landlord needs to have what is called a "fault ground." In other words, the tenant must have committed some fault. Examples of faults include not paying the rent, damaging the rental unit, and disturbing other tenants. By far the most common fault is not paying the rent when it is due. Non-fault grounds are discussed in Chapter 10. Also covered in Chapter 10 is one fault ground that can be used only at the end of the term of the tenancy—namely, persistent late payment of the rent.

NON-PAYMENT OF RENT VERSUS PERSISTENT LATE PAYMENT OF RENT

When a tenant fails to pay the rent on time, the landlord is wise to serve a notice of termination immediately. The RTA allows tenants to pay the rent late and stop the termination and eviction process. Inexperienced landlords can lose a lot of rent when they voluntarily allow tenants time to pay and then are required by the RTA to give their tenants yet more time. One solution is to start the RTA process with the notice of termination for non-payment immediately after the rent is due. Usually the rent is due on the first of each month. If it is not paid, the notice can and should be given on the second or the third day of the month. If a tenant has always been prompt with the rent before, a landlord of a small building may want to call the tenant as a reminder that the rent is overdue. However, landlords impose unnecessary delays on themselves when they delay giving the notice of termination.

Some tenants pay their rent late every month. During the term of the tenancy, all the landlord can do is give the notice of termination for non-payment of rent. If the notice leads to the payment of the rent, that is the end of the matter for that month. The landlord will often want to terminate the tenancy because the late payment is a nuisance and an administrative burden. However, the landlord cannot terminate the tenancy if the tenant pays the rent before the eviction process is completed. However, a landlord can terminate the tenancy for persistent late payment of rent at the end of a tenancy. That process is discussed in Chapter 10.

Table 9.1   Grounds for Early Termination

Description	RTA section
Non-payment of rent	s. 59
Misrepresenting income in public housing	s. 60
Committing an illegal act or carrying on an illegal business	s. 61
Causing undue damage	s. 62
Causing wilful damage	s. 63
Interfering with the reasonable enjoyment of the complex by the landlord or other tenants	s. 64
Impairing the safety of any person	s. 66
Permitting overcrowding contrary to health, safety, or housing standards required by law	s. 67

GROUNDS FOR TERMINATING TENANCIES

In Ontario, residential tenants have "security of tenure"; this means that to evict a tenant, a landlord needs to have one of the reasons specified in the RTA (see ss. 37(1), 38, and 39). The landlord cannot end a tenancy or evict a tenant merely because the tenant has not complied with the tenancy agreement. A particular breach of the agreement may also be a reason specified in the RTA, but it is the fact that the tenant's conduct falls within the statutory list of reasons that allows the landlord to terminate the tenancy. Table 9.1 sets out the grounds for early termination under the RTA.

NOTICE PERIODS, REMEDYING BREACHES, AND SECOND BREACHES

Table 9.2 sets out the notice periods for the various grounds of early termination.

The RTA allows a tenant to remedy some of the breaches—namely, causing undue damage, interference with the reasonable enjoyment of the property by the landlord or other tenants, and overcrowding. The remedies are for the tenant to pay for or to make the repair, to cease the interference, or to eliminate the overcrowding. If the tenant remedies the breach within seven days of receiving the notice, the landlord cannot proceed with an eviction. By repairing the damage, stopping the interference, or removing the people who created the overcrowding situation, the tenancy is restored to good standing. However, if the tenant commits another breach within six months, the tenant does not have the right to avoid termination by remedying the second breach, and there is a shorter notice period. The second breach may be any breach that can result in termination (other than failure to pay rent, which is dealt with separately); the second breach does not need to be the same as the first breach.

For example, consider a tenant who likes to play her stereo loudly late at night. The landlord serves a notice of termination on the grounds that she has substantially interfered with the reasonable enjoyment of the other tenants. The tenant stops playing the stereo too loudly. The landlord cannot then proceed with termination of the tenancy. If, five months later, the tenant accidentally breaks the glass of the main entrance door to the building, this undue damage constitutes a second

Table 9.2   Notice Periods for Early Termination

Eviction grounds	Form Number	Tenant has right to remedy*	Notice period (1st breach)	Notice period (2nd breach)**	Sections of the RTA
Illegal act involving production of or trafficking in illegal drugs	N6	No	10 days	n/a	s. 61(2)
Illegal act	N6	No	20 days	14 days***	ss. 61(1), 68(2)
Misrepresenting income in public housing	N6	No	20 days	14 days***	ss. 60(2), 68(2)
Wilful damage	N7	No	10 days	n/a	s. 63(1)
Undue damage	N5	Yes	20 days	14 days	ss. 62(2), 68(2)
Interfering with reasonable enjoyment	N5	Yes	20 days	14 days	ss. 64(2), 68(2)
Interfering with reasonable enjoyment of small landlord	N5	No	10 days	n/a	s. 65(1)
Act impairing safety	N7	No	10 days	n/a	s. 66(2)
Overcrowding	N5	Yes	20 days	14 days	ss. 67(2), 68(2)

    *   Tenant has 7 days to correct the behaviour/repair or make satisfactory arrangements to repair the damage.

   **   Within six months after first notice became void.

 *** If within the previous six months the tenant received a notice to terminate for undue damage, breach of reasonable enjoyment, or overcrowding, the notice period for an illegal act or misrepresenting income can be as short as 14 days.

breach of the RTA within six months of the first breach. The landlord can give a notice of termination effective in 14 days, and the tenant does not have the right to avoid the termination by paying for the repair of the door. (As we will see in the section on seeking s. 83 relief (relief from forfeiture), the tenant may be able to maintain the tenancy if the board decides to exercise its discretion in her favour. Therefore, a landlord may just insist on payment for the repair of the glass and not proceed with a termination application.)

In this example, a landlord who has served a notice of termination on the tenant after the first breach is in a better position to evict the tenant than a landlord who has not served notice after the first breach. A breach is considered a second breach only if notice of termination was given for the first breach. Therefore, if a tenant commits a significant breach, landlords who want to maintain all their rights should not merely give the tenant a warning; rather, the landlord should give the tenant a notice of termination using the approved form. By giving the first notice of termination, a landlord's rights to proceed with the termination are enhanced if the tenant commits a further breach.

TIME LIMITS

For all the fault grounds of termination, the landlord must give a notice of termination within a reasonable period of time after the breach. Usually the landlord will want to give the notice immediately after finding out about the breach. Often landlords find out about breaches because of complaints from other tenants. After receiving a complaint, it is good practice for the landlord to make some inquiries to see whether the complaint is valid. In the stereo example, one way to check is to ask other tenants if they also heard loud music, when, and from what apartment. If a complaint appears to be valid, the landlord should give a notice of termination.

The tenant may choose to stop the objectionable behaviour after receiving the notice of termination. For first breaches by causing undue damage, interfering with reasonable enjoyment, or permitting overcrowding, the landlord cannot proceed once the tenant has remedied the problem. For illegal acts, misrepresenting income (in public housing), impairing safety, or wilfully causing damage, the tenant will not reinstate the tenancy by remedying the breach, and the landlord can proceed to apply for eviction.

The landlord must apply to the Landlord and Tenant Board ("the board") within 30 days of the termination date specified in the notice (s. 69(2)). If the landlord does not apply within 30 days, the notice of termination becomes void, and the landlord cannot enforce it. The 30-day time limit does not apply to termination for non-payment of rent (s. 69(3)).

CHECKING LANDLORD'S NOTICE OF TERMINATION

Often a landlord contacts a lawyer or a paralegal after having given a notice of termination to a tenant. Immediately on being retained, the legal representative should check whether the notice has been correctly filled out and served. If not, the landlord should be informed of the problem and advised that a correct notice should be given to the tenant. If a notice of termination is invalid for even a minor reason, a termination application can be defeated. Therefore, it is important to ensure as early as possible that the notice of termination is correct (and has been correctly served).

If service was defective, the representative or the landlord may sometimes know (or can sometimes find out) whether the tenant received the notice in time. For example, the tenant may have spoken to the landlord about the notice and may have said when he or she received the notice. In these cases, the landlord can give evidence of what the tenant said, and the board has the power to validate the service (s. 191(2)).

A defect in the contents of the notice may or may not make the notice invalid. If you see a defect in the notice, you should tell your client what the problem is. Then it is for your client to decide whether to give a corrected notice or to proceed using the original notice. The following is a list of factors relevant to that decision:

- your opinion on the likelihood of the board's rejecting the notice, whether or not the tenant points out the potential defect;
- the landlord's opinion on the likelihood of the tenant's challenging the notice;
- your opinion on the likelihood of the board's rejecting the notice because of the tenant's challenge;
- the effect of losing the application because of the notice issue;
- whether it is too late to proceed with a corrected notice; and
- how much time will be lost by serving a corrected notice.

In most cases it is best to correct the technical error and start afresh.

CHOOSING THE GROUNDS TO USE

Sometimes the ground of termination for a tenant's objectionable behaviour is obvious. On other occasions, the objectionable behaviour can fall within several grounds. For example, suppose a tenant in a high-rise apartment building comes home drunk late one night, deliberately smashes and punches a hole through the apartment building door, and then wakes several tenants by banging on their doors. This behaviour constitutes causing undue damage (smashing the door), causing **wilful** damage (purposely smashing the door), an illegal act (mischief to private property or "vandalism"), and interfering with the reasonable enjoyment of other tenants (waking them up late at night). The choice of which notice (or notices) of termination to give depends on the following factors:

wilful
intentional or deliberate

- Does the landlord want to proceed to an eviction or merely have the tenant behave in an acceptable manner?

- Has the tenant committed a previous breach within six months (for which the tenant has been given a notice of termination)?

- Does the behaviour really constitute one ground and include another ground only incidentally?

- Does the nature and quality of the act make it reasonable to deal with it as an illegal act? Has a criminal charge been laid?

- How strong is the evidence for the various grounds?

In the example given, if this is a second breach and the first breach can be established easily, the landlord can best proceed on the grounds of undue damage and interference with reasonable enjoyment. On a second breach, the tenant cannot restore the tenancy by repairing the damage or discontinuing the offensive conduct. Avoiding the illegal act or wilful damage grounds eliminates the need to prove that the tenant intended to smash the door.

However, if this is a first breach and the landlord is satisfied with receiving payment for the repair of the door, the landlord can best proceed with the eviction on the ground of undue damage and/or the ground of wilful damage.[1] If the landlord wants to evict the tenant, you should proceed with interference with reasonable enjoyment, undue damage, wilful damage, and an illegal act. The tenant cannot remedy the illegal act, and the eviction application can proceed even if the tenant pays for the repair and stops disturbing the other tenants.

---

1 Section 62 allows a landlord to terminate a tenancy if the tenant wilfully or negligently causes undue damage. In this text we refer to s. 62 notices as "undue damage" notices. If the landlord gives a notice under this section, so long as the tenant repairs or pays for the repair of the damage, the tenancy can usually continue. Section 63 allows a landlord to give shorter notice to terminate without an opportunity for the tenant to repair the damage if the damage is wilful (that is, if the damage was not caused by negligence as in an accident), or if the tenant is using the rental unit in a way that is inconsistent with residential use and can be expected to cause major damage (for example, a marijuana grow operation or handling dangerous chemicals). In this text we refer to s. 63 notices as "wilful damage" notices.

There are three reasons not to proceed with the illegal act or wilful damage grounds alone. First, to do so reduces the chance of receiving money for the door repair. Second, it may be difficult to establish that the tenant committed the illegal act, which involves deliberate destruction of property rather than **negligent** or accidental damage. Third, if the landlord is not successful in the eviction application, then the "illegal act" does not constitute a first breach. (The landlord wants a notice that constitutes a first breach so that he or she gains the right to proceed on a second breach within six months.)

negligent
failing to take proper care

GENERAL COMMENTS ON THE TERMINATION NOTICES (FORMS N4 TO N7)

The notices of termination have certain features in common. They all require the tenant's name and address, the landlord's name and address, the address of the rental unit, and the date of termination. Figure 9.1 is a blank notice for non-payment of rent (Form N4). The N5, N6, and N7 forms are shown later as Figures 9.5, 9.6, and 9.7, respectively.

If known, the tenant's name should be given in full. If there is more than one tenant, the names of all the tenants should be listed. You should check with the landlord that there is no dispute about who the proper tenants are. If there is a dispute, you need to list as the tenants the people the landlord says are the tenants. You may also want to add "and any other occupants if found to be tenants by the board." If the tenant is known by several names, then state all the names. Before the names other than the presumed legal name, you should add the phrase "also known as" or "aka." Sometimes—for example, in an unlawful assignment—a landlord will not know the name of the tenant or occupant. In that case, identify the tenant(s) as "Tenant" or "Tenants" or "Occupant 1 and Occupant 2."

In the various addresses on the form, you should include the postal code. There are lines for the address of the rental unit separate from the lines for the name and address of the tenant. This is because a tenant may reside at an address different from the address of the rental unit. Both sections need to be filled in correctly.

CHOOSING THE TERMINATION DATE

The first substantive entry on most notices of termination is the termination date. There are a number of factors relevant to the selection of the termination date.

For most terminations for faults other than non-payment of rent, the minimum notice period is generally 20 days for a first breach and 14 days for a second breach. (See Table 9.2 above.) Remember that the second breach need not be for the same reason as the first breach. An illegal act, wilfully causing damage (that is, s. 63 damage), and misrepresentation of income in public housing do not count as a first breach. However, if the first breach is for undue damage, interference with reasonable enjoyment, or overcrowding, a second breach on any of the five grounds carries a 14-day minimum notice period, rather than the standard 20-day notice period for a first breach. For impairing safety, illegal drug production or trafficking, and wilfully causing damage, the minimum notice period is 10 days, whether the breach in question is a first or a second breach.

Figure 9.1   Blank Form N4

	Notice To End a Tenancy Early For Non-payment of Rent
	Form N4

To: (Tenant's name)	**From:** (Landlord's name)

This is a legal notice that could lead to you being evicted from your home.

Address of the Rental Unit

Street Number   Street Name

Street Type (e.g. Street, Avenue, Road)   Direction (e.g. East)   Unit/Apt./Suite

Municipality (city, town, etc.)   Province [O N]   Postal Code

This information is from your landlord:

I am giving you this notice because I believe you owe me $ ☐☐ , ☐☐☐ . ☐☐ **in rent.**

See the table on the next page for the details about how I calculated this amount.

I can apply to the Landlord and Tenant Board to have you evicted if you do not:

- **pay this amount* by** ☐☐ / ☐☐ / ☐☐☐☐   This date is called the **termination date**.

or   dd   mm   yyyy

- **move out by the termination date**

* If another rent payment comes due on or before the date you make the above payment to your landlord, you must also pay this extra amount.

WHAT YOU NEED TO KNOW
The following information is provided by the Landlord and Tenant Board

The termination date	The date that the landlord gives you in this notice to pay or move out must be at least: • 14 days after the landlord gives you the notice, if you rent by the month or year, or • 7 days after the landlord gives you the notice, if you rent by the day or week.
What if you agree with the notice	If you agree that you owe the amount that the landlord is claiming, you should pay this amount by the termination date in this notice. If you do so, this notice becomes void and the landlord cannot apply to the Board to evict you. If you do not pay the amount owing, and the landlord applies to the Board to evict you, you will likely have to pay the landlord's filing fee of $170.00, plus what you owe. **If you move out** by the date in this notice, your tenancy will end on the termination date. However, you may still owe money to your landlord. Your landlord will not be able to apply to the Board but they may still take you to Court for this money.
What if you disagree with the notice	If you disagree with what the landlord has put in this notice, you do not have to move out. You could talk to your landlord. You may also want to get legal advice. If you cannot work things out, and the landlord applies to the Board, you will be able to go to a hearing and explain why you disagree:

10101

Figure 9.1   Concluded

How you will know if the landlord applies to the Board
The earliest date that the landlord can apply to the Board is the day after the termination date in this notice. If the landlord does apply, the Board will schedule a hearing and send you a letter. The landlord must also give you a copy of the Notice of Hearing and the application.

What you can do if the landlord applies to the Board
- Get legal advice immediately; you may be eligible for legal aid services.
- Talk to your landlord about working out a payment plan.
- Go to the hearing where you can respond to your landlord's claims; in most cases, before the hearing starts you can also talk to a Board mediator about mediating a payment plan.

How to get more information
For more information about this notice or about your rights, you can contact the Landlord and Tenant Board. You can reach the Board by phone at **416-645-8080** or toll-free at **1-888-332-3234**. You can also visit the Board's website at **www.LTB.gov.on.ca**.

This table is completed by the landlord to show how they calculated the total amount of rent claimed on page 1:

Rent Period From: (dd/mm/yyyy) To: (dd/mm/yyyy)	Rent Charged $	Rent Paid $	Rent Owing $

Total Rent Owing $

Signature ☐ Landlord ☐ Agent

Signature   Date (dd/mm/yyyy)

First Name

Last Name

Company Name (if applicable)

Mailing Address

Unit/Apt./Suite   Municipality (city, town, etc.)   Province

Postal Code   Phone Number   Fax Number

E-mail Address

10101

To determine the date of termination, you also need to know how the notice of termination will be served. If it is to be mailed, you must allow five more days for the mail. If it is to be served by means other than mail, you must allow sufficient time for the landlord or the process server to serve the notice. The easiest way to serve the notice of termination is for the landlord or process server to place the notice in the tenant's mailbox or in the place where mail is normally delivered. Therefore, you should check whether the landlord has legal access to the tenant's mailbox. If the landlord does not have legal access to the mailbox, you will probably need to allow two or three days for personal service. Some people also allow one or two days as a safety margin. This avoids a problem if a landlord picks up the notice, intending to serve it that day, but serves it the next day instead. It also allows a small margin of safety in case the days have been miscounted. Applications to terminate for breaches other than non-payment of rent can be brought and heard earlier than the termination date; therefore, it is not particularly important to minimize the notice period for these other applications.

SIGNATURE AND AGENT INFORMATION

Individual issues involved in filling in the notice forms will be covered below with reference to each of the forms. However, there are further general matters that relate to the standard signature and agent information block at the end of each notice.

Where a date is requested on the form, it should be provided. Failure to do so does not necessarily make the notice invalid, but it creates difficulty in identifying the notice if several notices are given. In many cases, several notices of termination are given before one is finally made the subject of an application.

Whether the signature on the form is that of the landlord or the agent is a matter of choice. If the termination is on the basis of matters within the knowledge of the landlord and the landlord is a human being (rather than a corporation), it is better for you if the landlord signs the notice. This is most important when the notice is given for termination for personal use, demolition, conversion, repair, or renovation, because it is an offence to obtain possession of a rental unit by giving a notice of termination in bad faith. As the landlord's agent, you want to ensure that you are not charged with an offence if a question arises about the validity of the notice. Apart from this concern, the agent can sign the notice if it is more convenient than having the landlord sign it. For non-payment of rent, or when acting for a corporate landlord, it is common for the agent to sign most notices in order to expedite the processing of the notice. If you sign as the agent, you should fill in the agent information section. If the landlord signs the notice, you can still fill in the agent information section if the landlord wants you to do so.

Whoever signs the notice should sign the form with a pen, not a pencil. Because the form is computerized, it is easy to set up the forms to be filled in on your computer. If you do that, the signature on the form should be an original one, not an electronic signature.

FORM N4: TERMINATING A TENANCY FOR NON-PAYMENT OF RENT

The notice to terminate a tenancy early for non-payment of rent is Form N4. When completing Form N4, pay particular attention to the termination date. Where a landlord is terminating for grounds other than non-payment, the landlord can apply to the board before the termination date. However, this is not the case in an application for termination for non-payment of rent. Therefore, you need to allow enough time for the notice to be served, but if you allow more than 1 or 2 days extra time, the landlord will be losing rent unnecessarily. If a daily or weekly tenancy is being terminated for non-payment of rent, the termination date can be set 7 days after the notice is served. For all other tenancies, a termination date in a notice for non-payment of rent cannot be set earlier than 14 days after the notice is served. In a notice for non-payment, you want to stay close to the 14 days, because the application for termination cannot be brought until after the date fixed for termination in the notice.

In stating on Form N4 the amount of rent that the tenant must pay to avoid having to move out, you should not take into account the tenant's deposit for the last month's rent.[2] The landlord is entitled to that deposit as security to ensure that the tenant will pay the last month's rent. If the landlord applies the deposit earlier than the actual last month of the tenancy, the landlord is giving up that security.

Figures 9.2 and 9.3 show how to complete Form N4. The sample form at Figure 9.2 is for a tenant who has not paid any of her $902.15 November rent. The form is completed on November 2 for service on November 2 or 3. The termination date is November 17—namely, 14 days after November 3. Figure 9.3 is for a tenant who paid part of his November rent and none of his December rent. It is completed on December 3 for service on December 4 or 5. The termination date is December 19—namely, 14 days after December 5.

Tenants are sometimes able to persuade unsophisticated landlords to apply the last month's rent to rent arrears. In most cases, a landlord can require the tenant to replenish the last month's rent deposit. Therefore, even if the landlord has agreed to apply the deposit for last month's rent to rent arrears, and the deposit has been used up, you will serve the landlord better by disregarding the deposit in determining the rent that the tenant needs to pay to maintain the tenancy. You should obtain your client's instructions on this point, but we recommend that you advise the landlord to insist on the payment of the full rent due, leaving the last month's rent intact. You may think that the landlord cannot now insist on the payment of the full rent due because he or she has agreed to apply the last month's rent. However, usually the tenant will have given the landlord nothing in exchange for the landlord's agreement. Because the making of an enforceable contract requires a promise or an act by both parties, the landlord is not bound by his or her agreement. In

---

2   A landlord cannot take a deposit from a tenant as security for damage to a unit. The only deposit a landlord can take is one month's rent for the purpose of paying the last month's rent. This is known as "a deposit for last month's rent," "a deposit for LMR," or "LMR."

Figure 9.2 Completed Form N4

Notice To End a Tenancy Early For Non-payment of Rent

Form N4

To: (Tenant's name)

From: (Landlord's name)

This is a legal notice that could lead to you being evicted from your home.

Address of the Rental Unit

Street Number

Street Name

Street Type (e.g. Street, Avenue, Road)

Direction (e.g. East)

Unit/Apt./Suite

Municipality (city, town, etc.)

Province: O N

Postal Code

This information is from your landlord:

I am giving you this notice because I believe you owe me $ ___,9 0 2 . 1 5 in rent.

See the table on the next page for the details about how I calculated this amount.

I can apply to the Landlord and Tenant Board to have you evicted if you do not:

- **pay this amount* by** 1 7 / 1 1 / 2 0 1 1   This date is called the **termination date**.
  dd / mm / yyyy

or

- **move out by the termination date**

* If another rent payment comes due on or before the date you make the above payment to your landlord, you must also pay this extra amount.

WHAT YOU NEED TO KNOW

The following information is provided by the Landlord and Tenant Board

The termination date

The date that the landlord gives you in this notice to pay or move out must be at least:
- 14 days after the landlord gives you the notice, if you rent by the month or year, or
- 7 days after the landlord gives you the notice, if you rent by the day or week.

What if you agree with the notice

If you agree that you owe the amount that the landlord is claiming, you should pay this amount by the termination date in this notice. If you do so, this notice becomes void and the landlord cannot apply to the Board to evict you. If you do not pay the amount owing, and the landlord applies to the Board to evict you, you will likely have to pay the landlord's filing fee of $170.00, plus what you owe.

If you move out by the date in this notice, your tenancy will end on the termination date. However, you may still owe money to your landlord. Your landlord will not be able to apply to the Board but they may still take you to Court for this money.

What if you disagree with the notice

If you disagree with what the landlord has put in this notice, you do not have to move out. You could talk to your landlord. You may also want to get legal advice. If you cannot work things out, and the landlord applies to the Board, you will be able to go to a hearing and explain why you disagree.

10101

Version. 15/10/2009   This form has been approved by the Landlord and Tenant Board   Page 1 of 2

Figure 9.2   Concluded

How you will know if the landlord applies to the Board	The earliest date that the landlord can apply to the Board is the day after the termination date in this notice. If the landlord does apply, the Board will schedule a hearing and send you a letter. The landlord must also give you a copy of the Notice of Hearing and the application.
What you can do if the landlord applies to the Board	• Get legal advice immediately; you may be eligible for legal aid services. • Talk to your landlord about working out a payment plan. • Go to the hearing where you can respond to your landlord's claims; in most cases, before the hearing starts you can also talk to a Board mediator about mediating a payment plan.
How to get more information	For more information about this notice or about your rights, you can contact the Landlord and Tenant Board. You can reach the Board by phone at **416-645-8080** or toll-free at **1-888-332-3234**. You can also visit the Board's website at **www.LTB.gov.on.ca**.

This table is completed by the landlord to show how they calculated the total amount of rent claimed on page 1:

Rent Period From: (dd/mm/yyyy)	Rent Period To: (dd/mm/yyyy)	Rent Charged $	Rent Paid $	Rent Owing $
01/11/2011	30/11/2011	,902.15	, 0.00	,902.15
/ /	/ /	, .	, .	, .
/ /	/ /	, .	, .	, .
			Total Rent Owing $	, .

Signature   ☐ Landlord   ☒ Agent

Signature	Date (dd/mm/yyyy)
	November 2, 2011

First Name

Last Name

Company Name (if applicable)

Mailing Address

Unit/Apt./Suite   Municipality (city, town, etc.)   Province

Postal Code   Phone Number ( )   Fax Number ( )

E-mail Address

10101

Figure 9.3   Completed Form N4

Notice To End a Tenancy Early For Non-payment of Rent
Form N4

To: (Tenant's name)

From: (Landlord's name)

This is a legal notice that could lead to you being evicted from your home.

Address of the Rental Unit

Street Number

Street Name

Street Type (e.g. Street, Avenue, Road)

Direction (e.g. East)

Unit/Apt./Suite

Municipality (city, town, etc.)

Province: O N

Postal Code

This information is from your landlord:

I am giving you this notice because I believe you owe me $ 1,454.15 in rent.

See the table on the next page for the details about how I calculated this amount.

I can apply to the Landlord and Tenant Board to have you evicted if you do not:

- **pay this amount* by 19 / 12 / 2011** This date is called the **termination date**.
  dd   mm   yyyy

or

- **move out by the termination date**

* If another rent payment comes due on or before the date you make the above payment to your landlord, you must also pay this extra amount.

WHAT YOU NEED TO KNOW
The following information is provided by the Landlord and Tenant Board

The termination date
The date that the landlord gives you in this notice to pay or move out must be at least:
- 14 days after the landlord gives you the notice, if you rent by the month or year, or
- 7 days after the landlord gives you the notice, if you rent by the day or week.

What if you agree with the notice
If you agree that you owe the amount that the landlord is claiming, you should pay this amount by the termination date in this notice. If you do so, this notice becomes void and the landlord cannot apply to the Board to evict you. If you do not pay the amount owing, and the landlord applies to the Board to evict you, you will likely have to pay the landlord's filing fee of $170.00, plus what you owe.

If you move out by the date in this notice, your tenancy will end on the termination date. However, you may still owe money to your landlord. Your landlord will not be able to apply to the Board but they may still take you to Court for this money.

What if you disagree with the notice
If you disagree with what the landlord has put in this notice, you do not have to move out. You could talk to your landlord. You may also want to get legal advice. If you cannot work things out, and the landlord applies to the Board, you will be able to go to a hearing and explain why you disagree.

10101

Version. 15/10/2009   This form has been approved by the Landlord and Tenant Board   Page 1 of 2

Figure 9.3   Concluded

How you will know if the landlord applies to the Board	The earliest date that the landlord can apply to the Board is the day after the termination date in this notice. If the landlord does apply, the Board will schedule a hearing and send you a letter. The landlord must also give you a copy of the Notice of Hearing and the application.
What you can do if the landlord applies to the Board	• Get legal advice immediately; you may be eligible for legal aid services. • Talk to your landlord about working out a payment plan. • Go to the hearing where you can respond to your landlord's claims; in most cases, before the hearing starts you can also talk to a Board mediator about mediating a payment plan.
How to get more information	For more information about this notice or about your rights, you can contact the Landlord and Tenant Board. You can reach the Board by phone at **416-645-8080** or toll-free at **1-888-332-3234**. You can also visit the Board's website at **www.LTB.gov.on.ca**.

This table is completed by the landlord to show how they calculated the total amount of rent claimed on page 1:

Rent Period From: (dd/mm/yyyy)	To: (dd/mm/yyyy)	Rent Charged $	Rent Paid $	Rent Owing $
01/11/2011	30/11/2011	,952.00	,450.00	,502.00
01/12/2011	31/12/2011	,952.15	,0.00	,925.15
/ /	/ /	, .	, .	, .

Total Rent Owing $ 1,454.15

Signature   ☒ Landlord   ☐ Agent

Signature	Date (dd/mm/yyyy) December 19, 2011

First Name

Last Name

Company Name (if applicable)

Mailing Address

Unit/Apt./Suite   Municipality (city, town, etc.)   Province

Postal Code   Phone Number   (   )   Fax Number   (   )

E-mail Address

10101

contract law, in order for a contract to be valid and enforceable, there must be "**consideration**" for the making of the contract.

The next part of the form requires you to fill in the rent period or periods for which there is rent owing. Generally, a landlord applies any rent received against the earliest arrears so that the rent period for which rent is owing is the latest time for which rent is unpaid. However, in some situations, rent will have been overlooked for a month, or there will have been some dispute, and it is clear that the unpaid rent is for the whole month or for a part of a month earlier than the immediately past period. In this case, you should fill in the rent period for which it appears the rent was unpaid.

Suppose that the landlord and tenant agreed that the tenant would paint the fence around the backyard in August and could take $300 off the rent for doing so. The tenant paid the landlord $460, instead of the usual rent of $760 per month, but failed to paint the fence. The landlord noticed the unpainted fence on October 4 and decided to serve the notice of termination by mail that day. The landlord must choose a termination date allowing 5 days for mailing and 14 days for the tenant to pay, making a total of 19 days. The earliest possible termination date (with service by mail) is October 23.

Most of the forms come with instructions, notes, or both to help you understand how to use them. The N4 form provides a checklist that the landlord does not provide to the tenant, and information on the form itself for tenants labelled "what you need to know." The N5, N6, and N7 forms do not have checklists, but they do contain notes on the second page of the form to inform both landlord and tenant.

As a learning exercise, and when you are first working with the forms, you should read the checklist (found at Figure 9.4) and the notes carefully. The first paragraph of the notes usually indicates the minimum time period for the effective date of termination (for example, 14 days in a notice for non-payment of rent). This is a valuable check to ensure that you are choosing a proper termination date.

The next paragraph in the notes is unique to Form N4 because it tells tenants that they can stop an eviction by paying the arrears of rent, compensation, and costs to the landlord or into the board before an order becomes enforceable. Technically, the rent in arrears is any rent that was due before the termination date in the notice. Compensation equals the amount of the rent, calculated on a daily basis, after the termination date set out in the notice and until the date of payment. Compensation, which used to be called "compensation for use and occupation," is more relevant when the tenancy is actually terminated than when the tenancy is reinstated by the tenant. To reinstate the tenancy, the tenant's obligation is to pay all of the rent, including the rent for the full rental period (usually a month) for which the rent is due on the first of the month.

consideration
something of value given by both parties that induces each of them to enter into an agreement

Figure 9.4   Form N4 Checklist

Landlord
and
Tenant
Board

Form N4 - Checklist
Notice to End a Tenancy Early for Non-payment of Rent

Before you serve the attached notice to your tenant(s), make sure you can answer **YES** to each of the following questions. If not, your notice may be invalid. If you file an application to the Landlord and Tenant Board based on an invalid notice, your application may be dismissed and you will have to start over.

☐   **Did you fill in the correct termination date?**
If your tenant pays rent by the **month** or **year**, you must give **at least 14 days** notice. If your tenant pays rent by the **day** or **week**, you must give **at least 7 days** notice.

When counting the days, do not include the date you are giving the notice to the tenant. For example, if you give the notice to the tenant by hand on March 3rd, the first day of the 14-day notice period is March 4th; in this example, the earliest termination date would be March 17th. **If you are giving the notice to the tenant by mail or courier, you have to add extra days in calculating the termination date.** Read the Instructions to this form to see how much time you have to add.

☐   **Did you name each tenant who lives in the rental unit?**
If there is more than one tenant living in the rental unit, fill in the names of all the tenants.

☐   **Did you fill in the complete address of the rental unit?**
Be sure that you have provided the full address - including the correct unit number and postal code.

☐   **Did you check your math?**
Make sure you've correctly calculated the amount you believe the tenant owes. Check the calculations in the table on page 2 to be sure the Total Rent Owing is correct. Then check that this amount matches the amount you put in the box on page 1.

☐   **Did you include only rent amounts?**
This form is only for non-payment of **rent**. Rent includes the basic rent for the rental unit, plus any amount the tenant pays you separately for services (such as parking or cable). If the tenant is paying all or a portion of a utility bill directly to the utility company or indirectly through the landlord, this is not considered rent. See the Instructions for more information.

You should **not** use this form to tell the tenant they have failed to pay amounts other than rent (such as the last month's rent deposit or an NSF cheque charge).

☐   **Did you sign and date the notice?**

You should remove this checklist before you give the tenant the notice.

DEFENDING A NOTICE TO TERMINATE FOR NON-PAYMENT OF RENT

There are four ways for a tenant to defend an application to terminate a tenancy based on non-payment of rent:

1. by showing there was an error on the notice or the application, or with service of the notice or application;
2. by showing that the rent was paid;
3. by seeking s. 83 relief; and
4. by raising a tenant claim.

Showing That There Was an Error on the Notice

The board will dismiss any application based on a serious error on the notice. Applications are routinely dismissed when the notice has any of the following errors:

- the termination date for a monthly tenancy is less than 14 days after the notice was served;
- the tenant is misnamed (although a minor typo in the spelling of the name will usually not invalidate the notice);
- the unit is misidentified (although a minor typo will usually not invalidate the notice); and
- the outstanding rent period listed on the notice is wrong (for example, including the "rent period from" date but leaving out the "rent period to" date).

Showing That the Rent Was Paid

A tenant is able to void a notice to terminate for non-payment of rent by paying all the outstanding rent before the landlord applies to the board for an eviction based on that order. The outstanding rent is the amount of rent set out in the notice along with any other rent that becomes due.

Suppose the rent is $950 and is to be paid on the first of each month. If the tenant fails to pay the June rent and a notice of termination is given on June 2 with a termination date of June 14, the tenant can void the notice by paying $950 on or before June 14.

Suppose in the same example, the landlord waits until June 25 to give the notice of termination. The tenant could void the notice by paying $950 before June 30. However, if the notice is not voided before July 1, the tenant would have to pay $1,900 to void the notice (that is, $950 for June rent + $950 for July rent).

Once the landlord applies to the board, a tenant needs to pay the outstanding rent plus the application fee to void the notice. Payment can be made either to the landlord or to the board. As of February 2011, the application fee was $170, and that fee is paid by landlords when they file an eviction application.

Occasionally there will be a dispute over whether the tenant has paid all or part of the outstanding rent. Sometimes there will be a dispute over the amount of rent to be paid under the lease. These disputes are resolved through negotiation or mediation or are decided by the board at the hearing of the application.

For example, suppose the landlord and tenant agreed that the tenant would paint the fence around the backyard in May and the tenant could take off his costs in painting the fence from the June rent. The landlord might believe that the agreement means that the tenant can deduct only the $100 for the paint, while the tenant might believe that the agreement means that the tenant can deduct both the $100 for the paint plus $750 for labour.

Disputes over the amount of rent also arise when a tenant challenges the calculation of the rent. The landlord may try to justify an increase in rent through the withdrawal of a discount, through an above-guidance increase or where the unit is partially exempt from rent control. Meanwhile, the tenant may claim that rent should be reduced because of a reduction in services or that the landlord did not provide a rent reduction that is required under the RTA (see Chapter 19). These disputes are also resolved through mediation or are decided by the board at the hearing of the application.

In the case of tenants in social housing units, the board will not determine or review decisions concerning how much of the rent will be subsidized and how much the tenant is responsible for paying (s. 203). Hence, the board will accept the evidence of the social housing provider regarding the amount of rent that is to be paid by the tenant.

Finally, it is possible for landlords and tenants to dispute whether a rent payment was actually made. For example, a tenant may claim to have given the landlord cash and the landlord may deny it. In such a case, the issue would normally be resolved in a hearing, where an adjudicator would decide who is telling the truth.

Suppose the tenant claims to have put the rent in an envelope in the landlord's drop box and the landlord denies receiving it. In such a case, if the payment was made by cheque it would easily be resolved by the tenant replacing the cheque, and if necessary putting a stop payment on the first cheque. However, if the alleged payment was made by cash, the issue would normally be resolved in a hearing.

Seeking Section 83 Relief (Relief from Forfeiture)

Even if a landlord proves all the necessary elements of a claim for eviction, the board may refuse to grant an eviction unless it would be unfair to refuse, or the board may postpone the eviction (s. 83(1)). In determining whether it is unfair to refuse the eviction, the board looks at all the factors in the situation that affect both the landlord and the tenant. If the landlord has rented the premises to a new tenant, the board takes into account the effect of a refusal to evict on the new tenant as well.

In the case of an eviction for non-payment of rent, the RTA requires the board to provide tenants with an opportunity to void the order by paying all the outstanding rent and costs before the order becomes enforceable, usually within 11 days of the release of the order (s. 74(3)). Furthermore, tenants have one opportunity during their tenancy to void an order for eviction for non-payment of rent even after the order becomes enforceable by paying all the rent and costs before the **sheriff** actually executes the eviction order. As a result, in most cases, further relief from **forfeiture** is unfair to the landlord.

sheriff
officer who enforces orders of the courts or the board

forfeiture
losing a right because of failing to comply with one's obligations

The factors that are often examined for a non-payment of rent application include the amount of rent outstanding (the board is more likely to refuse the eviction if only a small part of one month's rent is owing than if entire months are outstanding), the likelihood of the tenant paying the outstanding amount in a timely manner (for example, if the tenant did not pay the rent while unemployed but is now fully employed with an income sufficient to pay the rent), and whether failure to pay the rent was not entirely the tenant's fault (for example, a personal tragedy or unexpected non-receipt of support payments).

The board will be more willing to allow relief from forfeiture for non-payment of rent for a tenant in a social housing rental unit because the tenant may have great difficulty paying for a rental unit in the private market without government assistance.

If a tenant claims relief from forfeiture, a landlord can lead evidence to contradict a tenant's claims. For example, a landlord may provide evidence that the excuse given for the non-payment of rent is not true. For example, the landlord could summons the person paying support to give evidence that it was paid on time. Alternatively, landlords can explain their own special circumstances. For example, the landlord may need the outstanding rent to pay the mortgage and a delay in the payment of rent could lead to the landlord breaching his or her obligations to the bank.

Relief from forfeiture is also available if the landlord fails to meet his or her obligations, or if the eviction is retaliatory—that is, in retaliation for something the tenant did. Section 83(3) of the RTA directs the board to refuse to grant an eviction if

- the landlord is in serious breach of the landlord's obligations;
- the reason for the application is that the tenant complained to a government body;
- the reason for the application is that the tenant has enforced his or her legal rights;
- the reason for the application is that the tenant is organizing a tenants' association or is a member of one; or
- the reason for the application is that the tenant has children and the presence of the children does not constitute overcrowding.

These situations are referred to as "retaliatory evictions." The section provides that an eviction shall be refused where "the reason" is a retaliatory reason, and not "a reason." Therefore, so long as the landlord can establish that the main reason for the eviction is other than one of the reasons listed above, then the fact that one of the reasons listed above exists—for example, the tenant complained to the building inspector—will not require the board member to refuse to allow the eviction.

In order to prevail, the factual circumstances in favour of the tenant must be compelling. For example, where a tenant is in arrears of rent for two months and the reason for the application is non-payment of rent, the fact that the tenant is the president of a tenants' association does not require the board to refuse the eviction unless the landlord regularly tolerates other tenants being in arrears for two months rent.

The board can also order the eviction to be postponed for a period of time. For example, if the eviction is to take place in the middle of June, the board may allow the tenant with school-aged children to remain in the unit until the school year ends at the end of June.

Raising a Tenant Claim

Section 82 of the RTA provides that at the hearing of a landlord's non-payment of rent eviction application, tenants can raise any issue, and the issue will be addressed as if they had filed their own tenant application. These issues could include maintenance complaints, allegations of harassment, or a challenge of the legality of the rent.

Tenants are not obliged to give notice of their allegations under this section. However, under the **rules of natural justice**, a landlord would be entitled to an adjournment to respond to allegations for which they are unprepared. In addition, if the first time the complaint is raised to the landlord is at the hearing, a board member will be more likely to find that the complaint is not serious.

Some tenants may wish to use s. 82 as a tactic to attempt to delay the eviction application by forcing the landlord to seek an adjournment to investigate the claim and to be prepared to respond fully. However, if the application is found to be frivolous, the board may order costs against the tenant at the conclusion of the hearing.

If a tenant does proceed to raise a s. 82 argument, the tenant will have the burden to prove his or her claim. Any board findings or decision about a s. 82 argument will be *res judicata* and cannot be raised in a separate application. As a result, tenants should not raise s. 82 arguments if they are not properly prepared to present sufficient evidence to support their claim.

Usually a party who wants an adjournment should ask for it before the hearing starts. However, if a landlord suspects that a tenant's claim made under s. 82 is frivolous, the landlord may want to proceed with the hearing, and ask for an adjournment only if the tenant's claim seems to be something more serious than the landlord thought. An adjournment would allow the landlord to bring a witness or investigate the facts.

rules of natural justice
the legal principle that parties affected by a decision are entitled to be given a fair opportunity to present their case to an unbiased decision maker

res judicata
latin for "the thing has been decided"; once a claim is heard and decided by a court or tribunal, it cannot be heard again

FORM N5: TERMINATING A TENANCY FOR DAMAGE, INTERFERENCE, OR OVERCROWDING

Form N5, the notice to terminate a tenancy early, covers the grounds of termination that can be remedied by a tenant: undue damage, interference with the reasonable enjoyment of the landlord or other tenants, and overcrowding. Note that the termination date differs depending on whether the breach is a first or second breach. This was explained earlier in this chapter and is also explained on page 2 of Form N5. Figure 9.5 is a blank Form N5. You choose the ground of termination that applies to your case and mark the appropriate box in part A. As described earlier, you may choose more than one ground. In part B, you must fill in the details of the facts that you allege are sufficient to terminate the tenancy. The size of the box in part B gives you some idea of the amount of detail that is required. You do not need to fill the box completely. In an exceptional case, you might fill the box

Figure 9.5   Blank Form N5

Notice to Terminate a Tenancy Early
Form N5

Read the instructions carefully before completing this form.

To: (Tenant's name and address)

From: (Landlord's name and address)

Address of the Rental Unit:

Termination Date

You must move out of the rental unit identified above on or before _____
(day/month/year)

Part A

Reasons for this Notice

I am giving you this notice because:

☐ 1. You, your guest or another occupant of the rental unit has wilfully or negligently damaged the rental unit or the residential complex.

☐ 2. You, your guest or another occupant of the rental unit has substantially interfered with:
- the reasonable enjoyment of the residential complex by the landlord or another tenant, or
- another lawful right, privilege or interest of the landlord or another tenant.

☐ 3. The number of people living in the rental unit is more than permitted by health, safety or housing standards.

Part B

Details About the Reasons for this Notice

The landlord must provide details about the events that led to giving you this notice, including information about the dates and times these events occurred.

40501

Figure 9.5 Continued

The landlord must complete Part C or Part D.

Part C: First Notice of Termination

☐ **This is your first notice of termination within the last six months**

> **If you correct the problem, as set out below, within seven days of when you receive this notice, this notice will be void and you will not have to move out.**
>
> **If you do not correct the problem within seven days, I can apply to the Board on the eighth day after you receive this notice, to have you evicted.**

If this notice is for Reason #1, you can correct the problem by:
- repairing the damaged property,
- paying me $_____, which is the reasonable cost of repairing the damaged property,
- replacing the damaged property if it is not reasonable to repair it,
- paying me $_____, which is the reasonable cost of replacing the damaged property, if it is not reasonable to repair it, or
- making arrangements satisfactory to me to either,
  - repair or replace the damaged property, or
  - pay me the reasonable cost of repairing or replacing the damaged property.

If this notice is for Reason #2, you can correct the problem by stopping the activities listed in Part B.

If this notice is for Reason #3, you can correct the problem by reducing the number of people living in the unit to _____ .

Part D: Second Notice of Termination

☐ **This is your second notice of termination within the last six months**

The first notice I gave you was for Reason # ____, and you voided that notice by correcting the problem within seven days of the day you received that notice.

> **Because this is your second notice within the last six months, there is nothing you can do to correct the problem and void this notice. I can apply to the Board immediately for an eviction order.**

Important Information

1. **The termination date**: If this is a **first notice** (Part C above), the termination date on page 1 cannot be earlier than the **20th** day after the landlord gives the tenant this notice. If this is a **second notice** (Part D above), the termination date on page 1 cannot be earlier than the **14th** day after the landlord gives the tenant this notice.

2. **If the tenant moves out by the termination date in this notice**, the tenancy will end on the termination date. However, if the reason that the landlord has served this notice is because the tenant has damaged the rental unit or complex, the tenant may still be ordered to pay the landlord for the damage.

3. **If the tenant disagrees with what the landlord claims in this notice**, the tenant does not have to move out of the rental unit. However, the landlord may apply to the Board for an order terminating the tenancy and evicting the tenant.

4. **The landlord's application to the Board:** If the landlord applies, the Board will schedule a hearing. The landlord must give the tenant a copy of the application and the Notice of Hearing.

5. **If you have any questions** about the law related to terminating tenancies and how it applies to this notice, you may contact the Landlord and Tenant Board at **416-645-8080** or toll-free at **1-888-332-3234**. Or, you may visit the Board's website at **www.LTB.gov.on.ca** for further information.

40501

Figure 9.5   Concluded

Part E: Signature

Signature   ☐ Landlord   ☐ Agent

First Name

Last Name

Phone Number

(   )

Signature

Date (dd/mm/yyyy)

Agent Information (if applicable)

Name	Company Name (if applicable)

Mailing Address	Phone Number

Municipality (city, town, etc)	Province	Postal Code	Fax Number

FOR OFFICE USE ONLY: File Number   –   F L and even attach a separate sheet of paper. In the latter case, write a phrase in the box, such as "see attachment."

In the box or the attachment, you need to state some specifics of the actions that give rise to the claim for termination. These should include a description of the tenant's specific actions and the dates or approximate dates on which they occurred. You do not necessarily have to provide the names or apartment numbers of tenants who have complained to the landlord. However, there needs to be enough detail in the notice so that the tenant knows "the specific allegation against her in order to (1) be in a position to know the case that must be met; (2) to decide whether to dispute the allegations made against her before the [board]; or (3) to stop the conduct or activities or correct the omission within seven days and thereby void the notice."[3] In part B, you might write, for example, "On or about April 25, 2011 the tenant created a disturbance in the halls after 2 a.m. by yelling and swearing in a loud voice and banging on the doors of other tenants' apartments." If it also applies, you could add, "The tenant often plays her stereo loudly after 11 p.m. on weeknights and between midnight and 3 or 4 a.m. on weekends."

If you have decided to use multiple grounds, and thus tick multiple reasons in part A, you may want to present the information in part B to match the breakdown in part A. This makes it easier for the tenant and the board to understand how the tenant is supposed to go about correcting the problem as indicated in part C. If yours is the first notice of termination within the last six months, and it is for damages, you need to indicate the reasonable cost of the repairs in part C. If the reason for termination is overcrowding, you need to state the number of people who are permitted to live in the rental unit. This varies from municipality to municipality, according to the local occupancy standards. The occupancy standards are often found in the municipality's property standards **bylaws**. If yours is the second notice within the last six months, you need to tick the relevant box in part D. Ticking that box is important in order to give the proper information to the tenant.

bylaws
rules about public behaviour, usually enacted by a municipality

DEFENDING A NOTICE TO TERMINATE FOR DAMAGE, INTERFERENCE, OR OVERCROWDING

There are four main ways for a tenant to defend an application to terminate a tenancy based on damage, interference, or overcrowding:

1. showing there was an error on the notice or the application, or with service of the notice or application;

2. disputing that the damage, interference, or overcrowding took place;

3. if based on a first notice, claiming that the damage, interference, or overcrowding was corrected; and

4. seeking s. 83 relief (relief from forfeiture).

---

3 *Re Metro Capital Management Group*, 2002 CarswellOnt 8691 (Div. Ct.), more commonly known as *Ball v. Metro*.

Showing That There Was an Error on the Notice

The board will dismiss any application based on a serious error in the notice. In addition to the errors listed under the above non-payment of rent section, applications are often dismissed because the description of the damage or interference was not specific enough. Tenants are entitled to be given enough detail in the notice to be able to properly address or respond to the alleged damage or interference. Failure to provide sufficient detail will invalidate the notice. For example, the board will typically dismiss an application if the sole detail a landlord gives in a notice to terminate is "tenant makes loud noises." The tenant is entitled to know what sort of noises are coming from the unit. Should the tenant lower the volume of conversations, lower the volume on the television, or stop the dog from barking? The tenant is also entitled to know where the noises are coming from. Are the alleged noises coming from the rental unit, the laundry room, or the garage? The tenant is also entitled to know when the noises occur. Is the problem that the tenant vacuums after a certain hour? Or is the problem that neighbours complain that the shower is loud when the tenant gets ready to work a night shift?

Disputing That the Damage, Interference, or Overcrowding Took Place

The landlord and the tenant may have very different views of what constitutes damage and what constitutes interference with the landlord or other tenants' enjoyment of the rental complex. There may even be different views on whether overcrowding takes place, as a landlord may argue that a friend who spends much of the day and night at the rental unit is an occupant, while a tenant may argue that the friend is a guest and does not count as an occupant for the overcrowding rules.

Tenants are responsible for the repair of undue damage to the rental unit or residential complex caused by the wilful or negligent conduct of the tenant, another occupant, or a guest of the tenant. In an application by a landlord to evict a tenant for causing damage, tenants can challenge

- whether the damage was undue damage (for example, a small scratch on a countertop is not undue damage, but breaking a countertop in two is);
- whether the wilful or negligent damage was caused by the tenant or by someone unrelated to the tenant (for example, a witness may see a person who looks like the tenant breaking a window in the lobby); and
- whether the damage was caused by the tenant or was caused by normal wear and tear.

Tenants may not substantially interfere with the reasonable enjoyment of the residential complex for all usual purposes by the landlord or another tenant. Reasonable people can disagree over whether a particular action substantially interferes with someone's reasonable enjoyment. In an application by a landlord to evict a tenant for causing serious interference, tenants can challenge

- whether the conduct occurred (for example, the landlord alleges that Jerome makes many female tenants uncomfortable in the building by making inappropriate comments in the hallways and by staring at the female tenants; Jerome may deny having made any comments or having stared at anyone; alternatively, Jerome may admit that he makes comments but deny that they are inappropriate); and

- whether the interference was substantial (for example, a tenant may admit that they play music loudly but claim that the noise is only a minor inconvenience to the other tenants).

Claiming That the Damage, Interference, or Overcrowding Was Corrected

As discussed earlier, the RTA allows a tenant to remedy these breaches by repairing the damage, stopping the interference, or removing the people who created the overcrowding situation. However, a landlord and tenant may disagree on whether the tenant remedied the breach.

Consider a tenant who punched a hole in the common hallway. After receiving a notice to terminate from the landlord, the tenant patches the hole and paints the area but does not match the paint very well to the rest of the wall. If the landlord brings an application to terminate, the tenant could argue that the damage was repaired. The board would need to decide whether the repair was sufficient.

Also consider a tenant who likes to play her stereo at the loudest volume setting late at night. After receiving a notice to terminate from the landlord demanding that she "stop playing her stereo loudly late at night," the tenant begins to turn down her radio to a slightly lower volume setting in the evening and turns it off at midnight. If the landlord brings an application to terminate, the board would need to decide whether the slightly lower volume means that the stereo is no longer being played loudly, and whether turning off the radio at midnight means that she is not playing it "late at night." This example shows that the landlord should ideally be more specific by requiring the tenant to stop playing the stereo loudly "after 11 p.m." or "after 10 p.m." instead of "late at night."

Seeking Section 83 Relief (Relief from Forfeiture)

Just as with a non-payment of rent application, even if a landlord proves all the necessary elements of a claim for eviction, the board may refuse to grant an eviction unless it would be unfair to refuse, or the board may postpone the eviction (s. 83(1)).

In the case of an eviction for damage, interference, or overcrowding, the factors involved primarily focus on the tenant's involvement in the fault and the tenant's circumstances. For example, the tenancy can be terminated for a disturbance that may not be the direct fault of the tenant. Consider two people living together who are disturbing the other tenants because they have loud arguments. If by the time of the hearing they have separated, and one wants to remain as a tenant, the board will probably consider whether the separation is likely to be permanent and whether the landlord has any legitimate reason to be concerned that the remaining tenant cannot pay the rent. If the separation is permanent, the disturbance will stop. If the remaining tenant can pay the rent, there is no unfairness in allowing the tenancy to continue.

FORM N6: TERMINATING A TENANCY FOR AN ILLEGAL ACT OR MISREPRESENTATION OF INCOME

Form N6 is used for notice to terminate a tenancy early for an illegal act or misrepresentation of income. Figure 9.6 shows a blank N6 form. The landlord needs to tick the box with the reason that notice is given and provide details about the reason on page 1 of the form. Misrepresentation of income is a ground of termination only in **public housing** or some form of social housing as listed in s. 7(1), paragraph 1, 2, 3, or 4.

public housing
rental housing provided by a government body at reduced rents to people with low incomes

An illegal act does not need to be a *Criminal Code* offence. Breach of a municipal bylaw or a provincial offence qualifies as an illegal act. To terminate the tenancy, the illegal act must take place in the rental unit or elsewhere at the residential complex.

The tenant has no right to remedy either an illegal act or a misrepresentation of income. However, in determining the notice period, you must have regard to whether a notice is a first or second notice of termination within the past six months. For the notice that you are preparing to be a second notice, the first notice must be a Form N5 notice, not a Form N6 notice.

To indicate that this notice is a second notice, and to use the 14-day termination period, the landlord must be able to prove that the first notice was validly given. The landlord cannot give out a notice without justification and then claim that any other notice is a second notice within six months. However, in a hearing based on the second notice, there is not likely to be a detailed examination of whether the first notice would have justified termination of the tenancy; rather, if the tenant challenges the first notice, the landlord needs to show that there is a reasonable degree of validity to that notice.

If there was a previous notice for an illegal act or misrepresentation of income that was not acted on, the current Form N6 is not considered to be a second notice, and you must allow a 20-day termination period. This is set out on page 2 of Form N6, where you are required to tick off the notice as either a first notice or a second notice. In either case, the tenant does not have the opportunity to correct the problem.

A shorter termination period is also available where the illegal act involves the production of or trafficking in an illegal drug. In those cases landlords can give as short as a 10-day termination period (s. 61(2)). In addition, when issuing an eviction order in drug cases, the board will order that the sheriff execute the enforcement of the order as soon as possible. Similar expedited orders are given for the other grounds for termination that require the minimum 10 days notice of termination—that is, impaired safety (s. 66), wilful damage (s. 63), and substantial interference with the landlord who resides in a small building (s. 65).

Note that the landlord's burden of proving an illegal act is not as onerous as the government's burden of proving an illegal act for the purpose of a criminal prosecution. The landlord needs to establish that it is more likely than not that the tenant committed the illegal act; rather than having to prove the illegal act beyond a reasonable doubt. The case law makes it clear that there is no need for a conviction for the landlord to succeed in the eviction application.

Figure 9.6   Blank Form N6

Notice to Terminate a Tenancy Early
Illegal Act or Misrepresentation of Income
Form N6

Read the instructions carefully before completing this form.

To: (Tenant's name and address)	From: (Landlord's name and address)

Address of the Rental Unit:

Termination Date

You must move out of the rental unit identified above on or before _____

(day/month/year)

Reason for this Notice

I am giving you this notice because:

☐ 1. I believe that you or another occupant of the rental unit has committed an illegal act or is carrying on an illegal business at the residential complex involving:
   - the production of an illegal drug,
   - trafficking in an illegal drug, or
   - possession of an illegal drug for the purposes of trafficking,
   or that you have permitted someone else to do so.

☐ 2. I believe that you or another occupant of the rental unit has committed an illegal act or is carrying on an illegal business, other than an illegal act or business described in reason #1 above, at the residential complex, or that you have permitted someone else to do so.

☐ 3. You live in a rent-geared-to-income unit and have misrepresented your income or that of family members who live in the rental unit.

Details About the Reason for this Notice

The landlord must provide details about the events that led to giving you this notice, including information about the dates and times these events occurred.

40601

Figure 9.6   Continued

About the Termination Date...

☐ **If this notice is for reason #1 only:**
- the termination date the landlord puts in this notice cannot be earlier than the tenth day after this notice is given, and
- there is no opportunity for you to correct the problem and void this notice.

If this notice is for reason #1 <u>and</u> reason #2 or #3:
- the earliest termination date the landlord can put in this notice will depend on whether this is the first or second notice of termination. See below.

☐ **If this notice of termination is for reason #2 or reason #3 and this is your first notice of termination within the last six months:**
- the termination date the landlord puts in this notice cannot be earlier than the **20th** day after this notice is given, and
- there is no opportunity for you to correct the problem and void this notice.

☐ **If this notice is for reason #2 or reason #3 and this is your second notice of termination within the last six months:**
- the termination date the landlord puts in this notice cannot be earlier than the **14th** day after this notice is given provided the following conditions apply:
  - the first notice of termination (a Form N5) was given because:
    - you damaged the rental unit or the residential complex,
    - you interfered with the reasonable enjoyment of others at the residential complex or
    - the unit was overcrowded, and
  - you voided that notice by correcting the problem within seven days of receiving the notice.
- there is no opportunity for you to correct the problem and void this notice.

Important Information

1. **If the tenant moves out by the termination date in this notice**, the tenancy will end on the termination date. However, if the reason that the landlord has served this notice is because the tenant of a Rent-Geared-to-Income unit has misrepresented their income or that of family members who live in the rental unit, the tenant may still be ordered to pay the landlord for the additional amount of money that the tenant would have been required to pay if the tenant had not misrepresented their income.

2. **If the tenant disagrees with what the landlord claims in this notice**, the tenant does not have to move out of the rental unit. However, the landlord may apply to the Board for an order terminating the tenancy and evicting the tenant.

3. **The landlord's application to the Board:** The landlord may file their application as soon as they have given the tenant this notice. If the landlord applies, the Board will schedule a hearing. The landlord must give the tenant a copy of the application and the Notice of Hearing.

4. **If you have any questions** about the law related to terminating tenancies and how it applies to this notice, you may contact the Landlord and Tenant Board at **416-645-8080** or toll-free at **1-888-332-3234**. Or, you may visit the Board's website at **www.LTB.gov.on.ca** for further information.

40601

Figure 9.6   Concluded

Signature   ☐ Landlord   ☐ Agent

First Name

Last Name

Phone Number

(⬚⬚⬚) ⬚⬚⬚ ⬚⬚⬚⬚

Signature	Date (dd/mm/yyyy)

Agent Information (if applicable)

Name	Company Name (if applicable)	
Mailing Address	**Phone Number**	
Municipality (city, town, etc.)	**Province**	**Postal Code**	**Fax Number**

FOR OFFICE USE ONLY: File Number ⬚⬚⬚ - ⬚⬚⬚⬚⬚ F L ⬚⬚

Delivery Method :   ☐ In Person   ☐ Mail   ☐ Fax   ☐ Courier   ☐ Email

40601

FORM N7: TERMINATING A TENANCY EARLY FOR IMPAIRED SAFETY, WILFUL DAMAGE, OR SERIOUS INTERFERENCE WITH RESIDENT LANDLORD'S REASONABLE ENJOYMENT

Form N7 is used for the grounds of termination, other than illegal act, that only require a minimum 10-day notice of termination. These include impaired safety, wilful damage of the rental unit or residential complex, using the rental unit in a manner inconsistent with its use as residential premises, and interfering with the landlord's reasonable enjoyment of the building. The last ground applies only where the landlord lives in the building and the building has three or fewer residential units. Figure 9.7 shows a completed Form N7.

The details in the N7 notice must be specified in the box provided for that purpose. It is best to provide the name of the person who did the act that gave rise to the application, if the name is known. However, if the name is not known, perhaps because the person was a guest of a tenant, you should describe the person by gender, size, apparent age, and any other identifying physical features. If you know or suspect that the person was a guest of the tenant, you should state that fact. The details on the notice should also set out the specific act that is complained of and the time and date, or approximate time and date, on which it occurred. For claims of serious impairment of safety, the details should clearly show why safety was seriously impaired by the act in question. Typical acts that impair safety include throwing beer bottles or other items off a balcony, blocking fire escapes, jamming open fire doors for extended periods or setting garbage on fire. For wilful damage, the details should clearly show how the damage was deliberately caused. You may need to attach a sheet of paper to give sufficient details of the act complained of.

If a tenant wilfully causes damage to the rental unit or residential complex, the landlord can choose whether to proceed with an N5 damage claim (under s. 62) or an N7 damage claim (under s. 63). The two biggest differences are that the N7 notice does not provide an opportunity for the tenant to void the notice by repairing or paying for the damage, and that the landlord must prove that the tenant deliberately caused the damage.

The RTA permits a landlord who lives in a building containing three or fewer units to give a 10-day notice of termination if the tenant substantially interferes with the landlord's reasonable enjoyment of the building (s. 65). Unlike notices for termination where the landlord does not live in the building or where the building has four or more units, tenants do not have an opportunity to correct their behaviour. Furthermore, under s. 84 of the RTA, unless the board grants relief from forfeiture, the sheriff is asked to expedite the enforcement of such eviction orders.

Figure 9.7   Completed Form N7

10-Day Notice to Terminate a Tenancy Early
Form N7

Read the instructions carefully before completing this form.

To: (Tenant's name and address)	From: (Landlord's name and address)
Joseph Thornton Apartment 406—65 Smythe Avenue London, ON N7B 5R5	Elizabeth Voles c/o Mary Voles 425 Main Street West London, ON N6A 4P4

Address of the Rental Unit:

same as above

425 Main Street West
London, ON N6A 4P4

Termination Date

You must move out of the rental unit identified above on or before September 15, 2011
(day/month/year)

Reason for this Notice

I am giving you this notice because:

☒ 1. You, your guest or another occupant of the rental unit has seriously impaired the safety of another person, and this event occurred in the residential complex.

☐ 2. You, your guest or another occupant of the rental unit has wilfully damaged the rental unit or the residential complex.

☐ 3. You, your guest or another occupant of the rental unit has used the rental unit or the residential complex in a manner that is inconsistent with its use as residential premises and this has caused or can be expected to cause serious damage.

☐ 4. You and I live in the same building and you, your guest or another occupant of the rental unit has substantially interfered with my reasonable enjoyment of the building or has substantially interfered with another of my lawful rights, privileges or interests. **Note:** This reason applies only if the building has three or fewer residential units.

Details About the Reason for this Notice

The landlord must provide details about the events that led to giving you this notice, including information about the dates and times these events occurred.

On September 2, 2011, the tenant Joe Thornton, or his guests, threw beer bottles off the balcony of his apartment onto a walkway leading from the side entrance to the parking area. This happened at approximately 4 p.m.

40701

Figure 9.7 Concluded

Important Information

1. **The termination date** cannot be earlier than ten days after this notice is given.

2. **If the tenant moves out by the termination date in this notice**, the tenancy will end on the termination date. However, if the reason that the landlord has served this notice is because the tenant has damaged the rental unit or complex, the tenant may still be ordered to pay the landlord for the damage.

3. **If the tenant disagrees with what the landlord claims in this notice**, the tenant does not have to move out of the rental unit. However, the landlord may apply to the Board for an order terminating the tenancy and evicting the tenant.

4. **The landlord's application to the Board:** The landlord may apply as soon as they have given the tenant this notice. If the landlord applies, the Board will schedule a hearing. The landlord must give the tenant a copy of the application and the Notice of Hearing.

5. **If you have any questions** about the law related to terminating tenancies and how it applies to this notice, you may contact the Landlord and Tenant Board at **416-645-8080** or toll-free at **1-888-332-3234**. Or, you may visit the Board's website at **www.LTB.gov.on.ca** for further information.

Signature   ☒ Landlord   ☐ Agent

First Name

| M | A | R | Y | | | | | | | | | | | | | | | | | | | | | | | | | |

Last Name

| V | O | L | E | S | | | | | | | | | | | | | | | | | | | | | | | | | | | |

Phone Number

(5 1 9) 6 6 4 3 0 3 0

Signature	Date (dd/mm/yyyy)
	04/09/2011

Agent Information (if applicable)

Name	Company Name (if applicable)
MARY VOLES	Property Manager

Mailing Address	Phone Number
425 Main Street West	519-664-3030

Municipality (city, town, etc.)	Province	Postal Code	Fax Number
London	ON	N6A 4P4	n/a

FOR OFFICE USE ONLY: File Number ☐☐☐ – ☐☐☐☐☐ F L ☐☐
Delivery Method : ☐ In Person   ☐ Mail   ☐ Fax   ☐ Courier   ☐ Email

40701

DEFENDING A NOTICE TO TERMINATE FOR AN ILLEGAL ACT, IMPAIRED SAFETY, WILFUL DAMAGE (S. 62), OR INTERFERING WITH THE REASONABLE ENJOYMENT OF LANDLORDS IN THEIR HOMES

Defending a notice to terminate for these allegations is very similar to defending an application based on a notice to terminate for damage or serious interference.

A tenant cannot void a first notice by correcting the wrongful behaviour in these cases. However, if you are representing the tenant you should consider bringing evidence that the tenant has stopped or corrected the behaviour for the purpose of seeking relief from forfeiture under s. 83. Consider also an illegal act in the residential complex by a tenant's child who is a young adult. If the offender has been removed from the premises, the tenant gives evidence that he or she will not permit the wayward child to reside there again, and the board believes that evidence, the board may well allow the tenancy to continue under s. 83(1). An illegal act may also be a minor one, such as theft in splitting a cable television transmitter. If the tenant complies with all other obligations, the board may relieve against the eviction for an illegal act under s. 83(1).

The board may be more open to s. 83 arguments if the tenant can demonstrate that his or her action was a single event that he or she is willing to try to rectify and is not likely to reoccur. For instance, if a tenant broke his window one night trying to get into his own unit when he returned from a night of partying and realized that he forgot his keys, the board would be much more inclined to grant relief from forfeiture if the tenant pays for the damage.

STEPS TO TAKE AFTER COMPLETING THE NOTICE OF TERMINATION

After completing the notice of termination, you must ensure that it is given to the tenant. That is usually done by mail, by courier, or by giving it to your client or a process server to give to the tenant. Unless you are dealing with a process server who has served RTA notices before, you must inform the process server of the allowable means for serving the notice. Once service has been completed, immediately prepare or obtain a certificate of service from the person who served the notice. (See Figure 9.8.) You may want to fill out the certificate, apart from the means of service, and give it to the landlord or the process server with the notice. You must make sure that the landlord or process server signs and sends the certificate of service back to you because you will be required to prove to the board that notice was given to the tenant. We recommend that you also staple a copy of the document to the certificate of service.

Figure 9.8 Certificate of Service

Landlord and Tenant Board
Ontario

Certificate of Service

File Number (if applicable): ☐☐☐ – ☐☐☐☐☐

Address of Rental Unit:

Unit / Apt. / Suite:

Street Address:

Municipality (City, Town, etc):

Postal Code:

I, _____ , certify that on ☐☐ / ☐☐ / ☐☐☐☐ ,

dd   mm   yyyy

I gave a copy of the following document(s):

☐ Notice of Termination Form # ____
☐ Application Form #_____
☐ Notice of Hearing

☐ Motion to Set Aside an Ex Parte Order
☐ Request to Review an Order
☐ Other _____
(insert name of document)

to the following person(s):

☐ the tenant   ☐ the landlord   ☐ other

_____
(insert the name of the person you gave the document to)

☐ more than one tenant, who is a party to the same application, on the same date and in the same way. (If you check this box, attach a list of the names and addresses of the people you served.)

by the following method of service:

☐ handing the document(s) to the person(s)
☐ handing the document(s) to an authorized employee of the landlord.
☐ handing the document(s) to an adult person in the tenant's rental unit.
☐ leaving the document(s) in the mailbox, or place where mail is normally delivered.
☐ placing the document(s) under the door of the rental unit or through a mail slot in the door.
☐ sending the document(s) by courier to the person(s).
☐ sending the document(s) by fax to fax number: _____
☐ sending the document(s) by mail or Xpresspost to the last known address of the person(s), at :

☐ a different method of service (provide details)

Notes:

1. The only document that can be properly served by posting it to the door of the rental unit is a notice of intent to enter a rental unit given under section 27 of the *Residential Tenancies Act*, unless a Member orders otherwise pursuant to Rule 5.2 of the Landlord and Tenant Board's Rules of Practice.

2. It is an offence under the *Residential Tenancies Act* to file false or misleading information with the Landlord and Tenant Board.

Signature   ☐ Landlord   ☐ Tenant   ☐ Agent   ☐ Other

First Name

Last Name

Phone Number
(☐☐☐) ☐☐☐ ☐☐☐☐

Signature (The person who served the documents must sign the form)

Date (dd/mm/yyyy)

For Office Use Only:
Delivery Method: ☐ In Person   ☐ Mail   ☐ Fax   ☐ Courier   ☐ Email   F L ☐☐

The Landlord and Tenant Board collects the personal information requested on this form under section 185 of the *Residential Tenancies Act, 2006*. This information will be used to determine applications under this Act. After an application is filed, all information may become available to the public. Any questions about this collection may be directed to a Customer Service Representative at 416-645-8080 or toll-free at 1-888-332-3234.

50201

Version. 31/01/2007

KEY TERMS

bylaws

consideration

forfeiture

negligent

public housing

res judicata

rules of natural justice

sheriff

wilful

REVIEW QUESTIONS

1. What is the most common reason landlords end tenancies early?

2. a. Name three other grounds landlords can use to end a tenancy early.

   b. For the grounds you named, can the tenant reinstate the tenancy by remedying the fault?

3. If after receiving an N4 notice the tenant fails to pay their next month's rent, must the landlord serve a new N4 notice?

4. If a landlord comes to you after giving a tenant notice of termination, what is the first thing you should do on the case?

5. Suppose a landlord wants to evict a tenant on the basis of a long list of things the tenant has done wrong. What factors do you look at to decide what notice or notices of termination to give?

6. What are the differences between an N5 notice for damage and an N7 notice for damage?

7. What are the differences between an N5 notice for interfering with the landlord's reasonable enjoyment and an N7 notice for interfering with the landlord's reasonable enjoyment?

8. Can a landlord give a notice to terminate to a tenant who has been arrested for shoplifting?

DISCUSSION ISSUES

1. A fire in an apartment causes $40,000 in damage to the unit and will make the unit uninhabitable for many weeks. The fire marshall tells the landlord that the fire was probably caused by careless smoking in bed, but cannot be certain. What should the landlord do if he wants to terminate the tenancy?

2. Tenants in neighbouring units are complaining to the landlord about two tenant spouses arguing loudly inside their unit late at night. What should the landlord do?

Terminating the Tenancy Agreement: No-Fault Grounds

10

In Ontario, residential tenants have "security of tenure": to evict a tenant, a landlord must have a reason specified in the *Residential Tenancies Act, 2006* (RTA) (ss. 37(1), 38, and 39). The landlord cannot end a tenancy or evict a tenant merely because the landlord wants to do so or because the lease comes to an end. Table 10.1 sets out the valid grounds for termination at the end of a term, as well as the notice periods required.

The form for a notice of termination at the end of a term of tenancy is Form N8, which is set out at the end of the chapter in Figure 10.1.

The RTA prevents landlords from terminating tenancies for improper reasons or if the termination is unfair. This matter is discussed below, under the heading "Relief from Forfeiture." The considerations raised there apply to all the grounds for termination set out in this chapter.

In this chapter we will deal with each ground of termination in turn. We first set out the conditions the landlord must meet. We then set out how the tenant can defend against the landlord's claim. If you are acting for the tenant, you should check the facts and determine what defence the tenant may have, if any. If you are

Table 10.1 Grounds for Termination at End of Term

Description	RTA section	Notice period
Personal or family use (use by the landlord, the landlord's spouse, or the child or parent of the landlord or the landlord's spouse)	s. 48(1)	60 days
Personal or family use by the purchaser of a 1-, 2-, or 3-unit building	s. 49(1)	60 days
Occupation by a caregiver who will provide services to the landlord or a family member living in the residential complex	s. 48(1)(d) s. 49(1)(d)	60 days 60 days
Demolition	s. 50(1)(a)	120 days
Conversion to a use other than residential	s. 50(1)(b)	120 days
Renovations or repairs that require vacant possession and a building permit	s. 50(1)(c)	120 days
Persistent late payment of rent	s. 58(1)1	60 days*
Ceasing to meet income qualifications in public housing	s. 58(1)2	60 days*
Cessation of employment where tenant was landlord's employee	s. 58(1)3	60 days*
Agreement collateral to agreement to buy a proposed condominium unit	s. 58(1)4	60 days*

*   For the grounds under s. 58, the notice period is normally 60 days, but it is 28 days in the case of a daily or weekly tenancy.

acting for the landlord, you should establish the conditions the landlord needs to meet and be ready to respond to any defence the tenant raises.

PERSONAL OR FAMILY USE

For termination for personal or family use, the notice period is 60 days before the end of the term or a period of tenancy (s. 48(2)).[1] The landlord cannot bring a tenancy to an early end based on this ground. The same notice period applies to termination when a purchaser wishes to occupy a unit (s. 49(3)). The RTA appears to allow a landlord to evict a tenant for a purchaser only if the residential complex contains three or fewer residential units or is a condominium unit (s. 49(2)). (If the complex contains four or more units and is not a condominium, it appears that the purchaser must complete the purchase and then proceed to evict as the landlord rather than as the purchaser.)[2]

In both cases, the "family use" can be by the owner's or purchaser's spouse or by a child or parent of the owner, purchaser, or spouse, or by a caregiver to the owner or to one of the listed family members (ss. 48(1) and 49(1)). The case law has established that grandchildren and grandparents do not fall within the section. Clearly nephews, nieces, cousins, or other relatives who are not listed do not fall within the section.

The RTA requires the landlord's or purchaser's intention to occupy to be in good faith—that is, honest, true, and not for any improper motive. In other words, if a tenant can show that the landlord's real reason for giving the notice is to get rid of the tenant, not to occupy the unit, the landlord is not entitled to the eviction. When filing an application for termination, the person who requires the rental unit must file with the Landlord and Tenant Board ("the board") an affidavit sworn by the person who intends to move in that he or she in good faith requires the rental unit for his or her own personal use (s. 72(1)). A sample affidavit is illustrated by Figure 10.2 at the end of the chapter. If an eviction for family use is contested, it is usual for the applicant, as well as for the person who will be moving into the unit (such as the child or parent), to testify at the hearing.

You may wonder what the RTA means when it refers to the situation in which the landlord "requires" the rental unit for personal or family use. The case law has decided that the landlord does not need to establish that the requirement for possession is a need or is reasonable, only that the landlord genuinely wants to occupy the premises as a residence or have it available for a listed family member. For example, the landlord is entitled to give a notice for personal possession of a four-bedroom house for the landlord's 22-year-old child, provided that the parent and child have a genuine intention that the child reside in the house. However, as discussed later in this chapter, if you are representing the tenant and challenging

---

1   There are special rules if a property has been occupied by the tenant at the time of a condominium conversion (s. 51). See the brief section on severance and condominium conversion later in this chapter.

2   There is some case law under the *Landlord and Tenant Act* that could allow a purchaser to give a notice of termination (even for a building of four or more units). However, that case law has probably been superseded by ss. 49(1) and (2) of the RTA.

the genuineness of the intention, you will want to address whether the desire to move into the specific rental unit seems like a natural use of the unit.

In the case of **co-operatives** or buildings owned by corporations, the application for personal use will be allowed only if the building in question contains four or fewer rental units, or if the landlord or a member of the landlord's family has previously been a genuine occupant of the unit (s. 72(2)).

The RTA has given a right to a tenant who receives a notice of termination for personal or family use to terminate the tenancy earlier than the date set by the landlord by giving 10 days' notice of the tenant's earlier date of termination (ss. 48(3) and (4) and ss. 49(4) and (5)).

co-operative
ownership of a building by several people together, where each person has the right to occupy one unit in the building, and exclude the other owners from that unit

DEFENDING A NOTICE TO TERMINATE FOR PERSONAL USE

There are three main ways to defend an application to terminate a tenancy based on personal possession by the landlord or a new purchaser:

1. showing there was an error on the notice or the application, or with service of the notice or application;

2. challenging the good faith of the notice; and

3. seeking s. 83 relief.

Showing That There Was an Error on the Notice

The board will dismiss any application based on a serious error in the notice. Applications for personal use are routinely dismissed when the notice has any of the following errors:

- the termination date for a monthly tenancy is less than 60 days after the notice was served;

- the termination date is not the last day of a rental period (for example, the landlord listed the termination date for a normal lease as August 1 rather than July 31);

- the lease term is not at an end on the termination date (for example, the termination date is July 31, 2011, but six months previously the landlord and tenant had agreed that the lease would be renewed for a full year from January 2011 to December 2011);

- the tenant is misnamed (although a minor typo in the spelling of the name will usually not invalidate the notice); and

- the unit is misidentified (although a minor typo will usually not invalidate the notice).

Challenging the Good Faith of the Notice

On receipt of a notice to terminate for personal possession, tenants often question whether the landlord genuinely wants to move into the unit or whether the purpose of the notice is essentially to get rid of the particular tenant. If the tenant can show that the landlord does not really intend to move into the unit (and thus has been dishonest in his or her affidavit), the tenant will be successful in having the application dismissed.

At a hearing, a landlord needs to prove to the board that the landlord (or whoever will be moving in) has a genuine intention to move into the unit. In most cases the landlord wants to use the rental unit as his or her home for the foreseeable future. In other cases the landlord, in good faith, wants the rental unit for only a number of months until other permanent living accommodations are obtained. In these cases the landlord will usually be successful at the hearing. However, if the landlord wants the unit only for a few days or weeks, the tenant will likely succeed.

If you are representing the tenant, in your cross-examination[3] of the landlord, you should ask questions to determine whether it seems sensible that the landlord wants the unit: questions like whether the quality, size, and location of the unit is similar to the landlord's current living accommodations, and if they are different, why the landlord wants those changes.

In addition to challenging the eviction application, if a tenant moves out in accordance with the notice for personal possession and the landlord (or other named person) does not move into the unit within a reasonable time after the tenant vacated, the tenant can bring an application claiming that the notice was given in bad faith (s. 57(1)). A successful application would result in damages for moving costs and any increased rent paid by the tenant in new accommodations (s. 57(3)1). The board can also impose an administrative fine on the landlord (s. 57(3)3).

Tenants should note that the fact that a landlord does not move into the unit is not definitive proof that the landlord gave the notice in bad faith. If the landlord can establish a genuine intention to move into the unit when the landlord gave the notice (and at the hearing if any), but that circumstances changed, the landlord should succeed in the defence of a tenant application. This will apply especially if the landlord treated the tenant fairly—for example, by offering to let the tenant move back in. In an application under s. 57, the board is entitled to determine that the notice was given in bad faith, even though the board determined before the eviction that the notice was given in good faith (s. 57(4)).

Seeking Section 83 Relief (Relief from Forfeiture)

Even if a landlord proves all the necessary elements of a claim for eviction, the board may refuse to grant an eviction unless it would be unfair to refuse, or the board may postpone the eviction (s. 83(1)). In determining whether it is unfair to allow the eviction, the board looks at all the factors in the situation that affect both the tenant and landlord, including the family member who is to move in.

Tenants may lead any evidence that suggests that it is fairer for them to stay in the unit than for the landlord to move into the unit. This could include the fact that the tenant is elderly, the unit is particularly suited to the tenant's needs, or the location of the unit is particularly suited to the needs of the tenant's children. If the tenant does not speak English, the tenant's agent can point to the suitability of the location of the rental unit within the tenant's ethnic community. Tenants with

---

3   Cross-examination and the entire hearing process are described in more detail in Chapter 12.

low income in units with low rent can point to their difficulty in obtaining other suitable housing. The length of time that tenants or their family have lived in the rental unit can also be a consideration. However, a landlord can lead evidence to contradict a tenant's claims. For example, a landlord can provide evidence that there are other apartments available in the vicinity. These factors affecting the tenant are considered together with the factors affecting the landlord.

Landlords can explain their own special circumstances to justify their entitlement to take possession of the unit. These circumstances may include the length of time that the landlord's family lived in the building, or in the vicinity of the building at an earlier date, or the fact that a special connection with the building exists as a result of factors peculiar to the landlord. For example, a building might be near the church a landlord attends regularly, or near a social club that an elderly family member wants to walk to. A landlord's income and ability to obtain other accommodation may also be relevant, as is a landlord's intention to have his or her child occupy the complex for the purpose of managing, maintaining, or cleaning it.

Relief from forfeiture is also available if the landlord has failed to meet his or her obligations, or if the eviction is retaliatory—that is, in retaliation for something the tenant did. Section 83(3) of the RTA directs the board to refuse to grant an eviction if

- the landlord is in serious breach of the landlord's obligations;
- the reason for the application is that the tenant complained to a government body;
- the reason for the application is that the tenant has enforced his or her legal rights;
- the reason for the application is that the tenant is organizing a tenants' association or is a member of one; or
- the reason for the application is that the tenant has children and the presence of the children does not constitute overcrowding.

These situations are referred to as "retaliatory evictions." The section provides that an eviction shall be refused where "the reason" is a retaliatory reason, and not "a reason." Therefore, as long as the landlord can establish that the main reason for the eviction is other than one of the reasons listed above, then the fact that one of the reasons listed above exists—for example, the tenant complained to the building inspector—will not require the board member to refuse to allow the eviction. The decision of the board will depend on whether the board believes that the no-fault ground advanced is the main reason for the application, or whether the prohibited ground is the main reason for the application, based on all the facts of the case.

DEMOLITION

A landlord may terminate a tenancy if the landlord requires possession of the rental unit in order to demolish it (s. 50(1)(a)). The notice period is at least 120 days before the end of a period of tenancy (s. 50(2)). After receiving notice of termination for demolition, the tenant may terminate early on at least 10 days notice of the tenant's earlier date of termination (ss. 50(4) and (5)). If the residential complex contains five or more units, and the demolition was not ordered to be carried out by a government agency, the landlord must provide the tenant with another rental unit acceptable to the tenant or pay the tenant three months rent as compensation for having to move (s. 52). The board will not order the eviction until that compensation has been paid (s. 83(4)).

CONVERSION TO A NON-RESIDENTIAL USE

A landlord may terminate a tenancy if the landlord requires possession of the rental unit in order to convert its use to a purpose other than a residential premises (s. 50(1)(b)). The notice period is at least 120 days before the end of a period of tenancy (s. 50(2)). After receiving notice of termination for conversion, the tenant may terminate at an earlier date on at least 10 days notice of that earlier date (ss. 50(4) and (5)). If the residential complex contains five or more units, the landlord must provide the tenant with another rental unit acceptable to the tenant or pay the tenant three months rent as compensation (s. 52). The board will not order the eviction until that compensation has been paid (s. 83(4)).

REPAIRS OR RENOVATIONS

A landlord may terminate a tenancy if the landlord requires possession of the rental unit in order to perform repairs or renovations that require vacant possession and a building permit (s. 50(1)(c)). The notice period is at least 120 days before the end of a period of tenancy (s. 50(2)). After receiving notice of termination for repairs or renovations, the tenant may terminate early on at least 10 days notice of the tenant's earlier date of termination (ss. 50(4) and (5)).

right of first refusal (to rent)
a right to be allowed to rent before the renovated unit is offered to other prospective tenants

The notice of termination for repairs or renovations must inform the tenant of his or her **right of first refusal** to return to the premises once it is ready for occupancy, and how the tenant may exercise that right (s. 50(3)). To exercise the right of first refusal, the tenant must give the landlord notice in writing before vacating the rental unit (s. 53(2)). A tenant who exercises a right of refusal may reoccupy the rental unit at the rent that would have been lawful if there had been no interruption in the tenant's tenancy (s. 53(3)). To preserve the right of first refusal, the tenant must inform the landlord, in writing, of any change of address (s. 53(4)).

If the residential complex contains five or more residential units, and the tenant gives the landlord notice of exercising the right of first refusal, the tenant is entitled to compensation equal to the rent for the lesser of three months and the period the unit is under repair or renovation. Before the board will order the eviction, the landlord must pay the tenant an amount equal to the rent for the period of time the landlord estimates is required to complete the repair or renovation or three months, whichever is less (s. 54(2)). The board will not order the eviction until that compensation has been paid (s. 83(5)).

For example, if the landlord gives notice of termination on August 15, specifying a termination date of December 31, for a renovation expected to take six months, the tenant can leave any time before December 31 if the tenant has given at least 10 days notice in writing. Before leaving, the tenant may choose to give written notice of an intention to return once the renovations have been completed. On returning, the rent will be the previous rent, plus whatever guideline increase would have applied had the tenant remained throughout, plus whatever above-guideline increase is approved by the board. The tenant is entitled to receive three months rent as compensation, whether or not the tenant is planning to return.

If the residential complex contains five or more residential units, and the tenant does not give notice of exercising his or her right of first refusal, and the repair or renovation is not ordered to be carried out by a government agency, the landlord must offer the tenant another rental unit acceptable to the tenant or pay the tenant the amount equal to three months rent as compensation (s. 54(1)). The board will not order the eviction until that compensation has been paid (s. 83(5)).

By giving notice of exercising the right of first refusal, the tenant allows the landlord to pay less compensation if the repair or renovation will take less than three months. However, the tenant gains the right to return to the repaired or renovated rental unit after the renovation without a significant rent increase. The landlord can raise the rent only under the rules that apply if there is no turnover of tenants. See Chapter 17 on rent increases by application.

Owners of residential complexes of one to four units need not pay the tenant any compensation when they terminate for extensive repair or renovations.

DEFENDING APPLICATIONS BASED ON TERMINATIONS FOR DEMOLITION, CONVERSION, OR MAJOR REPAIRS OR RENOVATIONS

Similar defences to those used for personal or family use can be used in an application for termination for demolition, conversion, or major repairs or renovations.

In addition, in defending a notice for termination based on repair or renovation, a tenant can challenge whether the landlord actually requires vacant possession. In some cases there can be no doubt that vacant possession is required (for example, electricity must be shut off for many months; the side of the building will be removed and exposed to the elements for many weeks; or dangerous machinery will be used in the rental unit for long periods of time). In other cases the ability to live in a rental unit under major repair or renovation will depend on the individual tenant. Whether a building permit is required is a question of fact to be determined by the municipality; the board will very rarely interfere with this decision. However, whether vacant possession is required to complete the repairs and renovation is a question that the board will answer. The desire of a tenant to live in the unit during the renovation is a factor that the board will consider in answering that question.

In defending a notice to terminate for conversion to non-residential use, a tenant can effectively defend such a conversion application by proving that the landlord's intended use is not in compliance with the zoning of the property or the landlord's **legal non-conforming right** under planning law.

As well, just as with a notice given in bad faith for personal possession, a tenant can bring a tenant application if a landlord does not perform the work to the rental unit set out in the notice within a reasonable period of time (s. 57(1)(c)). However, the tenant has to prove that the notice was given in bad faith. In order to successfully defend the tenant application, the landlord would have to show why the plans were changed and that the tenant was treated fairly.

legal non-conforming right
the right of an owner to continue a pre-existing use of a property after a zoning bylaw comes into force that prohibits the use

PERSISTENT LATE PAYMENT

Persistent late payment of rent often arises where tenants are experiencing financial difficulties or are careless in meeting their financial obligations.

For persistent late payment of the rent, the notice period is normally 60 days. However, in the case of a daily or weekly tenancy, the notice period is 28 days (ss. 58(2) and 44). According to the case law, eviction on this ground requires that the late payment be very persistent, but does not require that the payment be very late. To allow an eviction, the board normally requires that late payment be consistent in the past few months and that it has occurred at least 9 or 10 of the last 12 months. However, the payment need be late only by a few days each time.

It is important to find out why the rent payments are late. If they are late because the tenant is in financial trouble, the board will tend to be sympathetic. More often than evicting the tenant, the board will "put the tenant on terms." In other words, the board will order the tenant to pay the rent on time for the next 6, 9, or 12 months and order that on default of such timely payment, the landlord can apply without notice for termination under s. 78. If the rent payments are late because the tenant has been careless, the board may also put the tenant on terms. If the rent payments are late because the tenant wants to make trouble for the landlord, the board will be less willing to excuse the late payment. However, the board may still put the tenant on terms rather than order an eviction.

The process to be followed if the tenant fails to comply with the terms is set out in Chapter 15.

EMPLOYMENT THAT HAS BEEN TERMINATED

Where occupation of the residential rental is conditional on the tenant's employment by the landlord and the employment ends, the landlord may terminate the tenancy (s. 58(1)3). According to the case law, the tenant cannot avoid eviction by claiming that the termination of employment is wrongful under employment law. The notice period is normally 60 days (ss. 58 and 44(2), (3), and (4)). However, in the case of a daily or weekly tenancy, the notice period is 28 days (ss. 58 and 44(1)). Note also that if the tenant's employment was on a farm, the tenant has even less protection because such living accommodation is exempt from the RTA entirely (s. 5(b)). Also exempt is living accommodation in a project used at least in part for non-residential purposes if the occupancy is conditional on the occupant's continuing to be an employee of the enterprise carried out in the project (s. 5(h)). Finally, if the tenant was occupying a superintendent's premises, different rules apply. (See the section on termination of superintendent's employment in Chapter 15.)

CEASING TO MEET QUALIFICATIONS IN PUBLIC HOUSING

Apart from the limits that it sets on rent increases, the RTA applies to most housing that is publicly operated or publicly subsidized. Landlords of such housing have a special ground of termination—namely, that the tenant has ceased to meet the qualifications for the housing unit. This usually occurs when the tenant earns more income or acquires more assets than permitted by the rules governing the particular public housing units in question. However, a change in family size arising, for example, when children leave home could also disqualify a family from occupying its large unit. In that case, the public housing authority will usually allow the family to move to a smaller unit.

Termination because of ceasing to meet qualifications occurs at the end of the tenant's term, whereas termination and eviction for misrepresenting income can occur during the tenant's term (early termination).

Units that are subject to this ground for termination are rental units

- in a complex owned, operated, or administered by or on behalf of the Ontario Housing Corporation, the government of Canada, or an agency of either of them (ss. 58(1)2 and 7(1)1);
- in a complex described in the point above that is now operated by a local housing corporation or a service manager pursuant to a transfer under the *Social Housing Reform Act* (ss. 58(1)2 and 7(1)2);
- in a non-profit housing project developed under a prescribed federal or provincial program (ss. 58(1)2 and 7(1)3); and
- provided by a non-profit housing co-operative to tenants who are not members of the co-operative (ss. 58(1)2 and 7(1)4).

The notice period is usually 60 days (ss. 58 and 44(2), (3), and (4)). However, in the case of a daily or weekly tenancy, the notice period is 28 days (ss. 58 and 44(1)).

COLLATERAL AGREEMENT TO PURCHASE A PROPOSED CONDOMINIUM UNIT

When a developer builds a condominium, the building is usually ready to be occupied before the condominium declaration can be registered, and only the registration of the declaration permits the closing of sales of the units. Therefore, developers sell proposed condominium units and include **collateral** agreements that allow purchasers to occupy the units they have bought as tenants until the declaration is registered and the purchase can be completed. For a variety of reasons, the purchase may not be completed. Therefore, the RTA provides that if the agreement of purchase and sale is terminated, the landlord (the developer) can terminate the tenancy (s. 58(1)4). This allows the developer to sell the unit to a purchaser who wants to occupy the unit. For this ground of termination to apply, the RTA requires that the agreement of purchase and sale of the proposed condominium unit was made in good faith. In other words, it was made with the genuine intention to sell the unit; it was not made by the developer to gain this eviction right.

collateral
as part of

SEVERANCES AND CONDOMINIUM CONVERSIONS

There is a special rule for residential complexes that are created as a result of a **severance** (ss. 55 and 56). There are also special rules if a residential complex becomes subject to a condominium declaration after June 17, 1998 (s. 51). The details of these special rules are beyond the scope of this text.

severance
a consent under the *Planning Act* to the division of land into two or more separate pieces of land

CONCLUSION

Except for persistent late payment of rent, the grounds for termination at the end of the term of tenancy are all no-fault grounds. They are designed to allow landlords some degree of freedom to use or develop their property as they want (or repair it as necessary), while protecting tenants from being evicted for reasons other than those that are accepted as legitimate under the RTA.

KEY TERMS

collateral

co-operative

legal non-conforming right

right of first refusal (to rent)

severance

REVIEW QUESTIONS

1. What is security of tenure?
2. If a landlord decides that a tenant is annoying because the tenant votes for the wrong political party, can the landlord evict the tenant?
3. If a landlord wants to evict a tenant so that the landlord's son or daughter can move in while attending college, can the landlord evict the tenant?
4. Can a landlord evict a tenant so that the landlord's nephew or niece can move in while attending college?
5. A landlord is trying to evict a tenant so the landlord can move in. How can a tenant try to defeat the landlord's claim?
6. What would you find out from a tenant to try to obtain s. 83 relief (relief from forfeiture)?
7. Can a landlord of a six-unit building give a notice to terminate for personal possession?
8. Does a landlord have to compensate a tenant who moves out of their rental unit so that major repairs or renovations can be completed?

DISCUSSION ISSUES

1. Ever since entering her one-year lease six months ago, the tenant has been late paying her rent by a week or two every single month. The landlord needs the rent to pay his mortgage. What can the landlord do?
2. The owner of an 80-year-old house wants vacant possession to modernize the electrical system (the plugs currently are not grounded), and to replace all the original floors, kitchen cupboards, and bathroom fixtures. The tenant who has been there for 15 years doesn't want to move, and doesn't mind the house as it is. Can the tenant be forced to move?

Figure 10.1   Notice of Termination at End of Term

**Notice To Terminate a Tenancy
at the End of a Term
Form N8**

Read the Instructions carefully before completing this form.

To: (Tenant's name and address)

From: (Landlord's name and address)

Address of the Rental Unit:

Termination Date

You must move out of the rental unit identified above on or before _____ (day/month/year)

Reason for this Notice

I am giving you this notice because:

☐ 1.   You have been persistently late in paying rent.

☐ 2.   You no longer qualify to live in public or subsidized housing.

☐ 3.   The unit was made available to you as a condition of your employment and your employment has ended.

☐ 4.   Your tenancy was created in good faith as a result of an Agreement of Purchase and Sale for a proposed condominium unit and the agreement has been terminated.

☐ 5.   You are occupying the unit solely to receive rehabilitative or therapeutic services and the period of tenancy agreed to has ended.

Note: the landlord can only give a notice for this reason if no other tenant receiving these types of services is allowed to live in the complex for more than four years.

Details about the Reason for this Notice

The landlord must provide details about the events that led to giving you this notice, including information about the dates and times these events occurred.

Attach additional sheets if necessary.

40801

Version. 22/05/2007   This form has been approved by the Landlord and Tenant Board   Page 1 of 2

Figure 10.1   Concluded

Important Information

1. **The termination date** cannot be earlier than 28 days after the date the landlord gives the tenant this notice for a weekly or daily tenancy. Also, the date must be on the last day of the rental period. For all other types of tenancies the termination date cannot be earlier than 60 days after the date the landlord gives the tenant this notice and must be the last day of the rental period or, if the tenancy is for a fixed term, the last day of the fixed term.

2. **If the tenant moves out by the termination date in this notice**, the tenancy will end on the termination date.

3. **If the tenant disagrees with what the landlord claims in this notice**, the tenant does not have to move out of the rental unit. However, the landlord may apply to the Board for an order terminating the tenancy and evicting the tenant.

4. **The landlord's application to the Board:** The landlord may file their application as soon as they have given the tenant this notice. If the landlord applies, the Board will schedule a hearing. The landlord must give the tenant a copy of the application and the Notice of Hearing.

5. **If you have any questions** about the law related to terminating tenancies and how it applies to this notice, you may contact the Landlord and Tenant Board at **416-645-8080** or toll-free at **1-888-332-3234**. Or, you may visit the Board's website at **www.LTB.gov.on.ca** for further information.

Signature   ☐ Landlord   ☐ Agent

First Name

Last Name

Phone Number

( )

Signature

Date (dd/mm/yyyy)

Agent Information (if applicable)

Name

Company Name (if applicable)

Mailing Address

Phone Number

Municipality (city, town, etc.)

Province

Postal Code

Fax Number

FOR OFFICE USE ONLY: File Number ☐☐☐ - ☐☐☐☐☐ F L ☐☐

Delivery Method :   ☐ In Person   ☐ Mail   ☐ Fax   ☐ Courier   ☐ Email

40801

Figure 10.2   Sample Affidavit for Personal Possession

Landlord
and
Tenant
Board
Ontario

AFFIDAVIT

File Number: ☐☐☐ – ☐☐☐☐☐

I, ___Julia Huong___ of the City/Town/Municipality of ___Trillium ON___ make an oath or affirm and say as follows:

I recently purchased the duplex at 123 Main Street in Trillium ON. I intend to move into Unit 1 of 123 Main Street as soon as possible because I require the unit for my personal residence for the foreseeable future.

Sworn (or affirmed) before me at the ___City___ of ___Oakville___,

this ___15th___ day of ___June___, 20___11___.

_____
Signature of Commissioner

_____
Signature of Deponent

For Office Use Only:
Delivery Method: ☐ In Person   ☐ Mail   ☐ Fax   ☐ Courier   ☐ Email   F L ☐☐

50101

Version. 31/01/2007

Processing Applications Under the RTA

11

A person who applies to the Landlord and Tenant Board ("the board") is known as "the applicant." The person against whom the application is made is known as "the respondent." Applicants and respondents are collectively known as "parties" or "parties to an application."

ISSUING APPLICATIONS

Under the *Residential Tenancies Act, 2006* (RTA), an application must be in the form approved by the board (s. 185(1)). The forms are available on paper from your local board office or by downloading them from the board website, www.ltb.gov.on.ca.) Agents can be authorized to sign applications for a landlord, and the board may require a copy of the written authorization (s. 185(2)).

A party may combine several applications for hearing at the same time (s. 186). This allows a landlord to apply for eviction and arrears of rent in the same procedure, for example. (The application forms accommodate this common situation.) Note, however, that an application for an above-guideline rent increase cannot be combined with any other application (s. 186(3)).

Two or more tenants of a residential complex may file a tenant's application together if they both sign it (s. 186(2)). Such a joint application would be appropriate if both tenants are applying about similar maintenance problems in common areas, either with or without complaints about in-unit deficiencies.

When the application is for termination of the tenancy, the landlord must file a copy of the notice of termination and a certificate of service of the notice with the application. If the application is for a second breach within six months,[1] the landlord must file the first notice of termination and a certificate of service of that notice along with the current ones. When the application is for something other than termination, there may be other documents that must be filed with the application. For example, in an application for an above-guideline rent increase, the applicant is required to file the supporting invoices and proof of payment for the major repair or renovation work being claimed in the application.

---

1   Rules regarding a second breach within six months are explained in Chapter 9.

For virtually all tenant applications, tenants are not required to file any documents with the application. However, as a matter of good practice, if the tenant application is based on a complaint about a notice or document given to the tenant by the landlord, the tenant should file that notice or document.

There are fees for filing an application, which are payable in cash, by certified cheque or money order made out to the minister of finance, by credit card, or, in some locations, by debit card.

FILING DOCUMENTS AT THE LANDLORD AND TENANT BOARD

The board provides services and receives documents through two different types of offices—namely, regional offices and ServiceOntario centres. At the time of writing, there were three regional offices in Toronto and one each in Mississauga, Hamilton, London, Ottawa, and Sudbury. Those are the major urban areas where most landlord and tenant disputes take place. The regional offices process the files and organize the hearings for the area around the offices. For example, the Toronto East office serves the Regional Municipality of Durham as well as Scarborough. Regional offices have customer service representatives available during regular business hours. Customer service representatives can provide people with information about the board and the law.

There are also 67 ServiceOntario offices located across Ontario, including all the major municipalities smaller than London, many towns in the South, and many places in the North. For an up-to date list of the ServiceOntario centres, see the section called office locations on the website of the board at www.ltb.gov.on.ca. The ServiceOntario centres do not have staff of the board working behind the counters. They cannot provide people with information about the law, but they can accept documents. You can file applications and supporting documents in person at any of the ServiceOntario centres (Rule 6.1). If you want to file documents by mail or fax, you must send them to a regional office, and should send them to the appropriate regional office for the rental unit involved (Rules 6.2 and 6.3).

Landlords and tenants often need to give documents to the board. In most cases the first document the board receives from a party is an application. That is called filing an application. When a party files an application and pays the relevant application fee at a regional office, the board will almost always issue a notice of hearing. If a party is filing just one application at a board office (or sometimes two applications), the board staff person will usually prepare the application while the party waits so that they can take it away with them. If a party files multiple applications, the board will prepare the applications and make them available the next business day (or sometimes two days later).

Parties are able to submit applications by fax or by mail. You should mail or fax the document to the regional office for the rental unit involved. To file by fax, the application fee would need to be paid through a credit card. Otherwise cash or a certified cheque or money order may be used. Parties do not usually file applications by mail because that would delay the receipt of the application. If the board has not issued a single application while the party waits, the board will sometimes fax it to the applicant to save them making a trip to the board office to pick it up.

You should check what the board will do when you leave an application with the regional office or a ServiceOntario centre.

FRENCH LANGUAGE SERVICES

Parties are entitled to services from the board in French in the parts of the province designated under the *French Languages Services Act*. Rule 7 sets out the details of the provision of French language services.

HEARING DATES AND NOTICES OF HEARING

When an application is filed, the board gives the applicant a notice of hearing. In the district offices, the board gives hearing dates on most working days. Hearings at other locations are held only on certain days of the month. Subject to the board's workload and the hearing location, hearings can be set as soon as 11 to 14 days after the application is filed. However, because of backlogs at the board, hearings are often scheduled three to six weeks after the application is filed. (An applicant may want to ask for a date later than the date offered to allow more time for service, to permit more time between the date a dispute must be filed and the hearing date, or for other reasons personal to applicants.) If an applicant specifically requests it, and the service requirements permit it, the board can sometimes give a hearing date as soon as six days later. An applicant who obtains such a hearing date must **serve** the application and notice of hearing immediately, and not by mail.[2]

The board offices can issue notices of hearing while an applicant waits; however, the board typically asks agents and applicants with three or more applications to leave the applications and the fees, and to pick up the notices of hearing later that day or within the next day or two. The exact procedure and timing for bulk applications depend on the office involved and can vary from time to time with the office's workload.

Once an applicant is given the notice of hearing, each of the respondents must be served promptly with a copy of the application along with the notice of hearing. To prove that service has been completed, the applicant must file with the board a certificate of service.

The board sends notices to respondents advising them that an application has been filed against them, but it does not send a copy of the application or any details. If landlords or tenants receive such a letter but have not been served, they should contact the board to get a copy of the application and notice of hearing so that a hearing does not take place without their knowledge.

serve
deliver a legal document to a person the document affects

---

2   As of February 2011, the applicant is required to serve the notice of hearing and application. However, legislation is pending that would place the obligation to serve the documents on the board rather than on the applicant. The board would almost certainly serve the documents by mail, not by hand. That would mean that all hearings would need to be at least 10 days after the issuance of the notice of hearing. This allows 5 days for mailing and 5 days' notice for applications concerning impaired safety or illegal acts. Most other applications will require at least 15 days—5 days for mailing and 10 days' notice.

DISCLOSURE

disclosure
revealing information or
giving copies of documents

Tenants and landlords can ask for more **disclosure** about applications or disputes. In dealing with parties who are represented by lawyers or agents, it is good practice to ask the representative directly for the disclosure you require. This can include an exchange of witness lists, a brief indication of the evidence the witnesses are expected to give ("will say statements"), and the exchange of any documents that will be relied on. Naturally, if you ask for disclosure, you are expected to give disclosure. The exchange of information makes for a more efficient hearing and reduces the likelihood that an adjournment will be needed to reply to unexpected evidence.

Sometimes experts are called as witnesses. For example, when the condition of a building is at issue, an engineer may be called as a witness to give opinion evidence. If you intend to rely on an expert's opinion, you should voluntarily provide a report (or letter) from the expert, or at least a statement of what the expert is expected to say. The expert's report should be disclosed as soon as it is available. It should be disclosed 10 days before the hearing if there is that much time after the dispute is filed; if not, the expert's report should be disclosed as soon as possible.

PAYING MONEY INTO OR OUT OF THE BOARD

The board may order a respondent to pay a specified amount of money into the board (s. 195(1)). However, the board's policy is to deliver speedy hearings in order to avoid the need for this payment. For a landlord, the power to order payment into the board is most important when dealing with adjournment requests.[3] These requests must receive consideration, and many are granted. The board will generally order the tenant to pay only the amount that will become due during the adjournment. Each adjudicator may exercise his or her discretion based on the facts of the case.

If a respondent fails to pay the money into the board after being ordered to do so, the board may refuse to consider the respondent's evidence and submissions (s. 195(4)). It is important for applicants to press for the s. 195(4) remedy so that orders for payment are effective.

Respondents may pay money into the board voluntarily, but the board does not encourage them to do so.

If, before the board makes an eviction order, the tenant pays the landlord or the board all the rent in arrears, and any new rent that has come due, plus the fee for making the application, the landlord's application for eviction for non-payment is discontinued (s. 74(2)). If the board makes an order for termination and eviction, it will specify the rental arrears, the amount of NSF cheque charges and administration charges allowed, and the costs ordered by the board (ss. 74(3) and (4)). The order becomes void if the required payment is made before the enforcement date set out in the order (s. 74(5)).

If the landlord has applied for termination and eviction on grounds other than non-payment, as well as on grounds of non-payment, the application will proceed on the other grounds. If the board made an order for eviction based on non-pay-

---

3   See the discussion of rescheduling and adjourning hearings in the next section of this chapter.

ment and another ground of termination, the order for termination on the other ground remains valid.

RESCHEDULING OR ADJOURNING A HEARING

"Rescheduling" occurs when the board staff changes the hearing date by setting a new date that is earlier or later than the one originally set. If a hearing is rescheduled, the board usually issues a new notice of hearing. "Adjourning" occurs when an adjudicator, on the date set for the hearing, hears a request to adjourn and postpones the hearing to another date. In this case, the board often does not issue a new notice of hearing. Rule 12 addresses rescheduling hearings. Guideline 1 addresses both rescheduling hearings and adjourning hearings.

Parties may request the rescheduling of a hearing if they realize that it will be difficult to attend on the date set in the notice of hearing or if they will have difficulty assembling their case by that date. Parties should request the rescheduling as soon as possible and should seek the agreement of all other parties involved.

If one party asks another party for consent to adjourn, there are four possible responses:

- agree to adjourn;
- agree to adjourn subject to conditions, such as time limits or payment of money into the board;
- oppose the adjournment and argue against the request; or
- present no opposition and be ready to proceed, but not agree to the request or argue against the request.

In most circumstances, the board will not interfere with the request if the parties agree to reschedule or adjourn a hearing. As soon as possible, and no later than the morning of the day before the scheduled hearing date, the party requesting the rescheduling should deliver to the board a written request for rescheduling

- confirming that the other parties agree to the rescheduling, if applicable;
- indicating the dates on which the party requesting the rescheduling is available; and
- indicating the date preferences of the other parties.

All parties should telephone the board to ensure that the written request was received and that a new date and time has been scheduled.

If the other parties do not consent, a party can still seek a rescheduling or adjournment. The requesting party will have notified the other parties of the request by asking for their consent to reschedule. As soon as the other parties indicate that they do not agree to the request, the requesting party should decide whether it is possible to proceed with the hearing on the scheduled date (perhaps by rescheduling other commitments). If the requesting party still wants the rescheduling, the party or representative should notify the board of the request and the reasons, and inform the other parties immediately. This can best be done by sending the other parties a copy of the requesting party's letter to the board. The opposing parties can then reply to the board, stating their position on the request for rescheduling.

On receiving the written request and the reply, the board makes a decision on the request to reschedule. The board may require the parties to attend and speak to the adjournment request as a preliminary matter at the scheduled hearing date.

The board does not have a procedure for hearing a motion to decide on a disputed request for rescheduling before a scheduled date. Requests for adjournments are heard at the scheduled hearing time. The adjudicator who decides on the adjournment request is not required to conduct the hearing on the proposed adjourned date; therefore, any date can be chosen that is suitable to the parties and if a room is available.

If the parties do not agree to reschedule a hearing, the adjudicator considers the reasons for the adjournment request and whether there is prejudice to either party if the hearing is adjourned or not. A request for adjournment will generally be granted if it is made for a good reason and if there have not been previous reschedulings or adjournments. Good reasons include:

- medical problems specific to the scheduled date (in which case presumably a representative will be making the adjournment request);
- the absence of needed witnesses (despite reasonable efforts to have them attend);
- the desire to have the case heard with a related case that is scheduled later;
- a party's need for more time to retain a representative (because the party tried diligently before the hearing but failed to retain a representative for the hearing date); and
- the inability of a party's representative to attend on the hearing date because of a fixed prior commitment, such as a hearing in another case (a social engagement or other unimportant meeting is not likely to be accepted).

A party opposing the adjournment request needs to be specific regarding why an adjournment would result in significant prejudice. Examples of prejudice include:

- urgency in the need for certain repairs;
- a continued threat to the safety of other tenants; and
- the fact that an adjournment of more than a few days could cause the landlord to lose significantly more rent. (In this case, the landlord should ask that if the adjournment request is granted, the adjournment should be conditional on the payment of money into the board within a day or two, with an eviction order to be issued if the payment is not made.)

A party may make a request to adjourn a hearing after the hearing has begun. This can happen if

- one of the parties did not receive an expert's report in time to challenge its contents;
- unexpected evidence on an important issue requires a party to call new witnesses; or
- the hearing cannot be completed at the time originally set.

The original adjudicator must conduct the reconvened hearing because that person has already heard evidence and is **seized** of the case. Therefore, the hearing must be adjourned to a time when that adjudicator is available.

CONDITIONS IN ORDERS

The board may include in an order any conditions it considers fair in the circumstances (s. 204(1)). The most common exercise of this power involves conditions in an order allowing an adjournment. Conditions may include an order that a party pay money into the board to receive the adjournment or that the party receive no further adjournments. This latter condition makes the new date peremptory—that is, absolutely fixed—to the party seeking the adjournment. (Note: the word is "peremptory," not "pre-emptory," although many people make this mistake.)

seized
having begun to hear evidence in an application, the specific adjudicator must continue to hear the case until its resolution

KEY TERMS

disclosure
seized
serve

REVIEW QUESTIONS

1. a. What are the two types of Landlord and Tenant Board offices?

    b. What is done at each of them?

2. Suppose a tenant applies against the landlord. How does the tenant find out the hearing date? How does the landlord find out the hearing date?

3. What is disclosure? If you are acting for a party in an application to the board and the other party asks for disclosure, what should you do?

4. If you want disclosure and the other party won't give it to you, what can you do?

5. What is the difference between scheduling a hearing and adjourning a hearing?

6. What are some valid reasons to reschedule a hearing?

Negotiations, Mediation, and Hearings

12

The greatest number of applications under the *Residential Tenancies Act, 2006* (RTA) are for termination and eviction because of non-payment of rent. If a tenant can pay the current rent and can pay off the arrears over time, negotiation or mediation can be a useful way of resolving a landlord's claim. Applications for termination on other grounds and applications for remedies other than termination can also be successfully settled to the benefit of both parties.

NEGOTIATIONS

Parties can sometimes resolve disputes and applications through negotiations that lead to settlement. As a party's representative, you should be alert to the possibility of settlement. Settlements allow each party to retain control and gain some certainty over the outcome. The range of matters that can be settled include:

- the amount of rent in arrears;
- the payment schedule for arrears;
- the amount of rent abatement for maintenance problems; and
- the amount of a rent reduction for reduced or discontinued services and facilities.

The key to successful negotiation is to know the strengths and weaknesses of your client's case and the range of possible and likely outcomes from a hearing. Ask yourself, "What is the best alternative and the worst alternative to a settlement of the claim?" If you think negotiations may succeed, you should advise your client of your evaluation and obtain your client's instructions to negotiate.

Work out with your client an opening position, decide what would be a good result, and know your client's bottom line (that is, the most your client authorizes you to concede). It is a good idea to obtain written confirmation of your client's bottom line so that there is no misunderstanding and no dispute with the client later. Confirmation may take the form of a simple note in your handwriting, signed by your client. It will protect you (and your firm) from any allegation that you made a settlement that your client did not authorize. Your firm may tell you that it is not essential to have written authority from specified trustworthy clients of long standing. However, it is easy to obtain written authority by fax, and an email can easily confirm instructions in a telephone conversation.

Figure 12.1   Bargaining Ranges

Example 1:

Landlord's bargaining range   Tenant's bargaining range

No overlap of bargaining range: agreement unlikely

Example 2:

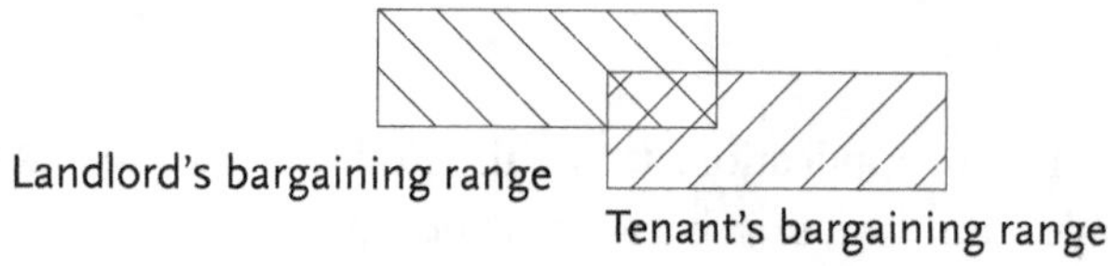

Landlord's bargaining range

Tenant's bargaining range

Overlap: agreement likely

Once you have your client's instructions, you can talk to the opposing party's representative (or to the party directly if there is no representative). You can do this by telephone or in person. In these negotiations, each representative usually talks about the merits of each client's case. Here you can learn useful information about the opposing case. After the initial statements, one representative or the other usually makes an offer, which is generally at his or her client's end of the reasonable range of possible results. The other representative then makes a counteroffer, which also is generally at his or her client's end of the reasonable range. If an offer is significantly outside what you think is the reasonable range, you may want to say that and to discuss the range of possible results in more detail. For a negotiation to result in a settlement, there must be an overlap of bargaining ranges (see Figure 12.1). Part of your job is to find out whether that overlap exists.

If the first counteroffer is within your view of the reasonable range, you will probably make another offer. The goal is to obtain a settlement as favourable to your client as possible, provided that settlement is better for your client than the risk, expense, and probable outcome of a hearing.

In the course of the negotiations, you may need to telephone your client for instructions. You may want to do that even if you are still negotiating within the range of your authority because it indicates to the other party that you are at or near the limit of your authority. In the negotiations, you may learn of **allegations** by the opposing party that are damaging to your client's case. You will then want to check with your client whether the allegations could be true, and whether there is any evidence available to you to answer or counter the allegations. New allegations or facts may change the likely outcome of the case and your client's instructions. You should arrange for your client to be available by telephone or in person when you are negotiating. You may need your client's new instructions confirmed by fax or email.

When the parties are close to settlement, one or another representative may ask for time for a client to consider the latest offer: a few hours or overnight is perfectly

allegations
statements about facts that may or may not be true

acceptable. If necessary, an interim agreement can be made to reschedule or adjourn a hearing pending settlement discussions. Sometimes a hearing is adjourned when an agreement has been reached in principle between the representatives, but the parties need time to prepare and sign the written version of the settlement agreement.

A settlement agreement should always be reduced to writing and signed by the parties. (A representative can sign for a party but is wise to do so only after obtaining written instructions.) Sometimes the representatives work out the details of the language of parts of a settlement agreement while obtaining further instructions.

Some terms in a settlement can be resolved by the representatives' knowledge of what is reasonable to ask or expect. For example, in a maintenance or service-reduction claim in a multi-unit building, the landlord will almost always demand confidentiality, and there is usually no reason for the tenant to refuse to give it. On the other hand, a tenant should refuse to agree not to complain about new problems that might arise in the future, and it is unreasonable for a landlord to make such a demand.

IMPLEMENTING A NEGOTIATED SETTLEMENT

Once a settlement has been reached, it can be implemented by the applicant's withdrawing the claim, or by a consent order of the board. On some occasions a hearing can be adjourned for a date in the future or even without a new date. However, the board is reluctant to allow open-ended delays. In the case of an adjournment, the party who has agreed in the settlement to make repairs or to pay money will have time to carry out those obligations. This is often done when it is the landlord who is required to make repairs or pay money. Once the settlement has been implemented, the application is withdrawn or dismissed on consent. If for some reason the party who is required to withdraw or consent to a dismissal does not do so, when the hearing proceeds the party who complied with the settlement can show that the settlement has been implemented. In such a case, costs can be awarded. (See Chapter 13.)

If a settlement calls for a tenant or a landlord to pay money, the opposing party will usually want to have the settlement made into an order at the time the settlement is made. In some cases an order made on consent where a tenant is required to pay money or else be evicted may provide that a landlord can apply under s. 78 of the RTA if the tenant does not meet specified conditions in the original consent order. If the tenant then fails to comply with these terms of settlement, the landlord can apply under s. 78 of the RTA without notice to the tenant and obtain an eviction order quickly. (See Chapter 15.)

For an application based on non-payment of rent, if the parties reach an agreement to settle (that is, a repayment schedule) without the use of the board's mediation service, then under s. 206 the board can issue an order for the payment of money without holding a hearing. This would avoid the need for the landlord to appear at the hearing. However, the board cannot issue an eviction order under s. 206, nor allow a future application under s. 78. If a tenant fails to meet payment obligations, the landlord would apply to reopen the application to have a hearing and to seek an eviction order. The board will schedule such an application on a priority basis to limit the prejudice to the landlord if the tenant does not abide by the agreement. However, in most circumstances it would be much more practical for the landlord to have the matter proceed to a brief hearing, or to involve the mediation service, so that the board can order the payment of the money agreed upon and the recourse to s. 78.

MEDIATION

Mediation is negotiation with the assistance of a neutral person called a mediator. At various district offices, the board has a number of mediators who assist parties in reaching settlements. A mediator is particularly helpful for an unrepresented party. One role of the mediator is to balance the relative power of the parties, so that an unrepresented party who may not be prepared to negotiate with a represented party's agent or lawyer may be prepared to negotiate with the assistance of a mediator. The suggestions and principles discussed above regarding negotiations all apply in mediation.

Parties or their representatives can ask a mediator to try to mediate an application by telephone. More commonly, mediations occur at the time set for the hearing. If a mediation fails to result in a settlement, the hearing proceeds on the same day. In an exceptional case, the parties may want to arrange to use the services of a board mediator on a day before the hearing. In some instances, a mediator will book an appointment for a mediation. Mediators do not usually arrange appointments but are available when they are on site. To see a mediator on a day before the scheduled hearing date, one of the parties should call the board office and speak to a mediator to see whether an appointment can be arranged (or, failing that, to see whether a mediator will likely be available on the day and time that the parties would like to attend). If an appointment has not been booked, the best times for parties to try to see mediators are between 2:00 and 4:00 p.m. At these times, the mediators will likely have dealt with most of the initial mediations arising from a block of hearings and may be available to deal with the walk-in mediation clients.

Mediators can help to keep a rambling or angry party focused. They can also point out problems and weaknesses with each party's case and give some guidance regarding the possible outcomes. Mediators have no power to impose a decision on the parties. It is the parties themselves who control whether a settlement can be reached.

Except for one restriction on the amount of a rent increase, a settlement mediated by a board mediator can include provisions that would otherwise contravene the RTA (ss. 104(2) and (3)).

Unlike a settlement reached by the parties alone, a settlement mediated by a board mediator can result in a consent order that provides that the landlord can apply under s. 78 of the RTA if the tenant does not meet specified conditions of the settlement. In that case, the landlord can apply without notice to the tenant and obtain an eviction order quickly if the tenant fails to meet the settlement terms. This cannot be done if the earlier settlement was achieved through negotiations between the parties without a mediator unless the settlement was incorporated into an order made after at least a brief hearing.

EXCHANGING INFORMATION

If negotiations are not attempted or do not produce a settlement and it appears that the application will be defended, the parties' representatives should exchange information about the evidence they will call at the hearing, so that there are no major surprises. Representatives who are prepared to admit certain facts should confirm the facts admitted in writing. Admissions and indications of the relevant issues and evidence allow representatives to bring only the witnesses who are needed to the hearing. This saves witness fees and shortens the hearing.

Sometimes a representative may refuse to disclose a client's case. You are entitled to know enough about the case you have to meet in order to be able to meet it. Sometimes the application or a dispute states enough for you to know the opposing party's case. If the facts are insufficient to disclose the case you must respond to, you can ask the board to direct the opposing party to provide further details of the claim or dispute. To avoid delaying the hearing, the request should be made at the earliest possible opportunity.

You can also ask the board to direct the opposing party to file a particular document or documents or other evidence necessary for the determination of the issues (s. 201(1)(d)). An opposing party, or someone related to an opposing party, can also be made to bring documents or evidence to a hearing by means of a summons.

FORCING WITNESSES TO ATTEND A HEARING: THE SUMMONS

Parties are entitled to force witnesses to attend to give evidence or to produce documents. To do this, a party asks the board to issue a **summons** to the witness. The board has a form for making the request for a summons. The party must state the name of the witness, the witness's address, the witness's relevant evidence, and the documents that the party wants the witness to bring. Representatives of parties are expected to prepare a draft summons stating the hearing time, date, and location; the witness's name and address; and the documents the witness is to bring to the hearing. The form of summons required to be used may be obtained from the board's offices.

summons
a document that the board will prepare or sign that requires a person to attend a hearing to give evidence

Even if witnesses are "friendly," some may require a summons to be served on them. For example, because of a policy of ensuring fairness as well as the appearance of fairness, a municipal property standards officer is generally not able to appear at a hearing unless summonsed. Also, an employer may require a summons to allow an employee to take time off work. Witnesses may be willing to disclose documents and discuss their evidence more fully with you once you have given them a summons.

The party who has obtained the summons must give a copy of it to the witness. In court proceedings, the person serving a summons must also give the witness the necessary conduct money at the same time. However, the board allows the conduct money to be given to the witness when he or she appears at the hearing. Technically, the conduct money should be paid in cash, but a witness will usually accept the payment of the conduct money by a cheque from a law firm or legal clinic. As of February 2011, conduct money is $50 for each day of attendance plus a travel allowance. The travel allowance is $3 if the witness resides in the city of the hearing; if not, kilometrage is payable at 24 cents per kilometre each way for the distance between the witness's residence and the place of the hearing. (If the witness lives more than 300 kilometres from the hearing location, the witness is entitled to $75 per night, and the travel allowance is the minimum return airfare plus 24 cents per kilometre each way from the witness's residence to the airport and from the airport to the hearing.) Employees of some government agencies do not want the conduct money because of the paperwork involved in turning it in to their employer. Therefore, check with them ahead of time.

As a matter of courtesy, a party or representative should tell witnesses the time they need to attend well in advance of the hearing. For example, if the witness under summons is your third witness, you may suggest an arrival time of 11:00 a.m. or after the lunch break because you will not reach the witness's evidence earlier. As much as possible, the timing should be worked out to minimize the inconvenience to each witness. Beware, however, that you must be prepared to proceed if the earlier witnesses fail to appear or are finished sooner than expected. As a matter of courtesy to the board and the other party or representative, you should have witnesses ready to testify as the hearing proceeds. If a hearing lasts more than one day, a summons may state that the witness is required to attend on the first day, but the party may tell the witness to attend on a later day. In that case, only the conduct money for the attendance required by the party needs to be paid.

affidavit
a document in a board or court proceeding in which a person sets out facts, and signs before a public official while swearing that the facts are true

If the evidence of a witness is uncontroversial, a party can obtain a letter or **affidavit** from the witness and provide that to the board. This method of giving evidence should be used only if the evidence is not crucial or if the other party or representative has agreed to it ahead of time. The other party or representative should agree if the evidence is not controversial or if receiving the evidence in writing helps his or her case. (Some cases may be assisted by a written format that takes the human element out of the evidence.)

If an important witness lives a long way from the location of the hearing (for example, in British Columbia), a party can ask the board to schedule the hearing when the witness will be in Ontario for other reasons. Alternatively, the party can take an affidavit from the witness and offer the other party the opportunity to have an agent conduct a cross-examination where the witness lives. The affidavit and the transcript can then be admitted in evidence. It would be even better to videotape an examination of the witness conducted by the parties' agents in British Columbia or to hold an electronic hearing. (See the following section.)

THE HEARING

Hearings are usually oral and conducted in person. They are scheduled to start at specific times during the day: usually 9:00 a.m., 11:00 a.m., or 1:00 p.m. A number of hearings are often scheduled for the same time block because the bulk of them are expected to be resolved by consent orders or by mediation or to be short enough to allow several hearings to be held within the following two- or four-hour period. The hearing is subject to the *Statutory Powers Procedure Act* (SPPA) (RTA s. 184(1)). The SPPA governs some aspects of procedure in board hearings, and you should obtain a copy of it and read it carefully. The SPPA establishes that the parties have a right to know the issues, to present evidence, and to cross-examine the witnesses presented by the other parties.

The board may make its own inquiries (ss. 201(1)(a) and (c)), which is the same power that adjudicators and rent officers had under previous legislation. If the board makes inquiries, it can consider the information obtained if it informs the parties of the additional information and gives the parties an opportunity to explain or refute it (s. 201(2)). The board will not generally go looking for information. It is the parties' job to bring the necessary evidence to the board hearing.

The board may hold an electronic hearing. Such a hearing can be held by video conference. More commonly, a hearing or a part of a hearing can be held by telephone conference. The board can require a party to pay for the cost of the electronic hearing. If the board proposes to hold an electronic hearing, a party can object in writing by a date set out in the notice. The party's objection would need to set out how the electronic hearing would cause the party significant prejudice.

Alternatively, the board may hold a written hearing. Under the written hearing process, the parties are required to file their evidence and submissions to the board in writing. The adjudicator will consider all relevant material presented and make his or her decision without holding a meeting between the parties. Written hearings are not appropriate where facts may be in dispute or where credibility of the parties or witness is in issue. Written hearings are typically used for above-guideline rent increases due to increased municipal taxes or utilities and for applications to vary the amount of a rent reduction due to decreasing municipal taxes. For other types of applications an applicant can request a written hearing, but, absent unusual circumstances, the request would likely be denied. A party can object to having the application resolved by a written hearing by filing an objection in writing within 27 days after the notice of written hearing is issued. To succeed, the party's objection would need to convince the board that the facts are in dispute, credibility is in issue, or a party is unable to participate in a written hearing.

The following information relates to oral hearings, which are the usual kinds of hearings. The board member assigned to conduct the hearing and issue a decision on the application is called "the adjudicator." The adjudicator has usually read the application and any written dispute before the hearing starts. This gives the adjudicator an idea of how complicated the application and defence are likely to be. We will consider two different levels of complexity.

Informal Hearings

When at least one of the parties is unrepresented, the hearings before the board tend to be relatively informal.

Suppose the case is a straightforward non-payment of rent case where the tenant does not deny the non-payment, but asks for relief from forfeiture. The adjudicator will strongly suggest mediation so that the landlord and the tenant can work out payment terms. If they cannot work out mutually agreeable payments terms, the hearing may proceed with the landlord seeking termination. At the hearing, the adjudicator will ask the landlord to state his or her case. The landlord or the landlord's representative can simply say that the rent is in arrears by a specified number of dollars, and payment was last received on a particular date for the rent (or part of the rent) due for a particular month. The adjudicator will then ask the tenant if there is any dispute as to the amount of rent owing or any reason why an eviction should not be granted. If there is disagreement, the adjudicator will probably try to sort out the disagreement by asking each party questions until the disagreement is resolved or the two positions are clear. The adjudicator will then clarify the status of the deposit for last month's rent.

The adjudicator will often ask the tenant when he or she can pay the arrears. If the tenant says "never," the adjudicator will clarify anything about the application that remains unclear and either order termination or state that an order will be issued in a few days. If the tenant proposes a payment plan, the adjudicator will ask for the landlord's comments. The landlord will explain why the tenant's payment plan is for too long or why an eviction is desirable despite the proposed payment plan. The landlord may complain that the tenant has failed to live up to previous settlements or has been the subject of complaints from other tenants.[1] The adjudicator will then likely order that the tenant can remain in the rental unit if the tenant meets a schedule of payments that the adjudicator will set out in the order.

Disputed Claims and Formal Hearings

If there is a real dispute about the facts, the adjudicator will ask the applicant to present his or her case. Before the applicant testifies, the adjudicator usually asks the applicant whether he or she wishes to swear an oath or to affirm that his or her evidence is true. An oath involves swearing to tell the truth on a Bible or other key religious document (such as the Koran). An affirmation leaves out the religious content and requires the telling of the truth under the law. Lying to the board or giving contradictory evidence are serious offences whether or not the witness has been sworn or affirmed. If the adjudicator does not take the initiative to swear or affirm the witness, the representative should ask that the witness be "sworn or affirmed." The adjudicator reads either the oath or the affirmation and the witness responds "yes."

The Applicant's Case

The adjudicator then hears the applicant's version of the facts. At this time, the evidence is presented to establish the facts relied on by the applicant. Most evidence is the statements from a witness about what the witness has seen or heard or what documents were delivered or signed. Argument about the meaning of what was said or written and submissions about the law are left to a later stage, after the evidence of all parties has been heard.

---

1   An applicant is usually restricted to making allegations relevant to the grounds put forward in the application. However, when a respondent wants relief from forfeiture (as discussed in Chapters 9 and 10), that relief is discretionary and will not be granted unless it is fair in all the circumstances. An adjudicator is therefore allowed to consider whether the tenant is a good tenant in respects other than the payment of the rent.

Usually the agent for the applicant will start the applicant's case by calling the applicant as the first witness. In the following text it is assumed that the first witness is the applicant. Be aware that in some cases it will not be the applicant themselves. The same sequence of direct examination, cross-examination, and re-examination applies to all witnesses.

If the applicant is represented, the adjudicator expects the applicant's representative to ask the applicant questions to bring out his or her version of the facts. This is known as "direct examination." For uncontroversial facts, the questions may suggest the answers. These questions are called "leading questions." Examples of facts that are usually uncontroversial are the occupation of the applicant, the address of the property, the ownership of the property, and the identity of the landlord and tenant. The following would usually be appropriate leading questions, which you would ask in different cases:

- I understand that you are the owner of 123 Elm Street. Is that correct?
- The tenant of the unit in question is Jane Smith?
- You are the tenant of apartment 6, 425 Maple Road, Oshawa?
- Your landlord is Mohammed Singh?
- I understand that you are a university student. Correct?

Questions concerning relevant facts that may be in dispute should not suggest the answers. These questions are open-ended or "non-leading questions." Good examples of non-leading questions are:

- Did something unusual happen that day?
- When you went into the living room, what did you see?
- What did you do next?
- When you arrived to move in, what was the condition of the unit?

The respondent or the respondent's representative can object if leading questions are asked about facts that are in dispute. This is done by saying, "Objection. The agent is leading the witness." The adjudicator may then hear the agent's position on whether the question is leading or may simply tell the agent to stop leading the witness.

Objections can also be made on other grounds. The most important one is relevancy. To make that objection, you would say something like, "Objection. I fail to see the relevance of that question." The adjudicator would then hear the other agent's position on whether the topic is relevant and then rule on whether the witness is to answer the question. If the adjudicator sees the relevance, the adjudicator may "allow the question." Sometimes an adjudicator will allow the question, but will request the agent asking it to proceed more quickly to the heart of the matter. If this does not happen, you may have to object again, or the adjudicator may prod the other agent to move on more quickly.

The applicant's representative needs to ensure that all the relevant facts of the applicant's story come out. The job of the respondent's representative is to object to irrelevant evidence and leading questions. You probably also want to make notes of the applicant's evidence while it is being given.

Cross-Examination

Once the applicant's representative is finished, usually indicated by the statement, "Those are all my questions," the respondent or the respondent's representative may put questions to the applicant. This is called "cross-examination." The purpose of cross-examination is to bring out facts that raise doubt about the applicant's version of the events, facts that show the applicant has reasons not to tell the truth (such as a hostile attitude toward the respondent), or facts that support the respondent's version of the events. On cross-examination you are allowed to suggest the answers you want by asking leading questions, and that is usually the best way to proceed. You may not like all the answers you receive on cross-examination, but you have an obligation to "put to the witness" any serious contradictions between what the witness has said and what your witnesses will say, so that the witness has the opportunity to explain the discrepancies.

During cross-examination, a party who is not cross-examining the witness can object to the cross-examiner's questions. Common objections are that a question is not relevant, that it assumes a fact not yet addressed in evidence, that it invites argument, or that it misstates what the witness or another witness said. The goal is to object before an improper question is answered. To object, a representative (or a party appearing without a representative) says, "objection" and states the reasons for the objection. For example, a representative may state, "Objection. I submit that the question is irrelevant. This is an application about harassment. It is irrelevant whether the landlord is losing money on the building." The party who asked the question can then reply to explain why the question is a proper one.

If the objection is sustained, the adjudicator does not allow the question. If the objection is overruled, the adjudicator allows the question. If an objection is made on grounds other than relevancy and is sustained, the cross-examiner can sometimes still ask questions about the issue. An example of a double-barrelled question is, "When did you stop entering the tenant's unit without proper notice?" The landlord's representative objects by saying something like, "Objection. The question assumes that the landlord has entered the tenant's unit without proper notice." The adjudicator should sustain the objection, and not allow the witness to answer that question. The cross-examiner may then ask, "Have you entered the tenant's unit without proper notice?" If the witness answers "yes," the cross-examiner can ask, "When did you stop?" Each question should usually address only one specific point. Questions should be short.

Re-examination

After the cross-examination is finished, the applicant's representative can ask the applicant any questions needed to clarify what the applicant said in cross-examination or to "answer" issues that arose in cross-examination. This is called "re-examination." The applicant's representative should *not* ask the applicant to repeat what he or she said before, and the questions should be non-leading. For example, "In response to Ms Smith's question, you said that you [whatever the witness said he or she did]. Why did you do that?"

Adjudicator's Questions

After the re-examination, the adjudicator may ask the applicant some questions. The adjudicator should then ask each representative, "Is there anything arising from that?" In other words, "Do you need to ask any questions to clarify or explain the answers the applicant gave me?" If the adjudicator forgets to ask, and there is something new to clarify or answer, either party's representative can say, "I have a question arising from that."

Remainder of the Applicant's Case

The applicant's representative can then call other witnesses to support the applicant's version of the events or to prove facts that are not within the personal knowledge of the applicant. (Although it is very uncommon, the applicant's representative can call the respondent as a witness in the applicant's case.) The process of direct examination, cross-examination, re-examination, and questions by the adjudicator is repeated with each witness. Once the applicant's representative has finished leading the evidence of the witnesses who support the applicant's case, the representative should say, "Those are all my witnesses."

The Respondent's Case

The respondent or the respondent's representative has a choice: to call no evidence and argue that the applicant has not made out his or her case, or to call evidence. In almost all cases, the respondent calls evidence to defend against the applicant's claim.

The respondent's case follows a similar course to the applicant's case. The respondent usually testifies first, and the respondent's testimony follows the sequence of direct examination, cross-examination, re-examination, and the adjudicator's questions. The rules about leading and non-leading questions apply. In other words, the questions of the respondent's representative to the respondent should be non-leading once any non-controversial matters have been covered. The applicant's questions to the respondent (in cross-examination) can be leading questions. The questions of the respondent's representative to the respondent on re-examination should be non-leading.

The respondent or the respondent's representative then calls any other witnesses who support the respondent's case. When finished the respondent's representative will say, "Those are all my witnesses."

Reply Evidence

The applicant may then call reply evidence to answer anything new that arose during the respondent's case. This evidence can come from the applicant, the applicant's witnesses, or from a new witness. However, it must be responsive to new matters raised in the respondent's case that the applicant could not reasonably have anticipated. If the evidence could have been called before, the adjudicator can refuse to hear it at the reply stage to prevent the applicant from "splitting the applicant's case."

The last part of a hearing is submissions. However, before we discuss those, let us consider a matter of hearing procedure designed to stop witnesses from tailoring their evidence to match the evidence of other witnesses.

Order Excluding Witnesses

In many cases, a representative may suspect that witnesses for the other side may tailor their evidence according to what they hear from earlier witnesses. In such a case, the representative should ask for an order excluding witnesses. This request should be made at the beginning of the hearing, before any evidence is called. The adjudicator will usually grant this order. The adjudicator will order that all witnesses except the applicant and respondent leave the hearing room while the evidence is being led and that no witness or party tell any other witness what was said in evidence. If this order is made, it is important that the parties, their representatives, and all the witnesses follow it.

A representative may sometimes accidentally violate the order by telling a witness what another witness has said in evidence. If this happens, the representative should inform the adjudicator of the error as soon as possible. Like everything else said to the adjudicator, such information must be given to the adjudicator in the presence of the other party's representation, or the other party, if he or she is not represented.

Often it is appropriate for witnesses to hear what other witnesses say in evidence. For example, expert witnesses should usually hear evidence of the facts on which they base their opinions. Expert witnesses are generally not included in an order excluding witnesses. An order excluding witnesses cannot prevent persons who are parties to the application (applicants or respondents) from hearing the evidence. However, on the advice of their representatives, parties may voluntarily leave the hearing room so that they do not hear other evidence. Alternatively, having parties testify before the other witnesses for their side ensures that their evidence is not "tainted" by hearing the evidence of others.

Submissions

The final stage of a hearing goes by a number of different names—submissions, argument, summing up, or summation. In the normal course of submissions, the applicant proceeds first, followed by the respondent. Then the applicant can reply to anything new in the respondent's submissions. Some adjudicators change the process by having the tenant speak last, or by not allowing the applicant to reply. The adjudicators may do this because unrepresented applicants usually do not restrict their reply to new matters raised by the respondent; instead they repeat what they said before, which is neither appropriate nor helpful. As a representative, you will likely be allowed to reply if the adjudicator knows that you will restrict your reply submissions to new points. In an appropriate case, when there is nothing new to reply to, you can earn the adjudicator's gratitude by saying, "I have no reply submissions."

The content of both parties' submissions should address two areas: first, they should summarize and draw out the implications of the evidence, and, second, they should state what the relevant law is and how it applies to the facts. Good submissions do not repeat the evidence, but they include reference to the important parts of the evidence. Good submissions make the most of the good parts of the evidence and explain away the bad parts. Good submissions for a party show how the pieces of the evidence fit together to justify that party's claims.

Often, the relevant law is clear, and in that case a brief reference to it is sufficient. If the relevant law is not clear, then representatives should argue for the interpretation of the law that will advance their client's case. This is done by setting out the issue clearly, quoting the relevant sections of the RTA and the regulations, and referring to the relevant guidelines. You can also refer the adjudicator to previous decisions of the board, of the Ontario courts, and of the courts of other provinces or common law jurisdictions (such as England, Australia, New Zealand, or the United States). See the discussion in Chapter 2 about the case law. That chapter explains what decisions are binding and what decisions are persuasive, what those terms mean, and the hierarchy of precedents. When referring to decisions of any decision-making body other than the board, be careful to show that the legislation is the same as the RTA in all relevant respects, or that the issue under the RTA is the same as the issue in the other case. You can also refer to what textbooks say about the interpretation and application of the RTA. See the discussion of texts also in Chapter 2.

It is important to learn how to put your arguments forcefully, but at the same time respectfully. If you are putting forward a particular interpretation or application of the law that is not obvious, but that is essential for your client to win the case, then you must press home the argument for that interpretation or application. This may often include showing that your interpretation of a section of the RTA is correct for various reasons, such as reasons of policy (the goals of the legislation) and consistency with other sections of the Act, as well as the common meaning of the words. If, however, your client has several routes to win the case, then you should be ready to move to the next point of your argument if the adjudicator hints or tells you to "move on."

You should have planned your submissions when you were planning the evidence you would call. In the days before the hearing you should make photocopies of any case law or texts you intend to rely on. You need at least three copies: one for yourself, one for the opposing party, and one for the adjudicator. Ideally you will highlight the key sections of the case law or texts you will rely on. If there are a number of cases and sections of texts, then you are wise to staple or bind the copies with a table of contents and tabs or page numbers through the whole package.

Once all the evidence has been put in, you need to adjust your submissions to fit the evidence that was actually given at the hearing. If there has been a significant amount of evidence, you may want to ask for a short recess to organize your argument, both on the evidence and on how the law applies to it. If a case takes more than a few hours, there will also be meal breaks or other breaks during which you can adjust your planned submissions to the evidence that has been given.

After the Submissions

After hearing the submissions, the adjudicator may adjourn the hearing pending the issuance of the order. In that case the adjudicator will consider the case and issue an order in writing. You are entitled to ask for reasons to be issued, and then the order will normally be issued with reasons, although the order can be issued with reasons to follow. Even without a request for reasons, adjudicators usually issue reasons if there has been a formal hearing.

Sometimes the adjudicator may just take a short recess and then return to the hearing room to deliver the decision. In that case you will want to make detailed notes of what the adjudicator says. Unless the adjudicator asks for further input on a particular point, it is improper to comment on the decision and very improper to argue with the adjudicator.

When the adjudicator is finished, from your place at the table, you can say "thank you," meaning thank you for hearing our evidence and my submissions, but you should not say anything else to the adjudicator. Throughout the hearing and at the end, you should never try to speak to the adjudicator unless in the presence of the opposing party or his or her representative.

KEY TERMS

affidavit
allegations
summons

REVIEW QUESTIONS

1. What is a bargaining range? Is a settlement more likely if the bargaining ranges overlap or if they don't?

2. What are the key issues in successful negotiating?

3. If a settlement is not reached in a negotiation, has anything been gained through the negotiation? If so, what?

4. How does mediation differ from negotiation?

5. What are the benefits of negotiating with the board's mediation service?

6. To summons a witness, what are the main things you have to do?

7. Create an outline of how a formal hearing is conducted.

8. What is a leading question?

9. When can a party's representative ask leading questions?

10. What does an agent talk about when making closing submissions?

The Order and Beyond

13

THE ORDER

Except in complicated cases, the Landlord and Tenant Board ("the board") usually prepares and issues orders within a few days after the hearing is completed. The order is mailed to all parties and their representatives, or on request, left in the board office for pickup. Reasons are not usually included. In more complicated cases, the board will often issue reasons. In any event, if the landlord or tenant asks at the hearing or within 30 days after the order is issued, the board is required to issue reasons.

Under the *Residential Tenancies Act, 2006* (RTA), an order for termination cannot generally be effective earlier than the date of termination set out in the notice of termination (s. 80(1)). However, if the order is made on an application based on a notice of termination alleging that the tenant impaired the safety of any person or that the tenant is wilfully causing damage to the unit or the residential complex, the board may terminate the tenancy earlier than the date of termination set out in the notice of termination (s. 80(2)).

COSTS

The board may order a party to an application to pay costs to another party (s. 204(2)). The board generally orders the respondent to pay the application fee incurred by a successful applicant. Fees of agents or lawyers are less often awarded. A successful party may also receive an order for the payment of the party's out-of-pocket costs of the hearing, including witness-conduct money.

Generally, agents' or lawyers' fees are awarded only against a party who is seen to have been at fault in an initial hearing, or who has been unsuccessful in a hearing to review an order. Agents' or lawyers' fees may be awarded against a party who has

- brought a frivolous or vexatious application or motion;
- initiated an application or any procedure in bad faith;
- taken unnecessary steps in a proceeding, thereby making the proceeding longer than it should have been;
- failed to take necessary steps, such as those required by the RTA or the rules;
- been guilty of misconduct at the hearing or in the proceeding;
- raised an issue that is irrelevant to the proceedings and continued to pursue that issue after an adjudicator has pointed out that it is irrelevant;

- asked for adjournments or delays without justification;
- failed to prepare adequately for the hearing;
- acted contemptuously toward an adjudicator or showed a lack of respect for the process or the board;
- failed to follow the directions of an adjudicator or upset the orderly conduct of the hearing; or
- unreasonably maligned another party or slurred the character of the other party.

Even when fees for a paid agent or a lawyer are awarded, they are for relatively small amounts.[1] If these fees are awarded, they are often awarded only for a portion of a hearing and perhaps a portion of the preparation time. For example, the board may award a party costs for the time that the other party wasted at the hearing, plus the preparation time to deal with the issue that was irrelevant.

The board can also order that its costs be paid by a party or a paid agent or counsel of a party (s. 204(3)). These costs orders are unusual and are awarded only if the board advises the party, or the agent or counsel, that it is considering such an order and hears submissions as to why the order should not be made.

CONDITIONS IN ORDERS

jurisdiction
the limits on what the board can decide and how it must go about making its decisions

The board may include in an order any conditions it considers fair in the circumstances (s. 204(1)). To be valid under our general law, the conditions must be related to the tenancy and the scope of the board's **jurisdiction**. For example, the board has no jurisdiction to order a party to get a haircut, but the board does have jurisdiction to order a party to keep the unit clean as a condition in another order, such as an order allowing the relief from forfeiture. An order can include a condition that a tenant pay the rent in arrears according to schedule, failing which the tenancy is terminated.

ENFORCING AN ORDER FOR EVICTION

writ of possession
an order of the court that directs the sheriff to evict a person and give possession of a property to a person named in the writ of possession

Once an eviction order is issued, it has the same effect as a **writ of possession** and may be enforced in the same manner (s. 85). As a writ of possession, the order is an order to the sheriff to give possession of certain premises to the landlord. The sheriff—that is, the court enforcement office—charges a fee for evicting a tenant. As of February 2011, the fee was $75 to file the order and $240 plus mileage for enforcing the eviction.

You should note that an order evicting a tenant expires six months after the date on which the order takes effect unless it is filed with the sheriff before it expires (s. 81).

---

1   As of February 2011, the Rules of Practice limit representation fees to $75 per hour for the services of a lawyer or paid agent, to a total of $500. However, a number of board decisions have ordered higher costs awards in extreme circumstances.

The process varies somewhat among different municipalities and counties, and you should check the process in your municipality. In most jurisdictions, the sheriff serves a written notice to vacate and gives the tenant seven more days to vacate. It is the responsibility of the landlord or the landlord's agent to inform the sheriff if the tenant has not vacated by the date set out in the sheriff's notice to vacate. If the sheriff is advised that the tenant has not vacated pursuant to the notice, the sheriff sends one or more officers to force the tenant to leave. It is the landlord's responsibility to arrange for a locksmith to attend at that time to change the locks to ensure that the tenant cannot get back into the unit. It is essential that the tenant not obtain a copy of the key to the new lock.

Sometimes the tenant will not have removed his or her belongings from the unit. The landlord must make the evicted tenant's property available for retrieval at a location near the rental unit between the hours of 8 a.m. to 8 p.m. during the 72-hour period after the eviction order is enforced (s. 41(3)). Usually, the landlord leaves the property in the rental unit and allows the tenant to retrieve it from there. After the 72 hours has passed, the landlord may sell, use, or dispose of the abandoned property immediately (ss. 41(1) and (2)). A landlord is not liable to pay the proceeds of sale to the tenant or to return the tenant's property (s. 41(4)).[2] A landlord and a tenant may agree on different terms for the disposal of the tenant's property, either in the tenancy agreement or later (s. 41(5)). Therefore, you should check the lease for terms concerning abandoned property. In addition, if it appears that there are valuables left in the unit, a landlord would be wise to take additional steps before disposing of the items to minimize potential claims by the tenant or others. For example, the landlord should attempt to notify the tenant that the landlord will be disposing of the items after a certain date. The landlord should catalogue the property, have the property appraised, and conduct a PPSA (*Personal Property Security Act*) search to determine whether there are any liens registered against the property.

ENFORCING AN ORDER FOR THE PAYMENT OF MONEY

Once the board makes an order for the payment of money, the next step is to obtain the money your client is owed by enforcing the order.

If you are acting for a tenant, you may start the process by writing a letter demanding the money from the landlord within a short period, such as seven days. If you are an employee of a law firm, you may want to have the money paid to the law firm in trust, so that your fees can be paid out to the firm and the balance sent on to the client. In this case, you need to send a **direction** from your client to the landlord to pay the money owing to the law firm in trust.

direction
a document telling someone to do something

2　Although the RTA states that a landlord is not liable to any person for selling, retaining, or otherwise disposing of a tenant's property in accordance with s. 41, the courts have held that landlords may be the involuntary bailees of goods left behind by tenants. Similar liability could arise when the items left behind did not belong to the tenant.

If you are acting for a landlord against a tenant who was fighting a point of principle, you may want to start the enforcement process with a letter demanding the payment that the board has ordered. In the letter, you should specify a short time limit for receiving the money, such as seven days. If you are acting against parties who are resisting payment because they have no money or because they detest your client, it is probably wise not to spend time on a letter, but rather to begin the court enforcement steps immediately. Even if you do send a letter and no money is forthcoming, you then enforce the order through the court system, which is described next.

The board will have sent you two certified copies of the order. Under s. 184(1) of the RTA and s. 19(1) of the *Statutory Powers Procedures Act* (SPPA), a party is entitled to file a certified copy of the order with the **Superior Court of Justice** and to have it enforced as if it were an order of the court. In order to do this, file one copy of the certified order with the local registrar of the Superior Court of Justice at the court house in the area where the **debtor** lives. File the second certified copy with the sheriff's office in any jurisdiction in which the debtor has assets. Pursuant to s. 19(2) of the SPPA, you need to notify the board that you have filed the order with the court within 10 days of filing it.

Superior Court of Justice
the highest trial court in Ontario in which individual judges decide important civil cases and serious crimes

debtor
a person who owes another person money

Section 19(3) of the SPPA provides that on receiving a certified copy of the board's order for the payment of money, the sheriff shall enforce the order as if it were an execution issued by the Superior Court of Justice. After the payment of the appropriate fee, the sheriff registers the order with the local registration office. Approximately one week after registering the order with the sheriff's office, you should complete an execution search in order to ensure that the sheriff has registered the order. The execution search is done by going to the sheriff's office and filling out a form. (It is the same search that is done as part of a real estate closing.)

By registering the order with the registrar and the sheriff, you are entitled to use the remedies in rule 60 of the Ontario *Rules of Civil Procedure* in order to collect the money. Subrule 60.07 sets out the procedure for seizing and selling personal assets and real estate through the sheriff's office. Subrule 60.08 allows you to "seize" moneys payable to the debtor by way of garnishment. Garnishment is a court process whereby people who owe money to the debtor (for example, employers) are required to pay the money to the sheriff instead of to the debtor. The sheriff in turn pays the money to your client. Garnishment can be used not only for existing debts but also for money that will be owing to the debtor in the future (for example, a tax refund from the Canada Revenue Agency).

A procedure exists that allows you to determine the location of the debtor's assets and the persons who owe or will owe the debtor money. Subrule 60.18 allows you to examine the debtor under oath to find out the location of the debtor's assets and sources of cash. Of course, other sources of information should also be used. The most important of these sources is your client's knowledge of the debtor. For example, a landlord's rental application may disclose a tenant's employer, and the rental application or returned cheques show a tenant's bank account. The money in a bank account may be seized or garnished because a bank account is technically a debt due from the bank to the depositor. Debtors often change their bank accounts to avoid creditors. Therefore, you should choose a date to garnish a bank account when there is likely to be a worthwhile amount of money in it. The best days are immediately after the debtor has been paid or collected rents, or immediately before the first of the month (when there should be money in the account to pay rent). Credit checks from local credit agencies are also useful sources of information.

Your clients will not always get the money owed to them. For example, a tenant's only source of income may be a form of public assistance that is exempt from garnishment, or a landlord may have insufficient assets to pay all of his or her creditors. In the latter case, money seized or garnished is distributed in equal shares by the sheriff pursuant to the *Creditor's Relief Act*. Finally, a debtor may declare bankruptcy. That places your client on a creditor's list so that your client shares the debtor's assets with the debtor's other creditors pursuant to the distribution regime in the *Bankruptcy and Insolvency Act*.

Therefore, one of the most important steps in enforcing an order is to decide whether the amount to be collected and the likelihood of collection justify the costs of collection. If the likelihood of success seems low, you may wish to register the board's order with the sheriff and the registrar, and let the order sit with them in the hope that another creditor will take enforcement proceedings. If this occurs, your client can collect his or her share of the proceeds paid by the sheriff without having to incur the cost of any extra work. Unless the debtor becomes bankrupt, the registration of the order with the sheriff remains in force for six years and can be renewed after that time.

You need to remember the fees that you or your employer want to collect when developing an enforcement plan. The expense and difficulty of collecting money should also be borne in mind when negotiating claims, both before and after an order is made. It can be sensible to accept part payment in full satisfaction of a party's debt in order to obtain some payment and avoid further delay and expense.

REVIEW OF AN ORDER

The board has the power to review a decision. This power is found in s. 209 of the RTA, which incorporates by reference s. 21.2 of the SPPA. The procedure for the review of an order is addressed in the rules and guidelines of the board (Rule 29 and Guideline 8).

A party to an order, or any person directly affected by an order, may request that the order be reviewed. The request must be made in writing within 30 days of the issuance of the order. The request must be signed by the person who makes it or that person's representative, and it must be accompanied by the appropriate fee. As of February 2011, the fee for a request for review was $50. A request should include the board's order number; the address of the rental unit or residential complex concerned; the name, address, and telephone number of the person requesting the review; the reason why the order should be reviewed; and the amendment or replacement order requested.

The party requesting a review may also request a stay of the order—that is, a suspension of the order and a temporary stoppage of the enforcement process. To request a stay, a party should set out the prejudice that he or she will suffer if the order is not stayed. If an order terminates a tenancy, a tenant seeking a review of the termination must seek a stay in order to have the termination reviewed. Once an order for eviction has been enforced or the tenant has moved out "voluntarily," the board will not review the termination and eviction; however, the board may review any other portions of the order, such as an order for the payment of money.

The party who requests a review must give a copy of the request for review and the request for a stay, if any, to the other parties to the review.

The first step in the review procedure is a preliminary review of the request, the order, and any written reasons. The review is conducted by a different adjudicator from the adjudicator who made the decision under review. The board may question any party who has requested the review of an order in writing or by telephone to clarify the basis for the request. After the preliminary review, the board may decide to deny the request for review without a hearing.

Alternatively, the board may decide to conduct a full review. The board may decide that the issues to be considered in the full review are those raised in the request or may decide that there are other issues that should be reviewed.

The board may decide to conduct a full review by way of an oral or electronic hearing or by written submissions. The board may issue a notice of hearing or a notice of review by written submissions to determine whether there was an error in the proceedings or in the order. If an error is found, the board may decide to hear the application again either in respect of specified issues or in total. Parties who receive a notice of review by written submissions may request that the review be determined by a hearing, explaining their reasons in writing. They must file the written request promptly. Any party may waive service of the notice of hearing or notice of review by written submissions.

The board will not accept any subsequent review request from a party who has made one already. The board may review an order, even if it has previously reviewed the order, if the request is made by another party on different grounds.

APPEAL OF AN ORDER

Divisional Court
a branch of the Superior Court of Justice in which trial justices sit in groups of three to hear appeals from boards

Any person affected by an order of the board may appeal the order to the **Divisional Court**, but only on a question of law (s. 210(1)). The appeal does not require the permission of the board or the court; it is a matter of right, but it is limited to questions of law, rather than questions of fact or questions of mixed law and fact. The time limit for making this appeal is 30 days from the date the board's order was issued (s. 210(1)).

An appeal is governed by the *Rules of Civil Procedure* of the Superior Court of Justice. The appeal process is complicated and time consuming. Parties usually retain a lawyer for an appeal to the Divisional Court, although they can act for themselves if they want. Non-lawyer agents are not allowed to represent parties in appeals to the Divisional Court. Even advising a party about an appeal to the Divisional Court would be practising law and therefore something that an agent is prohibited from doing. Appeals to the Divisional Court are expensive—usually costing thousands of dollars in legal fees.

respondent
the person who is on the other side of an appeal made by an appellant

appellant
the person who makes an appeal

Unless an order is obtained on a motion to the Divisional Court extending the time for service or allowing service by a different method, the notice of appeal (and certificate of evidence) required to start the appeal must be given personally to all **respondents** and to the board within 30 days of the order. The **appellant** must file the notice of appeal, obtain a transcript of the hearing, and prepare an appeal book.

The appeal book consists of a copy of all documents in the proceeding that have not been excluded through the process of the exchange of certificates of evidence. The appellant must also prepare a factum, which consists of a statement of the facts and a statement of the law to be argued on the appeal.

The appeal is heard by a panel of three judges of the Superior Court of Justice sitting as the Divisional Court. These appeals are heard only in the main city in each judicial region every two to six months, depending on the number of cases. There is a delay from the time that all the documents have been prepared to the time that the appeal is heard, which ranges from two to ten months.

The board is entitled to be heard on an appeal (s. 210(3)). However, it makes representations only if the appeal involves a significant point of jurisdiction or procedure or a major point of law that could adversely affect its operations.

On an appeal, the Divisional Court may **affirm**, **rescind**, amend, or replace the decision or order, or remit the matter to the board with its opinion (s. 210(4)). The Divisional Court may also make any other order that it considers proper, including any order with respect to costs (s. 210(5)).

affirm
approve and leave in place

rescind
cancel

After a decision of the Divisional Court, a party is entitled to seek permission to appeal to the Ontario Court of Appeal. The board is also entitled to seek permission to appeal, and to appeal as if it were a party to the appeal (s. 211).

Instead of appealing a decision of the board, a party may also make an application for judicial review to the Divisional Court. This application is a special form of "appeal" that is available if the board makes an error regarding its jurisdiction or breaches the rules of natural justice. The rules of natural justice include the right of a party to a proceeding to be heard, to summons witnesses and lead evidence, and to cross-examine the witnesses and challenge the evidence of the other parties to the application. There is a substantial amount of complicated case law governing what errors by a board entitle a party to apply successfully for judicial review. Parties should not attempt to make such an application without retaining a lawyer.

KEY TERMS

affirm

appellant

debtor

direction

Divisional Court

jurisdiction

rescind

respondent

Superior Court of Justice

writ of possession

REVIEW QUESTIONS

1. What are costs?

2. When will the Landlord and Tenant Board order a party to pay costs?

3. In what circumstances can a paralegal be ordered to pay costs to the board?

4. What does a landlord do to have an eviction order enforced?

5. Outline how a former tenant can enforce an order for payment against a landlord.

6. What is the process for having an order reviewed?

7. To what body are board orders appealed?

8. To launch an appeal, what does an appellant have to allege is wrong with a board order?

DISCUSSION ISSUES

1. Over the past year, an unrepresented landlord has filed four separate applications against a tenant alleging that he is interfering with the landlord's reasonable enjoyment of the residential complex. The first application was dismissed because the landlord made an error completing the N5 form, the second application was dismissed because the landlord did not properly serve another one of the N5 forms, and the third application was dismissed because the landlord did not adequately prove his case. What issues can be raised regarding costs?

2. The board has just issued an order terminating the tenancy for non-payment of rent. The tenant, who is currently working but has had difficulty holding down a job, did not appear at the hearing. The tenant calls the landlord's paralegal, asking whether he can save his tenancy by entering into a payment plan to pay off the arrears over the next few months. What are questions the paralegal should ask of the tenant, and what advice should the paralegal give her client?

Parting with Possession by the Tenant

14

TERMINATION BY THE TENANT

We have seen in Chapters 9 and 10 that to terminate a tenancy a landlord needs to have a specific cause for termination that is recognized by the *Residential Tenancies Act, 2006* (RTA). A tenant does not need such a cause to terminate a tenancy at the end of the term of the tenancy. However, a tenant does have to comply with certain procedural requirements.

The most important requirement is that the tenant give a written notice of termination (s. 43(1)). Tenants who are not familiar with Ontario law often fail to give a notice of termination, believing that the end of their lease is enough to bring their tenancy to an end. This is not the case. To end a tenancy, either the landlord or the tenant must give the other notice of termination.

A tenant's notice must

- identify the rental unit,
- state the date the tenancy is to terminate, and
- be signed by the tenant or the tenant's agent (s. 43(1)).

The notice should be in the form N9 as approved by the Landlord and Tenant Board ("the board"), but if the notice contains the required information (as set out above), it will almost certainly be sufficient.

The length of notice required depends on the type and term of the tenancy.

A periodic tenancy is one that renews automatically for a particular calendar period—for example, a month or a year. A tenancy for a fixed term is a tenancy from one date to another date. Even if the tenancy is for one year, if it is defined by the dates on which it begins and ends, then it is a fixed-term tenancy; it is not a yearly periodic tenancy.

If no notice of termination is given, a periodic tenancy for a week or a month renews for the period of the tenancy, such as a week or a month (s. 38(2)). If no notice of termination is given, a tenancy for a fixed term of any length renews as a monthly tenancy (s. 38(1)). If no notice of termination is given, a periodic tenancy for a year renews as a monthly tenancy (s. 38(3)).

The required notice period is 60 days for a fixed-term tenancy, a monthly tenancy, or a yearly tenancy (s. 44). For a daily tenancy or a weekly tenancy, the required notice period is 28 days (s. 44(1)). The date specified for termination must be the end of a fixed-term tenancy or the end of a period of a periodic tenancy.

People commonly refer to the required notice period as two months. However, January and February, and February and March, consist of 59 days (except in leap years). Tenants are deemed to have given 60 days' notice if they give notice for February 28 by January 1, or if they give notice for March 31 by February 1 (s. 44(5)). However, landlords are not relieved from such possible miscounting. A landlord's notice of termination for February 28 must be given by December 31, and a landlord's notice of termination for March 31 must be given by January 31.

If a tenant fails to comply with the notice requirements, the landlord can hold the tenant to a tenancy for an extended term, usually one month. If a tenant's notice is only a few days short of the required length, a landlord is wise to point out the problem to the tenant and agree to a termination on the date the tenant requests. Such an agreement should be in writing and signed by the tenant and the landlord. Ideally the parties would use the N11 form. Once a valid termination is arranged, the landlord can then rent the unit with a reasonable expectation that the original tenant will not **overhold**. If there is no such agreement, and the tenant vacates after giving an invalid notice, arrears of rent will be owing for the period that ends on the earliest valid termination date that could have been specified on the day that the notice was delivered (s. 88(1)). For example, if a tenant on a typical month-to-month lease gave notice on April 3rd that he or she was leaving on June 14th, the notice would not be valid because the termination date must be the last day of a month. If that tenant left by June 14th, he or she will owe all of June's rent—that is, on April 3rd, the earliest properly terminated tenancy date is June 30.

If a tenant's notice falls significantly short of the requirements, the landlord may want to take a harder line with the tenant. In that case, the landlord would notify the tenant that the notice is insufficient and that the tenant is obliged by the tenancy agreement (or its renewal by operation of law) to continue to rent the unit until proper notice is given. This usually results in the tenant's calling to find out what he or she can do. The landlord can then offer to terminate if the tenant pays an amount to compensate for the early termination including the loss of rent revenue and the costs of finding a new tenant—for example, an extra month's rent. If the tenant does vacate without such an agreement, the landlord would be able to proceed with an action at Small Claims Court for all losses due to the early termination. Landlords are required to minimize their losses by renting the unit in question as soon as they are reasonably able to rent it (s. 16).

Tenants can also "step out" of some or all of their obligations by subletting or assigning their tenancy, following the proper procedures.

overhold
a situation where the tenant remains in a rental unit after the tenancy has been terminated

THE DIFFERENCE BETWEEN A SUBLET AND AN ASSIGNMENT

Under the RTA, almost all tenancies can be sublet or assigned, including statutory month-to-month tenancies.[1] The main exceptions are social housing units and tenancies of superintendents' units, which cannot be assigned or sublet by the superintendent–tenant. The RTA distinguishes between assignments and sublets, setting different rules for each situation.

Subletting occurs when the tenant gives possession of the rental unit to a new tenant for a limited time, after which the original tenant returns to reoccupy the premises. The original tenant must intend to return before the end of the term of the tenancy agreement with the landlord. A landlord can refuse a tenant permission to sublet to a prospective subtenant only for a good reason, such as the failure of the prospective subtenant to pass a reference check.

Assignment occurs when the original tenant assigns the balance of the tenancy agreement to a new tenant, and the original tenant does not intend to return to the unit.

If the landlord did not have the right to refuse consent to an assignment, tenants could pass on desirable units with below-**market rents** to relatives, friends, or unrelated parties. However, a landlord may refuse an assignment (before a prospective assignee is presented for approval) for any reason, or for no reason at all (s. 95(2)). A tenant's remedy is the right to terminate the tenancy (s. 95(4)). Ideally, a landlord should communicate such a refusal to a tenant before the tenant finds a prospective assignee. After a tenant presents a prospective assignee, the landlord can still refuse consent to the assignment of the rental unit, but if the refusal is general rather than specific to a prospective assignee, the tenant then has the right to terminate the tenancy (ss. 95(3)(c) and (4)(c)). If within seven days of the request the landlord does not reply to the request to assign the rental unit (either in principle or to a potential assignee), then the tenant has the right to terminate the tenancy (ss. 95(4)(b) and (d)).

Alternatively, the landlord can consent to assignment in principle and retain control of the choice of assignee to whom the tenant may assign the tenancy. The refusal of specific assignees must be based on legitimate reasons, such as the failure of a prospective assignee to pass a credit or reference check (s. 95(5)).

Tenants may attempt to pass on desirable rental units without obtaining the landlord's consent. A landlord has only 60 days from discovering an unauthorized subtenant or assignee to apply to evict the unauthorized occupant. See the discussion under the heading "Landlord's Remedy for an Unauthorized Sublet" later in this chapter. In managing units with below-market rents, landlords should take care to determine the identity of the tenants and occupants in order to be in a position to enforce their rights.

market rent
the rent that a landlord can expect to receive for a particular rental unit or type and size of rental units

---

1 A statutory month-to-month tenancy arises where the last day of the term of a tenancy agreement for a fixed term has passed and the tenant remains in possession. Under the RTA, the tenant has the right to remain in possession as a tenant on a month-to-month basis until the tenant gives proper notice of termination to the landlord, or the landlord evicts the tenant on grounds permitted by the RTA.

In an assignment, the original tenant assigns the balance of the tenancy agreement to a new tenant, and the original tenant does not return to the unit. The new tenant (the assignee) becomes liable to the landlord for the tenant's obligations under the tenancy agreement, including the payment of the rent (s. 95(8)(a)). The former tenant ceases to be liable to the landlord for the tenant's obligations, including the payment of rent, after the effective date of the assignment (s. 95(8)(b)). The landlord cannot claim against a former tenant for breaches of obligation by the assignee after the effective date of the assignment. The former tenant has no right to return to the rental unit.

In a sublet, a tenant gives a subtenant the right to occupy the rental unit for a specific limited period of time, and the tenant has the right to resume occupancy (s. 97(1)). During the period of the subtenancy, the tenant remains liable to the landlord for the tenant's obligations, including the payment of rent and the repair of damage (s. 97(4)(a)). The subtenant is liable to the tenant for the subtenant's obligations under the subletting agreement (s. 97(4)(b)). The RTA contemplates that the subtenant pays rent to the tenant, and the tenant continues to pay rent to the landlord. It appears that if the subtenant pays rent directly to the landlord, such payment is as a matter of convenience only, and the landlord is not entitled to apply for arrears of rent against the subtenant.

In the case of a failure to pay rent, the landlord applies against the tenant for an order for the payment of the arrears of rent and for an order to evict the tenant and the subtenant. The landlord would generally be wise to give notice of that application to the subtenant, as well as to the tenant, whether or not it is required under the RTA or the rules. In fact, it appears that notice of the application can be given to the tenant by handing it to the subtenant (an apparently adult person) in the rental unit (s. 191(1)(c)). However, to be safe, it would be better to serve the tenant by a means by which the landlord can be sure that the tenant will receive the notice, such as personal service or by mail to the tenant's place of business or residence when that is not the rental unit.

SUBLETTING

Subletting Process

The process of subletting involves the tenant's requesting the landlord's permission to sublet the rental unit to another specific person. The landlord may require the tenant to pay the landlord's reasonable out-of-pocket expenses, such as the cost of a credit check (s. 97(3)). The landlord may, and should, interview the prospective subtenant and take an application as if the subtenant were a new tenant applying to rent the unit. The landlord must respect the provisions of the *Human Rights Code* (HRC). This means that the landlord must not discriminate on the grounds of race, ancestry, place of origin, colour, ethnic origin, citizenship, religion, sex (that is, gender), sexual orientation, age, marital status, family status, pregnancy, handicap, or receipt of public assistance (HRC, s. 2(1)).

The landlord may, and should, perform a reference check to determine whether the proposed subtenant is likely to be a suitable tenant.

Practical Advice for Landlords and Tenants

As a practical matter, the landlord should ensure that the tenant is aware that, in subletting, the tenant remains responsible for the payment of the rent and the fulfillment of all other tenant's obligations during the term of the tenancy. The landlord should also ensure that the subletting agreement between the tenant and the subtenant is in writing and includes a termination date before the end of the tenant's tenancy, which gives the tenant the right to occupy the unit on that date. If this is not provided in the sublet agreement, the situation may be one of assignment, rather than sublet.

The RTA makes it illegal for a tenant to sublet a rental unit for more than the **lawful rent**, to collect a fee for subletting, or to require a person to pay for goods or services as a condition of subletting (ss. 134(3) and 234(l)).

lawful rent
the rent that a landlord is permitted to charge a tenant

Applications to the Board

If the landlord has unreasonably delayed in replying to a tenant's request, or if a landlord has refused a sublet or assignment request, the tenant or former tenant may apply to the board for an order that the landlord has arbitrarily or unreasonably withheld consent to a sublet or assignment (s. 98). If the board finds that the landlord has unlawfully withheld consent to the sublet or assignment, the board may

- order that the sublet is authorized,
- authorize another sublet proposed by the tenant,
- order that the tenancy is terminated, or
- order an abatement of the tenant's rent (s. 98(3)).

The board may establish terms and conditions for a sublet or assignment (s. 98(4)). If the board authorizes a sublet or assignment, the legal effect is the same as if the landlord consents to the sublet (s. 98(5)).

The situations in which a tenant applies to the board vary. If, after a landlord's refusal or undue delay, a subtenant still wants the rental unit and the tenant wants to sublet to that person, the tenant may apply for an order authorizing the sublet. Alternatively, if the potential subtenant is no longer interested and the tenant has found another subtenant, the tenant may apply to the board to authorize the sublet to the second prospective subtenant. (By doing so, the tenant can avoid future delays and the possibility of "losing" the new subtenant.) If the tenant has put forward a subtenant who is refused and the tenant has not been able to find a second subtenant, the tenant may seek termination of the tenancy or an abatement of rent. In principle, if the board decides against the landlord and the tenant could have lived elsewhere rent free, the board can order a full abatement of the tenant's rent during the period of the proposed subtenancy, since the tenant would have had the rent paid by the subtenant if the subtenancy had been approved.

Regaining Possession at the End of a Sublet

If the subtenant fails to vacate the unit at the end of the subtenancy, the tenant may apply to the board for an order evicting the subtenant (s. 101(1)). Such an application must be made within 60 days after the end of the subtenancy (s. 101(2)). In addition, the landlord may apply to the board for an order evicting the subtenant (s. 101(1)). That application must also be made within 60 days after the end of the subtenancy (s. 101(2)). No notice of termination is required from the tenant or the landlord to the subtenant, and no ground of termination is required other than the mere fact that the subtenancy has come to an end (s. 97(5)). This makes sense because if the subtenant stays in occupancy, the subtenant becomes an assignee, and the landlord can refuse to allow an assignment of the tenancy.

Landlord's Remedy for an Unauthorized Sublet

If a tenant sublets a rental unit without obtaining the landlord's consent, the landlord may apply to the board for an order evicting the would-be subtenant and the tenant (s. 100(1)). The landlord must apply within 60 days of discovering the unauthorized occupancy (s. 100(2)). It appears that, in the landlord's application for eviction, the unauthorized subtenant cannot raise a defence that the landlord unreasonably withheld consent to the sublet because s. 98(1) allows only the tenant or former tenant to apply to the board for an order authorizing the sublet. However, the unauthorized subtenant may ask the former tenant to apply to the board for an order authorizing the sublet, and then ask the board to hear the two applications together.

If within 60 days of discovering the unauthorized occupancy, or within 60 days after the end of the subtenancy period, the landlord does not apply to the board and does not negotiate a new tenancy with the overholding subtenant, and if the tenant does not apply to evict the subtenant, the unauthorized subtenant is deemed to have received an assignment with the landlord's consent and becomes the tenant of the unit for all purposes (s. 104(4)).

ASSIGNMENT

Assignment Process

The RTA contemplates that the tenant may apply for the landlord's consent to an assignment in one of two ways. First, the tenant may ask for the landlord's consent to assign in principle (that is, without putting forward a specific assignee). The landlord can refuse without justifying the refusal (ss. 95(3) and (5)). If the landlord refuses consent or does not respond to the tenant's request within seven days, the tenant may terminate the tenancy (s. 95(4)). The tenant's notice to terminate must be given within 30 days of the request to assign and be effective at least 30 days after it is given (ss. 95(4) and 96). In the case of a daily or weekly tenancy, the notice must be effective at least 28 days after it is given (ss. 96 and 44(1)).

Second, the tenant may ask for the landlord's consent to assign the rental unit to a specific assignee. The landlord can refuse consent to any assignment without justifying the refusal (s. 95(3)(c)). If the landlord refuses consent generally or does not respond to the tenant's request within seven days, the tenant may terminate the tenancy. The tenant's notice to terminate must be given within 30 days of the request to assign and be effective at least 30 days after it is given (ss. 95(4) and 96). In the case of a daily or weekly tenancy, the notice must be effective at least 28 days after it is given (s. 44(1)).

Instead of giving a general refusal of consent to assignment, a landlord can evaluate a prospective assignee. The landlord may require the tenant to pay the landlord's reasonable out-of-pocket expenses, such as the cost of a credit check (s. 95(7)). The landlord may, and should, interview the prospective assignee and take an application as if the subtenant were a new tenant applying to rent the unit. The landlord must respect the provisions of the *Human Rights Code*, as described earlier in this chapter under the heading "Subletting Process." The landlord may, and should, perform credit and reference checks to determine whether the proposed assignee is likely to be a suitable tenant. In performing credit checks, the landlord is prohibited from applying an income-to-rent test. For example, the landlord cannot legally refuse to approve assignments to people for the sole reason that the rent would be more than 30 percent of their income. The landlord can consider a potential assignee's income level along with credit references and employment history (HRC, O. reg. 290/90). Based on all the relevant factors, the landlord can consent or refuse to consent to the assignment to the potential assignee (s. 95(3)(b)), but a refusal must be reasonable (s. 95(5)).

The RTA makes it illegal for a tenant to collect a fee for assigning a tenancy or to require a person to pay for goods or services as a condition of assignment (ss. 134(3) and 234(1)).

Application to the Board

If a landlord has refused an assignment to a potential assignee, the tenant may apply to the board for an order that the landlord has arbitrarily or unreasonably withheld consent to the assignment (s. 98(1)). If the board finds that the landlord has unlawfully withheld consent to an assignment to a potential assignee, it may

- order that the assignment is authorized,
- authorize another assignment proposed by the tenant,
- order that the tenancy is terminated, or
- order an abatement of the tenant's rent (s. 98(3)).

The board may establish terms and conditions for an assignment (s. 98(4)). If the board authorizes an assignment, the legal effect is the same as if the landlord consents to the assignment (s. 98(5)).

The situations in which a tenant applies to the board vary. If, after a landlord's refusal or undue delay, the assignee still wants the rental unit and the tenant wants to assign to that person, the tenant may apply for an order authorizing the assignment. Alternatively, if the assignee is no longer interested and the tenant has found another assignee, the tenant may apply to the board to authorize the assignment to the second potential assignee. (By doing so, the tenant can avoid future delays and the possibility of "losing" the new assignee.) If the tenant has put forward an assignee, the landlord has refused, and the tenant has not been able to find another potential assignee, the tenant will likely seek a termination of the tenancy and an abatement of the rent until the date of termination.

Landlord's Remedies for Unauthorized Assignment

If a tenant assigns a rental unit without obtaining the landlord's consent to the transfer, the landlord may negotiate a new tenancy agreement with the assignee, which may include a new rent (ss. 104(1) and (3)). Alternatively, the landlord may apply to the board for an order evicting the person to whom occupancy of the rental unit was transferred (s. 100(1)). The landlord must complete the tenancy agreement or apply within 60 days of discovering the unauthorized occupancy (ss. 104(3) and 100(2)). It appears that the would-be assignee cannot raise a defence that the landlord unreasonably withheld consent to the assignment in the landlord's application for eviction, since s. 98(1) provides only for the tenant or former tenant to apply for an order authorizing the assignment. However, the unauthorized assignee may ask the former tenant to apply to the board for an order authorizing the assignment, and then ask the board to hear the two applications together.

If the landlord does not negotiate a new tenancy agreement or apply within 60 days of discovering the unauthorized occupancy, the unauthorized assignee is deemed to be an authorized assignee, and "steps into the shoes" of the tenant for all purposes (s. 104(4)).

DEATH OF THE TENANT

Generally, if a tenant of a rental unit dies and there are no other tenants of the rental unit, the tenancy is terminated 30 days after the death of the tenant (s. 91(1)). However, if the deceased tenant had a spouse, unless the spouse vacates the unit within that 30-day period, the spouse will become tenant and will be responsible for any unpaid rent even if he or she was not named on the lease. (s. 3(1) of O.Reg. 516/06).

If a tenancy is terminated because of the death of a tenant, the landlord may immediately dispose of or sell any property of the deceased tenant that is unsafe or unhygienic (s. 92(1)(a)). However, the landlord is required to preserve any of the tenant's other property for the 30 days until the tenancy is terminated (s. 91(2)(a)).

executor
a person who is appointed in a will to administer the property of the person who made the will after that person dies

The landlord is also required to provide the tenant's **executor** or **administrator** access to the rental unit for the purpose of removing the deceased's property (s. 91(2)(b)). If there is no executor or administrator, the landlord is required to provide access to a member of the tenant's family for that purpose (s. 91(2)(b)).

After 30 days, the landlord may sell, use, or dispose of any remaining property of the deceased tenant (s. 92(1)(b)). Within six months after the tenant's death, if the executor or administrator (or a family member) claims property of the tenant that the landlord is using, the landlord must return it to the tenant's estate (s. 92(4)). Within six months after the tenant's death, if the executor or administrator (or a family member) claims property of the tenant that the landlord has sold, the landlord must pay the proceeds of the sale to the tenant's estate less any arrears of rent and the reasonable out-of-pocket expenses of moving, storing, securing, and selling the tenant's property (s. 92(3)). The landlord and the executor or administrator may agree to other terms than the terms set out in s. 92 (s. 92(5)).

administrator
a person who is appointed by the court to administer the property of a person who has died without naming an executor in a will

ABANDONED UNITS AND PROPERTY

A landlord may retake possession of a rental unit if the tenant has abandoned the unit (s. 39(a)). To signal that the landlord has retaken possession, it is wise to physically change the locks. A rental unit is not considered abandoned if the tenant is not in arrears of rent, even if none of the tenant's belongings is in the unit. The landlord does not need to apply to the board for an order terminating the tenancy but may apply to the board for such an order if the landlord chooses to (s. 79). The landlord should apply if there is any doubt as to whether the tenant has abandoned the rental unit.

The landlord's rights to deal with the property of a tenant who has abandoned the rental unit depend on the situation through which the rental unit has come to be abandoned.

If the tenant vacates after an eviction order is enforced by the sheriff, the landlord must hold the property for at least another 72 hours (see Chapter 13, Enforcing an Order for Eviction).

If the tenant has vacated the unit in accordance with a notice of termination (by landlord or tenant), an agreement to terminate, or the termination of a superintendent's unit, the landlord may sell, use, or dispose of abandoned property immediately (s. 41(1)). A landlord is not liable to pay the proceeds of sale to the tenant or to return the tenant's property (s. 41(4)). A landlord and a tenant may agree on different terms for the disposal of the tenant's property, either in the tenancy agreement or later (s. 41(5)).

If the tenant has abandoned the rental unit, other than as described above, the landlord may dispose of any unsafe or unhygienic items immediately (s. 42(2)). The landlord has the right to dispose of other abandoned property if the landlord obtains an order from the board under s. 79, or if the landlord gives the tenant and the board notice of the landlord's intention to dispose of the property (s. 42(1)). Notice to the tenant can be given by mail to the last-known address of the tenant, which is usually the abandoned unit. The landlord may sell, use, or otherwise dispose of any other items of abandoned property 30 days after the notice or the order (s. 42(3)).

Within the 30 days, a tenant may notify the landlord of the tenant's intention to remove the property, and the landlord must make the property available to the tenant at a reasonable time and at a place reasonably close to the rental unit (ss. 42(4) and (5)). The landlord may require the tenant to pay any arrears of rent and reasonable out-of-pocket expenses of moving, storing, and securing the tenant's property before allowing the tenant to remove the property (s. 42(6)).

Within six months of the notice or the order, the tenant may claim the property sold by the landlord. The landlord is then required to pay the tenant the amount by which the proceeds of sale exceed the landlord's out-of-pocket expenses of moving, storing, securing, or selling the property and any arrears of rent (s. 42(7)). Apart from the obligations stated above, the landlord is not liable to anyone for selling, retaining, or disposing of the tenant's property (s. 42(8)).

Landlords should exercise care when disposing of property because, although they are protected when they dispose of the tenant's property, they may not be protected from the ordinary legal rules if they dispose of property that belongs to someone other than the tenant. The disposal of furniture or entertainment equipment that the tenant has rented or bought under a conditional sales agreement can lead to a serious problem.

THE UNAUTHORIZED OCCUPANT

An occupant may be unauthorized because a subtenant does not vacate at the end of the subtenancy or because a proposed assignment or sublet is not approved by the landlord or authorized by the board.

If the landlord discovers an unauthorized occupant, the landlord has 60 days to

- negotiate a new tenancy agreement with an unauthorized assignee (s. 104),
- negotiate a new tenancy agreement with an unauthorized subtenant (s. 104), or
- apply to evict an unauthorized assignee or subtenant or an overholding subtenant (ss. 100 and 101).

If the landlord fails to negotiate a new tenancy agreement or apply to the board within 60 days, the unauthorized occupation is deemed to be an assignment of the rental unit with the consent of the landlord, and the unauthorized occupant becomes the tenant (s. 104(4)).

KEY TERMS

administrator   market rent
executor   overhold
lawful rent

REVIEW QUESTIONS

1. What does an Ontario tenant have to do to end a tenancy?
2. Can a tenant terminate their tenancy before their fixed term ends?
3. How much notice does a tenant need to give to terminate their tenancy?
4. What is the difference between assigning and subletting?
5. What does a tenant need to do to assign a tenancy?
6. What are a landlord's rights when a tenant wants to assign a tenancy?
7. If a tenant sublets a tenancy, and then the subtenant overholds, can the tenant apply to the board for relief and, if so, what relief?
8. If a tenant sublets a tenancy, and then the subtenant overholds, can the landlord apply for relief, and if so, what relief?
9. Suppose a tenant dies. What happens to the tenancy?
10. Suppose a tenant abandons the rental unit without receiving any termination notice from the landlord, but leaves furniture behind. What are the landlord's rights and obligations?

Additional Grounds for Termination

15

Apart from the situation where a landlord begins the process by giving a notice of termination to the tenant, there are other situations in which a landlord may want to apply for an order to terminate a tenancy and evict a tenant. Some of these applications are made without notice to the tenant, while other applications are made with notice to the tenant (or the occupant against whom the application is made). Table 15.1 sets out these grounds for application under the *Residential Tenancies Act, 2006* (RTA).

AGREEMENT TO TERMINATE OR TENANT'S NOTICE TO TERMINATE

When a tenant has entered into an agreement to terminate or has given a notice of termination, a landlord can apply to the Landlord and Tenant Board ("the board") before the termination date specified in the tenant's notice or in the agreement. However, the order will not be effective before that termination date (s. 77(5)). In making the application, a landlord must include an affidavit verifying the agreement or the notice of termination (s. 77(2)). The landlord must make the application no later than 30 days after the termination date (s. 77(3)).

When acting for a landlord, you must attach a copy of the notice that the tenant gave to the landlord or the agreement to terminate (if there is a written agreement). You must also attach the landlord's affidavit confirming the receipt of the notice or confirming the making of and the contents of the agreement to terminate. You do

Table 15.1   Additional Grounds for Applications to Terminate

Description	RTA section	Form number
Applications without notice		
Agreement to terminate (need not be in writing)	s. 77(1)	L3
Notice of termination by tenant	s. 77(1)	L3
Agreement to settle an application with termination in default	s. 78	L4
Previous board order allowing landlord to terminate if tenant did not meet specified conditions	s. 78	L4
Applications with notice		
Landlord's belief that tenant has abandoned rental unit	s. 79	L2
Termination of superintendent's employment	s. 94	L2
Unauthorized transfer of possession	s. 100	A2
Overholding by subtenant after end of subtenancy	s. 101	A2

not need to give notice of the application to the tenant. No hearing date is set because the board usually processes the application without holding a hearing. In applications made without notice, representatives have a special obligation to ensure that affidavits fully disclose all relevant facts.

While a written agreement is much preferred, an oral agreement to terminate a tenancy can form the basis of an application. However, it is often difficult to prove the existence of an oral agreement if one party denies that an agreement was made. A confirming letter is very helpful in establishing the existence of an oral agreement. Therefore, if an oral agreement is made, parties should confirm it in writing as soon as possible. In relying on an oral agreement, you need to take particular care to reflect all parts of the agreement accurately in the affidavit. If there is a confirming letter, it should be attached to the affidavit. The board's findings will take into account the credibility of the parties, and you can aid the landlord's credibility by being frank in the initial affidavit, as you are required to be.

If the tenant disagrees with the order terminating the tenancy, the tenant may make a motion within 10 days to the board to have the eviction order set aside (s. 77(6)). The making of the motion stays the order, and s. 77(7) provides that the order shall not be enforced during the stay. The board will hold a hearing to determine whether the tenant gave notice of termination or the landlord and tenant reached an agreement to terminate the tenancy. If the board finds that there was a termination, the board will likely lift the stay and confirm the eviction. However, if the tenant can convince the board that it would be fair to do so, the board can delay or refuse to grant the eviction (ss. 77(8)(b) and (c)).

BREACH OF CONDITIONS IN AN ORDER OR MEDIATED SETTLEMENT

If a landlord applies under s. 78 because a tenant has not met conditions in an order or mediated settlement, the landlord must include a copy of the order or settlement and an affidavit setting out the conditions that have not been met and how they have not been met (s. 78(2)). The statement may be as simple as, "The tenant was supposed to pay me $900 by August 10, 2011, and did not do so." You do not need to give notice of the application to the tenant. The board usually processes the application without holding a hearing. The landlord must make this application no later than 30 days after the failure of the tenant to meet a condition (s. 78(5)).

In making the application the landlord may also claim additional arrears of rent that have arisen after the previous order or settlement, NSF cheque charges, NSF administration charges, and compensation (for the use of the rental unit after a termination date) (s. 78(3)). If the landlord claims those amounts, the landlord's affidavit must set out the information to justify those claims and any payments made under the mediated settlement (if there was a settlement rather than an order) (s. 78(4)).

If the tenant disagrees with the order terminating the tenancy and awarding any other additional claims, the tenant may make a motion within 10 days to the board to have the eviction order set aside (s. 78(9)). The making of the motion stays the order, and s. 78(10) provides that the order shall not be enforced during the stay. The board will hold a hearing to determine whether the order is justified. If the board finds that the previous conditions were breached in a material way for which the tenant does not have a good excuse, the board will likely lift the stay and confirm the eviction. However, if the tenant can convince the board that it would be fair to do so, the board can delay or refuse to grant the eviction (ss. 77(11)(b) and (c)).

ABANDONED UNIT

If a landlord believes a tenant has abandoned a rental unit, the landlord may apply for an order terminating the tenancy under s. 79. If acting for the landlord, you must give the tenant notice of this application, which can be done by mailing a copy of the application and the notice of hearing to the tenant's last known address, which may well be the rental unit. This application is useful for the landlord because it provides protection from a claim by the tenant that the landlord has unlawfully regained possession of the rental unit, which is an offence under the Act. Obtaining a board order also allows a landlord greater rights in the disposition of a tenant's property, although the same rights can be obtained by giving a notice to the tenant. See the section in Chapter 14 under the heading "Abandoned Units and Property." Although the RTA sets no time limit for making this application, the landlord should apply quickly to minimize lost revenue.

TERMINATION OF SUPERINTENDENT'S EMPLOYMENT

The RTA defines "superintendent's premises" as a rental unit used by a janitor, manager, security guard, or superintendent and located in the residential complex with respect to which the person is so employed (s. 2(1)). When a landlord terminates the employment of one of the above-listed employees, the tenancy terminates on the same day unless otherwise agreed (s. 93(1)). The former employee is required to vacate the unit within seven days after the tenancy ends (s. 93(2)). The seven-day period is rent-free to the former employee (s. 93(3)). The case law has determined that the termination of the tenancy occurs on the termination of the employment whether or not the termination of the employment is lawful or wrongful under Ontario employment law. If the tenant does not vacate within the seven-day period, the landlord may apply to the board under s. 94.

If acting for the tenant, you should determine what, if any, agreement was made about the termination of the tenancy agreement when the employment agreement was made. In particular, if the tenant was living in the unit prior to becoming an employee, it may be an implied term of the employment agreement that the tenancy will not terminate on the termination of the employment. Based on that argument, the board may be willing to allow the tenant to remain in those circumstances.

UNAUTHORIZED SUBLET OR ASSIGNMENT

If a tenant attempts to assign or sublet a rental unit without a landlord's consent, the landlord can apply to the board for an order evicting the person to whom occupancy of the rental unit is transferred (s. 100(1)). The landlord's application under this section must be made no later than 60 days after the landlord has discovered the unauthorized occupancy (s. 100(2)). If the landlord does not file within 60 days of discovering the occupancy, there is a deemed assignment of the rental unit with the landlord's consent. When applying to evict the unauthorized occupant, the landlord may also apply for compensation for the use of the rental unit by the unauthorized occupant (s. 100(3)).

OVERHOLDING SUBTENANT

If a subtenant continues to occupy a rental unit after the end of a subtenancy, a landlord may apply to the board for an order evicting the subtenant (s. 101). The tenant who sublet the unit can also apply for an order evicting an overholding subtenant (s. 100(1)). Whether made by the landlord or the original tenant, the application must be made within 60 days after the end of the subtenancy. No notice of termination is required. The proceeding begins with the eviction application itself.

When applying to evict the overholding subtenant, the landlord may also apply for compensation for the use of the rental unit by the unauthorized occupant (s. 102). The overholding subtenant may offer the landlord money for occupying the rental unit. A landlord does not create a tenancy agreement with the unauthorized occupant by accepting compensation unless the landlord and unauthorized occupant agree (s. 103(2)), in which case the landlord will not be able to continue with the eviction application. In advising the landlord who has been offered or has accepted money in that situation, you should advise the landlord to accept the money, but at the same time to give the tenant a note saying that no new tenancy is being created by the acceptance of the "compensation for use and occupation." The landlord should keep a copy of the note. The landlord should not refer to the money as "rent," since rent is paid and accepted as payment for a tenancy.

REVIEW QUESTIONS

For the following questions, assume that all the tenants have month-to-month tenancies.

1. Suppose that, in a conversation on May 5, Jason tells his landlord, Emiko, that he will be moving out of his apartment on June 30, and Emiko is happy to see Jason end his tenancy. What should Emiko do?

2. Suppose that on September 25, Bianca gives her landlord, Omar, written notice of termination for November 30, but on November 30, Bianca doesn't move out. What can Omar do to regain possession of the apartment?

3. a. You are consulted by a superintendent, Andrew, who has just been fired by his employer and landlord. What rights and obligations does Andrew have concerning the rental unit he occupies?
   b. Would it matter if under Ontario labour law Andrew was entitled to more notice than he received?
   c. Would it matter if Andrew had lived in the rental unit for several years before he took on the job as superintendent?

DISCUSSION ISSUES

Tenant Beth wants to move away for the summer and decides to sublet her 2-bedroom rental unit to Jane from May through August. Beth, Jane and the landlord sign a sublet agreement. In the middle of August Jane decides she doesn't want to leave. What can Jane do? What can Beth do?

Increasing the Rent

16

This chapter deals with the annual rent increases to which a landlord is automatically entitled and the validation of initially illegal rent increases under the *Residential Tenancies Act, 2006* (RTA). The topics covered are the rent-increase guideline, the 12-month rule, the rule concerning the 90-day written notice of rent increase, and rent increases for new tenants 12 or more months after occupancy began. Chapter 17 covers the various rent increases a landlord can take if an application is approved by the Landlord and Tenant Board ("the board") as well as the various rent increases a landlord can take when an agreement is made with a tenant. Chapter 18 covers tenant applications about the amount of the rent.

THE GUIDELINE

Rent control restricts the amount of rent that could otherwise be charged in a free-market environment. Rent control has been in place in Ontario since 1975.

At an appropriate rent-increase date, a landlord in Ontario always has the ability to raise the rent in accordance with a guideline that is announced each year by the government. The guideline for the calendar year is determined using the Consumer Price Index for Ontario, averaged over a 12-month period.

During the entire history of peacetime rent control, landlords in Ontario have been allowed to take a guideline rent increase every 12 months without any specific government approval. The percentage has ranged from 0.7 per cent to 8.0 per cent, depending on the level of inflation and the legislation of the time. See Appendix E for a table of the guideline rent increases since peacetime rent control was first imposed in 1975. The guideline for each year is announced in July or August of the preceding year. The guideline increase can be taken only at an appropriate increase date and only with the required notice.

For rent increases that take effect in 2011, the guideline increase is 0.7 per cent. The calculation of a guideline increase is illustrated in example 16.1.

Example 16.1	**Guideline Rent Increase for 2011**
Current rent:	$850.00
Current guideline:	0.7%
Permitted new rent:	$855.95

There is no requirement that a new rent based only on a guideline increase be approved by the board. Tenants are required to pay the new rent, provided that proper notice of the rent increase is given and there are at least 12 months between rent increases. If tenants are unwilling to pay the new rent, they can try to negotiate a lower rent with the landlord or terminate the tenancy on appropriate notice to the end of its term. (Appropriate notice would be 60 days to the end of a tenancy for a fixed term or a month-to-month tenancy, or 28 days to the end of a daily or weekly tenancy.)

THE 12-MONTH RULE

There must be at least 12 months between rent increases imposed on a tenant in a rental unit (s. 119(1)(a)). If there has been no previous rent increase imposed on a tenant in a unit—for example, because the tenant has recently rented the unit—a landlord can increase the rent only after 12 months have passed since the rental unit was first rented to that tenant (s. 119(1)(b)).

WRITTEN NOTICE OF RENT INCREASE

To increase rent, a landlord must generally give a tenant a written notice of rent increase at least 90 days before the intended increase is to take effect (s. 116(1)). Except for units exempt from the guideline, the form to be used is form N1. For units exempt from the guideline, the form to be used is form N2. See the section on partial exemptions in Chapter 3 for the kinds of units which are exempt from the guideline. (The most common exemption is buildings no part of which was occupied before November 1, 1991.)

The notice of rent increase does not need to be given if the rent is increased because the landlord and the tenant have agreed that the landlord will provide an additional prescribed service (s. 123(2)). See Chapter 17 for further discussion on this topic.

WHAT IS LAWFUL RENT?

When a landlord and tenant first enter into a tenancy agreement, the parties agree upon a rent acceptable to both of them, which becomes the "lawful rent" (s. 113). This procedure is known as "vacancy decontrol." However, the RTA really provides "vacancy decontrol–recontrol" because the future rent increases are not allowed to exceed the guideline increase, unless an application is successful or an agreement is made subsequently under the agreement provisions of the RTA (or the unit is exempt from the guideline).

Some landlords use discounts to show a higher "lease rent" or "face rent" than the actual rent that a tenant is required to pay each month. The increase 12 months after a post-RTA tenant has moved in is based on the lawful rent first charged. Provided that any discount is within the discount rules (described in Appendix G), the lawful rent is the lease rent or face rent, not the discounted rent. Therefore, the landlord can effectively raise the rent by the amount of the discount *plus* the guideline increase. The policy behind the discount rules is to encourage landlords to provide lower rents even if they think the lower market will be temporary.

DISCOUNTS

The RTA sets out two types of discounts. A "prompt-payment" discount is used as an incentive for the tenant to pay rent on time. If the rent is paid late, the tenant is not entitled to the discount for that month. A "marketing discount" allows land-lords to provide rent-free or rent-lowered periods as a marketing tool.

VALIDATION OF INITIALLY ILLEGAL RENT INCREASES

Unless a tenant makes an application challenging the rent within one year of an alleged illegal increase, the rent charged and the rent increase taken are deemed to be lawful (s. 136). Section 136 stops claims based on defects in notices after one year has passed. A tenant can claim money paid in excess of that permitted by the RTA only within one year of the excess payment (s. 135(4)).

It was thought that s. 136 also prevented claims for other illegal rent increases—for example, rent increases given with no written notice. However, the Court of Appeal took a different view in *Turnbull's Grove Inc. v. Price* (2007), 85 OR (3d) 641. The facts in that case are complicated, but the court held that a rent increase that is void is not saved by the limitation period. Increases given without written notice are void. The validation of rents occurs for rent increases that would have been voidable—for example, an increase given with notice, but for an amount in excess of what was permitted. Section 135(4) would still limit the amount of rent rebate the tenant could claim to the amount paid during the 12 months before the application, but the rent could be rolled back if the increase under consideration was void.

Other applications may also have the effect of validating illegal rent increases. Under the doctrine known as *res judicata*, which means "a thing already judicially determined," issues that have been addressed in an application between the parties cannot be reopened. For example, suppose a tenant fell into arrears of rent, the landlord applied, and the board made an order requiring the tenant to pay certain amounts of rent to reinstate the tenancy. The tenant could not later challenge the validity of the rent, regardless of whether the last increase was taken with or without notice. (The tenant could challenge the validity of the rent in the landlord's application, but not in a subsequent proceeding.)

REVIEW QUESTIONS

1. a. What is the name for the rent increase that a landlord can take each year without any approval?

    b. To take that increase, what does a landlord need to do?

2. What was the amount of the increase a landlord could take without any approval in 2011?

3. What is the amount of the increase a landlord can take without any approval in the year you are studying this chapter?

4. Suppose Pedro rented an apartment to Angela last year for $1,000 with the first month rent-free. Does that discount affect the lawful rent? On what rent can Pedro base the increase this year?

Increasing the Rent by Application

17

Under the *Residential Tenancies Act, 2006* (RTA), a landlord may apply to the Landlord and Tenant Board ("the board") for an order allowing an above-guideline rent increase for any or all of the rental units in a residential complex if the landlord experiences one or more of the following situations:

1. an extraordinary increase in operating costs for

   a. municipal taxes and charges or

   b. utilities;

2. capital expenditures for the residential complex or one or more of the rental units; or

3. costs related to security services provided at the residential complex by persons not employed by the landlord (s. 126(1)).

This chapter describes the more important rules applying to each of the categories listed above, the procedure for obtaining an above-guideline rent increase by application, and the limits on the increases that can be awarded in these applications.

EXTRAORDINARY OPERATING COST INCREASES

The operating costs that qualify for above-guideline rent increases are municipal taxes and charges, hydro, water and sewage, and heating costs. An increase in the costs of any of these items is "extraordinary" if it is greater than the prescribed amounts (s. 126(2)). Electricity (commonly known in Ontario as "hydro"), water and sewage, and heating costs are referred to as utilities. In the application for an above-guideline rent increase, the landlord must report and document any increased costs claimed. Extraordinary increases are offset by unusual decreases.

In documenting the costs, the landlord must provide written evidence of the costs for the entire relevant time period and evidence of payment of those costs. The board accepts invoices or utility company printouts as proof of the costs. For municipal taxes, the relevant time period consists of the two calendar years that end at least 91 days before the first date of the intended rent increase. For utilities, the relevant time period for the first application under the RTA consists of the 24 months (chosen by the landlord) that end at least 91 days before the first date of the intended rent increase. The board compares the costs for the first of the two years with the costs for the second of the two years.

Note that extraordinary increases in municipal taxes and charges or in utilities do not allow a landlord to agree with a tenant to an above-guideline rent increase.

To gain an above-guideline rent increase for any of these cost increases, the landlord must apply to the board, and an order approving the increase must be issued.

COSTS NO LONGER BORNE: OPERATING COSTS

If a landlord increases the rent charged to a tenant pursuant to an above-guideline increase that is in whole or in part based on an increase in utilities, the landlord must give the tenant information about the cost of the utilities for the subsequent five years (RTA s. 128(2) and O. Reg. 516/06, s. 35). If the utility costs fall, the landlord needs to reduce the rent charged to the tenant in accordance with the regulations (s. 128(3); see O. Reg. 516/06, s. 35).

The requirement to provide information and, if necessary, reduce the rent is applicable only to continuing tenants who were subject to an above-guideline increase (s. 128(3)).

CAPITAL EXPENDITURES

A capital expenditure is an expenditure on a major renovation, repair, replacement, or new addition, the expected benefit of which extends for at least one year. Common examples of capital expenditures are roof replacements, concrete repairs, garage repairs, window replacements, and appliance replacements. The rules for capital expenditures are somewhat similar to the various rules that have been in place over the last 20 years. A landlord is not entitled to an increase in the rents by the whole cost of the capital expenditure; rather, the capital expenditure is amortized over the anticipated useful life of the item. The regulations include a table that sets out the useful lives for virtually all capital expenditures. In amortizing the cost over the useful life, the board includes an allowance for interest to reflect the fact that the landlord spends the money in one year but recovers it over an extended period. Table 17.1 sets out examples of four different capital expenditures and the above-guideline increase each generates if an application is made when the interest rate used for the amortization is 6.0 percent.

The total allowance will depend on the type of work done because different work is amortized over different periods of time. However, where a number of capital expenditures are done in the same time period, they tend to have different amortization periods, and the allowances tend to average out. As a rough rule of thumb, for an average mix of work, Table 17.2 shows the percentages of rent that must be spent in order to generate the corresponding percentage of above-guideline increase.

The actual results vary with the nature of the work performed and depend on a number of other factors involved in the application, including the current interest rate. Each case is fact specific. It is important that the calculation be done at the planning stage so that a landlord has a realistic expectation of the rent increase that will be generated by a capital expenditure.

Landlords can perform a capital expenditure personally and claim the reasonable value of their labour.

Not every capital expenditure will be approved by the board as grounds to justify a rent increase—only those expenditures that are deemed eligible. In an application by a landlord based on capital expenditures, a capital expenditure is eligible only if

Table 17.1   Sample Capital Expenditure Allowances

Total monthly rent:	$8,000 (units)
	$333 (parking)
Total annual rent:	$100,000
Interest rate:	6.0% per year

Capital expenditure	Lifespan	Cost	Annual allowance	Above-guideline increase (% of rent)
Caulking	10	$ 3,000	$ 398	0.40
Built-up roof	15	$12,000	$1,209	1.21
Hot water tank	20	$ 3,000	$ 256	0.26
Soffits and fascia	25	$ 3,000	$ 230	0.23
Total		$21,000	$2,093	2.10

Table 17.2   Rent Increase Allowances Based on Amount of Rent Spent on Capital Expenditures (CMHC interest rate 7.0% per year)

Capital expenditures (% of annual rent)	Above-guideline increase (% of annual rent)		
	First year	Second year	Third year
10	1.4	0	0
20	2.7	0	0
30	3.0	1.0	0
40	3.0	2.5	0
50	3.0	3.0	0.8

- it is necessary to protect or restore the physical integrity of the residential complex or part of it;

- it is necessary to maintain maintenance, health, safety, or other housing-related standards required by law;

- it is necessary to maintain the provision of a plumbing, heating, mechanical, electrical, ventilation, or air conditioning system;

- it provides access for persons with disabilities;

- it promotes energy or water conservation; or

- it maintains or improves the security of the residential complex or part of it (s. 126(7)).

The replacement of an item or system is not an eligible capital expenditure if the item or system did not require major repair or replacement unless the replacement promotes access for persons with disabilities, promotes energy or water conservation, or promotes security for the complex (s. 126(8)). For example, cosmetic upgrades are not eligible for above-guideline rent increases.

SECURITY SERVICES

A landlord can apply for an above-guideline rent increase for the operating costs related to security services provided for the residential complex by persons not employed by the landlord (s. 126(1)3). Such an application can be combined with an application for capital expenditures associated with the increased security, even if the landlord's own employees have done the work involved in the capital expenditure.

Note that a landlord cannot claim operating cost increases for security services provided by its own employees merely by establishing a separate corporation or business to provide that security service. The board is required to ascertain the real substance of all transactions and activities; in so doing, it may disregard the separate corporate existence of the participants (s. 202). The regulations also include provisions dealing with related companies or people (O. Reg. 516/06, s. 25). Also note that a new security service is a service that can form the basis of an agreement by tenants to an above-guideline rent increase.

PROCEDURE

An application for an above-guideline rent increase must be made at least 90 days before the effective date of the first intended rent increase (s. 126(3)). An application may include any or all of the rental units in a residential complex (s. 126(1)). If the landlord applies for fewer than all of the units in the complex, or if the costs apply differently to the different units in the complex, the board allocates the costs among the rental units affected.

The landlord files the application and all the supporting documentation with the board, which issues a notice of hearing to the landlord. The landlord then serves the application and the notice of hearing on all of the affected tenants.

At the date and time appointed for the hearing, the board will usually offer mediation to those tenants who are present. Mediation is explained in Chapter 12. For mediation to take place for an application for an above-guideline rent increase, all the tenants present need to agree to it, although that agreement is usually reached. Likewise for a mediated agreement to be implemented, all tenants present need to agree to the amount of rent increase. Such an agreement is usually reached. The board's mediators explain the above-guideline rent increase rules, and the fact that landlords are entitled to certain amounts of rent increases if they have performed major repairs or experienced unusual utility cost or tax increases. The board will not approve an increase that is higher than the landlord's claims justify. That protects the tenants who are not present. The upper limit on the rent increase also makes mediation a no-lose proposition for the tenants. For a landlord, mediation is superior to a hearing because it usually leaves the tenants feeling better when it is over. (In its very nature, an adjudication or hearing can leave the parties angry with each other and feeling that they were not believed or were attacked.)

This paragraph sets out the rules that apply if a hearing is conducted. The board may conduct inquiries before, during, or after a hearing (s. 201(1)), although inquiries are not usually made after a hearing. During the hearing, the adjudicator will question the landlord about any concerns the adjudicator has with the application. The board may direct a landlord, or in rare circumstances a tenant, to file additional evidence that it considers necessary to make its decision (s. 201(1)(d)).

If the landlord fails to comply with such a direction, the board may refuse to consider the landlord's submission and evidence regarding the issue raised in the direction, or it may dismiss the landlord's application (s. 201(3)). The board may consider relevant information it obtains independently of the parties, provided that it first informs the parties of the additional information and gives them an opportunity to explain or refute it (s. 201(2)). The board may also view premises (s. 201(1)(e)). If the adjudicator intends to do this, the adjudicator must give the parties an opportunity to view the premises with the adjudicator (s. 201(4)).

If the landlord is found to be in serious breach of its duty to maintain the rental complex in a good state of repair, the board shall dismiss the application or force the landlord to complete specified repairs before charging the above-guideline increase granted in the order (ss. 126(12) and (13)).

The board wants to process applications for an above-guideline rent increase before the first intended date of the increase. In cases where this does not occur, the tenant is obliged to pay only the greatest amount of rent that the landlord could charge without applying for a rent increase until the landlord receives an order approving the application (s. 126(5)). Normally that is the guideline increase. However, the tenant may voluntarily choose to pay the amount set out in the landlord's notice of rent increase (s. 126(6)).

If the order is made three months or more after the first effective date applied for, the board may order a tenant to pay the amount owing retroactively (because of the delay) in monthly installments, not exceeding 12 monthly installments (ss. 205(2) and (4)). The tenant may pay according to the authorized installments even if the tenancy is terminated (s. 205(3)).

EXTENT OF RENT INCREASE AND PHASE-IN

For extraordinary increases in municipal taxes and charges, or in utility costs, there is no limit on the amount of the above-guideline rent increase that can be ordered. However, the above-guideline rent increase for capital expenditures or security services is limited to 3 percent of the previous lawful rent. If the board finds that the landlord is entitled to more than 3 percent above the guideline rate, the board will order a 3 percent increase in the first year and other increases in the following two years in amounts not to exceed 3 percent of the lawful rent for the previous year, until the total increase has been taken, or 3 years have passed, whichever comes first (s. 126(11)). (However, in a mediation, the tenants sometimes seek an increase of less than 3 percent in the first year. For example, if the landlord's claims justify a total above-guideline increase of 4 percent, then after a hearing the board would order a 3 percent increase in the first year, followed by a 1 percent increase in the second year. In mediation, the parties may agree to a 2.5 percent increase in the first year, followed by a 1.5 percent increase in the second year, and the board will order that instead.)

The board's orders do not set out the amount of the new rent for the various units. An order of the board sets out the percentage rent increase that may be taken (s. 126(10)). A landlord may give an increase as high as the amount set out in the order, but must still comply with the other rules regarding rent increases, as discussed in Chapter 16.

An order of the board ceases to be of any effect when a new tenant enters into a new tenancy agreement with the landlord if the new tenancy agreement takes effect within the 90-day period before the first effective date of a rent increase (s. 126(14)). This is because the landlord is entitled to set a new market rent with the new tenants.

COSTS NO LONGER BORNE: CAPITAL EXPENDITURES

A tenant whose rent is increased because of an above-guideline increase for capital expenditures is entitled to have the rent reduced by the same percentage at the end of the average useful life of the capital expenditures allowed (s. 129). When the board issues an order for an above-guideline increase based on capital expenditures, the board will specify in the order a date on which the landlord must reduce the rent for affected tenants. That date will be the end of the average period over which the capital expenditures were amortized. Usually this date will be between 10 and 20 years after the above-guideline increase is issued.

The requirement to reduce the rent is only applicable to continuing tenants who were subject to an above-guideline increase (s. 129(c)).

SPECIALIZED REPRESENTATIVES

In Ontario's largest cities, there are lawyers and rent review consultants who specialize in applications for above-guideline rent increases. There can be a considerable amount of money at stake in these applications and they can be very complex. For these two reasons, there may be concerns about liability for errors or omissions in processing these applications. Therefore, your employer or a landlord may want to refer these cases to specialists in this field.

REVIEW QUESTIONS

1. a. Over the past two years Rashida has been having you act for her to evict several tenants. Lately Rashida has been complaining that her costs are going up a lot. Her insurance, heat, and hydro costs all went up more than 10 percent last year, but her rents went up only 2 percent. Is there anything you can suggest to her?

    b. Is there anything else you would think to ask her about?

    c. What would you do or suggest to Rashida about how to proceed?

2. a. A tenant, Mani, comes to your office. He has received a rent increase notice for an increase of 10 percent. He wants to know if his landlord can actually charge him a 10 percent increase. What would you tell him?

    b. Suppose Mani also tells you that he pays for his own heat, hydro, and water. Would that affect your advice to him?

Increasing the Rent by Agreement

18

In taking rent increases, a landlord is always subject to the limit of what a tenant is willing to pay, in that the tenant can give a notice to terminate and vacate the unit on 60 days' notice at the end of term (or 28 days' notice for a daily or weekly tenancy). Professional property managers and landlords keep a careful eye on the rents that their competitors are charging, and their own vacancy rates and turnover rates, in order to set their asking rents as high as they can while still keeping their building almost full. There are various techniques for setting rents, most of which fall in the category of marketing. Most of those techniques apply primarily to setting rents for new tenants. This text does not deal with marketing considerations because they are not relevant for law clerks, lawyers, or others who represent the interests of landlords before the Landlord and Tenant Board ("the board").

The *Residential Tenancies Act, 2006* (RTA) allows for landlords and continuing tenants to agree to above-guideline rent increases in the following circumstances. First, a landlord may increase rent if the landlord and the tenant agree that the landlord will provide a parking space or a new or additional service or facility listed in the regulations (s. 123(1)). Such an increase can take place at any time agreed upon between the landlord and the tenant (s. 123(2)). See below for more details.

Second, at a regular rent increase date and with the tenant's agreement, the landlord can increase the rent by up to 3 percent more than the guideline if the landlord carries out (or agrees to carry out) a specified capital expenditure or provides (or agrees to provide) a new or additional service (s. 121). Such an agreement must be made using a form approved by the board. Various conditions apply, which are discussed below.

AGREED INCREASE FOR PRESCRIBED SERVICES AND FACILITIES

Under s. 123, a landlord may increase rent if the landlord and the tenant agree that the landlord will provide a parking space or a new or additional service or facility listed in the regulations. At any time, and without giving a notice of rent increase, a landlord may increase the prescribed rent if the landlord and tenant agree that the landlord will provide one or more of the following additional services or facilities:

- a parking space (s. 123),
- cable television,
- satellite television,
- an air conditioner,

- extra electricity for an air conditioner,
- extra electricity for a washer or dryer in the rental unit,
- blockheater plug-ins,
- lockers or other storage space,
- heat,
- electricity,
- water or sewage services (excluding capital work),
- floor space,
- property taxes with respect to a site for a mobile home or a land lease home (O. Reg. 516/06, s. 16(1)), or
- such other services and facilities as may be prescribed by regulation from time to time.

Amount of Increase

O. Reg. 516/06, s. 16, prescribes that the amount by which the rent may generally be increased is "the actual cost to the landlord of the service [or] facility ... (other than floor space) that is the subject of the agreement or, where the actual cost to the landlord cannot be established or where there is no cost to the landlord, a reasonable amount based on the value of the service [or] facility."

If the additional facility is floor space, then generally the increase in rent must be proportionate to the change in floor space, except that where the amount would be unreasonable given the nature and quality of the floor space added or taken away, the increase in rent must be a reasonable amount based on the nature and quality of the floor space and the amount of the change in the floor space (O. Reg. 156/06, ss. 16(3) and (4)). The exception relates to high-cost floor space, such as bathroom or kitchen space, or low-cost floor space, such as unfinished areas or sun porches.

There are special rules if the service or facility was previously added and removed in accordance with an agreement under previous versions of s. 123 as found in previous rent control legislation. See O. Reg. 516/06, s. 16(5). See Chapter 19 for the rules about rent reductions due to the removal of a service or facility.

Details of the Agreement

The regular notice of rent increase does not need to be given if the rent is increased because the landlord and the tenant have agreed that the landlord will provide an additional prescribed service (s. 123(2)).

An agreement under s. 123 is void if it has been entered into as a result of coercion or as a result of a false, incomplete, or misleading representation by the landlord (s. 124).

The agreement to increase the rent because of the addition of a prescribed service or facility does not need to be in writing or in any particular form. However, for their own protection, landlords and tenants should sign a written agreement so that the amount of the rent increase, the service or facility in question, and the total new rent are spelled out clearly.

The 12-month rule, requiring 12 months between rent increases, does not apply to an increase for an additional parking space or an additional prescribed service that the landlord and tenant agree will be added (s. 123(2)). In other words, an increase for a parking space or other prescribed service does not affect the timing of the next rent increase (s. 119(2)).

AGREED INCREASE FOR CAPITAL EXPENDITURES OR ADDITIONAL SERVICES

At an appropriate rent-increase date (that is, at least 12 months after a previous increase in rent, other than an increase for the addition of a prescribed service or facility under s. 123), a landlord and a tenant may agree to an above-guideline rent increase if the landlord has carried out or agrees to carry out a specified capital expenditure in exchange for the rent increase, or if the landlord provides or agrees to provide a new or additional service in exchange for the rent increase (s. 121(1)). A "capital expenditure" is an expenditure on a major renovation, repair, replacement, or new addition, the expected benefit of which extends for at least one year. Examples include replacing appliances or cupboards, or renovating a bathroom or kitchen.

An additional service or facility may be any service or facility, including but not limited to the prescribed services that allow agreements under s. 123. Some examples of non-prescribed services are security services, recreation services, and cleaning services.

The increase is limited to 3 percent more than the guideline (s. 121(3)). However, the increase does not need to be justified by the amount spent by the landlord to carry out the capital expenditure. For example, a capital expenditure that would justify only a 1.5 percent increase above the guideline in an application may be the subject of a 3 percent above-guideline increase by agreement under s. 130. On the other hand, a capital expenditure that would justify a 2.5 percent increase may be used as the basis for an agreed increase of 1 percent above the guideline.

Details of the Agreement

An agreement under s. 121 must be in the form approved by the board for this purpose (s. 121(2)). The agreement must set out the new rent. It must also inform the tenant of the tenant's right to cancel the agreement within five days of signing it and the date the agreement is to take effect (ss. 121(2) and (4)). That date must be no earlier than six days after the agreement is signed (s. 121(5)).

Agreements under this section can be made after the landlord has given a notice of rent increase for a lower or higher amount than the amount of the agreement, provided that the agreed rent increase under s. 121 is to take effect on or before the date of the rent increase in the notice (s. 121(7)).

On the form evidencing the agreement it is important to specify as accurately as possible the work to be done, or the service to be added, in exchange for the payment of additional rent. If you need more space than the form provides, write, "See schedule attached," and attach the particulars on a separate page labeled "schedule" and stapled to the form. A tenant can apply to roll back the above-guideline rent increase if a landlord fails to comply with the agreement to make the capital expenditure or provide the new or additional service (s. 122(1)). A tenant is entitled to make that application within two years after the rent increase becomes effective (s. 122(2)). The tenant's right to apply because a landlord has failed to comply with such an agreement overrides the deeming of rent as legal one year after it has first been charged under s. 136 (s. 136(3)).

REVIEW QUESTIONS

1. a. Give some examples of services and facilities that a landlord can add, with the agreement of the tenant, in exchange for a rent increase?

    b. How much of a rent increase is allowed?

2. a. Suppose Marcello wants his landlord, Salma, to paint his kitchen and provide a new stove, but Salma says she can't afford to make those improvements within the guideline rent increase. Can Marcello and Salma agree to a higher increase for the work and stove? If so, what do they have to do?

    b. Suppose Marcello changes his mind three days later. Does he have to go through with the agreement?

    c. Instead, suppose Marcello goes ahead with the agreement and pays Salma the higher rent, but Salma doesn't paint the kitchen. What, if any, recourse does Marcello have? Does Marcello face a time limit?

Rent Reductions and Rebates

19

RENT REDUCTIONS FOR REMOVING A SERVICE OR FACILITY

Under the *Residential Tenancies Act, 2006* (RTA), the landlord is required to reduce the rent charged to a tenant if the landlord and the tenant agree that the landlord will cease to provide parking or any of the prescribed services or facilities listed in Chapter 18 (s. 125). If the service or facility was provided in accordance with a previous agreement under s. 123 (or one of the equivalent sections in previous legislation), the rent decrease is to be

- the most recent separate charge for the service or facility, or
- if there is no separate charge, the amount of the original increase for the service or facility adjusted by the percentage increase in the total rent since the service or facility was first provided (O. Reg. 516/06, s. 16(5)).

Example 19.1

In year 1, the rent is $1,000.00.

Sometime during year 1, the landlord and tenant agree to add a parking space and $50.00 to the rent as a separate charge: $50.00 is the average charge for other parking spaces and is chosen because no actual cost can be established.

The rent becomes:	unit	$1,000.00
	parking	$ 50.00
	total rent	$1,050.00

In year 2, the landlord takes an increase of 2 percent on the unit rent and $5.00 on the parking ($5.00 is 10 percent of the parking charge, but assume that the total increase, $25.00, or 2.38 percent, is within the guideline).

The rent becomes:	unit	$1,020.00
	parking	$ 55.00
	total rent	$1,075.00

Later in year 2, the landlord and the tenant agree that the tenant will give up the parking space. The rent decrease is $55.00; therefore, the rent is $1,020.00 after the decrease.

Example 19.2

In year 1, the rent is $1,000.00.

Sometime during year 1, the landlord and tenant agree to add a parking space and $50.00 to the rent: $50.00 is the average charge for other parking spaces and is chosen because no actual cost can be established. The landlord does not show the parking as a separate charge. The rent becomes $1,050.00.

In year 2, the landlord increases the rent to $1,075.00 (2.38 percent).

Later in year 2, the landlord and the tenant agree that the tenant will give up the parking space. The rent decrease is $51.19 ($50 + 2.38 percent); therefore, the rent is $1,023.81 after the decrease.

If the removed service or facility was not added under s. 132 (or one of the equivalent sections of previous legislation), the amount of the decrease is to be calculated the same way as the amount of the increase. See Chapter 18.

If the landlord and tenant have been unable to agree on the appropriate reduction, the tenant may enforce the right to a reduction by applying to the Landlord and Tenant Board ("the board") under s. 130 within one year after a reduction or discontinuance in a service or facility.

RENT REDUCTIONS FOR REDUCTIONS IN SERVICES AND FACILITIES

If, whether by choice or circumstances, a landlord unilaterally discontinues or reduces a service or facility for a rental unit or the residential complex, a tenant may apply for an order reducing the rent (s. 130(1)). If the tenant moves out of the unit after the discontinuance or reduction occurs (thereby becoming a former tenant), the former tenant can apply for a rent reduction (s. 130(2)).

The board may

* reduce the rent charged for a specified period of time if there has been a temporary reduction in a service,
* reduce the rent charged permanently, or
* order a rebate of rent to a tenant (s. 130(3)).

According to O. Reg. 516/06, s. 39(7), if the discontinuance or reduction is temporary and its duration is reasonable, taking into account the effect on the tenant, the board will not reduce the rent. Otherwise, if the service or facility was provided in accordance with a previous agreement under s. 123 (or the equivalent sections in previous legislation), the rent decrease is to be

* the most recent separate charge for the service or facility, or
* if there is no separate charge, the amount of the original increase for the service or facility adjusted by the percentage increase in the total rent since the service or facility was first provided (O. Reg. 516/06, s. 39(5)).

See Chapter 18 for examples of how this calculation is made.

If the discontinued service or facility was not added under s. 123 (or the equivalent sections in previous legislation), and the discontinuance of the service or facility was reasonable, then the amount of the decrease is to be calculated the same way as the amount of the increase. Specifically, the rent must be reduced by an amount that is equal to what would be a reasonable charge for the service or facility based on

- the cost of the service or facility to the landlord, or
- if the cost cannot be determined or if there is no cost, on the value of the service or facility (O. Reg. 516/06, s. 39(2)).

If the discontinued service or facility was not added under s. 123 (or the equivalent sections in previous legislation), and the discontinuance of the service or facility was *not* reasonable, then the rent decrease shall take into account

- the value of the service or facility, including the cost to the tenant of replacing the discontinued service or facility, and
- the effect of the discontinuance on the tenant (O. Reg. 516/06, s. 39(3)).

According to O. Reg. 516/06, s. 39(4), the rent reduction shall not be less than it would have been if the amount were determined based on the cost of the service or facility as determined under O. Reg. 516/06, s. 39(2).

The determination of whether a service or facility removal is reasonable or unreasonable depends on the facts of each case. Suppose the landlord removes a rooftop deck from tenant access. Such a removal tends to be considered reasonable if a new city bylaw prohibited such decks or if there were safety concerns. Such a removal tends to be considered unreasonable if the landlords barred most tenants from the deck, but attached it as a facility available only for a penthouse rental unit, which was then rented at an increased premium rent.

If a service or facility is reduced, the amount of the reduction of rent must be a reasonable proportion of the amount that would be determined if the service or facility were discontinued. The reasonable proportion is determined based on the degree of the reduction of the service or facility (O. Reg. 516/06, s. 39(6)).

If the rent charged is reduced permanently, the reduced rent forms the basis for future guideline or other rent increases under the RTA. An order permanently reducing the rent takes effect on the day that the discontinuance or reduction of the service or facility first occurred (s. 130(4)). The board determines that date and sets it out in the order. The tenant, or former tenant, has one year after the reduction or discontinuance of the service or facility to make the application (s. 130(5)).

The board has no power to add other tenants in the residential complex to a tenant's application for rent reduction, even if the application relates to common areas, services, or facilities. However, the board will accept applications that are signed by groups of tenants as long as each applicant signs the application form individually (s. 186(2)). Thus, tenants' associations and others may still organize group applications for rent reductions.

A tenant cannot apply for a rent reduction because of a reduction in the cost of utilities in a residential complex unless the landlord has charged the tenant a rent increase for the increase in utility costs. However, a tenant who paid an above-guideline increase because of an increase in the cost of utilities may be entitled to a rent reduction if the cost of utilities falls in a subsequent year (see Chapter 17).

RENT REDUCTIONS FOR MUNICIPAL TAX DECREASES

As with most taxes, property taxes are ultimately borne by the consumer of the product being taxed—in the case of apartments, the consumers are residential tenants. Historically, rental apartments in Ontario have been subject to higher property taxes than single-family homes. As part of a long-term program to reduce or eliminate that higher taxation, the province decided that the benefit of any tax savings that a building experiences should flow to residential tenants immediately and by legal requirement. The mechanism for achieving a "flow through" of tax savings on rental buildings is found in s. 131.

The rent for a rental unit in a residential complex is automatically reduced when there is a reduction in municipal property taxes that exceeds 2.49 percent (s. 131 and O. Reg. 516/06, s. 41(1)). If a rent reduction is required under s. 131, it takes effect on December 31 of the year in which the decrease was experienced. This means that if a landlord experienced a tax decrease from 2009 to 2010 greater than 2.49 percent of the taxes, then the rent for the rental units would be decreased on December 31, 2010. In more practical terms, and for most tenants the rent decrease can be said to occur on January 1, 2011. However, the technical date matters for tenants who are subject to a rent increase on January 1. For them the rent decrease occurs before and separately from the rent increase.

The reduced rent becomes the "lawful rent." However, subject to the usual limits on rent increases, the landlord is entitled to increase the rent at the next appropriate rent increase date after the reduction. For the December 31, 2010 reduction, the next rent increase can be as early as January 1, 2011, but that increase is based on the lower rent that applies after the decrease.

CALCULATION OF THE RENT REDUCTION DUE TO A TAX DECREASE

There are two different rent reduction calculations and rules depending on whether the rental property has seven or more units, or six or fewer units. The *Assessment Act* defines "multi-residential property" as land and buildings used for residential purposes that have seven or more self-contained units (other than condominiums, co-operatives, group homes, care homes, recreational properties, or land leases). For the purpose of property taxation, if there are seven or more private rental units on a single property tax roll, the property is multi-residential, whether the property is a high-rise apartment, a walk-up apartment, or row housing.

Multi-Residential Properties

Multi-residential properties have historically paid higher tax rates than owner-occupied houses and other residential property. In many cities across Ontario, multi-residential properties are taxed at more than twice the rate charged on residential property.

To calculate the automatic rent reduction for a multi-residential property,

1. determine the percentage by which the municipal property tax for the complex in the current year has decreased from the previous year; and

2. if the percentage is 2.5 percent or greater, multiply that percentage figure by 20 percent.

If the percentage is less than 2.49 percent, there is no automatic rent reduction (although, as described below, tenants may be able to apply for a reduction).

The calculation of an automatic rent reduction for a multi-residential property is illustrated in example 19.3.

Example 19.3 Automatic Rent Reduction for Multi-Residential Property

2010 taxes:	$100,000
2011 taxes:	$ 95,000
Decrease:	$ 5,000
Decrease as a percentage of 2010 taxes:	5%

Since 5% is greater than 2.49%, there is an automatic rent reduction.

Rent reduction percentage: 5 percent × 20% = 1%

If a tenant is paying $1,000 per month, the rent is reduced by $10 to $990 per month.

The foregoing methodology, which is set out by regulation, assumes that the municipal property taxes represent 20 percent of the annual revenue of a multi-residential complex. That percentage reflects the average ratio of property tax to rent in Ontario for multi-residential properties. Given that ratio, a 5 percent decrease in the taxes is the same amount of money as a 1 percent decrease in the rents.

Municipalities are required to give notice to tenants of residential complexes with seven or more units if a tax decrease exceeds 2.49 percent (s. 131(3) and O. Reg. 516/06, ss. 41(5) to (8)). The notice must be in a form approved by the board (s. 131(4)) and must

- inform the tenants that the rent is reduced;
- set out the percentage by which the rent is reduced and the date the reduction takes effect;
- inform the tenants that if the rent is not reduced in accordance with the notice, they may apply to the board under s. 135 for the return of money illegally collected; and
- advise the landlord and the tenants of their right to apply for an order under s. 132 to vary the calculation converting the tax decrease into the rent decrease (s. 131(4)).

Residential Properties

Although municipalities are not obliged to send rent reduction notices to tenants in residential buildings (that is, properties of six or fewer units on a single assessment roll number) that have seen tax decreases, the automatic rent reduction rules still apply.

The calculation of an automatic rent reduction for a residential property is illustrated in example 19.4.

Example 19.4   Automatic Rent Reduction for Residential Property

2010 taxes:	$2,700
2011 taxes:	$2,430
Decrease:	$ 270
Decrease as a percentage of 2010 taxes:	10%

Since 10% is greater than 2.49%, there is an automatic rent reduction.

Rent reduction percentage: 10% × 15 percent = 1.5%

If a tenant is paying $1,500.00 per month, the rent is reduced by $22.50 to $1,477.50 per month.

Over the course of 12 months, the rent will have been reduced by $270 (that is, $22.50 × 12 months).

The foregoing methodology, which is set out by regulation, assumes that the municipal property taxes represent 15 percent of the annual revenue of a residential complex. That percentage reflects the average ratio of property tax to rent in Ontario for smaller rented residential complexes.

The reason a tax decrease triggers a rent reduction of only 15 percent of the percentage tax decrease (or 20 percent for a multi-residential complex) is that taxes are only one component of rent. The rest of the rent goes to pay for the landlord's other costs, including things such as maintenance, repairs, utilities, insurance, employee costs, and financing, as well as for return on investment).

The city of Toronto has issued notices of rent reduction to all tenants even if the property has six or fewer units. That is not required by provincial law, and most other municipalities do not issue rent reduction notices to the smaller buildings. In most cities, tenants can check whether there has been a tax decrease by contacting the Tax Office of the city's finance department.

APPLICATIONS TO VARY AUTOMATIC RENT REDUCTIONS

If there is a rent reduction because of a municipal tax decrease, the tax reduction in dollars is roughly equivalent to the rent decrease in dollars. As stated above, an initial calculation is made that assumes that taxes represent either 15 or 20 percent of the total annual rent (depending on whether the complex has seven or more rental units). For a multi-residential property, if the taxes represent more than 20 percent of rent, the calculation favours the landlord, and the tenants can apply individually to vary the calculation (s. 132(1)). If taxes represent less than 20 percent of rent, the calculation favours the tenants, and the landlord can apply to vary the calculation (s. 132(1)). Likewise, if the taxes for a residential property are more or less than 15 percent, the landlord or tenants can apply to vary the automatic rent reduction calculation.

Applications to vary can also be brought by the landlord or by individual tenants where

- there are municipal charges, other than property taxes levied by the municipality on the property (for example, garbage levy charges and recycling charges);
- there is a manifest error in the rent reduction notice; or
- the municipal property tax has increased or decreased between the period that the rent reduction notice was issued and March 31 of the following year.

REVIEW QUESTIONS

1. Under what circumstances is a landlord required to reduce the rent?

2. How is a rent reduction calculated if the landlord gets rid of storage lockers?

3. a. How do landlords and tenants resolve disputes over how much a rent should be reduced due to the removal of a service?

   b. Does every tenant have to agree on how much the reduction should be?

4. If the property taxes for a rental unit fall, is the tenant entitled to a rent reduction, or are there some further conditions to determine whether the tenant is entitled to a rent reduction?

5. How do tenants find out if they are entitled to a rent reduction for municipal tax decreases?

Offences Under the RTA

20

The *Residential Tenancies Act, 2006* (RTA) has created a number of offences. These new offences can lead to prosecutions under the *Provincial Offences Act* (POA) in the same manner as offences under the previous legislation or other provincial legislation. The offences are considered to be quasi-criminal offences, rather than crimes.

The process usually begins with a complaint by a tenant to the Landlord and Tenant Board ("the board"). The board will refer the complaint for investigation by the Enforcement Branch of the Ministry of Municipal Affairs and Housing under ss. 227 and 229. The Enforcement Branch often contacts landlords to tell them that they are investigating a complaint and to ask for their side of the story. If you learn that a client of yours has received such a communication, you should refer your client to a lawyer or other agent who is very knowledgeable about the RTA for advice on how to respond. Often the right explanation and response will result in the Enforcement Branch not proceeding with a charge.

After the investigation is over, the prosecution begins with the issuance of a summons by the provincial offences court to the person being charged. The summons requires the person to appear to answer the charge or charges. The person charged is entitled to disclosure of the facts alleged to make up the offence. Unless the person pleads guilty, a trial is held, after which the court finds the person guilty or not guilty of the offence. After a finding of guilt, the court hears submissions as to sentence and announces the penalty.

In addition, the RTA includes a system for penalizing landlords for breaches of the Act that does not involve a prosecution under the POA. Instead, in some applications by a tenant for relief, such as an application alleging that a landlord gave notice of termination in bad faith, the board can impose an "administrative fine" on the landlord. The RTA permits the board to impose such a fine for breaches of the Act committed by the landlord or the landlord's superintendents or agents.

This chapter lists the offences that can be prosecuted under the POA, identifies the fines that can be imposed for committing the offences, describes the regime of administrative fines, and comments on landlords' liability for the actions of their superintendents and agents.

THE OFFENCES

Offences under the RTA are set out in ss. 233, 234, 235, 236, and 237.

Under s. 233, a person is guilty of an offence if the person knowingly

(a) withholds the reasonable supply of a vital service, care service or food or interferes with the supply in contravention of section 21;

(b) alters or causes to be altered the locking system on any door giving entry to a rental unit or the residential complex in a manner that contravenes section 24 or 35;

(c) restricts reasonable access to the residential complex by political candidates or their authorized representatives in contravention of section 28;

(d) seizes any property of the tenant in contravention of section 40;

(e) fails to afford a tenant a right of first refusal in contravention of section 51 or 53;

(f) recovers possession of a rental unit without complying with the requirements of sections 52, 54 and 55;

(g) coerces a tenant to sign an agreement referred to in section 121;

(h) harasses, hinders, obstructs or interferes with a tenant in the exercise of,

　(i) securing a right or seeking relief under this Act or in a court,

　(ii) participating in a proceeding under this Act, or

　(iii) participating in a tenants' association or attempting to organize a tenants' association;

(i) harasses, coerces, threatens or interferes with a tenant in such a manner that the tenant is induced to vacate the rental unit;

(j) harasses, hinders, obstructs or interferes with a landlord in the exercise of,

　(i) securing a right or seeking relief under this Act or in a court, or

　(ii) participating in a proceeding under this Act;

(k) obtains possession of a rental unit improperly by giving a notice to terminate in bad faith; or

(l) coerces a tenant of a mobile home park or land lease community to enter into an agency agreement for the sale or lease of their mobile home or land lease home or requires an agency agreement as a condition of entering into a tenancy agreement.

Note that almost all the charges are for things that a landlord might do. This is not because landlords are more likely to do wrong than tenants; rather it is because much of the RTA is about limiting what landlords can do. It also flows from the fact that the most common bad tenant behaviour is the non-payment of rent, and this is not an offence. In addition, other tenant misbehaviour is already a crime under the *Criminal Code*. For example, wilfully damaging someone's property is mischief under s. 430 of the *Criminal Code*.

There are several offences that can be committed by tenants under the RTA. One is the offence of changing the locks of a rental unit in violation of s. 35. Another, set out in s. 233(j), is the offence of harassing, hindering, obstructing, or interfering with a landlord in the exercise of

　(i) securing a right or seeking relief under this Act or in a court, or

　(ii) participating in a proceeding under this Act.

Tenants who sublet become landlords to their subtenants, and in that role the original tenants are subject to almost all the restrictions and offences directed at landlords. Tenants who assign their tenancies face restrictions similar to the restrictions on landlords, which prevent landlords from charging premiums or similar charges (s. 134(3)).

Section 234 provides as follows:

A person is guilty of an offence if the person,

(a) enters a rental unit where such entry is not permitted by section 26, 27 or 142 or enters without first complying with the requirements of section 26, 27 or 142;

(b) fails to make an evicted tenant's property available for retrieval in accordance with subsection 41(3);

(c) gives a notice to terminate a tenancy under section 48 or 49 in contravention of section 51;

(d) requires or receives a security deposit from a tenant contrary to section 105;

(e) fails to pay to the tenant annually interest on the rent deposit held in respect of their tenancy in accordance with section 106;

(f) fails to apply the rent deposit held in respect of a tenancy to the rent for the last month of the tenancy in contravention of subsection 106(10);

(g) fails to repay an amount received as a rent deposit as required by subsection 107(1) or (2);

(h) fails to provide a tenant or former tenant with a receipt in accordance with section 109;

(i) fails to provide the notice in the form required under section 114 or gives false information in the notice;

(j) requires a tenant to pay rent proposed in an application in contravention of subsection 126(5);

(k) fails to provide information on the total cost of utilities in accordance with subsection 128(2);

(l) charges or collects amounts from a tenant, a prospective tenant, a subtenant, a potential subtenant, an assignee or a potential assignee in contravention of section 134;

(m) gives a notice of rent increase or a notice of increase of a charge in a care home without first giving an information package contrary to section 140;

(n) does anything to prevent a tenant of a care home from obtaining care services from a person of the tenant's choice contrary to clause 147(a);

(o) interferes with the provision of care services to a tenant of a care home contrary to clause 147(b);

(p) increases a charge for providing a care service or meals to a tenant in a care home in contravention of section 150;

(q) interferes with a tenant's right under section 156 to sell or lease his or her mobile home;

(r) restricts the right of a tenant of a mobile home park or land lease community to purchase goods or services from the person of his or her choice in contravention of section 160;

(s) charges an illegal contingency fee in contravention of subsection 214(1);

(t) fails to comply with any or all of the items contained in a work order issued under section 225;

(u) obstructs or interferes with an inspector exercising a power of entry under section 230 or 231 or with an investigator exercising a power of entry under section 231;

(v) furnishes false or misleading information in any material filed in any proceeding under this Act or provided to the Board, an employee or official of the Board, an inspector, an investigator, the Minister or a designate of the Minister;

(w) unlawfully recovers possession of a rental unit;

(x) charges rent in an amount greater than permitted under this Act; or

(y) contravenes an order of the Board that,

(i) orders a landlord to do specified repairs or replacements or other work within a specified time, or

(ii) orders that a landlord, a superintendent or an agent of a landlord may not engage in any further activities listed in paragraphs 2 to 6 of subsection 29(1) against any of the tenants in a residential complex.

In addition, s. 235(1) states the following:

Any landlord or superintendent, agent or employee of the landlord who knowingly harasses a tenant or interferes with a tenant's reasonable enjoyment of a rental unit or the residential complex in which it is located is guilty of an offence.

Even if the offence itself is not committed, the RTA makes it an offence to attempt to commit one of these offences (s. 236). A director or officer of a corporate landlord commits an offence if he or she knowingly concurs in the offence (s. 237).

The time limit for commencing prosecutions is generally two years from the date of the offence (s. 239(2)).

FINES FOR THE OFFENCES

For committing an offence, an individual is liable to a fine of up to $25,000, while a corporation is liable to a fine of up to $100,000. Under ordinary sentencing principles, the maximum fine is to be given only to the worst offender (in terms of previous convictions) for the worst offence. If the landlord's conduct was calculated to obtain a financial gain, the amount of the potential gain is also a factor in determining the amount of the fine.

ADMINISTRATIVE FINES

In addition to the regime of enforcement through prosecution under the POA, the RTA includes a regime of administrative fines. A tenant or a former tenant can apply for an order that the landlord or the landlord's superintendent or agent has committed a prohibited act under certain sections of the RTA. See Table 20.1 for a list of the prohibited acts, along with the sections prohibiting the conduct, the sections permitting the application, and the section permitting the board to impose the administrative fine.

If the board determines that the landlord or the landlord's superintendent or agent has committed a prohibited act, the board may, among other remedies,

order that the landlord pay to the Board an administrative fine not exceeding the greater of $25,000 [because that is now the monetary jurisdiction of the Small Claims Court] (s. 31(1)(d)).

Table 20.1 Prohibited Conduct Subject to Administrative Fines

Prohibited conduct	RTA section that prohibits the conduct	RTA section that allows tenant's application	RTA section of related offence
Withholding reasonable supply of vital service, care service, or food	s. 21	s. 29(1)	s. 233(a)
Interfering with reasonable enjoyment of rental unit or residential complex	s. 22	s. 29(1)	s. 235(1)
Harassing, obstructing, coercing, threatening, or interfering with tenant	s. 23	s. 29(1)	s 235(h)
Altering locking system on door of unit or complex without giving replacement keys	ss. 24, 35(1)	s. 29(1)	s. 233(b)
Illegally entering rental unit	s. 25	s. 29(1)	s. 234(a)
Giving notice for personal use in bad faith (s. 48)	s. 37	s. 57(1)(a)	s. 233(k)
Purchaser's giving notice for personal use in bad faith (s. 49)	s. 37	s. 57(1)(b)	s. 233(k)
Giving notice for demolition, conversion, or repair in bad faith and not carrying through (s. 50)	s. 37	s. 57(1)(c)	s. 233(k)

If the board determines that the tenant was induced to vacate the rental unit by the prohibited conduct, the board can also order that the landlord pay a sum of money to compensate the tenant for

(a) all or any portion of any increased rent which the tenant has incurred or will incur for a one-year period after the tenant has left the rental unit; and

(b) reasonable out-of-pocket moving, storage and other like expenses which the tenant has incurred or will incur. (s. 31(2))

The prohibited conduct that can lead to those orders is set out in Table 20.1.

LIABILITY OF LANDLORDS FOR ACTS OF SUPERINTENDENTS AND AGENTS

Under the quasi-criminal offence sections, it is the person who actually commits the offence who is liable to punishment. However, a landlord can be found to have committed an offence by directing someone else to perform a prohibited act, and thus be liable to a fine under the offence sections. In addition, the language of the RTA allows an administrative fine to be imposed on a landlord when the landlord's superintendent or agent engages in prohibited conduct with or without the landlord's knowledge or approval. The administrative fine is a civil remedy, although it is paid to the board.

A landlord may be able to avoid an administrative fine for conduct of a superintendent or agent if the landlord can show that the superintendent or agent performed the prohibited act against the landlord's explicit or implied direction. To ensure that this defence is available, landlords should bring the list of prohibited conduct to the attention of all their employees and agents, and document that they have told their employees and agents to refrain from this conduct. It is good practice for landlords to instruct all new employees and agents to avoid prohibited conduct when they are hired or engaged and to repeat the instruction to them once a year. Landlords should have each employee sign an acknowledgment of receipt of these instructions.

A landlord can be subject either to an administrative fine or to prosecution under the POA, but not to both. Although this rule is not set out in the RTA, it flows from our general law that prevents a second prosecution for the same offence once a person has been either convicted or acquitted of an offence. (After a POA prosecution, a tenant may still apply for all the other relief under s. 31, but the board may not impose an administrative fine in addition to giving compensatory relief to the tenant.)

A POA prosecution of a superintendent or agent does not bar the imposition of an administrative fine on the landlord. However, a landlord may raise the defence that the superintendent or agent performed the prohibited act without the landlord's knowledge or approval, as discussed above.

REVIEW QUESTIONS

1. Can a tenant be charged under the *Provincial Offences Act*?

2. What is the difference between offences under s. 233 and offences under s. 234?

3. What is the maximum fine that can be imposed for an offence under the RTA?

4. Can a tenant bring a tenant application on the same grounds as the grounds on which a landlord was found guilty by the Provincial Offences Court?

Conclusion

21

Working in the area of residential tenancies in Ontario is a constant challenge. The steps you take have a significant impact on people's lives. The law is frequently changing, and you must stay abreast of all of the changes, large and small.

Often an eviction application results in the tenant being given another chance by the landlord or the Landlord and Tenant Board ("the board"). In these situations, the disputes involve parties who must learn to get along in an ongoing relationship, sometimes living in the same building.

The *Residential Tenancies Act, 2006* (RTA) encourages landlords and tenants to try to understand each other's needs and interests, and to work out resolutions of their conflicts. This might be the case where a tenant is seeking a new or additional service (perhaps a washer–dryer in the unit), or the landlord is seeking to recover money spent in restoring or improving an aging building. Under the RTA, landlords and tenants are free to enter into certain agreements that suit their needs. Whenever you are negotiating or mediating, put yourself in the position of the opposing parties: if you were in their shoes, what would be a reasonable outcome?

We encourage you to become familiar with the mediation and voluntary agreement opportunities available under the RTA. These can often lead to a "win–win" result.

Under the RTA, tenants are protected from landlords' attempts to impose additional charges or higher rents illegally. Once a tenancy has commenced, the tenant is protected and can enforce his or her rights swiftly in an application to the board.

Similarly, landlords are protected from tenants who try to take advantage of them. Tenants cannot transfer possession of a rental unit to strangers. Landlords can apply to remove strangers quickly or to require them to enter into new tenancy agreements if the landlord agrees to accept them as tenants.

A word of advice to those of you who are embarking upon a path that will bring you into frequent contact with those in the landlord–tenant field: Be mindful that in everything you do, your reputation precedes you. As a representative of a party involved in a board proceeding or negotiation, your most valuable asset is your integrity. Once you have earned a reputation as a knowledgeable, honest, fair, and firm representative of your client's interests, your path will be smooth. You will have earned the respect of those you will be dealing with at the board and in the residential tenancy industry.

Always be prepared. Know the facts of your case. Be sure the paperwork is accurate and complete. Present your documents in a neat and orderly manner. The easier you make it for an opposing representative or party to understand the merit of your proposal, the more likely you are to achieve a good result from negotiation or mediation. The easier you make it for an adjudicator to decide in your favour, the more likely you are to succeed at a hearing.

Residential tenancy law in Ontario is complex. It changes often, with the addition or amendment of regulations, rules, and guidelines. Cases are being decided continually. You must ask questions and seek out information. Learn how to find the answers you need. Attend seminars to update your knowledge. Get involved with your local and provincial landlord or tenant associations. They are a valuable source of information and contacts.

Above all, approach your work in this field with enthusiasm.

APPENDIXES

Residential Tenancies Act, 2006

SO 2006, c. 17

Amended by: 2006, c. 17, s. 261.

Consolidation Period: From January 1, 2011 to the e-Laws currency date.

Last amendment: 2010, c. 8, s. 39.

CONTENTS

PART I　INTRODUCTION

Purposes of Act

1. The purposes of this Act are to provide protection for residential tenants from unlawful rent increases and unlawful evictions, to establish a framework for the regulation of residential rents, to balance the rights and responsibilities of residential landlords and tenants and to provide for the adjudication of disputes and for other processes to informally resolve disputes.

Interpretation

2(1) In this Act,

"Board" means the Landlord and Tenant Board;

"care home" means a residential complex that is occupied or intended to be occupied by persons for the purpose of receiving care services, whether or not receiving the services is the primary purpose of the occupancy;

"care services" means, subject to the regulations, health care services, rehabilitative or therapeutic services or services that provide assistance with the activities of daily living;

"guideline," when used with respect to the charging of rent, means the guideline determined under section 120;

"land lease community" means the land on which one or more occupied land lease homes are situate and includes the rental units and the land, structures, services and facilities of which the landlord retains possession and that are intended for the common use and enjoyment of the tenants of the landlord;

"land lease home" means a dwelling, other than a mobile home, that is a permanent structure where the owner of the dwelling leases the land used or intended for use as the site for the dwelling;

"landlord" includes,

　　(a) the owner of a rental unit or any other person who permits occupancy of a rental unit, other than a tenant who occupies a rental unit in a residential complex and who permits another person to also occupy the unit or any part of the unit,

　　(b) the heirs, assigns, personal representatives and successors in title of a person referred to in clause (a), and

　　(c) a person, other than a tenant occupying a rental unit in a residential complex, who is entitled to possession of the residential complex and who attempts to enforce any of the rights of a landlord under a tenancy agreement or this Act, including the right to collect rent;

"Minister" means the Minister of Municipal Affairs and Housing;

"Ministry" means the Ministry of Municipal Affairs and Housing;

"mobile home" means a dwelling that is designed to be made mobile and that is being used as a permanent residence;

"mobile home park" means the land on which one or more occupied mobile homes are located and includes the rental units and the land, structures, services and facilities of which the landlord retains possession and that are intended for the common use and enjoyment of the tenants of the landlord;

"municipal taxes and charges" means taxes charged to a landlord by a municipality and charges levied on a landlord by a municipality and includes taxes levied on a landlord's property under Division B of Part IX of the *Education Act* and taxes levied on a landlord's property in unorganized territory, but "municipal taxes and charges" does not include,

(a) charges for inspections done by a municipality on a residential complex related to an alleged breach of a health, safety, housing or maintenance standard,

(b) charges for emergency repairs carried out by a municipality on a residential complex,

(c) charges for work in the nature of a capital expenditure carried out by a municipality,

(d) charges for work, services or non-emergency repairs performed by a municipality in relation to a landlord's non-compliance with a by-law,

(e) penalties, interest, late payment fees or fines,

(f) any amount spent by a municipality under subsection 219(1) or any administrative fee applied to that amount under subsection 219(2), or

(g) any other prescribed charges;

"non-profit housing co-operative" means a non-profit housing co-operative under the *Co-operative Corporations Act*;

"person," or any expression referring to a person, means an individual, sole proprietorship, partnership, limited partnership, trust or body corporate, or an individual in his or her capacity as a trustee, executor, administrator or other legal representative;

"prescribed" means prescribed by the regulations;

"regulations" means the regulations made under this Act;

"rent" includes the amount of any consideration paid or given or required to be paid or given by or on behalf of a tenant to a landlord or the landlord's agent for the right to occupy a rental unit and for any services and facilities and any privilege, accommodation or thing that the landlord provides for the tenant in respect of the occupancy of the rental unit, whether or not a separate charge is made for services and facilities or for the privilege, accommodation or thing, but "rent" does not include,

(a) an amount paid by a tenant to a landlord to reimburse the landlord for property taxes paid by the landlord with respect to a mobile home or a land lease home owned by a tenant, or

(b) an amount that a landlord charges a tenant of a rental unit in a care home for care services or meals;

"rental unit" means any living accommodation used or intended for use as rented residential premises, and "rental unit" includes,

(a) a site for a mobile home or site on which there is a land lease home used or intended for use as rented residential premises, and

(b) a room in a boarding house, rooming house or lodging house and a unit in a care home;

"residential complex" means,

(a) a building or related group of buildings in which one or more rental units are located,

(b) a mobile home park or land lease community,

(c) a site that is a rental unit,

(d) a care home, and,

includes all common areas and services and facilities available for the use of its residents;

"residential unit" means any living accommodation used or intended for use as residential premises, and "residential unit" includes,

(a) a site for a mobile home or on which there is a land lease home used or intended for use as a residential premises, and

(b) a room in a boarding house, rooming house or lodging house and a unit in a care home;

"Rules" means the rules of practice and procedure made by the Board under section 176 of this Act and section 25.1 of the *Statutory Powers Procedure Act*;

"services and facilities" includes,

(a) furniture, appliances and furnishings,

(b) parking and related facilities,

(c) laundry facilities,

(d) elevator facilities,

(e) common recreational facilities,

(f) garbage facilities and related services,

(g) cleaning and maintenance services,

(h) storage facilities,

(i) intercom systems,

(j) cable television facilities,

(k) heating facilities and services,

(l) air-conditioning facilities,

(m) utilities and related services, and

(n) security services and facilities;

"spouse" means a person,

(a) to whom the person is married, or

(b) with whom the person is living in a conjugal relationship outside marriage, if the two persons,

(i) have cohabited for at least one year,

(ii) are together the parents of a child, or

(iii) have together entered into a cohabitation agreement under section 53 of the *Family Law Act*;

"subtenant" means the person to whom a tenant gives the right under section 97 to occupy a rental unit;

"superintendent's premises" means a rental unit used by a person employed as a janitor, manager, security guard or superintendent and located in the residential complex with respect to which the person is so employed;

"tenancy agreement" means a written, oral or implied agreement between a tenant and a landlord for occupancy of a rental unit and includes a licence to occupy a rental unit;

"tenant" includes a person who pays rent in return for the right to occupy a rental unit and includes the tenant's heirs, assigns and personal representatives, but "tenant" does not include a person who has the right to occupy a rental unit by virtue of being,

    (a) a co-owner of the residential complex in which the rental unit is located, or

    (b) a shareholder of a corporation that owns the residential complex;

"utilities" means heat, electricity and water;

"vital service" means hot or cold water, fuel, electricity, gas or, during the part of each year prescribed by the regulations, heat.

Interpretation, sublet

(2) For the purposes of this Act, a reference to subletting a rental unit refers to the situation in which,

    (a) the tenant vacates the rental unit;

    (b) the tenant gives one or more other persons the right to occupy the rental unit for a term ending on a specified date before the end of the tenant's term or period; and

    (c) the tenant has the right to resume occupancy of the rental unit after that specified date.

Interpretation, abandoned

(3) For the purposes of this Act, a tenant has not abandoned a rental unit if the tenant is not in arrears of rent.

Rental unit, clarification

(4) A rented site for a mobile home or a land lease home is a rental unit for the purposes of this Act even if the mobile home or the land lease home on the site is owned by the tenant of the site.

Application of Act

3(1) This Act applies with respect to rental units in residential complexes, despite any other Act and despite any agreement or waiver to the contrary.

Conflicts, care homes

(2) In interpreting a provision of this Act with regard to a care home, if a provision in Part IX conflicts with a provision in another Part of this Act, the provision in Part IX applies.

Conflicts, mobile home parks and land lease communities

(3) In interpreting a provision of this Act with regard to a mobile home park or a land lease community, if a provision in Part X conflicts with a provision in another Part of this Act, the provision in Part X applies.

Conflict with other Acts

(4) If a provision of this Act conflicts with a provision of another Act, other than the *Human Rights Code*, the provision of this Act applies.

Provisions conflicting with Act void

4. Subject to section 194, a provision in a tenancy agreement that is inconsistent with this Act or the regulations is void.

Exemptions from Act

5. This Act does not apply with respect to,

    (a) living accommodation intended to be provided to the travelling or vacationing public or occupied for a seasonal or temporary period in a hotel, motel or motor hotel, resort, lodge, tourist camp, cottage or cabin establishment, inn, campground, trailer park, tourist home, bed and breakfast vacation establishment or vacation home;

    (b) living accommodation whose occupancy is conditional upon the occupant continuing to be employed on a farm, whether or not the accommodation is located on that farm;

    (c) living accommodation that is a member unit of a non-profit housing co-operative;

    (d) living accommodation occupied by a person for penal or correctional purposes;

    (e) living accommodation that is subject to the *Public Hospitals Act*, the *Private Hospitals Act*, the *Long-Term Care Homes Act 2007*, the *Ministry of Correctional Services Act* or the *Child and Family Services Act*;

    (f) short-term living accommodation provided as emergency shelter;

    (g) living accommodation provided by an educational institution to its students or staff where,

        (i) the living accommodation is provided primarily to persons under the age of majority, or all major questions related to the living accommodation are decided after consultation with a council or association representing the residents, and

        (ii) the living accommodation does not have its own self-contained bathroom and kitchen facilities or is not intended for year-round occupancy by full-time students or staff and members of their households;

    (h) living accommodation located in a building or project used in whole or in part for non-residential purposes if the occupancy of the living accommodation is conditional upon the occupant continuing to be an employee of or perform services related to a business or enterprise carried out in the building or project;

    (i) living accommodation whose occupant or occupants are required to share a bathroom or kitchen facility with the owner, the owner's spouse, child or parent or the spouse's child or parent, and where the owner, spouse, child or parent lives in the building in which the living accommodation is located;

    (j) premises occupied for business or agricultural purposes with living accommodation attached if the occupancy for both purposes is under a single lease and the same person occupies the premises and the living accommodation;

    (k) living accommodation occupied by a person for the purpose of receiving rehabilitative or therapeutic services agreed upon by the person and the provider of the living accommodation, where,

(i) the parties have agreed that,

(A) the period of occupancy will be of a specified duration, or

(B) the occupancy will terminate when the objectives of the services have been met or will not be met, and

(ii) the living accommodation is intended to be provided for no more than a one-year period;

(l) living accommodation in a care home occupied by a person for the purpose of receiving short-term respite care;

(m) living accommodation in a residential complex in which the Crown in right of Ontario has an interest, if,

(i) the residential complex was forfeited to the Crown in right of Ontario under the *Civil Remedies Act, 2001,* the *Prohibiting Profiting from Recounting Crimes Act, 2002* or the *Criminal Code* (Canada), or

(ii) possession of the residential complex has been or may be taken in the name of the Crown under the *Escheats Act*; and

(n) any other prescribed class of accommodation.

Other exemptions
Homes for special care, developmental services

6(1) Paragraphs 6, 7 and 8 of subsection 30(1) and sections 51, 52, 54, 55, 56, 104, 111 to 115, 117, 119 to 134, 136, 140 and 149 to 167 do not apply with respect to,

(a) accommodation that is subject to the *Homes for Special Care Act*; or

(b) accommodation that is a supported group living residence or an intensive support residence under the *Services and Supports to Promote the Social Inclusion of Persons with Developmental Disabilities Act, 2008.*

Rules relating to rent

(2) Sections 104, 111, 112, 120, 121, 122, 126 to 133, 165 and 167 do not apply with respect to a rental unit if,

(a) it was not occupied for any purpose before June 17, 1998;

(b) it is a rental unit no part of which has been previously rented since July 29, 1975; or

(c) no part of the building, mobile home park or land lease community was occupied for residential purposes before November 1, 1991.

Exemptions related to social, etc., housing

7(1) Paragraphs 6, 7 and 8 of subsection 30(1), sections 51, 52, 54, 55, 56 and 95 to 99, subsection 100(2) and sections 101, 102, 104, 111 to 115, 117, 120, 121, 122, 126 to 133, 140, 143, 149, 150, 151, 159, 165 and 167 do not apply with respect to a rental unit described below:

1. A rental unit located in a residential complex owned, operated or administered by or on behalf of the Ontario Housing Corporation, the Government of Canada or an agency of either of them.

2. A rental unit in a residential complex described in paragraph 1 whose ownership, operation or management is transferred under the *Social Housing Reform Act, 2000* to a service manager or local housing corporation as defined in that Act.

3. A rental unit located in a non-profit housing project or other residential complex, if the non-profit housing project or other residential complex was developed or acquired under a prescribed federal, provincial or municipal program and continues to operate under,

   i. Part VI of the *Social Housing Reform Act, 2000,*

   ii. an operating agreement, as defined in the *Social Housing Reform Act, 2000,* or

   iii. an agreement made between a housing provider, as defined in the *Social Housing Reform Act, 2000,* and one or more of,

      A. a municipality,

      B. an agency of a municipality,

      C. a non-profit corporation controlled by a municipality, if an object of the non-profit corporation is the provision of housing,

      D. a local housing corporation, as defined in the *Social Housing Reform Act, 2000,* or

      E. a service manager, as defined in the *Social Housing Reform Act, 2000.*

4. A rental unit that is a non-member unit of a non-profit housing co-operative.

5. A rental unit provided by an educational institution to a student or member of its staff and that is not exempt from this Act under clause 5(g).

6. A rental unit located in a residential complex owned, operated or administered by a religious institution for a charitable use on a non-profit basis.

Exemption re 12-month rule

(2) Section 119 does not apply with respect to,

(a) a rental unit described in paragraph 1, 2, 3 or 4 of subsection (1) if the tenant occupying the rental unit pays rent in an amount geared-to-income due to public funding; or

(b) a rental unit described in paragraph 5 or 6 of subsection (1).

Exemption re notice of rent increase

(3) Sections 116 and 118 do not apply with respect to increases in rent for a rental unit due to increases in the tenant's income if the rental unit is as described in paragraph 1, 2, 3 or 4 of subsection (1) and the tenant pays rent in an amount geared-to-income due to public funding.

Exception, subs. (1), par. 1

(4) Despite subsection (1), the provisions of this Act set out in that subsection apply with respect to a rental unit described in paragraph 1 of that subsection if the tenant occupying the rental unit pays rent to a landlord other than the Ontario Housing Corporation, the Government of Canada or an agency of either of them.

Same, subs. (1), par. 2

(5) Despite subsection (1), the provisions of this Act set out in that subsection apply with respect to a rental unit described in paragraph 2 of that subsection if the tenant occupying the rental unit pays rent to a landlord other than a service manager or local housing corporation as defined in the *Social Housing Reform Act, 2000* or an agency of either of them.

Same, subs. (1), par. 5

(6) Despite subsection (1), the provisions of this Act set out in that subsection apply with respect to a rent increase for rental units described in paragraph 5 of that subsection if there is a council or association representing the residents of those rental units and there has not been consultation with the council or association respecting the increase.

Rent geared-to-income

8(1) If a tenant pays rent for a rental unit in an amount geared-to-income due to public funding and the rental unit is not a rental unit described in paragraph 1, 2, 3 or 4 of subsection 7(1), paragraph 6 of subsection 30(1) and Part VII do not apply to an increase in the amount geared-to-income paid by the tenant.

Same, assignment, subletting

(2) Sections 95 to 99, subsection 100(2), sections 101 and 102, subsection 104(3) and section 143 do not apply to a tenant described in subsection (1).

Application to determine issues

9(1) A landlord or a tenant may apply to the Board for an order determining,

(a) whether this Act or any provision of it applies to a particular rental unit or residential complex;

(b) any other prescribed matter.

Order

(2) On the application, the Board shall make findings on the issue as prescribed and shall make the appropriate order.

PART II   TENANCY AGREEMENTS

Selecting prospective tenants

10. In selecting prospective tenants, landlords may use, in the manner prescribed in the regulations made under the *Human Rights Code*, income information, credit checks, credit references, rental history, guarantees, or other similar business practices as prescribed in those regulations.

Information to be provided by landlord

11(1) If a tenancy agreement is entered into, the landlord shall provide to the tenant information relating to the rights and responsibilities of landlords and tenants, the role of the Board and how to contact the Board.

Form

(2) The information shall be provided to the tenant on or before the date the tenancy begins in a form approved by the Board.

Tenancy agreement
Name and address in written agreement

12(1) Every written tenancy agreement entered into on or after June 17, 1998 shall set out the legal name and address of the landlord to be used for the purpose of giving notices or other documents under this Act.

Copy of tenancy agreement

(2) If a tenancy agreement entered into on or after June 17, 1998 is in writing, the landlord shall give a copy of the agreement, signed by the landlord and the tenant, to the tenant within 21 days after the tenant signs it and gives it to the landlord.

Notice if agreement not in writing

(3) If a tenancy agreement entered into on or after June 17, 1998 is not in writing, the landlord shall, within 21 days after the tenancy begins, give to the tenant written notice of the legal name and address of the landlord to be used for giving notices and other documents under this Act.

Failure to comply

(4) Until a landlord has complied with subsections (1) and (2), or with subsection (3), as the case may be,

(a) the tenant's obligation to pay rent is suspended; and

(b) the landlord shall not require the tenant to pay rent.

After compliance

(5) After the landlord has complied with subsections (1) and (2), or with subsection (3), as the case may be, the landlord may require the tenant to pay any rent withheld by the tenant under subsection (4).

Commencement of tenancy

13(1) The term or period of a tenancy begins on the day the tenant is entitled to occupy the rental unit under the tenancy agreement.

Actual entry not required

(2) A tenancy agreement takes effect when the tenant is entitled to occupy the rental unit, whether or not the tenant actually occupies it.

"No pet" provisions void

14. A provision in a tenancy agreement prohibiting the presence of animals in or about the residential complex is void.

Acceleration clause void

15. A provision in a tenancy agreement providing that all or part of the remaining rent for a term or period of a tenancy or a specific sum becomes due upon a default of the tenant in paying rent due or in carrying out an obligation is void.

Minimize losses

16. When a landlord or a tenant becomes liable to pay any amount as a result of a breach of a tenancy agreement, the person entitled to claim the amount has a duty to take reasonable steps to minimize the person's losses.

Covenants interdependent

17. Except as otherwise provided in this Act, the common law rules respecting the effect of a serious, substantial or fundamental breach of a material covenant by one party to a contract on the obligation to perform of the other party apply with respect to tenancy agreements.

Covenants running with land

18. Covenants concerning things related to a rental unit or the residential complex in which it is located run with the land, whether or not the things are in existence at the time the covenants are made.

Frustrated contracts

19. The doctrine of frustration of contract and the *Frustrated Contracts Act* apply with respect to tenancy agreements.

PART III   RESPONSIBILITIES OF LANDLORDS

Landlord's responsibility to repair

20(1) A landlord is responsible for providing and maintaining a residential complex, including the rental units in it, in a good state of repair and fit for habitation and for complying with health, safety, housing and maintenance standards.

Same

(2) Subsection (1) applies even if the tenant was aware of a state of non-repair or a contravention of a standard before entering into the tenancy agreement.

Landlord's responsibility re services

21(1) A landlord shall not at any time during a tenant's occupancy of a rental unit and before the day on which an order evicting the tenant is executed, withhold the reasonable supply of any vital service, care service or food that it is the landlord's obligation to supply under the tenancy agreement or deliberately interfere with the reasonable supply of any vital service, care service or food.

Non-payment

(2) For the purposes of subsection (1), a landlord shall be deemed to have withheld the reasonable supply of a vital service, care service or food if the landlord is obligated to pay another person for the vital service, care service or food, the landlord fails to pay the required amount and, as a result of the non-payment, the other person withholds the reasonable supply of the vital service, care service or food.

Landlord not to interfere with reasonable enjoyment

22. A landlord shall not at any time during a tenant's occupancy of a rental unit and before the day on which an order evicting the tenant is executed substantially interfere with the reasonable enjoyment of the rental unit or the residential complex in which it is located for all usual purposes by a tenant or members of his or her household.

Landlord not to harass, etc.

23. A landlord shall not harass, obstruct, coerce, threaten or interfere with a tenant.

Changing locks

24. A landlord shall not alter the locking system on a door giving entry to a rental unit or residential complex or cause the locking system to be altered during the tenant's occupancy of the rental unit without giving the tenant replacement keys.

Privacy

25. A landlord may enter a rental unit only in accordance with section 26 or 27.

Entry without notice
Entry without notice, emergency, consent

26(1) A landlord may enter a rental unit at any time without written notice,

> (a) in cases of emergency; or
>
> (b) if the tenant consents to the entry at the time of entry.

Same, housekeeping

(2) A landlord may enter a rental unit without written notice to clean it if the tenancy agreement requires the landlord to clean the rental unit at regular intervals and,

> (a) the landlord enters the unit at the times specified in the tenancy agreement; or
>
> (b) if no times are specified, the landlord enters the unit between the hours of 8 a.m. and 8 p.m.

Entry to show rental unit to prospective tenants

(3) A landlord may enter the rental unit without written notice to show the unit to prospective tenants if,

> (a) the landlord and tenant have agreed that the tenancy will be terminated or one of them has given notice of termination to the other;
>
> (b) the landlord enters the unit between the hours of 8 a.m. and 8 p.m.; and
>
> (c) before entering, the landlord informs or makes a reasonable effort to inform the tenant of the intention to do so.

Entry with notice

27(1) A landlord may enter a rental unit in accordance with written notice given to the tenant at least 24 hours before the time of entry under the following circumstances:

1. To carry out a repair or replacement or do work in the rental unit.
2. To allow a potential mortgagee or insurer of the residential complex to view the rental unit.
3. To allow a person who holds a certificate of authorization within the meaning of the *Professional Engineers Act* or a certificate of practice within the meaning of the *Architects Act* or another qualified person to make a physical inspection of the rental unit to satisfy a requirement imposed under subsection 9(4) of the *Condominium Act, 1998*.
4. To carry out an inspection of the rental unit, if,
   > i. the inspection is for the purpose of determining whether or not the rental unit is in a good state of

repair and fit for habitation and complies with health, safety, housing and maintenance standards, consistent with the landlord's obligations under subsection 20(1) or section 161, and

ii. it is reasonable to carry out the inspection.

5. For any other reasonable reason for entry specified in the tenancy agreement.

Same

(2) A landlord or, with the written authorization of a landlord, a broker or salesperson registered under the *Real Estate and Business Brokers Act, 2002*, may enter a rental unit in accordance with written notice given to the tenant at least 24 hours before the time of entry to allow a potential purchaser to view the rental unit.

Contents of notice

(3) The written notice under subsection (1) or (2) shall specify the reason for entry, the day of entry and a time of entry between the hours of 8 a.m. and 8 p.m.

Entry by canvassers

28. No landlord shall restrict reasonable access to a residential complex by candidates for election to any office at the federal, provincial or municipal level, or their authorized representatives, if they are seeking access for the purpose of canvassing or distributing election material.

Tenant applications

29(1) A tenant or former tenant of a rental unit may apply to the Board for any of the following orders:

1. An order determining that the landlord has breached an obligation under subsection 20(1) or section 161.

2. An order determining that the landlord, superintendent or agent of the landlord has withheld the reasonable supply of any vital service, care service or food that it is the landlord's obligation to supply under the tenancy agreement or deliberately interfered with the reasonable supply of any vital service, care service or food.

3. An order determining that the landlord, superintendent or agent of the landlord has substantially interfered with the reasonable enjoyment of the rental unit or residential complex for all usual purposes by the tenant or a member of his or her household.

4. An order determining that the landlord, superintendent or agent of the landlord has harassed, obstructed, coerced, threatened or interfered with the tenant during the tenant's occupancy of the rental unit.

5. An order determining that the landlord, superintendent or agent of the landlord has altered the locking system on a door giving entry to the rental unit or the residential complex or caused the locking system to be altered during the tenant's occupancy of the rental unit without giving the tenant replacement keys.

6. An order determining that the landlord, superintendent or agent of the landlord has illegally entered the rental unit.

Time limitation

(2) No application may be made under subsection (1) more than one year after the day the alleged conduct giving rise to the application occurred.

Order, repair, comply with standards

30(1) If the Board determines in an application under paragraph 1 of subsection 29(1) that a landlord has breached an obligation under subsection 20(1) or section 161, the Board may do one or more of the following:

1. Terminate the tenancy.

2. Order an abatement of rent.

3. Authorize a repair or replacement that has been or is to be made, or work that has been or is to be done, and order its cost to be paid by the landlord to the tenant.

4. Order the landlord to do specified repairs or replacements or other work within a specified time.

5. Order the landlord to pay a specified sum to the tenant for,

   i. the reasonable costs that the tenant has incurred or will incur in repairing or, where repairing is not reasonable, replacing property of the tenant that was damaged, destroyed or disposed of as a result of the landlord's breach, and

   ii. other reasonable out-of-pocket expenses that the tenant has incurred or will incur as a result of the landlord's breach.

6. Prohibit the landlord from charging a new tenant under a new tenancy agreement an amount of rent in excess of the last lawful rent charged to the former tenant of the rental unit, until the landlord has,

   i. completed the items in work orders for which the compliance period has expired and which were found by the Board to be related to a serious breach of a health, safety, housing or maintenance standard, and

   ii. completed the specified repairs or replacements or other work ordered under paragraph 4 found by the Board to be related to a serious breach of the landlord's obligations under subsection 20(1) or section 161.

7. Prohibit the landlord from giving a notice of a rent increase for the rental unit until the landlord has,

   i. completed the items in work orders for which the compliance period has expired and which were found by the Board to be related to a serious breach of a health, safety, housing or maintenance standard, and

   ii. completed the specified repairs or replacements or other work ordered under paragraph 4 found by the

Board to be related to a serious breach of the landlord's obligations under subsection 20(1) or section 161.

8. Prohibit the landlord from taking any rent increase for which notice has been given if the increase has not been taken before the date an order under this section is issued until the landlord has,

    i. completed the items in work orders for which the compliance period has expired and which were found by the Board to be related to a serious breach of a health, safety, housing or maintenance standard, and

    ii. completed the specified repairs or replacements or other work ordered under paragraph 4 found by the Board to be related to a serious breach of the landlord's obligations under subsection 20(1) or section 161.

9. Make any other order that it considers appropriate.

Advance notice of breaches

(2) In determining the remedy under this section, the Board shall consider whether the tenant or former tenant advised the landlord of the alleged breaches before applying to the Board.

Other orders re s. 29

31(1) If the Board determines that a landlord, a superintendent or an agent of a landlord has done one or more of the activities set out in paragraphs 2 to 6 of subsection 29(1), the Board may,

    (a) order that the landlord, superintendent or agent may not engage in any further activities listed in those paragraphs against any of the tenants in the residential complex;

    (b) order that the landlord, superintendent or agent pay a specified sum to the tenant for,

        (i) the reasonable costs that the tenant has incurred or will incur in repairing or, where repairing is not reasonable, replacing property of the tenant that was damaged, destroyed or disposed of as a result of the landlord, superintendent or agent having engaged in one or more of the activities listed in those paragraphs, and

        (ii) other reasonable out-of-pocket expenses that the tenant has incurred or will incur as a result of the landlord, superintendent or agent having engaged in one or more of the activities listed in those paragraphs;

    (c) order an abatement of rent;

    (d) order that the landlord pay to the Board an administrative fine not exceeding the greater of $10,000 and the monetary jurisdiction of the Small Claims Court;

    (e) order that the tenancy be terminated;

    (f) make any other order that it considers appropriate.

Same

(2) If in an application under any of paragraphs 2 to 6 of subsection 29(1) it is determined that the tenant was induced by the conduct of the landlord, the superintendent or an agent of the landlord to vacate the rental unit, the Board may, in addition to the remedies set out in subsection (1), order that the landlord pay a specified sum to the tenant for,

    (a) all or any portion of any increased rent which the tenant has incurred or will incur for a one-year period after the tenant has left the rental unit; and

    (b) reasonable out-of-pocket moving, storage and other like expenses which the tenant has incurred or will incur.

Order, s. 29(1), par. 5

(3) If the Board determines, in an application under paragraph 5 of subsection 29(1), that the landlord, superintendent or agent of the landlord has altered the locking system on a door giving entry to the rental unit or the residential complex, or caused the locking system to be altered, during the tenant's occupancy of the rental unit without giving the tenant replacement keys, and if the Board is satisfied that the rental unit is vacant, the Board may, in addition to the remedies set out in subsections (1) and (2), order that the landlord allow the tenant to recover possession of the rental unit and that the landlord refrain from renting the unit to anyone else.

Effect of order allowing tenant possession

(4) An order under subsection (3) shall have the same effect, and shall be enforced in the same manner, as a writ of possession.

Expiry of order allowing tenant possession

(5) An order under subsection (3) expires,

    (a) at the end of the 15th day after the day it is issued if it is not filed within those 15 days with the sheriff who has territorial jurisdiction where the rental unit is located; or

    (b) at the end of the 45th day after the day it is issued if it is filed in the manner described in clause (a).

Eviction with termination order

32. If the Board makes an order terminating a tenancy under paragraph 1 of subsection 30(1) or clause 31(1)(e), the Board may order that the tenant be evicted, effective not earlier than the termination date specified in the order.

PART IV   RESPONSIBILITIES OF TENANTS

Tenant's responsibility for cleanliness

33. The tenant is responsible for ordinary cleanliness of the rental unit, except to the extent that the tenancy agreement requires the landlord to clean it.

Tenant's responsibility for repair of damage

34. The tenant is responsible for the repair of undue damage to the rental unit or residential complex caused by the wilful or negligent conduct of the tenant, another occupant of the rental unit or a person permitted in the residential complex by the tenant.

Changing locks

35(1) A tenant shall not alter the locking system on a door giving entry to a rental unit or residential complex or cause the locking system to be altered during the tenant's occupancy of the rental unit without the consent of the landlord.

Landlord application

(2) If a tenant alters a locking system, contrary to subsection (1), the landlord may apply to the Board for an order determining that the tenant has altered the locking system on a door giving entry to the rental unit or the residential complex or caused the locking system to be altered during the tenant's occupancy of the rental unit without the consent of the landlord.

Order

(3) If the Board in an application under subsection (2) determines that a tenant has altered the locking system or caused it to be altered, the Board may order that the tenant provide the landlord with keys or pay the landlord the reasonable out-of-pocket expenses necessary to change the locking system.

Tenant not to harass, etc.

36. A tenant shall not harass, obstruct, coerce, threaten or interfere with a landlord.

PART V   SECURITY OF TENURE AND TERMINATION OF TENANCIES

Security of Tenure

Termination only in accordance with Act

37(1) A tenancy may be terminated only in accordance with this Act.

Termination by notice

(2) If a notice of termination is given in accordance with this Act and the tenant vacates the rental unit in accordance with the notice, the tenancy is terminated on the termination date set out in the notice.

Termination by agreement

(3) A notice of termination need not be given if a landlord and a tenant have agreed to terminate a tenancy.

When notice void

(4) A tenant's notice to terminate a tenancy is void if it is given,

(a) at the time the tenancy agreement is entered into; or

(b) as a condition of entering into the tenancy agreement.

When agreement void

(5) An agreement between a landlord and tenant to terminate a tenancy is void if it is entered into,

(a) at the time the tenancy agreement is entered into; or

(b) as a condition of entering into the tenancy agreement.

Application of subss. (4) and (5)

(6) Subsections (4) and (5) do not apply to rental units occupied by students of one or more post-secondary educational institutions in a residential complex owned, operated or administered by or on behalf of the post-secondary educational institutions.

Same

(7) Subsections (4) and (5) do not apply to rental units in a residential complex with respect to which the landlord has entered into an agreement with one or more post-secondary educational institutions providing,

(a) that the landlord, as of the date the agreement is entered into and for the duration of the agreement, rents the rental units which are the subject of the agreement only to students of the institution or institutions;

(b) that the landlord will comply with the maintenance standards set out in the agreement with respect to the rental units which are the subject of the agreement; and

(c) that the landlord will not charge a new tenant of a rental unit which is a subject of the agreement a rent which is greater than the lawful rent being charged to the former tenant plus the guideline.

Same

(8) The maintenance standards set out in the agreement and referred to in clause (7)(b) shall not provide for a lower maintenance standard than that required by law.

Same

(9) If the landlord breaches any of clauses (7)(a), (b) and (c), the agreement referred to in subsection (7) is terminated and the exemption provided by subsection (7) no longer applies.

Same

(10) The landlord shall be deemed to have not breached the condition in clause (7)(a) if,

(a) upon a tenant ceasing to be a student of a post-secondary educational institution that is a party to the agreement with the landlord, the landlord takes action to terminate the tenancy in accordance with an agreement with the tenant to terminate the tenancy or a notice of termination given by the tenant; or

(b) a tenant sublets the rental unit to a person who is not a student of a post-secondary educational institution that is a party to the agreement with the landlord.

Same

(11) Either party to an agreement referred to in subsection (7) may terminate the agreement on at least 90 days written notice to the other party and, upon the termination of the agreement, the exemption provided by subsection (7) no longer applies.

Deemed renewal where no notice

38(1) If a tenancy agreement for a fixed term ends and has not been renewed or terminated, the landlord and tenant shall be deemed to have renewed it as a monthly tenancy agreement containing the same terms and conditions that are in the expired tenancy agreement and subject to any increases in rent charged in accordance with this Act.

Same

(2) If the period of a daily, weekly or monthly tenancy ends and the tenancy has not been renewed or terminated, the landlord and tenant shall be deemed to have renewed it for another day, week or month, as the case may be, with the same terms and conditions that are in the expired tenancy agreement and subject to any increases in rent charged in accordance with this Act.

Same

(3) If the period of a periodic tenancy ends, the tenancy has not been renewed or terminated and subsection (2) does not apply, the landlord and tenant shall be deemed to have renewed it as a monthly tenancy, with the same terms and conditions that are in the expired tenancy agreement and subject to any increases in rent charged in accordance with this Act.

Restriction on recovery of possession

39. A landlord shall not recover possession of a rental unit subject to a tenancy unless,

(a) the tenant has vacated or abandoned the unit; or

(b) an order of the Board evicting the tenant has authorized the possession.

Distress abolished

40. No landlord shall, without legal process, seize a tenant's property for default in the payment of rent or for the breach of any other obligation of the tenant.

Disposal of abandoned property if unit vacated

41(1) A landlord may sell, retain for the landlord's own use or otherwise dispose of property in a rental unit or the residential complex if the rental unit has been vacated in accordance with,

(a) a notice of termination of the landlord or the tenant;

(b) an agreement between the landlord and the tenant to terminate the tenancy;

(c) subsection 93(2); or

(d) an order of the Board terminating the tenancy or evicting the tenant.

Where eviction order enforced

(2) Despite subsection (1), where an order is made to evict a tenant, the landlord shall not sell, retain or otherwise dispose of the tenant's property before 72 hours have elapsed after the enforcement of the eviction order.

Same

(3) A landlord shall make an evicted tenant's property available to be retrieved at a location close to the rental unit during the prescribed hours within the 72 hours after the enforcement of an eviction order.

Liability of landlord

(4) A landlord is not liable to any person for selling, retaining or otherwise disposing of a tenant's property in accordance with this section.

Agreement

(5) A landlord and a tenant may agree to terms other than those set out in this section with regard to the disposal of the tenant's property.

Enforcement of landlord obligations

(6) If, on application by a former tenant, the Board determines that a landlord has breached an obligation under subsection (2) or (3), the Board may do one or more of the following:

1. Order that the landlord not breach the obligation again.
2. Order that the landlord return to the former tenant property of the former tenant that is in the possession or control of the landlord.
3. Order that the landlord pay a specified sum to the former tenant for,
   i. the reasonable costs that the former tenant has incurred or will incur in repairing or, where repairing is not reasonable, replacing property of the former tenant that was damaged, destroyed or disposed of as a result of the landlord's breach, and
   ii. other reasonable out-of-pocket expenses that the former tenant has incurred or will incur as a result of the landlord's breach.
4. Order that the landlord pay to the Board an administrative fine not exceeding the greater of $10,000 and the monetary jurisdiction of the Small Claims Court.
5. Make any other order that it considers appropriate.

Disposal of property, unit abandoned

42(1) A landlord may dispose of property in a rental unit that a tenant has abandoned and property of persons occupying the rental unit that is in the residential complex in which the rental unit is located in accordance with subsections (2) and (3) if,

(a) the landlord obtains an order terminating the tenancy under section 79; or

(b) the landlord gives notice to the tenant of the rental unit and to the Board of the landlord's intention to dispose of the property.

Same

(2) If the tenant has abandoned the rental unit, the landlord may dispose of any unsafe or unhygienic items immediately.

Same

(3) The landlord may sell, retain for the landlord's own use or otherwise dispose of any other items if 30 days have passed after obtaining the order referred to in clause (1)(a) or giving the notice referred to in clause (1)(b) to the tenant and the Board.

Tenant's claim to property

(4) If, before the 30 days have passed, the tenant notifies the landlord that he or she intends to remove property referred to

in subsection (3), the tenant may remove the property within that 30-day period.

Same

(5) If the tenant notifies the landlord in accordance with subsection (4) that he or she intends to remove the property, the landlord shall make the property available to the tenant at a reasonable time and at a location close to the rental unit.

Same

(6) The landlord may require the tenant to pay the landlord for arrears of rent and any reasonable out-of-pocket expenses incurred by the landlord in moving, storing or securing the tenant's property before allowing the tenant to remove the property.

Same

(7) If, within six months after the date the notice referred to in clause (1)(b) is given to the tenant and the Board or the order terminating the tenancy is issued, the tenant claims any of his or her property that the landlord has sold, the landlord shall pay to the tenant the amount by which the proceeds of sale exceed the sum of,

(a) the landlord's reasonable out-of-pocket expenses for moving, storing, securing or selling the property; and

(b) any arrears of rent.

No liability

(8) Subject to subsections (5) and (7), a landlord is not liable to any person for selling, retaining or otherwise disposing of the property of a tenant in accordance with this section.

Notice of Termination — General

Notice of termination

43(1) Where this Act permits a landlord or tenant to give a notice of termination, the notice shall be in a form approved by the Board and shall,

(a) identify the rental unit for which the notice is given;

(b) state the date on which the tenancy is to terminate; and

(c) be signed by the person giving the notice, or the person's agent.

Same

(2) If the notice is given by a landlord, it shall also set out the reasons and details respecting the termination and inform the tenant that,

(a) if the tenant vacates the rental unit in accordance with the notice, the tenancy terminates on the date set out in clause (1)(b);

(b) if the tenant does not vacate the rental unit, the landlord may apply to the Board for an order terminating the tenancy and evicting the tenant; and

(c) if the landlord applies for an order, the tenant is entitled to dispute the application.

Period of notice

Period of notice, daily or weekly tenancy

44(1) A notice under section 47, 58 or 144 to terminate a daily or weekly tenancy shall be given at least 28 days before the date the termination is specified to be effective and that date shall be on the last day of a rental period.

Period of notice, monthly tenancy

(2) A notice under section 47, 58 or 144 to terminate a monthly tenancy shall be given at least 60 days before the date the termination is specified to be effective and that date shall be on the last day of a rental period.

Period of notice, yearly tenancy

(3) A notice under section 47, 58 or 144 to terminate a yearly tenancy shall be given at least 60 days before the date the termination is specified to be effective and that date shall be on the last day of a yearly period on which the tenancy is based.

Period of notice, tenancy for fixed term

(4) A notice under section 47, 58 or 144 to terminate a tenancy for a fixed term shall be given at least 60 days before the expiration date specified in the tenancy agreement, to be effective on that expiration date.

Period of notice, February notices

(5) A tenant who gives notice under subsection (2), (3) or (4) which specifies that the termination is to be effective on the last day of February or the last day of March in any year shall be deemed to have given at least 60 days notice of termination if the notice is given not later than January 1 of that year in respect of a termination which is to be effective on the last day of February, or February 1 of that year in respect of a termination which is to be effective on the last day of March.

Effect of payment

45. Unless a landlord and tenant agree otherwise, the landlord does not waive a notice of termination, reinstate a tenancy or create a new tenancy,

(a) by giving the tenant a notice of rent increase; or

(b) by accepting arrears of rent or compensation for the use or occupation of a rental unit after,

(i) the landlord or the tenant gives a notice of termination of the tenancy,

(ii) the landlord and the tenant enter into an agreement to terminate the tenancy, or

(iii) the Board makes an eviction order or an order terminating the tenancy.

Where notice void

46(1) A notice of termination becomes void 30 days after the termination date specified in the notice unless,

(a) the tenant vacates the rental unit before that time; or

(b) the landlord applies for an order terminating the tenancy and evicting the tenant before that time.

Exception

(2) Subsection (1) does not apply with respect to a notice based on a tenant's failure to pay rent.

Notice by Tenant
Tenant's notice to terminate, end of period or term

47. A tenant may terminate a tenancy at the end of a period of the tenancy or at the end of the term of a tenancy for a fixed term by giving notice of termination to the landlord in accordance with section 44.

Notice by Landlord at End of Period of Term
Notice, landlord personally, etc., requires unit

48(1) A landlord may, by notice, terminate a tenancy if the landlord in good faith requires possession of the rental unit for the purpose of residential occupation by,

(a) the landlord;

(b) the landlord's spouse;

(c) a child or parent of the landlord or the landlord's spouse; or

(d) a person who provides or will provide care services to the landlord, the landlord's spouse, or a child or parent of the landlord or the landlord's spouse, if the person receiving the care services resides or will reside in the building, related group of buildings, mobile home park or land lease community in which the rental unit is located.

Same

(2) The date for termination specified in the notice shall be at least 60 days after the notice is given and shall be the day a period of the tenancy ends or, where the tenancy is for a fixed term, the end of the term.

Earlier termination by tenant

(3) A tenant who receives notice of termination under subsection (1) may, at any time before the date specified in the notice, terminate the tenancy, effective on a specified date earlier than the date set out in the landlord's notice.

Same

(4) The date for termination specified in the tenant's notice shall be at least 10 days after the date the tenant's notice is given.

Notice, purchaser personally requires unit

49(1) A landlord of a residential complex that contains no more than three residential units who has entered into an agreement of purchase and sale of the residential complex may, on behalf of the purchaser, give the tenant of a unit in the residential complex a notice terminating the tenancy, if the purchaser in good faith requires possession of the residential complex or the unit for the purpose of residential occupation by,

(a) the purchaser;

(b) the purchaser's spouse;

(c) a child or parent of the purchaser or the purchaser's spouse; or

(d) a person who provides or will provide care services to the purchaser, the purchaser's spouse, or a child or parent of the purchaser or the purchaser's spouse, if the person receiving the care services resides or will reside in the building, related group of buildings, mobile home park or land lease community in which the rental unit is located.

Same, condominium

(2) If a landlord who is an owner as defined in clause (a) or (b) of the definition of "owner" in subsection 1(1) of the *Condominium Act, 1998* owns a unit, as defined in subsection 1(1) of that Act, that is a rental unit and has entered into an agreement of purchase and sale of the unit, the landlord may, on behalf of the purchaser, give the tenant of the unit a notice terminating the tenancy, if the purchaser in good faith requires possession of the unit for the purpose of residential occupation by,

(a) the purchaser;

(b) the purchaser's spouse;

(c) a child or parent of the purchaser or the purchaser's spouse; or

(d) a person who provides or will provide care services to the purchaser, the purchaser's spouse, or a child or parent of the purchaser or the purchaser's spouse, if the person receiving the care services resides or will reside in the building, related group of buildings, mobile home park or land lease community in which the rental unit is located.

Period of notice

(3) The date for termination specified in a notice given under subsection (1) or (2) shall be at least 60 days after the notice is given and shall be the day a period of the tenancy ends or, where the tenancy is for a fixed term, the end of the term.

Earlier termination by tenant

(4) A tenant who receives notice of termination under subsection (1) or (2) may, at any time before the date specified in the notice, terminate the tenancy, effective on a specified date earlier than the date set out in the landlord's notice.

Same

(5) The date for termination specified in the tenant's notice shall be at least 10 days after the date the tenant's notice is given.

Notice, demolition, conversion or repairs

50(1) A landlord may give notice of termination of a tenancy if the landlord requires possession of the rental unit in order to,

(a) demolish it;

(b) convert it to use for a purpose other than residential premises; or

(c) do repairs or renovations to it that are so extensive that they require a building permit and vacant possession of the rental unit.

Same

(2) The date for termination specified in the notice shall be at least 120 days after the notice is given and shall be the day a period of the tenancy ends or, where the tenancy is for a fixed term, the end of the term.

Same

(3) A notice under clause (1)(c) shall inform the tenant that if he or she wishes to exercise the right of first refusal under section 53 to occupy the premises after the repairs or renovations, he or she must give the landlord notice of that fact in accordance with subsection 53(2) before vacating the rental unit.

Earlier termination by tenant

(4) A tenant who receives notice of termination under subsection (1) may, at any time before the date specified in the notice, terminate the tenancy, effective on a specified date earlier than the date set out in the landlord's notice.

Same

(5) The date for termination specified in the tenant's notice shall be at least 10 days after the date the tenant's notice is given.

Conversion to condominium, security of tenure

51(1) If a part or all of a residential complex becomes subject to a registered declaration and description under the *Condominium Act, 1998* or a predecessor of that Act on or after June 17, 1998, a landlord may not give a notice under section 48 or 49 to a person who was a tenant of a rental unit when it became subject to the registered declaration and description.

Proposed units, security of tenure

(2) If a landlord has entered into an agreement of purchase and sale of a rental unit that is a proposed unit under the *Condominium Act, 1998* or a predecessor of that Act, a landlord may not give a notice under section 48 or 49 to the tenant of the rental unit who was the tenant on the date the agreement of purchase and sale was entered into.

Non-application

(3) Subsections (1) and (2) do not apply with respect to a residential complex if no rental unit in the complex was rented before July 10, 1986 and all or part of the complex becomes subject to a registered declaration and description under the *Condominium Act, 1998* or a predecessor of that Act before the day that is two years after the day on which the first rental unit in the complex was first rented.

Assignee of tenant not included

(4) Despite subsection 95(8), a reference to a tenant in subsection (1), (2) or (5) does not include a person to whom the tenant subsequently assigns the rental unit.

Conversion to condominium, right of first refusal

(5) If a landlord receives an acceptable offer to purchase a condominium unit converted from rented residential premises and still occupied by a tenant who was a tenant on the date of the registration referred to in subsection (1) or an acceptable offer to purchase a rental unit intended to be converted to a condominium unit, the tenant has a right of first refusal to purchase the unit at the price and subject to the terms and conditions in the offer.

Same

(6) The landlord shall give the tenant at least 72 hours notice of the offer to purchase the unit before accepting the offer.

Exception

(7) Subsection (5) does not apply when,

(a) the offer to purchase is an offer to purchase more than one unit; or

(b) the unit has been previously purchased since that registration, but not together with any other units.

Compensation, demolition or conversion

52. A landlord shall compensate a tenant in an amount equal to three months rent or offer the tenant another rental unit acceptable to the tenant if,

(a) the tenant receives notice of termination of the tenancy for the purposes of demolition or conversion to non-residential use;

(b) the residential complex in which the rental unit is located contains at least five residential units; and

(c) in the case of a demolition, it was not ordered to be carried out under the authority of any other Act.

Tenant's right of first refusal, repair or renovation

53(1) A tenant who receives notice of termination of a tenancy for the purpose of repairs or renovations may, in accordance with this section, have a right of first refusal to occupy the rental unit as a tenant when the repairs or renovations are completed.

Written notice

(2) A tenant who wishes to have a right of first refusal shall give the landlord notice in writing before vacating the rental unit.

Rent to be charged

(3) A tenant who exercises a right of first refusal may reoccupy the rental unit at a rent that is no more than what the landlord could have lawfully charged if there had been no interruption in the tenant's tenancy.

Change of address

(4) It is a condition of the tenant's right of first refusal that the tenant inform the landlord in writing of any change of address.

Tenant's right to compensation, repair or renovation

54(1) A landlord shall compensate a tenant who receives notice of termination of a tenancy under section 50 for the purpose of repairs or renovations in an amount equal to three months rent or shall offer the tenant another rental unit acceptable to the tenant if,

(a) the tenant does not give the landlord notice under subsection 53(2) with respect to the rental unit;

(b) the residential complex in which the rental unit is located contains at least five residential units; and

(c) the repair or renovation was not ordered to be carried out under the authority of this or any other Act.

Same

(2) A landlord shall compensate a tenant who receives notice of termination of a tenancy under section 50 for the purpose of repairs or renovations in an amount equal to the rent for the lesser of three months and the period the unit is under repair or renovation if,

(a) the tenant gives the landlord notice under subsection 53(2) with respect to the rental unit;

(b) the residential complex in which the rental unit is located contains at least five residential units; and

(c) the repair or renovation was not ordered to be carried out under the authority of this or any other Act.

Tenant's right to compensation, severance

55. A landlord of a residential complex that is created as a result of a severance shall compensate a tenant of a rental unit in that complex in an amount equal to three months rent or offer the tenant another rental unit acceptable to the tenant if,

(a) before the severance, the residential complex from which the new residential complex was created had at least five residential units;

(b) the new residential complex has fewer than five residential units; and

(c) the landlord gives the tenant a notice of termination under section 50 less than two years after the date of the severance.

Security of tenure, severance, subdivision

56. Where a rental unit becomes separately conveyable property due to a consent under section 53 of the *Planning Act* or a plan of subdivision under section 51 of that Act, a landlord may not give a notice under section 48 or 49 to a person who was a tenant of the rental unit at the time of the consent or approval.

Former tenant's application where notice given in bad faith

57(1) The Board may make an order described in subsection (3) if, on application by a former tenant of a rental unit, the Board determines that,

(a) the landlord gave a notice of termination under section 48 in bad faith, the former tenant vacated the rental unit as a result of the notice or as a result of an application to or order made by the Board based on the notice, and no person referred to in clause 48(1)(a), (b), (c) or (d) occupied the rental unit within a reasonable time after the former tenant vacated the rental unit;

(b) the landlord gave a notice of termination under section 49 in bad faith, the former tenant vacated the rental unit as a result of the notice or as a result of an application to or order made by the Board based on the notice, and no person referred to in clause 49(1)(a), (b), (c) or (d) or 49(2)(a), (b), (c) or (d) occupied the rental unit within a reasonable time after the former tenant vacated the rental unit; or

(c) the landlord gave a notice of termination under section 50 in bad faith, the former tenant vacated the rental unit as a result of the notice or as a result of an application to or order made by the Board based on the notice, and the landlord did not demolish, convert or repair or renovate the rental unit within a reasonable time after the former tenant vacated the rental unit.

Time limitation

(2) No application may be made under subsection (1) more than one year after the former tenant vacated the rental unit.

Orders

(3) The orders referred to in subsection (1) are the following:

1. An order that the landlord pay a specified sum to the former tenant for,
   i. all or any portion of any increased rent that the former tenant has incurred or will incur for a one-year period after vacating the rental unit, and
   ii. reasonable out-of-pocket moving, storage and other like expenses that the former tenant has incurred or will incur.
2. An order for an abatement of rent.
3. An order that the landlord pay to the Board an administrative fine not exceeding the greater of $10,000 and the monetary jurisdiction of the Small Claims Court.
4. Any other order that the Board considers appropriate.

Previous determination of good faith

(4) In an application under subsection (1), the Board may find that the landlord gave a notice of termination in bad faith despite a previous finding by the Board to the contrary.

Notice at end of term or period, additional grounds

58(1) A landlord may give a tenant notice of termination of their tenancy on any of the following grounds:

1. The tenant has persistently failed to pay rent on the date it becomes due and payable.
2. The rental unit that is the subject of the tenancy agreement is a rental unit described in paragraph 1, 2, 3 or 4 of subsection 7(1) and the tenant has ceased to meet the qualifications required for occupancy of the rental unit.
3. The tenant was an employee of an employer who provided the tenant with the rental unit during the tenant's employment and the employment has terminated.
4. The tenancy arose by virtue of or collateral to an agreement of purchase and sale of a proposed unit within the meaning of the *Condominium Act, 1998* in good faith and the agreement of purchase and sale has been terminated.

Period of notice

(2) The date for termination specified in the notice shall be at least the number of days after the date the notice is given that is set out in section 44 and shall be the day a period of the tenancy ends or, where the tenancy is for a fixed term, the end of the term.

Notice by Landlord Before End of Period or Term
Non-payment of rent

59(1) If a tenant fails to pay rent lawfully owing under a tenancy agreement, the landlord may give the tenant notice of termination of the tenancy effective not earlier than,

(a) the 7th day after the notice is given, in the case of a daily or weekly tenancy; and

(b) the 14th day after the notice is given, in all other cases.

Contents of notice

(2) The notice of termination shall set out the amount of rent due and shall specify that the tenant may avoid the termination of the tenancy by paying, on or before the termination date specified in the notice, the rent due as set out in the notice and any additional rent that has become due under the tenancy agreement as at the date of payment by the tenant.

Notice void if rent paid

(3) The notice of termination is void if, before the day the landlord applies to the Board for an order terminating the tenancy and evicting the tenant based on the notice, the tenant pays,

(a) the rent that is in arrears under the tenancy agreement; and

(b) the additional rent that would have been due under the tenancy agreement as at the date of payment by the tenant had notice of termination not been given.

Termination for cause, misrepresentation of income

60(1) A landlord may give a tenant notice of termination of the tenancy if the rental unit is a rental unit described in paragraph 1, 2, 3 or 4 of subsection 7(1) and the tenant has knowingly and materially misrepresented his or her income or that of other members of his or her family occupying the rental unit.

Notice

(2) A notice of termination under this section shall set out the grounds for termination and shall provide a termination date not earlier than the 20th day after the notice is given.

Termination for cause, illegal act

61(1) A landlord may give a tenant notice of termination of the tenancy if the tenant or another occupant of the rental unit commits an illegal act or carries on an illegal trade, business or occupation or permits a person to do so in the rental unit or the residential complex.

Notice

(2) A notice of termination under this section shall set out the grounds for termination and shall provide a termination date not earlier than,

(a) the 10th day after the notice is given, in the case of a notice grounded on an illegal act, trade, business or occupation involving,

(i) the production of an illegal drug,

(ii) the trafficking in an illegal drug, or

(iii) the possession of an illegal drug for the purposes of trafficking; or

(b) the 20th day after the notice is given, in all other cases.

Definitions

(3) In this section,

"illegal drug" means a controlled substance or precursor as those terms are defined in the *Controlled Drugs and Substances Act* (Canada);

"possession" has the same meaning as in the *Controlled Drugs and Substances Act* (Canada);

"production" means, with respect to an illegal drug, to produce the drug within the meaning of the *Controlled Drugs and Substances Act* (Canada);

"trafficking" means, with respect to an illegal drug, to traffic in the drug within the meaning of the *Controlled Drugs and Substances Act* (Canada).

Termination for cause, damage

62(1) A landlord may give a tenant notice of termination of the tenancy if the tenant, another occupant of the rental unit or a person whom the tenant permits in the residential complex wilfully or negligently causes undue damage to the rental unit or the residential complex.

Notice

(2) A notice of termination under this section shall,

(a) provide a termination date not earlier than the 20th day after the notice is given;

(b) set out the grounds for termination; and

(c) require the tenant, within seven days,

(i) to repair the damaged property or pay to the landlord the reasonable costs of repairing the damaged property, or

(ii) to replace the damaged property or pay to the landlord the reasonable costs of replacing the damaged property, if it is not reasonable to repair the damaged property.

Notice void if tenant complies

(3) The notice of termination under this section is void if the tenant, within seven days after receiving the notice, complies with the requirement referred to in clause (2)(c) or makes arrangements satisfactory to the landlord to comply with that requirement.

Termination for cause, damage, shorter notice period

63(1) Despite section 62, a landlord may give a tenant notice of termination of the tenancy that provides a termination date not earlier than the 10th day after the notice is given if the tenant, another occupant of the rental unit or a person whom the tenant permits in the residential complex,

> (a) wilfully causes undue damage to the rental unit or the residential complex; or

> (b) uses the rental unit or the residential complex in a manner that is inconsistent with use as residential premises and that causes or can reasonably be expected to cause damage that is significantly greater than the damage that is required in order to give a notice of termination under clause (a) or subsection 62(1).

Notice

(2) A notice of termination under this section shall set out the grounds for termination.

Non-application of s. 62(2) and (3)

(3) Subsections 62(2) and (3) do not apply to a notice given under this section.

Termination for cause, reasonable enjoyment

64(1) A landlord may give a tenant notice of termination of the tenancy if the conduct of the tenant, another occupant of the rental unit or a person permitted in the residential complex by the tenant is such that it substantially interferes with the reasonable enjoyment of the residential complex for all usual purposes by the landlord or another tenant or substantially interferes with another lawful right, privilege or interest of the landlord or another tenant.

Notice

(2) A notice of termination under subsection (1) shall,

> (a) provide a termination date not earlier than the 20th day after the notice is given;

> (b) set out the grounds for termination; and

> (c) require the tenant, within seven days, to stop the conduct or activity or correct the omission set out in the notice.

Notice void if tenant complies

(3) The notice of termination under subsection (1) is void if the tenant, within seven days after receiving the notice, stops the conduct or activity or corrects the omission.

Termination for cause, reasonable enjoyment of landlord in small building

65(1) Despite section 64, a landlord who resides in a building containing not more than three residential units may give a tenant of a rental unit in the building notice of termination of the tenancy that provides a termination date not earlier than the 10th day after the notice is given if the conduct of the tenant, another occupant of the rental unit or a person permitted in the building by the tenant is such that it substantially interferes with the reasonable enjoyment of the building for all usual purposes by the landlord or substantially interferes with another lawful right, privilege or interest of the landlord.

Notice

(2) A notice of termination under this section shall set out the grounds for termination.

Non-application of s. 64(2) and (3)

(3) Subsections 64(2) and (3) do not apply to a notice given under this section.

Termination for cause, act impairs safety

66(1) A landlord may give a tenant notice of termination of the tenancy if,

> (a) an act or omission of the tenant, another occupant of the rental unit or a person permitted in the residential complex by the tenant seriously impairs or has seriously impaired the safety of any person; and

> (b) the act or omission occurs in the residential complex.

Same

(2) A notice of termination under this section shall provide a termination date not earlier than the 10th day after the notice is given and shall set out the grounds for termination.

Termination for cause, too many persons

67(1) A landlord may give a tenant notice of termination of the tenancy if the number of persons occupying the rental unit on a continuing basis results in a contravention of health, safety or housing standards required by law.

Notice

(2) A notice of termination under this section shall,

> (a) provide a termination date not earlier than the 20th day after the notice is given;

> (b) set out the details of the grounds for termination; and

> (c) require the tenant, within seven days, to reduce the number of persons occupying the rental unit to comply with health, safety or housing standards required by law.

Notice void if tenant complies

(3) The notice of termination under this section is void if the tenant, within seven days after receiving the notice, sufficiently reduces the number of persons occupying the rental unit.

Notice of termination, further contravention

68(1) A landlord may give a tenant notice of termination of the tenancy if,

> (a) a notice of termination under section 62, 64 or 67 has become void as a result of the tenant's compliance with the terms of the notice; and

> (b) within six months after the notice mentioned in clause (a) was given to the tenant, an activity takes place, conduct occurs or a situation arises that constitutes grounds for a notice of termination under section 60, 61, 62, 64 or 67, other than an activity, conduct or a situation that is described in subsection 61(1) and that involves an illegal act, trade, business or occupation described in clause 61(2)(a).

Same

(2) The notice under this section shall set out the date it is to be effective and that date shall not be earlier than the 14th day after the notice is given.

Application by Landlord — After Notice of Termination

Application by landlord

69(1) A landlord may apply to the Board for an order terminating a tenancy and evicting the tenant if the landlord has given notice to terminate the tenancy under this Act or the *Tenant Protection Act, 1997*.

Same

(2) An application under subsection (1) may not be made later than 30 days after the termination date specified in the notice.

Exception

(3) Subsection (2) does not apply with respect to an application based on the tenant's failure to pay rent.

No application during remedy period

70. A landlord may not apply to the Board for an order terminating a tenancy and evicting the tenant based on a notice of termination under section 62, 64 or 67 before the seven-day remedy period specified in the notice expires.

Immediate application

71. Subject to section 70 and subsection 74(1), a landlord who has served a notice of termination may apply immediately to the Board under section 69 for an order terminating the tenancy and evicting the tenant.

Landlord or purchaser personally requires premises

72(1) The Board shall not make an order terminating a tenancy and evicting the tenant in an application under section 69 based on a notice of termination under section 48 or 49 unless the landlord has filed with the Board an affidavit sworn by the person who personally requires the rental unit certifying that the person in good faith requires the rental unit for his or her own personal use.

Same

(2) The Board shall not make an order terminating a tenancy and evicting the tenant in an application under section 69 based on a notice of termination under section 48 or 49 where the landlord's claim is based on a tenancy agreement or occupancy agreement that purports to entitle the landlord to reside in the rental unit unless,

(a) the application is brought in respect of premises situate in a building containing not more than four residential units; or

(b) one or more of the following people has previously been a genuine occupant of the premises:

(i) the landlord,

(ii) the landlord's spouse,

(iii) a child or parent of the landlord or the landlord's spouse, or

(iv) a person who provided care services to the landlord, the landlord's spouse, or a child or parent of the landlord or the landlord's spouse.

Demolition, conversion, repairs

73. The Board shall not make an order terminating a tenancy and evicting the tenant in an application under section 69 based on a notice of termination under section 50 unless it is satisfied that,

(a) the landlord intends in good faith to carry out the activity on which the notice of termination was based; and

(b) the landlord has,

(i) obtained all necessary permits or other authority that may be required to carry out the activity on which the notice of termination was based, or

(ii) has taken all reasonable steps to obtain all necessary permits or other authority that may be required to carry out the activity on which the notice of termination was based, if it is not possible to obtain the permits or other authority until the rental unit is vacant.

Non-payment of rent

74(1) A landlord may not apply to the Board under section 69 for an order terminating a tenancy and evicting the tenant based on a notice of termination under section 59 before the day following the termination date specified in the notice.

Discontinuance of application

(2) An application by a landlord under section 69 for an order terminating a tenancy and evicting the tenant based on a notice of termination under section 59 shall be discontinued if, before the Board issues the eviction order, the Board is satisfied that the tenant has paid to the landlord or to the Board,

(a) the amount of rent that is in arrears under the tenancy agreement;

(b) the amount of additional rent that would have been due under the tenancy agreement as at the date of payment by the tenant had notice of termination not been given; and

(c) the landlord's application fee.

Order of Board

(3) An order of the Board terminating a tenancy and evicting the tenant in an application under section 69 based on a notice of termination under section 59 shall,

(a) specify the following amounts:

(i) the amount of rent that is in arrears under the tenancy agreement,

(ii) the daily amount of compensation that must be paid under section 86, and

(iii) any costs ordered by the Board;

(b) inform the tenant and the landlord that the order will become void if, before the order becomes enforceable, the tenant pays to the landlord or to the Board the amount required under subsection (4) and specify that amount; and

(c) if the tenant has previously made a motion under subsection (11) during the period of the tenant's tenancy agreement with the landlord, inform the tenant and the landlord that the tenant is not entitled to make another motion under that subsection during the period of the agreement.

Payment before order becomes enforceable

(4) An eviction order referred to in subsection (3) is void if the tenant pays to the landlord or to the Board, before the order becomes enforceable,

(a) the amount of rent that is in arrears under the tenancy agreement;

(b) the amount of additional rent that would have been due under the tenancy agreement as at the date of payment by the tenant had notice of termination not been given;

(c) the amount of NSF cheque charges charged by financial institutions to the landlord in respect of cheques tendered to the landlord by or on behalf of the tenant, as allowed by the Board in an application by the landlord under section 87;

(d) the amount of administration charges payable by the tenant for the NSF cheques, as allowed by the Board in an application by the landlord under section 87; and

(e) the costs ordered by the Board.

Notice of void order

(5) If, before the eviction order becomes enforceable, the tenant pays the amount specified in the order under clause (3) (b) to the Board, an employee of the Board shall issue a notice to the tenant and the landlord acknowledging that the eviction order is void under subsection (4).

Determination that full amount paid before order becomes enforceable

(6) If, before the eviction order becomes enforceable, the tenant pays the amount due under subsection (4) either in whole to the landlord or in part to the landlord and in part to the Board, the tenant may make a motion to the Board, without notice to the landlord, for an order determining that the tenant has paid the full amount due under subsection (4) and confirming that the eviction order is void under subsection (4).

Evidence

(7) A tenant who makes a motion under subsection (6) shall provide the Board with an affidavit setting out the details of any payments made to the landlord and with any supporting documents the tenant may have.

No hearing

(8) The Board shall make an order under subsection (6) without holding a hearing.

Motion by landlord

(9) Within 10 days after an order is issued under subsection (6), the landlord may, on notice to the tenant, make a motion to the Board to have the order set aside.

Order of Board

(10) On a motion under subsection (9), the Board shall hold a hearing and shall,

(a) if satisfied that the tenant paid the full amount due under subsection (4) before the eviction order became enforceable, refuse to set aside the order made under subsection (6);

(b) if satisfied that the tenant did not pay the full amount due under subsection (4) before the eviction order became enforceable but that the tenant has since paid the full amount, refuse to set aside the order made under subsection (6); or

(c) in any other case, set aside the order made under subsection (6) and confirm that the eviction order is not void under subsection (4).

Payment after order becomes enforceable

(11) A tenant may make a motion to the Board, on notice to the landlord, to set aside an eviction order referred to in subsection (3) if, after the order becomes enforceable but before it is executed, the tenant pays an amount to the landlord or to the Board and files an affidavit sworn by the tenant stating that the amount, together with any amounts previously paid to the landlord or to the Board, is at least the sum of the following amounts:

1. The amount of rent that is in arrears under the tenancy agreement.
2. The amount of additional rent that would have been due under the tenancy agreement as at the date of payment by the tenant had notice of termination not been given.
3. The amount of NSF cheque charges charged by financial institutions to the landlord in respect of cheques tendered to the landlord by or on behalf of the tenant, as allowed by the Board in an application by the landlord under section 87.
4. The amount of administration charges payable by the tenant for the NSF cheques, as allowed by the Board in an application by the landlord under section 87.
5. The costs ordered by the Board.

Exception

(12) Subsection (11) does not apply if the tenant has previously made a motion under that subsection during the period of the tenant's tenancy agreement with the landlord.

Motion under subs. (11) stays eviction order

(13) An order under subsection (3) is stayed when a motion under subsection (11) is received by the Board and shall not be enforced under this Act or as an order of the Superior Court of Justice during the stay.

Order of Board

(14) Subject to subsection (15), if a tenant makes a motion under subsection (11), the Board shall, after a hearing,

(a) make an order declaring the order under subsection (3) to be void, if the tenant has paid the amounts set out in subsection (11); or

(b) make an order lifting the stay of the order under subsection (3), if the tenant has not paid the amounts set out in subsection (11).

Enforcement costs

(15) If, on a motion under subsection (11), the Board determines that the landlord has paid any non-refundable amount under the *Administration of Justice Act* for the purpose of enforcing the order under subsection (3), the Board shall specify that amount in the order made under clause (14)(a) and shall provide in the order that it is not effective unless,

(a) the tenant pays the specified amount into the Board by a date specified in the order; and

(b) an employee of the Board issues a notice under subsection (16).

Notice of payment

(16) If subsection (15) applies to an order made under clause (14)(a) and the tenant pays the amount specified in the order into the Board by the date specified in the order, an employee of the Board shall issue a notice to the tenant and the landlord acknowledging that the eviction order is void.

Failure to pay

(17) If subsection (15) applies to an order made under clause (14)(a) and the tenant does not pay the amount specified in the order into the Board by the date specified in the order, the stay of the order under subsection (3) ceases to apply and the order may be enforced.

Order for payment

(18) If the Board makes an order under clause (14)(b), the Board may make an order that the tenant pay to the landlord any non-refundable amount paid by the landlord under the *Administration of Justice Act* for the purpose of enforcing the order under subsection (3).

Illegal act

75. The Board may issue an order terminating a tenancy and evicting a tenant in an application referred to under section 69 based on a notice of termination under section 61 whether or not the tenant or other person has been convicted of an offence relating to an illegal act, trade, business or occupation.

Application based on animals

76(1) If an application based on a notice of termination under section 64, 65 or 66 is grounded on the presence, control or behaviour of an animal in or about the residential complex, the Board shall not make an order terminating the tenancy and evicting the tenant without being satisfied that the tenant is keeping an animal and that,

(a) subject to subsection (2), the past behaviour of an animal of that species has substantially interfered with the reasonable enjoyment of the residential complex for all usual purposes by the landlord or other tenants;

(b) subject to subsection (3), the presence of an animal of that species has caused the landlord or another tenant to suffer a serious allergic reaction; or

(c) the presence of an animal of that species or breed is inherently dangerous to the safety of the landlord or the other tenants.

Same

(2) The Board shall not make an order terminating the tenancy and evicting the tenant relying on clause (1)(a) if it is satisfied that the animal kept by the tenant did not cause or contribute to the substantial interference.

Same

(3) The Board shall not make an order terminating the tenancy and evicting the tenant relying on clause (1)(b) if it is satisfied that the animal kept by the tenant did not cause or contribute to the allergic reaction.

Application by Landlord — No Notice of Termination
Agreement to terminate, tenant's notice

77(1) A landlord may, without notice to the tenant, apply to the Board for an order terminating a tenancy and evicting the tenant if,

(a) the landlord and tenant have entered into an agreement to terminate the tenancy; or

(b) the tenant has given the landlord notice of termination of the tenancy.

Same

(2) The landlord shall include with the application an affidavit verifying the agreement or notice of termination, as the case may be.

Same

(3) An application under subsection (1) shall not be made later than 30 days after the termination date specified in the agreement or notice.

Order

(4) On receipt of the application, the Board may make an order terminating the tenancy and evicting the tenant.

Same

(5) An order under subsection (4) shall be effective not earlier than,

(a) the date specified in the agreement, in the case of an application under clause (1)(a); or

(b) the termination date set out in the notice, in the case of an application under clause (1)(b).

Motion to set aside order

(6) The respondent may make a motion to the Board, on notice to the applicant, to have the order under subsection (4) set aside within 10 days after the order is issued.

Motion stays order

(7) An order under subsection (4) is stayed when a motion to have the order set aside is received by the Board and shall not be enforced under this Act or as an order of the Superior Court of Justice during the stay.

Order of Board

(8) If the respondent makes a motion under subsection (6), the Board shall, after a hearing,

(a) make an order setting aside the order under subsection (4), if,

> (i) the landlord and tenant did not enter into an agreement to terminate the tenancy, and

> > (ii) the tenant did not give the landlord notice of termination of the tenancy;

(b) make an order setting aside the order under subsection (4), if the Board is satisfied, having regard to all the circumstances, that it would not be unfair to do so; or

(c) make an order lifting the stay of the order under subsection (4), effective immediately or on a future date specified in the order.

Application based on previous order, mediated settlement

78(1) A landlord may, without notice to the tenant, apply to the Board for an order terminating a tenancy or evicting the tenant if the following criteria are satisfied:

1. The landlord previously applied to the Board for an order terminating the tenancy or evicting the tenant.
2. A settlement mediated under section 194 or order made with respect to the previous application,
   i. imposed conditions on the tenant that, if not met by the tenant, would give rise to the same grounds for terminating the tenancy as were claimed in the previous application, and
   ii. provided that the landlord could apply under this section if the tenant did not meet one or more of the conditions described in subparagraph i.
3. The tenant has not met one or more of the conditions described in subparagraph 2 i.

Same

(2) The landlord shall include with the application a copy of the settlement or order and an affidavit setting out what conditions of the settlement or order have not been met and how they have not been met.

Order for payment

(3) In an application under subsection (1), the landlord may also request that the Board make an order for payment under subsection (7) if the following criteria are satisfied:

1. The landlord applied for an order for the payment of arrears of rent when the landlord made the previous application described in paragraph 1 of subsection (1).
2. A settlement mediated under section 194 or order made with respect to the previous application requires the tenant to pay rent or some or all of the arrears of rent.

Affidavit

(4) If the landlord makes a request under subsection (3), the affidavit included with the application under subsection (2) must also provide the following information:

1. The amount of any additional arrears of rent arising after the date of the settlement or order.

2. The amount of NSF cheque charges, if any, claimed by the landlord that were charged by financial institutions after the date of the settlement or order in respect of cheques tendered to the landlord by or on behalf of the tenant, to the extent the landlord has not been reimbursed for the charges.
3. The amount of NSF administration charges, if any, claimed by the landlord in respect of NSF cheques tendered by or on behalf of the tenant after the date of the settlement or order, to the extent the landlord has not been reimbursed for the charges.
4. If a settlement was mediated under section 194 with respect to the previous application,
   i. the amount and date of each payment made under the terms of the settlement and what the payment was for,
   ii. the amount of arrears of rent payable to the landlord under the terms of the settlement,
   iii. the amount of NSF cheque charges payable to the landlord under the terms of the settlement,
   iv. the amount of NSF administration charges payable to the landlord under the terms of the settlement, and
   v. the amount that the terms of the settlement required the tenant to pay to the landlord as reimbursement for the fee paid by the landlord for the application referred to in paragraph 1 of subsection (1).
5. The amount of any rent deposit, the date it was given and the last period for which interest was paid on the rent deposit.

Time for application

(5) An application under this section shall not be made later than 30 days after a failure of the tenant to meet a condition described in subparagraph 2 i of subsection (1).

Order terminating tenancy

(6) If the Board finds that the landlord is entitled to an order under subsection (1), the Board may make an order terminating the tenancy and evicting the tenant.

Order for arrears

(7) If an order is made under subsection (6) and the landlord makes a request under subsection (3), the Board may order the payment of the following amounts:

1. The amount of any compensation payable under section 86.
2. The amount of arrears of rent that arose after the date of the settlement or order referred to in paragraph 2 of subsection (3).
3. Such amount as the Board may allow in respect of NSF cheque charges claimed by the landlord that were charged by financial institutions, after the date of the settlement or order referred to in paragraph 2 of subsection (3), in respect of cheques tendered by or on behalf of the tenant and for which the landlord has not been reimbursed.

4. Such amount as the Board may allow in respect of NSF administration charges claimed by the landlord that were incurred after the date of the settlement or order referred to in paragraph 2 of subsection (3) in respect of NSF cheques tendered by or on behalf of the tenant and for which the landlord has not been reimbursed, not exceeding the amount per cheque that is prescribed as a specified amount exempt from the operation of section 134.

5. If a settlement was mediated under section 194 with respect to the previous application,

   i. the amount of arrears of rent payable under the terms of the settlement that has not been paid,

   ii. the amount payable under the terms of the settlement in respect of NSF cheque charges that were charged by financial institutions in respect of cheques tendered by or on behalf of the tenant and for which the landlord has not been reimbursed,

   iii. the amount payable under the terms of the settlement in respect of NSF administration charges for which the landlord has not been reimbursed, not exceeding the amount per cheque that is prescribed as a specified amount exempt from the operation of section 134, and

   iv. the amount payable under the terms of the settlement as reimbursement for the fee paid by the landlord for the previous application, to the extent that the amount payable did not exceed that fee and to the extent that the amount payable has not been paid.

Credit for rent deposit

(8) In determining the amount payable by the tenant to the landlord, the Board shall ensure that the tenant is credited with the amount of any rent deposit and interest on the deposit that would be owing to the tenant on the termination of the tenancy.

Motion to set aside order

(9) The respondent may make a motion to the Board, on notice to the applicant, to have an order under subsection (6), and any order made under subsection (7), set aside within 10 days after the order made under subsection (6) is issued.

Motion stays order

(10) An order under subsection (6) or (7) is stayed when a motion to have the order set aside is received by the Board and shall not be enforced under this Act or as an order of the Superior Court of Justice during the stay.

Order of Board

(11) If the respondent makes a motion under subsection (9), the Board shall, after a hearing,

(a) make an order setting aside the order under subsection (6), and any order made under subsection (7), if any of the criteria set out in subsection (1) are not satisfied;

(b) make an order setting aside the order under subsection (6), and any order made under subsection (7), if the Board is satisfied, having regard to all the circumstances, that it would not be unfair to set aside the order under subsection (6); or

(c) make an order lifting the stay of the order under subsection (6), and any order made under subsection (7), effective immediately or on a future date specified in the order.

Same

(12) In an order under clause (11)(b), the Board may amend a settlement mediated under section 194 or an order made with respect to the previous application if it considers it appropriate to do so.

Abandonment of rental unit

79. If a landlord believes that a tenant has abandoned a rental unit, the landlord may apply to the Board for an order terminating the tenancy.

Eviction Orders

Effective date of order

80(1) If a notice of termination of a tenancy has been given and the landlord has subsequently applied to the Board for an order evicting the tenant, the order of the Board evicting the tenant may not be effective earlier than the date of termination set out in the notice.

Exception, notice under s. 63 or 66

(2) Despite subsection (1), an order evicting a tenant may provide that it is effective on a date specified in the order that is earlier than the date of termination set out in the notice of termination if,

(a) the order is made on an application under section 69 based on a notice of termination under clause 63(1)(a) and the Board determines that the damage caused was significantly greater than the damage that was required by that clause in order to give the notice of termination; or

(b) the order is made on an application under section 69 based on a notice of termination under clause 63(1)(b) or subsection 66(1).

Expiry date of order

81. An order of the Board evicting a person from a rental unit expires six months after the day on which the order takes effect if it is not filed within those six months with the sheriff who has territorial jurisdiction where the rental unit is located.

Tenant issues in application for non-payment of rent

82(1) At a hearing of an application by a landlord under section 69 for an order terminating a tenancy and evicting a tenant based on a notice of termination under section 59, the Board shall permit the tenant to raise any issue that could be the subject of an application made by the tenant under this Act.

Orders

(2) If a tenant raises an issue under subsection (1), the Board may make any order in respect of the issue that it could have made had the tenant made an application under this Act.

Power of Board, eviction

83(1) Upon an application for an order evicting a tenant, the Board may, despite any other provision of this Act or the tenancy agreement,

(a) refuse to grant the application unless satisfied, having regard to all the circumstances, that it would be unfair to refuse; or

(b) order that the enforcement of the eviction order be postponed for a period of time.

Mandatory review

(2) If a hearing is held, the Board shall not grant the application unless it has reviewed the circumstances and considered whether or not it should exercise its powers under subsection (1).

Circumstances where refusal required

(3) Without restricting the generality of subsection (1), the Board shall refuse to grant the application where satisfied that,

(a) the landlord is in serious breach of the landlord's responsibilities under this Act or of any material covenant in the tenancy agreement;

(b) the reason for the application being brought is that the tenant has complained to a governmental authority of the landlord's violation of a law dealing with health, safety, housing or maintenance standards;

(c) the reason for the application being brought is that the tenant has attempted to secure or enforce his or her legal rights;

(d) the reason for the application being brought is that the tenant is a member of a tenants' association or is attempting to organize such an association; or

(e) the reason for the application being brought is that the rental unit is occupied by children and the occupation by the children does not constitute overcrowding.

No eviction before compensation, demolition or conversion

(4) The Board shall not issue an eviction order in a proceeding regarding termination of a tenancy for the purposes of demolition, conversion to non-residential rental use, renovations or repairs until the landlord has complied with section 52, 54 or 55, as the case may be.

No eviction before compensation, repair or renovation

(5) If a tenant has given a landlord notice under subsection 53(2) and subsection 54(2) applies, the Board shall not issue an eviction order in a proceeding regarding termination of the tenancy until the landlord has compensated the tenant in accordance with subsection 54(2).

Expedited eviction order

84. Subject to clause 83(1)(b), the Board shall, in an order made under section 69 based on a notice given under subsec-tion 61(1) that involves an illegal act, trade, business or occupation described in clause 61(2)(a) or based on a notice given under section 63, 65 or 66, request that the sheriff expedite the enforcement of the order.

Effect of eviction order

85. An order evicting a person shall have the same effect, and shall be enforced in the same manner, as a writ of possession.

Compensation for Landlord
Compensation, unit not vacated

86. A landlord is entitled to compensation for the use and occupation of a rental unit by a tenant who does not vacate the unit after his or her tenancy is terminated by order, notice or agreement.

Application

87(1) A landlord may apply to the Board for an order for the payment of arrears of rent if,

(a) the tenant has not paid rent lawfully required under the tenancy agreement; and

(b) the tenant is in possession of the rental unit.

Tenant issues

(2) Section 82 applies, with necessary modifications, to an application under subsection (1).

Compensation, overholding tenant

(3) If a tenant is in possession of a rental unit after the tenancy has been terminated, the landlord may apply to the Board for an order for the payment of compensation for the use and occupation of a rental unit after a notice of termination or an agreement to terminate the tenancy has taken effect.

Amount of arrears of rent or compensation

(4) In determining the amount of arrears of rent, compensation or both owing in an order for termination of a tenancy and the payment of arrears of rent, compensation or both, the Board shall subtract from the amount owing the amount of any rent deposit or interest on a rent deposit that would be owing to the tenant on termination.

NSF cheque charges

(5) On an application by a landlord under this section, the Board may include the following amounts in determining the total amount owing to a landlord by a tenant in respect of a rental unit:

1. The amount of NSF cheque charges claimed by the landlord and charged by financial institutions in respect of cheques tendered to the landlord by or on behalf of the tenant, to the extent the landlord has not been reimbursed for the charges.

2. The amount of unpaid administration charges in respect of the NSF cheques, if claimed by the landlord, that do not exceed the amount per cheque that is prescribed as a specified payment exempt from the operation of section 134.

Arrears of rent when tenant abandons or vacates without notice

88(1) If a tenant abandons or vacates a rental unit without giving notice of termination in accordance with this Act and no agreement to terminate has been made or the landlord has not given notice to terminate the tenancy, a determination of the amount of arrears of rent owing by the tenant shall be made in accordance with the following rules:

1. If the tenant vacated the rental unit after giving notice that was not in accordance with this Act, arrears of rent are owing for the period that ends on the earliest termination date that could have been specified in the notice, had the notice been given in accordance with section 47, 96 or 145, as the case may be.

2. If the tenant abandoned or vacated the rental unit without giving any notice, arrears of rent are owing for the period that ends on the earliest termination date that could have been specified in a notice of termination had the tenant, on the date that the landlord knew or ought to have known that the tenant had abandoned or vacated the rental unit, given notice of termination in accordance with section 47, 96 or 145, as the case may be.

Where landlord has given notice under s. 48, 49 or 50

(2) If a notice of termination has been given by the landlord under section 48, 49 or 50 and the tenant vacates the rental unit before the termination date set out in the notice without giving a notice of earlier termination or after giving a notice of earlier termination that is not in accordance with subsection 48(3), 49(4) or 50(4), as the case may be, a determination of the amount of arrears of rent owing by the tenant shall be made as if arrears of rent are owing for the period that ends on the earlier of the following dates:

1. The date that is 10 days after,
   i. the date the tenant gave notice of earlier termination, if the tenant vacated the rental unit after giving a notice of earlier termination that was not in accordance with subsection 48(3), 49(4) or 50(4), as the case may be, or
   ii. the date the landlord knew or ought to have known that the tenant had vacated the rental unit, if the tenant vacated the rental unit without giving a notice of earlier termination.

2. The termination date set out in the landlord's notice of termination.

New tenancy

(3) Despite subsections (1) and (2), if the landlord enters into a new tenancy agreement with a new tenant with respect to the rental unit, the tenant who abandoned or vacated the rental unit is not liable to pay an amount of arrears of rent that exceeds the lesser of the following amounts:

1. The amount of arrears of rent determined under subsection (1) or (2).

2. The amount of arrears of rent owing for the period that ends on the date the new tenant is entitled to occupy the rental unit.

Minimization of losses

(4) In determining the amount of arrears of rent owing under subsections (1), (2) and (3), consideration shall be given to whether or not the landlord has taken reasonable steps to minimize losses in accordance with section 16.

Compensation for damage

89(1) A landlord may apply to the Board for an order requiring a tenant to pay reasonable costs that the landlord has incurred or will incur for the repair of or, where repairing is not reasonable, the replacement of damaged property, if the tenant, another occupant of the rental unit or a person whom the tenant permits in the residential complex wilfully or negligently causes undue damage to the rental unit or the residential complex and the tenant is in possession of the rental unit.

Same

(2) If the Board makes an order requiring payment under subsection (1) and for the termination of the tenancy, the Board shall set off against the amount required to be paid the amount of any rent deposit or interest on a rent deposit that would be owing to the tenant on termination.

Compensation, misrepresentation of income

90. If a landlord has a right to give a notice of termination under section 60, the landlord may apply to the Board for an order for the payment of money the tenant would have been required to pay if the tenant had not misrepresented his or her income or that of other members of his or her family, so long as the application is made while the tenant is in possession of the rental unit.

Death of Tenant

Death of tenant

91(1) If a tenant of a rental unit dies and there are no other tenants of the rental unit, the tenancy shall be deemed to be terminated 30 days after the death of the tenant.

Reasonable access

(2) The landlord shall, until the tenancy is terminated under subsection (1),
   (a) preserve any property of a tenant who has died that is in the rental unit or the residential complex other than property that is unsafe or unhygienic; and
   (b) afford the executor or administrator of the tenant's estate, or if there is no executor or administrator, a member of the tenant's family reasonable access to the rental unit and the residential complex for the purpose of removing the tenant's property.

Landlord may dispose of property

92(1) The landlord may sell, retain for the landlord's own use or otherwise dispose of property of a tenant who has died that is in a rental unit and in the residential complex in which the rental unit is located,

> (a) if the property is unsafe or unhygienic, immediately; and

> (b) otherwise, after the tenancy is terminated under section 91.

Same

(2) Subject to subsections (3) and (4), a landlord is not liable to any person for selling, retaining or otherwise disposing of the property of a tenant in accordance with subsection (1).

Same

(3) If, within six months after the tenant's death, the executor or administrator of the estate of the tenant or, if there is no executor or administrator, a member of the tenant's family claims any property of the tenant that the landlord has sold, the landlord shall pay to the estate the amount by which the proceeds of sale exceed the sum of,

> (a) the landlord's reasonable out-of-pocket expenses for moving, storing, securing or selling the property; and

> (b) any arrears of rent.

Same

(4) If, within the six-month period after the tenant's death, the executor or administrator of the estate of the tenant or, if there is no executor or administrator, a member of the tenant's family claims any property of the tenant that the landlord has retained for the landlord's own use, the landlord shall return the property to the tenant's estate.

Agreement

(5) A landlord and the executor or administrator of a deceased tenant's estate may agree to terms other than those set out in this section with regard to the termination of the tenancy and disposal of the tenant's property.

Superintendent's Premises

Termination of tenancy

93(1) If a landlord has entered into a tenancy agreement with respect to a superintendent's premises, unless otherwise agreed, the tenancy terminates on the day on which the employment of the tenant is terminated.

Same

(2) A tenant shall vacate a superintendent's premises within one week after his or her tenancy is terminated.

No rent charged for week

(3) A landlord shall not charge a tenant rent or compensation or receive rent or compensation from a tenant with respect to the one-week period mentioned in subsection (2).

Application to Board

94. The landlord may apply to the Board for an order terminating the tenancy of a tenant of superintendent's premises and evicting the tenant if the tenant does not vacate the rental unit within one week of the termination of his or her employment.

PART VI   ASSIGNMENT, SUBLETTING AND UNAUTHORIZED OCCUPANCY

Assignment of tenancy

95(1) Subject to subsections (2), (3) and (6), and with the consent of the landlord, a tenant may assign a rental unit to another person.

Landlord's options, general request

(2) If a tenant asks a landlord to consent to an assignment of a rental unit, the landlord may,

> (a) consent to the assignment of the rental unit; or

> (b) refuse consent to the assignment of the rental unit.

Landlord's options, specific request

(3) If a tenant asks a landlord to consent to the assignment of the rental unit to a potential assignee, the landlord may,

> (a) consent to the assignment of the rental unit to the potential assignee;

> (b) refuse consent to the assignment of the rental unit to the potential assignee; or

> (c) refuse consent to the assignment of the rental unit.

Refusal or non-response

(4) A tenant may give the landlord a notice of termination under section 96 within 30 days after the date a request is made if,

> (a) the tenant asks the landlord to consent to an assignment of the rental unit and the landlord refuses consent;

> (b) the tenant asks the landlord to consent to an assignment of the rental unit and the landlord does not respond within seven days after the request is made;

> (c) the tenant asks the landlord to consent to an assignment of the rental unit to a potential assignee and the landlord refuses consent to the assignment under clause (3)(c); or

> (d) the tenant asks the landlord to consent to an assignment of the rental unit to a potential assignee and the landlord does not respond within seven days after the request is made.

Same

(5) A landlord shall not arbitrarily or unreasonably refuse consent to an assignment of a rental unit to a potential assignee under clause (3)(b).

Same

(6) Subject to subsection (5), a landlord who has given consent to an assignment of a rental unit under clause (2)(a) may subsequently refuse consent to an assignment of the rental unit to a potential assignee under clause (3)(b).

Charges

(7) A landlord may charge a tenant only for the landlord's reasonable out-of-pocket expenses incurred in giving consent to an assignment to a potential assignee.

Consequences of assignment

(8) If a tenant has assigned a rental unit to another person, the tenancy agreement continues to apply on the same terms and conditions and,

(a) the assignee is liable to the landlord for any breach of the tenant's obligations and may enforce against the landlord any of the landlord's obligations under the tenancy agreement or this Act, if the breach or obligation relates to the period after the assignment, whether or not the breach or obligation also related to a period before the assignment;

(b) the former tenant is liable to the landlord for any breach of the tenant's obligations and may enforce against the landlord any of the landlord's obligations under the tenancy agreement or this Act, if the breach or obligation relates to the period before the assignment;

(c) if the former tenant has started a proceeding under this Act before the assignment and the benefits or obligations of the new tenant may be affected, the new tenant may join in or continue the proceeding.

Application of section

(9) This section applies with respect to all tenants, regardless of whether their tenancies are periodic, fixed, contractual or statutory, but does not apply with respect to a tenant of superintendent's premises.

Tenant's notice to terminate, refusal of assignment

96(1) A tenant may give notice of termination of a tenancy if the circumstances set out in subsection 95(4) apply.

Same

(2) The date for termination specified in the notice shall be at least a number of days after the date of the notice that is the lesser of the notice period otherwise required under this Act and 30 days.

Subletting rental unit

97(1) A tenant may sublet a rental unit to another person with the consent of the landlord.

Same

(2) A landlord shall not arbitrarily or unreasonably withhold consent to the sublet of a rental unit to a potential subtenant.

Charges

(3) A landlord may charge a tenant only for the landlord's reasonable out-of-pocket expenses incurred in giving consent to a subletting.

Consequences of subletting

(4) If a tenant has sublet a rental unit to another person,

(a) the tenant remains entitled to the benefits, and is liable to the landlord for the breaches, of the tenant's obligations under the tenancy agreement or this Act during the subtenancy; and

(b) the subtenant is entitled to the benefits, and is liable to the tenant for the breaches, of the subtenant's

obligations under the subletting agreement or this Act during the subtenancy.

Overholding subtenant

(5) A subtenant has no right to occupy the rental unit after the end of the subtenancy.

Application of section

(6) This section applies with respect to all tenants, regardless of whether their tenancies are periodic, fixed, contractual or statutory, but does not apply with respect to a tenant of superintendent's premises.

Tenant application

98(1) A tenant or former tenant of a rental unit may apply to the Board for an order determining that the landlord has arbitrarily or unreasonably withheld consent to the assignment or sublet of a rental unit to a potential assignee or subtenant.

Time limitation

(2) No application may be made under subsection (1) more than one year after the day the alleged conduct giving rise to the application occurred.

Order re assignment, sublet

(3) If the Board determines that a landlord has unlawfully withheld consent to an assignment or sublet in an application under subsection (1), the Board may do one or more of the following:

1. Order that the assignment or sublet is authorized.
2. Where appropriate, by order authorize another assignment or sublet proposed by the tenant.
3. Order that the tenancy be terminated.
4. Order an abatement of the tenant's or former tenant's rent.

Same

(4) The Board may establish terms and conditions of the assignment or sublet.

Same

(5) If an order is made under paragraph 1 or 2 of subsection (3), the assignment or sublet shall have the same legal effect as if the landlord had consented to it.

Eviction with termination order

(6) If an order is made terminating a tenancy under paragraph 3 of subsection (3), the Board may order that the tenant be evicted, effective not earlier than the termination date specified in the order.

Tenant's notice, application re subtenant

99. The following provisions apply, with necessary modifications, with respect to a tenant who has sublet a rental unit, as if the tenant were the landlord and the subtenant were the tenant:

1. Sections 59 to 69, 87, 89 and 148.
2. The provisions of this Act that relate to applications to the Board under sections 69, 87, 89 and 148.

Unauthorized occupancy

100(1) If a tenant transfers the occupancy of a rental unit to a person in a manner other than by an assignment authorized under section 95 or a subletting authorized under section 97, the landlord may apply to the Board for an order terminating the tenancy and evicting the tenant and the person to whom occupancy of the rental unit was transferred.

Time limitation

(2) An application under subsection (1) must be made no later than 60 days after the landlord discovers the unauthorized occupancy.

Compensation

(3) A landlord who makes an application under subsection (1) may also apply to the Board for an order for the payment of compensation by the unauthorized occupant for the use and occupation of the rental unit, if the unauthorized occupant is in possession of the rental unit at the time the application is made.

Application of s. 87(5)

(4) Subsection 87(5) applies, with necessary modifications, to an application under subsection (3).

Overholding subtenant

101(1) If a subtenant continues to occupy a rental unit after the end of the subtenancy, the landlord or the tenant may apply to the Board for an order evicting the subtenant.

Time limitation

(2) An application under this section must be made within 60 days after the end of the subtenancy.

Compensation, overholding subtenant

102. A tenant may apply to the Board for an order for compensation for use and occupation by an overholding subtenant after the end of the subtenancy if the overholding subtenant is in possession of the rental unit at the time of the application.

Compensation, unauthorized occupant

103(1) A landlord is entitled to compensation for the use and occupation of a rental unit by an unauthorized occupant of the unit.

Effect of payment

(2) A landlord does not create a tenancy with an unauthorized occupant of a rental unit by accepting compensation for the use and occupation of the rental unit, unless the landlord and unauthorized occupant agree otherwise.

Miscellaneous new tenancy agreements
Assignment without consent

104(1) If a person occupies a rental unit as a result of an assignment of the unit without the consent of the landlord, the landlord may negotiate a new tenancy agreement with the person.

Overholding subtenant

(2) If a subtenant continues to occupy a rental unit after the end of the subtenancy and the tenant has abandoned the rental unit, the landlord may negotiate a new tenancy agreement with the subtenant.

Lawful rent

(3) Sections 113 and 114 apply to tenancy agreements entered into under subsection (1) or (2) if they are entered into no later than 60 days after the landlord discovers the unauthorized occupancy.

Deemed assignment

(4) A person's occupation of a rental unit shall be deemed to be an assignment of the rental unit with the consent of the landlord as of the date the unauthorized occupancy began if,

(a) a tenancy agreement is not entered into under subsection (1) or (2) within the period set out in subsection (3);

(b) the landlord does not apply to the Board under section 100 for an order evicting the person within 60 days of the landlord discovering the unauthorized occupancy; and

(c) neither the landlord nor the tenant applies to the Board under section 101 within 60 days after the end of the subtenancy for an order evicting the subtenant.

PART VII RULES RELATING TO RENT
General Rules
Security deposits, limitation

105(1) The only security deposit that a landlord may collect is a rent deposit collected in accordance with section 106.

Definition

(2) In this section and in section 106,

"security deposit" means money, property or a right paid or given by, or on behalf of, a tenant of a rental unit to a landlord or to anyone on the landlord's behalf to be held by or for the account of the landlord as security for the performance of an obligation or the payment of a liability of the tenant or to be returned to the tenant upon the happening of a condition.

Rent deposit may be required

106(1) A landlord may require a tenant to pay a rent deposit with respect to a tenancy if the landlord does so on or before entering into the tenancy agreement.

Amount of rent deposit

(2) The amount of a rent deposit shall not be more than the lesser of the amount of rent for one rent period and the amount of rent for one month.

Same

(3) If the lawful rent increases after a tenant has paid a rent deposit, the landlord may require the tenant to pay an additional amount to increase the rent deposit up to the amount permitted by subsection (2).

Qualification

(4) A new landlord of a rental unit or a person who is deemed to be a landlord under subsection 47(1) of the *Mortgages Act* shall

not require a tenant to pay a rent deposit if the tenant has already paid a rent deposit to the prior landlord of the rental unit.

Exception

(5) Despite subsection (4), if a person becomes a new landlord in a sale from a person deemed to be a landlord under subsection 47(1) of the *Mortgages Act*, the new landlord may require the tenant to pay a rent deposit in an amount equal to the amount with respect to the former rent deposit that the tenant received from the proceeds of sale.

Interest

(6) A landlord of a rental unit shall pay interest to the tenant annually on the amount of the rent deposit at a rate equal to the guideline determined under section 120 that is in effect at the time payment becomes due.

Deduction applied to rent deposit

(7) The landlord may deduct from the amount payable under subsection (6) the amount, if any, by which the maximum amount of the rent deposit permitted under subsection (2) exceeds the amount of the rent deposit paid by the tenant and the deducted amount shall be deemed to form part of the rent deposit paid by the tenant.

Transition

(8) Despite subsection (6), the first interest payment that becomes due under subsection (6) after the day this subsection comes into force shall be adjusted so that,

  (a) the interest payable in respect of the period ending before the day this subsection comes into force is based on the annual rate of 6 per cent; and

  (b) the interest payable in respect of the period commencing on or after the day this subsection comes into force shall be based on the rate determined under subsection (6).

Deduction of interest from rent

(9) Where the landlord has failed to make the payment required by subsection (6) when it comes due, the tenant may deduct the amount of the payment from a subsequent rent payment.

Rent deposit applied to last rent

(10) A landlord shall apply a rent deposit that a tenant has paid to the landlord or to a former landlord in payment of the rent for the last rent period before the tenancy terminates.

Rent deposit, prospective tenant

107(1) A landlord shall repay the amount received as a rent deposit in respect of a rental unit if vacant possession of the rental unit is not given to the prospective tenant.

Exception

(2) Despite subsection (1), if the prospective tenant, before he or she would otherwise obtain vacant possession of the rental unit, agrees to rent a different rental unit from the landlord,

  (a) the landlord may apply the amount received as a rent deposit in respect of the other rental unit; and

  (b) the landlord shall repay only the excess, if any, by which the amount received exceeds the amount of the rent deposit the landlord is entitled to receive under section 106 in respect of the other rental unit.

Post-dated cheques, etc.

108. Neither a landlord nor a tenancy agreement shall require a tenant or prospective tenant to,

  (a) provide post-dated cheques or other negotiable instruments for payment of rent; or

  (b) permit automatic debiting of the tenant's or prospective tenant's account at a financial institution, automatic charging of a credit card or any other form of automatic payment for the payment of rent.

Receipt for payment

109(1) A landlord shall provide free of charge to a tenant or former tenant, on request, a receipt for the payment of any rent, rent deposit, arrears of rent or any other amount paid to the landlord.

Former tenant

(2) Subsection (1) applies to a request by a former tenant only if the request is made within 12 months after the tenancy terminated.

General Rules Governing Amount of Rent
Landlord's duty, rent increases

110. No landlord shall increase the rent charged to a tenant for a rental unit, except in accordance with this Part.

Landlord not to charge more than lawful rent

111(1) No landlord shall charge rent for a rental unit in an amount that is greater than the lawful rent permitted under this Part.

Lawful rent where prompt payment discount

(2) The lawful rent is not affected by a discount in rent at the beginning of, or during, a tenancy of up to 2 per cent of the rent that could otherwise be lawfully charged for a rental period if the discount is provided for paying rent on or before the date it is due and the discount meets the prescribed conditions.

Lawful rent where another discount

(2.1) The lawful rent is not affected if one of the following discounts is provided:

1. A discount in rent at the beginning of, or during, a tenancy that consists of up to three months rent in any 12-month period if the discount is provided in the form of rent-free periods and meets the prescribed conditions.
2. A prescribed discount.

Lawful rent where both discounts provided

(2.2) For greater certainty, the lawful rent is not affected if discounts described in subsections (2) and (2.1) are both provided.

Same

(3) Subject to subsections (2) and (2.1), where a landlord offers a discount in rent at the beginning of, or during, a tenancy, the lawful rent shall be calculated in accordance with the prescribed rules.

Lawful rent where higher rent for first rental period

(4) Where the rent a landlord charges for the first rental period of a tenancy is greater than the rent the landlord charges for subsequent rental periods, the lawful rent shall be calculated in accordance with the prescribed rules.

Lawful rent when this section comes into force

112. Unless otherwise prescribed, the lawful rent charged to a tenant for a rental unit for which there is a tenancy agreement in effect on the day this section comes into force shall be the rent that was charged on the day before this section came into force or, if that amount was not lawfully charged under the *Tenant Protection Act, 1997*, the amount that it was lawful to charge on that day.

Lawful rent for new tenant

113. Subject to section 111, the lawful rent for the first rental period for a new tenant under a new tenancy agreement is the rent first charged to the tenant.

Notice to new tenant, order under par. 6, 7 or 8 of s. 30(1) in effect

114(1) If an order made under paragraph 6, 7 or 8 of subsection 30(1) is in effect in respect of a rental unit when a new tenancy agreement relating to the rental unit is entered into, the landlord shall, before entering into the new tenancy agreement, give to the new tenant written notice about the lawful rent for the rental unit in accordance with subsection (3).

Same

(2) If an order made under paragraph 6, 7 or 8 of subsection 30(1) takes effect in respect of a rental unit after a new tenancy agreement relating to the rental unit is entered into but before the tenancy agreement takes effect, the landlord shall, before the tenancy agreement takes effect, give to the new tenant written notice about the lawful rent for the rental unit in accordance with subsection (3).

Contents of notice

(3) A notice given under subsection (1) or (2) shall be in the form approved by the Board and shall set out,

    (a) information about the order made under paragraph 6, 7 or 8 of subsection 30(1);

    (b) the amount of rent that the landlord may lawfully charge the new tenant until the prohibition in the order made under paragraph 6, 7 or 8 of subsection 30(1) ends;

    (c) the amount of rent that the landlord may lawfully charge the new tenant after the prohibition in the order made under paragraph 6, 7 or 8 of subsection 30(1) ends;

    (d) information about the last lawful rent charged to the former tenant; and

    (e) such other information as is prescribed.

Order takes effect after tenancy agreement

(4) If an order made under paragraph 6, 7 or 8 of subsection 30(1) takes effect in respect of a rental unit after a new tenancy agreement relating to the rental unit takes effect, the landlord shall promptly give to the new tenant written notice about the lawful rent for the rental unit in accordance with subsection (5), unless the order was made on the application of the new tenant.

Contents of notice

(5) A notice given under subsection (4) shall be in the form approved by the Board and shall set out,

    (a) information about the order made under paragraph 6, 7 or 8 of subsection 30(1); and

    (b) such other information as is prescribed.

Application by new tenant

115(1) A new tenant who was entitled to notice under section 114 may apply to the Board for an order,

    (a) determining the amount of rent that the new tenant may lawfully be charged until the prohibition in the order made under paragraph 6, 7 or 8 of subsection 30(1) ends;

    (b) determining the amount of rent that the new tenant may lawfully be charged after the prohibition in the order made under paragraph 6, 7 or 8 of subsection 30(1) ends; and

    (c) requiring the landlord to rebate to the new tenant any rent paid by the new tenant in excess of the rent that the tenant may lawfully be charged.

Time for application

(2) No order shall be made under subsection (1) unless the application is made not later than one year after the new tenancy agreement takes effect.

Failure to comply with s. 114

(3) If, in an application under subsection (1), the Board finds that the landlord has not complied with section 114, the Board may order the landlord to pay to the Board an administrative fine not exceeding the greater of $10,000 and the monetary jurisdiction of the Small Claims Court.

Information to be filed

(4) If an application is made under subsection (1), the landlord shall file with the Board information as prescribed within the time prescribed.

Application of s. 135

(5) Section 135 does not apply to a new tenant with respect to rent paid by the new tenant in excess of the rent that the tenant could lawfully be charged if an application could have been made under subsection (1) for an order requiring the rebate of the excess.

Notice of Rent Increase
Notice of rent increase required
116(1) A landlord shall not increase the rent charged to a tenant for a rental unit without first giving the tenant at least 90 days written notice of the landlord's intention to do so.

Same
(2) Subsection (1) applies even if the rent charged is increased in accordance with an order under section 126.

Contents of notice
(3) The notice shall be in a form approved by the Board and shall set out the landlord's intention to increase the rent and the amount of the new rent.

Increase void without notice
(4) An increase in rent is void if the landlord has not given the notice required by this section, and the landlord must give a new notice before the landlord can take the increase.

Compliance by landlord, no notice required
117(1) Despite section 116 but subject to subsections (3) and (4), if an order was issued under paragraph 6 of subsection 30(1) and a new tenancy agreement was entered into while the order remained in effect, no notice of rent increase is required for the landlord to charge an amount that the landlord would have been entitled to charge in the absence of the order.

Same
(2) Despite section 116 but subject to subsections (3) and (4), if an order was issued under paragraph 8 of subsection 30(1), no notice of rent increase is required for the landlord to take a rent increase that the landlord would have been entitled to take in the absence of the order.

Limitation
(3) Subsections (1) and (2) apply only where the landlord,

    (a) has completed the items in work orders for which the compliance period has expired and which were found by the Board to be related to a serious breach of a health, safety, housing or maintenance standard; and

    (b) has completed the specified repairs or replacements or other work ordered under paragraph 4 of subsection 30(1) found by the Board to be related to a serious breach of the landlord's obligations under subsection 20(1) or section 161.

Effective date
(4) The authority under subsection (1) or (2) to take an increase or charge an amount without a notice of rent increase is effective on the first day of the rental period following the date that the landlord completed,

    (a) the items in work orders for which the compliance period has expired and which were found by the Board to be related to a serious breach of a health, safety, housing or maintenance standard; and

    (b) the specified repairs or replacements or other work ordered under paragraph 4 of subsection 30(1) found by the Board to be related to a serious breach of the landlord's obligations under subsection 20(1) or section 161.

Date of annual increase
(5) In determining the effective date of the next lawful rent increase under section 119,

    (a) an amount charged under subsection (1) shall be deemed to have been charged at the time the landlord would have been entitled to charge it if the order under paragraph 6 of subsection 30(1) had not been issued; and

    (b) an increase taken under subsection (2) shall be deemed to have been taken at the time the landlord would have been entitled to take it if the order under paragraph 8 of subsection 30(1) had not been issued.

Deemed acceptance where no notice of termination
118. A tenant who does not give a landlord notice of termination of a tenancy under section 47 after receiving notice of an intended rent increase under section 116 shall be deemed to have accepted whatever rent increase would be allowed under this Act after the landlord and the tenant have exercised their rights under this Act.

12-Month Rule
12-month rule
119(1) A landlord who is lawfully entitled to increase the rent charged to a tenant for a rental unit may do so only if at least 12 months have elapsed,

    (a) since the day of the last rent increase for that tenant in that rental unit, if there has been a previous increase; or

    (b) since the day the rental unit was first rented to that tenant, if clause (a) does not apply.

Exception
(2) An increase in rent under section 123 shall be deemed not to be an increase in rent for the purposes of this section.

Guideline
Guideline increase
120(1) No landlord may increase the rent charged to a tenant, or to an assignee under section 95, during the term of their tenancy by more than the guideline, except in accordance with section 126 or 127 or an agreement under section 121 or 123.

Guideline
(2) The guideline for a calendar year is the percentage change from year to year in the Consumer Price Index for Ontario for prices of goods and services as reported monthly by Statistics Canada, averaged over the 12-month period that ends at the end of May of the previous calendar year, rounded to the first decimal point.

Publication of guideline
(3) The Minister shall determine the guideline for each year in accordance with subsection (2) and shall have the guideline published in *The Ontario Gazette* not later than August 31 of the preceding year.

Transition

(4) The guideline for the calendar year in which this section comes into force shall be deemed to be the guideline established for that year under the *Tenant Protection Act, 1997*.

Same

(5) If this section comes into force on or after September 1 in a calendar year, the guideline for the following calendar year shall be deemed to be the guideline established for the following year under the *Tenant Protection Act, 1997*.

Agreements to Increase or Decrease Rent

Agreement

121(1) A landlord and a tenant may agree to increase the rent charged to the tenant for a rental unit above the guideline if,

    (a) the landlord has carried out or undertakes to carry out a specified capital expenditure in exchange for the rent increase; or

    (b) the landlord has provided or undertakes to provide a new or additional service in exchange for the rent increase.

Form

(2) An agreement under subsection (1) shall be in the form approved by the Board and shall set out the new rent, the tenant's right under subsection (4) to cancel the agreement and the date the agreement is to take effect.

Maximum increase

(3) A landlord shall not increase rent charged under this section by more than the guideline plus 3 per cent of the previous lawful rent charged.

Right to cancel

(4) A tenant who enters into an agreement under this section may cancel the agreement by giving written notice to the landlord within five days after signing it.

Agreement in force

(5) An agreement under this section may come into force no earlier than six days after it has been signed.

Notice of rent increase not required

(6) Section 116 does not apply with respect to a rent increase under this section.

When prior notice void

(7) Despite any deemed acceptance of a rent increase under section 118, if a landlord and tenant enter into an agreement under this section, a notice of rent increase given by the landlord to the tenant before the agreement was entered into becomes void when the agreement takes effect, if the notice of rent increase is to take effect on or after the day the agreed to increase is to take effect.

Tenant application

122(1) A tenant or former tenant may apply to the Board for relief if the landlord and the tenant or former tenant agreed to an increase in rent under section 121 and,

    (a) the landlord has failed in whole or in part to carry out an undertaking under the agreement;

    (b) the agreement was based on work that the landlord claimed to have done but did not do; or

    (c) the agreement was based on services that the landlord claimed to have provided but did not do so.

Time limitation

(2) No application may be made under this section more than two years after the rent increase becomes effective.

Order

(3) In an application under this section, the Board may find that some or all of the rent increase above the guideline is invalid from the day on which it took effect and may order the rebate of any money consequently owing to the tenant or former tenant.

Additional services, etc.

123(1) A landlord may increase the rent charged to a tenant for a rental unit as prescribed at any time if the landlord and the tenant agree that the landlord will add any of the following with respect to the tenant's occupancy of the rental unit:

1. A parking space.
2. A prescribed service, facility, privilege, accommodation or thing.

Application

(2) Subsection (1) applies despite sections 116 and 119 and despite any order under paragraph 6 of subsection 30(1).

Coerced agreement void

124. An agreement under section 121 or 123 is void if it has been entered into as a result of coercion or as a result of a false, incomplete or misleading representation by the landlord or an agent of the landlord.

Decrease in services, etc.

125. A landlord shall decrease the rent charged to a tenant for a rental unit as prescribed if the landlord and the tenant agree that the landlord will cease to provide anything referred to in subsection 123(1) with respect to the tenant's occupancy of the rental unit.

Landlord Application for Rent Increase

Application for above guideline increase

126(1) A landlord may apply to the Board for an order permitting the rent charged to be increased by more than the guideline for any or all of the rental units in a residential complex in any or all of the following cases:

1. An extraordinary increase in the cost for municipal taxes and charges or utilities or both for the residential complex or any building in which the rental units are located.
2. Eligible capital expenditures incurred respecting the residential complex or one or more of the rental units in it.

3. Operating costs related to security services provided in respect of the residential complex or any building in which the rental units are located by persons not employed by the landlord.

Interpretation

(2) In this section,

"extraordinary increase" means extraordinary increase as defined by or determined in accordance with the regulations.

When application made

(3) An application under this section shall be made at least 90 days before the effective date of the first intended rent increase referred to in the application.

Information for tenants

(4) If an application is made under this section that includes a claim for capital expenditures, the landlord shall make information that accompanies the application under subsection 185(1) available to the tenants of the residential complex in accordance with the prescribed rules.

Rent chargeable before order

(5) If an application is made under this section and the landlord has given a notice of rent increase as required, until an order authorizing the rent increase for the rental unit takes effect, the landlord shall not require the tenant to pay a rent that exceeds the lesser of,

(a) the new rent specified in the notice; and

(b) the greatest amount that the landlord could charge without applying for a rent increase.

Tenant may pay full amount

(6) Despite subsection (5), the tenant may choose to pay the amount set out in the notice of rent increase pending the outcome of the landlord's application and, if the tenant does so, the landlord shall owe to the tenant any amount paid by the tenant exceeding the amount allowed by the order of the Board.

Eligible capital expenditures

(7) Subject to subsections (8) and (9), a capital expenditure is an eligible capital expenditure for the purposes of this section if,

(a) it is necessary to protect or restore the physical integrity of the residential complex or part of it;

(b) it is necessary to comply with subsection 20(1) or clauses 161(a) to (e);

(c) it is necessary to maintain the provision of a plumbing, heating, mechanical, electrical, ventilation or air conditioning system;

(d) it provides access for persons with disabilities;

(e) it promotes energy or water conservation; or

(f) it maintains or improves the security of the residential complex or part of it.

Exception

(8) A capital expenditure to replace a system or thing is not an eligible capital expenditure for the purposes of this section if the system or thing that was replaced did not require major repair or replacement, unless the replacement of the system or thing promotes,

(a) access for persons with disabilities;

(b) energy or water conservation; or

(c) security of the residential complex or part of it.

Same

(9) A capital expenditure is not an eligible capital expenditure with respect to a rental unit for the purposes of this section if a new tenant entered into a new tenancy agreement in respect of the rental unit and the new tenancy agreement took effect after the capital expenditure was completed.

Order

(10) Subject to subsections (11) to (13), in an application under this section, the Board shall make findings in accordance with the prescribed rules with respect to all of the grounds of the application and, if it is satisfied that an order permitting the rent charged to be increased by more than the guideline is justified, shall make an order,

(a) specifying the percentage by which the rent charged may be increased in addition to the guideline; and

(b) subject to the prescribed rules, specifying a 12-month period during which an increase permitted by clause (a) may take effect.

Limitation

(11) If the Board is satisfied that an order permitting the rent charged to be increased by more than the guideline is justified and that the percentage increase justified, in whole or in part, by operating costs related to security services and by eligible capital expenditures is more than 3 per cent,

(a) the percentage specified under clause (10)(a) that is attributable to those costs and expenditures shall not be more than 3 per cent; and

(b) the order made under subsection (10) shall, in accordance with the prescribed rules, specify a percentage by which the rent charged may be increased in addition to the guideline in each of the two 12-month periods following the period specified under clause (10)(b), but that percentage in each of those periods shall not be more than 3 per cent.

Serious breach

(12) Subsection (13) applies to a rental unit if the Board finds that,

(a) the landlord,

(i) has not completed items in work orders for which the compliance period has expired and which are found by the Board to be related to a serious breach of a health, safety, housing or maintenance standard,

(ii) has not completed specified repairs or replacements or other work ordered by the Board under paragraph 4 of subsection 30(1) and found by the Board to be related to a serious breach of the landlord's obligations under subsection 20(1) or section 161, or

(iii) is in serious breach of the landlord's obligations under subsection 20(1) or section 161; and

(b) the rental unit is affected by,

(i) one or more items referred to in subclause (a)(i) that have not been completed,

(ii) one or more repairs or replacements or other work referred to in subclause (a)(ii) that has not been completed, or

(iii) a serious breach referred to in subclause (a)(iii).

Same

(13) If this subsection applies to a rental unit, the Board shall,

(a) dismiss the application with respect to the rental unit; or

(b) provide, in any order made under subsection (10), that the rent charged for the rental unit shall not be increased pursuant to the order until the Board is satisfied, on a motion made by the landlord within the time period specified by the Board, on notice to the tenant of the rental unit, that,

(i) all items referred to in subclause (12)(a)(i) that affect the rental unit have been completed, if a finding was made under that subclause,

(ii) all repairs, replacements and other work referred to in subclause (12)(a)(ii) that affect the rental unit have been completed, if a finding was made under that subclause, and

(iii) the serious breach referred to in subclause (12)(a)(iii) no longer affects the rental unit, if a finding was made under that subclause.

Order not to apply to new tenant

(14) An order of the Board under subsection (10) with respect to a rental unit ceases to be of any effect on and after the day a new tenant enters into a new tenancy agreement with the landlord in respect of that rental unit if that agreement takes effect on or after the day that is 90 days before the first effective date of a rent increase in the order.

Two ordered increases

127. Despite clause 126 (11)(b), if an order is made under subsection 126(10) with respect to a rental unit and a landlord has not yet taken all the increases in rent for the rental unit permissible under a previous order pursuant to clause 126(11)(b), the landlord may increase the rent for the rental unit in accordance with the prescribed rules.

Reductions of Rent

Utilities

128(1) If the Board issues an order under subsection 126(10) permitting an increase in rent that is due in whole or in part to an extraordinary increase in the cost of utilities,

(a) the Board shall specify in the order the percentage increase that is attributable to the extraordinary increase; and

(b) the Board shall include in the order a description of the landlord's obligations under subsections (2) and (3).

Information for tenant

(2) If a landlord increases the rent charged to a tenant for a rental unit pursuant to an order described in subsection (1), the landlord shall, in accordance with the prescribed rules, provide that tenant with information on the total cost of utilities for the residential complex.

Rent reduction

(3) If a landlord increases the rent charged to a tenant for a rental unit pursuant to an order described in subsection (1) and the cost of utilities for the residential complex decreases by more than the prescribed percentage in the prescribed period, the landlord shall reduce the rent charged to that tenant in accordance with the prescribed rules.

Application

(4) This section ceases to apply to a tenant of a rental unit in respect of a utility if the landlord ceases to provide the utility to the rental unit in accordance with this Act or an agreement between the landlord and that tenant.

Capital expenditures

129. If the Board issues an order under subsection 126(10) permitting an increase in rent that is due in whole or in part to eligible capital expenditures,

(a) the Board shall specify in the order the percentage increase that is attributable to the eligible capital expenditures;

(b) the Board shall specify in the order a date, determined in accordance with the prescribed rules, for the purpose of clause (c); and

(c) the order shall require that,

(i) if the rent charged to a tenant for a rental unit is increased pursuant to the order by the maximum percentage permitted by the order and the tenant continues to occupy the rental unit on the date specified under clause (b), the landlord shall, on that date, reduce the rent charged to that tenant by the percentage specified under clause (a); and

(ii) if the rent charged to a tenant for a rental unit is increased pursuant to the order by less than the maximum percentage permitted by the order and the tenant continues to occupy the rental unit on the date specified under clause (b), the landlord shall, on that date, reduce the rent charged to that tenant by a percentage determined in accordance with the prescribed rules that is equal to or lower than the percentage specified under clause (a).

Reduction in services

130(1) A tenant of a rental unit may apply to the Board for an order for a reduction of the rent charged for the rental unit due to a reduction or discontinuance in services or facilities provided in respect of the rental unit or the residential complex.

Same, former tenant

(2) A former tenant of a rental unit may apply under this section as a tenant of the rental unit if the person was affected

by the discontinuance or reduction of the services or facilities while the person was a tenant of the rental unit.

Order re lawful rent

(3) The Board shall make findings in accordance with the prescribed rules and may order,

(a) that the rent charged be reduced by a specified amount;

(b) that there be a rebate to the tenant of any rent found to have been unlawfully collected by the landlord;

(c) that the rent charged be reduced by a specified amount for a specified period if there has been a temporary reduction in a service.

Same

(4) An order under this section reducing rent takes effect on the day that the discontinuance or reduction first occurred.

Same, time limitation

(5) No application may be made under this section more than one year after a reduction or discontinuance in a service or facility.

Municipal taxes

131(1) If the municipal property tax for a residential complex is reduced by more than the prescribed percentage, the lawful rent for each of the rental units in the complex is reduced in accordance with the prescribed rules.

Effective date

(2) The rent reduction shall take effect on the date determined by the prescribed rules, whether or not notice has been given under subsection (3).

Notice

(3) If, for a residential complex with at least the prescribed number of rental units, the rents that the tenants are required to pay are reduced under subsection (1), the local municipality in which the residential complex is located shall, within the prescribed period and by the prescribed method of service, notify the landlord and all of the tenants of the residential complex of that fact.

Same

(4) The notice shall be in writing in a form approved by the Board and shall,

(a) inform the tenants that their rent is reduced;

(b) set out the percentage by which their rent is reduced and the date the reduction takes effect;

(c) inform the tenants that if the rent is not reduced in accordance with the notice they may apply to the Board under section 135 for the return of money illegally collected; and

(d) advise the landlord and the tenants of their right to apply for an order under section 132.

Same

(5) A local municipality that gives a notice under this section shall, on request, give a copy to the Board or to the Ministry.

Application for variation

132(1) A landlord or a tenant may apply to the Board under the prescribed circumstances for an order varying the amount by which the rent charged is to be reduced under section 131.

Same

(2) An application under subsection (1) must be made within the prescribed time.

Determination and order

(3) The Board shall determine an application under this section in accordance with the prescribed rules and shall issue an order setting out the percentage of the rent reduction.

Same

(4) An order under this section shall take effect on the effective date determined under subsection 131(2).

Application, reduction in municipal taxes

133(1) A tenant of a rental unit may apply to the Board for an order for a reduction of the rent charged for the rental unit due to a reduction in the municipal taxes and charges for the residential complex.

Order

(2) The Board shall make findings in accordance with the prescribed rules and may order that the rent charged for the rental unit be reduced.

Effective date

(3) An order under this section takes effect on a date determined in accordance with the prescribed rules.

Illegal Additional Charges
Additional charges prohibited

134(1) Unless otherwise prescribed, no landlord shall, directly or indirectly, with respect to any rental unit,

(a) collect or require or attempt to collect or require from a tenant or prospective tenant of the rental unit a fee, premium, commission, bonus, penalty, key deposit or other like amount of money whether or not the money is refundable;

(b) require or attempt to require a tenant or prospective tenant to pay any consideration for goods or services as a condition for granting the tenancy or continuing to permit occupancy of a rental unit if that consideration is in addition to the rent the tenant is lawfully required to pay to the landlord; or

(c) rent any portion of the rental unit for a rent which, together with all other rents payable for all other portions of the rental unit, is a sum that is greater than the rent the landlord may lawfully charge for the rental unit.

Same

(2) No superintendent, property manager or other person who acts on behalf of a landlord with respect to a rental unit shall, directly or indirectly, with or without the authority of the landlord, do any of the things mentioned in clause (1)(a), (b) or (c) with respect to that rental unit.

Same

(3) Unless otherwise prescribed, no tenant and no person acting on behalf of the tenant shall, directly or indirectly,

(a) sublet a rental unit for a rent that is payable by one or more subtenants and that is greater than the rent that is lawfully charged by the landlord for the rental unit;

(b) collect or require or attempt to collect or require from any person any fee, premium, commission, bonus, penalty, key deposit or other like amount of money, for subletting a rental unit, for surrendering occupancy of a rental unit or for otherwise parting with possession of a rental unit; or

(c) require or attempt to require a person to pay any consideration for goods or services as a condition for the subletting, assignment or surrender of occupancy or possession in addition to the rent the person is lawfully required to pay to the tenant or landlord.

Money Collected Illegally

Money collected illegally

135(1) A tenant or former tenant of a rental unit may apply to the Board for an order that the landlord, superintendent or agent of the landlord pay to the tenant any money the person collected or retained in contravention of this Act or the *Tenant Protection Act, 1997*.

Prospective tenants

(2) A prospective tenant may apply to the Board for an order under subsection (1).

Subtenants

(3) A subtenant may apply to the Board for an order under subsection (1) as if the subtenant were the tenant and the tenant were the landlord.

Time limitation

(4) No order shall be made under this section with respect to an application filed more than one year after the person collected or retained money in contravention of this Act or the *Tenant Protection Act, 1997*.

Rent deemed lawful

136(1) Rent charged one or more years earlier shall be deemed to be lawful rent unless an application has been made within one year after the date that amount was first charged and the lawfulness of the rent charged is in issue in the application.

Increase deemed lawful

(2) An increase in rent shall be deemed to be lawful unless an application has been made within one year after the date the increase was first charged and the lawfulness of the rent increase is in issue in the application.

S. 122 prevails

(3) Nothing in this section shall be interpreted to deprive a tenant of the right to apply for and get relief in an application under section 122 within the time period set out in that section.

PART VIII   SUITE METERS AND APPORTIONMENT OF UTILITY COSTS

Suite meters

137(1) In this section,

"meter" has the same meaning as in Part III of the *Energy Consumer Protection Act, 2010*;

"suite meter" has the same meaning as in Part III of the *Energy Consumer Protection Act, 2010*;

"suite meter provider" has the same meaning as in Part III of the *Energy Consumer Protection Act, 2010*.

Interruption in supply

(2) A landlord who has the obligation under a tenancy agreement to supply electricity may interrupt the supply of electricity to a rental unit when a suite meter is installed if,

(a) the suite meter is installed by a suite meter provider;

(b) the supply of electricity is interrupted only for the minimum length of time necessary to install the suite meter; and

(c) the landlord provides adequate notice to the tenant in accordance with the prescribed rules.

Termination of obligation to supply electricity

(3) Subject to subsections (4) and (5), if a meter or a suite meter is installed in respect of a rental unit, a landlord who has the obligation under a tenancy agreement to supply electricity to the rental unit may terminate that obligation by,

(a) obtaining the written consent of the tenant in the form approved by the Board;

(b) providing adequate notice of the termination of the obligation to the tenant in accordance with the prescribed rules; and

(c) reducing the rent, in the prescribed circumstances and in accordance with the prescribed rules, by an amount that accounts for the cost of electricity consumption and related costs.

Information for tenants

(4) A landlord shall not terminate an obligation to supply electricity under subsection (3) unless, before obtaining the written consent of the tenant, the landlord has provided the tenant with the prescribed information.

Limitation

(5) Where the primary source of heat in the unit is generated by means of electricity, a landlord may terminate an obligation to supply electricity under subsection (3) in the prescribed circumstances, solely if the landlord meets the prescribed conditions.

Revising agreements

(6) The tenant may, within the prescribed time and in the prescribed circumstances, request that the landlord adjust the rent reduction provided under subsection (3) based on the

prescribed rules and the landlord shall adjust the rent and provide a rebate based on the prescribed rules.

Information for prospective tenants

(7) Except under the prescribed circumstances, if a suite meter is installed in respect of a rental unit, the landlord shall, before entering into a tenancy agreement with a prospective tenant for the unit, provide the prospective tenant with the following information in the form approved by the Board:

1. The most recent information available to the landlord for the prescribed period from the suite meter provider concerning electricity consumption in the rental unit.
2. If the rental unit was vacant during any part of the period to which the information referred to in paragraph 1 applies, a statement of the period that the rental unit was vacant.
3. Such other information as is prescribed.

Other circumstances where information required

(8) If a meter or a suite meter is installed in respect of a rental unit, a landlord shall, before entering into a tenancy agreement with a prospective tenant for a rental unit, provide the prospective tenant with the information required under subsection (7) or with such portion of the information required under subsection (7) as may be prescribed, in such other circumstances as are prescribed.

Electricity conservation and efficiency obligations

(9) If a suite meter is installed in respect of a rental unit and the obligation of the landlord to supply electricity has been terminated, the landlord shall, in accordance with the prescribed rules,

    (a) ensure that any appliances provided for the rental unit by the landlord satisfy the prescribed requirements relating to electricity conservation and efficiency;

    (b) ensure that other aspects of the rental unit satisfy the prescribed requirements relating to electricity conservation and efficiency; and

    (c) ensure that other prescribed requirements relating to electricity conservation and efficiency are complied with.

Same, other prescribed circumstances

(10) If a meter or a suite meter is installed in respect of a rental unit, a landlord shall comply with the electricity conservation and efficiency obligations referred to in subsection (9) in such other circumstances as are prescribed.

Tenant's application

(11) A tenant or a former tenant of a rental unit may apply to the Board in the prescribed circumstances for an order determining whether the landlord has breached an obligation under this section.

Order, general

(12) If the Board determines in an application under subsection (11) that a landlord has breached an obligation under subsection (2), (6), (7), (8), (9) or (10), the Board may do one or more of the following:

1. Order an abatement of rent.
2. Authorize a repair or replacement that has been or is to be made, or work that has been or is to be done, and order its cost to be paid by the landlord to the tenant.
3. Order the landlord to do specified repairs or replacements or other work within a specified time.
4. Order that the rent charged be reduced by a specified amount and order the appropriate rebate.
5. Make any other order that it considers appropriate.

Order, breach of subs. (3), (4) or (5)

(13) If the Board determines in an application under subsection (11) that a landlord has breached an obligation under subsection (3), (4) or (5), the Board may, in addition to the remedies set out in subsection (12), do one or more of the following:

1. Terminate the tenancy.
2. Order that the landlord assume the obligation to supply electricity to the rental unit and set the new rent that can be charged.

Eviction with termination order

(14) If the Board makes an order terminating a tenancy under paragraph 1 of subsection (13), the Board may order that the tenant be evicted, effective not earlier than the termination date specified in the order.

Determination re capital expenditures

(15) Except under the prescribed circumstances, for the purpose of section 126, a capital expenditure is not an eligible capital expenditure if,

    (a) a meter or a suite meter was installed in respect of a residential complex before the capital expenditure was made;

    (b) the capital expenditure failed to promote the conservation of electricity or the more efficient use of electricity; and

    (c) the purpose for which the capital expenditure was made could reasonably have been achieved by making a capital expenditure that promoted the conservation of electricity or the more efficient use of electricity.

Charges, fees and security deposits

(16) Where a meter or suite meter is installed in respect of a rental unit and the tenant is responsible for the payment for the supply of electricity, sections 134 and 135 have no application to charges, fees or security deposits that are required to be paid for the supply of electricity and any amount paid for the supply of electricity shall not be considered to be an amount of consideration or a service that falls within the definition of "rent" in subsection 2(1).

Interference with a vital service, reasonable enjoyment

(17) Where a meter or a suite meter is installed in respect of a rental unit and the tenant is responsible for the payment for the supply of electricity and a landlord, landlord's agent or a suite meter provider is attempting to enforce the rights or obligations afforded them under this section or under section 31 of the *Electricity Act, 1998*, electricity is deemed not to be a vital service within the meaning of section 21 and any interference with the supply of electricity is deemed not to be an interference with the tenant's reasonable enjoyment within the meaning of sections 22 and 235.

Lease provisions void

(18) A provision in a tenancy agreement which purports to provide that a tenant has consented or will consent to the termination of the obligation of the landlord to supply electricity to the rental unit on a future date or otherwise purports to provide terms which are inconsistent with the provisions contained in this section is void.

Apportionment of utility costs

138(1) A landlord of a building containing not more than six rental units who supplies a utility to each of the rental units in the building may, with the written consent of the tenant, charge the tenant a portion of the cost of the utility in accordance with the prescribed rules if,

(a) the landlord provides adequate notice to the tenant in accordance with the prescribed rules; and

(b) the rent for the rental unit is reduced in accordance with the prescribed rules.

Not a service

(2) If a landlord charges a tenant a portion of the cost of a utility in accordance with subsection (1), the utility shall not be considered a service that falls within the definition of "rent" in subsection 2(1).

Termination of tenancy prohibited

(3) If a landlord charges a tenant a portion of the cost of a utility in accordance with subsection (1), the landlord shall not serve a notice of termination under section 59 or make an application to the Board for an order under section 69 or 87 if the notice or application is based on the tenant's failure to pay the utility charge.

Information for prospective tenants

(4) If a landlord charges tenants a portion of the cost of a utility, the landlord shall, before entering into a tenancy agreement with a prospective tenant, provide the prospective tenant with the following information:

1. The portion of the cost of the utility that is applicable to the rental unit that would be occupied by the prospective tenant, expressed as a percentage of the total cost of the utility.
2. The total cost of the utility for the building for the prescribed period for which the landlord has information on the cost of the utility.

3. If any part of the building was vacant during any part of the period to which the information referred to in paragraph 2 applies, a statement of which part of the building was vacant and of the period that it was vacant.
4. Such other information as is prescribed.

Utility conservation and efficiency obligations

(5) If a landlord charges a tenant a portion of the cost of a utility, the landlord shall, in accordance with the prescribed rules,

(a) ensure that any appliances provided by the landlord satisfy the prescribed requirements relating to conservation and efficient use of the utility;

(b) ensure that other aspects of the rental unit satisfy the prescribed requirements relating to conservation and efficient use of the utility; and

(c) ensure that other prescribed requirements relating to conservation and efficient use of the utility are complied with.

Tenant's application

(6) A tenant or a former tenant of a rental unit may apply to the Board in the prescribed circumstances for an order determining whether the landlord has breached an obligation under this section.

Order, general

(7) If the Board determines in an application under subsection (6) that a landlord has breached an obligation under subsection (4) or (5), the Board may do one or more of the following:

1. Order an abatement of rent.
2. Authorize a repair or replacement that has been or is to be made, or work that has been or is to be done, and order its cost to be paid by the landlord to the tenant.
3. Order the landlord to do specified repairs or replacements or other work within a specified time.
4. Order that the rent charged be reduced by a specified amount and order the appropriate rebate.
5. Make any other order that it considers appropriate.

Order, breach of subs. (1)

(8) If the Board determines in an application under subsection (6) that a landlord has breached an obligation under subsection (1), the Board may, in addition to the remedies set out in subsection (7), do one or more of the following:

1. Terminate the tenancy.
2. Order that the landlord assume the obligation to supply the utility to the rental unit and set the new rent that can be charged.

Eviction with termination order

(9) If the Board makes an order terminating a tenancy under paragraph 1 of subsection (8), the Board may order that

the tenant be evicted, effective not earlier than the termination date specified in the order.

Determination re capital expenditures

(10) For the purpose of section 126, a capital expenditure is not an eligible capital expenditure if,

(a) the landlord charged tenants a portion of the cost of a utility before the capital expenditure was made;

(b) the capital expenditure failed to promote the conservation or more efficient use of the utility; and

(c) the purpose for which the capital expenditure was made could reasonably have been achieved by making a capital expenditure that promoted the conservation or more efficient use of the utility.

PART IX   CARE HOMES
Responsibilities of Landlords and Tenants
Agreement required

139(1) There shall be a written tenancy agreement relating to the tenancy of every tenant in a care home.

Contents of agreement

(2) The agreement shall set out what has been agreed to with respect to care services and meals and the charges for them.

Compliance

(3) If, on application by a tenant, the Board determines that subsection (1) or (2) has not been complied with, the Board may make an order for an abatement of rent.

Information to tenant

140(1) Before entering into a tenancy agreement with a new tenant in a care home, the landlord shall give to the new tenant an information package containing the prescribed information.

Effect of non-compliance

(2) The landlord shall not give a notice of rent increase or a notice of increase of a charge for providing a care service or meals until after giving the required information package to the tenant.

Tenancy agreement: consultation, cancellation
Tenancy agreement: right to consult

141(1) Every tenancy agreement relating to the tenancy of a tenant in a care home shall contain a statement that the tenant has the right to consult a third party with respect to the agreement and to cancel the agreement within five days after the agreement has been entered into.

Cancellation

(2) The tenant may cancel the tenancy agreement by written notice to the landlord within five days after entering into it.

Entry to check condition of tenant

142(1) Despite section 25, a landlord may enter a rental unit in a care home at regular intervals to check the condition of a tenant in accordance with the tenancy agreement if the agreement requires the landlord to do so.

Right to revoke provision

(2) A tenant whose tenancy agreement contains a provision requiring the landlord to regularly check the condition of the tenant may unilaterally revoke that provision by written notice to the landlord.

Assignment, subletting in care homes

143. A landlord may withhold consent to an assignment or subletting of a rental unit in a care home if the effect of the assignment or subletting would be to admit a person to the care home contrary to the admission requirements or guidelines set by the landlord.

Notice of termination

144(1) A landlord may, by notice, terminate the tenancy of a tenant in a care home if,

(a) the rental unit was occupied solely for the purpose of receiving rehabilitative or therapeutic services agreed upon by the tenant and the landlord;

(b) no other tenant of the care home occupying a rental unit solely for the purpose of receiving rehabilitative or therapeutic services is permitted to live there for longer than the prescribed period; and

(c) the period of tenancy agreed to has expired.

Period of notice

(2) The date for termination specified in the notice shall be at least the number of days after the date the notice is given that is set out in section 44 and shall be the day a period of the tenancy ends or, where the tenancy is for a fixed term, the end of the term.

Termination, care homes

145(1) Despite section 44, a tenant of a care home may terminate a tenancy at any time by giving at least 30 days notice of termination to the landlord.

Care services and meals

(2) A tenant who terminates a tenancy under subsection (1) may require the landlord to stop the provision of care services and meals before the date the tenancy terminates by giving at least 10 days notice to the landlord.

Same

(3) The tenant has no obligation to pay for care services and meals that would otherwise have been provided under the tenancy agreement after the date the landlord is required to stop the provision of care services and meals under subsection (2).

Same

(4) The estate of a tenant has no obligation to pay for care services and meals that would otherwise have been provided under the tenancy agreement more than 10 days after the death of the tenant.

Notice of termination, demolition, conversion or repairs

146(1) A landlord who gives a tenant of a care home a notice of termination under section 50 shall make reasonable efforts to find appropriate alternate accommodation for the tenant.

Same

(2) Sections 52 and 54 do not apply with respect to a tenant of a care home who receives a notice of termination under section 50 and chooses to take alternate accommodation found by the landlord for the tenant under subsection (1).

External care providers

147. A landlord shall not,

(a) do anything to prevent a tenant of a care home from obtaining care services from a person of the tenant's choice that are in addition to care services provided under the tenancy agreement; or

(b) interfere with the provision of care services to a tenant of a care home, by a person of the tenant's choice, that are in addition to care services provided under the tenancy agreement.

Transferring Tenancy
Transferring tenancy
Application

148(1) A landlord may apply to the Board for an order transferring a tenant out of a care home and evicting the tenant if,

(a) the tenant no longer requires the level of care provided by the landlord; or

(b) the tenant requires a level of care that the landlord is not able to provide.

Order

(2) The Board may issue an order under clause (1)(b) only if it is satisfied that,

(a) appropriate alternate accommodation is available for the tenant; and

(b) the level of care that the landlord is able to provide when combined with the community based services provided to the tenant in the care home cannot meet the tenant's care needs.

Mandatory mediation

(3) If a dispute arises, the dispute shall be sent to mediation before the Board makes an order.

Same

(4) If the landlord fails to participate in the mediation, the Board may dismiss the landlord's application.

Rules Related to Rent and Other Charges
Rent in care home

149. If there is more than one tenancy agreement for a rental unit in a care home, the provisions of Part VII apply, subject to subsection 6(2), with respect to each tenancy agreement as if it were an agreement for a separate rental unit.

Notice of increased charges

150(1) A landlord shall not increase a charge for providing a care service or meals to a tenant of a rental unit in a care home without first giving the tenant at least 90 days notice of the landlord's intention to do so.

Contents of notice

(2) The notice shall be in writing in the form approved by the Board and shall set out the landlord's intention to increase the charge and the new charges for care services and meals.

Effect of non-compliance

(3) An increase in a charge for a care service or meals is void if the landlord has not given the notice required by this section, and the landlord must give a new notice before the landlord can take the increase.

Certain charges permitted

151(1) Nothing in subsection 134(1) limits the right of a landlord to charge a tenant of a rental unit in a care home for providing care services or meals to the tenant so long as the landlord has complied with the requirements of sections 140 and 150.

Same

(2) Nothing in subsection 134(3) limits the right of a tenant or a person acting on behalf of a tenant to charge a subtenant of a rental unit in a care home for providing care services or meals to the subtenant.

PART X MOBILE HOME PARKS AND LAND LEASE COMMUNITIES
General
Application

152(1) This Part applies with respect to tenancies in mobile home parks.

Same; land lease communities

(2) This Part applies with necessary modifications with respect to tenancies in land lease communities, as if the tenancies were in mobile home parks.

Interpretation

153. A reference in this Part to a tenant's mobile home shall be interpreted to be a reference to a mobile home owned by the tenant and situated within a mobile home park of the landlord with whom the tenant has a tenancy agreement.

Responsibilities of Landlords and Tenants
Park rules

154(1) If a landlord establishes rules for a mobile home park,

(a) the landlord shall provide a written copy of the rules to each tenant; and

(b) the landlord shall inform each tenant in writing of any change to the rules.

Failure to comply

(2) Until a landlord has complied with clause (1)(a) or (b), as the case may be,

(a) the tenant's obligation to pay rent is suspended; and

(b) the landlord shall not require the tenant to pay rent.

After compliance

(3) After the landlord has complied with clause (1)(a) or (b), as the case may be, the landlord may require the tenant to pay any rent withheld by the tenant under subsection (2).

Information about property assessment

155(1) If a tenant is obligated to pay a landlord an amount to reimburse the landlord for property taxes paid by the landlord with respect to a mobile home owned by the tenant and the landlord obtains information from the Municipal Property Assessment Corporation with respect to the value of the mobile home for assessment purposes, the landlord shall promptly provide the tenant with a copy of that information.

Suspension of tenant's obligation to pay

(2) A tenant's obligation to pay the landlord an amount to reimburse the landlord for property taxes paid by the landlord with respect to a mobile home owned by the tenant is suspended, and the landlord shall not require the tenant to pay that amount, if,

(a) the landlord has failed to comply with subsection (1) with respect to the most recent information obtained by the landlord from the Municipal Property Assessment Corporation; or

(b) the landlord has not, in the previous 12 months, obtained written information from the Municipal Property Assessment Corporation with respect to the value of the mobile home for assessment purposes.

Exception

(3) Clause (2)(b) does not apply if the landlord has made reasonable efforts in the previous 12 months to obtain written information from the Municipal Property Assessment Corporation with respect to the value of the mobile home for assessment purposes but has been unable to obtain the information.

After compliance

(4) The landlord may require the tenant to pay any amount withheld by the tenant under subsection (2) after,

(a) complying with subsection (1), if clause (2)(a) applied; or

(b) obtaining written information from the Municipal Property Assessment Corporation with respect to the value of the mobile home for assessment purposes and complying with subsection (1), if clause (2)(b) applied.

Tenant's right to sell, etc.

156(1) A tenant has the right to sell or lease his or her mobile home without the landlord's consent.

Landlord as agent

(2) A landlord may act as the agent of a tenant in negotiations to sell or lease a mobile home only in accordance with a written agency contract entered into for the purpose of beginning those negotiations.

Same

(3) A provision in a tenancy agreement requiring a tenant who owns a mobile home to use the landlord as an agent for the sale of the mobile home is void.

Landlord's right of first refusal

157(1) This section applies if a tenancy agreement with respect to a mobile home contains a provision prohibiting the tenant from selling the mobile home without first offering to sell it to the landlord.

Same

(2) If a tenant receives an acceptable offer to purchase a mobile home, the landlord has a right of first refusal to purchase the mobile home at the price and subject to the terms and conditions in the offer.

Same

(3) A tenant shall give a landlord at least 72 hours notice of a person's offer to purchase a mobile home before accepting the person's offer.

Landlord's purchase at reduced price

(4) If a provision described in subsection (1) permits a landlord to purchase a mobile home at a price that is less than the one contained in a prospective purchaser's offer to purchase, the landlord may exercise the option to purchase the mobile home, but the provision is void with respect to the landlord's right to purchase the mobile home at the lesser price.

Advertising a sale
For sale signs

158(1) A landlord shall not prevent a tenant who owns a mobile home from placing in a window of the mobile home a sign that the home is for sale, unless the landlord does so in accordance with subsection (2).

Alternative method of advertising a sale

(2) A landlord may prevent a tenant who owns a mobile home from placing a for sale sign in a window of a mobile home if all of the following conditions are met:

1. The prohibition applies to all tenants in the mobile home park.
2. The landlord provides a bulletin board for the purpose of placing for sale advertisements.
3. The bulletin board is provided to all tenants in the mobile home park free of charge.
4. The bulletin board is placed in a prominent place and is accessible to the public at all reasonable times.

Assignment

159(1) If a tenant has sold or entered into an agreement to sell the tenant's mobile home and the tenant asks the landlord to consent to the assignment of the site for the mobile home to the purchaser of the mobile home,

(a) clause 95(3)(c) does not apply; and

(b) the landlord may not refuse consent to the assignment unless, on application under subsection (2), the

Board determines that the landlord's grounds for refusing consent are reasonable.

Time for application

(2) The landlord may apply to the Board, within 15 days after the tenant asks the landlord to consent to the assignment, for a determination of whether the landlord's grounds for refusing consent are reasonable.

Contents of application

(3) The landlord shall set out in the application the landlord's grounds for refusing consent.

Deemed consent

(4) If the landlord does not apply to the Board in accordance with subsections (2) and (3), or the Board determines that the landlord's grounds for refusing consent are not reasonable, the landlord shall be deemed to have consented to the assignment.

Restraint of trade prohibited

160(1) A landlord shall not restrict the right of a tenant to purchase goods or services from the person of his or her choice, except as provided in subsection (2).

Standards

(2) A landlord may set reasonable standards for mobile home equipment.

Responsibility of landlord

161. In addition to a landlord's obligations under section 20, a landlord is responsible for,

(a) removing or disposing of garbage or ensuring the availability of a means for removing or disposing of garbage in the mobile home park at reasonable intervals;

(b) maintaining mobile home park roads in a good state of repair;

(c) removing snow from mobile home park roads;

(d) maintaining the water supply, sewage disposal, fuel, drainage and electrical systems in the mobile home park in a good state of repair;

(e) maintaining the mobile home park grounds and all buildings, structures, enclosures and equipment intended for the common use of tenants in a good state of repair; and

(f) repairing damage to a tenant's property, if the damage is caused by the wilful or negligent conduct of the landlord.

Termination of Tenancies

Mobile home abandoned

162(1) This section applies if,

(a) the tenant has vacated the mobile home in accordance with,

(i) a notice of termination of the landlord or the tenant,

(ii) an agreement between the landlord and tenant to terminate the tenancy, or

(iii) an order of the Board terminating the tenancy or evicting the tenant; or

(b) the landlord has applied for an order under section 79 and the Board has made an order terminating the tenancy.

Notice to tenant

(2) The landlord shall not dispose of a mobile home without first notifying the tenant of the landlord's intention to do so,

(a) by registered mail, sent to the tenant's last known mailing address; and

(b) by causing a notice to be published in a newspaper having general circulation in the locality in which the mobile home park is located.

Landlord may dispose of mobile home

(3) The landlord may sell, retain for the landlord's own use or dispose of a mobile home in the circumstances described in subsection (1) beginning 60 days after the notices referred to in subsection (2) have been given if the tenant has not made a claim with respect to the landlord's intended disposal.

Same

(4) If, within six months after the day the notices have been given under subsection (2), the tenant makes a claim for a mobile home which the landlord has already sold, the landlord shall pay to the tenant the amount by which the proceeds of sale exceed the sum of,

(a) the landlord's reasonable out-of-pocket expenses incurred with respect to the mobile home; and

(b) any arrears of rent of the tenant.

Same

(5) If, within six months after the day the notices have been given under subsection (2), the tenant makes a claim for a mobile home which the landlord has retained for the landlord's own use, the landlord shall return the mobile home to the tenant.

Same

(6) Before returning a mobile home to a tenant who claims it within the 60 days referred to in subsection (3) or the six months referred to in subsection (5), the landlord may require the tenant to pay the landlord for arrears of rent and any reasonable expenses incurred by the landlord with respect to the mobile home.

No liability

(7) Subject to subsection (4) or (5), a landlord is not liable to any person for selling, retaining or otherwise disposing of a tenant's mobile home in accordance with this section.

Death of mobile home owner

163. Sections 91 and 92 do not apply if the tenant owns the mobile home.

Termination under s. 50

164(1) If a notice of termination is given under section 50 with respect to a tenancy agreement between the landlord and a tenant who owns a mobile home, the date for termination specified in the notice shall, despite subsection 50(2), be at least one year after the date the notice is given and shall be the day a period of the tenancy ends or, where the tenancy is for a fixed term, the end of the term.

Same

(2) If a notice of termination is given under section 50 with respect to a tenancy agreement between the landlord and a tenant who owns a mobile home and the tenant is entitled to compensation under section 52, 54 or 55, the amount of the compensation shall, despite those sections, be equal to the lesser of the following amounts:

1. One year's rent.
2. $3,000 or the prescribed amount, whichever is greater.

Rules Related to Rent and Other Charges
Assignment of existing tenancy agreement

165. Despite subsection 95(8), if a tenancy agreement for a site for a mobile home is assigned and the assignee purchases or enters into an agreement to purchase the former tenant's mobile home, the landlord may increase the rent payable by the assignee under the tenancy agreement by not more than the prescribed amount.

Entrance and exit fees limited

166. A landlord shall not charge for any of the following matters, except to the extent of the landlord's reasonable out-of-pocket expenses incurred with regard to those matters:

1. The entry of a mobile home into a mobile home park.
2. The exit of a mobile home from a mobile home park.
3. The installation of a mobile home in a mobile home park.
4. The removal of a mobile home from a mobile home park.
5. The testing of water or sewage in a mobile home park.

Increased capital expenditures

167(1) If the Board finds that a capital expenditure is for infrastructure work required to be carried out by the Government of Canada or Ontario or a municipality or an agency of any of them, despite subsection 126(11), the Board may determine the number of years over which the rent increase justified by that capital expenditure may be taken.

Definition

(2) In this section,

"infrastructure work" means work with respect to roads, water supply, fuel, sewage disposal, drainage, electrical systems and other prescribed services and things provided to the mobile home park.

PART XI　THE LANDLORD AND TENANT BOARD
Board

168(1) The Ontario Rental Housing Tribunal is continued under the name Landlord and Tenant Board in English and Commission de la location immobilière in French.

Board's jurisdiction

(2) The Board has exclusive jurisdiction to determine all applications under this Act and with respect to all matters in which jurisdiction is conferred on it by this Act.

Composition

169(1) The members of the Board shall be appointed by the Lieutenant Governor in Council.

Remuneration and expenses

(2) The members of the Board who are not public servants employed under Part III of the *Public Service of Ontario Act, 2006* shall be paid the remuneration fixed by the Lieutenant Governor in Council and the reasonable expenses incurred in the course of their duties under this Act, as determined by the Minister.

Public servant members

(3) Members of the Board may be persons who are appointed or transferred under the *Public Service of Ontario Act, 2006*.

Chair and vice-chair

170(1) The Lieutenant Governor in Council shall appoint one member of the Board as Chair and one or more members as vice-chairs.

Same

(2) The Chair may designate a vice-chair who shall exercise the powers and perform the duties of the Chair when the Chair is absent or unable to act.

Chair, chief executive officer

(3) The Chair shall be the chief executive officer of the Board.

Quorum

171. One member of the Board is sufficient to conduct a proceeding under this Act.

Conflict of interest

172. The members of the Board shall file with the Board a written declaration of any interests they have in residential rental property, and shall be required to comply with any conflict of interest guidelines or rules of conduct established by the Chair.

Expiry of term

173. Despite section 4.3 of the *Statutory Powers Procedure Act*, if the term of office of a member of the Board who has participated in a hearing expires before a decision is given, the term shall be deemed to continue for four weeks, but only for the purpose of participating in the decision and for no other purpose.

Power to determine law and fact

174. The Board has authority to hear and determine all questions of law and fact with respect to all matters within its jurisdiction under this Act.

Members, mediators not compellable

175. No member of the Board or person employed as a mediator by the Board shall be compelled to give testimony or produce documents in a civil proceeding with respect to matters that come to his or her knowledge in the course of exercising his or her duties under this Act.

Rules and Guidelines Committee

176(1) The Chair of the Board shall establish a Rules and Guidelines Committee to be composed of the Chair, as Chair of the Committee, and any other members of the Board the Chair may from time to time appoint to the Committee.

Committee shall adopt rules

(2) The Committee shall adopt rules of practice and procedure governing the practice and procedure before the Board under the authority of this section and section 25.1 of the *Statutory Powers Procedure Act*.

Committee may adopt guidelines

(3) The Committee may adopt non-binding guidelines to assist members in interpreting and applying this Act and the regulations made under it.

Means of adoption

(4) The Committee shall adopt the rules and guidelines by simple majority, subject to the right of the Chair to veto the adoption of any rule or guideline.

Make public

(5) The Board shall make its rules, guidelines and approved forms available to the public.

Information on rights and obligations

177. The Board shall provide information to landlords and tenants about their rights and obligations under this Act.

Employees

178. Employees may be appointed for the purposes of the Board in accordance with the regulations.

Professional assistance

179. The Board may engage persons other than its members or employees to provide professional, technical, administrative or other assistance to the Board and may establish the duties and terms of engagement and provide for the payment of the remuneration and expenses of those persons.

Reports
Annual report

180(1) At the end of each year, the Board shall file with the Minister an annual report on its affairs.

Further reports and information

(2) The Board shall make further reports and provide information to the Minister from time to time as required by the Minister.

Tabled with Assembly

(3) The Minister shall submit any reports received from the Board to the Lieutenant Governor in Council and then shall table them with the Assembly if it is in session or, if not, at the next session.

Board may set, charge fees

181(1) The Board, subject to the approval of the Minister, may set and charge fees,

(a) for making an application under this Act or requesting a review of an order under section 21.2 of the *Statutory Powers Procedure Act*;

(b) for furnishing copies of forms, notices or documents filed with or issued by the Board or otherwise in the possession of the Board; or

(c) for other services provided by the Board.

Same

(2) The Board may treat different kinds of applications differently in setting fees and may base fees on the number of residential units affected by an application.

Make fees public

(3) The Board shall ensure that its fee structure is available to the public.

Fee refunded, review

182. The Board may refund a fee paid for requesting a review of an order under section 21.2 of the *Statutory Powers Procedure Act* if, on considering the request, the Board varies, suspends or cancels the original order.

PART XII   BOARD PROCEEDINGS

Expeditious procedures

183. The Board shall adopt the most expeditious method of determining the questions arising in a proceeding that affords to all persons directly affected by the proceeding an adequate opportunity to know the issues and be heard on the matter.

SPPA applies

184(1) The *Statutory Powers Procedure Act* applies with respect to all proceedings before the Board.

Exception

(2) Subsection 5.1(2) of the *Statutory Powers Procedure Act* does not apply with respect to an application under section 132 or 133 or an application solely under paragraph 1 of subsection 126(1).

Exception

(3) Subsection 5.1(3) of the *Statutory Powers Procedure Act* does not apply to an application under section 126, 132 or 133.

Form of application

185(1) An application shall be filed with the Board in the form approved by the Board, shall be accompanied by the prescribed information and shall be signed by the applicant.

Application filed by representative

(2) An applicant may give written authorization to sign an application to a person representing the applicant under the authority of the *Law Society Act* and, if the applicant does so, the Board may require such representative to file a copy of the authorization.

Combining applications

186(1) A tenant may combine several applications into one application.

Same

(2) Two or more tenants of a residential complex may together file an application that may be filed by a tenant if each tenant applying in the application signs it.

Same

(3) A landlord may combine several applications relating to a given tenant into one application, so long as the landlord does not combine an application for a rent increase with any other application.

Parties

187(1) The parties to an application are the landlord and any tenants or other persons directly affected by the application.

Add or remove parties

(2) The Board may add or remove parties as the Board considers appropriate.

Service
Service of application

188(1) An applicant to the Board shall give the other parties to the application a copy of the application within the time set out in the Rules.

Service of notice of hearing

(2) Despite the *Statutory Powers Procedure Act*, an applicant shall give a copy of any notice of hearing issued by the Board in respect of an application to the other parties to the application.

Certificate of service

(3) A party shall file with the Board a certificate of service in the form approved by the Board in the circumstances set out in the Rules.

Notice by Board

189(1) Where an application is made to the Board, the Board shall notify the respondent in writing that an application has been made and, where possible, shall provide the respondent with information relating to the hearing and such other information as is prescribed.

Exception

(2) Subsection (1) does not apply in the circumstances prescribed.

Board may extend, shorten time

190(1) The Board may extend or shorten the time requirements related to making an application under section 126, subsection 159(2) or section 226 in accordance with the Rules.

Same

(2) The Board may extend or shorten the time requirements with respect to any matter in its proceedings, other than the prescribed time requirements, in accordance with the Rules.

How notice or document given

191(1) A notice or document is sufficiently given to a person other than the Board,

(a) by handing it to the person;

(b) if the person is a landlord, by handing it to an employee of the landlord exercising authority in respect of the residential complex to which the notice or document relates;

(c) if the person is a tenant, subtenant or occupant, by handing it to an apparently adult person in the rental unit;

(d) by leaving it in the mail box where mail is ordinarily delivered to the person;

(e) if there is no mail box, by leaving it at the place where mail is ordinarily delivered to the person;

(f) by sending it by mail to the last known address where the person resides or carries on business; or

(g) by any other means allowed in the Rules.

When notice deemed valid

(2) A notice or document that is not given in accordance with this section shall be deemed to have been validly given if it is proven that its contents actually came to the attention of the person for whom it was intended within the required time period.

Mail

(3) A notice or document given by mail shall be deemed to have been given on the fifth day after mailing.

How notice or document given to Board

192(1) A notice or document is sufficiently given to the Board,

(a) by hand delivering it to the Board at the appropriate office as set out in the Rules;

(b) by sending it by mail to the appropriate office as set out in the Rules; or

(c) by any other means allowed in the Rules.

Same

(2) A notice or document given to the Board by mail shall be deemed to have been given on the earlier of the fifth day after mailing and the day on which the notice or the document was actually received.

Time

193. Time shall be computed in accordance with the Rules.

Board may mediate

194(1) The Board may attempt to mediate a settlement of any matter that is the subject of an application or agreed upon by the parties if the parties consent to the mediation.

Settlement may override Act

(2) Despite subsection 3(1) and subject to subsection (3), a settlement mediated under this section may contain provisions that contravene any provision under this Act.

Restriction

(3) The largest rent increase that can be mediated under this section for a rental unit that is not a mobile home or a land lease home or a site for either is equal to the sum of the guideline and 3 per cent of the previous year's lawful rent.

Successful mediation

(4) If some or all of the issues with respect to an application are successfully mediated under this section, the Board shall dispose of the application in accordance with the Rules.

Hearing

(5) If there is no mediated settlement, the Board shall hold a hearing.

Money paid to Board

195(1) Where the Board considers it appropriate to do so, the Board may, subject to the regulations,

> (a) require a respondent to pay a specified sum into the Board within a specified time; or

> (b) permit a tenant who is making an application for an order under paragraph 1 of subsection 29(1) to pay all or part of the rent for the tenant's rental unit into the Board.

Rules re money paid

(2) The Board may establish procedures in the Rules for the payment of money into and out of the Board.

No payment after final order

(3) The Board shall not, under subsection (1), authorize or require payments into the Board after the Board has made its final order in the application.

Effect of failure to pay under cl. (1)(a)

(4) If a respondent is required to pay a specified sum into the Board within a specified time under clause (1)(a) and fails to do so, the Board may refuse to consider the evidence and submissions of the respondent.

Effect of payment under cl. (1)(b)

(5) Payment by a tenant under clause (1)(b) shall be deemed not to constitute a default in the payment of rent due under a tenancy agreement or a default in the tenant's obligations for the purposes of this Act.

Board may refuse to proceed if money owing

196(1) Upon receiving information that an applicant owes money to the Board as a result of having failed to pay any fine, fee or costs,

> (a) if the information is received on or before the day the applicant submits an application, an employee of the Board shall, in such circumstances as may be specified in the Rules, refuse to allow the application to be filed;

> (b) if the information is received after the application has been filed but before a hearing is held, the Board shall stay the proceeding until the fee, fine or costs have been paid and may discontinue the application in such circumstances as may be specified in the Rules;

> (c) if the information is received after a hearing with respect to the application has begun, the Board shall not issue an order until the fine, fee or costs have been paid and may discontinue the application in such circumstances as may be specified in the Rules.

Definition

(2) In subsection (1),

"fine, fee or costs" does not include money that is paid in trust to the Board pursuant to an order of the Board and that may be paid out to either the tenant or the landlord when the application is disposed of.

Where Board may dismiss

197(1) The Board may dismiss an application without holding a hearing or refuse to allow an application to be filed if, in the opinion of the Board, the matter is frivolous or vexatious, has not been initiated in good faith or discloses no reasonable cause of action.

Same

(2) The Board may dismiss a proceeding without holding a hearing if the Board finds that the applicant filed documents that the applicant knew or ought to have known contained false or misleading information.

Joinder and severance of applications
Applications joined

198(1) Despite the *Statutory Powers Procedure Act*, the Board may direct that two or more applications be joined or heard together if the Board believes it would be fair to determine the issues raised by them together.

Applications severed

(2) The Board may order that applications that have been joined be severed or that applications that had been ordered to be heard together be heard separately.

Application severed

199. The Board may order that an application be severed and each severed part dealt with as though it were a separate application under this Act if,

> (a) two or more applications are combined under section 186 in the application;

> (b) the application is made by more than one tenant under subsection 186 (2); or

> (c) the Board believes it would be appropriate to deal separately with different matters included in the application.

Amendment and withdrawal of applications
Amend application

200(1) An applicant may amend an application to the Board in accordance with the Rules.

Withdraw application

(2) Subject to subsection (3), an applicant may withdraw an application at any time before the hearing begins.

Same, harassment

(3) An applicant may withdraw an application under paragraph 4 of subsection 29(1) only with the consent of the Board.

Same

(4) An applicant may withdraw an application after the hearing begins with the consent of the Board.

Other powers of Board

201(1) The Board may, before, during or after a hearing,

(a) conduct any inquiry it considers necessary or authorize an employee of the Board to do so;

(b) request a provincial inspector or an employee of the Board to conduct any inspection it considers necessary;

(c) question any person, by telephone or otherwise, concerning the dispute or authorize an employee of the Board to do so;

(d) permit or direct a party to file additional evidence with the Board which the Board considers necessary to make its decision;

(e) view premises that are the subject of the hearing; or

(f) on its own motion and on notice to the parties, amend an application if the Board considers it appropriate to do so and if amending the application would not be unfair to any party.

Same

(2) In making its determination, the Board may consider any relevant information obtained by the Board in addition to the evidence given at the hearing, provided that it first informs the parties of the additional information and gives them an opportunity to explain or refute it.

Same

(3) If a party fails to comply with a direction under clause (1)(d), the Board may,

(a) refuse to consider the party's submissions and evidence respecting the matter regarding which there was a failure to comply; or

(b) if the party who has failed to comply is the applicant, dismiss all or part of the application.

Parties may view premises with Board

(4) If the Board intends to view premises under clause (1)(e), the Board shall give the parties an opportunity to view the premises with the Board.

Findings of Board

202. In making findings on an application, the Board shall ascertain the real substance of all transactions and activities relating to a residential complex or a rental unit and the good faith of the participants and in doing so,

(a) may disregard the outward form of a transaction or the separate corporate existence of participants; and

(b) may have regard to the pattern of activities relating to the residential complex or the rental unit.

Determinations related to housing assistance

203. The Board shall not make determinations or review decisions concerning,

(a) eligibility for rent-geared-to-income assistance as defined in the *Social Housing Reform Act, 2000* or the amount of geared-to-income rent payable under that Act; or

(b) eligibility for, or the amount of, any prescribed form of housing assistance.

Conditions in order

204(1) The Board may include in an order whatever conditions it considers fair in the circumstances.

Order re costs

(2) The Board may order a party to an application to pay the costs of another party.

Same

(3) The Board may order that its costs of a proceeding be paid by a party or the party's paid representative.

Same

(4) The amount of an order for costs shall be determined in accordance with the Rules.

Same

(5) Subsections (2) to (4) apply despite section 17.1 of the *Statutory Powers Procedure Act*.

Order payment

205(1) The Board may include in an order the following provision:

The landlord or the tenant shall pay to the other any sum of money that is owed as a result of this order.

Payment of order by instalments

(2) If the Board makes an order for a rent increase above the guideline and the order is made three months or more after the first effective date of a rent increase in the order, the Board may provide in the order that if a tenant owes any sum of money to the landlord as a result of the order, the tenant may pay the landlord the amount owing in monthly instalments.

Same

(3) If an order made under subsection (2) permits a tenant to pay the amount owing by instalments, the tenant may do so even if the tenancy is terminated.

Same

(4) An order providing for monthly instalments shall not provide for more than 12 monthly instalments.

Agreement to settle matter

206(1) Where a landlord has made an application under section 69 for an order terminating a tenancy and evicting the tenant based on a notice of termination under section 59 or an application for payment of arrears of rent, or both, the Board may make an order including terms of payment without holding a hearing if,

(a) the parties have reached a written agreement resolving the subject-matter of the application;

(b) the agreement has been signed by all parties; and

(c) the agreement is filed with the Board before the hearing has commenced.

Contents of order

(2) In an order under subsection (1), the Board may, based on the agreement reached by the parties, order,

(a) payment of any arrears and NSF cheque charges or related administration charges that are owing;

(b) payment of the fee paid by the landlord for the application to the Board; and

(c) payment of any rent that becomes due during the period in which the arrears are required to be paid.

Restriction

(3) In an order under subsection (1), the Board shall not order that the tenancy be terminated or include a provision allowing for an application under section 78.

Request by landlord

(4) A landlord may file a request to reopen the application if the tenant fails to comply with the terms of the order and shall, in the request, indicate which terms were not complied with and the manner in which the tenant failed to meet the terms of the order.

Request by landlord or tenant

(5) A landlord or tenant may file a request to reopen the application within 30 days after the order was made on the basis that the other party coerced them or deliberately made false or misleading representations which had a material effect on the agreement and the order issued under subsection (1).

Timing

(6) A request under subsection (4) shall not be made later than 30 days after a failure of the tenant to meet a term of the order.

Copy of request, notice of hearing

(7) The party filing the request must give the other parties to the application a copy of the request to reopen the application and the notice of hearing within the time set out in the Rules.

Condition

(8) If a request to reopen is made under subsection (4), the Board shall not proceed to hear the merits of the application unless the Board is satisfied that the tenant failed to comply with a term of the order.

Same

(9) If a request to reopen is made under subsection (5), the Board shall not proceed to hear the merits of the application unless the Board is satisfied that there was coercion or deliberate false or misleading representations which had a material effect on the agreement and the order issued under subsection (1).

Monetary jurisdiction; deduction of rent; interest
Monetary jurisdiction of Board

207(1) The Board may, where it otherwise has the jurisdiction, order the payment to any given person of an amount of money up to the greater of $10,000 and the monetary jurisdiction of the Small Claims Court.

Same

(2) A person entitled to apply under this Act but whose claim exceeds the Board's monetary jurisdiction may commence a proceeding in any court of competent jurisdiction for an order requiring the payment of that sum and, if such a proceeding is commenced, the court may exercise any powers that the Board could have exercised if the proceeding had been before the Board and within its monetary jurisdiction.

Same

(3) If a party makes a claim in an application for payment of a sum equal to or less than the Board's monetary jurisdiction, all rights of the party in excess of the Board's monetary jurisdiction are extinguished once the Board issues its order.

Minimum amount

(4) The Board shall not make an order for the payment of an amount of money if the amount is less than the prescribed amount.

Order may provide deduction from rent

(5) If a landlord is ordered to pay a sum of money to a person who is a current tenant of the landlord at the time of the order, the order may provide that if the landlord fails to pay the amount owing, the tenant may recover that amount plus interest by deducting a specified sum from the tenant's rent paid to the landlord for a specified number of rental periods.

Same

(6) Nothing in subsection (5) limits the right of the tenant to collect at any time the full amount owing or any balance outstanding under the order.

Post-judgment interest

(7) The Board may set a date on which payment of money ordered by the Board must be made and interest shall accrue on money owing only after that date at the post-judgment interest rate under section 127 of the *Courts of Justice Act*.

Notice of decision

208(1) The Board shall send each party who participated in the proceeding, or the person who represented the party, a copy of its order, including the reasons if any have been given, in accordance with section 191.

Same

(2) Section 18 of the *Statutory Powers Procedure Act* does not apply to proceedings under this Act.

Order final, binding

209(1) Except where this Act provides otherwise, and subject to section 21.2 of the *Statutory Powers Procedure Act*, an order of the Board is final and binding.

Power to review

(2) Without limiting the generality of section 21.2 of the *Statutory Powers Procedure Act*, the Board's power to review a decision or order under that section may be exercised if a party to a proceeding was not reasonably able to participate in the proceeding.

Appeal rights

210(1) Any person affected by an order of the Board may appeal the order to the Divisional Court within 30 days after being given the order, but only on a question of law.

Board to receive notice

(2) A person appealing an order under this section shall give to the Board any documents relating to the appeal.

Board may be heard by counsel

(3) The Board is entitled to be heard by counsel or otherwise upon the argument on any issue in an appeal.

Powers of Court

(4) If an appeal is brought under this section, the Divisional Court shall hear and determine the appeal and may,

(a) affirm, rescind, amend or replace the decision or order; or

(b) remit the matter to the Board with the opinion of the Divisional Court.

Same

(5) The Divisional Court may also make any other order in relation to the matter that it considers proper and may make any order with respect to costs that it considers proper.

Board may appeal Court decision

211. The Board is entitled to appeal a decision of the Divisional Court on an appeal of a Board order as if the Board were a party to the appeal.

Substantial compliance sufficient

212. Substantial compliance with this Act respecting the contents of forms, notices or documents is sufficient.

Electronic documents

213. Any document referred to in this Act and specified in the regulations or in the Rules may be created, signed, filed, provided, issued, sent, received, stored, transferred, retained or otherwise dealt with electronically if it is done in accordance with the regulations or the Rules.

Contingency fees, limitation

214(1) No agent who represents a landlord or a tenant in a proceeding under this Act or who assists a landlord or tenant in a matter arising under this Act shall charge or take a fee based on a proportion of any amount which has been or may be recovered, gained or saved, in whole or in part, through the efforts of the agent, where the proportion exceeds the prescribed amount.

Same

(2) An agreement that provides for a fee prohibited by subsection (1) is void.

PART XIII MUNICIPAL VITAL SERVICES BY-LAWS

Definition

215. In this Part,

"vital services by-law" means a by-law passed under section 216.

By-laws respecting vital services

216(1) The council of a local municipality may pass by-laws,

(a) requiring every landlord to provide adequate and suitable vital services to each of the landlord's rental units;

(b) prohibiting a supplier from ceasing to provide the vital service until a notice has been given under subsection 217(1);

(c) requiring a supplier to promptly restore the vital service when directed to do so by an official named in the by-law;

(d) prohibiting a person from hindering, obstructing or interfering with or attempting to hinder, obstruct or interfere with the official or person referred to in subsection 218(1) in the exercise of a power or performance of a duty under this section or sections 217 to 223;

(e) providing that a person who contravenes or fails to comply with a vital services by-law is guilty of an offence for each day or part of a day on which the offence occurs or continues;

(f) providing that every director or officer of a corporation that is convicted of an offence who knowingly concurs in the commission of the offence is guilty of an offence;

(g) authorizing an official named in the by-law to enter into agreements on behalf of the local municipality with suppliers of vital services to ensure that adequate and suitable vital services are provided for rental units.

Exception

(2) A vital services by-law does not apply to a landlord with respect to a rental unit to the extent that the tenant has expressly agreed to obtain and maintain the vital services.

Contents of vital services by-law

(3) A vital services by-law may,

(a) classify buildings or parts of buildings for the purposes of the by-law and designate the classes to which it applies;

(b) designate areas of the local municipality in which the by-law applies;

(c) establish standards for the provision of adequate and suitable vital services;

(d) prohibit a landlord from ceasing to provide a vital service for a rental unit except when necessary to alter or repair the rental unit and only for the minimum period necessary to effect the alteration or repair;

(e) provide that a landlord shall be deemed to have caused the cessation of a vital service for a rental unit if the landlord is obligated to pay the supplier for the vital service and fails to do so and, as a result of the non-payment, the vital service is no longer provided for the rental unit.

Notice by supplier

217(1) A supplier shall give notice of an intended discontinuance of a vital service only if the vital service is to be discontinued for the rental unit because the landlord has breached a contract with the supplier for the supply of the vital service.

Same

(2) The notice shall be given in writing to the clerk of the local municipality at least 30 days before the supplier ceases to provide the vital service.

Inspection

218(1) An official named in a vital services by-law or a person acting under his or her instructions may, at all reasonable times, enter and inspect a building or part of a building with respect to which the by-law applies for the purpose of determining compliance with the by-law or a direction given under subsection 221(1).

Same

(2) Despite subsection (1), the official or person shall not enter a rental unit,

(a) unless he or she has obtained the consent of the occupier of the rental unit after informing him or her that he or she may refuse permission to enter the unit; or

(b) unless he or she is authorized to do so by a warrant issued under section 231.

Services by municipality

219(1) If a landlord does not provide a vital service for a rental unit in accordance with a vital services by-law, the local municipality may arrange for the service to be provided.

Lien

(2) The amount spent by the local municipality under subsection (1) plus an administrative fee of 10 per cent of that amount shall, on registration of a notice of lien in the appropriate land registry office, be a lien in favour of the local municipality against the property at which the vital service is provided.

Not special lien

(3) Subsection 349(3) of the *Municipal Act, 2001* does not apply with respect to the amount spent and the fee, and no special lien is created under that subsection.

Certificate

(4) The certificate of the clerk of the local municipality as to the amount spent is proof, in the absence of evidence to the contrary, of the amount.

Interim certificate

(5) Before issuing a certificate referred to in subsection (4), the clerk shall send an interim certificate by registered mail to the registered owner of the property that is subject to the lien and to all mortgagees or other encumbrancers registered on title.

Appeal

220. An affected owner, mortgagee or other encumbrancer may, within 15 days after the interim certificate is mailed, appeal the amount shown on it to the council of the local municipality.

Payments transferred

221(1) If the local municipality has arranged for a vital service to be provided to a rental unit, an official named in the vital services by-law may direct a tenant to pay any or all of the rent for the rental unit to the local municipality.

Effect of payment

(2) Payment by a tenant under subsection (1) shall be deemed not to constitute a default in the payment of rent due under a tenancy agreement or a default in the tenant's obligations for the purposes of this Act.

Use of money

222(1) The local municipality shall apply the rent received from a tenant to reduce the amount that it spent to provide the vital service and the related administrative fee.

Accounting and payment of balance

(2) The local municipality shall provide the person otherwise entitled to receive the rent with an accounting of the rents received for each individual rental unit and shall pay to that person any amount remaining after the rent is applied in accordance with subsection (1).

Immunity

223(1) No proceeding for damages or otherwise shall be commenced against an official or a person acting under his or her instructions or against an employee or agent of a local municipality for any act done in good faith in the performance or intended performance of a duty or authority under any of sections 215 to 222 or under a by-law passed under section 216 or for any alleged neglect or default in the performance in good faith of the duty or authority.

Same

(2) Subsection (1) does not relieve a local municipality of liability to which it would otherwise be subject.

PART XIV   MAINTENANCE STANDARDS

Prescribed standards and complaints
Application of prescribed standards

224(1) The prescribed maintenance standards apply to a residential complex and the rental units located in it if,

(a) the residential complex is located in unorganized territory;

(b) there is no municipal property standards by-law that applies to the residential complex; or

(c) the prescribed circumstances apply.

Minister to receive complaints

(2) The Minister shall receive any written complaint from a current tenant of a rental unit respecting the standard of maintenance that prevails with respect to the rental unit or the residential complex in which it is located if the prescribed maintenance standards apply to the residential complex.

Complaints to be investigated

(3) Upon receiving a complaint under this section, the Minister shall cause an inspector to make whatever inspection the Minister considers necessary to determine whether the landlord has complied with the prescribed maintenance standards.

Cost of inspection

(4) The Minister may charge a municipality and the municipality shall pay the Minister for the cost, as prescribed, associated with inspecting a residential complex in the municipality, for the purposes of investigating a complaint under this section and ensuring compliance with a work order under section 225.

Same

(5) If a municipality fails to make payment in full within 60 days after the Minister issues a notice of payment due under subsection (4), the notice of payment may be filed in the Superior Court of Justice and enforced as if it were a court order.

Inspector's work order

225(1) If an inspector is satisfied that the landlord of a residential complex has not complied with a prescribed maintenance standard that applies to the residential complex, the inspector may make and give to the landlord a work order requiring the landlord to comply with the prescribed maintenance standard.

Same

(2) The inspector shall set out in the order,

(a) the municipal address or legal description of the residential complex;

(b) reasonable particulars of the work to be performed;

(c) the period within which there must be compliance with the terms of the work order; and

(d) the time limit for applying under section 226 to the Board for a review of the work order.

Review of work order

226(1) If a landlord who has received an inspector's work order is not satisfied with its terms, the landlord may, within 20 days after the day the order is issued, apply to the Board for a review of the work order.

Order

(2) On an application under subsection (1), the Board may, by order,

(a) confirm or vary the inspector's work order;

(b) rescind the work order, if it finds that the landlord has complied with it; or

(c) quash the work order.

PART XV   ADMINISTRATION AND ENFORCEMENT

Duties of Minister

227. The Minister shall,

(a) monitor compliance with this Act;

(b) investigate cases of alleged failure to comply with this Act; and

(c) where the circumstances warrant, commence or cause to be commenced proceedings with respect to alleged failures to comply with this Act.

Delegation

228. The Minister may in writing delegate to any person any power or duty vested in the Minister under this Act, subject to the conditions set out in the delegation.

Investigators and inspectors

229. The Minister may appoint investigators for the purpose of investigating alleged offences and may appoint inspectors for the purposes of sections 224 and 225.

Inspections

230(1) Subject to subsection (6), an inspector may, at all reasonable times and upon producing proper identification, enter any property for the purpose of carrying out his or her duty under this Act and may,

(a) require the production for inspection of documents or things, including drawings or specifications, that may be relevant to the inspection;

(b) inspect and remove documents or things relevant to the inspection for the purpose of making copies or extracts;

(c) require information from any person concerning a matter related to the inspection;

(d) be accompanied by a person who has special or expert knowledge in relation to the subject-matter of the inspection;

(e) alone or in conjunction with a person possessing special or expert knowledge, make examinations or take tests, samples or photographs necessary for the purposes of the inspection; and

(f) order the landlord to take and supply at the landlord's expense such tests and samples as are specified in the order.

Samples

(2) The inspector shall divide the sample taken under clause (1)(e) into two parts and deliver one part to the person from whom the sample is taken, if the person so requests at the time the sample is taken and provides the necessary facilities.

Same

(3) If an inspector takes a sample under clause (1)(e) and has not divided the sample into two parts, a copy of any report on the sample shall be given to the person from whom the sample was taken.

Receipt

(4) An inspector shall provide a receipt for any documents or things removed under clause (1)(b) and shall promptly return them after the copies or extracts are made.

Evidence

(5) Copies of or extracts from documents and things removed under this section and certified as being true copies of or extracts from the originals by the person who made them are admissible in evidence to the same extent as and have the same evidentiary value as the originals.

Where warrant required

(6) Except under the authority of a warrant issued under section 231, an inspector shall not enter any room or place actually used as a dwelling without requesting and obtaining the consent of the occupier, first having informed the occupier that the right of entry may be refused and entry made only under the authority of a warrant.

Warrant

231(1) A provincial judge or justice of the peace may at any time issue a warrant authorizing a person named in the warrant to enter and search a building, receptacle or place if the provincial judge or justice of the peace is satisfied by information on oath that there are reasonable grounds to believe that an offence has been committed under this Act and the entry and search will afford evidence relevant to the commission of the offence.

Seizure

(2) In a warrant, the provincial judge or justice of the peace may authorize the person named in the warrant to seize anything that, based on reasonable grounds, will afford evidence relevant to the commission of the offence.

Receipt and removal

(3) Anyone who seizes something under a warrant shall,

(a) give a receipt for the thing seized to the person from whom it was seized; and

(b) bring the thing seized before the provincial judge or justice of the peace issuing the warrant or another provincial judge or justice to be dealt with according to law.

Expiry

(4) A warrant shall name the date upon which it expires, which shall be not later than 15 days after the warrant is issued.

Time of execution

(5) A warrant shall be executed between 6 a.m. and 9 p.m. unless it provides otherwise.

Other matters

(6) Sections 159 and 160 of the *Provincial Offences Act* apply with necessary modifications with respect to any thing seized under this section.

Protection from personal liability

232(1) No proceeding for damages shall be commenced against an investigator, an inspector, a member of the Board, a lawyer for the Board or an officer or employee of the Ministry or the Board for any act done in good faith in the performance or intended performance of any duty or in the exercise or intended exercise of any power under this Act or for any neglect or default in the performance or exercise in good faith of such a duty or power.

Crown liability

(2) Despite subsections 5(2) and (4) of the *Proceedings Against the Crown Act*, subsection (1) does not relieve the Crown of any liability to which it would otherwise be subject.

PART XVI   OFFENCES

Offences requiring knowledge

233. A person is guilty of an offence if the person knowingly,

(a) withholds the reasonable supply of a vital service, care service or food or interferes with the supply in contravention of section 21;

(b) alters or causes to be altered the locking system on any door giving entry to a rental unit or the residential complex in a manner that contravenes section 24 or 35;

(c) restricts reasonable access to the residential complex by political candidates or their authorized representatives in contravention of section 28;

(d) seizes any property of the tenant in contravention of section 40;

(e) fails to afford a tenant a right of first refusal in contravention of section 51 or 53;

(f) recovers possession of a rental unit without complying with the requirements of sections 52, 54 and 55;

(g) coerces a tenant to sign an agreement referred to in section 121;

(h) harasses, hinders, obstructs or interferes with a tenant in the exercise of,

(i) securing a right or seeking relief under this Act or in a court,

(ii) participating in a proceeding under this Act, or

(iii) participating in a tenants' association or attempting to organize a tenants' association;

(i) harasses, coerces, threatens or interferes with a tenant in such a manner that the tenant is induced to vacate the rental unit;

(j) harasses, hinders, obstructs or interferes with a landlord in the exercise of,

(i) securing a right or seeking relief under this Act or in a court, or

(ii) participating in a proceeding under this Act;

(k) obtains possession of a rental unit improperly by giving a notice to terminate in bad faith; or

(l) coerces a tenant of a mobile home park or land lease community to enter into an agency agreement for the sale or lease of their mobile home or land lease home or requires an agency agreement as a condition of entering into a tenancy agreement.

Other offences

234. A person is guilty of an offence if the person,

(a) enters a rental unit where such entry is not permitted by section 26, 27 or 142 or enters without first complying with the requirements of section 26, 27 or 142;

(b) fails to make an evicted tenant's property available for retrieval in accordance with subsection 41(3);

(c) gives a notice to terminate a tenancy under section 48 or 49 in contravention of section 51;

(d) requires or receives a security deposit from a tenant contrary to section 105;

(e) fails to pay to the tenant annually interest on the rent deposit held in respect of their tenancy in accordance with section 106;

(f) fails to apply the rent deposit held in respect of a tenancy to the rent for the last month of the tenancy in contravention of subsection 106(10);

(g) fails to repay an amount received as a rent deposit as required by subsection 107(1) or (2);

(h) fails to provide a tenant or former tenant with a receipt in accordance with section 109;

(i) fails to provide the notice in the form required under section 114 or gives false information in the notice;

(j) requires a tenant to pay rent proposed in an application in contravention of subsection 126(5);

(k) fails to provide information on the total cost of utilities in accordance with subsection 128(2);

(l) charges or collects amounts from a tenant, a prospective tenant, a subtenant, a potential subtenant, an assignee or a potential assignee in contravention of section 134;

(l.1) terminates the obligation to supply electricity without the tenant's consent in contravention of subsection 137(3);

(l.2) charges a tenant a portion of the cost of the utility without the consent of the tenant in contravention of subsection 138(1);

(m) gives a notice of rent increase or a notice of increase of a charge in a care home without first giving an information package contrary to section 140;

(n) does anything to prevent a tenant of a care home from obtaining care services from a person of the tenant's choice contrary to clause 147(a);

(o) interferes with the provision of care services to a tenant of a care home contrary to clause 147(b);

(p) increases a charge for providing a care service or meals to a tenant in a care home in contravention of section 150;

(q) interferes with a tenant's right under section 156 to sell or lease his or her mobile home;

(r) restricts the right of a tenant of a mobile home park or land lease community to purchase goods or services from the person of his or her choice in contravention of section 160;

(s) charges an illegal contingency fee in contravention of subsection 214(1);

(t) fails to comply with any or all of the items contained in a work order issued under section 225;

(u) obstructs or interferes with an inspector exercising a power of entry under section 230 or 231 or with an investigator exercising a power of entry under section 231;

(v) furnishes false or misleading information in any material filed in any proceeding under this Act or provided to the Board, an employee or official of the Board, an inspector, an investigator, the Minister or a designate of the Minister;

(w) unlawfully recovers possession of a rental unit;

(x) charges rent in an amount greater than permitted under this Act; or

(y) contravenes an order of the Board that,

(i) orders a landlord to do specified repairs or replacements or other work within a specified time,

(ii) orders that a landlord, a superintendent or an agent of a landlord may not engage in any further activities listed in paragraphs 2 to 6 of subsection 29(1) against any of the tenants in a residential complex, or

(iii) orders a landlord not to breach an obligation under subsection 41(2) or (3) again.

Harassment, interference with reasonable enjoyment

235(1) Any landlord or superintendent, agent or employee of the landlord who knowingly harasses a tenant or interferes with a tenant's reasonable enjoyment of a rental unit or the residential complex in which it is located is guilty of an offence.

Exception

(2) For the purposes of subsection (1), the carrying out of repairs, maintenance and capital improvements does not constitute harassment or interference with a tenant's reasonable enjoyment of a rental unit or the residential complex in which it is located unless it is reasonable to believe,

(a) that the date or time when the work is done or the manner in which it is carried out is intended to harass the tenant or interfere with the tenant's reasonable enjoyment; or

(b) that the repairs, maintenance or capital improvements were carried out without reasonable regard for the tenant's right to reasonable enjoyment.

Attempts

236. Any person who knowingly attempts to commit any offence referred to in section 233, 234 or 235 is guilty of an offence.

Directors and officers

237. Every director or officer of a corporation who knowingly concurs in an offence under this Act is guilty of an offence.

Penalties

238(1) A person, other than a corporation, who is guilty of an offence under this Act is liable on conviction to a fine of not more than $25,000.

Same

(2) A corporation that is guilty of an offence under this Act is liable on conviction to a fine of not more than $100,000.

Limitation

239(1) No proceeding shall be commenced respecting an offence under clause 234(v) more than two years after the date on which the facts giving rise to the offence came to the attention of the Minister.

Same

(2) No proceeding shall be commenced respecting any other offence under this Act more than two years after the date on which the offence was, or is alleged to have been, committed.

Evidence

Proof of filed documents

240(1) The production by a person prosecuting a person for an offence under this Act of a certificate, statement or document that appears to have been filed with or delivered to the Board by or on behalf of the person charged with the offence shall be received as evidence that the certificate, statement or document was so filed or delivered.

Proof of making

(2) The production by a person prosecuting a person for an offence under this Act of a certificate, statement or document that appears to have been made or signed by the person charged with the offence or on the person's behalf shall be received as evidence that the certificate, statement or document was so made or signed.

Proof of making, Board or Minister

(3) The production by a person prosecuting a person for an offence under this Act of any order, certificate, statement or document, or of any record within the meaning of section 20 of the *Statutory Powers Procedure Act*, that appears to have been made, signed or issued by the Board, the Minister, an employee of the Board or an employee of the Ministry, shall be received as evidence that the order, certificate, statement, document or record was so made, signed or issued.

True copies

(4) Subsections (1) to (3) apply, with necessary modifications, to any extract or copy of a certificate, statement, document, order or record referred to in those subsections, if the extract or copy is certified as a true extract or copy by the person who made the extract or copy.

PART XVII REGULATIONS

Regulations

241(1) The Lieutenant Governor in Council may make regulations,

1. prescribing circumstances under which one or more rental units that form part of a residential complex, rather than the entire residential complex, are care homes for the purposes of the definition of "care home" in subsection 2(1);

2. prescribing services that are to be included or not included in the definition of "care services" in subsection 2(1);

3. prescribing charges not to be included in the definition of "municipal taxes and charges" in subsection 2(1);

4. prescribing persons that are to be included or are not to be included in the definition of "tenant" in subsection 2(1) and exempting any such persons from any provision of the Act specified in the regulation;

5. prescribing, for the purposes of the definition of "vital service" in subsection 2(1), the part of each year during which heat is a vital service;

6. prescribing classes of accommodation for the purposes of clause 5(n);

7. prescribing federal, provincial or municipal programs for the purpose of paragraph 3 of subsection 7(1);

8. providing that specified provisions of this Act apply with respect to any specified housing project, housing program, rental unit, residential complex or other residential accommodation or any class of them;

9. exempting any housing project, housing program, rental unit, residential complex or other residential accommodation or any class of them from any provision of this Act;

10. prescribing grounds of an application for the purposes of clause 9(1)(b);

11. respecting the rules for making findings for the purposes of subsection 9(2);

12. prescribing for the purposes of section 22, paragraph 3 of subsection 29(1) and subsection 31(1),

    i. standards and criteria to be applied by the Board in determining if a landlord, superintendent or agent of a landlord has substantially interfered with the reasonable enjoyment of a rental unit or residential complex in carrying out maintenance, repairs or capital improvements to the unit or complex, and

    ii. criteria to be applied by the Board in determining whether to order an abatement of rent under subsection 31(1) when a landlord, superintendent or agent of a landlord is found to have substantially interfered with the reasonable enjoyment of a rental unit or residential complex in carrying out maintenance, repairs or capital improvements to the unit or complex and rules for calculating the amount of the abatement;

13. prescribing the hours during which a landlord is required to make an evicted tenant's property available to be retrieved under subsection 41(3);

14. prescribing conditions applicable to discounts referred to in subsection 111 (2) or paragraph 1 of subsection 111(2.1);

15. prescribing discounts for the purpose of paragraph 2 of subsection 111(2.1);

16. prescribing rules for the purpose of subsection 111(3) for calculating the lawful rent which may be charged where a landlord provides a tenant with a discount in rent at the beginning of, or during, a tenancy, and prescribing different rules for different types of discounts;

17. prescribing rules for the purpose of subsection 111(4) for the calculation of lawful rent where the rent a landlord charges for the first rental period of a tenancy is greater than the rent the landlord charges for any subsequent rental period;

18. prescribing the circumstances under which lawful rent for the purposes of section 112 will be other than that provided for in section 112 and providing the lawful rent under those circumstances;

19. prescribing information to be included in a notice under clause 114(3)(e);

20. prescribing information to be filed and the time in which it is to be filed for the purposes of subsection 115(4);

21. respecting rules for increasing or decreasing rent charged for the purposes of sections 123 and 125;

22. prescribing services, facilities, privileges, accommodations and things for the purposes of paragraph 2 of subsection 123(1);

23. defining or describing the method for determining what constitutes "extraordinary increase" for the purpose of section 126;

24. prescribing rules governing making information available under subsection 126(4);

25. prescribing the rules for making findings for the purposes of subsection 126(10);

26. prescribing rules governing the time period to be specified in an order under clause 126(10)(b);

27. prescribing rules for the purpose of clause 126(11)(b);

28. prescribing rules for the purposes of section 127;

29. prescribing rules for the purposes of subsection 128(2);

30. prescribing a percentage, a period and rules for the purposes of subsection 128(3);

31. prescribing rules governing the determination of the date to be specified in an order under clause 129(b);

32. prescribing rules governing the determination of the percentage by which rent is required to be reduced under subclause 129(c)(ii);

33. prescribing the rules for making findings for the purposes of subsection 130(3);

34. prescribing percentages and rules for the purposes of subsection 131(1);

35. prescribing rules for the purposes of subsection 131(2);

36. prescribing a number of rental units, a period and methods of service for the purposes of subsection 131(3);

37. prescribing circumstances for the purposes of subsection 132(1);

38. prescribing a period of time for the purposes of subsection 132(2);

39. prescribing rules for the purposes of subsection 132(3);

40. prescribing the rules for making findings for the purposes of subsection 133(2) and for determining the effective date for an order under subsection 133(3);

41. exempting specified payments from the operation of section 134;

42. prescribing rules governing the provision of notice for the purposes of clause 137(2)(c);

43. prescribing rules governing the provision of a notice for the purposes of clause 137(3)(b);

44. prescribing the circumstances and the rules governing the reduction of rent for the purposes of clause 137(3)(c);

45. prescribing the information to be provided to the tenant for the purposes of subsection 137(4);

45.1 prescribing the circumstances and conditions to be met for the purposes of subsection 137(5);

45.2 prescribing the time, the circumstances and the rules for the purposes of subsection 137(6);

45.3 prescribing the circumstances under which a landlord is exempt from complying with subsection 137(7);

45.4 prescribing a period for the purposes of paragraph 1 of subsection 137(7);

46. prescribing information to be provided to a prospective tenant for the purposes of paragraph 3 of subsection 137(7);

47. prescribing the portions of information to be provided and prescribing other circumstances for the purposes of subsection 137(8);

48. prescribing the rules and the requirements for the purposes of clauses 137(9)(a), (b) and (c);

48.1 prescribing other circumstances for the purposes of subsection 137(10);

49. prescribing circumstances in which a tenant may apply to the Board under subsection 137(11);

49.1 prescribing the circumstances under which subsection 137(15) would not apply;

50. prescribing rules governing charging tenants a portion of the cost of a utility for the purposes of subsection 138(1);

51. prescribing rules governing the provision of a notice for the purposes of clause 138(1)(a);

52. prescribing rules governing the reduction of rent for the purposes of clause 138(1)(b);

52. prescribing rules governing the reduction of rent for the purposes of clause 138(1)(b);

52.1 prescribing a period for the purposes of paragraph 2 of subsection 138(4);

53. prescribing information to be provided to a prospective tenant for the purposes of paragraph 4 of subsection 138(4);

54. prescribing the rules and the requirements for the purposes of clauses 138(5)(a), (b) and (c);

55. prescribing circumstances in which a tenant may apply to the Board under subsection 138(6);

56. prescribing the information that shall be contained in an information package for the purposes of section 140;

57. prescribing a period for the purpose of clause 144(1)(b);

58. prescribing an amount for the purposes of paragraph 2 of subsection 164(2);

59. prescribing an amount for the purposes of section 165;

60. prescribing services and things for the purposes of section 167;

61. respecting the appointment, including the status, duties and benefits, of employees of the Board for the purposes of section 178;

62. prescribing information to be filed with an application to the Board for the purposes of subsection 185(1);

63. prescribing information to be provided under subsection 189(1);

64. prescribing circumstances for the purposes of subsection 189(2);

65. prescribing time requirements that cannot be extended or shortened for the purposes of subsection 190(2);

66. restricting the circumstances in which the Board may, under section 195, require a person to make a payment into the Board;

67. governing the management and investment of money paid into the Board, providing for the payment of interest on money paid into the Board and fixing the rate of interest so paid;

68. prescribing forms of housing assistance for the purposes of clause 203(b);

69. prescribing an amount for the purposes of subsection 207(4);

70. governing electronic documents for the purposes of section 213, including specifying the types of documents that may be dealt with electronically for the purposes of that section, regulating the use of electronic signatures in such documents and providing for the creating, filing, providing, issuing,

sending, receiving, storing, transferring and retaining of such documents;

71. prescribing an amount for the purposes of subsection 214(1);

72. prescribing maintenance standards for the purposes of section 224;

73. prescribing other criteria for determining areas in which maintenance standards apply for the purposes of clause 224(1)(c);

74. respecting the amount or the determination of the amount the Minister may charge a municipality for the purposes of subsection 224(4), including payments to inspectors, overhead costs related to inspections and interest on overdue accounts;

75. making a regulation made under paragraph 25, 26, 66 or 67 applicable, with necessary modifications, to an application to which subsection 242(6) or (7) applies, and providing that the regulation applies despite any regulations made under the *Tenant Protection Act, 1997*;

76. defining "serious" as it is used in any provision of this Act and defining it differently for different provisions;

77. defining any word or expression used in this Act that has not already been expressly defined in this Act;

78. prescribing any matter required or permitted by this Act to be prescribed.

Same

(2) A regulation made under subsection (1) may be general or particular in its application.

PART XVIII   TRANSITION

Applications made under Tenant Protection Act, 1997

242(1) Despite the repeal of the *Tenant Protection Act, 1997* but subject to the other provisions of this section, that Act shall be deemed to be continued in force for the purpose only of continuing and finally disposing of applications that were made under that Act before that Act was repealed, including any appeals, motions or other steps in those applications.

Default orders

(2) Sections 177 and 192 of the *Tenant Protection Act, 1997* do not apply to an application referred to in subsection 192(1) of that Act unless, before that Act was repealed, an order was made with respect to the application without holding a hearing.

Powers on eviction applications

(3) Section 83 of this Act applies, with necessary modifications, and section 84 of the *Tenant Protection Act, 1997* does not apply, to an application made under the *Tenant Protection Act, 1997* before that Act was repealed for an order evicting a tenant, unless the final order in the application was made before that Act was repealed.

Eviction orders for arrears of rent

(4) If, pursuant to subsection (1), subsections 72(4) to (10) of the *Tenant Protection Act, 1997* apply to an eviction order,

subsections 74(11) to (18) of this Act also apply, with necessary modifications, to the eviction order.

Eviction and other orders for arrears of rent

(5) Section 82 of this Act applies, with necessary modifications, to an application by a landlord under section 69 of the *Tenant Protection Act, 1997* for an order terminating a tenancy and evicting a tenant based on a notice of termination under section 61 of that Act, and to an application by a landlord under subsection 86(1) of that Act, unless the final order in the application was made before that Act was repealed.

Breach of landlord's responsibility to repair

(6) Section 195 of this Act applies, with necessary modifications, and section 182 of the *Tenant Protection Act, 1997* does not apply, to an application made under subsection 32(1) of that Act before it was repealed for an order determining that a landlord breached the obligations under subsection 24(1) or 110(1) of that Act, unless a final order was made under subsection 34(1) or 110(3) of that Act before it was repealed.

Application for above guideline increase

(7) Subsections 126(12) and (13) of this Act apply, with necessary modifications, to an application made under section 138 of the *Tenant Protection Act, 1997*, unless a final order was made under subsection 138(6) or (10) of that Act before it was repealed.

Proceedings before other bodies under earlier legislation

243. Section 223 of the *Tenant Protection Act, 1997* continues to apply, despite the repeal of that Act.

Orders, etc., under former Act

244. Subject to section 242, a reference in this Act to an order, application, notice, by-law or other thing made, given, passed or otherwise done under a provision of this Act includes a reference to an order, application, notice, by-law or thing made, given, passed or done under the corresponding provision of the *Tenant Protection Act, 1997*.

Information from former Rent Registry

245(1) The Board shall provide any information it received under subsection 157(3) of the *Tenant Protection Act, 1997* to members of the public on request.

Application

(2) Subsection (1) does not apply after the first anniversary of the date this section comes into force.

Use of certain forms

246. Despite the repeal of the *Tenant Protection Act, 1997*, the form of a notice of rent increase, notice of increased charges in a care home or notice of termination that could have been used under that Act may be used for the corresponding purpose under this Act any time within two months after this section comes into force.

Regulations Under the RTA

ONTARIO REGULATION 516/06
GENERAL

Consolidation Period: From January 1, 2011 to the e-Laws currency date.

This is the most current consolidation of this law available on e-Laws.

There may be more recent events that are not included in this notice.

Last amendment: O. Reg. 395/10.

CONTENTS

PART I   INTERPRETATION AND EXEMPTIONS

Definition of "care home"

1(1) One or more rental units that form part of a residential complex are care homes for the purpose of the definition of "care home" in subsection 2(1) of the Act if the rental units are occupied or intended to be occupied by persons for the purpose of receiving care services, whether or not receiving the care services is the primary purpose of the occupancy.

(2) Subsection (1) applies even if a third party rents the rental unit from the landlord and provides or arranges to provide both the rental unit and care services to the tenant.

Definition of "care services"

2(1) As part of health care services, rehabilitative services, therapeutic services and services that provide assistance with the activities of daily living, the following are included in the definition of "care services" in subsection 2(1) of the Act:

1. Nursing care.
2. Administration and supervision of medication prescribed by a medical doctor.
3. Assistance with feeding.
4. Bathing assistance.
5. Incontinence care.
6. Dressing assistance.
7. Assistance with personal hygiene.
8. Ambulatory assistance.
9. Personal emergency response services.

(2) The following services are included in the definition of "care services" in subsection 2(1) of the Act if they are provided along with any service set out in subsection (1):

1. Recreational or social activities.
2. Housekeeping.
3. Laundry services.
4. Assistance with transportation.

Definition of "tenant"

3(1) If a tenant of a rental unit dies and the rental unit is the principal residence of the spouse of that tenant, the spouse is included in the definition of "tenant" in subsection 2(1) of the Act unless the spouse vacates the unit within the 30-day period described in subsection 91(1) of the Act.

(2) If a tenant vacates a rental unit without giving a notice of termination under the Act and without entering into an agreement to terminate the tenancy, and the rental unit is the principal residence of the spouse of that tenant, the spouse is included in the definition of "tenant" in subsection 2(1) of the Act.

(3) Subsection (2) does not apply if any one or more of the following criteria are satisfied:

1. The rental unit is in a building containing not more than three residential units and the landlord resides in the building.
2. The spouse vacates the rental unit no later than 60 days after the tenant vacated the rental unit.
3. The tenant who vacated the rental unit was not in arrears of rent and the spouse fails to advise the landlord, before an order is issued under section 100 of the Act, that he or she intends to remain in the rental unit.
4. The tenant who vacated the rental unit was in arrears of rent, the landlord gives the spouse a notice in a form approved by the Board within 45 days after the date the tenant vacated the unit, and the spouse fails, within 15 days after receiving the notice,
   i. to advise the landlord that he or she intends to remain in the rental unit, or
   ii. to agree in writing with the landlord to pay the arrears of rent.
5. The tenant who vacated the rental unit was in arrears of rent, the landlord does not give the spouse a notice referred to in paragraph 4 within 45 days after the date the tenant vacated the unit, and the spouse fails, before an order is issued under section 100 of the Act,
   i. to advise the landlord that he or she intends to remain in the rental unit, or
   ii. to agree in writing with the landlord to pay the arrears of rent.

(4) Subsections (1) and (2) do not apply to,
   (a) a rental unit described in section 7 of the Act;
   (b) a rental unit that is in a care home to which Part IX of the Act applies; or
   (c) a rental unit to which section 6 of this Regulation applies.

Definition of "vital service"

4(1) For the purpose of the definition of "vital service" in subsection 2(1) of the Act, September 1 to June 15 is prescribed as the part of the year during which heat is a vital service.

(2) For the purposes of subsection (1), heat shall be provided so that the room temperature at 1.5 metres above floor level and one metre from exterior walls in all habitable space and in any area intended for normal use by tenants, including recreation rooms and laundry rooms but excluding locker rooms and garages, is at least 20 degrees Celsius.

(3) Subsection (2) does not apply to a rental unit in which the tenant can regulate the temperature and a minimum temperature of 20 degrees Celsius can be maintained by the primary source of heat.

Prescribed programs

5. The following federal, provincial or municipal programs are prescribed for the purposes of paragraph 3 of subsection 7(1) of the Act:

1. Non-Profit Low Rental Housing Program established under the *National Housing Act* (Canada).
2. Non-Profit 2% Write-Down Non-Profit Housing Program established under the *National Housing Act* (Canada).
3. Non-Profit Full Assistance Housing Programs administered before January 1, 2001 by the Ministry, not including the Municipal Non-Profit Housing Program, but including,
   i. JobsOntario Homes,
   ii. The Ontario Non-Profit Housing Program (P-3000),
   iii. The Ontario Non-Profit Housing Program (P-3600),
   iv. The Ontario Non-Profit Housing Program (P-10,000),
   v. Homes Now, and
   vi. Federal/Provincial Non-Profit Housing Program (1986-1993).
4. Municipal Non-Profit Housing Program (1978-1985).
5. Municipal Assisted Housing Program (Toronto Housing Company).
6. Urban Native Fully Targeted Housing Program established under the *National Housing Act* (Canada).
7. Urban Native 2% Write-Down and Additional Assistance Program established under the *National Housing Act* (Canada).

Exemptions from certain provisions

6(1) Section 8, paragraphs 6, 7 and 8 of subsection 30(1), sections 51, 52, 54, 55, 56 and 95 to 99, subsection 100(2) and sections 101, 102, 104, 111 to 115, 117, 120, 121, 122, 126 to 133, 140, 143, 149, 150, 151, 159, 165 and 167 of the Act do not apply to rental units that meet the criteria set out in subsection (2) and that were developed or acquired under the following initiatives:

1. Canada-Ontario Affordable Housing Program—Rental and Supportive Housing.
2. Canada-Ontario Affordable Housing Program—Northern Housing.
3. Residential Rehabilitation Assistance Program.
4. Supporting Communities Partnership Initiative.
5. Municipal capital facility by-laws for housing or other council-approved municipal housing programs.

(2) Subsection (1) applies to a rental unit described in that subsection if,

(a) the unit is subject to an agreement related to the provision of housing services between the landlord and one or more of,

(i) a municipality,

(ii) an agency of a municipality,

(iii) a non-profit corporation controlled by a municipality, if an object of the non-profit corporation is the provision of housing,

(iv) a local housing corporation, as defined in the *Social Housing Reform Act, 2000*, or

(v) a service manager as defined in the *Social Housing Reform Act, 2000*;

(b) the unit is identified as a subsidized unit that was developed or acquired under an initiative listed in subsection (1), and as being subject to an agreement described in clause (a), in,

(i) the tenancy agreement, or

(ii) a written notice that was given by the landlord to the tenant, if the tenancy agreement was entered into before January 31, 2007; and

(c) the tenant, at the time the tenancy agreement was entered into, was on or was eligible to be on a social housing waiting list.

(3) Section 8, paragraphs 6, 7 and 8 of subsection 30(1), sections 51, 52, 54, 55, 56 and 95 to 99, subsection 100(2) and sections 101, 102, 104, 111 to 115, 117, 120, 121, 122, 126 to 133, 140, 143, 149, 150, 151, 159, 165 and 167 of the Act do not apply to rental units that were developed or acquired, and that continue to operate, under the Rural and Native Rental Housing Program established under the *National Housing Act* (Canada).

(4) Section 119 of the Act does not apply to a rental unit that is exempt under subsection (1) or (3) if the tenant occupying the unit pays rent in an amount geared-to-income due to public funding.

(5) Sections 116 and 118 of the Act do not apply to increases in rent for a rental unit due to increases in the tenant's income if the rental unit is exempt under subsection (1) or (3) and the tenant pays rent in an amount geared-to-income due to public funding.

(6) Paragraph 2 of subsection 58(1) and subsection 60(1) of the Act apply to a rental unit described in subsection (1) or (3) of this section, even though the rental unit is not a rental unit described in paragraph 1, 2, 3 or 4 of subsection 7(1) of the Act.

Rental unit in care home

7(1) Subsections 37(4) and (5) of the Act do not apply to a rental unit in a care home if,

(a) the rental unit is occupied for the purpose of receiving rehabilitative or therapeutic services agreed upon by the tenant and the landlord;

(b) the period of occupancy agreed to by the tenant and the landlord is no more than four years;

(c) the tenancy agreement stipulates that the tenancy may be terminated and the tenant evicted when the objectives of the services have been met or will not be met; and

(d) the unit is subject to an agreement for the provision of housing services between the landlord and a service manager as defined in the *Social Housing Reform Act, 2000*.

(2) If a landlord makes an application under subsection 77(1) of the Act and the application is based on a notice or agreement to which, pursuant to subsection (1), subsections 37(4) and (5) of the Act do not apply, the expression "the termination date specified in the agreement or notice" in subsection 77(3) of the Act means the earlier of the following dates:

1. The last day of the period of occupancy referred to in clause (1)(b).

2. The day that is 60 days after the day the tenant received notice from the landlord that the objectives of the services have been met or will not be met.

(3) For greater certainty, for the purposes of clause (1)(c) and subsection (2), the objectives of the services will not be met if the tenant has repeatedly and substantially withdrawn from participation in the services.

PART II   MATTERS RELATING TO RENT

Reasonable enjoyment during repairs

Definition

8(1) In this section,

"work" means maintenance, repairs or capital improvements carried out in a rental unit or a residential complex.

(2) For the purposes of section 22, paragraph 3 of subsection 29(1) and subsection 31(1) of the Act, this section applies to the Board in making a determination,

(a) as to whether a landlord, superintendent or agent of a landlord, in carrying out work in a rental unit or residential complex, substantially interfered with the reasonable enjoyment of the unit or complex for all usual purposes by a tenant or former tenant, or by a member of the household of a tenant or former tenant; and

(b) whether an abatement of rent is justified in the circumstances.

(3) In making a determination described in subsection (2),

(a) the Board shall consider the effect of the carrying out of the work on the use of the rental unit or residential complex by the tenant or former tenant, and by members of the household of the tenant or former tenant; and

(b) the Board shall not determine that an interference was substantial unless the carrying out of the work constituted an interference that was unreasonable in the circumstances with the use and enjoyment of the rental unit or residential complex by the tenant or former tenant, or by a member of the household of the tenant or former tenant.

(4) If the Board finds that the landlord, superintendent or agent of the landlord, in carrying out work in a rental unit or residential complex, substantially interfered with the reasonable enjoyment of the unit or complex for all usual purposes by a tenant or former tenant, or by a member of the household of a tenant or former tenant, the Board shall not order an abatement of rent if all of the following conditions are satisfied:

1. The landlord gave notice to the tenant or former tenant at least 60 days before the commencement of the work, or, in cases of emergency, as soon as was reasonable in the circumstances, concerning the work to be carried out.

2. The landlord gave notice to any prospective tenant of a rental unit at the first opportunity to do so before the landlord entered into a new tenancy agreement with that tenant.

3. The notice describes the nature of the work to be carried out, the expected impact on tenants and members of their households and the length of time the work is expected to take.

4. The notice was reasonably accurate and comprehensive in the circumstances at the time it was given.

5. If there was a significant change in the information provided under paragraph 3, the landlord provided to the tenant or former tenant an update to the notice in a timely manner.

6. The work,
   i. is necessary to protect or restore the physical integrity of the residential complex or part of it,
   ii. is necessary to comply with maintenance, health, safety or other housing related standards required by law,
   iii. is necessary to maintain a plumbing, heating, mechanical, electrical, ventilation or air conditioning system,
   iv. provides access for persons with disabilities,
   v. promotes energy or water conservation, or
   vi. maintains or improves the security of the residential complex.

7. If required under the *Building Code Act, 1992*, a permit was issued in respect of the work.

8. The work was carried out at reasonable times, or if a municipal noise control by-law was in effect, during the times permitted under the noise control by-law.

9. The duration of the work was reasonable in the circumstances.
10. The landlord took reasonable steps to minimize any interference resulting from noise associated with the work.

(5) If the Board finds that the landlord, superintendent or agent of the landlord, in carrying out work in a rental unit or residential complex, substantially interfered with the reasonable enjoyment of the unit or complex for all usual purposes by a tenant or former tenant, or by a member of the household of a tenant or former tenant, and an abatement of rent is not prohibited under subsection (4), the Board shall consider the following in determining whether it is appropriate to order an abatement of rent and the amount of the abatement:

1. The nature, duration and degree of interference with the reasonable enjoyment of the rental unit or residential complex that was caused by the carrying out of the work.
2. Whether the tenant or former tenant is responsible for any undue delay in the carrying out of the work.
3. The steps taken by the landlord during the work to minimize interference with the reasonable enjoyment of the rental unit or residential complex.
4. Whether the tenant or former tenant took advantage of any service provided by the landlord or arrangement made by the landlord that would minimize interference with the reasonable enjoyment of the rental unit or residential complex.
5. Whether a failure to carry out the work could, within a reasonable period of time, reasonably be expected to result in,
    i. interference with the reasonable enjoyment of the rental unit or residential complex for all usual purposes by a tenant or member of his or her household,
    ii. a reduction or discontinuation of a service or facility,
    iii. damage or additional damage to the rental unit, the residential complex or anything in the unit or complex,
    iv. a risk to any person's health or personal safety, or
    v. a breach of section 20 or section 161 of the Act by the landlord.

(6) Except as permitted under subsection (7), no abatement of rent shall exceed 25 per cent of the monthly rent for each month or part of a month during which there was substantial interference with the reasonable enjoyment of the rental unit or residential complex for all usual purposes by the tenant or former tenant, or by a member of the household of the tenant or former tenant.

(7) The Board may order an abatement of rent that exceeds 25 per cent of the monthly rent for a rental unit if,

(a) the Board considers a larger abatement to be warranted in the circumstances because the interference with the reasonable enjoyment of the rental unit or residential complex far exceeded the level that would normally be expected, taking into consideration all of the relevant circumstances; and

(b) the Board is satisfied that,

(i) the work is not work described in paragraph 6 of subsection (4),

(ii) the work was carried out at unreasonable times or at a time that is not permitted under any applicable noise control by-law,

(iii) the work was carried out in a manner that contravened a condition or requirement of a building permit issued under the *Building Code Act, 1992,*

(iv) the work was carried out over a period of time far in excess of the amount of time that normally would be required, after taking into consideration any exceptional circumstances beyond the control of the landlord, including weather-related delays, delays in obtaining necessary government approvals or permits and delays caused by market shortages of suitable goods or services or qualified labour at reasonable costs, or

(v) the landlord refused to take reasonable steps during the work to minimize interference with the reasonable enjoyment of the rental unit or residential complex for all usual purposes by the tenant or former tenant, or by a member of the household of the tenant or former tenant.

(8) The Board shall not order an abatement of rent that exceeds 100 per cent of the monthly rent for each month or part of a month during which the Board determines that the work substantially interfered with the reasonable enjoyment of the rental unit or residential complex for all usual purposes by the tenant or former tenant, or by a member of the household of the tenant or former tenant.

Receipt

9. A document constitutes a receipt for the purposes of section 109 of the Act if it includes, at a minimum,

(a) the address of the rental unit to which the receipt applies;

(b) the name of the tenants to whom the receipt applies;

(c) the amount and date for each payment received for any rent, rent deposit, arrears of rent, or any other amount paid to the landlord and shall specify what the payment was for;

(d) the name of the landlord of the rental unit; and

(e) the signature of the landlord or the landlord's authorized agent.

Prescribed conditions under s. 111(2) and (2.1), par. 1 of the Act

10(0.1) The only condition prescribed for the purpose of subsection 111(2) of the Act is that the discount must be provided for in a written or oral agreement.

(1) The following conditions are prescribed for the purpose of paragraph 1 of subsection 111(2.1) of the Act:

1. The discount must be provided for in a written agreement.

2. If the rent is paid monthly and the discount is equal to the rent for one month or less, the entire discount must be taken during one rental period.

3. If the rent is paid monthly and the discount is equal to the rent for a period greater than one month but not more than two months, the discount equal to the rent for one month must be taken during one rental period and the balance within one other rental period.

4. If the rent is paid monthly and the discount is equal to the rent for a period greater than two months but not more than three months, the discount equal to the rent for two months must be taken for two rental periods and the balance within one other rental period.

5. If the rent is paid daily or weekly, the discount must be taken in periods that are at least one week in duration.

(2) REVOKED.

Prescribed discounts under s. 111(2.1), par. 2 of the Act

11(1) The following discounts are prescribed for the purposes of paragraph 2 of subsection 111(2.1) of the Act:

1. A discount provided for in a written agreement, if the total amount of the discount that is provided during the first eight months of the 12-month period does not exceed the rent for one month.

2. A discount provided for in a written agreement, if,
    i. the total amount of the discount that is provided in the 12-month period does not exceed the rent for two months,
    ii. the total amount of the discount that is provided in the first seven months of the 12-month period does not exceed the rent for one month, and
    iii. any discount that is provided in the last five months of the 12-month period is provided in only one of those months and does not exceed the rent for one month.

3. A discount provided under a tenancy agreement that operates under the Strong Communities Housing Allowance Program—Toronto Pilot, if the landlord sets out the discounted rent and the undiscounted rent in the written tenancy agreement and in a written notice to the tenant accompanying any notice of rent increase given to the tenant under section 116 of the Act.

(2) In this section,

"the 12-month period" means,

   (a) the 12-month period following the commencement of the tenancy,

   (b) the 12-month period following any rent increase taken after the 12-month period described in clause (a), other than a rent increase taken under section 123 of the Act, or

   (c) where clauses (a) and (b) do not apply, the 12-month period following the most recent anniversary of a rent increase taken in accordance with section 116 of the Act or, where no rent increase has been taken in accordance with section 116 of the Act, the commencement of the tenancy.

Calculation of lawful rent

12(1) The rules set out in this section apply in calculating lawful rent under subsection 111(3) of the Act.

(2) The lawful rent for any rental period in the 12-month period shall be calculated in the following manner:

1. Add the sum of the rents that are actually charged or to be charged in each of the rental periods in the 12-month period to the largest eligible discount determined under subsection (6).

2. Divide the amount determined under paragraph 1 by the number of rental periods in the 12-month period.

3. Add to the amount determined under paragraph 2 any rent increases under section 123 of the Act and subtract from that amount any rent decreases under section 125 of the Act.

(3) Despite subsection (2), if a landlord provides a discount in rent that is greater than 2 per cent of the rent that could otherwise be lawfully charged for a rental period for paying rent on or before the date it is due, the lawful rent shall be calculated by dividing the discounted rent by 0.98.

(4) Despite subsections (2) and (3), if the landlord provides a discount in rent described in subsection 111(2) of the Act and another discount, other than a discount described in subsection 111(2.1) of the Act, the lawful rent for any rental period in the 12-month period shall be calculated in the following manner:

1. Add the sum of the rents that are actually charged or to be charged in each of the rental periods in the 12-month period to the sum of the discounts described in subsection 111(2) of the Act actually provided or to be provided to the tenant during the 12-month period.

2. Add the amount determined under paragraph 1 to the largest eligible discount determined under subsection (6).

3. Divide the amount determined under paragraph 2 by the number of rental periods in the 12-month period.

4. Add to the amount determined under paragraph 3 any rent increases under section 123 of the Act and subtract from that amount any rent decreases under section 125 of the Act.

(5) Despite subsections (2) and (3), if the landlord provides a discount in rent that is greater than 2 per cent of the rent that could otherwise be lawfully charged for a rental period for paying rent on or before the date it is due, and the landlord also provides another discount in rent, other than a discount described in subsection 111(2.1) of the Act, the lawful rent for any rental period in the 12-month period shall be calculated in the following manner:

1. Divide the discounted rent by 0.98.
2. Multiply the amount determined under paragraph 1 by the number of rental periods in the 12-month period and add the result to the largest eligible discount determined under subsection (6).
3. Divide the amount determined under paragraph 2 by the number of rental periods in the 12-month period.
4. Add to the amount determined under paragraph 3 any rent increases under section 123 of the Act and subtract from that amount any rent decreases under section 125 of the Act.

(6) For the purpose of this section, the largest eligible discount shall be determined in accordance with the following rules:

1. In the case of a discount that is provided for in a written agreement, the largest eligible discount is the largest of the following amounts:
   i. The lesser of the following amounts:
      A. The sum of the discounts in rent during the first eight months of the 12-month period.
      B. The rent for one month.
   ii. The largest discount in rent during any month in the last five months of the 12-month period, plus the lesser of the following amounts:
      A. The sum of the discounts in rent during the first seven months of the 12-month period.
      B. The rent for one month.
   iii. The largest discount in rent during any month in the 12-month period, if,
      A. the rent is paid monthly, and
      B. the largest discount in rent during any month in the 12-month period is equal to the rent for less than one month.
   iv. The sum of the largest discount in rent during any month in the 12-month period and the second-largest discount in rent during any month in the 12-month period, if,
      A. the rent is paid monthly,
      B. the largest discount in rent during any month in the 12-month period is equal to the rent for one month, and
      C. the second-largest discount in rent during any month in the 12-month period is equal to the rent for less than one month.

   v. The sum of the largest discount in rent during any month in the 12-month period, the second-largest discount in rent during any month in the 12-month period, and the third-largest discount in rent during any month in the 12-month period, if,
      A. the rent is paid monthly,
      B. the largest discount in rent during any month in the 12-month period and the second-largest discount in rent during any month in the 12-month period are both equal to the rent for one month, and
      C. the third-largest discount in rent during any month in the 12-month period is equal to the rent for less than one month.
   vi. The rent for three months, if,
      A. the rent is paid monthly, and
      B. the largest discount in rent during any month in the 12-month period, the second-largest discount in rent during any month in the 12-month period, and the third-largest discount in rent during any month in the 12-month period are all equal to the rent for one month.
   vii. The lesser of the following amounts, if the rent is paid daily or weekly:
      A. The sum of the discounts in rent provided in the form of rent-free weeks during the 12-month period.
      B. The rent for 13 weeks.
2. In the case of a discount that is not provided for in a written agreement, the largest eligible discount is the largest discount in rent in one rental period in the 12-month period.

(7) Despite subsection (2), if a tenancy agreement operates under the Strong Communities Housing Allowance Program—Toronto Pilot, and the landlord does not comply with paragraph 3 of subsection 11(1), the lawful rent shall be the undiscounted rent that was permitted under the Act at the time when the tenancy agreement began to operate under the Program.

(8) In this section,

"the 12-month period" has the same meaning as in section 11.

Higher rent charged in first rental period

13. If the rent a landlord charges for the first rental period of a tenancy is greater than the rent the landlord charges for subsequent rental periods in the 12-month period beginning on the day the tenancy commenced, the lawful rent for each rental period in that 12-month period shall be calculated in the following manner:

1. Add all the rents actually charged or to be charged by the landlord during the 12-month period.
2. Subtract from that sum the rent for the first rental period.

3. Divide the amount determined under paragraph 2 by a number equal to the number of rental periods in the 12-month period minus 1.

Exclusions from calculation of rent

14. For the purpose of calculating lawful rent under sections 12 and 13, the rent actually charged or to be charged does not include,

(a) amounts which cannot be lawfully charged for a reason other than the operation of section 12 or 13;

(b) rent increases under section 123 of the Act during the 12-month period defined in subsection 11(2) of this Regulation; or

(c) rent decreases under section 125 of the Act during the 12-month period defined in subsection 11(2) of this Regulation.

Material to be filed

15. If an application is made by a new tenant under subsection 115(1) of the Act, the landlord shall file with the Board, at or before the hearing, an affidavit sworn by the landlord setting out the last lawful rent charged to the former tenant and any available evidence in support of the affidavit.

Prescribed services, facilities, etc.

16(1) The following services, facilities, privileges, accommodations or things are prescribed for the purposes of subsection 123(1) and section 125 of the Act:

1. Cable television.
2. Satellite television.
3. An air conditioner.
4. Extra electricity for an air conditioner.
5. Extra electricity for a washer or dryer in the rental unit.
6. Blockheater plug-ins.
7. Lockers or other storage space.
8. Heat.
9. Electricity.
10. Water or sewage services, excluding capital work.
11. Floor space.
12. Property taxes with respect to a site for a mobile home or a land lease home.

(1.1) In a circumstance in which clause 137(3)(c) or 138(1)(b) of the Act requires a landlord to reduce the rent for a rental unit, the rent reduction rules that are prescribed for the purposes of clause 137(3)(c) or 138(1)(b) of the Act apply instead of the requirements set out in subsections (2) to (5).

(2) If there is an agreement under subsection 123(1) or section 125 of the Act, the maximum increase in rent or minimum decrease in rent shall be the actual cost to the landlord of the service, facility, privilege, accommodation or thing, other than floor space, that is the subject of the agreement or, where the actual cost to the landlord cannot be established or where there is no cost to the landlord, a reasonable amount based on the value of the service, facility, privilege, accommodation or thing.

(3) If the agreement under subsection 123(1) or section 125 of the Act is to provide or cease to provide floor space, the maximum increase in rent or minimum decrease in rent shall be proportionate to the change in floor space.

(4) If an amount determined in accordance with subsection (3) would be unreasonable given the nature and quality of the floor space added or taken away, the maximum increase in rent or minimum decrease in rent shall be a reasonable amount based on the nature and quality of the floor space and the amount of the change in the floor space.

(5) Despite subsections (2), (3) and (4), where a service, facility, privilege, accommodation or thing was provided in accordance with a previous agreement under section 123 of the Act, section 132 of the *Tenant Protection Act, 1997*, section 46 of the *Rent Control Act, 1992* or subsection 96(4) of the *Residential Rent Regulation Act*, the minimum decrease in rent on ceasing to provide the service, facility, privilege, accommodation or thing shall be equal to,

(a) the most recent amount of the separate charge for the service, facility, privilege, accommodation or thing; or

(b) where there is no separate charge, the increase in rent which the landlord took when the service, facility, privilege, accommodation or thing was first provided, adjusted by the percentage increase in the rent being charged for the rental unit from the date the service, facility, privilege, accommodation or thing was first provided to the date the landlord ceased to provide it.

Exemptions from s. 134 of the Act

17. The following payments are exempt from section 134 of the Act:

1. Payment for additional keys, remote entry devices or cards requested by the tenant, not greater than the direct costs.
2. Payment for replacement keys, remote entry devices or cards, not greater than the direct replacement costs, unless the replacement keys, remote entry devices or cards are required because the landlord, on the landlord's initiative, changed the locks.
3. Payment of a refundable key, remote entry device or card deposit, not greater than the expected direct replacement costs.
4. Payment of NSF charges charged by a financial institution to the landlord.
5. Payment of an administration charge, not greater than $20, for an NSF cheque.
6. Payment by a tenant or subtenant in settlement of a court action or potential court action or an application or potential application to the Board.
7. Payment to a landlord or tenant of a mobile home park or land lease community at the commencement of a tenancy as consideration for the rental of a particular site.

8. Payment of a charge not exceeding $250 for transferring, at the request of the tenant,
    i. between rental units to which subsection 6(1) or (3) of this Regulation applies, if the rental units are located in the same residential complex, or
    ii. between rental units in a residential complex that is described in paragraph 1, 2, 3 or 4 of subsection 7(1) of the Act.
9. Payment of an amount to reimburse the landlord for property taxes paid by the landlord with respect to a mobile home or a land lease home owned by the tenant.

PART III   APPLICATION FOR RENT INCREASES ABOVE GUIDELINE

Definitions

18(1) In the Act and in this Part,

"capital expenditure" means an expenditure for an extraordinary or significant renovation, repair, replacement or new addition, the expected benefit of which extends for at least five years including,

(a) an expenditure with respect to a leased asset if the lease qualifies as determined under subsection (2), and

(b) an expenditure that the landlord is required to pay on work undertaken by a municipality, local board or public utility, other than work undertaken because of the landlord's failure to do it,

but does not include,

(c) routine or ordinary work undertaken on a regular basis or undertaken to maintain a capital asset in its operating state, such as cleaning and janitorial services, elevator servicing, general building maintenance, grounds-keeping and appliance repairs, or

(d) work that is substantially cosmetic in nature or is designed to enhance the level of prestige or luxury offered by a unit or residential complex;

"incurred" means, in relation to a capital expenditure,

(a) the payment in full of the amount of the capital expenditure, other than a holdback withheld under the *Construction Lien Act*,

(b) if the expenditure relates to a lease, the assumption, when the lease commences, of the obligations under it, or

(c) if the expenditure relates to work undertaken by a municipality, local board or public utility, when the work is completed;

"physical integrity" means the integrity of all parts of a structure, including the foundation, that support loads or that provide a weather envelope and includes, without restricting the generality of the foregoing, the integrity of,

(a) the roof, exterior walls, exterior doors and exterior windows,

(b) elements contiguous with the structure that contribute to the weather envelope of the structure, and

(c) columns, walls and floors that support loads.

(2) For the purposes of the definition of "capital expenditure" in subsection (1), a lease qualifies if substantially all the risks and benefits associated with the leased asset are passed to the lessee and, when the lease commences, any one or more of the following is satisfied:

1. The lease provides that the ownership of the asset passes to the lessee at or before the end of the term of the lease.
2. The lease provides that the lessee has an option to purchase the asset at the end of the term of the lease at a price that is less than what the market value of the asset will be at that time.
3. The term of the lease is at least 75 per cent of the useful life of the asset, as determined in accordance with section 27 but without regard to any part of section 27 that prevents the useful life from being determined to be less than 10 years.
4. The net present value of the minimum lease payments is at least 90 per cent of the asset's fair market value at the commencement of the lease where the net present value is determined using the interest rate determined under section 20.

Definitions

19(1) In this Part,

"base year" means,

(a) when determining rent increases due to an extraordinary increase in the cost for municipal taxes and charges, the last completed calendar year immediately preceding the day that is 90 days before the effective date of the first intended rent increase referred to in the application,

(b) when determining rent increases due to an extraordinary increase in the cost for utilities or due to operating costs related to security services, the annual accounting period of one year in length chosen by the landlord which is most recently completed on or before the day that is 90 days before the effective date of the first intended rent increase referred to in the application;

"local board" means a "local board" as defined in the *Municipal Affairs Act*;

"reference year" means the 12-month period immediately preceding the base year.

(2) Despite clause (b) of the definition of "base year" in subsection (1), if an order has previously been issued with respect to the residential complex under section 126 of the Act in which relief was granted for an extraordinary increase in costs for utilities or for operating costs related to security services, the base year shall begin and end on the same days of the year as the base year used in the previous order.

Interest rate

20. The interest rate for the purposes of subsection 18(2) and subsection 26(6) is the chartered bank administered conventional five-year mortgage interest rate on the last Wednesday of the month before the month in which the application is made, as reported by the Bank of Canada.

Factor to be applied

21(1) The factor to be applied for the purposes of paragraph 6 of subsection 29(2), paragraph 3 of subsection 29(3) and paragraph 2 of subsection 30(2) is determined by dividing the total rents of the rental units in the residential complex that are subject to the application and are affected by the operating cost by the total rents of the rental units in the residential complex that are affected by the operating cost.

(2) For the purpose of subsection (1), the rent for a rental unit that is vacant or that is otherwise not rented shall be deemed to be the average rent charged for the rental units in the residential complex.

Material to accompany application

22(1) An application under section 126 of the Act must be accompanied by the following material:

1. If the application is based on an extraordinary increase in the cost for municipal taxes and charges or utilities or both,
   i. evidence of the costs for the base year and the reference year and evidence of payment of those costs, and
   ii. evidence of all grants, other forms of financial assistance, rebates and refunds received by the landlord that effectively reduce those costs for the base year or the reference year.
2. If the application is based on capital expenditures incurred,
   i. evidence of all costs and payments for the amounts claimed for capital work, including any information regarding grants and assistance from any level of government and insurance, resale, salvage and trade-in proceeds,
   ii. details about each invoice and payment for each capital expenditure item, in the form approved by the Board, and
   iii. details about the rents for all rental units in the residential complex that are affected by any of the capital expenditures, in the form approved by the Board.
3. If the application is based on operating costs related to security services, evidence of the costs claimed in the application for the base year and the reference year and evidence of payment of those costs.

(2) Despite subsection (1), if any of the following material is unavailable at the time the application is made under section 126 of the Act but becomes available before the end of the hearing, the material must be provided to the Board before or during the hearing:

1. Evidence described in subparagraph 1 ii of subsection (1).
2. Information concerning grants and assistance referred to in paragraph 2 of subsection (1).
3. Information concerning insurance, resale, salvage and trade-in proceeds referred to in paragraph 2 of subsection (1).

(3) An application under section 126 of the Act must be accompanied by two additional photocopies of the application, by two additional photocopies of the material that accompanies the application under subsection (1), and by a compact disc containing the material that accompanies the application under subsection (1) in portable document format.

(4) If material is provided to the Board under subsection (2), it must be accompanied by two additional photocopies of the material and by an updated compact disc containing the material that accompanied the application under subsection (1) and the material provided under subsection (2) in portable document format.

(5) A landlord does not have to provide a compact disc under subsection (3) or (4) if,

(a) the residential complex to which the application relates contains six or fewer residential units and the residential complex is located in a rural or remote area; and

(b) the landlord cannot reasonably provide the compact disc.

(6) Subsections (3), (4) and (5) do not apply if the application referred to in subsection (1) is not based on capital expenditures.

Information for tenants

23(1) The rules set out in this section apply for the purposes of subsection 126(4) of the Act.

(2) Upon the request of a tenant subject to the application, the landlord shall provide the tenant with a compact disc containing the material provided to the Board under subsections 22(1) and (2) in portable document format, for a charge of not more than five dollars.

(3) Instead of providing the compact disc referred to in subsection (2), the landlord and the tenant may agree that the landlord will provide the tenant with,

(a) a photocopy of the material provided under subsections 22(1) and (2), for no more than the landlord's reasonable out-of-pocket costs for the photocopying; or

(b) an e-mail of the material provided under subsections 22(1) and (2) in portable document format, at no charge to the tenant.

(4) Despite subsection (2), if a landlord does not provide the Board with a compact disc pursuant to subsection 22(5), the landlord shall, upon the request of the tenant, provide the tenant with a photocopy of the material provided under subsections 22(1) and (2), for a charge of not more than five dollars.

(5) If the landlord has an office in or close to the residential complex, the landlord shall, during normal business hours and at no charge, make a photocopy of the material provided under subsections 22(1) and (2) available for viewing by tenants subject to the application.

(6) The landlord shall, in the application, inform every tenant subject to the application of the ways in which a tenant may obtain access under this section to the material provided under subsections 22(1) and (2).

Determination of capital expenditures, operating costs

24(1) In determining the amount of any capital expenditures or the amount of operating costs in an application under section 126 of the Act, the Board shall,

(a) include, for an application filed on or after July 1, 2010, any provincial sales tax and harmonized sales tax paid by the landlord in respect of the capital expenditures or operating costs, but not in respect of operating costs for utilities;

(b) exclude any penalties, interest or other similar charges for late payment of any amount paid by the landlord in respect of the capital expenditures or operating costs;

(c) exclude any amount that has already been included in calculating the amount of a capital expenditure or operating cost in the same application or for which the landlord has obtained relief in a previous order under the Act or under the *Tenant Protection Act, 1997*; and

(d) subtract the amount of all grants, other forms of financial assistance, rebates and refunds received by the landlord that effectively reduce the operating costs.

(1.1) In determining the amount of any capital expenditures or the amount of operating costs in an application under section 126 of the Act that is filed before July 1, 2010, the Board shall include the goods and services tax and provincial sales tax paid by the landlord in respect of the capital expenditures or operating costs.

(2) If a residential complex forms part of a larger project, the operating costs for the project and the amount of capital expenditures which benefit both the residential complex and the other parts of the project shall be allocated between the residential complex and the other parts of the project in accordance with one or more of the following factors:

1. The area of each part of the project.
2. The market value of each part of the project.
3. The revenue generated by each part of the project.

(3) If the allocation of operating costs and capital expenditures in accordance with subsection (2) would be unreasonable considering how much of the costs and expenditures are attributable to each part of the project, the operating costs and capital expenditures shall be allocated among the parts of the project in reasonable proportions according to how much of the costs and expenditures are attributable to each part of the project.

(4) In this section,

"harmonized sales tax" means any tax imposed under Part IX of the *Excise Tax Act* (Canada).

Non-arm's length transaction

25(1) If the landlord incurs a cost arising out of a transaction that is not an arm's length transaction, the Board shall consider only that part of the landlord's cost that is less than or equal to the costs that would arise from a similar market transaction.

(2) In this section,

"arm's length" means the persons involved are not related persons;

"control" means direct or indirect ownership or control either alone or with a related person of,

(a) more than 50 per cent of the issued share capital of a corporation having full voting rights under all circumstances, or

(b) issued and outstanding share capital of a corporation in an amount that permits or may permit the person to direct the management and policies of the corporation;

"family," in relation to a person, means,

(a) the person's spouse,

(b) the parents or other ancestors or the children or other descendants of the person or the person's spouse,

(c) the brothers and sisters of the person or the person's spouse, and the children and other descendants of those brothers and sisters,

(d) the aunts and uncles of the person and the person's spouse and the children and other descendants of those aunts and uncles,

(e) the spouses of the person's sons and daughters;

"related person," where used to indicate a relationship with any person, includes,

(a) a member of the family of such person,

(b) an employer or employee of such person,

(c) a partner of such person,

(d) a trust or estate in which such person has a beneficial interest,

(e) a trust or estate in which such person serves as a trustee or in a similar capacity,

(f) a trust or estate in which persons related to such person, as otherwise determined under this definition, have a beneficial interest,

(g) a corporation controlled by such person,

(h) a corporation controlled by such person and persons related to such person, or

(i) a corporation controlled by a person related to such person;

"similar market transaction" means an arm's length transaction that occurs or may reasonably be expected to occur under the same or comparable terms and conditions and in the same general geographic location.

(3) In this section, one corporation is related to another corporation if,

(a) one of the corporations is controlled by the other corporation;

(b) both of the corporations are controlled by the same person or group of related persons each member of which is related to every other member of the group;

(c) each of the corporations is controlled by one person and the person who controls one of the corporations and the person who controls the other corporation are related persons;

(d) one of the corporations is controlled by one person and that person is related to any member of a group of related persons that controls the other corporation;

(e) one of the corporations is controlled by one person and that person is related to each member of an unrelated group that controls the other corporation;

(f) any member of a group of related persons that controls one of the corporations is related to each member of an unrelated group that controls the other corporation; or

(g) each member of an unrelated group that controls one of the corporations is a related person to at least one member of an unrelated group that controls the other corporation.

Findings related to capital expenditures

26(1) The rules set out in this section apply to the Board in making findings relating to capital expenditures.

(2) A rent increase shall not be ordered in respect of a capital expenditure unless the work was completed during the 18-month period ending 90 days before the effective date of the first intended rent increase referred to in the application.

(3) The value of the landlord's own labour in carrying out the work involved in the capital expenditure is equal to the amount of time spent multiplied by a rate of pay that is reasonable given the landlord's experience and skill in the type of work done but,

(a) if the amount of time spent exceeds the amount of time that would be reasonable given the landlord's experience and skill, the latter amount of time shall be used in the calculation of the value of the landlord's own labour;

(b) only that part of the value of the landlord's own labour that does not exceed the amount a person in the business of doing such work would charge shall be considered; and

(c) the value of the landlord's own labour does not include any amount with respect to the management and administration of the work involved in the capital expenditure.

(4) The cost of a leased asset is the fair market value of the leased asset at the commencement of the lease.

(5) The amount of a capital expenditure is calculated as follows:

1. Add the following amounts:
   i. The purchase prices.
   ii. The cost of any leased assets.
   iii. The installation, renovation and construction costs.
   iv. The value of the landlord's own labour as determined under subsection (3).

2. Subtract from the amount determined under paragraph 1 any grant or other assistance from any level of government and any insurance, salvage, resale or trade-in proceeds related to the work undertaken or the item purchased.

(6) For each rental unit that is subject to the application, the percentage rent increase that is justified by capital expenditures shall be determined in accordance with the following rules.

1. Determine which capital expenditures affect the unit.

2. For each capital expenditure that affects the unit, multiply the amount of the capital expenditure determined under subsection (5) by the rent for the unit, and divide that result by the sum of the rents for all rental units in the residential complex that are affected by the capital expenditure.

3. If the Board is of the opinion that the amount determined under paragraph 2 for a capital expenditure does not reasonably reflect how the unit is affected by the capital expenditure,
   i. paragraph 2 does not apply, and
   ii. the Board shall determine an amount by another method that, in the opinion of the Board, better reflects how the unit is affected by the capital expenditure.

4. Add the amounts determined under paragraph 2 or 3, as the case may be, for all of the capital expenditures that affect the unit.

5. Amortize the amount determined under paragraph 4 over the weighted useful life of the capital expenditures that affect the unit, as determined in paragraph 6, in equal monthly instalments of blended principal and interest.

6. The weighted useful life of all capital expenditures that affect the unit shall be determined in accordance with the following rules:
   i. For each capital expenditure that affects the unit,
      A. divide the amount determined under paragraph 2 or 3, as the case may be, for the capital expenditure by the amount determined under paragraph 4, and
      B. multiply the amount determined under sub-subparagraph A by the useful life of the capital expenditure, as determined under section 27.

ii. Add the results determined under sub-subparagraph i B for all capital expenditures that affect the unit and round to the nearest full year.

7. The amortization under paragraph 5 shall be calculated using the interest rate determined under section 20.

8. The percentage rent increase that is justified for the unit by capital expenditures is determined by dividing the amortized amount determined under paragraph 5 by the monthly rent for the unit, and multiplying the result by 100.

Useful life of work or thing

27(1) The useful life of work done or a thing purchased shall be determined from the Schedule subject to the following rules:

1. Where the useful life set out in Column 2 of the Schedule is less than 10 years, the useful life of work done or a thing purchased shall be deemed to be 10 years.

2. If, when a thing is purchased, it has previously been used, the useful life of the thing shall be determined taking into account the length of time of that previous use.

3. If the work done or thing purchased does not appear in the Schedule, the useful life of the work or thing shall be determined with reference to items with similar characteristics that do appear in the Schedule.

4. Despite paragraphs 2 and 3, for the purposes of making a finding under this section, the useful life of work done or a thing purchased shall not be determined to be less than 10 years.

(2) If the useful life of work done or a thing purchased cannot be determined under subsection (1) because the work or thing does not appear in the Schedule and no item with similar characteristics appears in the Schedule, the useful life of the work or thing shall be what is generally accepted as the useful life of such work or thing but in no case shall the useful life be determined to be less than 10 years.

Municipal taxes or charges and utilities, extraordinary increase

28(1) An increase in the cost of municipal taxes and charges or utilities is extraordinary if it is greater than the guideline plus 50 per cent of the guideline.

(2) For the purposes of subsection (1), the guideline is the guideline for the calendar year in which the effective date of the first intended rent increase referred to in the application falls.

(3) Despite subsection (1), if the guideline is less than zero, any increase in the cost of municipal taxes and charges or utilities is deemed to be extraordinary.

Rules

29(1) The rules set out in this section apply to the Board in making findings related to extraordinary increases in the cost for municipal taxes and charges or utilities or both.

(2) Subject to subsection (4), the amount of the allowance for an extraordinary increase in the cost for municipal taxes and charges is calculated as follows:

1. Adjust the reference year costs for municipal taxes and charges by the guideline plus 50 per cent of the guideline determined in accordance with subsection 28(2).

2. If municipal taxes and charges for a tax year are increased as a result of an appeal of a tax assessment, add to the base year costs for municipal taxes and charges the amount of the increase resulting from the appeal.

3. If a tax notice respecting the reference year municipal taxes and charges is issued on or after November 1 in the base year, add to the base year costs for municipal taxes and charges the amount, if any, by which the reference year municipal taxes and charges exceed the municipal taxes and charges for the year preceding the reference year.

4. If a tax notice respecting the reference year municipal taxes and charges is issued on or after November 1 in the base year and if the reference year municipal taxes and charges are increased as a result of an appeal of a tax assessment, the amount of the increase resulting from the appeal,
    i. shall be included in determining the amount by which the reference year municipal taxes and charges exceed the municipal taxes and charges for the year preceding the reference year for the purpose of paragraph 3, and
    ii. shall not be added under paragraph 2.

5. Subtract the reference year costs for municipal taxes and charges, as adjusted under paragraph 1, from the base year costs for municipal taxes and charges, as adjusted under paragraphs 2, 3 and 4.

6. Multiply the amount determined in paragraph 5 by the factor determined under section 21.

(3) The amount of the allowance for an extraordinary increase in the cost for utilities shall be calculated as follows:

1. Adjust the reference year costs for each of heat, electricity and water by the guideline plus 50 per cent of the guideline determined in accordance with subsection 28(2).

2. Subtract the amount determined in paragraph 1 for heat from the base year costs for heat and do the same for electricity and water.

3. Multiply the amount determined in paragraph 2 for heat by the factor for heat determined under section 21 and do the same for electricity and water.

4. Add together the amounts determined under paragraph 3.

(4) The amount of the adjusted base year utility costs shall be calculated as follows:

1. Multiply the reference year costs for each of heat, electricity and water by 50 per cent of the guideline determined in accordance with subsection 28(2).

2. Subtract the amount determined under paragraph 1 for heat from the base year costs for heat and do the same for electricity and water.

3. Add together the amounts determined under paragraph 2.

(5) Despite section 28, if the guideline is less than zero per cent, for the purposes of the calculations in subsections (2), (3) and (4) the guideline is deemed to be zero per cent.

(6) An increase in municipal taxes and charges as a result of an appeal of a tax assessment shall not be considered under subsection (2) if the application for the rent increase was filed more than 12 months after the decision on the appeal was issued.

Operating costs related to security services

30(1) This section applies to the Board when making findings respecting operating costs related to security services.

(2) The amount of the allowance for operating costs related to security shall be calculated as follows:

1. Subtract the operating costs for security services in the reference year from the operating costs for security services in the base year.

2. Multiply the amount determined under paragraph 1 by the factor determined under section 21.

(3) The Board shall exclude from the calculation under subsection (2) any operating costs for security services that are no longer being provided to the tenant at the time the application is heard.

Calculation of percentage rent increase

31. The percentage rent increase above the guideline for each rental unit that is the subject of the application shall be calculated in the following manner:

1. Divide the amount of each allowance determined under subsection 29(2), subsection 29(3) and section 30 by the total rents for the rental units that are subject to the application and are affected by the operating cost.

2. If the Board is of the opinion that the amount determined under paragraph 1 for an allowance does not reasonably reflect how the rental units that are subject to the application are affected by the operating cost to which the allowance relates,
   i. paragraph 1 does not apply in respect of the allowance, and
   ii. the Board shall determine an amount by another method that, in the opinion of the Board, better reflects how the rental units that are subject to the application are affected by the operating cost to which the allowance relates.

3. Determine the percentage that each allowance referred to in paragraph 1 represents of the total rents for the rental units that are subject to the application and are affected by the operating cost by multiplying each of the amounts determined under paragraph 1 or 2, as the case may be, by 100.

4. Subject to paragraph 5, add together the percentages determined under paragraph 3 for each allowance referred to in paragraph 1 that relates to an operating cost that affects the rental unit.

5. In performing the addition required by paragraph 4, do not include the percentage determined under paragraph 3 for the allowance determined under subsection 29(3) if that percentage is less than 0.50.

6. Add the percentage determined under paragraph 4 and the percentage determined under paragraph 8 of subsection 26(6).

When rent increase may be taken

32(1) Subject to section 33 of this Regulation, if the Board orders a rent increase for a rental unit under subsection 126(10) of the Act, that rent increase may only be taken within 12 months of the first intended rent increase referred to in the application for a rental unit in the residential complex.

(2) Subject to section 33 of this Regulation, the rent increases provided for under subsection 126(11) of the Act may only be taken during the subsequent 12-month periods which begin and end on the same days of the year as the 12-month period referred to in subsection (1).

(3) Despite subsection (1), if the unit is subject to clause 126(13)(b) of the Act, the rent charged for the rental unit shall not be increased before the date specified by the Board under clause 126(13)(b) of the Act, and the increase may only be taken within 12 months after that date.

(4) Despite subsection (2), if the unit is subject to clause 126(13)(b) of the Act, the rent increases provided for under subsection 126(11) of the Act may only be taken during the subsequent 12-month periods which begin and end on the same days of the year as the 12-month period referred to in subsection (3).

When rent increase may be taken

33(1) If an order with respect to a rental unit that increases the lawful rent is made under section 126 of the Act with respect to capital expenditures or operating costs for security services before the time for taking any rent increases under one or more previous orders has expired, the landlord may annually increase the lawful rent being charged by no more than the guideline rent increase plus 3 per cent of the previous lawful rent, until such time as no rent increase with respect to capital expenditures or operating costs related to security services ordered under section 126 of the Act remains to be taken.

(2) If a landlord fails to take a rent increase in accordance with subsection (1) in any 12-month period in which the landlord was entitled to take such a rent increase, the landlord may not take that rent increase in any subsequent time period.

(3) If a landlord takes a rent increase in accordance with subsection (1) that is less than the amount the landlord was entitled to take, the landlord may not take the amount of the rent increase which the landlord failed to take in any subsequent time period.

(4) This section does not prevent a landlord from increasing the rent charged by more than 3 per cent of the previous lawful rent charged with respect to an extraordinary increase in the cost for municipal taxes and charges or utilities or both in accordance with an order under subsection 126(10) of the Act.

Sequence—components of the increase

34. For the purpose of making determinations under section 36 and subsection 38(2) of this Regulation, the following rules apply if a landlord was permitted to increase the rent pursuant to an order under subsection 126(10) of the Act based on more than one of the grounds in subsection 126(1) of the Act but the increase taken by the landlord was less than the maximum increase permitted by the order:

1. The increase taken by the landlord shall be deemed to have been taken for municipal taxes and charges, up to the percentage set out in the order for municipal taxes and charges.

2. If the increase taken by the landlord was greater than the percentage set out in the order for municipal taxes and charges, the balance of the increase shall be deemed to have been taken for eligible capital expenditures, up to the percentage set out in the order for eligible capital expenditures.

3. If the increase taken by the landlord was greater than the sum of the percentages set out in the order for municipal taxes and charges and for eligible capital expenditures, the balance of the increase shall be deemed to have been taken for utilities, up to the percentage set out in the order for utilities.

4. If the increase taken by the landlord was greater than the sum of the percentages set out in the order for municipal taxes and charges, for eligible capital expenditures and for utilities, the balance of the increase shall be deemed to have been taken for operating costs related to security services.

PART IV REDUCTIONS IN RENT—UTILITIES AND CAPITAL EXPENDITURES

Utilities

35(1) If the Board has issued an order under subsection 126(10) of the Act permitting an increase in rent that is due in whole or in part to an extraordinary increase in the cost of utilities, and the landlord has taken the increase in whole or in part, the landlord shall provide, in a form approved by the Board, information to a tenant who was subject to the order and continues to reside in the unit to which the order applied in accordance with the rules set out in this section.

(2) The information shall be provided on or before the anniversary of the first effective date of the rent increase set out in the order each year for five years following the first effective date.

(3) The information shall include,

(a) the total amount of the adjusted base year utility costs for the residential complex or building as set out in the order;

(b) the current utility costs;

(c) if the amount in clause (b) is less than the amount in clause (a), the determinations made under section 36; and

(d) if applicable, the percentage and dollar amount of the rent reduction and the date it takes effect.

(4) Subsection (1) ceases to apply to a tenant if the landlord has provided the tenant with rent reductions under subsection 128(3) of the Act and the total amount of those reductions is equal to the lesser of the following amounts:

1. The amount of the increase permitted under subsection 126(10) of the Act that is set out in the order as related to utilities.

2. The amount of the increase taken for utilities, as determined under section 34.

(5) Upon the request of a tenant who was subject to the order, the landlord shall provide a compact disc containing all utility bills used to justify current utility costs in portable document format.

(6) The landlord is only required to provide the information requested under subsection (5) upon a request made by the tenant within two years from the date the information under this section was given.

(7) The information referred to in subsection (5) shall be provided for a charge of not more than five dollars.

(8) Instead of providing the compact disc referred to in subsection (5), the landlord and the tenant may agree that the landlord will provide the tenant with,

(a) a photocopy of the information required under subsection (5), for no more than the landlord's reasonable out-of-pocket costs for the photocopying; or

(b) an e-mail of the information required under subsection (5) in portable document format at no charge to the tenant.

(9) A landlord does not have to provide a compact disc under subsection (5) if,

(a) the residential complex to which the application relates contains six or fewer residential units and the residential complex is located in a rural or remote area;

(b) the landlord cannot reasonably provide the compact disc; and

(c) that landlord provides the tenant with a photocopy of the information required under subsection (5), for a charge of not more than five dollars.

(10) In this section and section 36,

"current utility costs" means,

(a) the costs covering the most recent of the subsequent 12-month periods which begin and end on the same days of the year as the base year used in the previous order, multiplied, where applicable, by the allocation factor determined under subsection 24(2) or (3) and set out in the order, or

(b) the amount determined in accordance with subsection (11), if,

(i) the landlord no longer provides one or more utilities to the residential complex or to other parts of a larger project that the residential complex forms part of, and

(ii) an allocation factor was determined under section 24(2) or (3) and set out in the order.

(11) The amount referred to in clause (b) of the definition of "current utility costs" in subsection (10) shall be determined in accordance with the following rules:

1. If the landlord no longer provides one or more utilities to all or part of the non-residential portions of the project,

   i. multiply the total base year utility costs for the project as set out in the order by the percentage that was set out in the order for each utility that the landlord no longer provides to all or part of the non-residential portions of the project,

   ii. subtract the allocation factor determined under subsection 24(2) or (3) and set out in the order from 1, and

   iii. for each utility that the landlord no longer provides to all or part of the non-residential portions of the project, multiply the amount determined under subparagraph i by the amount determined under subparagraph ii.

2. If the landlord no longer provides one or more utilities to part of the non-residential portions of the project, the landlord shall, for each of those utilities, modify the amount determined under subparagraph 1 iii to reflect the proportion of the non-residential portion of the project to which he or she still provides the utility, in a manner consistent with the original methodology used to apportion the costs under subsection 24(2) or (3), as described in the order.

3. If the landlord no longer provides one or more utilities to all or part of the residential portions of the project, for each of those utilities,

   i. multiply the total base year utility costs for the project as set out in the order by the percentage that was set out in the order for the utility,

   ii. multiply the amount determined in subparagraph i by the allocation factor determined in subsection 24(2) or (3) and set out in the order, and

   iii. multiply the amount determined under subparagraph ii by the number of rental units for which

the landlord no longer provides the utility divided by the total number of rental units for which the landlord provided the utility at the time the increase was ordered.

4. Add the following amounts:

   i. The utility costs covering the most recent of the subsequent 12-month periods which begin and end on the same days of the year as the base year used in the previous order.

   ii. The amounts determined under subparagraph 1 iii, if any, for utilities that the landlord no longer provides to all the non-residential portions of the project.

   iii. The amounts determined under paragraph 2, if any, for utilities that the landlord no longer provides to part of the non-residential portions of the project.

   iv. The amounts determined under subparagraph 3 iii, if any, for utilities that the landlord no longer provides to all or part of the residential portions of the project.

5. Multiply the amount determined under paragraph 4 by the allocation factor determined in subsection 24(2) or (3) and set out in the order.

6. Subtract from the amount determined under paragraph 5 the sum of the amounts determined under subparagraph 3 iii, if any, for utilities that the landlord no longer provides to all or part of the residential portions of the project.

(12) If the order referred to in subsection (1) is based on an application filed on or after July 1, 2010, the current utility costs cannot include any provincial sales tax or harmonized sales tax paid by the landlord in respect of the utility.

(13) In this section,

"harmonized sales tax" means any tax imposed under Part IX of the *Excise Tax Act* (Canada).

Rent reductions under s. 128(3) of the Act

36(1) The following rules apply in determining the amounts of rent reductions under subsection 128(3) of the Act:

1. Subtract the current utility costs from the adjusted base year utility costs as set out in the order.

2. If the amount determined in paragraph 1 is zero or less, no rent reduction is required.

3. If the amount determined in paragraph 1 is greater than zero,

   i. divide the amount determined in paragraph 1 by the allowance that justified the increase that was set out in the order, and

   ii. multiply the amount from subparagraph i by the percentage increase in rent for utilities that was set out in the order.

4. Despite paragraph 1, if a reduction in utility costs was previously determined in accordance with this

subsection, the determination in paragraph 1 shall be made by subtracting the current utility costs from the utility costs used to justify the previous rent reduction.

(2) Despite subsection (1), the following rules apply in determining the amounts of rent reductions under subsection 128(3) of the Act if, in accordance with the Act or an agreement between the landlord and the affected tenants, the landlord ceases to provide one or more utilities to one or more rental units in the residential complex:

1. Subject to paragraphs 5 and 6, multiply the adjusted base year utility costs by the percentage that was set out in the order for each utility.

2. Subject to paragraph 6, multiply the allowance that justified the increase that was set out in the order by the percentage that was set out in the order for each utility.

3. The following rules apply to a rental unit to which the landlord has not ceased to provide any utilities:

    i. Calculate the sum of the amounts determined under paragraph 1.

    ii. If the amounts of one or more previous rent reductions were determined under this paragraph for the rental unit, subtract from the amount determined under subparagraph i the sum of all determinations previously made under subparagraph iii for the rental unit.

    iii. Subtract the current utility costs from the amount determined under subparagraph i or, if subparagraph ii applies, from the amount determined under subparagraph ii.

    iv. Calculate the sum of the amounts determined under paragraph 2.

    v. If the amount determined under subparagraph iii is zero or less, no rent reduction is required.

    vi. If the amount determined under subparagraph iii is greater than zero, the amount of the rent reduction under subsection 128(3) of the Act shall be determined in accordance with the following rules:

        A. Divide the amount determined under subparagraph iii by the amount determined under subparagraph iv.

        B. Multiply the amount determined under sub-subparagraph A by the percentage increase in rent for utilities that was set out in the order.

4. The following rules apply to a rental unit to which the landlord has ceased to provide one or more utilities:

    i. Calculate the sum of the amounts determined under paragraph 1 for the utilities that the landlord still provides to the rental unit.

    ii. If the amounts of one or more previous rent reductions were determined under this paragraph for the rental unit, subtract from the amount

determined under subparagraph i the sum of all determinations previously made under subparagraph iv.

iii. If the amounts of one or more previous rent reductions were determined under paragraph 3 for the rental unit, subtract the amount determined in accordance with the following rules from the amount determined under subparagraph i or, if subparagraph ii applies, from the amount determined under subparagraph ii:

    A. Calculate the sum of all amounts previously determined under subparagraph 3 iii for the rental unit.

    B. Calculate the sum of the percentages that were set out in the order for the utilities that the landlord has not ceased to provide to the rental unit.

    C. Multiply the amount determined under sub-subparagraph A by the percentage determined under sub-subparagraph B.

iv. Subtract the portion of the costs in the current utility costs attributable to the utilities no longer provided to the rental unit by the landlord from the current utility costs.

v. Subtract the amount determined under subparagraph iv from,

    A. the amount determined under subparagraph i, if neither subparagraph ii nor subparagraph iii applies,

    B. the amount determined under subparagraph ii, if subparagraph ii applies and subparagraph iii does not apply, or

    C. the amount determined under subparagraph iii, if subparagraph iii applies.

vi. Calculate the sum of the amounts determined under paragraph 2 for the utilities that the landlord still provides to the rental unit.

vii. For each utility set out in the order that is still provided to the rental unit by the landlord, multiply the percentage that was set out in the order for the utility by the percentage increase in rent for utilities that was set out in the order.

viii. If the amount determined under subparagraph v is zero or less, no rent reduction is required.

ix. If the amount determined under subparagraph v is greater than zero, the amount of the rent reduction under subsection 128(3) of the Act shall be determined in accordance with the following rules:

    A. Divide the amount determined under subparagraph v by the amount determined under subparagraph vi.

B. Multiply the amount determined under sub-subparagraph A by the sum of the percentages determined under subparagraph vii.

x. Despite subparagraph ix, if the amount determined under subparagraph v is greater than zero and the sum of the percentages of any previous rent reductions arising from the same order is less than the sum of the percentages determined under subparagraph vii, the amount of the rent reduction under subsection 128(3) of the Act shall be determined by subtracting from the amount determined under sub-subparagraph ix B the sum of the percentages of the previous rent reductions arising from the same order.

xi. Despite subparagraph ix, no rent reduction is required if the amount determined under subparagraph v is greater than zero and the sum of the percentages of any previous rent reductions arising from the same order is equal to or greater than the sum of the percentages determined under subparagraph vii.

5. If one or more rent reductions were previously determined in accordance with subsection (1), the reference in paragraph 1 to the adjusted base year utility costs shall be deemed to be a reference to the current utility costs used to determine the most recent of the previous rent reductions in accordance with subsection (1).

6. If a utility is no longer provided by the landlord to one or more rental units, the references in paragraphs 1 and 2 to the percentage that was set out in the order for that utility shall be deemed to be a reference to the percentage that was set out in the order for that utility multiplied by the number of rental units to which the landlord still provides the utility divided by the number of rental units to which the landlord provided the utility at the time of the application.

(3) Despite subsections (1) and (2), if the amount of a rent reduction determined under those subsections, expressed as a percentage of the current rent, is less than 0.50, no rent reduction is required.

(4) Despite subsections (1) and (2), if the amount of a rent reduction determined under those subsections, expressed as a percentage of the current rent, is 0.50 or more, the rent reduction shall be reduced, if necessary, so that the sum of the rent reduction and any previous rent reductions arising from the same order does not exceed the lesser of the following amounts:

1. The amount of the increase permitted under subsection 126(10) of the Act that is set out in the order as related to utilities.

2. The amount of the increase taken for utilities, as determined under section 34 of this Regulation.

(5) A rent reduction determined under this section takes effect on the first anniversary, on or after the latest date for providing information under subsection 35(2), of the date the increase permitted by the order was taken.

(6) If the date that a rent reduction takes effect under subsection (5) is the same as the date on which a rent increase takes effect, the rent reduction shall be deemed to take effect immediately before the rent increase.

Prescribed percentage, period

37(1) The prescribed percentage for the purposes of subsection 128(3) of the Act is the percentage decrease in utility costs that results in a percentage decrease in rent of 0.50 per cent or more as determined under subsections 36(1) and (2) of this Regulation.

(2) The prescribed period for the purposes of subsection 128(3) of the Act is the most recent 12-month period which begins and ends on the same days of the year as the base year used in the previous order.

Rules for prescribing a date for the purpose of s. 129 of the Act

38(1) The rules for determining a date for the purpose of clause 129(c) of the Act are as follows:

1. If the unit is subject to an order issued under subsection 126(10) of the Act and subsection 126(13) of the Act does not apply, the date shall be the day immediately before the anniversary, in the year determined by adding the weighted useful life as determined under paragraph 6 of subsection 26(6) of this Regulation to the year in which the landlord took the increase, of the date the landlord took the increase.

2. Despite paragraph 1, if a landlord was entitled to take an increase under clause 126(10)(b) of the Act but only took an increase or increases under clause 126(11)(b) of the Act, the date shall be the day immediately before the anniversary, in the year determined by adding the weighted useful life as determined under paragraph 6 of subsection 26(6) of this Regulation to the year that contains the first effective date set out in the order, of the first effective date set out in the order.

3. If the unit is subject to an order issued under subsection 126(10) of the Act, and was subject to subsection 126(13) of the Act, the date shall be the day immediately before the anniversary, in the year determined by adding the weighted useful life as determined under paragraph 6 of subsection 26(6) of this Regulation to the year that contains the first effective date set out in the order, of the first effective date set out in the order.

(2) The rules to determine the percentage for the purpose of subclause 129(c)(ii) of the Act are as follows:

1. If an order was issued by the Board under subsection 126(10) of the Act permitting an increase in rent that is due in whole to eligible capital expenditures, the

percentage reduction shall be equal to the percentage increase taken by the landlord.

2. If an order was issued by the Board under subsection 126(10) of the Act permitting an increase in rent that is due only in part to eligible capital expenditures, the percentage reduction shall be the percentage for eligible capital expenditures as determined under section 34 of this Regulation.

PART V REDUCTIONS IN RENT— SERVICES AND TAXES

Rules relating to reduction in services

39(1) The rules set out in this section apply in respect of making findings relating to a reduction of the rent charged under section 130 of the Act based on a discontinuance or reduction in services or facilities.

(1.1) In a circumstance in which clause 137(3)(c) or 138(1)(b) of the Act requires a landlord to reduce the rent for a rental unit, the rent reduction rules that are prescribed for the purposes of clause 137(3)(c) or 138(1)(b) of the Act apply instead of the requirements set out in subsections (2) to (7).

(2) If a service or facility is discontinued and the discontinuance was reasonable in the circumstances, the rent shall be reduced by an amount that is equal to what would be a reasonable charge for the service or facility based on the cost of the service or facility to the landlord or, if the cost cannot be determined or if there is no cost, on the value of the service or facility, including the cost to the tenant or former tenant of replacing the discontinued service or facility.

(3) If a service or facility is discontinued and the discontinuance was not reasonable in the circumstances, the rent shall be reduced by an amount that takes into account the following matters:

1. The value of the service or facility, including the cost to the tenant or former tenant of replacing the discontinued service or facility.
2. The effect of the discontinuance on the tenant or former tenant.

(4) The amount of the rent reduction determined under subsection (3) shall not be less that the amount of the reduction that would have been required under subsection (2) had the discontinuance been reasonable.

(5) Despite subsections (2), (3) and (4), if a service or facility was previously provided to the tenant or former tenant under an agreement under section 123 of the Act, section 132 of the *Tenant Protection Act, 1997*, section 46 of the *Rent Control Act, 1992* or subsection 96(4) of the *Residential Rent Regulation Act*, the reduction in rent on discontinuing the service or facility shall be equal to,

    (a) the most recent amount of the separate charge for the service or facility; or

    (b) where there is no separate charge, the increase in rent that the landlord took when the service or facility was first provided, adjusted by the percentage increase in rent being charged for the rental unit from the date the service or facility was first provided to the date the landlord discontinued the service or facility.

(6) If a service or facility is reduced, the amount of the reduction of rent shall be a reasonable proportion, based on the degree of the reduction of the service or facility, of the amount of the reduction in rent that would have been determined under subsections (2) to (5) had the service or facility been discontinued.

(7) If the discontinuance or reduction is temporary and its duration is reasonable, taking into account the effect on the tenant or former tenant, there shall be no reduction of rent.

Application of ss. 24 and 25

40. Sections 24 and 25 of this Regulation apply with necessary modifications to an application to the Board by a tenant under section 130 or 133 of the Act.

Reduction of municipal taxes

41(1) For the purpose of subsection 131(1) of the Act, the prescribed percentage is 2.49 per cent.

(2) For the purpose of section 131 of the Act,

"municipal property tax" means taxes charged to a landlord by a municipality and includes taxes levied on a landlord's property in unorganized territory and taxes levied under Division B of Part IX of the *Education Act*, but does not include,

    (a) charges for inspections done by a municipality on a residential complex related to an alleged breach of a health, safety, housing or maintenance standard,

    (b) charges for emergency repairs carried out by a municipality on a residential complex,

    (c) charges for work in the nature of a capital expenditure carried out by a municipality,

    (d) charges for work, services or non-emergency repairs performed by a municipality in relation to a landlord's non-compliance with a by-law,

    (e) penalties, interest, late payment fees or fines,

    (f) any amount spent by a municipality under subsection 219(1) of the Act or any administrative fee applied to that amount under subsection 219(2) of the Act, or

    (g) any other charges levied by the municipality.

(3) If the lawful rent for the rental units in a residential complex is to be reduced under subsection 131(1) of the Act, the reduction in rent shall be determined as follows:

1. Determine the percentage by which the municipal property tax for the residential complex in the year has been reduced from the municipal property tax for the residential complex in the previous year.
2. Determine the percentage by which the rent is to be reduced by multiplying the percentage determined under paragraph 1 by 20 per cent for properties that fall under the multi-residential property class as defined in section 4 of Ontario Regulation 282/98 (General) made under the *Assessment Act*, and 15 per cent otherwise.

(4) The prescribed date for the purposes of subsection 131(2) of the Act is December 31 of any year in which the municipal property tax reduction takes effect.

(5) The prescribed number of rental units for the purpose of subsection 131(3) of the Act is seven.

(6) The period within which notification of a rent reduction must be given for the purpose of subsection 131(3) of the Act is,

(a) between June 1 and September 15 for landlords; and

(b) between October 1 and December 15 for tenants.

(7) When the notice under subsection 131(3) of the Act is served on the landlord, it shall be addressed to the landlord or to the owner of the property for tax purposes and when it is served on the tenants, the notice for each tenant shall be addressed to the tenant or occupant of the tenant's rental unit.

(8) The notice under subsection 131(3) of the Act shall be served,

(a) by handing it to the person;

(b) if the person is a landlord, by handing it to an employee of the landlord exercising authority in respect of the residential complex to which the notice relates;

(c) if the person is a tenant, by handing it to an apparently adult person in the rental unit;

(d) by leaving it in the mail box where mail is ordinarily delivered to the person;

(e) if there is no mail box, by leaving it at the place where mail is ordinarily delivered to the person; or

(f) by sending it by mail, by courier or by facsimile to the last known address where the person resides or carries on business.

Application for variance

42(1) For the purpose of subsection 132(1) of the Act, a person may apply to the Board for an order varying the rent reduction determined under section 131 of the Act if,

(a) other charges that are in addition to the municipal property tax and that are not set out in clauses (a), (b), (c), (d), (e) and (f) of the definition of "municipal property tax" in subsection 41(2) were levied upon the landlord by the municipality in the base year;

(b) the percentage of the rent charged in the residential complex that the municipal property tax comprises is not 20 per cent for properties that fall under the multi-residential property class as defined in section 4 of Ontario Regulation 282/98 (General) made under the *Assessment Act*, and 15 per cent otherwise;

(c) there is an error in the notice of rent reduction with respect to the amount by which the municipal property tax is reduced or the amount by which the rent is to be reduced; or

(d) the municipal property tax is increased or decreased during the period from the day the notice of rent reduction was issued to March 31 of the year following the date the rent reduction takes effect.

(2) An application referred to in subsection (1) shall be made,

(a) if a notice of the rent reduction is required to be given under subsection 131(3) of the Act, on or before the later of,

(i) 90 days following the day on which the person who will be the applicant is given the notice of rent reduction, and

(ii) March 31 in the year following the year in which the rent reduction takes effect;

(b) if a notice of the rent reduction is not required to be given under subsection 131(3) of the Act, on or before the later of,

(i) 90 days following the day on which the tax notice effecting the reduction in the municipal property tax and forming the basis of the rent reduction is issued, and

(ii) March 31 in the year following the year in which the rent reduction takes effect.

Determination by Board
Definitions

43(1) In this section,

"base year" means the calendar year in which the rent reduction takes effect;

"reference year" means the calendar year immediately preceding the base year.

(2) The Board shall make a determination in respect of an application under clause 42(1)(a), (c) or (d) in the following manner:

1. Calculate the actual decrease, if any, in the municipal taxes and charges from the reference year to the base year.

2. Determine the percentage rent decrease for a rental unit that is subject to the application,

   i. if the total of the annual rents is not proven by the landlord or the tenant, in accordance with paragraphs 1 and 2 of subsection 41(3), and

   ii. otherwise, by dividing the amount determined under paragraph 1 by the total of the annual rents for all of the rental units in the residential complex and multiplying that quotient by 100.

(3) The Board shall make a determination in respect of an application under clause 42(1)(b) in the following manner:

1. Calculate the actual decrease, if any, in the municipal taxes and charges from the reference year to the base year.

2. Determine the percentage rent decrease for a rental unit that is subject to the application by dividing the amount determined under paragraph 1 by the total of the annual rents for all of the rental units in the residential complex and multiplying that quotient by 100.

Information to be filed with application

44. The following shall be filed with an application under section 132 of the Act:

1. Evidence of the amount of municipal taxes in the reference year and in the base year.

2. If the application is made under clause 42(1)(a), evidence of the other charges levied by the municipality in the reference year and in the base year.

3. If the application is made under clause 42(1)(b), evidence of the rents charged for the residential complex.

4. If notice of a reduction of rent has been given under subsection 131(3) of the Act, a copy of that notice.

Reduction in municipal taxes and charges
Definitions

45(1) In this section,

"base year" means the last completed calendar year immediately preceding the day on which an application under section 133 of the Act is filed with the Board;

"reference year" means the calendar year immediately preceding the base year.

(2) For the purpose of this section, the adjusted costs for municipal taxes and charges for the base year shall be calculated in the following manner:

1. If municipal taxes and charges for a tax year are decreased as a result of an appeal of a tax assessment, subtract from the base year costs for municipal taxes and charges the amount of the decrease resulting from the appeal.

2. If a tax notice respecting the reference year municipal taxes and charges is issued on or after November 1 in the base year,

   i. subtract from the base year costs for municipal taxes and charges the amount, if any, by which the municipal taxes and charges for the year preceding the reference year exceed the reference year municipal taxes and charges, and

   ii. if the reference year municipal taxes and charges are decreased as a result of an appeal of a tax assessment, the amount of the decrease resulting from the appeal shall be taken into account in determining the amount by which the municipal taxes and charges for the year preceding the reference year exceed the reference year municipal taxes and charges for the purpose of subparagraph i, and shall not be subtracted under paragraph 1.

3. A decrease in municipal taxes and charges as a result of an appeal of a tax assessment shall not be considered under paragraph 1 or 2 if,

   i. the decrease is for a tax year before 1996, or

   ii. the application for the rent reduction was filed more than 12 months after the decision on the appeal was issued.

(3) The following are prescribed as the rules for making findings on an application for a reduction in rent due to a reduction in the municipal taxes and charges for the residential complex:

1. If the reduction in municipal taxes and charges takes effect in the base year, the amount of the allowance is the amount by which the costs for the reference year exceed the costs for the base year.

2. Otherwise, the amount of the allowance is the amount by which the costs for the base year exceed the adjusted costs for the base year.

(4) The percentage rent decrease for a rental unit that is subject to an application under section 133 of the Act shall be calculated in the following manner:

1. Divide the amount of the allowance determined under subsection (3) by the total of the annual rents for the rental units in the residential complex.

2. Multiply the amount determined under paragraph 1 by 100.

(5) If the landlord or the tenant does not prove the total of the annual rents for the rental units in the residential complex, the percentage rent decrease shall be calculated in the following manner:

1. Divide the amount of the allowance determined under subsection (3) by the reference year costs.

2. Multiply the amount determined under paragraph 1 by 20 for properties that fall under the multi-residential property class as defined in section 4 of Ontario Regulation 282/98 (General) made under the *Assessment Act*, and 15 otherwise.

(6) A rent reduction order made under section 133 of the Act takes effect on the first day of the first rental period that commences on or after the date the application was filed with the Board.

PART VI   GENERAL

Hours for retrieval of property

46. For the purposes of subsection 41(3) of the Act, a landlord shall make an evicted tenant's property available between the hours of 8 a.m. and 8 p.m.

Contents of information package

47. The information package referred to in section 140 of the Act must contain the following information:

1. List of the different types of accommodation provided and the alternative packages of care services and meals available as part of the total charge.

2. Charges for the different types of accommodation and for the alternative packages of care services and meals.

3. Minimum staffing levels and qualifications of staff.

4. Details of the emergency response system, if any, or a statement that there is no emergency response system.

5. List and fee schedule of the additional services and meals available from the landlord on a user pay basis.

6. Internal procedures, if any, for dealing with complaints, including a statement as to whether tenants have any right of appeal from an initial decision, or a statement that there is no internal procedure for dealing with complaints.

Care homes
48. The prescribed period for the purposes of clause 144(1)(b) of the Act is four years.

Interpretation
49. For the purpose of clause 148(1)(a) of the Act, the expression "no longer requires the level of care provided by the landlord" includes circumstances where the tenant has repeatedly and substantially withdrawn from participation in some or all of the care services provided by the landlord that are set out in the tenancy agreement, and the tenant is not receiving substantially equivalent community based services.

Mobile homes
50. For the purpose of section 165 of the Act, the prescribed amount is the greater of,

(a) $50 per month; and

(b) the amount, including the guideline, that the landlord would have been entitled to take as a rent increase under an order under subsection 126(10) of the Act before the first anniversary of the commencement of the new tenancy had the former tenant remained the tenant.

Interpretation
51. For the purpose of section 167 of the Act, the definition of "infrastructure work" includes work with respect to fire hydrants and related systems, poles for telephone service, walkways, garbage storage and disposal areas, fencing, retaining walls and flood control systems.

PART VII   BOARD—ADMINISTRATION AND POWERS

Employees
52. Employees of the Board shall be appointed under the *Public Service Act*.

Information to accompany application
53. An application to the Board must be accompanied by the following information:

1. If the application is with respect to a notice of termination on any ground, a copy of the notice of termination and a certificate of service of the notice of termination, if notice was given by the landlord.

2. If the application is with respect to a notice of termination for demolition, conversion repair or severance, in addition to the information required by paragraph 1, evidence, where required, that the landlord paid the necessary compensation required under section 52, 54 or 55 of the Act or found acceptable alternative accommodation for the tenant.

3. If the application is with respect to a notice of termination due to a second contravention in six months, in addition to the information required by paragraph 1, a copy of the original notice of termination and a copy of the certificate of service of the original notice of termination.

4. If the application is made under section 77 of the Act with respect to an agreement to terminate the tenancy, a copy of the agreement.

5. If the application is with respect to a review of a work order under section 226 of the Act, a copy of the work order.

Board notice
54(1) The following information shall be included in the notice set out in subsection 189(1) of the Act:

1. The Board's file number for the application.

2. Where scheduled, the date of the hearing.

3. Contact information for the Board.

(2) An application filed under section 77 or 78 of the Act is prescribed for the purposes of subsection 189(2) of the Act.

Service of notice
55. Where an application is scheduled to be heard within seven days of the application being filed, the Board shall send the notice referred to in section 189 of the Act to the respondent by courier service or, where courier service to the rental unit is not available, the Board shall attempt to contact the respondent by telephone and send the notice by mail.

Restriction on altering time requirements
56. The following are time requirements that the Board may not extend or shorten under subsection 190(2) of the Act:

1. All time requirements related to notice requirements for terminating tenancies.

2. All deadlines for filing applications, other than those which the Board is expressly permitted to extend or shorten under subsection 190(1) of the Act.

3. The 24-hour notice required under subsection 27(1) of the Act.

4. The 72-hour period referred to in subsection 41(2) of the Act.

5. The six-month periods referred to in subsections 42(7), 92(3) and (4) and 162(4) and (5) of the Act.

6. The 30-day period referred to in subsection 46(1) of the Act.

7. The period described in subsection 77(5) of the Act during which an eviction order is not effective.

8. The period described in subsection 80(1) of the Act, subject to subsection 80(2) of the Act, during which an eviction order is not effective.

9. The 30-day period referred to in subsection 91(1) of the Act.

10. The seven-day period referred to in clause 95(4)(d) of the Act.

11. The 60-day period referred to in subsection 104(3) of the Act.

12. The 90-day notice period required by sections 116 and 150 of the Act.

13. The 12-month period referred to in subsection 119(1) of the Act.

14. The five-day period in which an agreement to increase the rent charged may be cancelled under subsection 121(4) of the Act.

15. The six-day period referred to in subsection 121(5) of the Act.

16. The one-year period after which rent and rent increases shall be deemed to be lawful under subsections 136(1) and (2) of the Act.

17. The five-day period in which a tenancy agreement may be cancelled, as described in section 141 of the Act.

18. The 10-day period referred to in subsection 145(2) of the Act.

19. The 30-day period referred to in subsection 206(6) of the Act.

20. The 60-day period referred to in paragraph 2 of subsection 3(3) of this Regulation.

21. The 45-day periods referred to in paragraphs 4 and 5 of subsection 3(3) of this Regulation.

Financial matters

57(1) The Board may establish bank accounts in the name of the Board into which it may place money paid to the Board.

(2) The Board may invest money paid to the Board in investments in which the Minister of Finance may invest public money under section 3 of the *Financial Administration Act*.

(3) The Board may employ a trust corporation to make the investments or to act as a custodian of the securities purchased as investments.

(4) Money paid into the Board shall bear interest at the rate of 0.25 per cent per year, compounded semi-annually.

Prescribed amount

58. The amount prescribed for the purpose of subsection 207(4) of the Act is five dollars.

Filings in electronic format

59(1) If the Board permits an application to be filed in an electronic format by electronic means, "sign" for the purposes of subsections 185(1) and (2) and 186(2) of the Act means to type one's name on the application, and "signed" and "signs" have a corresponding meaning.

(2) If the Board permits an application to be filed in an electronic format by electronic means, "shall be accompanied by the prescribed information" in subsection 185(1) of the Act shall be interpreted as requiring the mailing, faxing or delivery of the prescribed information such that it is received by the Board, or is deemed under the Act to have been given to the Board, within five days following the day on which the application was filed electronically with the Board.

Contingency fees

60. For the purpose of section 214 of the Act, the allowed amount of a contingency fee charged by an agent of a landlord or tenant is 10 per cent of the amount that has been or may be recovered, gained or saved, in whole or in part, over a one-year period through the efforts of the agent.

PART VIII   OTHER MATTERS

Transition

61. Section 32 of this Regulation applies with necessary modifications to an application to which subsection 242(7) of the Act applies despite any regulation made under the *Tenant Protection Act, 1997*.

62. OMITTED (REVOKES OTHER REGULATIONS).

63. OMITTED (PROVIDES FOR COMING INTO FORCE OF PROVISIONS OF THIS REGULATION).

SCHEDULE   USEFUL LIFE OF WORK DONE OR THING PURCHASED

Column 1 *Work done or thing purchased*	Column 2 *Useful life in years*
Sitework	
1. Fences	
i. Concrete	20
ii. Steel, Chain Link	15
iii. Metal, Wrought Iron	25
iv. Wood	15
2. Landscaping	
i. Dead Tree Removal	20
ii. New Trees	20
iii. Shrub Replacement	15
iv. Sodding	10
3. Parking Lot, Driveways and Walkways	
i. Asphalt	15
ii. Concrete	15
iii. Gravel	10
iv. Interlocking Brick	20
v. Repairs	5
Concrete	
1. Curbs and Patio Slabs	15
2. Foundation Walls	20
3. Garage Concrete Floor (Slab) and Rebar Repairs	10
4. Retaining Walls	25

Work done or thing purchased	*Useful life in years*
5. Stairs and porches	10
6. Balcony Slabs	10
Masonry	
1. Chimney	
i. Masonry (Brick, Block)	20
ii. Metalbestos Type	15
iii. Repairs, Masonry	15
2. Masonry	
i. Repairs, Tuck Pointing	15
ii. Replacement	20
3. Sandblasting	25
Metals	
1. Balcony Railings, Steel	15
Wood and Plastics	
1. Balcony Railings, Wood	10
2. Decks and Porches	20
3. Retaining Walls, Wood	15
Thermal and Moisture Protection	
1. Caulking	10
2. Eavestrough and Downpipes	
i. Aluminium, Plastic	15
ii. Galvanized	20
3. Garage Conc. Floor, Waterproofing	
i. Membrane	15
ii. Sealer	5
4. Insulation	20
5. Metal Flashing	
i. Aluminium	25
ii. Galvanized, Painted	15
iii. Steel, Prefinished	10
6. Roof	
i. Cedar Shakes	25
ii. Clay Tiles	25
iii. Built Up	15
iv. Inverted four-ply	20
v. Metal Panels	25
vi. Sarnafil	25
vii. Single ply	20
viii. Slate	25
ix. Sloped (Asphalt Shingles)	15
x. Repairs	5
7. Siding	
i. Asphalt Shingles	15
ii. Cedar	25
iii. Cedar Shakes	25
iv. Insulated Panel, Aluminium	25
v. Steel	25
vi. Masonite	20
vii. Plywood	10
viii. Stucco	20

Work done or thing purchased	*Useful life in years*
8. Soffits and Fascia	
i. Aluminium	25
ii. Gypsum	15
iii. Plywood	20
iv. Pre-finished Steel	25
v. Vinyl	25
vi. Wood	15
9. Waterproofing, Above Ground	15
Doors and Windows	
1. Aluminium Storm Doors and Windows	15
2. Doors	
i. Aluminium, Steel	20
ii. Patio	20
iii. Wood	20
3. Garage Door and Operator	10
4. Lock Replacement, Building	20
5. Window Framing	
i. Aluminium	20
ii. Wood	15
Finishes	
1. Carpets	
i. Common Areas	10
ii. Ensuite	10
2. Flooring	
i. Asphalt	10
ii. Ceramic Tile	10
iii. Hardwood	20
iv. Linoleum	10
v. Marble	25
vi. Parquet	20
vii. Quarry Tile	10
viii. Restaining	5
ix. Rubber Tiles	20
x. Sanding	5
xi. Vinyl Tile	10
3. Gypsum Board	
i. Repairs	5
ii. Replacement	20
4. Marble Wall Panels	25
5. Mirror Panels	10
6. Painting	
i. Exterior: Walls, Trim, Balconies	5
ii. Interior: Common Areas, Ensuite	10
7. Panelling	20
8. Suspended Ceilings	
i. Fibre	15
ii. Metal	25
9. Wallcovering, Vinyl	10

Work done or thing purchased	Useful life in years
Specialties	
1 Bicycle Racks	10
2. Building, Storage/Service	20
3. Lockers	
i. Recreational	15
ii. Storage	15
4. Mailboxes	15
5. Playground Equipment (Swings, etc.)	10
6. Satellite Dish	10
7. Saunas	
i. Heaters	10
ii. Walls	15
8. Steel Television Antennae	15
9. Swimming Pool	
i. Above Ground	10
ii. Ceramic Tile	15
iii. Concrete	20
iv. Heater	10
v. Painting	5
vi. Pump, Filter	15
vii. Vinyl	15
10. Whirlpool, Jacuzzi	15
Equipment	
1. Backhoe	10
2. Dehumidifiers	10
3. Floor Polishers	
i. Commercial	15
ii. Domestic	5
4. Front End Loader	10
5. Garbage Bins, Boxes	10
6. Garbage Compactors	15
7. Garbage Disposers	5
8. Garbage Huts	
i. Metal	20
ii. Wood	15
9. Humidifiers	10
10. Incinerator	15
11. Metal Scaffold	20
12. Power Lawnmower	10
13. Snow Blower	10
14. Tractors, Small	10
15. Trucks, Pick-up and Delivery	10
16. Vacuums, Commercial	10
Furnishings	
1. Appliances	
i. Clothes Dryer	15
ii. Dishwasher	10
iii. Microwave	10
iv. Refrigerator	15
v. Stove	15
vi. Washing Machine	15
2. Cabinets, Counters: Bath, Kitchen	25

Work done or thing purchased	Useful life in years
3. Drapes	10
4. Furniture	
i. Couches	10
ii. Folding Chairs and Tables	10
iii. Office	10
5. Pictures	15
6. Venetian Blinds	10
Conveying Systems	
1. Elevators	
i. Electrical Controls	15
ii. Interior Wall Panels	15
iii. New Installation	20
iv. Mechanical Retrofit (Cable System)	15
Mechanical	
1. Heating, Ventilation and Air Conditioning	
i. Boilers	
A. Gas Fired Atmospheric	15
B. Hot Water	15
C. Insulation	25
D. Retubing	20
E. Steam	25
ii. Central System (air conditioning)	15
iii. Chiller	25
iv. Cooling Tower	25
v. Corridor System	15
vi. Exhaust and Supply Fans	20
vii. Fan Coil Units	20
viii. Furnace	
A. Electric, Forced Air	25
B. Oil, Gas, Forced Air	25
C. Oil, Gas, Wall or Floor	20
ix. Heat Exchanger	15
x. Heat Pumps	15
xi. Heating System	
A. Electric	10
B. Hot Air	15
C. Hot Water	25
D. Steam	10
xii. Hot Water Tanks	
A. Commercial	20
B. Domestic	25
xiii. Sanitary Exhaust	
A. Central System	20
B. Individual System	15
xiv. Stair Pressurization Fans	20
xv. Units (Air Conditioners)	
A. Incremental	15
B. Sleeve, Window	10

Work done or thing purchased   *Useful life in years*

2. Mechanical
   i. Culvert (Metal, Concrete)   25
   ii. Drains, Stacks (Plastic)   20
   iii. Lawn Sprinklers
     (Underground)   10
   iv. Plumbing Fixtures
     A. Faucets   10
     B. Tubs, Toilets, Sinks   15
   v. Pumps
     A. Booster, Circulating   25
     B. Fire, Jockey   15
     C. Sump   15
   vi. Risers   25
   vii. Sanitary System   25
   viii. Septic Tank and Tile Bed   20
   ix. Storm System   25
   x. Valves, Access Doors,
     Fittings, etc.   15
   xi. Water Softener   15
   xii. Water Treatment   20
   xiii. Wells and Water System   20

Electrical
1. Electric Heating Cables
  (Garage Ramp)   10
2. Emergency Lighting
  (Battery Operated)   15
3. Emergency System
   i. Lighting   20
   ii. Generator   25
4. Fire Extinguishers   10
5. Fire System
  (Alarms, Smoke Detectors)   15
6. Intercom   15
7. Light Fixtures
   i. Exterior   15
   ii. Interior:
     Common Areas, Ensuite   10
8. Panel and Distribution   15
9. Power Line   25
10. Rewiring   25
11. Street Lighting   15
12. Surveillance System
   i. Cameras   15
   ii. Monitors   15
   iii. Switchers   15
13. Switches and Splitters   25
14. Temperature Control
   i. Electric
     A. Indoor   15
     B. Outdoor   15
   ii. Pneumatic   20
15. Transformer   25

O. Reg. 516/06, Sched.

ONTARIO REGULATION 517/06 MAINTENANCE STANDARDS

Consolidation Period: From January 31, 2007 to the e-Laws currency date.

No amendments.

CONTENTS

PART I   INTERPRETATION AND APPLICATION

Definitions

1. In this Regulation,

"exterior common areas" includes roads, pathways, parking areas, garbage storage areas, grounds for the use of tenants and, in a mobile home park or land lease community, the sites on which homes are situated;

"guard" means a barrier, that may or may not have openings through it;

"habitable space" means a room or area used or intended to be used for living, sleeping, cooking or eating purposes and includes a washroom.

Maintenance standards and compliance

2(1) This Regulation prescribes the maintenance standards for the purposes of subsection 224(1) of the Act.

(2) Except as otherwise provided, the landlord shall ensure that the maintenance standards in this Regulation are complied with.

Good workmanship

3. All repairs to and maintenance of a rental unit or residential complex shall be carried out in a manner and with the materials that are accepted as good workmanship in the trades concerned.

Municipal property standards by-laws applicable to exterior

4. If there is a municipal property standards by-law applicable only to the exterior of residential complexes or rental units, the maintenance standards in this Regulation that relate to the exterior of residential complexes or rental units do not apply to the residential complexes or rental units in the municipality that are subject to the by-law, but the maintenance standards in this Regulation that relate to the interior of residential complexes or rental units do apply to them.

PART II   STRUCTURAL ELEMENTS

Maintenance

5. The structural elements in a residential complex shall be maintained in a sound condition so as to be capable of safely sustaining their own weight and any load or force that may normally be imposed.

Structural soundness, etc.

6(1) Every floor of a basement, cellar or crawl space, and every slab at ground level, foundation wall, wall and roof shall be structurally sound, weathertight and damp-proofed and shall be maintained so as to reasonably protect against deterioration, including that due to weather, fungus, dry rot, rodents, vermin or insects.

(2) The site upon which a residential complex is situated shall be graded and drained to prevent the ponding of water on the surface, the erosion of soil and the entrance of water into a building or structure.

Roofs

7(1) Every roof shall be watertight.

(2) The roof and any cornice flashing, fascia, soffit, coping, gutter, rainwater leader, vent or other roof structure,

(a) shall be maintained to properly perform their intended function; and

(b) shall be kept clear of obstructions, hazards and dangerous accumulations of snow and ice.

Retaining walls, guards and fences

8. Retaining walls, guards and fences in exterior common areas shall be maintained in a structurally sound condition and free from hazards.

PART III   UTILITIES AND SERVICES
Plumbing
Maintenance

9(1) Plumbing and drainage systems in a residential complex, and their appurtenances, shall be maintained free from leaks, defects and obstructions and adequately protected from freezing.

(2) A residential complex shall be provided with a means of sewage disposal.

(3) The means of sewage disposal shall be maintained in a good state of repair.

Required fixtures

10(1) Subject to subsections (2), (3) and (4), every rental unit shall contain the following fixtures:

1. A toilet.
2. A kitchen sink.
3. A washbasin.
4. A bathtub or shower.

(2) Subsection (1) does not apply to rental units that share a fixture described in paragraph 1, 2 or 4 of subsection (1) if no more than two rental units share the fixture and access to the fixture from each rental unit is possible without,

(a) passing through another rental unit;

(b) travelling along an unheated corridor; or

(c) travelling outside the building containing the rental units.

(3) Subsection (1) does not apply to a boarding house or lodging house if,

(a) there is at least one toilet, one washbasin and one bathtub or shower for every five rental units;

(b) all tenants have access to a kitchen sink; and

(c) all fixtures mentioned in clauses (a) and (b) are available in each building containing rental units.

(4) Subsection (1) does not apply to a residential complex or rental unit that has never been provided with piped water.

(5) The fixtures required by this section shall be maintained in a good state of repair and in a safely operable condition and shall be supplied with a supply of potable water sufficient for normal household use at a flow and pressure sufficient for the intended use of the fixtures.

Hot and cold running water

11(1) Every kitchen sink, washbasin, bathtub and shower shall be provided, by safe equipment, with hot and cold running water.

(2) The ordinary temperature of the hot water provided must be at least 43 degrees Celsius.

Washroom requirements

12(1) Every washroom shall be enclosed and shall have,

(a) a water-resistant floor; and

(b) a door that can be,

(i) secured from the inside, and

(ii) opened from the outside in an emergency.

(2) The walls and ceiling around a bathtub or shower shall be water-resistant.

(3) In subsection (1),

"washroom" means an area containing a toilet, urinal, bathtub, shower or washbasin.

Toilets and urinals

13. No toilet or urinal shall be located in a room used for or intended to be used for sleeping or preparing, consuming or storing food.

Electrical
Supply of electrical power

14(1) A supply of electrical power shall be provided to all habitable space in a residential complex.

(2) The wiring and receptacles necessary to provide electrical power shall be maintained free of conditions dangerous to persons or property.

(3) Every kitchen shall have outlets suitable for a refrigerator and a cooking appliance.

(4) If a rental unit has a meter for electricity for the purpose of billing the tenants of that rental unit, the meter shall be properly maintained and kept accessible to the tenants.

(5) This section does not apply to a residential complex that has never been connected to an electrical power system.

Heating
Maintenance of room temperature

15(1) Heat shall be provided and maintained so that the room temperature at 1.5 metres above floor level and one metre from exterior walls in all habitable space and in any area intended for normal use by tenants, including recreation rooms and laundry rooms but excluding locker rooms and garages, is at least 20 degrees Celsius.

(2) Subsection (1) does not apply to a rental unit in which the tenant can regulate the temperature and a minimum temperature of 20 degrees Celsius can be maintained by the primary source of heat.

(3) Every residential complex shall have heating equipment capable of maintaining the temperature levels required by subsection (1).

(4) No rental unit shall be equipped with portable heating equipment as the primary source of heat.

(5) Only heating equipment approved for use by a recognized standards testing authority shall be provided in a room used or intended for use for sleeping purposes.

Fuel and utilities

16(1) Fuel supplied to a residential complex or rental unit shall be supplied continuously in adequate quantities.

(2) Utilities supplied to a residential complex or rental unit shall be supplied continuously.

(3) The supply of fuel and utilities may be interrupted for such reasonable period of time as may be required for the purpose of repair or replacement.

(4) Subsections (1) and (2) do not apply if the tenancy agreement makes the tenant responsible for the supply of fuel or utilities and the supply has been discontinued because of arrears in payment.

Maintenance of heating systems

17. Heating systems, including stoves, heating appliances, fireplaces intended for use, chimneys, fans, pumps and filtration equipment, shall be maintained in a good state of repair and in a safely operable condition.

Air supply and fuel storage

18(1) A space that contains heating equipment that burns fuel shall have a natural or mechanical means of supplying the air required for combustion.

(2) If heating equipment burns solid or liquid fuel, a storage place or receptacle for the fuel shall be provided in a safe place and maintained in a safe condition.

Lighting and Ventilation

Artificial lighting

19(1) Adequate artificial lighting shall be available at all times in all rooms, stairways, halls, corridors, garages, and basements of a residential complex that are accessible to tenants.

(2) Artificial lighting shall be provided in exterior common areas to permit these areas to be used or passed through safely, and to provide security.

(3) Subsections (1) and (2) do not apply to a residential complex that has never been connected to an electrical power system.

(4) Artificial lighting that has been installed in outbuildings normally used by tenants, including garages, shall be kept in operable condition.

(5) Artificial lighting shall be maintained in a good state of repair.

Ventilation

20. All habitable space shall be provided with natural or mechanical means of ventilation that is adequate for the use of the space.

Smoke, gases and toxic fumes

21(1) Chimneys, smoke-pipes, flues and gas vents shall be kept clear of obstructions and maintained so as to prevent the escape of smoke and gases into a building containing one or more rental units.

(2) Parking garages shall be maintained so as to prevent the accumulation of toxic fumes and the escape of toxic fumes into a building containing one or more rental units.

Rooms that require windows

22(1) Subject to subsections (2) and (3), every bedroom, living room and dining room shall have a window (which may be part of a door) to the outside of the building.

(2) A window is not required in a dining room if it has artificial lighting.

(3) A window is not required in a living room or dining room if,

    (a) there is an opening in a dividing wall to an adjoining room;

    (b) the adjoining room has a window to the outside; and

    (c) the total window area of the adjoining room is at least 5 per cent of the combined floor areas of the living room or dining room and the adjoining room.

Doors, windows and skylights

23(1) Every existing opening in the exterior surface of a building designed for a door or window shall be equipped with a door or window capable of performing the intended function.

(2) Doors, windows and skylights shall be maintained so that,

    (a) they are weathertight; and

    (b) any damaged or missing parts are repaired or replaced.

PART IV   SAFETY AND SECURITY

Guards

24(1) Guards shall be installed and maintained wherever,

    (a) there is a vertical drop of more than 600 millimetres (including along the open sides of stairs, ramps, balconies, mezzanines and landings); and

    (b) they would be required for a newly constructed or renovated area under the building code made under the *Building Code Act, 1992.*

(2) A guard required by subsection (1) shall provide reasonable protection from accidental falls for any person on the premises.

Window safety devices

25(1) This section applies with respect to every window in a rental unit that is in a storey above the storey that has,

    (a) its floor closest to ground level; and

    (b) its ceiling more than 1.8 metres above average ground level.

(2) At the request of the tenant, each window referred to in subsection (1) shall be equipped with a safety device to prevent any part of the window from opening so as to admit a sphere greater than 100 millimetres in diameter.

(3) The safety device required by subsection (2) shall not make the window incapable of being opened by an adult without a key or the use of tools.

Exterior common areas

26(1) Exterior common areas shall be maintained in a condition suitable for their intended use and free of hazards and, for these purposes, the following shall be removed:

1. Noxious weeds as defined in the regulations to the *Weed Control Act.*

2. Dead, decayed or damaged trees or parts of such trees that create an unsafe condition.

3. Rubbish or debris, including abandoned motor vehicles.

4. Structures that create an unsafe condition.

5. Unsafe accumulations of ice and snow.

(2) An inoperative motor vehicle or trailer that has remained in an exterior common area for more than a reasonable amount of time shall be removed.

(3) Wells and holes in exterior common areas shall be filled or safely covered and the wells shall also be protected from contamination.

Abandoned refrigerators, etc.

27(1) An abandoned or inoperable icebox, refrigerator or freezer shall not be left in a common area unless it is awaiting removal.

(2) An icebox, refrigerator or freezer that is awaiting removal shall have all its doors removed.

Surface of driveways, etc.

28. Driveways, ramps, parking garages, parking areas, paths, walkways, landings, outside stairs and any similar area shall be maintained to provide a safe surface for normal use.

Locking windows and doors

29(1) Every window and exterior door, including a balcony door, that is capable of being opened and that is accessible from outside a rental unit or a building containing a rental unit shall be equipped so that it can be secured from the inside.

(2) At least one entrance door in a rental unit shall be capable of being locked from outside the rental unit.

(3) If a rental unit-to-vestibule communication system together with a vestibule door locking release system is provided, it shall be maintained in a good state of repair and in a safely operable condition.

(4) Parking areas that are intended to be secured, shared locker rooms and shared storage rooms shall be provided with doors equipped with security devices that prevent access to persons other than the landlord and tenants.

(5) A mail delivery slot that enters directly into a rental unit, and any similar opening for deliveries, shall be located and maintained to prevent access to any door's or window's locking or securing mechanisms.

(6) Subsection (5) does not apply with respect to a mail delivery slot or other opening that has been sealed.

(7) Mail boxes provided by the landlord shall be properly maintained and capable of being secured.

PART V   MOBILE HOME PARKS AND LAND LEASE COMMUNITIES

Application

30(1) Sections 31 to 36 apply to mobile home parks and land lease communities.

(2) The other sections of this Regulation also apply to mobile home parks and land lease communities.

Water supply

31(1) A supply of potable water and water pressure that are sufficient for normal household use shall be available for each rental unit in a mobile home park or land lease community.

(2) An adequate supply of water and adequate water pressure shall be available for fire fighting.

(3) Fire hydrants owned by the landlord shall be regularly tested and maintained and kept free from accumulations of snow and ice.

Roads

32(1) Roads within a mobile home park or land lease community shall be,

(a) kept free of holes and cleared of snow and obstructions;

(b) maintained to control dust; and

(c) kept passable.

(2) Excavations made for repairs shall be filled in and the ground returned to its previous condition.

Mailboxes

33. Mailboxes and the approaches to them shall be kept free of snow and other obstructions.

Distance between mobile homes

34. Where the distance between mobile homes is three metres or more, that distance shall not be reduced to less than three metres through the addition of a deck or ramp or by any other means, unless a lesser distance provides an adequate degree of fire safety.

Sewage

35(1) Sewage holding tanks in a mobile home park or land lease community shall be emptied whenever necessary.

(2) Sewage connections and other components of a sewage system shall be provided in a mobile home park or land lease community and shall be permanently secured to prevent a discharge of sewage.

(3) In subsection (2),

"sewage system" means a municipal sanitary sewage system or a private sewage disposal system and includes a sewage system as defined in the building code made under the *Building Code Act, 1992* and a sewage works as defined in the *Ontario Water Resources Act*.

Electrical supply

36. Electrical supply and connections in a mobile home park or land lease community supplied by the landlord shall be maintained free of conditions dangerous to persons or property.

PART VI GENERAL MAINTENANCE

Floors, etc.

37. Every floor, stair, veranda, porch, deck, balcony, loading dock and every structure similar to any of them, and any covering, guard or surface finishing shall be maintained in a good state of repair.

Cabinets, etc.

38. Every cabinet, cupboard, shelf and counter top provided by the landlord of a rental unit shall be maintained in a structurally sound condition, free from cracks and deterioration.

Walls and ceilings

39(1) Interior cladding of walls and ceilings shall be maintained free from holes, leaks, deteriorating materials, mould, mildew and other fungi.

(2) A protective finish shall be applied to all repairs made to walls and ceilings.

Appliances

40(1) Appliances supplied by the landlord of the rental unit shall be maintained in a good state of repair and in a safely operable condition.

(2) In subsection (1),

"appliances" includes refrigerators, stoves, clothes washers, clothes dryers, dishwashers and hot water tanks.

Heat loss

41. Those portions of a residential complex used for human habitation, including common areas, shall be maintained to minimize heat loss through air infiltration.

Locker and storage rooms

42. Locker and storage rooms shall be kept free of dampness and mildew.

Elevators

43. Elevators intended for use by tenants shall be properly maintained and kept in operation except for such reasonable time as may be required to repair or replace them.

Common areas

44(1) All interior common areas and exterior common areas shall be kept clean and free of hazards.

(2) For the purpose of subsection (1),

"interior common areas" includes laundry rooms, garbage rooms, corridors, lobbies, vestibules, boiler rooms, parking garages, storage areas and recreation rooms.

Garbage

45(1) In a building containing more than one rental unit, one or more suitable containers or compactors shall be provided for garbage.

(2) Garbage in a container or compactor provided in accordance with subsection (1) shall be stored and either placed for pick-up or regularly disposed of so as not to cause a risk to the health or safety of any person.

(3) A container or compactor provided in accordance with subsection (1) shall be maintained in a clean and sanitary condition, shall be accessible to tenants and shall not obstruct an emergency route, driveway or walkway.

Rodents, etc.

46(1) A residential complex shall be kept reasonably free of rodents, vermin and insects.

(2) The methods used for exterminating rodents and insects shall be in accordance with applicable municipal or provincial law.

(3) Openings and holes in a building containing one or more rental units shall be screened or sealed to prevent the entry of rodents, vermin, insects and other pests.

Interior doors

47. Every existing interior door shall be maintained so that it is capable of performing its intended function and any damaged or missing parts shall be repaired or replaced.

PART VII INSPECTION CHARGES

Inspection charge

48. The Minister may charge a municipality $265 for each inspection made under subsection 224(3) of the Act or to ensure compliance with a work order under section 225 of the Act.

Invoice

49. The Minister shall send an invoice to the municipality requiring the payment of one or more charges and the invoice shall specify for each charge the date of the inspection, the address of the residential complex inspected and the date by which the municipality must pay.

50. OMITTED (REVOKES OTHER REGULATIONS).

51. OMITTED (PROVIDES FOR COMING INTO FORCE OF PROVISIONS OF THIS REGULATION).

Landlord and Tenant Board Rules of Practice*

The Board's Rules of Practice set out the procedural rules that must be followed under the *Residential Tenancies Act*.

TABLE OF CONTENTS

Amended: January 4, 2011

INTRODUCTION

Legislation

Subsection 176(2) of the *Residential Tenancies Act, 2006*
("the RTA")
Section 25.1 of the *Statutory Powers Procedure Act*
("the SPPA")

Subsection 176(2) of the RTA requires the Board to "adopt rules of practice and procedure" governing its practice and procedure, as permitted by section 25.1 of the *Statutory Powers Procedure Act*. Subsection 176(5) states that the Board must make its rules available to the public.

Section 25.1 of the SPPA provides that "a tribunal may make rules governing the practice and procedure before it."

Note: The Rules are set out in **bold** face. The commentary in *italics* is to assist the parties in understanding the application of the Rules and some of the procedures of the Board. Questions regarding the Rules may be directed to the Board by calling 1-888-332-3234, or 416-645-8080 from within the greater Toronto area.

Release Date: January 31, 2007

RULE 1   GENERAL RULES

Legislation

Section 4 of the *Statutory Powers Procedure Act*
("the SPPA")
Section 183 of the *Residential Tenancies Act, 2006*
("the RTA")

1.1 These Rules will be interpreted broadly to produce the fairest and most expeditious resolution of the application.

Under section 183 of the RTA, the Board shall adopt the most expeditious method of determining the questions arising in an application that affords to all parties directly affected by it an adequate opportunity to know the issues and to be heard on the matter. It is important that the Rules should be interpreted and applied in a manner that is consistent with the RTA.

1.2 Where a provision of the RTA or the SPPA, or of a regulation under either of them, applies directly to a particular issue, that provision will determine the issue, regardless of any Rule to the contrary.

If there is any situation in which one of these Rules would produce one result, but a specific provision of the RTA, the regulations or the SPPA would produce a different result, the legislation or regulations would apply. In other words, the RTA, the SPPA and the regulations prevail over these Rules.

1.3 Where something is not provided for in these Rules, the practice may be decided by referring to a similar provision in these Rules.

These Rules cannot deal with every situation. This Rule contemplates that a Member would seek guidance from other Rules on analogous subjects in deciding how to proceed.

1.4 No defect in an application, a document created after the application was filed, or in a step taken in the proceedings after the application was filed, will make the application invalid unless the rights of another party are substantially prejudiced by the defect, and the prejudice cannot be remedied.

If any part of a proceeding is tainted by a procedural error, this should not prevent the Board from determining the case on its merits. The same is true if there is a flaw in the application or any other document created for the purpose of the application. However, this Rule does not allow a Member to disregard any defect in a document created before the application was filed (e.g., a notice of rent increase or a notice of termination) or a step taken before that date (e.g., the service of such a notice). Further, this Rule would not apply if the error was detrimental to another party's rights in a significant way, and could not be remedied. If there is prejudice claimed on both sides, it is up to the Member to weigh the prejudice and balance the rights of the parties. This Rule is similar to a rule of the civil courts.

1.5 A Member may waive a Rule where appropriate, provided that the Rule does not have a non-waiver provision. If a Member waives a Rule, the Member shall give reasons for waiving the Rule in the order or decision. Rules that have a non-waiver provision, such as Rules 4.5, 13.22 and 26.6, may not be waived.

There will be situations where a Rule that is appropriate in most situations would not be fair or just in a specific case. For that reason, a party may request that a Rule be waived, or a Member may waive a Rule on his or her own initiative. For example, a Member may waive a Rule for the purpose of accommodating a party in accordance with the Human Rights Code. In most cases, a Rule would not be waived without inviting and considering submissions from the parties. This Rule is authorized by subsection 4(2) of the SPPA. Despite this Rule, Rules 4.5, 13.22 and 26.6 may not be waived.

1.6 After the application is filed, a party may waive service by the Board or by another party of a Notice of Hearing or any other document.

Under subsection 4(1) of the SPPA, a party may waive any procedural requirement of the "governing legislation." This Rule deals with only some of the procedural requirements to which subsection 4(1) would apply. It deals with a situation such as scheduling the hearing of a set aside motion, which will be heard very quickly if the landlord agrees to waive service of the Notice of Hearing. There are other rules in the RTA and in the Rules which require the Board to give a document to a party after the application has begun. Parties are allowed to waive service of these documents because they wish to expedite the proceedings or because they have been advised of them at the hearing or by telephone.

Amended: October 15, 2009

RULE 2   INITIATIVE OF THE BOARD

Legislation

Sections 16.1, 23 and 25.1 of the *Statutory Powers Procedure Act* ("the SPPA")

A number of rules in the SPPA give a Member the initiative to take procedural steps without a request from a party. For example, under section 16.1, the Member may make any interim decision or order in the proceedings, and impose conditions on the decision or order. Under section 23, a Member may make orders or directions which are proper to prevent abuse of its process.

2.1 Members may exercise any of their powers under these Rules or under the RTA on their own initiative or at the request of a party.

If a Rule applies to a case, it need not be raised by a party. The Member may decide on his or her own to apply the Rule.

2.2 The Member may decide the procedure to be followed for an application and may make specific procedural directions or orders at any time and may impose such conditions as are appropriate and fair.

Members should make procedural directions or orders to assist the parties and bring the proceedings to a fair and expeditious conclusion. The Member may decide that a procedural ruling should be made only with specific conditions, so long as those conditions are fair to all parties. For example, an adjournment may be granted, but the Member may require that the respondent pay a sum of money into the Board, or order that one party pay another party's costs, or direct that there may not be an adjournment of the next hearing date, except in the most extraordinary circumstances.

RULE 3   COMMUNICATIONS WITH THE BOARD

3.1 A party shall not attempt to speak directly to a Member outside the hearing.

The principle is that no party should give any evidence or submissions to a decision-maker, except in the presence of the other parties at a hearing to avoid the perception of bias.

Ordinarily, any communication with the Board in the absence of the other parties will have to be through an employee of the Board. However, a Board Member has the discretion to permit a party to speak to the Member in the hearing room in the absence of the other parties in limited circumstances relating to procedural matters only. For example, if a party attends the hearing on the day scheduled for the hearing after the matter has been disposed of in the party's absence, a Member may still allow the party to explain in the hearing room why they were unable to attend on time.

3.2 The Member may direct a party or representative communicating with the Board to provide a copy or notice of the communication to each other party.

In some cases, a communication with the Board should be disclosed to the other party. For example, if a party tells Board staff that an adjournment will be requested in advance of the hearing, they may be ordered to tell the other party. [The party should use one of the methods of service permitted by section 191 of the RTA or Rule 5.1, unless the Member specifies another method.]

Amended: January 4, 2011

RULE 4   COMPUTATION OF TIME

Legislation

Section 193 of the *Residential Tenancies Act, 2006* ("the RTA")

Sections such as 44, 59, 77 and 116 have deadlines for certain actions

Related Rules

Many Rules have deadlines for which it is necessary to count days.

Section 193 of the RTA provides that: *"Time shall be computed in accordance with the Rules."* It is important that parties understand the way in which the Board will count days in order to know the deadlines for giving documents to other parties such as applications and motions, and filing other documents with the Board, etc. These Rules are also important for landlords to understand since they apply to deadlines not related to an application, such as the time for giving a notice of termination or a notice of rent increase.

4.1 Subject to Rule 1.2, the time between two events is computed by excluding the day on which the first event occurs and including the day on which the second event occurs.

For example, if a landlord is counting 14 days that are required between the date a notice of termination will be given to a tenant, and the date of termination to be set out in the notice, they would

not count the date the notice will be given (the "first event") but will include the proposed date of termination (the "second event"). All weekend days and other holidays are counted. Thus, a notice given on the 10th of the month could be effective as early as the 24th.

"Business Days" and "Non-Business Days"

4.2 The following days are referred to as "non-business days" in these Rules:

> **(a) Saturday or Sunday;**
>
> **(b) a day proclaimed by the Governor General or Lieutenant Governor as a public holiday;**
>
> **(c) New Year's Day, Family Day, Good Friday, Easter Monday, Victoria Day, Canada Day, the civic holiday in August, Labour Day, Thanksgiving Day, Remembrance Day, Christmas Day and Boxing Day;**
>
> **(d) if New Year's Day, Canada Day or Remembrance Day fall on a Saturday or Sunday, the following Monday; and**
>
> **(e) if Christmas Day falls on a Saturday or Sunday, then the following Monday and Tuesday, and if on a Friday, then the following Monday.**

A "business day" is a day that the Board is open to the public for the filing of documents and conducting its business. This definition of "non-business days" is provided to assist the understanding of the following Rules.

4.3 If the time limit for filing a notice or document falls on a non-business day, the notice or document may be filed on the next business day.

For example, the deadline for filing a motion to set aside an ex parte order is ten days after the date the order is issued. Where the 10-day deadline falls on a Saturday or Sunday, the motion may be filed on the following Monday.

4.4 A notice or document may be given to another person on a non-business day and, in the case of a notice, it may become effective on a non-business day.

A party is permitted to give a document to another party on a non-business day. For example, a notice may be served on a Saturday, and days are counted from the Sunday. If the days counted to compute the effective date of a notice were to end on a Sunday, it would be effective on that day, even though it is a non-business day. This is somewhat different than the rules of court, but they recognize that some documents given under the RTA do not relate to proceedings, but to such situations as giving a notice of termination or a notice of rent increase.

4.5 Despite Rule 1.5, Rules 4.1 to 4.4 may not be waived or varied.

Rule 1.5 allows a Member to waive or vary any of these Rules in the circumstances of the application. However, the Rules concerning computation of time cannot be waived by the Member in any circumstances.

Amended: December 8, 2008

RULE 5 SERVING A DOCUMENT ON ANOTHER PARTY

Legislation

Section 191 of the *Residential Tenancies Act, 2006* ("the RTA")

Related Rules

Rules 4.1 to 4.5 (Computation of Time)
Rules 10.1 to 10.8 (Serving the Application or Motion & Notice of Hearing)
Rules 11.1 to 11.4 (Certificates of Service)

Section 191 of the RTA provides that a party may give another person a document by various means listed in subsection (1), including handing it to the person, mailing it to them, leaving it in a mail box or a place where mail is ordinarily delivered. It refers to giving a document to a "person" rather than a "party" because it includes all documents mentioned in the RTA, such as notices of termination and rent increase, which are not related to applications when they are given. Clause 191(1)(g) deems "any other means allowed in the Rules" to be sufficient service of the document.

These Rules also set out when a document is considered to have been given to another person, depending upon the method of service used. For service by mail, subsection 191(3) of the RTA provides that service is effective five days after mailing.

Other Permitted Methods of Service

5.1 A person may give a notice or document to another person by any of the following methods:

> **(a) by courier to that person;**
>
> **(b) if there is a fax machine where the person carries on business or in the residence of the person, by fax;**
>
> **(c) for service on a person who occupies the rental unit, by placing it under the door of the unit or through a mail slot in the door;**
>
> **(d) for service on a tenant of a notice under section 27 of the RTA, by any permitted method of service or posting it on the door of the rental unit;**
>
> **(e) if the document is an application or was created after the application was filed, by hand delivery, mail, courier or fax to the representative for a party; or**
>
> **(f) if the document is an application or was created after the application was filed, by any method directed or permitted by the Board in writing.**

Where a notice or document is given by a method other than the methods of service permitted by subsection 191(1) of the RTA or this rule, that notice or document will be deemed to have been validly given if it is proven that the information in the notice or document came to the attention of the person for whom it was intended.

Board Permitting Other Methods of Service

5.2 A Member may give written directions to a party, either on his or her own initiative or on that party's request, regarding one or both of the following:

(a) who shall be served with the application or any other document; or

(b) how an application or document shall be served.

If a party is unsure about how the requirements of the RTA should be interpreted in a particular case, they may ask in writing for a Member to issue written directions. The party may also want directions because they have had difficulty in serving documents on another party according to the methods permitted by the RTA and these Rules. Such a party may ask in writing that a Member issue written directions to serve the documents by another method, as permitted by Rule 5.1. Finally, the Member may, on their own initiative, direct service on additional parties who should have been served or direct the method of service if there has been some problem to date.

Using Courier Delivery

5.3 If a notice or document is delivered to another person by courier, it is deemed to be given on the day following the day it was given to the courier but, if that is a non-business day, it is deemed to be given on the next business day.

This Rule recognizes that couriers usually deliver documents the next day. If the party who mailed the document can prove that the other party received it earlier than the deemed date, see Rule 5.6. For example, if a party paid for "same day" courier service, and the delivery occurred on the same day the document was given to the courier, it would be found to be given that day.

Using Xpresspost

5.4 A notice or document given by Xpresspost is deemed to be given by mail.

Although Xpresspost is marketed as a courier-like service, a notice or document given by this method is deemed to be given by mail. Subsection 191(3) of the RTA specifies that a notice or document that is given by mail is deemed to have been given on the fifth day after mailing.

Using Fax

5.5 If a notice or document is given to another person by fax, it will be found to be given on the date imprinted on the fax.

If a fax is received by 11:59 P.M. on Monday, it will be found to have been given on Monday. After midnight, it will be found to be given on Tuesday.

Earlier Receipt

5.6 If the person who gave a notice or document to another person can prove that the person received it on an earlier date than the date deemed by the RTA or these Rules, the Board will find that it was given on the earlier date.

This Rule would apply if, at a hearing, the date of service is an issue. If the other party admits receiving the document earlier than five days after mailing, this would be accepted. If the party who gave the document can show in some other way that the other party received it earlier, the earlier date may be accepted.

RULE 6   FILING DOCUMENTS WITH THE BOARD

Legislation

Subsection 192(1) of the *Residential Tenancies Act, 2006* ("the RTA")

Related Rules

Rules 4.1 to 4.5 (Computation of Time)

Subsection 192(1) of the RTA states that: "*A notice or document is sufficiently given to the Board,*

(a) *by hand delivering it to the Board at the appropriate office as set out in the Rules;*

(b) *by sending it by mail to the appropriate office as set out in the Rules; or*

(c) *by any other means allowed in the Rules."*

6.1 A document may be delivered in person to any Board office or to a ServiceOntario Centre that accepts service on behalf of the Board.

For example, an application may be filed in person with the Toronto South Regional Office, even if the address to which it relates falls within the area that is the responsibility of the Toronto North Regional Office. The offices at which filing is permitted include all Board offices.

A document delivered to a ServiceOntario Centre that accepts service on behalf of the Board is considered filed under section 185 (under the authority of clause 192(1)(c) of the RTA). A ServiceOntario Centre is an office of the Ontario government which provides a wide range of general information about many ministries in one location.

To determine if a ServiceOntario Centre accepts service on behalf of the Board, call 416-326-1234 or toll free at 1-800-267-8097. This information is also available online at www.Ontario.ca.

6.2 A document that is filed by mail, courier or fax shall be sent to the Regional Office responsible for the area in which the residential complex referred to in the document is located.

A party should send a document to the Board office that is processing or will process the application. Sending the document to any other office is sufficient according to Rule 6.3, but the best practice is to send it to the correct office, avoiding possible delays or filing errors. This Rule recognizes courier and fax as acceptable methods of filing under clause 192(1)(c) of the RTA.

6.3 A document is sufficiently given if sent by mail, courier or fax to any other office of the Board, but not to a ServiceOntario Centre.

While the best practice, as contemplated by Rule 6.2, is to file documents with the office responsible for their processing, the Board will forward the documents to the responsible Regional Office as quickly as possible if they are sent to another office. Documents should not, however, be sent by mail, courier or fax to a ServiceOntario Centre.

When a Document is Considered Received

6.4 If a party files a document by mail addressed to a Board office, it is deemed to be filed on the fifth day following the day it was mailed or, if that is a non-business day, the next business day.

Subsection 192(2) of the RTA provides that a notice or document given by mail to the Board shall be deemed to have been given on the fifth day after mailing or, if earlier, the date it is actually received. A Member may not waive a provision in the RTA. For example, if a document was mailed to the Board on the 7th of the month, but was not delivered until the 20th, it is considered received on the 12th.

This Rule clarifies that the five days is computed taking into account whether or not the fifth day is a business day. A business day is a day that is not a weekend day or statutory holiday (see Rule 4.2). In the example, if the 12th was a Saturday, the document would be considered filed on the 14th (Monday). However, if the document was actually received earlier, it would be found to be received on the earlier date (see subsection 192(2) of the RTA).

6.5 If a document is filed by fax into a Board office, it will be considered received on the date imprinted by the fax machine.

For example, if a document was received by fax at 11:59 P.M. on March 3rd, it will be considered to be received on March 3rd. However, it is the responsibility of the person filing the document to ensure that the fax transmission was in fact received by the Board. No faxes should be sent to ServiceOntario Centres.

Amended: October 15, 2009

RULE 7   FRENCH LANGUAGE SERVICES

Legislation

The *French Language Services Act* ("the FLSA")

The FLSA sets out general requirements for the provision of French language services in the province of Ontario. This Rule sets out the Board's practice regarding its provision of these services.

7.1 Parties are entitled to communicate with and receive services from the Board in French where:

(a) the rental unit that is the subject of an application is located in a designated area of the province as set out in the Schedule to the *French Language Services Act*; or

(b) the party making the request for French language services resides in a designated area.

7.2 Where a party is entitled to French language services, hearings can proceed in both French and English, or fully in French if all parties in attendance consent.

With the assistance of an interpreter, parties may participate in a Board hearing in both French and English. In some cases, however, all of the parties may be capable and willing to proceed solely in French.

7.3 Where a party is entitled to French language services, they must inform the Board in writing as soon as possible before the hearing that they require French language services at the hearing.

It is important for parties who intend to request French language services at a Board hearing to do so as quickly as possible, so that the necessary arrangements can be made for an interpreter.

7.4 Where a party makes a request at a hearing for French language services, the Member presiding at the hearing will decide how to proceed.

Where a party fails to request French language services until the day of the hearing, it will be up to the Member to decide whether or not to adjourn the hearing to a later date so that arrangements can be made for an interpreter.

7.5 Where a party is entitled to and requests French language services, the Board will book and pay for the service of an interpreter.

Where a party qualifies for and requests French language services, the Board will make the necessary arrangements for the services of an interpreter and pay the related costs.

7.6 Where a party is entitled to and requests French language services at a hearing, the Board will attempt to schedule a French-speaking Member within a reasonable time to preside at the hearing.

7.7 Where a French-speaking Member cannot be scheduled to hear a matter within a reasonable time, the Board may schedule an English-speaking Member and arrange for the services of an interpreter at the hearing.

When a party makes a request for French language services at a hearing, the Board attempts to schedule a French-speaking Member. However, it is not always possible to provide this level of service within a reasonable time from the date the application was filed. In such cases, the Board will schedule an English-speaking Member and will ensure that an interpreter is present to assist the parties and the Member.

7.8 The Board will provide all of its correspondence and decisions in French to a party who is entitled to and has requested French language services.

Where a party has requested French language services, the Board will ensure that the party receives all correspondence initiated by the Board with respect to the application in French, including a French translation of the Member's decision.

7.9 The Board will not translate documents that are filed by parties or their representatives from French to English, nor from English to French.

7.10 Where a document is filed in either English or French, the Member may order the person to also provide it in the other language, translated by a qualified translator at the person's expense, if the Member considers it necessary for the fair determination of the matter.

Where a Member determines that it is necessary for a party to provide a translation of a document they have filed, the Member should consider that the services of a certified translator can be quite costly. Where a party uses the services of an uncertified translator, however, the Member may need to determine whether the translation is adequate.

Release Date: January 31, 2007

RULE 8   APPLICATION SCREENING RULES

Legislation

Section 185 of the *Residential Tenancies Act* ("the RTA")

Staff of the Landlord and Tenant Board will check applications when they are filed and inform the applicant if the application is incomplete, or if they note any errors that may potentially invalidate the application; the applicant will decide how they want to proceed.

Although staff will review applications, it is always the applicant's responsibility to ensure that their application is complete, accurate and in compliance with the RTA. Ultimately it will be up to the Member hearing the application to decide whether or not the application is valid.

Applications that will be Refused

8.1 Where the RTA requires an application, other than an application made under section 126, to be accompanied by prescribed information, staff will not accept the application if the prescribed information is not filed at the same time.

Subsection 185(1) of the RTA requires that an application be accompanied by the prescribed information. If the prescribed information is not filed along with the application, the application is not properly filed and it will be returned.

The only exception is for applications for an above guideline rent increase, made under section 126 of the RTA. Staff will not check these applications for the required information before the application is filed. The process staff will follow is set out in Rules 8.5.1 and 8.5.2 below.

8.2 Staff will not accept a landlord's application for compensation for arrears, damages and/or misrepresentation of income where the landlord has indicated that the tenant is not in possession of the rental unit.

An application for the payment of arrears (s.87), compensation for damages (s.89) and compensation for misrepresentation of income (s.90) can only be made to the Board if the tenant is still in possession of the rental unit at the time the application is filed.

8.3 Staff will not accept an application to terminate the tenancy and evict the tenant for non-payment of rent if the application is being filed on or before the termination date in the landlord's notice of termination.

The RTA states that an application to terminate a tenancy and evict a tenant cannot be made until the day following the termination date specified in the notice. If the application is filed on or before the termination date, it will be returned to the landlord and the landlord informed of the earliest date that they can file the application.

8.4 Staff will not accept an application to terminate the tenancy and evict the tenant based on a notice of termination under section 62, 64 or 67 of the RTA if the application is made before the seven-day remedy period specified in the notice expires.

Where a notice of termination gives the tenant a seven-day period to remedy the notice, the application to terminate the tenancy and evict the tenant cannot be made before the 8th day. An application that is filed before the seven-day remedy period expires will be returned.

8.5 Staff will not accept an application to terminate the tenancy and evict the tenant if it is filed later than 30 days after the termination date specified in the notice, unless it is an application based on the tenant's failure to pay rent.

Applications for an Above Guideline Rent increase (s. 126 of the RTA)

8.5.1 Staff will check an application made under section 126 to ensure that the landlord has included the following:

   (i) a completed application Form L5—Application for a Rent Increase Above the Guideline Order;

   (ii) if the application includes a claim under s.126(1)1:

      (a) a completed Schedule 1—Details of Operating Costs

      (b) supporting documents

   (iii) if the application includes a claim under s.126(1)2:

      (a) three copies of a completed Schedule 2—Details of Capital Expenditures;

      (b) three copies of a completed "Information about Rental Units in the Complex" form

      (c) three copies of completed "Capital Expenditures: Additional Details" forms

      (d) two additional copies of the L5 application form

      (e) three copies of any supporting documents for the application

      (f) a compact disk containing the information filed with the application in portable document format

   (iv) if the application includes a claim under s. 126(1)3

      (a) a completed Schedule 1—Details of Operating Costs

      (b) supporting documents

Although staff will check the application to ensure that the necessary forms have been filled out and that supporting documents have been filed, they will not check to confirm that there are supporting documents for each cost claimed, nor will they confirm any of the amounts claimed by the landlord against the supporting documents. Further, staff will not check for calculation errors.

8.5.2 If the information listed in Rule 8.5.1 is missing from an application made under section 126 of the RTA, staff will send the applicant a letter that:

    (i)   lists the information that is missing, and

    (ii) informs the applicant that a hearing will not be scheduled until the missing information is received.

After a landlord files an application for an above guideline rent increase, staff will check the application to ensure that the information set out in Rule 8.5.1 has been filed. If anything is missing, staff will let the applicant know in writing. The Board will not schedule a hearing for an application for an above guideline rent increase until all the required material has been filed.

Applications with Potential Errors

8.6 Unless the application is made under section 126 of the RTA, staff will inform the applicant of any information that is missing or that may be inaccurate and give them an opportunity to correct or complete the information before the application is considered "filed."

These errors include errors or incomplete information in the name and address of the parties and rental unit; not clearly indicating which grounds are being applied for; clerical errors in calculating the amounts claimed in the application and the application not being signed.

This rule does not apply to applications for an above guideline rent increase. The process Board staff will follow for this type of application is set out in Rules 8.5.1 and 8.5.2 above.

8.7(a) If there is a potential error which may invalidate the Notice of Termination, staff will contact the applicant and ask them how they wish to proceed.

    (b) Staff will return an application by mail if the applicant does not inform the Board how they wish to proceed within one business day from the time they were contacted.

If a landlord filed an application by fax, mail or courier and an error is noted that could invalidate the Notice of Termination, staff will call the landlord to inform them of this error and ask them how they wish to proceed. If staff are unable to reach the landlord, they will leave a message explaining the error and asking that the landlord contact the Board by the end of the following business day. Staff will also inform the landlord that if they do not do so, the application will be returned.

8.8 If the notice of termination specifies a termination date that is not at least the number of days required by the RTA for that type of notice, this error is considered to potentially invalidate the notice.

For example, if a termination notice is given for nonpayment of rent, the termination date for a daily or weekly tenancy must be at least 7 days and 14 days for monthly or yearly tenancies. These types of timeframes cannot be extended by the Board and thus, if the landlord has specified a termination date that is less than the number of days required, the notice would be invalid.

8.9 In addition to rule 8.8, other errors that potentially invalidate a notice of termination for non-payment of rent given under section 59 of the RTA may include:

    (a) Failing to identify the tenant of the rental unit;

    (b) Failing to identify the rental unit;

    (c) Indicating an amount other than rent in the total amount the tenant owes;

    (d) Indicating inconsistent amounts that the tenant owes within the notice;

    (e) Incorrectly calculating the amounts the tenant owes (in the table explaining how the arrears owing were calculated);

    (f) Failing to sign or fill in the landlord's or agent's name in the signature field of the notice form;

    (g) Failing to provide contact information for the landlord or agent.

8.10 Errors that could potentially invalidate a notice of termination for reasons other than nonpayment of rent under the RTA may include:

    (a) Failing to identify the tenant of the rental unit;

    (b) Failing to identify the rental unit;

    (c) Failing to indicate the reason for termination on a notice form that has more than one reason;

    (d) Failing to provide any details in the notice of termination where the form requires details explaining the reason to be provided;

    (e) Failing to give complete information in the notice as to how the tenant can remedy the problem where the notice of termination is under section 62, 64 or 67 of the RTA;

    (f) Failing to sign or fill in the landlord's or agent's name in the signature field of the notice form;

    (g) Failing to provide contact information for the landlord or agent.

8.11 Notwithstanding Rules 8.6 to 8.10, it will always be the applicant's decision whether or not to make any changes to the application or file it as is.

8.12 Notwithstanding Rules 8.1 to 8.10, the applicant is ultimately responsible for ensuring that the application is complete, accurate and in compliance with the RTA.

Amended: December 8, 2008

RULE 9   REFUSING TO ACCEPT OR PROCEED WITH AN APPLICATION

Legislation

Section 196 of the *Residential Tenancies Act* ("the RTA")

Where the Board learns of an applicant's failure to pay any fine, fee or costs payable to the Board on or before the date that person submits a new application, section 196 of the RTA states that staff may refuse to accept the application "in such circumstances as may be specified in the Rules." This Rule defines the circumstances where such refusal is appropriate.

*Where the Board learns of an applicant's failure to pay any fee, fine or costs **before** a hearing has been held, the RTA states that the proceeding shall be stayed until the fee, fine or costs have been paid. Where the Board learns of the applicant's failure to pay **after** a hearing has been held, the order shall not be issued until the fee, fine or costs have been paid.*

In addition to these provisions, the RTA allows a Board Member to discontinue an application "in such circumstances as may be specified in the Rules." These Rules establish those circumstances.

9.1 If an applicant has failed to pay to the Board any fine, fee or costs, staff shall refuse to accept any new application from that person until the fine, fee or costs have been paid unless the issues raised in the new application are of an urgent nature.

Although the RTA enables Board staff to refuse to accept a new application from an applicant who has failed to pay a fee, fine or costs to the Board, if the new application appears urgent staff will accept it. An application might be viewed as urgent if, for example, it deals with conduct which seriously impairs the safety of the landlord or other tenants or if it has been filed in an attempt to regain entry into a rental unit where the locks have been changed illegally.

9.2 With respect to Rule 9.1, applications pursuant to section 69 for an order terminating a tenancy and evicting a tenant due to rent arrears and applications pursuant to section 87 for an order for payment of rent arrears are not urgent.

9.3 Where an employee of the Board has accepted an application pursuant to Rule 9.1, a Member may determine that the issues raised in the application are not sufficiently urgent to have justified accepting it, and:

(a) shall stay the proceeding,

(b) shall inform the parties by notice that the applicant must pay the full amount owing by a specified date, not later than 15 days after the notice is issued, and

(c) may discontinue the application if the full payment is not made by the specified date.

Although staff may accept a new application from an applicant who owes money to the Board in accordance with Rule 9.1, a Member may find that the issues are not urgent. The Member may make this finding with or without inviting submissions from the parties. Where the Member finds that the application should not have been accepted, they will stay the proceeding and give the applicant a deadline by which to pay the outstanding monies. Where the applicant fails to pay by the deadline, the Member may discontinue the application.

9.4 Where the Board learns that the applicant has failed to pay a fine, fee or costs before a hearing is commenced, a Board Member shall inform the parties by notice that:

(a) the proceeding is stayed,

(b) a hearing will not be held unless the applicant pays the fee, fine or costs by a specified date not later than 15 days after the notice is issued, and

(c) the application may be discontinued if the full payment is not made by the specified date.

This Rule limits the amount of time the Board will hold on to a pending application once it is learned that the applicant owes money to the Board as a result of their failure to pay a fine, fee or costs. The impact of the applicant's failure to pay, on both the Board and the respondent, is such that reasonable measures must be taken promptly to ensure that the outstanding debt is satisfied before the application can proceed.

9.5 Where a hearing is commenced and the Board learns, before the hearing is completed or before an order is issued, that the applicant has failed to pay a fine, fee or costs, the Board Member hearing the application:

(a) shall stay the proceeding,

(b) shall inform the parties by notice that the hearing will not conclude or an order will not be issued unless the applicant pays the full amount owing by a specified date, not later than 15 days after the notice is issued, and

(c) may discontinue the application if the full payment is not made by the specified date.

Because an adjournment may result in a hearing being held over a number of days, it is possible that the Board will learn that an applicant owes money to the Board after the hearing has begun but before it is completed. In such cases, the Board Member will stay the proceeding and give the applicant a deadline to pay the outstanding fee, fine or costs and may discontinue the application where the full amount is not paid by the specified deadline.

9.6 Where an applicant has failed to pay an outstanding fine, fee or costs by the deadline specified by the Board Member, the Member may discontinue the application without refunding the filing fee unless discontinuing the application would be inappropriate in the particular circumstances.

The deadline specified by the Member provides the applicant with a reasonable amount of time to pay the outstanding fine, fee or costs to the Board. Although the Member may discontinue the application where full payment is not received by the deadline, the Member may decide that this would be inappropriate in light of the circumstances of the applicant(s) or respondent(s).

Release Date: January 31, 2007

RULE 10   SERVING THE APPLICATION OR MOTION & THE NOTICE OF HEARING

Legislation

Subsections 188(1) and (2) of the *Residential Tenancies Act, 2006,* ("the RTA")

Subsection 6(1) of the *Statutory Powers Procedure Act* ("the SPPA")

Related Rules

Rules 4.1 to 4.5 (Computation of Time)

Rules 5.1 to 5.6 (Serving a Document on Another Party)

Rules 11.1 to 11.4 (Certificates of Service)

Subsection 188(1) of the RTA states that "An applicant to the Board shall give the other parties to the application a copy of the application within the time set out in the Rules." Subsection 188(2) of the RTA requires the applicant to serve the Notice of Hearing on the respondent. Subsection 6(1) of the SPPA requires that the parties be "given reasonable notice of the hearing ..."

The Board may set a deadline for the applicant to serve (give) the Notice of Hearing and application or motion on the respondent(s). This is to ensure that the respondent will have adequate time to prepare for the hearing.

The rules for serving these documents are set out in Rules 5.1 to 5.4. In most cases, it is expected that the applicant will serve these documents on the respondent as soon as they have filed the application or motion and received the Notice of Hearing from the Board. However, if there is a delay in serving these documents, the applicant must have regard to these Rules.

An explanation of how to count days under the RTA is set out in Rules 4.1 to 4.5.

These Rules do not apply where an application is resolved by written hearing.

10.1 For any type of application under the RTA other than those mentioned in Rules 10.2, 10.3, 10.4 and 10.5, the applicant must give a copy of the application and the Notice of Hearing to the respondent as soon as possible but not later than ten days before the hearing date.

This Rule applies to applications such as, a tenant's rebate application, a harassment application or an application filed together by the tenants of more than one unit.

10.2 For an application under section 77 or 78 of the RTA which proceeds to a hearing, the applicant must give a copy of the application and the Notice of Hearing to the respondent as soon as possible but not later than ten days before the time set for the hearing, unless otherwise directed by the Board.

Ordinarily, an application under section 77 (eviction based on a tenant's notice to vacate or an agreement of the parties to terminate the tenancy) or section 78 (eviction based on a tenant's breach of the settlement of a previous eviction application) will result in an order without a hearing. For these applications, the landlord is not required to give the application to the tenant in most cases. However,

if the Member reviewing the application believes it should proceed to a hearing, the applicant will be asked to give the application and a Notice of Hearing to the tenant respondents. The usual rule is that ten days notice must be given by the landlord to the tenant, according to the usual service rules, but the Member may direct more or less notice depending on the circumstances.

10.3 Where an order is issued under section 206(1) and a party files a request to re-open the application under subsection 206(4) or 206(5), the party who files the request must give a copy of the request to re-open the application and the Notice of Hearing to the other parties as soon as possible but not later than five days before the hearing date.

When a request is filed to re-open an application that has been resolved by consent order, the hearing is scheduled promptly. As a result, the usual 10-day service of the request and notice of hearing do not apply.

10.4 For applications filed under sections 126, 132 or 148, the applicant must give a copy of the application and the Notice of Hearing to the respondent(s) as soon as possible but not later than 30 days before the hearing date.

The time to hearing is longer for certain applications than others. For example, an application to increase the rent above the guideline, an application to vary the amount of a rent reduction, or an application to transfer a tenant out of a care home. The Board recognizes that respondents may need more time to prepare for the hearing for this kind of application.

10.5 For applications filed under the following sections of the RTA, the applicant must give a copy of the application and the Notice of Hearing to the respondent as soon as possible but not later than five days before the hearing date:

(a) subsection 29(1), made solely or in part under paragraph 5

(b) subsection 41(6)

(c) section 69, based on notice given under:

(i) subsection 61(1) that involves an illegal act, trade, business or occupation described in clause 61(2)(a),

(ii) section 63,

(iii) section 65, or

(iv) section 66.

(d) section 94.

This rule applies to applications to the Board to deal with serious and time-sensitive matters such as the illegal lock-out of a tenant, the retrieval of property after the enforcement of an eviction by the Sheriff and the eviction of a tenant whose conduct may affect the safety of other tenants and the landlord. It also applies to applications to terminate the tenancy of a tenant of a superintendent's unit when their employment has ended. This is important to ensure that a landlord is able to provide accommodation to the new superintendent in a timely manner. Whenever possible, a hearing on these types of application will be scheduled within seven days of the receipt of the application. As a result, the applicant will be required to give these documents to the respondent at least five days before the hearing.

If an applicant believes that the matter should be heard more quickly, they can ask the Board to shorten the time for serving these documents under Rule 15.

10.6 If there is more than one applicant, the applicant who files the application with the Board must give a copy of the Notice of Hearing to the other applicants.

If there are several applicants, it is the responsibility of the applicant who files the application, and receives the Notice of Hearing, to give it to the other applicants. This should be done as quickly as possible to avoid any need to reschedule or adjourn the hearing.

10.7 A party who brings a motion to set aside an ex parte order, an order under subsection 74 (3), or an order under subsection 74(8) must give a copy of the motion and the Notice of Hearing to the other party(ies) at least 48 hours before the time set for the hearing, unless otherwise directed by the Board.

Where the Board issues an ex parte order, the respondent may file a motion to set aside the order within ten days of the date it was issued. Where the Board issues an order under subsection 74(8) to void an eviction order, the respondent/landlord also has ten days to file the set-aside motion. A tenant can also make a motion under subsection 74(11) to void an eviction order after the order becomes enforceable but before it is executed, provided the tenant files a sworn affidavit stating that the required amounts have been paid to the landlord and the Board.

The usual rule is that the party bringing the motion must give 48 hours notice to the other party(ies) by any of the permitted methods of service. However, the Member may direct the party bringing the motion to give more or less notice depending on the circumstances.

10.7.1 A landlord who files a motion under s.126(13)(b) must give a copy of the motion and the Notice of Hearing to the tenant(s) affected by the motion, at least 10 days before the time set for the hearing, unless otherwise directed by the Board.

Under s.126(13)(b) of the RTA, a Member can order that an increase justified in an Above Guideline Increase Application be deferred until the landlord has completed required repairs. The order will include a date by which the repairs must be completed. Once the landlord has completed the required repairs they must file a motion with the Board by the deadline set out in the order. A hearing will be scheduled and the landlord will have to serve the Notice of Hearing, along with a copy of the motion, on the tenants affected by the motion.

10.8 If a party fails to give the Notice of Hearing and application or motion to any other party(ies) in accordance with these Rules the Member may:

(a) proceed with the hearing if the Member finds that the other party(ies) suffered no prejudice whatsoever as a result of the party's failure to serve the documents or to serve them on time;

(b) adjourn the hearing to give the other party(ies) an adequate opportunity to prepare for the hearing; or

(c) dismiss the application or motion if the Member finds that the party deliberately failed to serve the documents in accordance with these Rules.

A Member may proceed with the application or motion if convinced that the party(ies) who were not served, or not served on time, have consented freely and without pressure from the party who filed the application or motion to proceed then with the hearing. The only other situation in which the hearing should proceed on the scheduled date is where the Member is convinced that the other party(ies) had sufficient time after they knew the details of the application or motion to prepare for the hearing.

The power to dismiss the application or motion should only be used in extraordinary circumstances. This would include a situation in which the party who filed the application or motion, or their agent, appears to have deliberately failed to serve the documents, or to serve them on time.

In most cases, an adjournment will be the appropriate way to resolve a party's failure to serve the documents according to these Rules.

The Member may also determine that any delay caused by the failure of the party who filed the application or motion to serve the other party(ies) promptly, without an appropriate reason, is unreasonable conduct as defined in the Guideline on "Costs."

Amended: December 8, 2008

RULE 11   CERTIFICATES OF SERVICE

Legislation

Subsection 188(3) of the *Residential Tenancies Act, 2006* ("the RTA")

Related Rules

Rules 4.1 to 4.5 (Computation of Time

Rules 5.1 to 5.6 (Serving a Document on
Another Party)

Rules 10.1 to 10.8 (Serving the Application or Motion &
Notice of Hearing)

Section 188 of the RTA provides that the applicant shall give the other parties to the application a copy of the application and a copy of the Notice of Hearing issued by the Board for the application. Subsection (3) provides that a party shall file a Certificate of Service in the form approved by the Board in the circumstances set out in these Rules.

11.1 The applicant must file with the Board a Certificate of Service signed by the individual who gave the application and Notice of Hearing to another party.

The Certificate of Service is a document in which an individual declares that they have given a copy of the application and Notice of Hearing to a respondent, or a document to another person (e.g., notice of termination). Thus, the certificate may only be completed by the individual who served the documents (e.g., applicant, property manager, superintendent, process server, friend, etc.). The applicant may not sign the certificate if they were not the individual who gave the documents. The individual must state when and how the documents were served. In some cases, more than one Certificate of Service will be filed for the same application, because there may have been more than one respondent. However, the individual may certify to serving more than one individual on the same date in the same certificate if they were served in the same manner.

The best practice is to serve the application and Notice of Hearing as quickly as possible, and file the certificate right after. If the respondent does not appear at the hearing, it will be important for the applicant to prove that the application and Notice of Hearing were served; otherwise, the Member may not make an order.

11.2 The applicant shall file any necessary Certificate of Service within five days after the application and Notice of Hearing are served.

Prompt filing of the Certificate of Service is important to ensure that the file is complete for the hearing day. Thus, failure to file a certificate may result in an order for costs against the applicant or their representative, even if the applicant is successful in the application.

11.3 If the applicant does not file the Certificate of Service before the hearing, the applicant may prove service of the application and Notice of Hearing by:

(a) filing a Certificate of Service at the beginning of the hearing; or

(b) by calling as a witness at the hearing the individual who gave the application and Notice of Hearing to the other party to the application.

The applicant is expected in all cases to file the Certificate of Service as soon as they have given the application and Notice of Hearing, well in advance of the hearing. However, where this is not possible, the applicant may prove the service of the documents in two ways. A certificate may be filed at the start of the hearing. The applicant may also bring the individual who served the documents to the hearing, and call them as a witness if service is questioned.

Of course, the party who was allegedly served may challenge the facts in a Certificate of Service and give evidence that they were not served, or were served on a different date or in a different way. The Member may also have questions about the statements made in the certificate or given by a witness at the hearing.

11.4 A Member may direct any party to an application to file a Certificate of Service with respect to any document which was given in relation to the proceedings.

Not only the application and Notice of Hearing must be served on another party. For most types of eviction application, the landlord must have earlier served a notice of termination. Also, these Rules require notice to be given to another party in various circumstances. In any of these situations, the Member may require a Certificate of Service to be filed before taking any action that would result from the service of that document.

RULE 12 RESCHEDULING A HEARING

Legislation
Section 183 of the *Residential Tenancies Act* (the RTA)

12.1 Where, prior to a hearing, that has not previously been adjourned, all parties to an application agree to having the hearing of the application rescheduled, the Board may cancel and reschedule the hearing.

This Rule deals with rescheduling before a matter has been adjourned. Before a party makes a rescheduling request to the Board for a hearing not previously adjourned by a Board Member, they must contact the other parties and obtain their consent. The rescheduling request must include confirmation that the consent of the other parties has been obtained. Where the other parties do not agree to the rescheduling, the issue may be raised at the originally scheduled hearing. [See Interpretation Guideline 1, "Adjourning and Rescheduling Hearings" for the Board's policy on adjournments and additional information about making a request.]

The Board usually cancels and reschedules a hearing where the parties agree, but the Board reserves the right to refuse to do so where the hearing has previously been rescheduled on the consent of the parties.

In any case where the Board reschedules a hearing, the Board may determine the length of time to be allotted to the rescheduled hearing.

12.1.1 Other than in exceptional circumstances, the Board will not grant a request to reschedule a hearing that has previously been adjourned unless the request to reschedule has been filed at least two full business days before the scheduled hearing.

Exceptional circumstances are circumstances relating to matters of an unexpected or urgent nature that may suddenly arise, for example, an unforeseen medical emergency or illness that will not allow the parties sufficient time to file a request to reschedule at least two full business days before the scheduled hearing.

12.1.2 Subject to Rule 12.1.1, where a hearing has previously been adjourned and a request to reschedule the hearing is filed, a Board Member will decide whether to:

(i) grant the rescheduling based solely upon the request;

(ii) deny the rescheduling based solely upon the request;

(iii) issue a direction to require written submissions and grant the rescheduling request or deny the rescheduling request after considering those submissions;

(iv) hold a hearing, either orally or electronically, to determine if the request should be granted or denied; or;

(v) require the parties to attend on the date fixed for the hearing to speak to the request.

In exercising their discretion to grant or deny the rescheduling request on the basis of the written agreement between the parties, a Board Member may consider, among other factors:

(i) whether the request to reschedule was made early enough to allow the Board to consider it without requiring the attendance of the parties; or

(ii) whether the request was made early enough to allow the Board to schedule another matter to be heard in place of the matter that is the subject of the rescheduling request.

The Board may refuse a request even where all the parties agree to the rescheduling. This might be the case where, for example, the request appears to be an attempt to delay the process.

If the request for rescheduling is denied, the Board expects the parties to be prepared to proceed with the hearing.

If the applicant does not attend the hearing, the application may be dismissed. If the respondent does not attend the hearing the Board may proceed in the respondent's absence.

12.1.3 In any case where the parties or their representatives request that the Board reschedule a hearing, they must provide the Board with a list of the dates for the three months following the date of the scheduled hearing on which each party or their representatives are not available to proceed if the hearing is rescheduled.

12.1.4 In any case where a rescheduling of the hearing is requested, the parties or their representatives must contact the Board to determine if the rescheduling request has been granted, and, if granted, the date for the rescheduled hearing.

12.2 A party who requests the rescheduling of a hearing must obtain the consent of all other parties, whether or not the notice of hearing and application have been served on the respondent(s).

Although the requestor must obtain the consent of all parties before making the rescheduling request, it is not a requirement that the application and notice of hearing be served before the rescheduling request is made. Where the applicant realizes, before they serve these documents, that they need to reschedule the hearing, the applicant will have to explain to the respondent that they have filed an application against them.

12.3 The Board may reschedule a hearing on its own initiative and the original hearing shall be cancelled.

It may be necessary from time to time for the Board to reschedule a hearing on its own initiative. In such cases, the parties and their representatives will be notified.

___

Amended: January 4, 2011

RULE 13   MEDIATION BY THE BOARD

Legislation

Sections 74, 78, 148, 175,194 and 195 of the *Residential Tenancies Act* ("the RTA")

Related Rules

Rule 14 (Settlements Reached Without Board Mediation)

The RTA gives special recognition to mediation of applications which is conducted by Mediators employed by the Board. Section 194 of the RTA permits the Board to attempt to mediate a settlement of any matter that is the subject of an application or agreed upon by the parties, if the parties consent to the mediation (except mandatory mediation under section 148 of the RTA for care home "transfers"). If a mediation is conducted by a Board Mediator, the agreement may include provisions that contravene the RTA. There is, however, a limitation on agreements reached through Board mediation, since negotiated rent increases cannot exceed 3% above the annual guideline.

Subparagraph 78(1)2.i of the RTA provides that the conditions imposed on the tenant in the order or mediated settlement described in paragraph 78(1)2 include only those conditions which, if not met by the tenant, would give rise to the same reasons for terminating the tenancy under the RTA as were claimed in the previous application. Thus, a term of settlement which is a condition for future termination without notice to the tenant must meet two tests; it must be the same reason that was raised in the eviction application that was settled and the reason must be one recognized by the RTA. For this reason, mediated settlements of eviction applications based only on rental arrears will not allow for a section 78 application based on late payment of future rents, once the arrears and costs have been paid.

The RTA provides that these Rules will set out the way in which the Board will dispose of an application if a Board mediated agreement resolves some or all of the issues raised by an application. If there is no mediated settlement, the Board is required to hold a hearing.

Mediators will not mediate agreements intended to modify an order of the Board, such as an agreement with terms that impose conditions on the enforceability of the order. A Board order is a final disposition of an application and as such, these types of agreements, commonly referred to as "side agreements" will not be mediated.

Pursuant to subsection 194(1) of the RTA, the Board may only mediate landlord and tenant disputes when an application has been made to the Board. The Board may decide not to mediate an application where there is little chance of success, where it will cause undue delay, or where there are minimal potential benefits.

When the parties to an application agree, a Board mediation may deal with and resolve issues which are not included in that application to satisfy the interests of the parties and to make more effective and long lasting agreements.

The Conduct of Board Mediations

13.1 A Mediator shall assist the parties in identifying their interests and in devising ways of satisfying those interests which may be agreeable to all parties.

Mediators are expected to elicit from each party their positions and interests relating to the issues. Mediators will assist the parties in focussing on their interests so as to find potential solutions to satisfy those interests.

13.2 If a Mediator ends a mediation before an agreement is reached between the parties, the application shall proceed to a hearing.

A Mediator may terminate a mediation for a number of reasons. It may become obvious that the mediation will be unsuccessful in settling the issues raised by the parties, or will take an unreasonable amount of time before a settlement becomes possible. One of the parties may become disorderly and refuse to follow the Mediator's requests to act in an orderly manner. A party may be attempting to delay the resolution of the application. A party may be badgering the other party or using inappropriate methods to obtain concessions, or misrepresent the facts, the law or the rules or practices of the Board. In any of these cases, the Mediator may bring the mediation to an end and send the parties to a hearing. Any settlement that the parties reach without the Mediator will be subject to Rules 14.1 to 14.3.

13.3 A Mediator shall explain to any party involved in a mediation the effect of any provision of the proposed agreement which may be inconsistent with the RTA or regulations before the party signs the agreement.

There may be disputes between parties to an application in which a resolution may involve an inconsistency with the rights and obligations set out in the RTA. It may be in the interests of both parties to make such an agreement. However, Board Mediators will not allow a party to give up their rights under the RTA without that party being aware of what they are giving up. The degree of explanation necessary will depend on factors such as whether the party is represented at the mediation session and the nature of the contravention. The explanation may be given in the presence of all parties or in individual "caucuses" with parties.

13.4 A Mediator may describe to the parties to the mediation, the provisions of the RTA, regulations, Rules, Guidelines, relevant case law or practices of the Board.

As many parties are not represented by a lawyer or agent, they will often be unfamiliar with the procedures for a mediation or a hearing. It is proper for a Mediator to answer questions about those procedures or inform the parties about the provisions of the RTA, the regulations, a Guideline or a past decision of the Courts, former Tribunal, or the Board which appears to be relevant.

13.5 A Mediator shall not offer a personal opinion or give advice to either party to the mediation regarding the merits of the application.

The role of a Mediator is to remain neutral, while assisting the parties to come to a settlement. They are an impartial facilitator of the discussions between the parties. They do not decide the case, nor express their personal opinion about the fairest outcome, if the case were adjudicated. In this role, it is not proper to give an opinion regarding the merits of the application or any other issue raised by the parties.

Representative's Authority at a Mediation

13.6 A representative who wishes to participate in a mediation without the party they represent shall do one of the following:

　　(a) file an agency authorization signed by the party specifically authorizing them to enter into a settlement on the party's behalf;

　　(b) if the representative is a lawyer entitled to practice in Ontario, give assurances that the party has authorized them to enter into a settlement on the party's behalf; or

　　(c) indicate that they have the verbal authorization to act on behalf of the absent party and obtain the consent of the other participating parties and the Mediator to mediate with such an authorization.

It is crucial to any settlement discussions in a mediation that all participants have authority to make an agreement. It is not satisfactory if a deal is reached, but a representative must have it ratified later by the party they represent. This leads to situations in which a representative can seek a settlement, and then use the client's approval as a means of trying to obtain better terms. However, if the circumstances are acceptable to the other party and the Mediator, the mediation may be conducted with the participation of the representative, even without written agency authorization. The representative must give assurances that the party has authorized them to enter into a settlement on the party's behalf. The representative must also be prepared to either sign the resulting mediated settlement as the party's authorized agent, or give consent to the terms of the settlement before a Member of the Board in the event of a joint submission for an Order of the Board on consent. If the representative is a lawyer, it is assumed that they would not misrepresent their instructions from the client, since they are subject to discipline by the Law Society.

Settlement Agreements

13.7 A Mediator may prepare a written agreement based on the parties' settlement.

This Rule recognizes that Mediators may involve themselves to the extent of assisting the parties to draft their agreement since the Board believes this helps to ensure that the parties understand their respective rights and responsibilities and promotes the clear and objective wording of agreements between parties, especially where one or both are not represented.

The Mediator will tell the parties that a written mediated agreement will not result in an order of the Board. The written agreement may be structured to provide virtually everything which could be contained in an order, including the possibility of re-opening the application according to these Rules if any party does not carry out their obligations under the agreement within one year. The written agreement may also allow for a new application for eviction being filed by the landlord without notice to the tenant pursuant to section 78 of the RTA if the tenant does not carry out specified obligations under the agreement.

13.8 If a party has paid money into the Board, the Mediator shall direct payment out of the funds in accordance with the agreement of the parties.

Under the terms of the RTA, the Board may establish procedures in its rules for the payment of money into and out of the Board. This Rule deals with any situation in which a party has either voluntarily paid money into the Board or was directed to pay money into the Board. It is important that the funds held by the Board are dealt with, and the mediated agreement must address this. If there is a full settlement, the parties must agree how much will be paid to each party. The Mediator will then use their signing authority in respect of the Board account to ensure that this agreement is carried out properly. If there is only a partial settlement, this issue may be one of those which proceeds to the hearing to be decided by the Member.

Disposing of an Application

13.9 If a written mediated settlement resolves the issues raised by an application the Mediator shall dispose of the application.

When all of the issues with respect to an application are successfully mediated and a mediated agreement is signed by each of the parties, the Mediator will dispose of the application by updating the Board's electronic records to reflect that the application was resolved by means of mediation. If mediation results in a joint submission for an order of the Board on consent, the resulting order will dispose of the application.

Section 148 of the RTA (care home transfers), provides that mediation is mandatory and that the Board may dismiss the landlord's application where the landlord fails to participate in the mediation. As a result, the Mediator must advise the Member hearing the application that mediation has been attempted, and when applicable, where the landlord has failed to participate in the mediation. The Mediator may advise the Member orally or in writing.

Partial Settlement Reached Through Board Mediation

13.10 If mediation results in the resolution of some but not all of the issues raised in the application, the Mediator may present a joint submission to the Board respecting the resolved issues, leaving the unresolved issues to be decided at the hearing in accordance with the RTA.

The parties may be able to resolve only one or some of the issues raised in the application. The Mediator will explain to the parties that the hearing of the unresolved issues in the application will proceed and an order will be issued, but the Member will not usually question the parties' agreement regarding the issues which have been settled through a Board mediation. So that the Member is clear about which issues are left to be resolved by the hearing, the Mediator may present, either orally or in writing in the form of a Joint Submission, those issues which were settled. A copy of the mediated agreement for these issues shall not be presented.

13.11 If the issues in the application are not resolved through mediation but the parties have agreed on some of the facts, a Mediator may assist the parties in preparing an "Agreed Statement of Facts" which shall be presented to the Member at the hearing.

There may be situations where the parties cannot resolve the application through mediation but they do agree to some of the facts. In such cases, and if the parties agree, the Mediator can draft an "Agreed Statement of Facts" for the parties to sign. It facilitates the hearing if the Member can be told which facts are not in dispute.

13.12 A mediated settlement of procedural matters only may result in an interim agreement being signed by the parties and this agreement will be kept as part of the Board's record. Such interim agreements will not be subject to the confidentiality provisions of Rule 13.20.

If the mediation takes place before the date of the hearing, the parties may agree to sign an interim agreement on procedural matters. Such interim agreements may include terms such as rescheduling the hearing to a different date, disclosure of issues, and payment in/out. Interim agreements must contain a provision where each party agrees to have a copy of the interim agreement placed on the Board's record for consideration by the Member when the application is decided at a hearing.

Re-opening the Application

13.13 Either party to an agreement resulting from mediation by the Board may request in writing that the application be re-opened due to the failure of the other party to meet any of the terms of the written mediated agreement.

If a party does not comply with any term of a written mediated agreement, the other party may ask to re-open the original application. A party may ask for an application to be re-opened if either monetary or non-monetary items were not complied with.

However, since the Member hearing the re-opening can only consider issues properly raised in the application, it may not be useful to ask to re-open if the part of the agreement which was breached relates to something outside the application (e.g., brought up at the mediation). Also, as the Member is limited to ordering remedies permitted by the RTA, re-opening for a breach of a provision of the agreement that could not be ordered may not have the desired effect.

This right to request re-opening of the application exists whether or not the agreement provides for the re-opening of the application. A hearing will be scheduled, but the Board may attempt to mediate a request to re-open if the parties consent.

13.14 Either party to an agreement resulting from mediation by the Board may request in writing that the application be re-opened on the basis that, during the mediation, the other party coerced them or deliberately made false or misleading representations which had a material effect on the agreement.

If a party claims that the mediation which resolved the application was affected by another party's coercion or misrepresentation of material facts, the application may be re-opened to review that issue. The first issue at the hearing will be whether there was any coercion, misrepresentation or the furnishing of misleading information. The seriousness of these allegations makes it unlikely that mediation of the request to re-open will be attempted as it would not likely be successful.

13.15 A request to re-open an application must state the alleged breach of the agreement and must be filed, with a copy of the agreement, within one year of the date the agreement was signed. However, with the consent of each party at the time of the signing of the agreement, the parties may agree to a longer re-opening period.

It is essential for the party requesting the re-opening of the application to file the agreement and set out in the request what part of the agreement was not met by the other party, and how it was not met. The request must be filed within one year of the date the agreement was signed. In some limited cases, for example, where there is an extended repayment period, the parties may agree at the time of the signing of the mediated agreement to a longer re-opening period. If the request is filed late, it must be accompanied by a request to extend the time for filing, explaining why it was late.

The procedural rules in the RTA and these Rules regarding applications apply with respect to a re-opened application. In deciding the re-opened application, the Member will usually take into consideration the terms of the agreement which were already met by each party, in deciding what remedies are then appropriate.

13.16 The person requesting that the application be re-opened shall give a copy of their request and the notice of hearing to all other parties to the application at least five days before the hearing.

Since the application is being re-opened, a hearing will be scheduled when the request is filed. A notice of hearing will be given to the party making the request. As with any application, it is their responsibility to advise the other party by giving them a copy of the notice of hearing. They must also give the other party a copy of their request (and, if applicable, a copy of the request for an extension of time). These documents must be served using one of the permitted methods of service (see Rules 5.1 to 5.2) at least five days before the scheduled hearing date.

Confidentiality of the Mediation Process

13.17 Anything said in a Board mediation and any offer to settle the application will be confidential and, where no agreement is reached, may not be used by one party against another in the same or any other proceedings.

It is essential to the mediation process that all parties trust that what they say in the mediation in order to try to settle the case is confidential and will not be used against them later in the hearing or in other Board or Court proceedings. A party should feel free to make any statement of fact or suggest that a fact in dispute may be true in the mediation without fear that it will be used as an admission (that is, the other party must still prove the fact if there is a hearing). Similarly, parties must be able to make and discuss offers to settle, without concern that the other party will raise those offers at the hearing.

By the same principle, parties should be able to make written proposals to settle, or draft proposed agreements. If the mediation does not result in a complete settlement, the document should not be used by one party against another later (whether or not the document was expressly "without prejudice").

13.18 Board Mediators shall not reveal information obtained in mediation to any other persons, including Board Members.

Board Mediators must respect the confidentiality of the mediation process.

13.19 Notwithstanding Rule 13.18, Board Mediators may discuss the issues raised and offers of settlement in collegial discussions for professional development purposes without revealing the names of the parties or other specifics about a case that may reveal the names of the parties.

13.20 Except where the parties agree otherwise, copies of any Board mediated agreements are confidential and:

(a) are the property of the parties; and

(b) any signed copy which has come into the possession of the Mediator will be returned to the parties or destroyed.

The Mediator will normally assist the parties in setting out in writing the terms of their agreement. However, the signed copies of the agreement belong to each party, and any copies in the possession of the Mediator will be destroyed. Signed copies which are given to the Mediator for any reason will be returned to the party for whom they were intended. It is the intention of the Board to preserve the interest of the parties in maintaining confidentiality regarding the terms of their agreements.

13.21 Unless the Mediator is required by law to disclose information provided during a mediation, any information provided to the Mediator:

(a) will not be disclosed to any other party without the consent of the party who provided it;

(b) will not be retained by the Board; and

(c) if it is a document, will be returned to the party who provided it,

unless the party who provided it asks that it be placed on the application file.

The information may have been provided verbally or in the form of documents. A document provided to a Mediator will be returned to the party who submitted it after the mediation is terminated, and no copy will be retained in the application file (unless the party requested it to be filed). However, some documents received during a mediation are intended to be evidence or submissions to be placed in the application, and will be considered if there is a hearing because the mediation is not successful.

Permission to give the documents or information to other parties would normally be obtained when the information was provided, but could be obtained later. Permission will always be obtained before the information or document is shared with other parties. Permission can be given by the party regarding specified information or documents in writing or orally (noted in the file).

Under section 175 of the RTA, a Member or Mediator cannot be compelled to give testimony or produce documents in a civil proceeding if the information came to their knowledge in the course of their duties under the RTA. This means that a Mediator cannot be called to a hearing of the Board or a Court to report what was said at a mediation session or in separate discussions with any party.

However, in extraordinary cases, the evidence of a Mediator may be compelled in Court (such as at a criminal trial, where the public interest requires the evidence). It is also possible that information will have to be produced to a member of the public under the provisions of the Freedom of Information and Protection of Privacy Act. *Further, the Board recognizes that it has an obligation to advise appropriate officials if any potential criminal act or intention is revealed in the course of the mediation.*

13.22 Despite Rule 1.5, Rules 13.17 to 13.21 may not be waived or varied.

Rule 1.5 allows a Member to waive or vary any of these Rules in the circumstances of the application. However, the Rules concerning confidentiality of the mediation process cannot be waived or varied by the Member in any circumstances.

Release Date: January 31, 2007

RULE 14   SETTLEMENTS REACHED WITHOUT BOARD MEDIATION

Legislation

Section 3 of the *Residential Tenancies Act* ("the RTA")
Section 206 of the RTA
Section 4.1 of the *Statutory Powers Procedure Act* ("the SPPA")

Related Rules

Rule 13 (Mediation by the Board)

There will be cases in which the parties, between themselves, resolve an application without any assistance from a Mediator employed by the Board. They may also retain the services of a private mediator or any other person to assist them in settling the dispute between them. These Rules deal with the consequences of such an agreement.

Section 3 of the RTA provides that the Act applies, regardless of any agreement or waiver to the contrary. Thus, parties may only settle an application by agreeing to terms or conditions which are consistent with the legislation. Section 4.1 of the SPPA permits an order to be issued without a hearing, on the consent of the parties, so long as the Act under which the order is issued permits this. The

power to issue a "consent order" under the RTA is restricted by section 3, in that no order may include terms which contravene the Act. This is further confirmed by subsection 194(2) of the RTA which allows a settlement to contain provisions which contravene the Act, but only where it was mediated by the Board.

If the parties settle the issues raised by the application, and part of the agreement is that the application will be withdrawn, the applicant may withdraw the application without the consent of the Board at any time prior to the commencement of the hearing (subject to the provisions of subsection 200(3) of the RTA). However, if any term of the agreement to settle is not in accordance with the Act, the fact that the parties agreed to it will not prevent the applicant from applying again or affect the result of any subsequent application.

If the parties settle the application, and part of the agreement is that an order should be issued in accordance with what the parties have agreed, these Rules will apply.

14.1 If the parties have settled an application without mediation by the Board, and all parties request that some or all of the terms of their agreement be made part of an order, a party may file the agreement at the beginning of the hearing.

A party may file an agreement to settle or "minutes of settlement" before the hearing date, but all of the parties should still attend the hearing. If a party files the agreement at the hearing, this should be done before any evidence is heard. The Member will then review the agreement in accordance with Rule 14.2.

14.2 If the Member is satisfied that the terms of the agreement:

> **(a) are in accordance with the provisions of the RTA, and**

> **(b) do not include any term which the RTA would not permit to be ordered for the application,**

an order may be issued in accordance with the agreement or, with the consent of the parties, another order may be issued that would be more appropriate, based on what the parties have agreed to and in compliance with this Rule.

Parties to an application may settle issues that are beyond the scope of the application in their agreement. Or, their settlement may include terms that would normally not be included in an order for that type of application.

The Member will ask the parties any questions necessary to satisfy themselves that the parties fully appreciate the consequences of their agreement and that it was voluntarily settled. This will be difficult in some cases without understanding all of the facts of the case. Nevertheless, in view of section 3 of the RTA, the Member should ensure that the parties' agreement is not inconsistent with any provision of the Act. In some cases, they may ask for evidence to confirm this.

If the Member believes that another order would be appropriate, based on the basic principles that the parties have agreed to, the Member may ask whether the parties consent to that order. If the Member decides not to adopt the agreed terms within an order, and the parties do not agree to any variation proposed by the Member, the hearing on the merits of the application will proceed, unless the applicant wishes to withdraw the application (and, if required, permission to withdraw is granted, such as in a harassment application).

14.3 If the parties to an application have settled, or are close to a settlement of the issues between them, they may request that a Board Mediator facilitate a mediated settlement of the application before the Board.

Only settlements resulting from mediation by the Board will dispose of the application without an order. Settlement of the issues raised by an application without the assistance of a Board Mediator may result in an agreement, but an order in accordance with the agreement will only be issued if the terms are not inconsistent with the Act.

If the parties have already settled some or all of the issues between them and approach a Board Mediator, the Mediator may agree to conduct a mediation with them in accordance with Rule 13. This will include eliciting from each party their interests and whether the terms they have already agreed to satisfy those interests.

The special provisions for settlements mediated by the Board recognizes that Mediators employed by the Board will have a role in ensuring that the mediation is fair and the parties realize what they may be giving up, if they are agreeing to settlements that may contravene the Act. If the parties have settled the application themselves or through an outside mediator, the Board cannot be sure that the parties were aware of their rights.

14.4 Rules 14.1 through 14.3 do not apply to agreements made under s.206 of the RTA.

Under section 206 of the RTA the Board may issue an order on consent without holding a hearing if the parties submit an agreement. In these cases, it is not necessary for the parties to appear before a Member at a hearing.

Amended: July 5, 2007

RULE 15   EXTENDING AND SHORTENING TIME

Legislation
Section 190 of the *Residential Tenancies Act, 2006*
("the RTA")

Related Rules
Rule 13.15 (Mediation by the Board:
  Re-opening Applications)
Rule 30.1 (Order Void or Stayed)
Rules 29.3-29.4 (Review of Orders: Time for Making
  a Request)

Regulation
Section 56 of Ontario Regulation 516/06

The RTA and the Board's Rules of Practice establish a number of deadlines for filing applications and other documents with the Board, and for serving documents to other parties. Subsection 190(1) of the RTA specifically authorizes the Board to extend or shorten the time for making an application under: section 126 (to increase the rent above guideline), subsection 159(2) (for a deter-

mination that the landlord's grounds for refusing consent to an assignment of a mobile home site are reasonable), and/or section 226 (to review a provincial work order). Subsection 190(2) permits the Board to extend or shorten time for other matters in proceedings in accordance with these Rules.

15.1 Subject to section 56 of O. Reg. 516/06, a party may make a request to extend or shorten time.

For example, a party may file a motion to set aside an ex parte order after the deadline if they submit a request for an extension of time when filing the motion. Under subsection 77(7) of the RTA, an ex parte order is stayed if a motion to set aside the order is received by the Board. When a motion is filed late, it will not stay the order unless a Member decides to extend the time for filing the motion. It is important to determine as quickly as possible whether the extension of time is granted.

A party may also request an extension of time where a Member has allowed a party to file a document by a certain date, and the party realizes that they may have difficulty meeting the deadline. In this case, the party should make the request for extension of time as soon as they become aware of the need for it.

A party may make a request to shorten the time requirement to serve a Notice of Hearing or for other procedural matters. However, the Board has no authority to extend or shorten those time requirements which are specified under the regulations (see section 56), such as notice requirements for terminating tenancies or the 12 month deeming rule for rent to be lawful under subsection 119(1) of the RTA.

A request pursuant to this Rule may include a request to extend the time to either request reasons or request a review of an order (see Rule 15.6 commentary).

15.2 A request to extend or shorten time must be in writing and must set out the reasons why additional time is requested.

Where a document is filed after the deadline, it is up to the party making the request to set out in writing the reasons why additional time is necessary. Documents, except for applications made under section 126, subsection 159(2) or section 226, will not be accepted without a written request for an extension of time.

15.3 Where the request to extend or shorten time is related to a document in a party's possession, the document must be filed along with the request.

For example, if a party is filing a request to review an order more than 30 days after the order was issued, the party must file the request to extend time along with the review request. This will avoid delays in processing the document if the request to extend or shorten time is granted.

15.4 Where the Board has denied a party's request to extend or shorten time, no subsequent request from the same party to extend or shorten the same time requirement will be considered.

Where a party has sought an extension of time (or an abridgement of time, as the case may be) to do a particular thing, such as file a set aside motion, a Member will decide whether or not to grant the request. If the request is denied, the same party may not file another request seeking the same remedy, even if different reasons are set out in the subsequent request.

15.5 A Member may extend or shorten the time for filing a document without obtaining or considering submissions from the other parties to the application.

It may be prejudicial to a party to delay the decision on the request to extend or shorten time by seeking submissions from the other parties to the application. In many cases, it will be necessary to decide the issue based only on the reasons given in the request. However, a Member may seek submissions from the other parties before deciding the issue.

15.6 A Member shall consider the following factors in deciding whether to extend or shorten any time requirement under the RTA or these Rules:

    (a) the length of the delay, and the reason for it;

    (b) any prejudice a party may experience;

    (c) whether any potential prejudice may be remedied;

    (d) whether the request is made in good faith; and

    (e) any other relevant factors.

The Board has the discretion to extend or shorten a time period set out in the RTA or the Rules, or refuse such a request. In most cases, the request will be to extend time, and the length of the delay requested is very relevant. So too are the reasons that the party explains as the need for the extension.

If the extension causes little or no prejudice to other parties, a close examination of the reason for and length of the extension will be less important.

Although subsection 190(2) of the RTA authorizes the Board to extend or shorten time requirements in accordance with these Rules, the regulations limit which time requirements under the RTA may be extended.

For example, a party may request an extension of time to file a request for review because they have requested reasons within a reasonable time, and those reasons were not issued in time to review those reasons and file the request for a review of the order within the 30 days prescribed by this rule.

15.7 A document for which a request to extend or shorten time is required is deemed not to be received until the request has been made and granted.

If the request to extend or shorten time is denied, the document will be returned to the party who submitted it, as the document will not be considered to have been accepted by the Board.

15.8 If the request to extend or shorten time is granted, the document will be deemed to have been received on the date on which the party filed it.

15.9 Rules 15.7 and 15.8 do not apply to applications made under section 126, subsection 159(2) and section 226 of the RTA.

A request to extend or shorten time made on an application filed under section 126 (for an above guideline increase), subsection 159(2) (for a determination that the landlord's grounds for refusing consent to an assignment of a mobile home site are reasonable) or section 226 (to review a work order) is typically handled as a preliminary matter at the hearing. In order to schedule a hearing, the application must be accepted.

Amended: July 5, 2007

RULE 16   AMENDING APPLICATIONS

Legislation

Section 200 and subsection 201(1) of the
Residential Tenancies Act, 2006 ("the RTA")

Subsection 200(1) of the RTA permits an applicant to amend an application in accordance with the Rules.

Subsection 201(1) also permits the Board to amend an application on its own motion and on notice to the parties where the Board considers it appropriate and as long as to do so would not be unfair to any party.

16.1 An applicant who wishes to amend the application before the hearing shall:

    (a) file the written request for the amendment and an amended application;

    (b) give a copy of the documents to all other parties;

    (c) file a certificate of service for the request and the amended application.

The applicant should give written notice of the amendment to the Board and the respondent(s) as soon as possible after the need for the amendment becomes known. The applicant should give this notice by filing both:

- *a written request describing the amendment requested, and*

- *a copy of the application marked "Amended" at the top of the first page, and clearly showing the requested amendment at the appropriate place in the application in a way that the respondent will understand it, initialling the changes. (Usually the applicant will photocopy the application, and highlight the amendment on this copy.)*

The applicant must give a copy of the written request and the amended application to each respondent. This should be given using one of the methods of service permitted by section 191 of the RTA and Rules 5.1 to 5.6. A certificate of service must be filed to prove that the documents were given to each respondent.

The applicant must decide whether the amendment is so minor that it should be raised at the beginning of the hearing, or whether notice should be given earlier to the respondents. The best practice is to give notice of the requested amendment to each respondent and the Board as much before the hearing as possible. The applicant must still convince the Member that the amendment is proper.

16.2 When an applicant files a request to amend an application, staff of the Board will process the amended application and, if necessary, issue a new Notice of Hearing. The decision about whether or not to grant the requested amendment will be made by a Member.

When an amended application is filed, staff will process it according to the usual application filing procedures. Where the amendment affects the information that appears on the Notice of Hearing, a new notice will be issued. The decision about whether or not to grant the amendment will be made by the Member at the hearing.

16.3 If a new Notice of Hearing is required, the hearing date in the new notice will remain the same as the existing Notice of Hearing unless the applicant has consent of all parties to reschedule. If a new Notice of Hearing is issued, the applicant must give a copy to each respondent.

If there no consent to reschedule and there is insufficient time for the applicant to provide the required amount of service of the new Notice of the Hearing, the matter will proceed as originally scheduled and it will be up to the Member at the hearing or who otherwise decides the application, to deal with any issues raised as a result of the insufficient service.

If a new Notice of Hearing is issued, the applicant should give it to the other parties using one of the methods of service permitted by section 191 of the RTA and Rules 5.1 to 5.6. A certificate of service must be filed to prove that the notice was given to each respondent.

16.4 A Member shall decide whether to permit an amendment taking into consideration the following factors:

   (a) whether the amendment was requested as soon as the need for it was known, if that was important in the circumstances;

   (b) any prejudice a party may experience as a result of the amendment;

   (c) whether the amendment is significant enough to warrant any delay that may be caused by the amendment;

   (d) whether the amendment is necessary and was requested in good faith; and

   (e) any other relevant factors.

The Board has the discretion to accept an amendment of an application, or refuse to permit it. Some amendments are necessary because they correct mistakes which are so significant that, without them, the respondent would not understand what they were to answer, or the hearing would deal with the wrong issues. Other amendments are less significant (e.g., a minor up-dating of information, or addition of information that does not change the relief requested). The Member should consider the need for the amendment, balancing this against any delay in requesting it (notifying the respondents) and any prejudice the respondents will suffer if they must respond to it. The Member may consider any other relevant factor when deciding the application.

The decision to accept or reject a proposed amendment will be made by the Member at the start of the hearing, and rarely if ever in advance.

16.5 Where the parties to an application resolve the application through mediation conducted by the Board and the parties agree to the requested amendment, the application will be considered amended.

For example, if the applicant has named a child of the tenant as one of the tenants in the application and both the applicant and respondent agree that the child's name should be removed from the application, the Mediator will make note of this amendment in the Board's file. In this case, the parties would not be required to appear before a Member to have a decision made on the amendment to the application.

Release Date: January 31, 2007

RULE 17   WITHDRAWING AN APPLICATION

Legislation

   Section 200 of the *Residential Tenancies Act, 2006*
   ("the RTA")

Related Rules

   Rule 22 (Written Hearings)

Subsection 200(2) of the RTA allows an applicant to withdraw an application without the consent of the Board if the request is made before the hearing begins. Subsection 200(4) provides that, once the hearing starts, the applicant may only withdraw the application with the consent of a Member. However, under subsection 200(3), a tenant who applies under paragraph 4 of subsection 29(1) of the RTA may not withdraw an application at any stage without the consent of the Board.

When a Hearing Begins

17.1 For the purposes of subsection 200(2) of the RTA, an oral or electronic hearing has begun when the parties first appear before a Member, even if the appearance is only to deal with a preliminary matter.

It is important to be certain when a hearing has begun in order to ascertain whether or not a Member's consent is required before an application can be withdrawn. Note that this definition of when a hearing has begun only applies for the purposes of determining whether or not consent is required, and does not necessarily mean that the Member who heard the preliminary matter is seized with the application.

17.2 For the purposes of subsection 200(2) of the RTA, a written hearing has begun when the respondents' deadline to file responses has passed.

When an application is being resolved by written hearing, deadlines are established for respondents to file responses to the application, and for the applicant to reply to those responses (see Rule 22.4).

Applicant's Responsibility to Notify Respondents

17.3 An applicant who withdraws an application shall promptly notify the Board and each other party.

It is the responsibility of the applicant to notify each respondent that the hearing has been cancelled because of the withdrawal, even if the Notice of Hearing has not been served.

The best practice is for the applicant to notify the Board and the other party or parties in writing of the withdrawal of the application. However, the Board will accept verbal notice of a withdrawal.

Amended: July 5, 2007

RULE 18   SEVERING AN APPLICATION

Legislation

Section 199 of the *Residential Tenancies Act* ("the RTA")

18.1 Where an application is created as the result of the severing of another application, any procedural requirements that were satisfied, or procedural issues resolved in the original application continue to apply to the severed application, unless a Member decides otherwise.

This Rule ensures that a party's rights are not prejudiced in situations where the Board determines that an application will be severed into a number of separate applications. For example, if the Member dealing with the original application grants a party's request to close the file to the public, the party who made the request would not have to make this request again where another application was created as a result of severing. However, a Member could determine that because of the severing, the issues raised which lead to the closing of the original file are now not applicable to all of the applications, and those applications where public access is no longer an issue could be opened to the public.

Release Date: January 31, 2007

RULE 19   DISCLOSURE RULES

Legislation

Section 5.4 of the *Statutory Powers Procedure Act* ("the SPPA")

Under section 5.4 of the SPPA, a tribunal may, at any stage of its proceedings up to the end of the hearing, make orders for the exchange of documents, the exchange of reports of expert witnesses, the provision of particulars and any other form of disclosure. The tribunal must adopt rules of practice in order to use this authority but cannot use these powers to require the production of privileged information.

Disclosure may be useful to facilitate a better hearing, especially if proper consideration is given to the type of proceedings, the knowledge of the parties about procedures, and the desire for an expeditious and fair procedure.

Note that the powers set out in these rules are in addition to the power the Board has to conduct inquiries or direct parties to file

additional evidence as set out in s.201 of the RTA. Further discussion of the Board's powers under s.201 may be found in the Board's Guideline 13—Other Powers of the Board.

19.1(1) A Member may, at any stage of the proceeding, before the hearing has been completed, direct or order a party to disclose and exchange documents or any other material relevant to the proceeding, within the time and according to the method that the Member directs or orders.

(2) A Member shall not direct or order the disclosure of privileged information.

(3) A party who breaches an order or direction for disclosure may not rely on the evidence that was not disclosed as directed or ordered, unless otherwise ordered.

The rules of natural justice provide parties with the right to know the case that they must meet at a hearing and the right to disclosure from an opposing party of all documents or other material relevant to the issues in the hearing. The scope of disclosure includes documents or other material that might enable the other party to advance its case or to damage the case of the adversary.

The Board strongly encourages cooperation from parties in voluntarily disclosing and exchanging all relevant documents or other material, before or on the day of the hearing. Where necessary, a Member will make an order or issue a direction, in order to assist a party in obtaining disclosure in a manner that ensures a fair hearing.

19.2 A landlord who applies for an above guideline rent increase based on paragraphs 1 or 3 of subsection 126(1) shall be prepared to disclose at the hearing the rent for each rental unit in the residential complex, and the date that rent was established for a new tenant under section 113 of the RTA or last increased for an existing tenant.

On an application for an above guideline rent increase based on an extraordinary increase in the cost for municipal taxes and charges or utilities or both, or based on operating costs related to security services the landlord does not have to file a detailed list of rents for all the rental units in the residential complex. They should, however, bring such a list to the hearing in case the total rent information for the complex is disputed by the tenant or questioned by the Member. In addition to the rent information (total rent charged for each unit, before any discounts, as of the month the application is made), the landlord should be prepared to give evidence as to the date that rent was established: if the rent was set for a new tenant, the date is when the tenancy began; if the rent was the result of an increase for an existing tenant, the date is when the rent last increased.

Where a landlord makes an application for a rent increase above the guideline based on capital expenditures incurred, they are required by paragraph 22(1)2 of O.Reg. 516/06 to file a detailed list of rents, among other materials, with the application.

Amended: December 8, 2008

RULE 20   PRE-HEARING CONFERENCES

Legislation

Section 5.3 of the *Statutory Powers Procedure Act*
  ("the SPPA")

Under section 5.3 of the SPPA, a Board may direct the parties to attend a pre-hearing conference. The Board must adopt rules of practice in order to be able to use this authority. The purpose of a conference is to discuss the preparations for the hearing and the hearing itself, including attempts to define and narrow the issues in dispute, disclose potential evidence and witness lists, and discuss the possibilities of mediation.

Generally speaking, the Board will direct a conference to be held only where it is anticipated that there will be a lengthy hearing of one or more days, and the hearing could be shortened or made more effective as a result of a pre-hearing conference.

Direction to Attend

20.1 A Member may direct a pre-hearing conference to be held to consider any or all of the following:

(a) which issues will be dealt with at the hearing and whether these can be clarified or simplified;

(b) whether any facts or evidence may be agreed upon by the parties;

(c) the dates by which any steps in the proceeding are to be taken or begun;

(d) the estimated duration of the hearing; and

(e) any other matter that may assist in the just and most expeditious disposition of the application.

A Member or staff member may conduct the pre-hearing conference, but it may only be held at the direction of a Member. There are various issues which could be considered. For example, the parties could make submissions concerning whether a party should be added or removed, the date by which any step should be taken or begun, the order of proceedings at the hearing and the estimated length of the hearing.

A pre-hearing conference is intended to deal with procedural issues, to the largest degree possible by consensus among the parties. However, where necessary, the conference may result in recommendations or, if a Member presided, a procedural order or direction.

Release Date: January 31, 2007

RULE 21   ELECTRONIC HEARINGS

Legislation

Section 5.2 of the *Statutory Powers Procedure Act* ("the SPPA")

Under subsection 5.2(2) of the SPPA, a tribunal may hold an electronic hearing rather than an "oral hearing" (a face to face hearing, or a hearing in person). "Electronic hearing" means a hearing held by conference call, video conferencing or some other means of electronic technology permitting persons to hear one another. An elec-

tronic hearing should not be held unless all parties, the Member and the witnesses can hear each other at all times.

According to subsection 5.2(2) of the SPPA, a tribunal will not hold an electronic hearing if a party satisfies it that holding an electronic hearing instead of an oral hearing is likely to cause the party significant prejudice.

When to Hold an Electronic Hearing

21.1 In deciding whether to hold an electronic hearing, the Board may consider any relevant factors, including:

(a) the number of parties to the proceeding;

(b) the suitability of the electronic technology for the subject matter of the hearing;

(c) whether the nature of the evidence is appropriate for an electronic hearing, including whether credibility is in issue and the extent to which facts are in dispute;

(d) the extent to which the matters in dispute are questions of law;

(e) the convenience of the parties; and

(f) the cost, efficiency and timeliness of proceedings.

Electronic hearings are most appropriate in cases in which there are few issues of fact to be decided, there will be few witnesses, and they are not likely to be cross-examined. However, cases with some factual issues can be heard electronically. This kind of hearing is well suited to dealing with submissions on procedural and legal issues.

There may be logistics which would make an electronic hearing difficult or unworkable, such as lack of facilities for viewing videos, no way of viewing photographs, or the lack of a fax machine to view documents that should be exchanged during the hearing.

In some cases, an electronic hearing on an early date may be preferred by the parties, and it may also be more convenient than travelling to a hearing facility and spending more time. In many cases, an electronic hearing will result in less public expense and will permit an earlier resolution of the application. This is not to say that the Board will hold most hearings electronically, but this option may be used in appropriate cases.

21.2 A party to an electronic hearing who objects to the type of hearing shall file an objection in writing with the Board by the date set out in the notice of electronic hearing, setting out how an electronic hearing would cause them significant prejudice.

For an electronic hearing (unlike a written hearing) a party's objection will not automatically convert the hearing into an oral one. It will be up to the Member who reviews the submissions to decide whether the electronic hearing would significantly prejudice the party who objects. The Member may, without hearing from the other parties, decide to convert the hearing to an oral hearing (a hearing in person) or to continue with the electronic hearing because there is no significant prejudice. The Member may also decide to invite submissions from the other parties before deciding this question.

Conditions for an Electronic Hearing

21.3 If directed by the Board, the party specified in the direction may be required to arrange for the facilities or equipment necessary for the electronic hearing, including paying any associated expenses.

Where an electronic hearing is scheduled at the request of a party, the Member may require that party to pay all or part of the cost of providing the necessary facilities.

Procedural directions specific to individual hearings could, for example, identify who will be responsible for setting up electronic hearings and paying for facilities, and in which locations video-conferences can be held. Usually conference calls will be arranged by and paid for by the Board, but one or more parties may be required to pay the costs of video-conferences.

Release Date: January 31, 2007

RULE 22   WRITTEN HEARINGS

Legislation

Section 5.1 of the *Statutory Powers Procedure Act* ("the SPPA")

Subsections 184(2) & (3) of the *Residential Tenancies Act* ("the RTA")

Related Rules

Rule 17 (Withdrawing an Application)

Rule 21 (Electronic Hearings)

Under section 5.1 of the SPPA, the Board may hold a written hearing rather than an "oral hearing" (a face to face hearing) or an "electronic hearing" (held by conference call, video conferencing or some other means of electronic technology permitting persons to hear one another). In a written hearing, the parties are required to file their evidence and make submissions to the Board in writing. The Board makes a decision based on the evidence and submissions filed without holding an oral hearing.

Written hearings are inexpensive and easy to arrange. However, they may not be suitable for applications where facts may be in dispute or credibility is an issue.

Subsection 5.1(2) of the SPPA as amended on February 14, 2000, sets out that if a party satisfies the Board that there is a good reason not to hold a written hearing, the Board will not do so. However, subsection 184(2) of the RTA sets out that if the application was made under sections 132 or 133 or if it was made solely under paragraph 1 of subsection 126(1) of the RTA, subsection 5.1(2) of the SPPA does not apply. For applications which relate to municipal property taxes or utilities, parties are not invited to make submissions regarding whether or not the application should be resolved by written hearing.

Subsection 5.1(3) of the SPPA sets out that in a written hearing, all parties are entitled to receive every document that the Board receives in a proceeding. However, under subsection 184(3) of the RTA applications related to municipal property taxes or rent increases above the guideline are exempt from this provision. As a result, the requirement for all parties to receive every document that the Board receives does not apply to applications under sections 126, 132 and 133. For these applications, the applicant is required to serve only the application and notice of hearing on the other parties. As well, the Board is not required to send copies of the documents filed with respect to an application to the parties.

If a party wants to review the documents, they can do so by requesting to view the application file at a Board office. Also, if the application was filed under section 126 and includes a claim for capital expenditures, landlords are required to make extra efforts to give tenants access to the supporting documents for the application. Additional information on these requirements may be found in the Board's Guideline 14—Above Guideline Rent Increase Applications.

When to Hold a Written Hearing

22.1 In deciding whether to hold a written hearing, the Board may consider any relevant factors, including:

> **(a) the suitability of a written hearing format considering the subject matter of the hearing;**
>
> **(b) whether the nature of the evidence is appropriate for a written hearing, including whether credibility is in issue and the extent to which facts are in dispute;**
>
> **(c) the extent to which the matters in dispute are questions of law;**
>
> **(d) the convenience of the parties;**
>
> **(e) the ability of the parties to participate in a written hearing; and**
>
> **(f) the cost, efficiency and timeliness of proceedings.**

The Board may schedule a written hearing if the application was made under sections 132 (an application to vary the amount of a rent reduction) or 133 (an application for a rent reduction for municipal taxes) or if it was made solely under paragraph 1 of subsection 126(1) of the RTA (an application for an above guideline rent increase due to increased municipal taxes or utilities). The evidence (in these applications) is generally straightforward and objective and in most cases parties will not dispute the facts or need to test credibility. As a result, these applications are ideally suited for written hearings.

*The Board may schedule written hearings for other applications such as applications to increase the rent above the guideline **not** based solely on the ground of increased taxes or utilities, or if a written hearing was requested by the applicant. However, a written hearing **may** not always be appropriate, for example, where credibility is an issue, and the Board will schedule an oral or electronic hearing instead.*

22.2 A party who objects to a written hearing shall file an objection in writing with the Board no later than 27 days after the notice of written hearing is issued, setting out why the party believes the application should not be resolved by a written hearing.

The 27 day period for objecting will be set out in the notice of written hearing. If a party files an objection within the 27 day deadline, the Board will consider whether to convert the hearing to either an oral or an electronic hearing. However, if the application was made under sections 132 or 133 or if it was made solely under paragraph 1 of subsection 126(1) of the RTA, the Board can proceed with the written hearing despite a party's objection. A 27 day period for objecting will not be set out in the notice of written hearing for these applications.

22.3 Whenever appropriate, the Board may continue a written hearing as:

   (a) an oral hearing;

   (b) an electronic hearing, after considering any objections made under Rule 21.2.

In some cases, a Member may decide after beginning a written hearing that an oral or an electronic hearing would be more appropriate. For example, the Member may decide that oral submissions are necessary to resolve facts in dispute. The Member may convert the written hearing to an oral or electronic hearing without inviting submissions from the parties. If the Member is considering an electronic hearing, and is aware of any objections to an electronic hearing, the Member will consider the objections before making the decision. Provisions for objecting to electronic hearings are set out in Rule 21.2.

Document Filing Procedure

22.4(1) The applicant shall serve a copy of the application and the notice of written hearing on each respondent no later than 20 days after the notice of written hearing is issued.

(2) If the application was made for an increase above the guideline under section 126 of the RTA, and if a party wishes to respond, they shall do so by filing a response with the Board no later than 50 days after the notice of written hearing is issued.

(3) For all other applications, if a party wishes to respond, they shall do so by filing a response with the Board no later than 34 days after the notice of written hearing is issued.

(4) A response shall:

   (a) set out the party's submissions;

   (b) set out any remedy or other relief requested; and

   (c) be accompanied by the evidence that explains or supports the response.

(5) If the application was made for an increase above the guideline under section 126 of the RTA, the applicant may reply to a response by filing a reply with the Board no later than 65 days after the notice of written hearing is issued.

(6) For all other applications, the applicant may reply to a response by filing a reply with the Board no later than 41 days after the notice of written hearing is issued.

In a written hearing, respondents to the application are entitled to respond to the evidence and submissions made by the applicant. Applicants are entitled to reply to any responses. The deadlines for responding, and for replying to responses are set out in the notice of written hearing. If the respondent or applicant responds or replies after the deadline for doing so has expired, the Member may decide not to consider the response or reply.

Pursuant to subsection 5.1(3) of the SPPA, all parties to the application being resolved by a written hearing are entitled to receive

copies of any document filed with the Board. Therefore, the applicant and respondents are required to serve a copy of any document they file with the Board in a written hearing on the other parties to the application. However, in accordance with subsection 184(3) of the the RTA, applications that are limited to claims regarding taxes or rent increases above the guideline are exempt from this provision.

22.5 If the application was made under sections 126, 132 or 133 of the RTA, then parties to the application are not required to serve copies of any documents filed with respect to the application on the other parties to the application, except as required by subsection 126(4) and the related regulations and Rule 22.4, sub rule (1).

Subsection 184(3) of the RTA states that if the application was made under sections 126, 132 or 133 then, subsection 5.1(3) of the SPPA does not apply. This means that for these applications, parties are not required to serve copies of the documents they file with the Board on the other parties (other than the requirement for the applicant to serve the application and the notice of hearing on the other parties).

Certificate of Service

22.6 The applicant must file with the Board a certificate of service according to Rule 11.1 no later than 25 days after the notice of written hearing is issued.

22.7 If the applicant fails to file the certificate of service by the date set out in Rule 22.6 the Board may dismiss the application.

Rule 11.1 requires an applicant to file a certificate of service demonstrating that they have given a copy of the application and the notice of hearing to the other parties to the application. The deadline for filing the certificate of service will be set out in the notice of written hearing.

Amended: July 5, 2007

RULE 23   REQUIRING A WITNESS TO ATTEND A HEARING

Legislation

Section 12 of the *Statutory Powers Procedure Act* ("the SPPA")

Section 12 of the SPPA permits the Board to issue a summons to require a witness to attend a hearing and give sworn or unsworn evidence and to produce documents, records, and things which are relevant and admissible.

23.1 Any Member may sign a summons to a witness.

This Rule clarifies that the Chair is not required to sign a summons, nor will it always be the Member who eventually hears the case. Since the RTA does not address who may issue a summons, clause 12(2)(b) of the SPPA provides the Chair will do so. The Rule allows any Member to sign the summons.

23.2 An applicant who requests the issuance of a summons to a witness shall provide a written request to the Board, stating the necessity and relevance of the summons. This request shall be made promptly after the applicant becomes aware of the need for the summons.

If a Member is satisfied by the written request that the evidence sought will be relevant and will likely be admissible, the Member will issue a summons. It is preferable that the summons be issued as soon before the hearing as possible so that it can be served on the witness in time to allow them to arrange to attend the hearing. The written request should set out the following:

- *the name of the witness and their address for service;*
- *a summary of the evidence to be given by the witness;*
- *an explanation of why the evidence of the witness would be relevant and necessary; and*
- *details of any documents or things which the witness should be required to bring to the hearing.*

If the party requesting the summons is represented by a lawyer or paid agent, the request should be accompanied by a drafted summons, ready to be signed by a Member.

23.3 A respondent who requests the issuance of a summons to a witness shall provide a written request, stating the necessity and relevance of the summons, promptly after being served with the notice of hearing.

The timing of making the request (same contents as listed under Rule 23.2) is different for a respondent since they do not become aware of the application until the notice of hearing is served on them by the applicant. Again, it is preferable to file the request as early as possible so that the summons may be served by the respondent on the witness as much before the hearing as possible.

23.4 The issuance or refusal to issue a summons may be reviewed by the Member presiding at the hearing.

In some cases, the Board may choose not to decide whether to issue a summons until the start of the hearing, after hearing the requesting party's explanation, and asking any questions. In other cases, where a summons has been issued before the hearing, the Member conducting the hearing may decide that the summons should be cancelled or amended, or if the witness is present, they may be excused from remaining. For example, the Member may decide that some of the documents which the witness was required to bring to the hearing will have no relevance to the facts in issue, and excuse that some were not produced.

23.5 The party who requested the summons shall be responsible for serving the summons on the witness, paying any associated expenses and fees, and enforcing the summons.

Subsection 12(3) of the SPPA requires that the summons be "served personally" on the witness, which means handing it to the person. The rules for serving by mail or leaving it with another person, etc. do not apply. Where a person fails to appear at a hearing pursuant to a summons, a party may seek to have the summons enforced

pursuant to section 12 of the SPPA. Section 12 provides that a judge of the Superior Court of Justice may issue a warrant against a person if the judge is satisfied that the person was served with a summons, the person failed to participate, attend or to remain in attendance in accordance with the summons, and the person's attendance or participation is material to the ends of justice. A party seeking to enforce a summons is encouraged to seek legal advice.

23.6 If the witness attends the hearing, the party who requested the summons shall pay to the witness the fees and allowances set out in the Tariff which is Appendix "B" of these Rules before the witness testifies.

A witness need not be paid until they attend the hearing.

23.7 A person effecting personal service of a summons need not produce the original signed document or have it in their possession.

Although there are many permitted methods of serving an application and notice of hearing, there is only one way to serve a summons. "Personal service" means handing the document to the potential witness (a specific individual, never a company, partnership, etc.), or at least approaching the individual and offering it to them. This Rule makes it clear that the person will be serving a copy of the summons and does not even need to take the signed original with them. This Rule is based on R16.02(2) of the Rules of Civil Procedure for the Courts.

Amended: October 15, 2009

RULE 24 RESTRICTING PUBLIC ACCESS TO THE HEARING

Legislation

Section 9 of the *Statutory Powers Procedure Act* ("the SPPA")

Under section 9 of the SPPA, a hearing shall be open to the public except where matters involving public security may be disclosed or where:

> *"intimate financial or personal matters or other matters may be disclosed at the hearing of such a nature, having regard to the circumstances, that the desirability of avoiding disclosure thereof in the interests of any person affected or in the public interest, outweighs the desirability of adhering to the principle that hearings be open to the public ... ."*

The public will have access to all Board hearings, unless otherwise ordered by a Member. In rare circumstances, a Member will be satisfied that the hearing must be closed in accordance with section 9 of the SPPA. For example, this may occur if there will be medical evidence in a hearing, such as one dealing with a care home transfer application (section 148 of the RTA).

The Board's position on public access is as follows: Hearings will be open to the public unless the Member believes that there is sufficient reason to deny the public access. While hearings are open to the public, the application file is not. This means that while a member of the public can attend a Board hearing, they will not be given access to the file. Only parties and their representatives can be given access to the file.

24.1 If a party wishes to request that the hearing be closed, they shall promptly notify the Board and every other party of the request and provide reasons for the request for the hearing to be closed.

The Board and every other party to the proceeding must know as soon as reasonably possible that a request to close the hearing will be made so that the Board can make any special arrangements required to prevent public access to the hearing. It is important that the party making the request explain the basis of the request to ensure that a Member will have a reasonable opportunity to decide if special arrangements are required.

24.2 If a Member decides that all or part of the hearing should be closed to the public, the Member may:

> **(a) decide which persons who are not parties may be present at the closed portions of the hearing;**
>
> **(b) direct any persons who will be present at the hearing to file an undertaking to maintain confidentiality;**
>
> **(c) issue an order for the parties and a copy for the public in which any personal information related to the closed portion of the hearing is severed.**

Once the Member has heard the submissions of the parties at the start of the hearing, the Member may decide that the evidence and submissions on one or more particular issues should be heard while excluding the public. The Member might also conclude that the entire hearing should be closed to the public. Of course, it is also possible that the request will be unsuccessful and the hearing will be open.

If the hearing will be closed, this Rule authorizes the Member to include specific directions about how the proceedings will be conducted. For example, during the portion of the hearing to be closed to the public, the Member can specify who should be in the hearing room. In a particularly sensitive case, those present can be required by the Member to sign an undertaking not to disclose what took place during the closed portion of the hearing. Further, the Member may decide to issue a "public" copy of the order, and the reasons if they are issued, in which references to the closed portion of the hearing are removed, although the parties would receive the complete order and reasons, if issued.

Amended: January 4, 2011

RULE 25 RECORDING OF PROCEEDINGS

Legislation

Subsection 9(2) and section 20 of the *Statutory Powers Procedure Act* ("the SPPA")

These Rules explain the practices of the Board regarding its own recording of hearings, as well as that by parties, journalists and other persons. Subsection 9(2) of the SPPA permits the Board to make orders or directions at an oral or electronic hearing to maintain order, and provides for certain actions which may be taken against a person who disobeys the Board's instructions.

25.1 Subject to Rule 25.5, no person shall make a visual or audio recording of any part of the proceeding unless authorized by the Member before or at the beginning of the hearing.

This Rule is intended to apply to parties, their agents, journalists or other persons. The Member may impose conditions on the recording to protect the integrity of the hearing.

25.2 If the Board records the hearing, the recording will form part of the record and any party may request a copy of the recording upon payment of the required fee.

The Board will record a hearing if circumstances permit. Accordingly, most Board hearings will be recorded. If requested, the Board will do a search for an audio recording of the hearing, and will provide a copy of a hearing recorded, for a fee. No guarantee of the existence or quality of a recording can be provided. Recordings made by the Board are not transcribed, but pursuant to section 20 of the SPPA, they are part of the "record" for the purposes of review of an order or for appeal.

25.3 The deadline for a party to request a copy of a recording of a hearing is ten years from the date the hearing was recorded.

This deadline is established because per Rule 25.4, the Board may dispose of any recording of a hearing ten years after the hearing was recorded.

25.4 The Board may erase or otherwise dispose of a recording of a hearing if ten years have passed since the hearing was recorded.

The Board reserves the right to dispose of any recording of a hearing ten years after it was made. However the Board may, if it chooses, retain a recording for a longer period of time if one of the hearings on it is still pending with the Board or with the Courts.

25.5 Any party may bring a verbatim reporter at their own expense for the purpose of creating a transcript, provided that the party notifies the Board in advance.

In particular cases, a party will wish to have a transcript of the hearing. As the Board will not produce transcripts, the party would have to arrange for their own professional reporter (e.g. a court reporter) to be present at the hearing. As long as the party advises the Board in advance, the Member will permit this. The reporter must, of course, be sufficiently experienced to properly record the hearing and not disrupt it. The Board will not pay for the reporter's fees or expenses.

Amended: December 8, 2008

RULE 26   ORDERS AND REASONS

Legislation

Section 208 of the *Residential Tenancies Act, 2006* ("the RTA")

Section 17 of the *Statutory Powers Procedure Act* ("the SPPA")

At the end of a hearing, the Member will adjourn the hearing pending the issuance of an order.

In view of subsection 17(1) of the SPPA, the written order is the official decision of the Board. The written order (and reasons, if issued) have legal status and are enforceable.

26.1 The Board shall send a copy of any order and/or reasons to each party to the application:

(a) by ordinary mail to the last known address of each party;

(b) by ordinary mail to the representative of the party; or

(c) by any other method directed or permitted by the Member.

The usual practice will be to mail a certified copy of the order to all parties and their representatives, not only to those who participated in the hearing. Generally, copies will not be sent by fax, although they may be picked up for a fee at the responsible Board Office. However, occasionally special circumstances will arise, and the Board may arrange a different method of service. Although in general copies of the order will be certified, orders that are not certified may be sent in cases such as above guideline rent increase applications.

26.2 If a party wishes the Member to issue written reasons for the order, the party must make the request:

i. orally at the hearing, or

ii. in writing within 30 days after the order is issued, unless the time for requesting written reasons has been extended in accordance with Rule 15.

The Member shall then issue the reasons for the order promptly.

(b) If the member has already issued the written reasons, the Member shall deny the request.

(c) Where the Member denies the request for written reasons, the Member shall notify the party who requested

the written reasons, in writing, of the denial and the reasons for the denial.

Subsection 17(1) of the SPPA requires a tribunal to issue written reasons for its orders upon the request of any party. The Board will exercise its authority to issue reasons on its own initiative in some cases, and will issue reasons when requested by a party under this Rule. However, in most cases, written reasons will not be issued. Parties who intend to request a review of an order or file an appeal are encouraged to ask for written reasons as soon as possible after the order is issued. Where the time has been extended by the Board for requesting a review of an order, or, by the Divisional Court for filing a Notice of Appeal, and, the parties did not request written reasons within 30 days after the order has been issued, the parties are expected to request written reasons as soon as possible after the extension of time for requesting a review or filing an appeal has been granted.

26.3 Despite Rule 26.2, a Member shall give reasons for departing from a guideline whether or not reasons are requested.

Interpretation Guidelines are intended to assist the parties in understanding the Board's usual interpretation of the law and to promote consistency in decision-making. A Member's reasons for not following a guideline should be clearly explained in the decision.

26.4 If an order is reviewed under section 21.2 of the *Statutory Powers Procedure Act*, and a reviewing Member determines that it is necessary to have reasons, the Member who issued the order under review shall issue reasons promptly, without having regard to the content of the request for a review of the order.

Many review requests (see Rule 29) can be decided without reasons, so a Member is only required to write reasons if a Member who is conducting the preliminary review or review hearing determines that reasons are necessary. See the commentary to Rule 15.1 and 15.6.

26.5 If an order has been appealed and the Member who issued the order is requested to issue reasons, the Member shall issue reasons promptly without having regard to the content of the appeal.

For an appeal, reasons, if requested, should be issued quickly in order to have a complete record available for the Divisional Court, and to allow the parties to understand the decision they are appealing. (Note: Under subsection 210(2) of the RTA a party who appeals an order must give copies of the Notice of Appeal and any other appeal documents to the Board.)

26.6 Despite Rule 1.5, Rule 26 cannot be waived.

Amended: January 4, 2011

RULE 27   ORDERING COSTS TO A PARTY OR BOARD COSTS

Legislation

Sections 74, 78, 206 and subsections 204(2) to (4) of the *Residential Tenancies Act, 2006* ("the RTA")

Interpretation Guideline

Guideline #3 Costs

Subsection 204(2) of the RTA gives the Board the discretion to order one party to pay another party's costs. Subsection 204(3) allows the Board to order that its costs of a proceeding be paid by a party or a party's paid representative. In accordance with subsection 204(4), the amount for an order for costs shall be set in these Rules.

The Interpretation Guideline on costs sets out the usual approach followed by the Board when ordering costs against a party, a party's agent or a party's legal representative. These Rules complement the approach suggested in the Guideline.

Ordering Application Fee as "costs"

27.1 If the applicant is successful, the Board may order the respondent to pay the application fee to the applicant as "costs."

This Rule will generally allow a successful applicant to obtain an order for recovery of the application fee they have paid. See Guideline #3—Costs regarding when an applicant should be considered to have been "successful." Note that there are some sections of the RTA that explicitly authorize or require the Board to issue an order for the payment of the application fee, or other fees, as costs. For example: sections 74, 78, and 206.

Ordering the Costs of Another Party

27.2 Pursuant to subsection 204(2) of the RTA, the Board may order a party to an application to pay the costs of another party. These costs may include an amount for:

    (a) representation/preparation fees; and

    (b) other out-of-pocket expenses.

Where the Board orders a party to pay the representation/preparation fees incurred by another party, these fees shall not exceed $100 per hour for the services of a paid agent or legal representative. The total amount ordered for representation/preparation fees shall not exceed $700 in respect of the proceedings as a whole. In addition, the total amount ordered for other out-of-pocket expenses shall not exceed $700 in respect of the proceedings as a whole.

This Rule sets the maximum amount which may be allowed if a Member decides it is appropriate to order one party to pay another party's costs. The Guideline on costs suggests this is appropriate only where a party has been responsible for unreasonable conduct. It also suggests situations in which a party is not entitled to costs even if there has been unreasonable conduct by another party.

With respect to representation/preparation fees, the intention of this Rule is to allow the recovery of these fees only for the portion of the hearing that was affected by the unreasonable conduct. For example, if the Member warned the respondent's legal representative that an issue they raised did not seem relevant to the application,

and yet they continued to pursue the issue unreasonably, the Member could order the respondent to pay costs to the applicant that correspond to the time wasted (up to the maximum set by this Rule).

A Member may also, in appropriate circumstances, order a party to pay another party's out-of-pocket expenses "thrown away" due to unreasonable conduct. Examples of such costs include: witness fees, travel expenses, child care-expenses, or lost income related to the hearing.

Ordering Board Costs

27.3 Pursuant to subsection 204(3) of the RTA, the Board may order that its costs of a proceeding be paid by a party or a paid agent or legal representative. These costs shall not exceed $100 per hour for the hearing or $700 in total in respect of the proceeding as a whole.

There are two limits on the amount of Board costs ordered. First, if the unreasonable conduct affects the hearing, the order shall not exceed $100 per hour. Second, the amount allowed in total for the proceeding cannot exceed $700, including any amount ordered for the hearing.

This Rule recognizes unreasonable conduct in any stage of the proceeding will be relevant in considering the Board's costs, not just unreasonable conduct at the hearing. In other words, there may be an order for Board costs even where the unreasonable conduct did not occur during the actual hearing.

Amended: January 4, 2011

RULE 28   AMENDING AN ORDER

Legislation

Section 21.1 of the *Statutory Powers Procedure Act* ("the SPPA")

Related Rules

Rule 15 (Extending and Shortening Time)

Rule 30 (Order Void or Stayed)

Interpretation Guidelines

Guideline 15—Amending Orders

Section 21.1 of the SPPA allows a tribunal, at any time, to correct a typographical error, error of calculation or similar error made in its decision or order. These types of errors may be construed as clerical errors.

A clerical error may be the result of a mistake or omission made by the Board in the process of writing an order or other decision. Or, a clerical error may be an error made by a party in preparing a document which is submitted to the Board that ends up being transcribed into an order or decision. A serious error, on the other hand, such as an error of procedure or fact or an unreasonable application of discretion, would be the subject of a request for the Board to review an order (see Rule 29).

See also Guideline 15 "Amending an Order."

28.1 A party to an order or any person directly affected by it may request that an order or any other decision be amended to correct a clerical error on or before the date that is 30 days after the order or decision is issued.

This Rule permits any party to an order to request that the order or other decision be amended to correct a clerical error. It also permits any other person directly affected by a particular order or other decision to request such an amendment.

The time limit to make the request recognizes the desire of the Board that its orders be considered final within a reasonable time. A request to extend this time limit may be made under Rule 15. The Member considering such a request would consider factors such as the reason for the delay, the length of the delay, and any evidence of prejudice suffered by any person.

28.2 A Member of the Board may, upon their own initiative, amend an order or decision they have issued, in order to correct a clerical error.

This Rule permits the Board to amend an order or decision. Generally, an order or decision will only be amended if a party requests it, but in some cases a Member may initiate an amendment where they believe it is appropriate and necessary.

Form and Contents of Request

28.3 A request to amend an order or other decision to correct a clerical error shall be made in writing and shall be signed by the person making the request.

The person requesting the amendment may use the form provided by the Board, but the form is not required. A letter will be sufficient if it at least contains the information required by Rule 28.4. The form or letter must be signed by the person making the request or their representative.

28.4 A request must include: the Board's order number, the address of the rental unit or residential complex concerned and the name, address and telephone number of the person requesting the amendment, a description of the error, and the requested change.

These are minimum requirements. If the person requesting the amendment is not a party, they should explain their interest in the matter. If they are also appealing the order, applying for judicial review or asking for a review of the order (see Rule 29), this should also be noted in the request.

Assigning a Member to the Request

28.5 Subject to Rule 28.6, a request to amend an order or other decision will be considered by the Member who issued the order or decision that is the subject of the request.

The Member who issued the original order is in the best position to know the reasons for their findings and the intent of the decision. Therefore, the Member who issued the order or decision that is the subject of the request will be responsible for determining whether or not a clerical error was made in the order or decision.

28.6 Where the Member who issued the order or decision that is the subject of an amendment request is on an extended absence from the Board, the request will be considered by the regional Vice-Chair.

This might be the case, for example, where a request to amend a clerical error is received while a Member is on vacation, or some other form of leave, or where a request is received after a Member's appointment to the Board has ended.

Considering the Request

28.7 The Member who considers the request to amend an order or other decision, may:

a) amend the order, without requesting submissions or holding a hearing, based solely upon the request to amend the order;

b) deny the amendment request, based solely upon the request to amend the order;

c) issue a direction letter to invite written submissions and amend the order or deny the request to amend the order after considering those submissions;

d) hold a hearing to determine if the order should be amended or the request to amend denied.

Ordinarily, a Member will decide whether or not a clerical error exists in the order or decision based solely on the contents of the request, without seeking submissions from the other parties.

If the Member determines, with or without seeking submissions, that a clerical error exists in the order or decision, and that it should be amended, an amended order that clearly explains why the order is being changed and what the changes are will be sent to all parties.

Where a decision to deny the request is made without seeking submissions, the Member will send a letter to the party who made the request, explaining why the request has been denied. If a decision to deny the request is made after seeking submissions, a denial letter will be sent to all parties to the application. Where the decision to deny the request is made after a hearing has been held, an order will be sent to all parties explaining the reasons for the denial.

A member may find that it is necessary to invite submissions from other parties before making a decision.

In deciding whether or not to seek submissions, the Member should consider whether a party might be prejudiced if the order is amended.

Submissions may be requested in writing, by means of a direction letter, or at a hearing. In some cases, a Member may decide, after considering the written submissions of the parties, that it is necessary to hold a hearing to allow the parties to make further submissions or to clarify the issue(s).

Request to Stay the Order

28.8 A party may request a stay of the order by setting out in writing the prejudice they may suffer if the order is not stayed pending the decision regarding the amendment.

Generally, a stay of the order will not be necessary unless the amendment request is received late in the process and the Member is unable to deal with the request immediately. For example, if a party believes that an order for eviction due to nonpayment of rent and for the payment of arrears contains an error in the amount owing, and the amendment request is made close to the enforceable date of the order, the tenant may request that the order be stayed so that the landlord cannot enforce the eviction. A stay may also be needed if the Member decides to seek submissions on the request.

When a Member decides to stay an order, they may at the same time require the requester of the amendment to pay an amount into the Board. See the Interpretation Guideline entitled "Payment into the Board."

If the Board stays the order, it will ordinarily be stayed until a final decision is made regarding the amendment of the clerical error. However, the Member may at any time decide that the stay is no longer appropriate and revoke it.

28.9 A Member may, upon the request of a party or upon their own initiative, stay an order pending the resolution of a request to amend the order or may revoke a stay, without obtaining submissions from any party or holding a hearing.

The Member who considers the request to amend the order to correct a clerical error may decide to stay the order, whether or not a party asks for a stay. At a later stage, it may become apparent that the stay is no longer appropriate, and a Member would then be authorized to revoke the stay that had previously been ordered.

The reason for not obtaining submissions or holding a hearing before a stay is issued is that it is necessary that the stay be in effect as quickly as possible to protect the status quo while the amendment request is being considered. Without the stay, the order could be enforced, which may render the request meaningless. Since the amendment request will generally be dealt with within a relatively short period of time, it would unduly lengthen the proceedings to add a period of submissions.

Where an order is stayed, the person who might be adversely affected if the order were not stayed is responsible to take a copy of that order to the Court Enforcement Office (see Rule 30.4).

Consequential Amendments

28.10 If an order is amended to correct a clerical error, the Member may also amend or update other provisions of the order as necessary.

Amended: July 5, 2007

RULE 29   REVIEW OF ORDERS

Legislation

Section 21.2 of the *Statutory Powers Procedure Act* ("the SPPA")

Section 181, 182, 184 and 209 of the *Residential Tenancies Act, 2006* ("the RTA")

Related Rules

Rule 15 (Extending and Shortening Time)

Rule 26.4 (Orders and Reasons)

Rule 28 (Amending an Order)

Rule 30 (Order Void of Stayed)

Interpretation Guidelines

Guideline 8—Review of Orders

Section 21.2 of the SPPA authorizes a tribunal which adopts rules of practice to review its own orders. The scope of and procedures for such reviews are set out in these Rules. A person affected by an order may request a review if they believe the Member made a serious error, such as an error of procedure or fact or an unreasonable application of discretion. A clerical error, on the other hand, such as a mistake made by the Board in writing an order, would be the subject of a request to amend an order (see Rule 28).

It is clear that the review of orders was a power which the Legislature contemplated for the Board. Section 184 of the RTA states that the SPPA applies to proceedings before the Board and section 209 sets out that orders of the Board are final and binding subject to the review provision of section 21.2 of the SPPA. Also, section 181(1)(a) allows the Board to charge fees for a request to review an order, and section 182 provides that the fee may be refunded in certain situations.

The following expressions are used interchangeably in these rules: "request for a review of an order," "request to review an order," and "review request."

Requests to Review an Order

29.1 A party to an order or any person directly affected by it may file a written request to review any order or any decision which finally disposes of an application in whole or part.

Any person named as a party by the order may file a written request to review the order. As well, any other person directly affected by the outcome of that particular order (but not merely a similar fact situation) may file a written request to review the order and thereby seek to be added as a party to the proceedings. For example, if two persons own a residential complex, but only one was named as the landlord and participated in the proceedings, the other landlord may seek a review of the order if the order affects his or her interests.

The Board expects that the parties or any other person directly affected by a particular order will exercise the opportunity to request a review of that order if they believe a serious error occurred. Generally, a Vice Chair will not consider initiating a review until the parties have exhausted their rights in this regard.

Any final order may be reviewed if there are proper grounds to do so (see the Interpretation Guideline entitled "Review of an Order").

The Board may also review any other decision which either terminates the proceedings or affects the rights of the parties in a final way. Interim orders cannot generally be the subject of a review request since it is not usually appropriate to interrupt and delay a proceeding before there is a final result. Interim orders that deal with matters such as adjournments, disclosure and interim payments are examples of orders that cannot be reviewed.

However, if the interim order finally disposes of a portion of an application or affects the interests of a party in a final way, a review may be considered by the Board. Examples include interim orders that terminate a tenancy, or interim orders that determine that a particular person is not a party to the proceeding.

29.1.1 Vice-Chair of the Board may initiate a review of any order or any decision.

The Board expects that the parties or any other person directly affected by a particular order will exercise the opportunity to request a review of that order if they believe a serious error occurred. Generally, a Vice Chair will not consider initiating a review until the parties have exhausted their rights in this regard. However, even if a party has already exercised their opportunity to request a review, the Vice Chair may decline a request to initiate a Board-initiated review. The Board-initiated review process is not intended to serve as a further review or appeal mechanism for parties who are dissatisfied with the result of their request to review an order.

A Vice Chair may initiate a review even if a party has not exercised the opportunity to request a review request if it comes to the Board's attention that a party's ability to participate in a hearing was affected by a Board administrative error. For example, if a party failed to attend a Board hearing because the Board provided the incorrect hearing date, the Board may initiate a review.

29.2 A request for a review of an order must provide sufficient information to support a preliminary finding that the order may contain a serious error or that a serious error may have occurred in the proceedings.

A description of what is a serious error is contained in the Board's Interpretation Guideline entitled "Review of an Order."

Time for Making a Request

29.3 A request to review an order shall be made to the Board on or before the date that is 30 days after the order is issued unless the review was initiated by a Vice-Chair.

This time limit recognizes the desire of the Board that its orders should be considered final within a reasonable time. The same time period is used as that within which a party must decide whether or not to appeal an order on a question of law. This will encourage parties to consider their options and act quickly.

A request to extend this time limit may be made under Rule 15. For example, if a person who alleges they should have been a party does not discover there was an order until long after it was issued, time would usually be extended to permit the request to be considered on its merits. The Member considering such a request would consider

factors such as the reason for the delay, the length of the delay, and any evidence of prejudice suffered by any person.

29.4 If an order is amended, a request to review the order shall be made on or before the date that is 30 days after the amended order is issued.

For example, if the name of a party is corrected through an amending order, and the person believes the name is still incorrect, the time period of 30 days to ask for a review starts to run on the date after the amending order was issued.

Form, Contents and Parties

29.5 A review request shall be made in writing, shall be signed by the person making the request and shall be accompanied by the required fee.

The person requesting the review should use the Board-approved form. A letter will be sufficient if it is clearly identified as a request for review, and if it at least contains the information specified in Rule 29.6. The form or letter must be signed by the person making the request or their representative and must be accompanied by the required fee.

29.6 A review request must include: the Board's order number; the address of the rental unit or residential complex concerned; the name, address and telephone number of the person requesting the review; the reason, in detail, why the order should be reviewed; the remedy requested; and, where an appeal of the order has been filed with the Divisional Court, an explanation as to why the stay resulting from the appeal should be lifted for the purpose of resolving the review request.

These are minimum requirements. The form or letter used to request the review may also ask for an extension of time to file the request (see Rule 15) and/or a stay of the order during the review process (see Rule 29.7). If the person requesting the review was not a party to the original proceedings, they should explain their interest in the matter, or if they were a party who did not attend the hearing, they should explain why. If the person requesting the review is also appealing the order, applying for judicial review or asking for an amendment of the order (see Rule 28), this should also be noted in the request.

29.7 A party requesting a review of an order may also request a stay of the order by setting out in writing the prejudice they may suffer if the order is not stayed pending the decision regarding the review.

In some cases, by the time the review is completed, the issue would no longer exist if the order has already been enforced. In cases where a Member decides to stay an order pending the resolution of the review, the Member may also be concerned that a party might be prejudiced by the delay caused by the review.

For example, if an order for eviction due to arrears of rent is stayed, the landlord cannot enforce the order and re-rent the unit, and if the current tenant continues to fall behind in rental payments during the time of the review the landlord is powerless to take action.

In these cases, when a Member decides to stay an order, they may at the same time require the requester of the review to pay an amount into the Board. See the Interpretation Guideline entitled "Payment into the Board."

If the Board stays the order, it will ordinarily be stayed until a final decision is made regarding the review. However, the Member may at any time decide that the stay is no longer appropriate and lift it.

29.8 The parties to the review request are the parties to the order being reviewed, the person requesting the review, and any other person added to the proceedings by the Board, but a Vice-Chair who initiated the review is not a party.

Rule 29.1 sets out that a person directly affected by the order may request a review, even if they were not a party to the original proceedings. The Member may also determine in the course of the review that a person directly affected by the proceedings should be added. See section 187 of the RTA.

Assigning a Member to the Review

29.9(a) A Member may not review an order that they issued.

(b) Subject to (c) and (d), a Member may not review an order related to an order they issued, even if the order to be reviewed was written by another Member.

(c) A Member may review an order that has been stayed by an interim order written by that Member.

(d) A Member may review an order where the Member has previously issued a related interim order without consideration of the merits of the application.

In order to avoid possible prejudice to the party requesting the review, a Member will not review their own order or related orders issued by any Member.

For example, a Landlord applies to evict a tenant who is in arrears of rent (an L1 application). The Board denies the eviction and issues an order that imposes conditions on the Tenant and provides that the Landlord can apply ex parte for an order terminating the tenancy and evicting the tenant if the tenant fails to meet those conditions (an L4 application). The Member who issued the original L1 order will not review any order resulting from the L4 application filed by the Landlord.

If a Member decides on a preliminary review of a request to review an order that there may have been a serious error, and issues an interim order staying the order pending the outcome of the hearing based on the review request, that Member may preside at the review hearing. Also, if the Member has previously issued an interim order addressing such matters as disclosure without consideration of the merits of the application, that Member may preside at a review hearing held in respect of the final order.

Preliminary Decisions Regarding a Request for a Review of an Order

29.10 After a preliminary review of a request to review an order, unless the Member determines that the order may contain a serious error or that a serious error may have occurred in the proceedings, the Member shall deny the review request without a hearing.

In most cases, a Member will conduct a preliminary review of the request to review an order. In a preliminary review, a Member determines whether the request for review discloses a potential serious error in the order or in the proceeding, and whether the issues raised are within the scope of the power to review. Ordinarily, a decision in a preliminary review will be based solely on the contents of the request and the order, without seeking submissions from the other party and without holding a hearing.

The Member shall deny the request immediately if the request for review does not identify a potential serious error in the order or in the proceeding, or if the issues raised are not within the scope of the power to review. If the review request is denied, the Member will issue a decision denying the request, including a brief statement of the reasons for the decision.

29.11(a) If, after a preliminary review of a request to review an order, the Member determines that the order may contain a serious error or that a serious error may have occurred in the proceedings, the Member shall send the matter to a hearing for a consideration as to whether or not the request discloses a serious error in the order or proceedings.

(b) If the matter that the Member is sending to a hearing pursuant to Rule 29.11(a) has been stayed by subsection 25(1) of the SPPA as a result of an appeal of the order to Divisional Court, the Member shall lift the stay of the order, pursuant to subsection 25(1)(b) of the SPPA, so that the Member at the hearing may determine whether or not the request discloses a serious error in the order or the proceedings.

(c) However, should the Member determine that the rights of the parties should be preserved pending the Board's decision regarding the request for a review of the order, the Member shall issue a Board stay of the order.

29.12 A Member may, upon the request of a party or upon their own initiative, without obtaining submissions or holding a hearing in that regard, stay an order or lift any stay, pending the outcome of the hearing of a review request.

The Member who conducts the preliminary review of the request to review an order when it is received may decide to stay the order, whether or not the party who made the request asked for a stay. Without the stay, the order could be enforced.

Note: where an order is stayed, the person who might be adversely affected if the order were not stayed is responsible to take a copy of that order to the Court Enforcement Office (see Rule 30.4).

At a later stage, it may become apparent that the stay ordered by the Board is no longer appropriate, in which case the Member would then lift the stay. Where the order for which a review request has been made has also been appealed to the Divisional Court, the Member, in order to conduct a review of the order, may decide to lift the stay of proceedings that is automatically imposed by the filing of the appeal.

The reason for not obtaining submissions or holding a hearing before a stay is ordered is that it is necessary that the stay be in effect as quickly as possible to protect the status quo while the review is being determined. Since the review proceedings will generally be disposed of within a relatively short period of time, it would unduly lengthen the proceedings to add a period of submissions about such preliminary issues as the ordering or lifting of a stay.

29.13 If a Vice-Chair initiated the review, that Vice-Chair shall determine whether or not the order should be stayed at the time the review is initiated and shall issue an interim order staying the order under review, if necessary, and may lift any stay as required, pending the outcome of the review hearing.

29.14 A Vice-Chair, prior to initiating any review of an order, shall conduct a preliminary review to determine if there may be a serious error in the order or in the proceedings and, having made that determination, that Vice-Chair, another Vice-Chair or a Member shall be assigned to conduct the review hearing without any other preliminary review.

A Board initiated review shall proceed directly to the review hearing.

Type of Hearing

29.15 A Member may conduct a hearing to consider a review request, or to consider any issues to be reviewed, by way of an oral, electronic or written hearing.

An oral hearing is one conducted in the presence of the Member and any parties and representatives who appear. An electronic hearing is conducted through a conference call or through audio-visual facilities, usually with the Member, parties and representatives at two or more locations, but able to hear everything said by all of the other participants. Electronic hearings may be held under Rule 21.

In a written hearing, the parties are required to file their evidence and make submissions to the Board in writing. The Member makes a decision based on the evidence and submissions filed without holding a meeting between the parties. Written hearings may be held under Rule 22.

An oral hearing would ordinarily be held when the issues to be reviewed involve the presentation of evidence because there is alleged to be an error of fact; that is, it is alleged that there is an error as to the facts found in the order. Depending on a number of factors, such as whether credibility of witnesses will be an issue, the hearing may be conducted by conference call or in person (i.e., an electronic or an oral hearing).

Where the Member believes that the issues raised by the request are straightforward, and involve arguments based on the facts found by the Member who made the order, the Member conducting the review may decide that the review may be conducted by written hearing.

Where the party requesting the review alleges an error of natural justice, the reviewing Member could ask for written submissions regarding that issue and, if convinced there was an error, proceed to hear the application from the beginning through an oral or electronic hearing.

Decisions Resulting from a Hearing of a Request for a Review of an Order

29.16 If, after holding a hearing to determine if a review request discloses a serious error in the order or proceedings, the Member determines that there is no serious error, the Member shall dismiss the request, lift any stay and confirm the order under review.

If, after hearing from the parties, the Member determines that there is no serious error, the Member shall issue an order dismissing the request for review.

29.17 If, after holding a hearing to determine if a review request discloses a serious error in the order or proceedings, the Member determines that there is a serious error, the Member will determine the issues to be reviewed.

If the Member determines that there is a serious error, the Member will proceed to hear the issues to be reviewed.

29.18 The Member may decide that the issues to be reviewed will be:

    (a) all or some of the issues raised in the request;

    (b) any other issues which the Member believes should be reviewed.

When the Member considers the issues raised in the request, they may decide that all of these issues should be reviewed, with submissions from both parties. However, they may decide that only one or more of the issues are within the scope of the review, and would then limit the issues to be reviewed.

In considering the issues raised in the request and the order or decision itself, the Member may come to the preliminary conclusion that those issues will lead to a need to review other parts of the order. In addition, the Member may find that there was another possible serious error in the proceedings or in the order.

29.19 After hearing the issues to be reviewed, the Member may confirm, vary, suspend or cancel the order under review, and lift any stay if necessary.

Subsequent Requests for Review

29.20 The Board shall accept only one review request from a party, and shall not accept a subsequent request from that same party to review the resulting review order or decision.

This Rule is based on the legal principle that a matter already decided cannot be decided again by a court or tribunal. It also encompasses the concept that a party should raise all grounds for possible serious error in their request.

29.21 The Board may review an order which has previously been reviewed, or may review a review order, if the request is made by another party upon different grounds or if the review is initiated by a Vice-Chair of the Board.

The request of a party for a review will not prevent a new request from a different party, unless the request is based on grounds already decided through the other review. However, if the request is made late, the requesting party must convince the Board that this further review should be allowed to proceed. The Board reserves the right to initiate a second review or review of a review order, on its own motion, in appropriate cases.

Withdrawing a Request

29.22 If a request to withdraw a review request is made at a hearing or after an interim order has been issued, the request may be withdrawn only with the consent of the Board.

The Board recognizes a party's right to withdraw a request to review. However, if the request is made at the hearing or after an interim order has been issued, the review request may be withdrawn only if the Member consents. If the Member allows the request to be withdrawn, they will also lift the stay of the original order, if it was stayed, and order payment out, if money was paid into the Board.

29.23 A party may withdraw a review request without the consent of the Board as long as the hearing of the request has not commenced, and no interim or other order has been issued regarding the request.

Amended: January 4, 2011

RULE 30   ORDER VOID OR STAYED

Legislation

Sections 74, 77 and 78 of the *Residential Tenancies Act, 2006*

Related Rules

Rule 28 (Amending an Order)
Rule 29 (Review of Orders)
Rule 31 (Paying money into and out of the Board)

There are a number of situations in which an action taken by a party to a Board proceeding impacts the enforcement of a prior Board decision. For example, a respondent may file a motion to set aside an ex parte order or make the payment required to void an eviction order.

30.1 Except where a set aside motion is filed under subsection 74(9), it is the responsibility of the party who files a set aside motion to immediately take a copy of the motion and Notice of Hearing to the Court Enforcement Office.

In most cases, the automatic legal effect of filing a set aside motion after an ex parte order has been issued is to stay the order. Before the applicant is notified of the set aside motion, they may take steps to enforce the order; however, once the motion is filed, the applicant cannot enforce the order.

For an eviction order, the respondent should take the set aside motion and Notice of Hearing to the Sheriff's Office after filing the motion with the Board. For an eviction order which also orders the payment of money, the respondent should take a copy of the motion and Notice of Hearing to the Sheriff's Office and the enforcement offices of the Superior Court of Justice and the Small Claims Court.

However, where a set aside motion is filed under subsection 74(9) about an order which voids an eviction order, there is no requirement to take the motion or Notice of Hearing to the Sheriff's Office. In this case, the order that voids the eviction order remains in effect; there is nothing to be enforced pending the Board's decision on the set aside motion.

30.2 Where a notice is issued under subsection 74(5) or subsection 74(16) which acknowledges that an eviction order is void, it is the responsibility of the tenant to immediately take a copy of that notice to the Court Enforcement Office.

If a tenant has paid the full amount required to void an eviction order (based on rent arrears) to the Board, an employee of the Board will issue a notice acknowledging that the eviction order is void. Once this notice is issued the landlord cannot enforce the eviction order. As soon as the tenant receives the notice from the Board, they are responsible for taking a copy of it to the Court Enforcement Office (Sheriff).

30.3 Where an order is issued under subsection 74(6) or under clause (a) of subsection 74(14) which confirms that an eviction order is void, it is the responsibility of the tenant to immediately take a copy of that order to the Court Enforcement Office.

If a tenant has paid the full amount required to void an eviction order based on rent arrears, before the order becomes enforceable, either in whole to the landlord or in part to the landlord and in part to the Board, and then files a motion in accordance with subsections 74(6) and 74(7) for an order confirming that the order is void, the Board can issue such an order. Once this order is issued the landlord cannot enforce the eviction order. As soon as the tenant receives the order from the Board, they are responsible for taking a copy of the order to the Court Enforcement Office (Sheriff).

The same holds true, in most cases, for an order that the Board issues on a tenant's motion under subsection 74(11) if, after the order becomes enforceable, the tenant pays the amount required under subsection 74(11) to void the eviction order based on rent arrears. However, where the Board determines that the landlord has already paid a non-refundable amount to enforce the eviction order, the Board will specify that the order voiding the eviction will not be effective unless the tenant pays to the Board a specified amount, by a specified date, to cover the landlord's enforcement costs.

30.4 Where an order is issued that stays the order under consideration, it is the responsibility of the person who might be adversely affected if the order were not stayed to immediately take a copy of that order to the Court Enforcement Office.

For example, if a tenant files a request to review an eviction order and includes a request for a stay, the Board can issue such a stay under Rule 29.12. Similarly, the Board can issue a stay under Rule 28.9 related to a request to amend an order. Once the stay is issued, the landlord cannot enforce the original order. As soon as the tenant receives the order from the Board, they are responsible for taking a copy of the order to the Court Enforcement Office (Sheriff). The Board is not responsible to ensure that the Sheriff's office receives a copy of the order.

Amended: July 5, 2007

RULE 31   PAYING MONEY INTO AND OUT OF THE BOARD

Legislation

Subsections 74(2) to (18) and section 195 of the *Residential Tenancies Act, 2006* ("the RTA")

Related Rules

Rule 13.8 (Mediation by the Board: Paying Out Under an Agreement)

Subsection 74(2) of the RTA states that if the Board is satisfied that a tenant has paid the sum owing and the application fee to the Board or to the landlord before the order is issued, the application will be discontinued.

Subsection 74(4) of the RTA states that if an eviction order has been issued but, before it becomes enforceable, the tenant voluntarily pays the amount specified in the order, the eviction order is void. The amount can be paid entirely to the Board, entirely to the landlord, or in part to the Board and in part to the landlord. These Rules establish procedures for the payment out of these monies.

Further, subsection 74(11) allows a tenant to void the order after the date the order becomes enforceable but before it is enforced, by paying everything owing, including the Sheriff's fees if applicable. The tenant must file a motion and a hearing will be held to determine if the order is void. A tenant is only allowed to void an eviction order in this manner once per tenancy.

Clause 195(1)(a) of the RTA provides that the Board may require the respondent to pay a specified amount into the Board within a specified time where the Board considers it appropriate to do so. Further, under subsection 195(4), if the respondent fails to pay in as required, the Board may refuse to consider their evidence and submissions.

Clause 195(1)(b) of the RTA allows the Board to permit a tenant who has made an application about maintenance to pay some or all of their rent into the Board. Subsection 195(5) states that if such a payment is allowed, it is not considered to be arrears of rent or a breach of the tenant's obligations.

Subsection 195(2) provides that the Board may establish procedures for payment into and out of the Board through these Rules. Interpretation Guideline #2 (Payment into the Board) provides guidance as to the reasons for which a Member might require payment, as well as what the consequences might be if the respondent fails to follow such a requirement.

Arrears of Rent: Voluntary Payments Made Before an Order is Issued

31.1 If, before an order is issued, a tenant voluntarily pays money to the Board which is at least the amount required to discontinue the application under subsection 74(2) of the RTA, a Member shall:

(a) **direct that the amount that would be required to discontinue the application be paid out to the landlord,**

(b) **direct that any excess be paid to the tenant, and**

(c) **order that the application is discontinued without holding a hearing.**

Where a landlord files an application to evict a tenant for non-payment of rent, and the tenant pays the rent arrears, any additional rent owing and the landlord's filing fee, the landlord's application will be discontinued and no hearing will be held. The amount that would be required to discontinue the application will be paid out to the landlord. If the tenant has paid in more than enough to discontinue the application, the extra amount will be paid back to the tenant.

Arrears of Rent: Payments Made Before an Eviction Order is Enforceable

31.2 If, after an order is issued, a tenant voluntarily pays money to the Board in accordance with subsection 74(4) of the RTA before the eviction order becomes enforceable, and the amount paid in is at least the amount that would be required to void the order according to subsection 74(4), a Regional Manager or Manager, Customer Service will:

(a) **direct that the amount that would be required to void the order be paid to the landlord,**

(b) **direct that any excess be paid to the tenant, and**

(c) **issue a Notice to the parties acknowledging that the eviction order that is based on arrears of rent is void.**

After the Board has issued an eviction order in a landlord's application based on non-payment of rent, the tenant has an opportunity to void the order before the date the landlord can enforce it. Where the tenant pays into the Board an amount that is sufficient to void the eviction order, staff of the Board will issue a notice acknowledging that the eviction order is void. The staff member will also direct that the amount that the tenant has paid in that would be sufficient to void the order will be paid out to the landlord. Where the tenant has paid in more than enough to void the order, the extra amount will be paid back to the tenant.

31.3 If, after an order is issued but before it becomes enforceable, a tenant voluntarily pays money to the Board in an amount that is less than the amount that would be required to void the order according to subsection 74(4), and the tenant does not file a motion under subsection 74(6), a Regional Manager or Manager, Customer Service will:

(a) **direct the money to be paid to the landlord, once the order has become enforceable, and**

(b) **issue a Notice to the parties confirming the amount that was paid out to the landlord, and that it was not sufficient to void the order.**

Where an eviction order has been issued based on non-payment of rent, the tenant can void the order by paying the amounts owing to the landlord and/or to the Board. Where the tenant pays the whole amount to the landlord, or part to the landlord and part to the Board, the tenant can make a motion to the Board for an order determining that the full amount has been paid and that the eviction order is void.

Where the tenant pays money into the Board but it is less than the amount required to void an eviction order and the tenant does not make a motion for an order confirming that the eviction order is void, staff of the Board will issue a notice to the parties informing them that the amount the tenant paid in was not sufficient to void the order. The staff member will direct that the money that the tenant has paid into the Board will be paid out to the landlord. The notice and direction will be issued after the date the order can be enforced.

31.4 If, after an order is issued but before it becomes enforceable, a tenant voluntarily pays money to the Board in an amount that is less than the amount that would be required to void the order according to subsection 74(4), and the tenant files a motion under subsection 74(6), a Member will, at the time of issuing an order on the motion, direct payment out to the landlord of any monies paid in.

Where the tenant makes a motion to the Board for a notice confirming that the eviction order is void, but the amount that the tenant has paid in to the Board is not sufficient to void the order, the Member will direct that any monies paid into the Board will be paid out to the landlord when it issues an order on the tenant's motion.

Arrears of Rent: Payments Made After Eviction Order Enforceable

31.5 If, after an order becomes enforceable, a tenant voluntarily pays money to the Board in an amount that is at least the amount that would be required to void the order and the tenant files a motion under subsection 74(11), a Member will, at the time of issuing an order on the motion:

(a) direct that the amount that would be required to void the order be paid to the landlord; and

(b) direct that any excess shall be paid to the tenant.

Even after the date an eviction order can be enforced, a tenant has an opportunity to void the order. Where a tenant pays to the Board an amount that is sufficient to void the eviction order and makes a motion to set aside the order, the Board will issue an order declaring that the eviction order is void. The Board will, at that time, also direct that the amount that would be sufficient to void the eviction order be paid out to the landlord; any extra amount that the tenant paid into the Board will be paid out to the tenant.

31.6 If, after an order becomes enforceable, a tenant voluntarily pays money to the Board in an amount that is less than the amount that would be required to void the order, and the tenant files a motion under subsection 74(11), a Member will, at the time of issuing an order on the motion, direct the money to be paid to the landlord.

Where a tenant makes a motion to the Board to set aside an eviction order after the date the order can be enforced, and pays money to the Board, but the amount is not sufficient to void the eviction order, the Board will lift the stay of the eviction order resulting from the tenant's motion. This means that the landlord will be able to enforce the eviction order. The Board will direct that the money the tenant has paid in to the Board be paid out to the landlord.

31.7 If, after an order becomes enforceable, a tenant voluntarily pays money to the Board but does not file a motion under subsection 74(11) a Regional Manager or Manager, Customer Service will:

(a) direct the money to be paid to the landlord; and

(b) issue a Notice to the parties confirming the amount that was paid out to the landlord, and that the order is not void.

Where a tenant pays to the Board an amount to void the eviction order but does not make a motion to set aside the order, staff of the Board will direct that the money be paid out to the landlord and will issue a notice to the parties informing them of the amount that was paid. The notice will also set out that the order is not void.

Enforcement Costs Set Out in an Order Issued Under Subsection 74(14)

31.8 If a tenant pays to the Board at least the amount specified pursuant to subsection 74(15) (enforcement costs) in an order issued under subsection 74(14) by the date set out in that order, a Regional Manager or Manager, Customer Service will:

(a) issue a Notice acknowledging that the eviction order that is based on arrears of rent is void;

(b) direct that the amount that would be required to void the order be paid to the landlord, and

(c) direct that any excess shall be paid to the tenant.

Where a tenant makes a motion to the Board to set aside an eviction order after the enforceable date in the order, a hearing will be held. The Board will determine whether the eviction order is void because the tenant has paid the required amounts and whether the landlord has paid any non-refundable enforcement fees with respect to the eviction order. Where the Board determines that the tenant has paid the required amounts and that the landlord has paid enforcement fees, the Board will issue an order setting out that the eviction order is void, provided that the tenant pays an amount into the Board to cover the enforcement fees by a specified date. Where the tenant pays that amount into the Board by the date set out in the order, staff of the Board will issue a notice acknowledging that the eviction order is void. The staff member will also direct that the amount the tenant has paid in to cover the enforcement costs will be paid out to the landlord; if the tenant has paid more than the required amount, any excess will be paid back to the tenant.

31.9 If an order is issued under subsection 74(14) that specifies an amount payable pursuant to subsection 74(15), and the tenant does not pay this specified amount into the Board by the date set out in the order, a Regional Manager or Manager, Customer Service will:

> **(a) issue a Notice confirming that the specified amount was not paid by the specified date, and that the order issued under clause (a) of subsection 74(14) is no longer stayed and may be enforced, and**

> **(b) direct that any money paid in to the Board be paid out to the landlord.**

Where the Board determines that the tenant has paid the amounts required to void an eviction order after the enforcement date, the Member can order the tenant to pay into the Board an amount to cover the costs the landlord has incurred to enforce the eviction order. Where the tenant does not pay the full amount by the deadline in the Board's order, staff of the Board will issue a notice informing the parties that the eviction order can be enforced. The staff member will also direct that any money the tenant has paid in will be paid out to the landlord.

Directed Payments

31.10 If a respondent pays money into the Board in accordance with a direction or order of a Member, a Member will direct payment out at the time of issuing an order.

If a respondent pays money into the Board as a result of a Member's direction or order requiring them to pay in that amount, the applicant is not entitled to have the money paid out to them in advance of an order being made. The requirement to pay into the Board may have arisen because of a delay of the hearing, and was in the nature of security for payment of any amount which the Board decides should be ordered against the respondent. Thus, payment out to the applicant would be premature before the hearing is completed and an order is issued. Payment out would be in accordance with the amount determined to be owing in the order.

Payment In on Maintenance Applications

31.11 Unless the tenant's request under clause (b) of subsection 195(1) is made at the hearing, it must be in writing, and must specify:

> **(a) the amount of rent the tenant is required to pay and the date rent payments are due under the tenancy agreement;**

> **(b) the amount of rent the tenant wishes to pay in and the rent period(s) or portion(s) of rent period(s) covered by that amount; and**

> **(c) the reasons why the tenant believes the Board should allow their request.**

When a tenant makes an application to the Board about maintenance, they can also make a request to pay their rent into the Board. The tenant can make this request orally at the hearing. At any other point in the application process, this request must be made in writing. To make the request in writing, the tenant should use the form approved by the Board; however, a letter will be sufficient if it at least contains the information required by this rule. The form or letter must be signed by the person making the request or their representative.

31.12 If the tenant's request under clause (b) of subsection 195(1) is made before the hearing for the application starts, the request will be decided *ex parte*.

Where a tenant makes a request to pay their rent into the Board on a maintenance application before the start of the hearing, the Member will make a decision on the request without seeking submissions from the other parties.

31.12.1 Where the Board has denied a tenant's request to pay in under Rule 31.12, no subsequent request from the tenant to pay into the Board will be considered before the hearing for the application starts.

If a tenant asks to pay into the Board on a maintenance application before the start of the hearing, a Member will decide whether or not to grant the request. If the request is denied, the tenant may not make another such request before the start of the hearing.

31.13 If the tenant's request under clause 195(1)(b) is made after the hearing for the application starts, the Member hearing the application will decide whether or not to grant the request ex parte or after receiving submissions (oral or written) from the other parties.

For information on when the Board considers it appropriate to allow a party to pay money into the Board, see the Interpretation Guideline #2, Payment into the Board.

31.14 If a Member decides to allow the tenant to pay some or all of their rent into the Board, the Member will issue an interim order which will be sent to all parties to the application.

31.15 If a tenant pays their rent into the Board pursuant to an interim order issued under Rule 31.14, the Member will direct payment out at the time of issuing an order, or if the application is resolved by mediation, the Mediator will direct payment out under Rule 13.8.

Amended: January 4, 2011

APPENDIX A   SERVICEONTARIO CENTRES

Atikokan
108 Saturn Avenue

Aurora
50 Bloomington Road West

Bancroft
50 Monck Street

Barrie
34 Simcoe Street

Belleville
199 Front Street
Century Place

Blind River
62 Queen Avenue

Brampton
7765 Hurontario Street

Brockville
7 King Street West

Chapleau
190 Cherry Street

Chatham
Civic Centre
315 King Street West

Cochrane
2 3rd Avenue

Cornwall
127 Sydney Street

Dryden
479 Government Road
Main Floor

Elliot Lake
50 Hillside Drive North

Espanola
148 Fleming Street, Suite 2

Fort Frances
922 Scott Street

Geraldton
208 Beamish Avenue West

Gore Bay
35 Meredith Street

Guelph
1 Stone Road West, Main Floor

Hawkesbury
692 Main Street East

Hearst
613 Front Street

Huntsville
207 Main Street West

Ignace
Corner Hwy. 17 and Hwy. 599

Iroquois Falls
260 Main Street

Kapuskasing
122 Government Road West

Kemptville
10 Campus Drive

Kenora
810 Robertson Street, Suite 104

Kingston
Ontario Government Centre
Beechgrove Complex
51 Heakes Lane, Main Floor

Kirkland Lake
10 Government Road East

Kitchener
City Hall, Main Floor
200 King Street West

Lindsay
322 Kent Street West

Manitouwadge
40 Manitou Road

Marathon
Peninsula Square, Centre Block
52 Peninsula Road, Suite 105

Minden
Highway 35 By-pass

Moosonee
Ontario Government Building
34 Revillion Road North

New Liskeard
280 Armstrong Street

Nipigon
Ontario Government Building
5 Wadsworth Drive

North Bay
447 McKeown Avenue
Suite 111

Oakville
Halton Region Administrative Centre
1151 Bronte Road

Ottawa
110 Laurier Avenue West

Owen Sound
1400 1st Avenue West

Parry Sound
7 Bay Street

Pembroke
31 Riverside Drive

Peterborough
Ontario Government Building
300 Water Street, Main Floor

Rainy River
408 Atwood Avenue

Red Lake
227 Howey Street

Renfrew
316 Plaunt Street South

Sarnia
Bayside Mall
150 Christina Street North

Sault Ste. Marie
70 Foster Drive, Main Lobby

Simcoe
40 Colborne Street South

Sioux Lookout
62 Queen Street

St. Catharines
301 St. Paul Street

Stratford
5 Huron Street

Sturgeon Falls
94 King Street, Unit 8

Thunder Bay
435 South James Street
Suite 114

Timmins (South Porcupine)
Ontario Government Building
Highway 101 East

Toronto (Downsview)
3737 Chesswood Drive

Wawa
48 Mission Road

Whitby
590 Rossland Road East

Windsor
400 City Hall Square East
Suite 205

Amended: October 1, 2008

APPENDIX B: WITNESS FEES

TARIFF A: Solicitors' Fees and Disbursements Allowable Under Rule 58.05 of the Rules of Civil Procedure: Disbursements

Attendance Money Allowed pursuant to

Rule 53.04(4) of the Rules of Civil Procedure

PART II   Disbursements

Attendance money actually paid to a witness who is entitled to attendance money, to be calculated as follows:

Item Amount

1. Attendance allowance for each day of necessary attendance $50
2. Travel allowance, where the hearing or examination is held,
   (a) in a city or town in which the witness resides, $3.00 for each day of necessary attendance;
   (b) within 300 kilometres of where the witness resides, 24¢ a kilometre each way between his or her residence and the place of hearing or examination;
   (c) more than 300 kilometres from where the witness resides, the minimum return airfare plus 24¢ a kilometre each way from his her residence to the airport and from the airport to the place of hearing or examination.
3. Overnight accommodation and meal allowance, where the witness resides elsewhere than the place of hearing or examination and is required to remain overnight, for each overnight stay $75

Landlord and Tenant Board Interpretation Guidelines*

TABLE OF CONTENTS

Amended: January 4, 2011

INTERPRETATION GUIDELINE #1
ADJOURNING AND RESCHEDULING HEARINGS

Interpretation Guidelines are intended to assist the parties in understanding the Board's usual interpretation of the law, to provide guidance to Members and promote consistency in decision-making. However, a Member is not required to follow a Guideline and may make a different decision depending on the facts of the case.

Section 184 of the *Residential Tenancies Act, 2006* ("the RTA") provides that the *Statutory Powers Procedure Act* applies to all proceedings before the Board; and the authority to adjourn hearings is found in section 21 of the *Statutory Powers Procedure Act* which provides that:

A hearing may be adjourned from time to time by a tribunal of its own motion or where it is shown to the satisfaction of the tribunal that the adjournment is required to permit an adequate hearing to be held.

This guideline identifies situations that may warrant the rescheduling or adjournment of a Board hearing.

Rescheduling and adjourning can be defined in the following way:

Rescheduling involves staff setting a new date for the hearing in advance of the date originally set for it, usually confirmed by a new Notice of Hearing;

Adjourning involves a Member's decision regarding when the hearing of an application will proceed and/or be completed.

General Approach of the Board

Section 183 of the RTA directs the Board to "adopt the most expeditious method of determining the questions arising in a proceeding that affords to all persons directly affected by the proceeding an adequate opportunity to know the issues and to be heard on the matter."

Parties should assume that all of their evidence and submissions will usually be heard on the date stated in the Notice of Hearing. This means that the parties should be prepared to present their evidence, call and question witnesses and make their submissions. The Board's decision will generally be made shortly afterwards.

Risks of Failing to Attend the Hearing or Prepare for It

Parties failing to appear at the hearing specified on the Notice take considerable risks. Section 7 of the *Statutory Powers Procedure Act* provides that a tribunal may proceed with a hearing in the absence of any party. In exceptional circumstances, a Member may exercise the jurisdiction to adjourn a case on the Board's motion in order to determine whether the party who did not appear will do so on a later date. However, parties should not expect such a decision.

Where an applicant fails to appear, the Member will normally proceed with the hearing, which means the applicant's case will be dismissed as abandoned, whether or not the respondent has attended.

Where the respondent fails to appear, the Member will normally proceed with the hearing, and may make a decision based on the evidence of the applicant.

Not preparing for a hearing based on the expectation that it will be postponed, even though the other party prefers to proceed, has substantial risks. If the Member decides to proceed with the hearing on the date set, the evidence presented will be considered, even if additional evidence should rightfully have been presented. Being unprepared strongly increases the risk of failure to prove one's case.

Finally, the only remedies for an incorrect order may be "review of the order" (reconsideration), judicial review or appeal; however, appeal is limited to questions of law, and both appeal and judicial review can be very expensive court procedures. It is highly advisable to deal with the application promptly at the start, rather than count on someone interceding later to reverse an order already issued.

Rescheduling Hearings

If a party realizes it will be difficult to attend a hearing or that they will not be prepared in time for a hearing, they may seek the rescheduling of the hearing date set out in the Notice of Hearing. They should request rescheduling as soon as possible after they realize it is necessary.

The Board will generally only reschedule a hearing if the party seeking the delay is able to obtain the agreement of the other party or parties (see Rule 12).

If a tenant requests rescheduling, they should deal with the landlord's representative, if there is one, or with the landlord directly. If there are multiple landlords, the agreement of each must be obtained.

When a landlord requests rescheduling, they should deal with the tenant's representative, if one exists, or with the tenant directly. If there is more than one tenant, the agreement of each must be obtained.

It is important that parties respond reasonably to requests from another party to reschedule. Although there are always a number of factors to take into account, if parties are unreasonable in their responses to requests to rescheduling, a Member may find that since rescheduling caused no prejudice to either party, the party who refused the request may be ordered to pay costs.

The party seeking the hearing's rescheduling should send or fax to the Board a written request for rescheduling indicating:

- confirmation that the other party or parties have agreed to the rescheduling;
- what dates the party requesting the rescheduling will be available (subject to the availability of a Member); and
- what dates, if any, the other party(ies) indicated they preferred for the rescheduled hearing.

This written request must be received by the Board no later than the morning of the day before the hearing and a copy should be sent to the other party(ies).

All parties should phone the Board no later than the afternoon of the day before the hearing to ensure that the written request was received, and that the hearing has in fact been rescheduled, and to what date, time and place.

In some cases, exceptional circumstances arise at the last moment (such as the death of a close family member) which prevent the party from meeting the procedures set out above. In such circumstances, the party should notify the Board by telephone as soon as they become aware of this, and inform the other party or their agent, as well. The case will remain on the list of hearings for the scheduled time, but the Member will be apprised of the telephone message and, if convinced that the circumstances are indeed exceptional, may adjourn the hearing without the party being present.

A party may request that a hearing be rescheduled because they are covered by section 1 of the *Human Rights Code*, and the Board is unable to accommodate their needs at the originally scheduled hearing. Such requests will be addressed by the Board in accordance with the Board's *Human Rights Policy*.

It may be necessary from time to time for the Board to reschedule a hearing on its own initiative. For example, the Board may determine that it is necessary to reschedule a hearing to a different date in order to ensure that a sign-language interpreter is available, if so required by one of the parties. In such cases, the parties and their representatives will be notified.

When Partial Mediation Is Achieved

When a Board Mediator assists the parties in mediation and a partial settlement is reached by the parties, an interim agreement may be signed by the parties. The parties to the interim agreement may agree to reschedule the hearing to a later date for a Member to determine the unresolved issues (see Rule 13.12).

Adjournments

Procedural Issues

If a party is unable to obtain consent to a rescheduling from the other parties in advance of the hearing date, the party or their agent must attend on the hearing date to request an adjournment from the Member. A request for an adjournment will normally be heard at the outset of the session for which the hearing is scheduled.

An adjournment is a procedural decision. If the request is made at the start of the hearing, the Member is not "seized" with the case, thus the same Member is not required to conduct the hearing on the adjourned date. However, if the request is made part way through a hearing, the Member will likely be seized with the case because they heard evidence. For instance, an applicant may discover that the respondent's case involves facts that they did not realize were going to be raised, and that evidence from a witness who is not present is necessary to counter the respondent's defence. In such a situation, the hearing must be adjourned to a time when the same Member can continue the hearing.

Balancing Rights Between the Parties

Section 183 of the RTA states that the Board should be expeditious, but should ensure that the parties are given "an adequate opportunity to know the issues and to be heard on the matter." The key question becomes how to balance the rights of the parties to ensure that matters are resolved quickly while not sacrificing their rights to a fair hearing. The determining factors a Member will weigh are very different depending on whether the parties agree to adjourn, or one party's request to adjourn is contested by one or more other parties.

Agreement to Adjourn

If the parties agree to adjourn the hearing, the Board will not interfere with this agreement in most circumstances. The hearing will be adjourned to a date set by the Board, although the parties may have an opportunity to offer some preferred dates.

However, sometimes the Member may decide it would not be in the public interest to proceed as the parties have arranged. Although the Member will not normally force the parties into a hearing immediately, the parties may be required to proceed on an earlier date than what was agreed upon.

Considerations Where There Is No Agreement

Parties are generally required to make themselves available to attend scheduled hearings by making whatever arrangements are necessary. The granting of adjournments is in the discretion of the Member hearing the application. However, if the parties cannot attend the scheduled hearing and are not able to reach an agreement regarding one party's wish to adjourn the hearing, the Member should weigh the prejudice that might be suffered by each party. The Member will consider the prejudice to a party having to appear repeatedly, without a good reason for having to do so. As discussed below, if a Member grants an adjournment, certain conditions may be imposed upon either party in order to alleviate the prejudice the other party may experience as a result of the adjournment.

Therefore, when appearing before the Member the parties should present specific reasons why they would be significantly prejudiced by an adjournment. For example, a delay may economically prejudice a party or may mean a lost opportunity. There may also be aggravating circumstances, such as an urgent need for certain repairs or the continued tenancy will be a threat to other tenants' safety.

The Member is also entitled to consider the conduct of the party opposing the adjournment. For example, if that party is the applicant, and they delayed serving the application until the last day permitted by the Rules, thus giving the respondent the minimum time contemplated, the request is more likely to be granted. Also, if the party opposing the request has shown bad faith or refused to provide information about their case to the respondent which would allow them to prepare quickly for the hearing, this should weigh in favour of an adjournment.

The Member must take into account the public interest in resolving the case as soon as possible. However, the public interest in an expeditious result is greater in some types of applications than in others. A claim for eviction because the tenant threatens the safety of the landlord or other tenants should be dealt with as swiftly as possible, as should a case in which the tenant claims there is ongoing harassment by the landlord or their staff.

Adjournment to Allow Representation

Section 10 of the *Statutory Powers Procedure Act* allows parties the right to be represented by a lawyer or agent at the hearing. However, the right to representation does not automatically guarantee an adjournment. Therefore, the onus is on a party notified of a hearing and wishing to be represented and to make all reasonable efforts to find a lawyer or agent able to represent them on the date on their Notice of Hearing. Nevertheless, a short adjournment may be allowed where a representative has been retained, but is unavailable on the date set for the hearing, or where the party can demonstrate that they have made reasonable efforts to retain a lawyer or agent before the hearing but have yet been unable to do so.

Adjournment to Permit Another Application

A respondent may also request an adjournment because they have filed or will be filing an application against the applicant. This should merit an adjournment only if the respondent's application will affect the outcome of the application being considered.

Adjournment Requests Respecting Court Proceedings

Some parties seek adjournments on the basis that a Court will rule on a similar issue between other parties in the future. This would generally be an invalid reason for permitting a case to remain undecided for a long period: it would be preferable to proceed with the hearing.

Adjournment on Consent for Mediation

A party sometimes hopes that a case may be settled, and that they need more time to resolve the issues with the other party. Although the Board encourages this, and in many cases offers mediation services, a hearing should not be delayed for this purpose, unless both parties agree.

Adjournment to Prepare Case

A respondent may request an adjournment because they may not know the case they must answer. If the respondent demonstrates that the information about the applicant's claims is unclear or not detailed enough to allow them to know what evidence they must present at the hearing, this may justify an adjournment. In deciding whether the claim is sufficiently complete and clear, the Member should evaluate the application, documents filed with it and any information the respondent already had.

A party may request an adjournment to acquire evidence required to prove the facts of the case. It may be a respondent who makes this request because they have received the application too close to the hearing date (though technically "on time" according to the rules for giving applications). Also, any party who has become aware of the other party's intended evidence, and wishes to review or obtain their own evidence to refute their position may request an adjournment.

Adjournment to Prepare for Section 82

In an application by a landlord for rent arrears (section 87 of the RTA) or for termination of the tenancy for rent arrears (section 59 of RTA), section 82 permits tenants to raise any issue that could be raised in a tenant application under the RTA. Where the tenant raises issues under section 82 that the landlord could not reasonably have anticipated and cannot address at the hearing with a short recess, the landlord may request an adjournment to another date for the purpose of investigating the tenant's allegations and obtaining relevant evidence.

Conditions for an Adjournment

The Member may decide that a condition should be attached to the granting of an adjournment. Examples of some conditions that may be included:

- an adjournment may be given on the condition that the party requesting it will disclose to the other party(ies) some further information about their position or a copy of evidence that the party will present to the Board when the hearing resumes;
- in a case involving a claim for the payment of money, the Member may decide that a respondent requesting an adjournment should pay the amount claimed by the applicant, or a lesser sum, into the Board as security for the payment of any order which may result from the application, or may come due before the next hearing date (see section 195 of the RTA and Guideline 3, entitled "Costs");
- the adjournment will be granted on a "peremptory" basis, which means that no further adjournment requests will be granted to the party that requested the adjournment, except in the most exceptional circumstances or where the other party consents to the subsequent adjournment request;
- a party opposing the adjournment may ask for costs incurred resulting from the adjournment and any such costs will be considered pursuant to Guideline 3 (also see subsection 204(2) of the RTA).

Amended: October 15, 2009

INTERPRETATION GUIDELINE #2
PAYMENT INTO THE BOARD

Interpretation Guidelines are intended to assist the parties in understanding the Board's usual interpretation of the law, to provide guidance to Members and promote consistency in decision-making. However, a Member is not required to follow a Guideline and may make a different decision depending on the facts of the case.

This Guideline is meant to help parties understand when a Member may: a) require a respondent to pay money into the Board and b) permit a tenant to pay all or part of their rent into the Board.

Subsection 195(1) of the *Residential Tenancies Act, 2006* ("the RTA") reads as follows:

> Where the Board considers it appropriate to do so, the Board may, subject to the regulations,[1]
>
> (a) require a respondent to pay a specified sum into the Board within a specified time; or
>
> (b) permit a tenant who is making an application for an order under paragraph 1 of subsection 29(1) to pay all or part of the rent for the tenant's rental unit into the Board.

The money paid into the Board is held in a special trust account. Once the application is decided, the Member will order the money paid out to the appropriate party.

Requiring Payment into the Board

A decision under paragraph 195(1)(a) would generally be made at the hearing after receiving submissions from the parties. As most cases will be heard expeditiously, orders to pay money into the Board would be most appropriate in cases where the hearing will be adjourned for some length of time.

In some cases, the amount owing may increase during the proceedings. The longer the adjournment, the more is at risk to the applicant. The applicant may want the Member to require the respondent to pay money into the Board in order to discourage the respondent from unnecessarily prolonging the proceedings.

Where the potential amount owing will increase during the proceedings, and the matter will be adjourned, the Board may require the respondent to pay into the Board:

- all or part of the amount that is owing or claimed to be owing as of the hearing date; and/or,
- the additional amount that will become owing.

It is generally more appropriate to require payment into the Board of the additional amount that will become owing during the delay, because otherwise the respondent's right to dispute the application may be negatively affected.

As an alternative, the Board may require one party to make a payment directly to the other party instead of paying into the

Board. However, the consequences of failing to comply in subsection 195(4) would not apply in this situation.

The applicant may want to ensure that there will be no problems collecting the amount ordered. However, in any application for the payment of money, the applicant may have problems collecting the amount ordered to be paid. If Members required money to be paid into the Board whenever a respondent wished to dispute the application, this would discourage some respondents from exercising their right to a hearing of the merits of the application. This would give an unfair advantage to parties with greater economic power, or to parties who claimed more than the amount they are owed. Therefore, it would not be appropriate to require payment into the Board for this reason.

Rules for Payment in and Payment Out

Subsection 195(2) of the RTA states that the Board may establish rules for the payment of money into and out of the Board. The rules for payment into and out of the Board may be found in Rule 31 of the Rules of Practice, Paying Money Into and Out of the Board.

Consequences of Failing to Pay Money into the Board

The consequences of failing to follow the requirement to pay money into the Board are set out in subsection 195(4):

> If a respondent is required to pay a specified sum into the Board within a specified time under clause (1)(a) and fails to do so, the Board may refuse to consider the evidence and submissions of the respondent.

Where the Member determines that there is no reasonable explanation for the respondent's failure to pay money into the Board, the Member may proceed with the hearing and refuse to hear the evidence and submissions of the respondent. The respondent would be entitled to be present at the hearing, to make procedural objections and to cross-examine witnesses. However, the respondent would not be entitled to present their own documents or witnesses nor to argue their case.

If the respondent can provide a reasonable explanation for their failure to comply with the requirement to pay money into the Board, the Member may proceed with the hearing and allow the respondent to participate.

Permitting Payment into the Board

The Board may permit a tenant who is making an application based on a landlord's breach of the duty to repair in subsection 20(1) or section 161 to pay all or part of their rent into the Board. This request may be made at the time the tenant files the application or at the hearing. For further information see Rule 31, Paying Money Into and Out of the Board, and Guideline 5, Breach of Maintenance Obligations.

The tenant will have to satisfy the Board that special circumstances exist that justify the payment in of rent. Special circumstances may include: where the tenant does not know who to pay or how to contact the landlord; the landlord refuses to accept the rent; or where the tenancy will be terminated and it

---

1   No regulation has been passed which affects this provision.

may be difficult for the tenant to enforce the order. There may be other factors and circumstances to consider.

Note that under subsection 195(5) of the RTA, when a tenant is permitted to pay into the Board, the payment is deemed not to constitute a default in the payment of rent under the tenancy agreement or the RTA.

Release Date: January 31, 2007

INTERPRETATION GUIDELINE #3
COSTS

Interpretation Guidelines are intended to assist the parties in understanding the Board's usual interpretation of the law, to provide guidance to Members and promote consistency in decision-making. However, a Member is not required to follow a Guideline and may make a different decision depending on the facts of the case.

Generally, when someone takes another person to court, they hope that they will collect from the other party some part of their expenses of the lawsuit. The Board has a discretionary power similar to that of the Courts to order "costs." The Board may order one of the parties to pay costs to another party or may order that the Board's costs be paid by a party, a paid agent or counsel to a party. However, the Board does not want to use its power to award costs in a way which would discourage landlords and tenants from exercising their statutory rights.

Subsections 2, 3 and 4 of section 204 of the *Residential Tenancies Act, 2006* ("the RTA") provide that:

(2) The Board may order a party to an application to pay the costs of another party.

(3) The Board may order that its costs of a proceeding be paid by a party or a paid agent or counsel to a party.

(4) The amount of an order for costs shall be determined in accordance with the Rules.

This Guideline sets out the Board's position on when it may be appropriate to order costs. Generally costs may be ordered where a party's conduct in the proceeding was unreasonable. Costs should not be confused with an administrative fine. An administrative fine is a remedy to be used by the Board to encourage compliance with the RTA and to deter landlords from engaging in similar activity in the future. For further information on administrative fines, see Guideline 16.

Submissions on Representation Costs and Board Costs

Before ordering a party to pay representation costs of another party or before ordering a party, agent or lawyer to pay the costs of the Board, a Member should ensure that the person who will be affected by the order for costs has an opportunity to make submissions on the matter.

However, if a party has received notice of a hearing and does not attend or if an agent or lawyer is on the record as representing a party and does not attend a hearing, a Member may proceed to make an order for costs without notifying the person affected of the intention to do so, provided that the failure to attend the hearing delayed the process unnecessarily or caused unnecessary expense to the other party.

Ordering Costs Against a Party or a Paid Representative

Costs Ordered in Most Cases

In most cases, the only costs allowed will be the application fee. This should be ordered if the applicant is successful in obtaining an order which allows the relief they asked for in the application, or substantially all of that relief. This includes cases which are resolved by an order based on an application for which no notice is required (section 77 of the RTA). Where appropriate, this cost will be ordered regardless of whether or not the applicant seeks such a remedy.

It is anticipated that return of the application fee will not usually be ordered in the situations listed below:

1. Applications to increase rents above the guideline; such applications involve many respondents and it would be impractical to order costs in these cases.
2. Applications to evict tenants based on their own notice or agreement to terminate where the application is made before the date of termination.
3. Applications to evict a tenant based on a no-fault ground (e.g. a landlord application for termination of the tenancy for the landlord's own use).

Other Costs

A party who wants to claim costs in addition to the application fee should be prepared to speak to the matter and to provide support for the claim. The other party will also be allowed to make submissions on the issue.

In most cases, costs should not be allowed for the other expenses incurred by the successful party such as travel, expert reports, etc. Neither the fees of a representative for preparation time, nor hearing time, should be allowed except in the circumstances set out below.

Further Costs Where a Party's Conduct Is Unreasonable

A Member has the discretion to require a party to pay, as costs, any representation or preparation expenses of another party where the conduct of the party was unreasonable. Conduct is unreasonable if it causes undue expense or delay and includes the following"

1. Bringing a frivolous or vexatious application or motion
2. Initiating an application or any procedure in bad faith
3. Taking unnecessary steps in a proceeding
4. Failing to take necessary steps, such as those required by the RTA or Rules
5. Any misconduct at the hearing or in the proceeding
6. Raising an issue which is irrelevant to the proceedings and continuing to pursue that issue after the Member has pointed out that it is irrelevant

7. Asking for adjournments or delays without justification
8. Failing to prepare adequately for the hearing
9. Acting contemptuously toward the Member or showing a lack of respect for the process or the Board
10. Failing to follow the directions of the Member or upsetting the orderly conduct of the hearing
11. Unreasonably maligning another party or slurring the character of the other party

Examples of failing to comply with the RTA or Rules would include the following situations:

- Failing to follow a procedural order or direction such as an order to serve another party with a document
- Serving another party in a way which was not appropriate
- Delaying the hearing by not taking actions required in the Rules

The amount ordered by a Member will usually be less than the actual cost since the Rules will set out maximum amounts for the Member to consider.

Generally, only fees for a representative's time spent at the hearing will be allowed. However, in some cases, a further amount for preparation time may be allowed if the unreasonable conduct led to the need for the representative to spend additional time preparing for the hearing.

Representation fees should not be allowed if the representative did not conduct themselves in a professional manner.

Generally speaking, the Member may refuse to allow representation fees if the conduct of the representative does not demonstrate an understanding of the following:

- Legislation, Regulations, Rules and Guidelines
- The position of their client
- The role of an agent appearing before a quasi-judicial Board
- Standards of proper behaviour and conduct in a hearing

Further Costs Where the Conduct of the Paid Representative of a Party Is Unreasonable

A Member has the discretion to order a party to pay costs to another party where the conduct of the party's representative was unreasonable. Conduct is unreasonable if it causes undue expense or delay and includes situations listed above under the heading "Further Costs Where a Party's Conduct Is Unreasonable." Unreasonable conduct may also include displaying an inadequate knowledge of the RTA and other relevant legislation.

In addition to making an award of costs, the Board may exclude from a hearing any person, other than a lawyer qualified to practice in Ontario, appearing as an agent on behalf of a party if it is found that the agent is not competent to properly represent or advise the party or does not understand and comply at the hearing with the duties and responsibilities of an advocate and adviser.

Cases Where Costs Should Not Be Allowed

As a general principle, a Member should not order costs of any kind in favour of a party if the conduct of that party was not proper. For example, if the applicant was responsible for an adjournment because they were not prepared, the Member might decide that they should not be awarded any costs. If both parties were responsible for unreasonable conduct, neither should be ordered to pay the costs to the other, although one or both may be ordered to pay the Board costs.

Amount of Costs

Rule 27 of the Board's Rules of Practice sets out the criteria for Members to consider when determining the amount of costs to order.

Ordering the Board's Costs

The Board expects parties and their paid representatives to act reasonably in pursuing their applications or defending their positions. This includes bringing applications only when there are substantial grounds. It also includes taking all required procedural steps, not taking unnecessary ones and acting in a courteous and orderly way at a hearing.

When a party or a paid representative acts improperly or unreasonably in a proceeding, the Board may order the party or their paid representative to pay to the Board an amount that will partly cover the expenses that the Board has incurred as a result of that conduct. If the unreasonable conduct was the fault of the party's representative, the Board will normally order that the paid representative pay the Board's costs.

Pursuant to section 196 and Rule 9, failure to pay costs ordered may result in the Board refusing to allow the filing of an application; a stay in proceedings; a delay in the issuance of an order; and/or a discontinuance of the proceeding. See Rule 9 "Refusing to Accept or Proceed with an Application" for further details.

General Approach

A Member has the discretion to order a party or a paid representative to pay the costs of the Board. This power, however, should be used sparingly. It was not the intent of the Legislature that this power should ever be used to obtain cost recovery for salaries, administration or other expenses of the Board.

In those rare situations in which a party or their representative is responsible for unreasonable conduct, this power allows the Board to accomplish two objectives:

- Recover some of the taxpayers' monies which funded the proceedings, and,
- Discourage inappropriate practices and conduct by parties and their representatives.

An award of Board costs is appropriate in cases in which the adjudicative costs to the public have been unjustifiably increased by the unreasonable conduct or omission of a party or their agent or lawyer.

Unreasonable conduct would include the situations listed above under the headings "Further Costs Where a Party's

Conduct Is Unreasonable" and "Further Costs Where the Conduct of the Paid Representative of a Party Is Unreasonable."

Ordering Board costs is not related to which party is successful. Since the reason such costs are awarded is to encourage proper conduct, it is conceivable that a successful party who adds unnecessary steps to the proceeding or behaves inappropriately at a hearing, may have to pay the Board's expenses for part of the proceeding.

The discretion for a Member to order Board costs to be paid by an agent or lawyer would only be used where, on the balance of probabilities, it is the behaviour of the agent or lawyer and not the client which is in issue.

Ordering Party Costs and Board Costs

An order for a party to pay both the representation/preparation fees of another party and to pay the Board's costs in the same case would only be made in exceptional circumstances.

This would usually include the following:

- A case in which a party clearly and knowingly misled the Board, such as filing an inflated claim for arrears, a false certificate of service, or an altered invoice
- A case where a party was reckless or indifferent about the truthfulness of their evidence, such as stating that the other party did not serve a document which they know they received
- Situations in which the party failed to comply with directions from the Member about the orderly conduct of the hearing
- Evidence of harassment of the other party to prevent the application or defence of the application

Generally, if the party who would pay the costs has been unsuccessful, it is more appropriate to order them to pay costs to the successful party. If the party whose conduct was unreasonable was the successful party, they should be ordered to pay Board costs.

Release Date: January 31, 2007

INTERPRETATION GUIDELINE #4
ABANDONMENT OF A RENTAL UNIT

Interpretation Guidelines are intended to assist the parties in understanding the Board's usual interpretation of the law, to provide guidance to Members and promote consistency in decision-making. However, a Member is not required to follow a Guideline and may make a different decision depending on the facts of the case.

Section 79 of the *Residential Tenancies Act, 2006* ("the RTA") states:

If a landlord believes that a tenant has abandoned a rental unit, the landlord may apply to the Board for an order terminating the tenancy.

Although section 79 explains how the landlord may receive an order terminating the tenancy in cases where the tenant has abandoned the unit, it is not mandatory for this type of order to be issued for the landlord to treat the unit as abandoned. However, there is a substantial risk in re-renting the unit without such an order unless it is clear that the tenant has vacated and does not intend to continue the tenancy.

This Guideline is intended to provide guidance in determining if the unit has been abandoned.

When May the Unit Be Considered to Be Abandoned?

Abandonment is a unilateral act by the tenant to relinquish their tenancy and give up possession of the rental unit without properly giving notice of the termination to the landlord. If the landlord is not sure whether or not a rental unit has been abandoned, they may file an application for determination of this issue with the Board; however, it should be noted the Board has no jurisdiction to issue an order for rent or compensation if a tenant is no longer in possession of the rental unit (see section 87). In this case, the landlord may seek a remedy by applying to Court.

Section 2(3) of the RTA provides that a rental unit is not considered abandoned where the tenant is not in arrears of rent. Even if there is evidence of abandonment, such as the furniture being removed, the landlord cannot treat the unit as abandoned before the end of the rental period if the rent is fully paid.

Evidence of Abandonment

If there is rent due, there must still be substantial evidence of abandonment before the landlord can re-rent the unit or deal with the tenant's property that is remaining in the unit. There are circumstances where the evidence is clear. For example, the tenant may tell the landlord or the superintendent that they are moving out. The tenant may be seen in the process of moving out of the building, and later the door of the unit is found open, showing that all furniture and personal effects were removed. Provided there is no evidence to the contrary, this evidence would support a finding that the tenant has abandoned the rental unit.

The evidence may also be cumulative; there may be several indications that the tenant has left the unit. For example, a neighbour has reported that they saw the tenant moving and the tenant advised the landlord that they intended to leave, or the tenant was known to have accepted a job in another city and the mail has not been collected for a number of weeks. In such circumstances, the landlord may be justified in considering the unit to be abandoned.

The landlord should make reasonable efforts to contact the tenant to determine if they have left the unit (for example, by writing the tenant or calling them at different times each day). The landlord should give the tenant a reason to reply to a letter and should keep notes of the times and dates that they telephoned. The failure of the tenant to respond to the letters and telephone calls should be consistent with the abandonment of a unit and not with a tenant who is on vacation or out of town on business.

If the unit has been abandoned, in accordance with subsection 42(1), the landlord may dispose of any of the tenant's property found in the unit provided that one of the following conditions is met:

1. The landlord applied to the Board and obtained an order terminating the tenancy based on the abandonment of the rental unit.
   OR
2. The landlord gave a notice to the tenant and to the Board stating that the landlord intends to dispose of the property if the tenant does not claim the property within 30 days of the notice being given.

If either of these conditions has been met, the landlord may immediately dispose of anything unsafe or unhygienic and, after 30 days following the issuance of the order or the giving of the notice, may dispose of any other tenant belongings. If a tenant does claim the belongings within the 30 day period, they must pay the landlord any arrears of rent and any reasonable costs of moving, storing and securing the property.

If the landlord sells the property, the tenant has 6 months—from the date of the order or from the date the landlord gave notice of their intention to dispose of the property—to claim the proceeds of the sale. The landlord is allowed to deduct from the proceeds of the sale any arrears of rent and any reasonable costs incurred in the moving, storing, securing or selling of the property.

Application to Determine if the Tenant has Abandoned the Unit

If the landlord applies to the Board under section 79, the application must be served on the tenant in accordance with section 191.

Release Date: January 31, 2007

INTERPRETATION GUIDELINE #5
BREACH OF MAINTENANCE OBLIGATIONS

Interpretation Guidelines are intended to assist the parties in understanding the Board's usual interpretation of the law, to provide guidance to Members and promote consistency in decision-making. However, a Member is not required to follow a Guideline and may make a different decision depending on the facts of the case.

This Guideline deals with the responsibility of landlords to maintain residential complexes and rental units and with the appropriate choice of remedies.[1]

---

[1] This guideline does not discuss the additional responsibilities under section 161 for mobile home parks or land lease communities. For a mobile home park or land lease community, the landlord has additional specific responsibilities under section 161, such as garbage removal, park roads maintenance and sewage disposal, etc. Although these obligations may also be enforced under subs. 29(1), they are not specifically addressed in this Guideline.

Section 20 of the *Residential Tenancies Act, 2006* ("the RTA") states as follows:

(1) A landlord is responsible for providing and maintaining a residential complex, including the rental units in it, in a good state of repair and fit for habitation and for complying with health, safety, housing and maintenance standards.

(2) Subsection (1) applies even if the tenant was aware of a state of non-repair or a contravention of a standard before entering into the tenancy agreement.

A tenant may apply to the Board under paragraph 1 of subsection 29(1) of the RTA for an order to determine if the landlord is in breach of these obligations. If the Board determines that a breach occurred, section 30 provides a number of available remedies that may be ordered, including ordering the work to be done, abatement of rent, and termination of the tenancy. The Board may also order the landlord to pay compensation to the tenant for the cost of repairing or replacing property damaged, destroyed or disposed of as a result of the landlord's breach, as well as other reasonable out-of-pocket expenses. The Board may also award general damages for breach of the tenancy agreement.

The Intention of the Legislation

The intention behind sections 20, 29 and 30 is to make landlords responsible for maintaining their complexes, and not to limit their obligations by transferring them by agreement to the tenant. If a tenant agreed in a lease to assume the responsibility to maintain any part of the unit or complex, beyond ordinary cleanliness and damage, this would not be enforceable.[2]

The statute should be interpreted in a way which encourages the best maintained complexes and units. The landlord is required to rectify maintenance deficiencies and meet applicable standards. When a deficiency is found, the breach of maintenance obligations will generally result in an order under section 30. In some situations, the landlord will also be ordered to compensate tenants for problems of which the landlord was aware, or could reasonably be expected to have knowledge of, but took no action to rectify.

It is not a proper defence to such an application that the landlord needs the money for other purposes, even for other repairs. If there are many repairs necessary in a complex, the Member could take into account that some work should come first, and delay an order for other repairs. However, the obligation to maintain residential premises is not subject to whether the landlord has available funds.

Obligation Extends to the Residential Complex

The residential complex extends beyond the rental unit occupied by the tenant, to include the facilities and common areas provided for tenants by the landlord. This includes the lobby,

---

[2] See *Fleischman v. Grossman Holdings Ltd.* (1976), 16 OR (2d) 746 (CA) regarding exclusionary clauses in leases and *Burt Dozet Management Inc. v. Goharzad*, [2001] OJ No. 695 (Div. Ct.).

hallways, stairwells, laundry facilities, parking areas, exterior grounds, recreational facilities, etc.[3]

Any physical facilities which the landlord can be found to have rented to the tenant, or permitted the tenant to use, should be maintained by the landlord. This may include facilities not immediately adjacent to the complex, but which the landlord has specifically agreed to provide (such as a swimming pool at a nearby building, parking in a separate lot, storage elsewhere, etc.).

In *Quann v. Pajelle Investments Ltd.*,[4] it was held that:

In our day and age, the urban lease of an apartment in a substantial building gives to the tenant a package of goods and services. Those goods and services include not only walls and ceilings but adequate heat, light, and ventilation, serviceable plumbing facilities, secure windows and doors, proper sanitation and maintenance, the rights guaranteed to the tenant ... . If the duty of the landlord is not fulfilled the tenant has the right to seek relief.

A landlord may assert that they have a good program of maintenance and repair, including preventative maintenance and a system of processing complaints. This is not a release of the landlord's responsibility to respond to a real problem. It is reasonable management practice to answer maintenance requests in the order of their urgency (e.g., water leaks come before a loose wall tile), but all legitimate requests must be answered within a reasonable time.

A Landlord's Right to Enter a Unit to Check Maintenance Issues

Paragraph 4 of subsection 27(1) the RTA permits a landlord to enter a rental unit to carry out an inspection where notice is provided 24 hours before the time the landlord intends to enter provided that:

i. The inspection is to determine whether or not the unit is in a good state of repair and fit for habitation and complies with health, safety, housing and maintenance standards consistent with the landlord's obligations under subsection 20(1) or section 161, and

ii. It is reasonable to carry out the inspection.

When Can an Application Be Made?

An application must be made by the current or former tenant within one year of the date the alleged breach occurred. When determining whether an application has been made "in time" pursuant to subsection 29(2) of the RTA, a Member will have to determine when the alleged breach occurred.

---

[3] In *Herbold v. Pajelle Investments Ltd.*, [1976] 2 SCR 520, the Supreme Court of Canada held that rented premises extend beyond the rental unit and include the facilities and common areas provided to the tenants. This has been further clarified in the TPA by the use of the terms "rental unit" and "residential complex."

[4] (1975), 7 OR (2d) 769 (Co. Ct.).

When a breach is a single event such as an illegal entry, the limitation period begins on the day the event happened. Where the breach is not a single event but is ongoing or recurring as may be the case with some maintenance obligations or with non-compliance with standards, then the breach occurs over a period of time and the limitation period runs from the date that the repair is completed or the standard is complied with. The landlord's obligation for maintenance is ongoing and continues until the landlord has fulfilled the obligation. In all cases the limitation period is one year.

The intention behind the limitation period found in section 29(2) of the RTA is that the applicant has only a certain amount of time to file the application and obtain a remedy, but may bring the application at any time within the limitation period. For instance, a unit or complex may have numerous problems which started at various times and gradually worsened to arrive at a state of non-repair which caused the tenant to apply. The fact that the tenant did not bring the application when the breach first arose does not affect the tenant's right to file an application. There is no provision in the RTA requiring the tenant to bring an application immediately upon the breach of an obligation by the landlord. However, the tenant may not include in an application any item which has been rectified by the landlord more than one year before the application was filed.

If the application is filed "in time" pursuant to subsection 29(2) and the breach is no longer occurring as of the date of the order, the Board may award a remedy (such as a rent abatement) for the timeframe calculated from one year prior to the application filing date to the date the breach ended . Where the breach is ongoing as of the date of the order, the potential remedy may provide for periods beyond the date of the order to the date that the breach is no longer occurring (*Goodman and Pearlman v. Menyhart and Menyhart*, [2009] OJ No. 1602, and *Toronto Community Housing Corp v. Allan Vlahovich*, [2010] OJ No. 1463). (Also see the section on **REMEDIES THAT MAY BE ORDERED**, further on in this Guideline).

The most recent decision that considered the proper application of subsection 29(2) was that of the Divisional Court in *Toronto Community Housing Corp. v. Vlahovich*, [2010] OJ No. 1463. In *Vlahovich*, the Court stated:

In light of the one year limitation period in s. 29(2), the Board can only make a determination that a landlord has breached an obligation under s. 20(1) during the one year period before the making of the application. Accordingly, the remedy that may be granted may only be granted in relation to breaches during that one year period.

In *Vlahovich*, the Divisional Court explained that, "properly understood" the earlier decision of the Divisional Court in *Goodman v. Menyhart*, [2009] OJ No. 1602, was not inconsistent with the Court's approach in *Vlahovich*. The Court emphasized that the Divisional Court panel in *Goodman v. Menyhart* had ordered that an abatement can extend back one year before the application had been made and no further. The Court in *Vlahovich* stated that in *Goodman v. Menyhart*, the only issue was whether the limitation period should extend back twelve months from the order of the Board or from the filing of the application. In that case, and, consistent with the reasoning in *Vlahovich*, the limitation period extended back one year from the filing of the application.

Rent Payment Into the Board

Clause (b) of subsection 195(1) indicates that where the Board considers it appropriate, the Board may permit a tenant who is making a maintenance application to pay some or all of their rent into the Board. Subsection 195(5) states that if such a payment is allowed, it is not considered to be arrears of rent or a breach of the tenant's obligations. As discussed in Guideline 2 "Payment Into the Board," such requests will only be granted in special circumstances.

See Rule 31, Paying Money into and Out of the Board for details on the procedures for requesting payment of rent into the Board.

What Issues Should Be Permitted at the Hearing

The applicant has an obligation to set out the nature of the issues being raised, so that the respondent has the opportunity to prepare for the hearing. The items alleged to be in need of maintenance or repair or failure to meet standards should be set out on the application form, as should any claims for compensation for damaged, destroyed or disposed of items. If no details are set out, the application could be dismissed, or the applicant may be allowed an amendment to provide details. In some cases this will cause an adjournment to allow the landlord to prepare to meet those issues.

Even if the tenant has been specific in the application about the items which require repair or are below standards, or about compensation claims, they may try to raise further items at the hearing. The Member will have to decide whether to permit these additional items, usually after hearing the tenant's explanation of why they were not raised before, and the landlord submissions about any prejudice they may suffer in responding to the new items. The new items must have a connection with the items raised initially.

Applying the Tests to Each Item

Each item raised by the tenant which was not remedied within the last year must be considered under all the tests in section 20. For example, with a complaint of lack of heat, the Member will have to consider whether this is failing to maintain a good state of repair, whether the premises are unfit for habitation because of the lack of heat, and whether the landlord has thus failed to comply with standards. If the problem alleged by the tenant falls into any of these categories, it will justify a finding of breach of obligations.

In general, where there is a conflict between what the Member believes would be required by "good state of repair and fit for habitation" and the standard imposed by the responsible public authority, and the landlord has met the standard, the Member should not find the landlord in breach of section 20.

Good State of Repair

The landlord's obligation under section 20 to provide and maintain the premises in a good state of repair is very broad. It would include anything that was capable of being repaired. The full extent of the obligation does not depend on the tenancy agreement.

Fit for Habitation

A number of cases have also considered the meaning of "fit for habitation." *Summers v. Salford Corp.*[5] is the leading case from Britain. The Court held that if the state of disrepair is such that by ordinary use, damage may naturally be caused to the occupier, either in respect of personal injury to life or limb or injury to health, the house is considered not reasonably fit for habitation.

This phrase "fit for habitation" is not the standard expected, and should not be used to limit or qualify "good state of repair." Generally, it is enough for any part of the premises to be unfit. Examples would include infestations of rodents or vermin, bathrooms with backed-up sewage, rooms with broken windows, etc.

Health, Safety, Housing and Maintenance Standards

Most standards are found in municipal property standards by-laws, but may also be provincial standards such as the fire code, elevator standards or the provincial standard under the RTA (see below). The tenant has the obligation to bring the standard to the attention of the Member, usually by filing a copy of the by-law, RTA or other document either before or at the hearing. However, the Member may on his or her own initiative refer to the standard.

If a notice of violation, work order or other order has been issued for this complex or unit, it represents a finding by a public official that the landlord has not complied with the standard. Once the tenant files a copy of the notice or order, a Member will be entitled to accept this as evidence of non-compliance with a standard. However, the landlord is entitled to have the issue determined by the Board if they dispute the notice or order. In such a case, the landlord must raise this dispute, file the document and bring forward evidence to prove their position.

A landlord may argue that the work order has not taken effect, and should not be considered, if the time for compliance has not yet expired. In fact, many work orders are issued after non-compliance with a standard has existed for some time. The fact that the landlord has been given more time by another authority to rectify the problem does not mean that there is no problem. The issue should not be dismissed on this basis. Of course, if the work order was the first way that the landlord discovered this problem existed, the fact that the compliance period has not yet expired for a non-urgent item may indicate a different remedy than a long-standing problem that was ignored.

A landlord may also argue that actions taken by the public authority pursuant to the work order, such as prosecution of a

---

[5] [1943] 1 All ER 68.

provincial offence, should be considered as penalty enough for the non-compliance with the standard. However, the Member must still determine whether there was non-compliance with a standard, although it may be taken into account that the landlord has paid a fine in deciding what remedy is appropriate.

If no complaint has been filed with the appropriate public authority, it is then necessary for the Board to hear evidence on the issue and come to its own conclusion. A notice of violation issued by a public authority is not necessary for a finding of a breach of section 20.

If the applicant submits that a maintenance condition does not meet a standard, but has no evidence at the hearing of the exact nature of the standard, the Member may consider the item under the other tests (good state of repair or fit for habitation). However, the landlord is entitled then to introduce the standard, and to show that they are meeting it.

Provincial Maintenance Standard
Work orders will also be issued by the Ministry of Municipal Affairs and Housing for municipalities which do not have their own property standards by-laws. These orders are authorized by the provincial maintenance standard set out in the regulations.[6]

Some tenants may wish to use the provincial maintenance standard, even though their own municipality has a property standards by-law. However, section 20 requires landlords to comply with standards and this must be read as meaning only those standards which are enforceable for that complex.

What Is Not Required by This Landlord Obligation
Landlords may choose to undertake programs of preventative maintenance. However, a tenant cannot insist that their landlord undertake specific preventative maintenance work as a necessary repair.

When landlords undertake repairs, there is often a dispute between the parties about whether the repairs were properly done. The tenant has no right to insist upon a standard of perfection regarding repairs. By the same token, a landlord is not entitled to rely upon repairs that were improperly done as a complete answer to the need for repairs, especially if the repairs had no effect or resulted in a need for further repairs.

Where the Problem Has Been Repaired/Rectified
The tenant must apply within one year after the breach of obligation existed, but the fact that a problem has been rectified before the application was filed does not exclude it from consideration. However, it would appear that the cases generally support the principle that, if the landlord responded within a reasonable time, and the response was appropriate to effect the repair, no abatement or other remedy should be ordered.

Timeliness of response depends on a great number of factors, but principally on the seriousness of the state of non-repair and its possible effects on the tenant and the availability of materials and possibly contractors to do the repairs. The tenant may also be alleging that the repairs attempted by the landlord

were ineffective or badly done, which has reduced the value of the unit or left the same problem unremedied. These issues must be addressed directly through evidence and decided by the Member.

Tenant Conduct That Will Result in Dismissing a Claim
Section 34 of the RTA provides that the tenant is responsible for the repair of any undue damages to the rental unit or residential complex caused by the wilful or negligent conduct of the tenant, other occupants of the rental unit or persons who are permitted in the residential complex by the tenant. Thus, if the landlord alleges that the repairs requested by the tenant were in fact the tenant's responsibility, this issue must be decided by the Member.

Similarly, it may be necessary to hear evidence regarding an allegation that the tenant or persons they permitted on the premises contributed to the severity of the maintenance problem, or aggravated its repair. The tenant may have unreasonably prevented the landlord from entering the unit to assess the problem or make the repairs. In such a case, the repair may still be ordered to be done by the landlord or the tenant, but the tenant's conduct may result in no abatement or other remedy.

Remedies That May Be Ordered
Assuming that the Member has heard the evidence and decided that there has been a breach of the landlord's obligations, there are a number of factors that should be considered before arriving at the remedy or remedies to be included in the order.

The Member should ask for submissions from the parties specifically about the remedies that are appropriate for each item. The applicant and respondent may have discussed the dispute and come to some conclusion concerning the type or amount of relief to be given, although a Member is not bound to follow a joint submission.

Whether Tenant Notified the Landlord
Subsection 30(2) of the RTA states that, in determining the remedy, the adjudicator shall consider whether the applicant advised the landlord of the alleged breaches before filing their application. If the tenant failed to notify the landlord before making the application, it does not mean that the application must be dismissed, or even that this item should be dismissed.

Although the best practice for a tenant is to notify a landlord in writing of any serious problem, this provision does not require the notice to be written. Where the tenant alleges there was oral notice, they must convince the Member through their testimony that notice was given to the landlord or an employee, and when.

However, failure to advise the landlord will affect the remedies to be ordered, unless the landlord knew about the problem already or should have known. An applicant should not be awarded less relief than another tenant if they reasonably believed other tenants had already complained or the problem should have been obvious to the landlord or their employees.

---

6 O. Reg. 517/06.

A. *Order the Landlord to Do the Work*

Section 30 permits the Member to order the landlord to do specified repairs or replacements or other work within a specified time.

Most tenants apply because they want the landlord to be ordered to do the repairs or replacements. Thus, where these applications are mediated or settled, the agreement will usually include the landlord's promise to do the agreed work by a certain date.

An order should be very specific about the repairs or replacements that are required and by what date. The time allowed should be realistic given the season and any other factors that may delay the work. A Member may order that a tenant can deduct an amount from future rent payments if a landlord fails to comply with the order within a specified period of time.

B. *Authorize the Tenant to Do the Repairs or Replacements*

Section 30 allows a Member to authorize a repair or replacement that has been or is to be made and order its cost to be paid by the landlord to the tenant.

This will be an appropriate remedy where the failure of the landlord to comply with their maintenance obligations has resulted in the tenant being forced to do the repair or replacement. For example, if a tenant has already paid to have their refrigerator repaired, the Member could authorize the repair and order the landlord to refund the tenant the cost they incurred (so long it is reasonable) by a specific date or to deduct the amount from the rent.

In general, if repairs or replacements have not been done yet, difficult repairs or replacements and those that must be done consistently with similar work in the complex should usually be done by the landlord.

Where the repairs or replacements could be properly done by the tenant, the best order may be a combination. For example, the landlord could be ordered to do specified work by a specific date, failing which, the tenant would be authorized to do the same work, and deduct a specified amount from the rent. It would usually be advisable to have evidence, through estimates, of the cost of the repairs or replacements.

Section 207 of the RTA allows the adjudicator to set out recovery provisions in the order in the event that the landlord does not pay the tenant the lump sum amount ordered.

C. *Order an Abatement of Rent*

Section 30 allows a Member to order an abatement of rent. This is a monetary award expressed in terms of past or future rent. It may be a lump sum payment the landlord is ordered to pay the tenant, which effectively orders the landlord to give back part of the rent paid. It may be an order to allow the tenant to pay less rent by a certain amount or percentage, or even to pay no rent, for a specified time period. It could also be a combination of these.

This remedy is not appropriate where the landlord was not aware of the problem until the application was filed, but they should be ordered to fix the problem. If the landlord has already rectified the problem, and did so within a reasonable time, an abatement is not appropriate.

There is no guidance in the RTA to assist the Member in determining the amount of an abatement of rent. In determining the amount to be ordered, the Member will consider the period of time that the problem existed and the severity of the problem in terms of its effect on the tenant.

The test should be the impact on the average tenant or the impact a reasonable person would expect this problem to have had on a tenant. If the tenant has a particular susceptibility to this particular problem, the landlord can only reasonably be liable to the tenant for more significant penalties if it can be shown that the landlord knew of the particular condition of the tenant.

This remedy should not be seen as punishment for landlord conduct or inaction. It is compensation to the tenant for the inadequate state of repair and any inconvenience or actual loss of use of the rental unit or common facilities.

Effect of the Rent Level on the Abatement

The usual approach will be to look at an abatement as a portion of the rent. In other words, a Member will assess what percentage of the package of shelter and services rented by the tenant is not available to the tenant. That will then be expressed as a dollar amount, and logically this will be greater if the rent is greater.

In a rental unit with a low rent, or a lower rent than for similar units nearby, the landlord may argue that the maintenance standard expected would be somewhat less, and there should be no abatement or a minimal one. However, it must be remembered that the RTA guarantees adequate maintenance even if the tenant accepted the unit "as is." This is what one Ontario Court Justice stated about this issue:

> It is clear from the existing jurisprudence that there is no magic formula for determining what is an appropriate amount for an abatement ... . And while a tenant cannot reasonably expect luxury accommodation for marginally economic rent, even at the low end of the market a tenant is entitled to certain minimum guarantees.[7]

The other side of this issue is whether a higher rent entitles a tenant to better maintenance, and thus faster repairs, a wider responsibility for repairs and higher abatements if repairs are not done. This would seem to be an expectation related to the contract, rather than a tenant protection intended by the statute. Section 20 should not be interpreted in this way.

Knowledge of the Landlord

A landlord may assert that they are not liable for the unexpected results of maintenance problems of which they were not aware or that they could not reasonably be expected to have knowledge

---

7   *Prenor Trust Company of Canada v. Karen Forrest*, [1993] OJ No. 1058 (Ont. Ct. J).

of. This is indeed the law, as established by two Ontario Court of Appeal decisions. The Court rejected the claim for damages to a tenant who fell through rotting steps, of which the landlord was unaware.[8] However, in a similar case in which the tenant had advised the landlord of the wobbling stairs, the Court found the landlord liable for damages.[9] These were claims for "damages" but the same principle applies to abatements.

Is There Liability for Abatement During Repairs or Replacements?

In some past decisions, the Court ordered landlords to pay an abatement of rent for the period of major repairs done for the tenant's benefit. This reflects the loss of use of part of the unit or services, and from one point of view this loss was directly caused (at least in some cases) from the landlord's failure to do work earlier. The opposite viewpoint is that such an abatement is counterproductive because the landlord will not have enough funds to do the work, and will discourage landlords from doing necessary improvements.

The Supreme Court of Canada set out the basic rule in *Herbold v. Pajelle Investments Ltd.*[10] The Court held that only in the most exceptional cases should an abatement of rent be granted for failure to provide common facilities and services during a short period required for necessary repairs and renovations. The Court noted that where there are long and important delays in providing these things which the landlord is responsible for providing, an abatement should be ordered. In *Greenbranch Investments Ltd. v. Goulborn*[11] the Court of Appeal held that repairs done by the landlord in that case did not deprive the tenants of the physical use and enjoyment of their premises.

Section 8 of O. Reg. 516/06 sets out criteria to be applied by the Board in determining whether there is substantial interference when a landlord does maintenance, repairs or capital improvements, criteria for determining whether to order an abatement of rent, and rules for calculating an abatement. These rules must be applied in an application for a finding that the landlord has substantially interfered with the reasonable enjoyment of the unit by the tenant, but they do not apply to an application for a finding that a landlord has failed to repair or maintain the unit or complex.

If a landlord has done little maintenance for an extended period, and a serious condition results that takes some time to rectify, the landlord should be responsible for the tenants' loss of use of their unit or common facilities during the repairs.

However, if the landlord has a reasonable program of maintenance, including preventative maintenance, and is acting responsibly to rectify a problem that requires extensive repairs, an abatement of rent should not be ordered.

This approach imposes greater liability on landlords who do not meet their maintenance obligations, while encouraging responsible landlords to undertake major projects.

Thus, although proving that there is good maintenance of a complex will not avoid a finding that specific maintenance problems exist and must be rectified, it will affect the abatement remedy. Thus, it is only where the tenant has claimed an abatement of rent and that remedy is available that evidence of a good maintenance program should be accepted.

D. Termination of the Tenancy and Eviction of the Tenant

These remedies should be used in serious cases and only where the tenant requests them or a public authority has required the unit to be vacated. These remedies may also be ordered on consent of both parties if, for example, they both feel the relationship cannot continue.

If the rental unit is not fit for human habitation, the tenancy should be terminated. For example, if this occurred due to a disaster such as flooding, and the landlord does not wish to restore the unit immediately and make provisions such as a hotel to bridge the time, the tenancy could be terminated retroactively to the date of the flooding, with an abatement ordered from that date on (similar to compensation in the other direction).

The Member may also choose this remedy if the condition of the unit is so poor as to threaten the safety of the tenants or threaten their well-being. However, ordinarily the landlord should have had a reasonable opportunity to rectify the situation before termination is ordered.

Where an eviction of the tenant is ordered, the effective date of the eviction may not be earlier than the termination date specified in the order.

E. Order the Landlord to Pay a Specified Sum to the Tenant

The Member may order the landlord to pay the reasonable costs the tenant has or will incur to replace property where the tenant's property has been damaged, destroyed or disposed of as a result of the landlord's breach. These costs should only be awarded where repairing the property is not a reasonable alternative.

The Member may order the landlord to pay the tenant compensation for other reasonable out-of-pocket expenses that the tenant has or will incur as a result of the landlord's breach. The Board may also, in an appropriate case, award general damages for breach of the tenancy agreement.

---

8   In *McQuestion v. Schneider* (1975), 8 OR (2d) 249 (CA), the Court rejected the tenant's argument that this duty to repair imposed a strict or absolute liability on the landlord.

9   In *Dye v. McGregor* (1978), 20 OR (2d) 1 (CA), the Court found that this notice was sufficient to establish some degree of want of repair and found the landlord liable.

10   [1976] 2 SCR 520.

11   [1972] OJ No. 956 (CA).

F. Prohibit Rent Increases

The Member may also prohibit the landlord from:

i. charging a new tenant an amount of rent in excess of the last lawful rent charged to the former tenant;

ii. giving a notice of a rent increase; or

iii. taking any rent increase for which notice has been given if the increase has not been taken before the date of any order the member may issue under this section.

Any of these remedies may be included in an order for the period until the landlord:

i. has completed the items in work orders for which the compliance period has expired and which were found by the Board to be related to a serious breach of a health, safety, housing or maintenance standard; and

ii. has completed the specified repairs or replacements or other work ordered under paragraph 4 of section 30 found by the Board to be related to a serious breach of the landlord's obligations under section 20(1) or section 161 of the RTA.

Note that a Member must find that a landlord has not completed the items in a work order or orders relating to a "serious" breach of the relevant standard or obligation. What constitutes a serious breach is discussed under "Serious Breach of Landlord Obligations" in Guideline 7, Relief from Eviction.

G. Any Other Order That Is Appropriate

Section 30 also permits the Board to make any other order that it considers appropriate.

The Board has the authority under the *Statutory Powers Procedure Act* to issue interim orders. This may be an appropriate remedy when the landlord has shown no inclination to do the work required, and the Member does not believe that an order to do the work will be respected. This would be especially applicable where authorizing the tenant to do the work would not be appropriate because of the nature of the repairs needed. The Member could issue an interim order assessing an abatement of rent of an appropriate amount for each month until the landlord completes the repairs. This will encourage the landlord to do the work expeditiously.

For cases in which the work should be done very quickly, the decision on the abatement could be delayed by adjourning the case for a short period, allowing the landlord to return on a later date to show the work is completed. The advantage of this approach is that it encourages the work to be done, while not putting the Member in the position of issuing a final order with conditions (which may be difficult to enforce for the tenant). Usually a date for the adjourned hearing should be set, but in appropriate cases the hearing could be adjourned without a date, allowing any party to bring it back on with seven days notice to the other parties.

Another option would be to order the landlord to do the specific repairs within a specific period, but also order that,

failing the work being done within that time, the tenant may recover the appropriate amount to do the work through deductions to the rent. Alternatively, if the landlord failed to do the work by the deadline, the tenant would be entitled to a rent abatement for each rental period until the work was completed.

The Member may also combine any of the above mentioned remedies where they believe it is appropriate to do so.

Amended: January 4, 2011

INTERPRETATION GUIDELINE #6
TENANTS RIGHTS

Interpretation Guidelines are intended to assist the parties in understanding the Board's usual interpretation of the law, to provide guidance to Members and promote consistency in decision-making. However, a Member is not required to follow a Guideline and may make a different decision depending on the facts of the case.

Under subsection 29(1) of the *Residential Tenancies Act, 2006* ("the RTA") a tenant may apply to the Board for an order determining that the landlord, superintendent or agent of the landlord:[1]

- has illegally entered the unit;
- has altered a locking system on a door giving entry to the unit or the complex, without giving the tenant replacement keys;
- has withheld or deliberately interfered with the reasonable supply of care service, food or of any vital service, other than the supply of electricity where a suite meter has been installed in accordance with section 137 of the RTA and the tenant is responsible for paying for electricity and the landlord, the landlord's agent or the suite meter provider is attempting to enforce its rights or obligations;
- has substantially interfered with the tenant's reasonable enjoyment of the premises;
- has harassed, obstructed, coerced, threatened or interfered with a tenant.

Section 31 of the RTA sets out the remedies which the Board may include in an order if a finding is made in respect to any of these matters (referred to as "the actions").

Under subsections (1), (2) and (3), these remedies include:

- ordering the landlord, superintendent or agent not to engage in any of those actions against any of the tenants in the complex;
- ordering an abatement of rent;
- ordering the landlord to pay an administrative fine to the Board up to $25,000;
- ordering the landlord, superintendent or agent to pay compensation to the tenant for property that has been

---

[1] For the exact text of these provisions, see the RTA.

damaged, destroyed or disposed of as a result of the action;

- ordering the landlord, superintendent or agent to pay other reasonable out-of-pocket expenses that the tenant has incurred or will incur;
- where the tenant has been illegally locked out, ordering the landlord to allow the tenant to recover possession of the rental unit, and to refrain from re-renting the unit in the interim;
- terminate tenancy and order eviction (see s. 32); and/or
- making any other order it considers appropriate.

If the conduct induced the tenant to vacate the unit, subsection (2) also permits the Board to order the landlord to pay a specified amount to the tenant as compensation for:

- increased rent the tenant incurs within 12 months, and
- reasonable moving and related expenses.

Section 8 of O. Reg. 516/06, made pursuant to section 241 of the RTA, sets out criteria to be applied by the Board in determining whether there is substantial interference when a landlord does maintenance, repairs or capital improvements; as well as criteria for determining whether to order an abatement of rent, and rules for calculating the abatement.

Subsection 31(3) permits the Board to order the landlord to allow the tenant to recover possession of the rental unit. If the landlord does not voluntarily comply with the Board's order by allowing the tenant to regain possession, the tenant can enforce the Board's order through the sheriff's office. In the case where the tenant does not regain possession, the Board's order will expire at the end of 15 days after the date it was issued if it has not been filed with the sheriff's office. Even where the tenant files the order with the appropriate sheriff's office the Board's order will expire at the end of the 45th day (see subsection 31(4) and (5) for exact wording of the RTA).

Applying Section 29(2)—One Year Limitation Period
An application must be made by the current or former tenant within one year of the date the alleged breach occurred. When determining whether an application has been made "in time" pursuant to subsection 29(2) of the RTA, a Member will have to determine when the alleged breach occurred.

When a breach is a single event such as an illegal entry, then the limitation period begins on the day the event happened. Where the breach is not a single event but is ongoing or recurring as may be the case with some instances of interference with reasonable enjoyment or the withdrawal or withholding of a vital service, then the breach occurs over a period of time and the limitation period runs from the date that the behaviour causing the interference with reasonable enjoyment ceases or the vital service is restored to the tenant. However, in all cases the limitation period is one year.

The intention behind the limitation period found in section 29(2) of the RTA is that the applicant has only a certain amount of time to file the application and obtain a remedy, but may bring the application at any time within the limitation period. The fact that the tenant did not bring the application when the breach first arose does not affect the tenant's right to file an application. There is no provision in the RTA requiring the tenant to bring an application immediately upon the breach of the Act. However, the tenant may not include in an application any issue which has been resolved by the landlord more than one year before the application was filed.

If the application is filed "in time" pursuant to subsection 29(2) and the breach is no longer occurring as of the date of the order, the Board may award a remedy (such as a rent abatement) for the timeframe calculated from one year prior to the application filing date to the date the breach ended . Where the breach is ongoing as of the date of the order, the potential remedy may provide for periods beyond the date of the order to the date that the breach is no longer occurring (*Goodman and Pearlman v. Menyhart and Menyhart*, [2009] OJ No. 1602, and *Toronto Community Housing Corp v. Allan Vlahovich*, [2010] OJ No. 1463). (For a discussion regarding remedies that can be ordered by the Board see the sections on remedies later in this Guideline.)

The most recent decision that considered the proper application of subsection 29(2) was that of the Divisional Court in *Toronto Community Housing Corp. v. Vlahovich*, [2010] OJ No. 1463. In *Vlahovich*, the Court stated:

> In light of the one year limitation period in s. 29(2), the Board can only make a determination that a landlord has breached an obligation under s. 20(1) during the one year period before the making of the application. Accordingly, the remedy that may be granted may only be granted in relation to breaches during that one year period.

In *Vlahovich*, the Divisional Court explained that, "properly understood" the earlier decision of the Divisional Court in *Goodman v. Menyhart*, [2009] OJ No. 1602, was not inconsistent with the Court's approach in *Vlahovich*. The Court emphasized that the Divisional Court panel in *Goodman v. Menyhart* had ordered that an abatement can extend back one year before the application had been made and no further. The Court in *Vlahovich* stated that in *Goodman v. Menyhart*, the only issue was whether the limitation period should extend back twelve months from the order of the Board or from the filing of the application. In that case, and, consistent with the reasoning in *Vlahovich*, the limitation period extended back one year from the filing of the application.

Where Notice Is Given in Bad Faith
Notice of termination of the tenancy can be given by the landlord:

- for the use of the rental unit by the landlord, the landlord's spouse, child or parent of the landlord or spouse of the landlord, or for a person providing care services to the landlord or the landlord's spouse, child or parent of the landlord or spouse of the landlord (see section 48 of the RTA);

- for the use of the rental unit by the purchaser, the purchaser's spouse, child or parent of the purchaser or spouse of the purchaser, or for a person providing care services to the purchaser or the purchaser's spouse, child or parent of the purchaser or spouse of the purchaser (see section 49 of the RTA);
- for the demolition, conversion or repairs of the rental unit (see section 50 of the RTA).

Under subsection 57(1) of the RTA, a former tenant may apply to the Board for an order determining that the landlord has given notice of termination in bad faith in the circumstances found in sections 48, 49 or 50 of the RTA. The former tenant may apply if they have vacated the rental unit as a result of the notice given by the landlord or an application or as a result of an order issued by the Board based on the notice. The application must be filed by the former tenant within one year after they vacated the rental unit.

Properly Naming Respondents

It is essential that the tenant name the appropriate persons as respondents. The tenant should name the landlord as a respondent in the application as well as any other person that they believe is responsible for the issues that they are raising in their application. If a person who the tenant alleges to be responsible is not named as a party to the application, and thus has no opportunity to respond to the allegations and make submissions on the possible remedies, no remedies will be ordered against that person.

For example, if the tenant names only the landlord as a respondent, but proves that a superintendent or agent of the landlord was responsible for the action, the Board can order remedies against the landlord but cannot order remedies against the superintendent or agent personally.

If the landlord is a corporation or similar entity, the Member must determine whether the persons who engaged in the actions against the tenant were acting on behalf of the landlord. A corporation may only act through human beings: namely, its officers and employees. The corporation may also enter into a contract with an agent to act on its behalf. Thus, if the individual who engaged in the action against the tenant was an officer, employee or agent of the corporation, the corporation is responsible as the landlord and the Member may order remedies against both the individual and the corporation.

If the tenant decides early in the hearing that another respondent should have been named, the Member must consider whether the tenant should have been aware that the other respondent should have been named in the application. The hearing would have to start again from the beginning if another respondent is added by the Member. However, if the other respondent is a corporation, one of whose employees, officers or agents was at the hearing already, it might not be necessary to re-start the hearing.

Remedies

If the Board determines that the landlord, superintendent or agent has violated the rights of the tenant under subsection 29(1), the Board may order any one or more of the remedies mentioned in subsection 31(1).

Abatement Orders

If the Board determines that the landlord, superintendent or agent has violated the rights of the tenant under subsection 29(1), the Board may order any one or more of the remedies mentioned in subsection 31(1).

If the Board determines that an abatement of rent is appropriate in the circumstances, the Board will determine the amount and/or duration of the abatement. To make this determination the Board will look at factors such as:

- The respondent's intentions in doing the action complained of by the tenant;
- Whether the respondent was motivated by malice toward the tenant;
- The extent of harm that the tenant suffered as a result of the respondent's actions;
- Whether the tenant contributed to or aggravated the situation;
- The frequency or duration of the actions or events, and if a landlord has taken or permitted an action against the tenant. For instance, if it was a single action which deprived the tenant of their tenancy, such as locking the tenant out of the unit, the Board should consider this among the most serious means of harming a tenant. If the actions occurred over a period of time, the Member should consider the number of occasions and the total period of time. The abatement may be expressed as a portion of the rent which would reflect the seriousness of the expected effects on a tenant. Normally, this would be allowed for the periods in which the actions occurred. For example, for a serious case of harassment, an abatement of twenty-five to fifty per cent of the rent may be appropriate. In cases of minor (but not trivial) harassment, an order of between five and fifteen percent abatement would be more appropriate.

When a Member finds that the respondent engaged in actions against the tenant, they should consider the effects those actions would have on an average tenant. However, if it is proven that the respondent was aware of particular circumstances of this applicant which would aggravate the effects of the actions, those circumstances should be considered. For example, cornering a person in a parking garage and raising one's voice may be annoying to most tenants; however, if the landlord knows the tenant is vulnerable and lives alone, such an incident may be seriously disturbing and may warrant a larger abatement of rent.

If a superintendent or agent is proven to have engaged in the actions, and not the landlord, an order for the landlord to pay an abatement may be made if the person who engaged in the actions was an employee, agent or officer of the landlord, whether or not acting properly under instructions from the landlord.

A superintendent or agent would not be ordered to pay an abatement of rent, since the tenant pays rent to the landlord; however, they may be ordered to pay compensation (see below under "Other Appropriate Orders").

Orders Prohibiting Actions Against Tenants

Normally the order will direct the respondent not to engage in any of the listed activities against any tenant in the complex. This remedy may be appropriate even if there is no evidence that the landlord has engaged in similar actions against another tenant or tenants. However, in an appropriate case, the Member may order the respondent not engage in a specific activity against the applicant tenant and members of their household.

The main test in deciding whether to order this relief is whether it is in the public interest to deter this respondent from any further occurrence of actions against tenants. This is particularly true if the actions against the tenant threatened the health or safety of the tenant or a member of their household.

Orders Terminating Tenancies

There are several situations in which a tenancy may be terminated by the order.

If the tenant was induced to move out of the unit by reason of the landlord's actions, and the Member finds that moving out was reasonable in the circumstances, the tenancy should be ordered terminated, usually as of the date they vacated the unit. This will prevent the landlord from applying to the Board for any further rent from the tenant. The Member should order the landlord to refund to the tenant all rent paid pertaining to the period of time after the effective date of termination, plus the rent deposit. For example, if the termination is June 15, and June rent and a rent deposit were paid, the landlord should refund 1½ months rent to the tenant. The authority for such an order is "Other Appropriate Orders" (see below).

If the tenant requests termination of the tenancy or if the parties agree, termination may be ordered. It is desirable if the parties agree on appropriate terms and timing of the termination. This would avoid unintended financial consequences to one or both of the parties. If the Board makes an order terminating the tenancy the Board may also order that the tenant be evicted.

If the tenant wants to stay in the unit, this request should be honoured unless there is clear danger to the occupants of the unit. If the health or safety of the tenant or a member of their household is threatened, the tenancy should be terminated.

If the respondent's actions put the tenant in a position that the tenancy cannot be safely continued, the request to terminate the tenancy should be granted. For example, the landlord cuts off a tenant's heat in the winter. In order not to put the tenant at a disadvantage compared to a tenant who moved out before applying, the Member might also order the respondent to pay the tenant's moving expenses, even if these have to be estimated.

Orders to Pay an Administrative Fine

An administrative fine is a remedy to be used by the Board to encourage compliance with the RTA and to deter landlords, superintendents and agents from engaging in similar actions in the future. This remedy is appropriate in serious cases where the landlord has shown a blatant disregard for the RTA and other remedies will not provide adequate deterrence and compliance.

For further information on administrative fines please see Guideline 16.

Other Appropriate Orders

The legislation allows the Board to make an order which may be appropriate, in addition to the other remedies set out in sections 30 and 31 of the RTA. Before making such an order the Member shall take into consideration the individual circumstances between the parties and will advise the parties of the order they may be considering. The Board will allow the parties an opportunity to make submissions on the order and will also consider the practicality and enforceability of the order.

Compensation for Future Rent and Moving Expenses

These remedies are limited to cases in which the applicant was induced to vacate the unit as a result of the landlord actions. For example, if the respondent's conduct was sufficient to justify a finding of serious interference with reasonable enjoyment, to a degree that would cause the average tenant to vacate, moving expenses and other reasonable out of pocket expenses can be ordered. This compensation is in addition to any abatement of rent or other remedies ordered.

The tenant may claim for "all or any portion of any increased rent which the tenant has incurred or will incur for a one year period after the tenant has left the rental unit." The first question then is whether the tenant has actually rented another unit, and what the rent for that unit is. If the rent is higher, the total amount that could be ordered is the difference over a 12 month period. However, if the tenant has rented a larger unit or a better unit, the Member would consider evidence of the rents for units in the neighbourhood similar to the unit which is subject of the application. The compensation could be limited to the lower amount.

However, the tenant is not required to make an exhaustive search of every possible rental unit. If the tenant rents a comparable unit, after a reasonable search, they should not be expected to have found the lowest rent possible. Further, the tenant cannot be expected to have rented another unit from the respondent, even at a lower rent.

In some cases, a tenant who has been forced to leave the rental unit as a result of the landlord's actions will be living in temporary accommodation at the time of hearing. The tenant may be paying little or no rent for this temporary accommodation. However, if the tenant can establish that they have found permanent accommodation after a reasonable search and intend to move into this accommodation, the tenant could make a claim for the increased rent they will incur once they move into the permanent accommodation. Such proof could include a rental application or a signed lease. However, the time limit for making such a claim is 12 months after the tenant vacated the rental unit which is the subject of the application.

In addition, the tenant may also claim "reasonable out of pocket moving, storage and other like expenses." These are costs which the tenant has already incurred which may be proven by bills or receipts, or will incur and may be proven by contracts or quotations. The term "other like expenses" would include other costs that were incurred or will be incurred in order to move into another unit, such as a fee to an apartment locating service or real estate service or expenses to move the telephone or cable service.

Interference Resulting from Maintenance, Repairs or Capital Improvements

Where the landlord has substantially interfered with a tenant's reasonable enjoyment of a unit or complex while carrying out maintenance, repairs or improvements, the remedy that the Board will normally consider is an abatement of rent. It is unlikely that the Board will consider it reasonable to order the landlord to stop doing the work. However, in some cases, it may be appropriate to consider an order for payment of the tenant's out-of-pocket expenses, an order terminating the tenancy or, where the tenant has been induced to move as a result of the activity, an order for payment of increased rent and moving expenses.

Section 241 of the RTA provides the authority to make regulations that set standards and criteria to be applied where tenants claim that landlords have substantially interfered with their reasonable enjoyment of the unit or complex in carrying out maintenance, repairs or capital improvements to the unit or complex. The section also authorizes regulations establishing criteria that must be applied by the Board in determining whether to order an abatement of rent in these applications.

These standards and criteria are found in section 8 of O. Reg. 516/06. The regulation requires the Board to consider the effect of the work on the tenant's use of the unit or the complex. The Member must determine that the effect was unreasonable in the circumstances, in order to find that there has been a substantial interference with the tenant's reasonable enjoyment of the unit or complex. If it is not found that the effect on the tenant was unreasonable in the circumstances, the application will be dismissed.

If it is determined that there has been a substantial interference, the regulation provides that the Board shall not grant the remedy of an abatement of rent, regardless of the effect of the work on the tenant, if the landlord has met the ten conditions set out in the regulation.

Where it is determined that there has been substantial interference and that an abatement is not prohibited, the Board will consider the five criteria set out in the regulation in determining whether it is appropriate to order an abatement and the amount of the abatement.

Any abatement ordered will not exceed 25% of the monthly rent for any month or part of a month in which there is substan-

tial interference unless the specific circumstances exist as set out in the regulation. In such case, the Board cannot order an abatement of rent that exceeds 100 per cent of the rent for each month or part of a month during which the Board determines that the work substantially interfered with the tenant's reasonable enjoyment of the rental unit or residential complex.

Amended: January 4, 2011

INTERPRETATION GUIDELINE #7 RELIEF FROM EVICTION: REFUSING OR DELAYING AN EVICTION

Interpretation Guidelines are intended to assist the parties in understanding the Board's usual interpretation of the law, to provide guidance to Members and promote consistency in decision-making. However, a Member is not required to follow a Guideline and may make a different decision depending on the facts of the case.

Even though a landlord proves their case in an application to evict a tenant, the Board must review and consider the circumstances of each case to determine whether or not the eviction should be refused or delayed. In some cases, the Board *must* refuse the eviction. These powers are referred to as "relief from eviction."

Legislation

Section 83 of the *Residential Tenancies Act, 2006* ("the RTA") states:

(1) Upon an application for an order evicting a tenant, the Board may, despite any other provision of this Act or the tenancy agreement,

   (a) refuse to grant the application unless satisfied, having regard to all the circumstances, that it would be unfair to refuse; or

   (b) order that the enforcement of the order of eviction be postponed for a period of time.

(2) If a hearing is held, the Board shall not grant the application unless it has reviewed the circumstances and considered whether or not it should exercise its powers under subsection (1).

(3) Without restricting the generality of subsection (1), the Board shall refuse to grant the application where satisfied that:

   (a) the landlord is in serious breach of the landlord's responsibilities under this Act or of any material covenant in the tenancy agreement;

   (b) the reason for the application being brought is that the tenant has complained to a government authority of the landlord's violation of a law dealing with health, safety, housing or maintenance standards;

   (c) the reason for the application being brought is that the tenant has attempted to secure or enforce his or her legal rights;

   (d) the reason for the application being brought is that the tenant is a member of a tenant's association or is attempting to organize such an association; or

(e) the reason for the application being brought is that the rental unit is occupied by children and the occupation by the children does not constitute overcrowding.

General Principles

The Board has a general discretion to refuse or delay an eviction under subsection 83(1), after considering all relevant circumstances. This authority arises upon any application for an order to evict a tenant. This general discretion does not automatically arise where an application is resolved without a hearing (e.g., in the case of an ex-parte order issued pursuant to subsection 78(6) of the RTA) or where a hearing is held for another purpose (e.g., in the case of a hearing of a set aside motion under subsection 74(11) of the RTA). Where a hearing is held on an application to evict a tenant, including a hearing that the tenant does not attend, and a hearing of an application that would normally by resolved by an ex parte order but has been sent to hearing (subsection 77(1) or 78(1) applications), the Board must review and consider the circumstances of both parties to determine whether or not the eviction should be delayed or refused prior to granting an application. The Board must consider the circumstances whether or not the tenant requests relief from eviction, and may pose questions to the landlord and/or tenant to better understand the circumstances.

Further, subsection 83(3) provides for mandatory relief from eviction in certain situations. If the Board finds that any of clauses (a) to (e) of subsection 83(3) applies, the Board must not grant the application to evict.

Discretionary Refusal of an Eviction

The Board must review and consider all the circumstances to determine whether or not to exercise its discretion to refuse an eviction. For example:

- in a case involving an allegation of tenant "fault" (such as eviction for arrears or illegal act), consider whether the reason is serious enough to justify an eviction,
- in a case involving a landlord's allegation of interference with reasonable enjoyment, consider whether refusing to evict the tenant would result in applications against the landlord by other tenants for interference with their reasonable enjoyment, or
- consider whether refusing to evict the tenant would result in an unreasonable financial hardship to the landlord.

In "having regard to all the circumstances" the Member shall consider the relevant circumstances of the tenant and landlord and the impact on other occupants in the residential complex in delaying or denying eviction. Therefore, if the tenant's request presents a possible reason for refusal, the landlord may then explain why the refusal to evict would be unfair to them or to other occupants in the residential complex.

Where the Board exercises its discretion to refuse to evict a tenant, the Board may attach conditions to such an order that one or both parties must follow.

Circumstances Justifying Discretionary Refusal

The tenant's conduct has been an important consideration in many past decisions. For example:

- If the tenant got far behind in their rent payments, but has recently made extra payments to catch up, and owes relatively little now, the discretion may be exercised in their favour.
- In a case of persistent late payment of rent, the tenant had financial problems when he became unemployed, but for months since he found another job, payment has been right on time. The eviction may be refused despite the earlier months of late payments, due to the tenant's good conduct. In such circumstances, the Member may order that on-time rent payments are to be made, by the tenant to the landlord, for a specified number of months following the hearing.
- A tenant is not excused from paying rent even if the landlord has greater financial resources (e.g., a public agency or large corporate landlord). Other relevant factors may include whether the current reason for eviction has been repeated, the impact this tenant is having on the landlord or other tenants, whether the tenant has taken positive steps to reduce or eliminate the reason for the eviction, and other indications of good faith on the part of either the landlord or the tenant.

Landlord actions or conduct which led to the eviction should also be considered. For example, if the landlord unreasonably prevented a tenant from repairing damage done by a guest or child, this would be relevant. If the landlord has excused many other tenants from a minor breach, an arbitrary eviction of one tenant for the same breach may be refused, depending on all of the other circumstances.

Discretionary Delay of an Eviction

The Board must review and consider the circumstances to determine whether or not to exercise its discretion to delay an eviction.

Although the time period is not set out in the RTA, Board orders commonly provide that a tenant has 11 days after an order for arrears of rent and termination of the tenancy is issued to pay all of the rent arrears and costs owing to the landlord. If the tenant does not make the necessary payment, the tenant can be evicted for failure to pay rent starting on the 12th day after the order is issued. This period of time takes into account such matters as the time it takes for the tenant to receive the order in the mail and acquire the rent money to pay to the landlord. Therefore, a decision of the Board to postpone the enforcement of an eviction order under clause 83(1)(b) of the RTA often means the order would provide that the order could not be filed with the Court Enforcement Office until more than 12 days after the date the order is issued.

Generally, the Member would take into account the time that it will normally take the landlord to enforce the order through the Court Enforcement Office.

Even if "all of the circumstances" did not justify refusal of the eviction, the Member may look at the same issues of unfairness to each party, and decide whether or not to delay the eviction. Eviction may appear to be unfair if no other accommodation is available to the tenant (e.g., a social housing tenant). However, a case in which the landlord is in a better financial position than the tenant does not justify refusal of the eviction. Ordinarily, the tenant's lack of resources will be considered as a reason to delay an eviction, not to refuse it. However, all circumstances must be considered.

The following are some examples that illustrate situations in which a delay may be considered:

- The tenant asserts that the market conditions in the locality are unusually "tight" and that it will take some time to find suitable accommodation.
- The tenant shows that they are affected by a severe medical condition which makes it difficult to find other accommodation, and there are no persons who can help him or her search for a vacant unit.
- The tenant's family is very large and they require at least five bedroom accommodation, similar to their current unit. There are very few such units in the local market, and none are in the current advertisements.

Mandatory Refusal of Eviction

Mandatory refusal applies to situations which the RTA provides are serious enough to justify refusal—regardless of any other circumstances.

If a tenant raises circumstances which might fall into subsection 83(3), the Member must decide whether it applies.[1] Further, once it is found that subsection (3) applies, the Member must refuse the eviction.[2]

Serious Breach of Landlord Obligations

The Board must refuse an eviction if the landlord is in serious breach of the landlord's responsibilities under the RTA or the tenancy agreement.

Many claims are related to the landlord's maintenance obligations. A health or safety concern due to lack of repair may be serious enough to justify refusal. Conditions which deprive the tenant of the full use of the premises will usually be serious, particularly if it affects the kitchen, bathroom or sleeping areas. Members must decide whether other repair problems constitute a "serious breach" of obligations, considering the landlord's actions to resolve the problems as well. Other factors such as how long the breach was on-going or the level of risk to the tenants may also be relevant.[3]

In cases related to the obligation to repair, the tenant's conduct may also be relevant. For example, if the tenant has never before complained to the landlord about a long-standing repair problem, they may have shown they did not consider it to be serious. Further, if the landlord was not aware of the problem, the Member may not consider it to be a serious breach of obligation. Further, the tenant should not have contributed to the problem, such as by obstructing the landlord's repair efforts.

In cases related to the obligation to repair, the age of the property and the landlord's intentions for the property may be factors for the Member to consider. For example, if the landlord is intending to demolish the property and the tenant was served a notice to terminate for that reason, the Member would consider these factors before deciding to refuse to evict.[4]

The tenant may raise a breach of another obligation of the landlord under the RTA. For example, the RTA imposes on landlords the obligation not to illegally enter a unit, nor to harass a tenant. The Member must decide the issue and, if satisfied that the facts presented show a serious breach, they must refuse the eviction. However, mandatory refusal of eviction is generally accepted to refer to serious breaches existing at the time of the hearing, not breaches from the past tht have been remedied.[5]

If the tenant raises a breach of the tenancy agreement, they must present facts to show that it was a serious breach and that it relates to a significant provision of the agreement.

Even if the breach is not found to be serious and there would be no mandatory refusal, the lack of repair or other breach of obligation may still be considered. It would be one of the circumstances of unfairness to consider in deciding whether discretionary refusal is appropriate.

Retaliatory Actions by the Landlord

The Member must refuse the eviction if the reason the landlord applied for eviction is described in clause (b) to (e) of subsection 83(3) (these clauses are quoted on page 1).

The tenant would explain what actions they took which they believe caused the landlord to seek the eviction. However, the tenant has a higher onus. They must prove that the reason for the application is one of the above motivations.[6] It is difficult to prove another person's state of mind. The landlord will assert that the reason stated in the application was the reason for the application.

The tenant may try to show from the landlord's conduct that the motivation was retaliatory. For example, the tenant may be able to show that the landlord has evicted other tenants who asserted their rights. The tenant might also show that the landlord ignored the same issue that is the basis for this eviction,

---

[1] See *Forgie v. Widdicombe Place*, [2002] OJ No. 2956 (Div. Ct.).

[2] See *Chin v. Hunt* (1986), 17 OAC 267 (Div. Ct.).

[3] *Sage v. Corporation of the County of Wellington* (April 25, 2005), London Docket No. 1471 (Div. Ct.).

[4] *MacNeil et al. v. 976445 Ontario Ltd.* (June 6, 2005), London Docket No. 04-1465 (Div. Ct.).

[5] Supra note 4.

[6] *MacNeil et al. v. 976445 Ontairo Ltd.* (June 6, 2005), London Docket No. 04-1465 (Div. Ct.).

for other tenants. A pattern of conduct may be considered by the Board, but it may also be explained by the landlord.

Even if the tenant does not establish to the Member's satisfaction that the reason for the application was retaliation and, thus refusal is not mandatory, the facts that supported the tenant's claim could be one of the circumstances considered in deciding whether there should be discretionary refusal of the eviction.

Applications Under Section 77

Under subsection 77(4) of the RTA, the Board may make an order terminating the tenancy and evicting the tenant without notice to the tenant and without a hearing (ex-parte), if the landlord has filed an application with the Board under subsection 77(1), based on either an agreement between the landlord and the tenant to terminate the tenancy or a notice of termination given by the tenant.

Decisions Made Ex Parte

An application (L3) filed by a landlord pursuant to subsection 77(1) of the Act is generally resolved by an ex parte order issued pursuant to subsection 77(4).

The tenant may file a motion pursuant to subsection 77(6) to set aside the ex parte order. The Board then holds a hearing to consider the tenant's motion. As a hearing concerning such a motion does not arise upon an application for an order to evict a tenant, subsection 83(1) does not apply. Instead, the Board exercises similar discretionary relief under subsection 77(8), which provides:

If the respondent makes a motion under subsection (6), the Board shall, after a hearing,

    (a) make an order setting aside the order under subsection (4), if

          i. the landlord and tenant did not enter into an agreement to terminate the tenancy, and

          ii. the tenant did not give the landlord notice of termination of the tenancy;

    (b) make an order setting aside the order under subsection (4), if the Board is satisfied, having regard to all the circumstances, that it would not be unfair to do so; or

    (c) make an order lifting the stay of the order under subsection (4), effective immediately or on a future date specified in the order.

When having regard to all the circumstances, pursuant to clause 77(8)(b) the Board should consider circumstances that occurred with regard to the signing of the agreement to terminate the tenancy and thereafter or circumstances that occurred after the giving of the notice of termination by the tenant to the landlord.

Decisions Made When a Hearing Is Held

In those cases where an application filed under subsection 77(1) is sent to hearing and therefore is not decided ex parte, subsection 83(2) provides that the Board shall not grant the application unless it has reviewed the circumstances and considered whether or not it should exercise its powers under subsection (1).

With respect to the exercise of discretion under section 83, Members hearing a subsection 77(1) application will consider the circumstances that occurred with regard to the signing of the agreement to terminate and thereafter or circumstances that occurred after the giving the notice of termination.

Applications Under Section 78

Under subsections 78(6) & (7) of the RTA, the Board may issue an order evicting the tenant and ordering the tenant to pay arrears of rent without a hearing (ex-parte), if the landlord has filed an application with the Board under subsection 78(1).

Decisions Made Ex Parte

An application (L4) filed by a landlord pursuant to subsection 78(1) of the Act is generally resolved by an ex parte order issued pursuant to subsections 78(6) & (7).

The tenant may file a motion pursuant to subsection 78(9), to set aside an ex parte order issued under subsections 78(6) & (7). The Board then holds a hearing to consider the tenant's motion. As a hearing concerning such a motion does not arise upon an application for an order to evict a tenant, subsection 83(1) does not apply. Instead, the Board exercises similar discretionary relief under clauses 78(11)(b) & (c).

Pursuant to clause 78(11)(b) the Board may make an order setting aside the ex parte order issued if the Board is satisfied, having regard to all the circumstances, that it would not be unfair to set aside the order.

This provision gives the Members discretion to grant relief to the tenant by setting aside the ex parte order, notwithstanding the fact that the tenant has breached a condition required in the conditional order or mediated agreement.

In their consideration of this provision, Members should take into account:

- Circumstances that occurred after the date of the mediated agreement or conditional order that caused the party to be unable to meet the terms of the agreement or order. (Circumstances that occurred prior to the issuance of the conditional order or the signing of the mediated agreement should have been considered at the time the conditional order was made or the mediated agreement was signed, with respect to the previous application.)
- The circumstances of both the landlord and tenant and the impact on other occupants in the residential complex in delaying or denying eviction.

It is also important to remember that setting aside the ex parte order results in the original mediated agreement or conditional order remaining in full force and effect. In some cases, it may be impossible for the tenant to fulfill the remaining conditions contained in the mediated agreement or conditional order (i.e. the deadline for payments has now passed), and/or the parties wish to consent to new conditions.

The matter may be resolved in one of the following ways:

- The parties can consent to be bound by a new mediated agreement containing new terms or conditions, and in addition agree that the ex parte order would be set aside by order of the Member which order would also acknowledge that the L4 application had been resolved through a mediated agreement.

- The parties can consent to be bound by a new hearing order to be issued by the Member containing new terms or conditions.
- The Member may, in an order, revise the terms of a Board mediated settlement or an order made with respect to the previous application if the Member considers it appropriate to do so, (e.g. a revised payment schedule). In exercising this authority, the Member may, subject to the consideration of fairness, wish to consider ordering new conditions that are as close as possible to the original conditions imposed in the original order or mediated agreement.

If the tenant's motion to set aside the ex parte order is denied and clause 78(11)(b) has not been applied, the Board may make an order lifting the stay of the ex-parte order effective immediately or on a future date. Clause 78(11)(c) directs the Member to lift the stay of the ex parte order, thus permitting the landlord to enforce the ex parte order. The discretion given to Members to lift the stay on a future date is similar to the relief from eviction provided by clause 83(1)(b) which gives the Member authority to postpone the enforcement of the eviction for a period of time.

In considering such relief, the Member should take into account the same criteria as set out for clause 78(11)(b).

Decisions Made When a Hearing Is Held

In those cases where an application filed under subsection 78(1) is sent to hearing for clarification, therefore is not decided ex parte, subsection 83(2) provides that the Board shall not grant the application unless it has reviewed the circumstances and considered whether or not it should exercise its powers under subsection (1).

With respect to the exercise of discretion under section 83, Members hearing a subsection 78(1) application will consider the circumstances that occurred with regard to the signing of the mediated agreement and thereafter or circumstances that occurred after the date of the hearing which resulted in the conditional order.

Amended: January 4, 2011

INTERPRETATION GUIDELINE #8
REVIEW OF AN ORDER

Interpretation Guidelines are intended to assist the parties in understanding the Board's usual interpretation of the law, to provide guidance to Members and promote consistency in decision-making. However, a Member is not required to follow a Guideline and may make a different decision depending on the facts of the case.

The authority of the Board to review its own orders comes from section 21.2 of the *Statutory Powers Procedure Act* ("the SPPA") and subsection 209(2) of the *Residential Tenancies Act, 2006* ("the RTA"). Subsection 209(2) of the RTA provides that the Board's power to review a decision or order under section 21.2 of the SPPA may be exercised if a party to a proceeding was not reasonably able to participate in the proceeding. The procedures for dealing with a request to review an order are found in the Rules of Practice (see Rule 29).

This Guideline provides guidance concerning the scope of the power to review.

The party may ask for a review of the order if they believe the Member made a "serious error" or where they were not reasonably able to participate in the proceeding relying on section 21.2 of the SPPA, subsection 209(2) of the RTA, and Rule 29 of the Rules of Practice. Although Rule 29 permits a Vice Chair to initiate a review, the Board does not contemplate that reviews will be initiated often by a Vice Chair. The Board expects a party or a person directly affected by the Board order to make a written request for review under Rule 29 first, and not merely to request the Vice Chair to initiate a review.

If the order subject to the review request was resolved by a hearing, the review will be decided by a Member other than the Member who heard the application. A Member may not review their own orders, or any order with regard to an application for which the Member issued an interim order, except an interim order that stays the order under review (see Rule 29.9).

Communication Between the Reviewing Member and the Original Hearing Member

Members are often required to review orders of another Member in the same office. A Reviewing Member must make their decision independently and the process must be free of the perception of undue or improper influence. In order to uphold and preserve the integrity and independence of the review process, a Member considering a review request or conducting a review hearing shall not have any communication with the original Hearing Member about the substance and merits of the review request prior to the final disposition of the review request. The Reviewing Member and the original Hearing Member may engage in the following communication:

1. The Reviewing Member may request in writing that the original Hearing Member issue reasons if the Reviewing Member determines that reasons are necessary to consider the review request. The original Hearing Member shall then inform the Reviewing Member in writing when reasons will be issued. The written communication between the Members forms part of the record.
2. If the Reviewing Member believes that the order under review may contain a clerical error, the order may be referred to the original Hearing Member in writing to consider whether there is a clerical error.

What Is a Serious Error?

A serious error may include one of the following:

- an error of jurisdiction (e.g., applying a provision of the RTA in a case to which it does not apply, or exercising a power outside the proper authority of the Board), whether or not it was raised at the original hearing
- an error of procedure which prejudiced a party (e.g., failing to comply with the rules of natural justice)
- if a party to a proceeding was not reasonably able to participate in the proceeding pursuant to subsection 209(2)
- an error of fact which was material to the decision, and which was clearly an unreasonable finding considering the evidence which was before the Member
- an error of fact which is material to the decision which is demonstrated by new evidence which was not before the Member (e.g., a witness who was out of the country on the day of the original hearing), so long as the Member reviewing the order is satisfied that there is a sufficient reason why the evidence was not presented in the original hearing
- an error in law, but the Board will not normally review a reasonable interpretation of the statute by a Member, even if the interpretation differs from that of the reviewing member
- an error in applying discretion allowed by the law which is unreasonable (e.g., the Member allowed remedies which were inappropriate in the circumstances or which were, in quantum or degree, beyond what would reasonably be allowed).

When Is a Party "Not Reasonably Able to Participate" in a Proceeding?

A party may not be reasonably able to participate in a proceeding in a variety of circumstances. In *Montgomery and Turgeon v. 737259 Ontario Ltd.*, the Divisional Court found that the phrase "being reasonably able to participate in the proceeding," as that phrase appeared in the *Tenant Protection Act, 1997*, s. 192(4), should not be interpreted so strictly as to unduly prevent the Ontario Rental Housing Tribunal or court from exercising its discretion when it is right and just to do so. In *Mandache et al. v. Dron*, also under the TPA, the Member found that the party's failure to attend a hearing as a result of their own negligence or the negligence of their paid agent did not mean the party lacked a proper opportunity to participate in the hearing. The party appealed this decision to the Divisional Court which dismissed the appeal on the basis that the appellant had not raised a question of law as required by s. 196 of the TPA, this result left the Tribunal's decision undisturbed.

Consistent with this guidance, the Board may determine that a party was not reasonably able to participate in a proceeding where:

- the party did not receive the notice of hearing and the application because of the party's brief absence during the time of service (e.g., where the party was out of town, in the hospital, detained in police custody);
- the notice of hearing and other documents are served incorrectly (e.g., to the wrong address or to the incorrect individual);
- the party was physically unable to attend and did not have the opportunity to have an agent attend on his or her behalf (e.g., sudden illness);
- the party was led to believe by the other party that there was no need to respond to the application or attend the proceeding because all issues had been settled; or
- the party attended the proceeding, but the member's conduct did not allow the party to be reasonably able to participate.

These are only examples of the types of circumstances in which the Board may determine that a party was not reasonably able to participate in a proceeding. The Board would need to consider the specific circumstances of a matter to determine whether a party was not reasonably able to participate in a particular proceeding. It will usually be insufficient for a party to state they did not participate in the proceeding because they did not understand the possible consequences of the proceedings. The Board expects parties to read a notice of hearing and other documents received in relation to a matter before the Board and to seek help if they cannot understand it.

In general, an assertion that a party had not been able to attend without explaining why in the review request can result in the request for review being denied without a hearing. Accordingly, the party requesting the review must describe the specific circumstances that prevented them from participating in the proceeding. A member may consider all the circumstances that are relevant, including the party's understanding of the proceeding, as well as matters such as the actions taken by the party in preparing their case, in obtaining representation, in contacting the Board or the other party, etc. A member then determines whether, if proven at a hearing, the circumstances described in the review request may lead the Board to find that the requester was not reasonably able to participate.

What Will Be Reviewed?

Under Rule 29.10, a Member will conduct a preliminary review of a request to review an order without holding a hearing and determine whether or not the order may contain a serious error or a serious error may have occurred in the proceedings.

Where the Member determines that there is a possibility of a serious error affecting the result of the case, a review hearing will be held. Otherwise, the Member will issue an order dismissing the request for review.

Where a review hearing is held, a Member will hear submissions on whether or not the request for review actually discloses a serious error. Where a Member determines that no serious error occurred, the request for review will be denied.

Where a Member determines that a serious error has occurred, parties requesting a review should understand that they will not automatically obtain a full rehearing of the application, and that the review may be limited to certain issues. The hearing may proceed with one or all of the following:

1. There may be a partial or full rehearing of the matter.
2. The Member will decide what, if any, issues will be reviewed. This may be some or all of the issues set out in the request and any potential errors identified by the reviewing Member.
3. The Member may or may not hear or rehear evidence and may simply decide to hear submissions.

Not Interfering with Discretion

The Board will not interfere with the proper exercise of discretion by a Member.

Discretion refers to decisions such as whether relief from eviction should be granted (see section 83) or what remedies should be ordered in a particular case. The reviewing Member should not interfere with the decision even if they may have exercised the discretion in a somewhat different way. A review is not for making minor adjustments to the discretion which was reasonable: for example, that an abatement was within the reasonable range of amounts which could have been ordered.

Error of Fact

Since a party cannot appeal an order to the Divisional Court, except on a point of law, it is important that the Board review alleged errors of fact. However, the Board may decline to review an order if the alleged error is trivial in amount or would not significantly change the result. This means that it is essential that the party requesting the review should specify in some detail not only what the error is, but how it would change the order if the Board agrees it is an error.

New Evidence

If a Member did not give proper consideration to the evidence before them, this should be reviewed. However, if the evidence was not presented by the party now making the request, the reviewing Member has a discretion to accept or refuse the new evidence. If the original Member improperly refused the evidence, it should now be admitted. If the party had no access to the evidence at the time of the hearing, and it is necessary to properly decide the case, the evidence may be permitted, allowing the other parties their respective rights.

Nevertheless there are some cases in which new evidence can be refused. If there is no reason why the evidence was not presented in the first instance, permission may be denied. Presenting a "case" in stages is inappropriate because it prejudices the other party and increases the costs and delays of proceedings. New evidence of little weight or related to issues which were not in dispute should not be accepted.

Interim Orders

A Member may make an interim to stay the order under review upon a party's request or on their own initiative. This will pre-

vent parties from enforcing the original order during the review, which in some cases would mean a review order would have no effect. The decision to stay the order may be further considered after submissions are heard at the review hearing. The stay may be lifted if, for example, it was requested only for delay.

Any other interim order which is appropriate may be made, such as one for disclosure, for certain work to be performed by a landlord, for payment into the Board by a landlord or tenant, etc.

Results of the Review

A request to review may be granted or denied. If the request is granted, section 21.2 of the SPPA allows the Board to "confirm, vary, suspend or cancel the decision or order." Thus, the reviewing Member may resolve the request in any of these manners:

- dismissing the original application and canceling the order;
- varying part of the original order or reasons;
- canceling the original order and replacing it with a new order; or
- confirming the original order.

Where appropriate, the reviewing Member may take into account any change in the facts of the case since the date the order was issued. For example, if any payment was made under the order or any work was done which it ordered, it would not be proper to ignore such changes. If more has been paid under an order than the review shows should have been owing, the reviewing Member may order repayment to set the matter right in accordance with the conclusions of the review order.

Under section 182 of the RTA, the reviewing member may order a refund of a fee paid for a request to review if, on considering the request, the Board varies, suspends or cancels the order.

What Happens Where an Appeal Is Filed with the Divisional Court?

Where an appeal from a Board decision has been filed in the Divisional Court, the appeal operates as a stay of the matter under subsection 25(1) of the SPPA. In this circumstance, clause 25(1)(b) permits the Board to lift the stay. If a party or a person directly affected by the order has filed a request for review, the requester should include in the written request an explanation why the Board should lift the stay and consider the request for review. The lifting of the stay is a discretionary power that the Board may exercise in the appropriate situation and parties should be prepared to make submissions on it if requested by the Member. In the situation where the Board decides to proceed with the review, the Board may make an interim order lifting the stay and may include in that order any conditions that it considers appropriate. Such conditions may include preserving the status quo between the parties until the matter is finally disposed of.

Amended: January 4, 2011

INTERPRETATION GUIDELINE #9
EVICTION FOR AN ILLEGAL ACT OR BUSINESS

Interpretation Guidelines are intended to assist the parties in understanding the Board's usual interpretation of the law, to provide guidance to Members and promote consistency in decision-making. However, a Member is not required to follow a Guideline and may make a different decision depending on the facts of the case.

This Guideline deals with eviction applications under the *Residential Tenancies Act, 2006* ("the RTA") that are based on an illegal act or business. Subsection 61(1) of the RTA provides:

> 61(1) A landlord may give a tenant notice of termination of the tenancy if the tenant or another occupant of the rental unit commits an illegal act or carries on an illegal trade, business or occupation or permits a person to do so in the rental unit or the residential complex.

Illegal Act or Business

The term "illegal" is not defined in the RTA but would include a serious violation of a federal, provincial or municipal law. If the illegality is trivial or technical, the act or business or occupation might not be considered serious enough to warrant eviction.

An illegal act will be serious if it has the potential to affect the character of the premises or to disturb the reasonable enjoyment of the landlord or other tenants.[1] The seriousness of this ground can be seen in the fact that there is no opportunity in section 61 for the tenant to avoid termination by rectifying the illegal act.

The fact that a tenant or another occupant may have devised a fraud in the unit, written a bad cheque or failed to file a tax return does not necessarily create a threat to the other tenants in the building or a problem for the landlord. By contrast, drug offences may bring the risk of harmful effects upon other occupants of the complex.

A contravention of the RTA would not, in itself, constitute an illegal act under section 61 of the RTA. If there is a remedy for the act elsewhere in the RTA, it would not be appropriate to evict for an illegal act. For example, a failure to pay rent would not be considered an illegal act for the purpose of section 61. Subletting or assigning the rental unit without the landlord's consent would not necessarily constitute an illegal act that justifies eviction.[2]

However, in one case the Divisional Court held that where the tenant listed her rental unit with a real estate agent and repeatedly sublet the unit to short-term occupants for a rent that greatly exceeded the lawful rent and without the landlord's consent, this pattern of activity constituted the conduct of an illegal business.[3] Such conduct is contrary to section 134 of the RTA and is an offence under section 234(l) of the RTA, but those sections do not provide a remedy for the landlord.

Permitting an Illegal Act or Business

A tenant may be evicted under section 61 if the tenant or other occupant "permits" a person to commit an illegal act in the rental unit or residential complex. It is not sufficient to prove that the tenant or other occupant allowed the person who committed the illegal act to be in the rental unit or residential complex.

A finding that the tenant or other occupant permitted an illegal act may be inferred from their knowledge of the illegal act. For instance, there may be sufficient evidence for the Member to conclude that the tenant or other occupant knew of the illegal act or was wilfully blind to the illegal act and therefore permitted it.[4]

Rental Unit or Residential Complex

Subsection 61(1) provides that the illegal act must have occurred in the rental unit or the residential complex. The definition of "residential complex" in section 2 of the RTA includes all common areas and services and facilities available for the use of its residents. This would include areas such as the laundry room, parking lot and recreational facilities.

The fact that a tenant or other occupant has been charged with robbing the convenience store across the street would not be a ground for the landlord to evict, whereas robbing other units in the complex would be sufficient.[5]

Notice Periods

Subsection 61(2) sets out notice periods for different types of illegal acts.

> (2) A notice of termination under this section shall set out the grounds for termination and shall provide a termination date not earlier than,
>> (a) the 10th day after the notice is given, in the case of a notice grounded on an illegal act, trade, business or occupation involving,
>>> (i) the production of an illegal drug;
>>> (ii) trafficking in an illegal drug;
>>> (iii) the possession of an illegal drug for the purposes of trafficking; or
>> (b) the 20th day after the notice is given, in all other cases.

Subsection 61(2)(b) allows a landlord to terminate a tenancy on 20 days notice where a tenant or another occupant commits an illegal act or carries on an illegal trade, business or occupation in the rental unit or residential complex, or the tenant or

---

1 *Samuel Property Management Ltd. v. Nicholson* (2002), 61 OR (3d) 470 (CA), at para. 28, citing *Swansea Village Co-operative v. Balcerzak* (1988), 63 OR (2d) 741 at 745 (Div. Ct.).

2 *Valleyview Apartments Ltd. and Estate of Max Rothbart* (1988), 65 OR (2d) 209 (Div. Ct.).

3 *Sutton Place Grande Limited v. Hammer and Griffiths,* [2002] OJ No. 1792 (Div. Ct.).

4 *Grant v. Metropolitan Toronto Housing Authority,* [2002] OJ No. 1162 (Div. Ct.).

5 *Peel Non-Profit v. Hogarth* (1990), 72 OR (2d) 702 (CA), aff'g. (1989), 68 OR (2d) 617 (Div. Ct.).

another occupant permits someone else to commit an illegal act or carry on an illegal activity in the unit or the complex.

Subsection 61(2)(a) provides a shorter 10-day notice period when the illegal activity involves the production of an illegal drug, trafficking in an illegal drug or the possession of an illegal drug for the purpose of trafficking. Further, an application to terminate a tenancy based on such a notice is processed more quickly than most other types of applications, with a shorter time to hearing due to the potentially serious implications for the landlord and other tenants.

A landlord may file an application based on an illegal act immediately after the notice of termination is given, but not later than 30 days after the termination date in the notice.

Notice Period for a Second Breach

If a landlord has given a notice of termination for damage under section 62, interference with reasonable enjoyment under section 64 or overcrowding under section 67, and the notice has become void as a result of the tenant's compliance, the landlord may give a 14-day notice instead of a 20-day notice if the tenant commits an illegal act within six months of when the first notice was given. But this does not apply if the second notice is for one of the three drug-related activities in subsection 61(2)(a) as the termination date in these cases is already a minimum of 10 days after the notice is given.

Drug Offences

The drug offences in subsection 61(2) include:

(i) the production of an illegal drug;

(ii) trafficking in an illegal drug;

(iii) the possession of an illegal drug for the purposes of trafficking.

Subsection 61(3) provides the following definitions:

(3) In this section,

"illegal drug" means a controlled substance or precursor as those terms are defined in the *Controlled Drugs and Substances Act (Canada)*;

"possession" has the same meaning as in the *Controlled Drugs and Substances Act (Canada)*;

"production" means, with respect to an illegal drug, to produce the drug within the meaning of the *Controlled Drugs and Substances Act (Canada)*;

"trafficking" means, with respect to an illegal drug, to traffic in the drug within the meaning of the *Controlled Drugs and Substances Act (Canada)*.

Meaning of "Illegal Drug"

Subsection 61(3) of the RTA states that an illegal drug means a controlled substance or precursor as those terms are defined in the *Controlled Drugs and Substances Act* (CDSA). The CDSA states that a "controlled substance" refers to those substances included in Schedule I, II, III, IV or V in the CDSA (such as Cannabis or Opium), and that "precursor" refers to a substance found in Schedule VI of that Act (such as Ephedrine).

Meaning of "Possession"

Subsection 61(3) of the Act states that possession has the same meaning as in the CDSA. The CDSA states that possession means possession within the meaning of subsection 4(3) of the *Criminal Code*. Subsection 4(3) of the *Criminal Code* states:

(3) For the purposes of this Act,

(a) a person has anything in possession when he has it in his personal possession or knowingly

(i) has it in the actual possession or custody of another person, or

(ii) has it in any place, whether or not that place belongs to or is occupied by him, for the use or benefit of himself or another person, and

(b) where one of two or more persons, with the knowledge and consent of the rest, has anything in his custody or possession, it shall be deemed to be in the custody and possession of each and all of them.

Note that simple possession of a drug is not enough to attract subsection 61(2) of the RTA which deals with possession "for the purposes of trafficking." Thus, where mere possession of a drug is alleged, the landlord should give a 20-day notice under subsection 61(2)(b) instead of a 10-day notice under subsection 61(2)(a).

Meaning of "Production"

Subsection 61(3) of the Act states that production means, with respect to an illegal drug, to produce the drug within the meaning of the CDSA. The CDSA states that "produce" means, in respect of a substance included in Schedule I to IV of that Act, to obtain the substance by any method or process including:

- manufacturing, synthesizing or using any means of altering the chemical or physical properties of the substance, or
- cultivating, propagating, or harvesting the substance or any living thing from which the substance may be extracted or otherwise obtained, and
- includes the offer to produce.

Meaning of "Trafficking"

Subsection 61(3) of the Act states that trafficking in an illegal drug means to traffic within the meaning of the CDSA. The CDSA states that "traffic" means, in respect of a substance in Schedule I to IV, to

- sell, administer, give, transfer, transport, send or deliver the substance,
- sell an authorization to obtain the substance, or
- offer to do either of the above

unless they are done under the authority of the regulations to the CDSA.

Meaning of "Possession for the Purposes of Trafficking"

The phrase "possession for the purposes of trafficking" in subsection 61(2)(iii) is not defined in the RTA or the CDSA. Subsection 5(2) of the CDSA simply states that "No person shall, for the purpose of trafficking, possess a substance included in Schedule I, II, III or IV."

In some cases, possession for the purposes of trafficking may be inferred from the surrounding circumstances. For instance, where the police find a large quantity of drugs, cash and weigh scales, the Member may be able to determine that the tenant or another occupant had possession of the drugs for the purpose of trafficking.

Burden of Proof

In Board proceedings the burden of proof is on a "balance of probabilities" which applies to all civil proceedings rather than "beyond a reasonable doubt" as in criminal proceedings.[6] The burden of proof is the level of proof required by the applicant to prove his or her case in order to be successful. In each case the Member will scrutinize the evidence to determine if the preponderance of evidence supports the conduct alleged by the applicant in the application.

An eviction can be ordered even though the tenant or other occupant carrying on the illegal act, trade, business or occupation has not been *charged* with an offence relating to the illegal act.[7] Conversely, the fact that a tenant or other occupant has been charged with an offence is not necessarily proof that an illegal act was committed.[8]

Furthermore, section 75 of the RTA provides that the Board may evict a tenant for an illegal act whether or not the tenant or other person has been *convicted* of an offence relating to the illegal act. Therefore, there is no need for a Member to adjourn the Board proceeding until the matter has been heard by a court of competent jurisdiction.

Relief from Eviction

The Member must consider whether a termination of the tenancy may be unfair having regard to all the circumstances: see subsection 83(1)(a) of the RTA and the Guideline on "Relief from Eviction." This means there will be a two step determination: first, whether the tenant has committed an illegal act that justifies eviction; and second, whether the eviction should, nevertheless, be refused or delayed having regard to the circumstances.

In determining whether to refuse or delay an eviction, the Member should weigh the seriousness of the illegal act against factors such as: the length of the tenancy, the financial circumstances of the tenant, whether there are children living in the unit, whether there have been other problems with the tenant, whether the tenant is likely to commit the illegal act again.[9] There may be other factors to consider.

---

6 *F.H. v. McDougall*, [2008] 3 SCR 41.

7 *Samuel Property Management Ltd. v. Nicholson* (2002), 61 OR (3d) 470 (CA).

8 *Greaves v. Toronto Community Housing Corporation* (December 14, 2004), Toronto Docket No. 411/03 (Div. Ct.).

9 *Metropolitan Toronto Housing Authority v. Pennant* (1991), 81 DLR (4th) 404 (Ont. Ct. Gen. Div.).

In addition, instead of terminating the tenancy the Member may impose conditions in the order pursuant to subsection 204(1) of the RTA. For example, if the tenant is keeping a dangerous animal in the rental unit, the tenant could be ordered to remove it. If the tenant is carrying on a business that is prohibited by a zoning by-law, the Member could impose a condition in the order that the tenant no longer conduct the business in the unit. If the tenant's guest committed an illegal act, relief from eviction could be considered with a condition that the tenant not permit that person into the building again. The order could provide that if the tenant does not comply with a condition specified in the order, the landlord may apply *ex parte* under section 78 of the RTA for eviction.

Amended: January 4, 2011

INTERPRETATION GUIDELINE #10 PROCEDURAL ISSUES REGARDING EVICTION APPLICATIONS

Interpretation Guidelines are intended to assist the parties in understanding the Board's usual interpretation of the law, to provide guidance to Members and promote consistency in decision-making. However, a Member is not required to follow a Guideline and may make a different decision depending on the facts of the case.

This Guideline deals with interpretation questions respecting the steps required to bring an eviction application under the *Residential Tenancies Act, 2006* ("the RTA") and what will be the result of failing to follow those procedures.

Adequacy of the Notice of Termination

The Notice of Termination (the Notice) is an essential step in the landlord's process of evicting a tenant[1] (except section 77 and 78 applications). The Board will not terminate a tenancy and order eviction of the tenant unless the tenant has received a valid Notice of Termination from the landlord and the landlord has successfully proved the ground claimed in the Notice at the hearing of the application.

If the document given to the tenant or the method or time of service are defective, in most cases this will result in dismissal of the application or the denial of the eviction portion of the application.

The Notice of Termination must specify a date of termination without doubt or condition. The landlord must set a date which allows at least the minimum period of Notice for that ground for eviction, or the longest period if there are several grounds set out in the same Notice. The Board has no authority to shorten the notice period required by the RTA in view of section 56 of the regulations (O. Reg. 516/06) and Rule 1.4 of the Rules of Practice. If a shorter notice period is given than is required, the application will be dismissed.

---

1 *Re Bransfield Construction Co. Ltd. and Cox*, [1973] 3 OR 989 (Div. Ct.).

The Divisional Court of Ontario has held that an unsigned Notice of Termination may be valid, so long as the landlord's name is shown.[2] However, other requirements may not be so easily resolved. An incorrect termination date in a Notice may render it invalid.[3] For example, stating a period of time but not a specific date (e.g., "14 days" rather than "April 16, 2001") may not be sufficient.[4]

If the Notice of Termination is confusing to the degree that a reasonable person could not understand precisely what it means, a Member would find it defective.[5] For example, in some cases this might include: uncertainty about whether the landlord is the person giving the Notice, vagueness about the reason for giving the Notice,[6] a lack of details about the reason, etc. A Notice which only specifies a reason which is not a ground for eviction under the RTA would be invalid; and even adding such a claim to a legitimate ground may confuse the Notice in some cases.

In the end, whether the Notice is adequate is a question of whether it communicates the necessary elements clearly enough that a tenant would be expected to understand it and the options they have. For example, Notices were found invalid which did not state the required information that the tenant need not vacate pursuant to the Notice.[7]

Adequacy of Service of the Notice of Termination

The Notice of Termination must be given to the tenant by a method set out in subsection 191(1) of the RTA and in Rule 5.1 of the Rules of Practice. If the landlord has used a different method (without specific permission through a direction signed by a Member), and the tenant does not voluntarily admit to receiving the Notice on time, an application for eviction may be dismissed. If the tenant acknowledges receipt of the Notice by the date required or if the landlord can prove that the tenant received it, this will be sufficient no matter how the Notice was served.

Substantial Compliance with Forms

Some landlords like to produce their own versions of the approved forms for Notices of Termination and Applications. These forms usually use the wording found on the Board's form

and are simply intended to allow computer inputting or other convenience to the landlord. So long as the landlord's form includes the information set out for the tenant in the Board form, the different form will usually be permitted. The Member who must rule on the adequacy of such a Notice may consider whether it substantially complies with the legal requirements as expressed in the form approved by the Board, taking into consideration the points mentioned above.

However, if the landlord seeks to communicate other messages in the form which are misleading about the tenant's rights or inconsistent with the provisions of the RTA, this may cause a Member to find it defective. Information may be provided which is not misleading, is not inconsistent with the law and does not confuse the essential information in the Notice.

Oral notice of termination cannot substantially comply with a requirement to give written notice. The statutory requirement to give written Notice cannot be waived by a Member.

Giving Multiple Notices of Termination

A landlord may believe there is more than one ground for eviction, and give a Notice with more than one ground or, more likely, two Notices of Termination together. The landlord may also find another ground for eviction while a Notice has not yet been resolved, and give another Notice for the new ground.

The RTA doesn't prohibit a landlord from starting eviction proceedings against a tenant relying on more than one ground and succeed on all or some of the grounds. For example, if the tenant is behind in the rent, and has damaged property in the complex, the landlord should be able to ask for eviction under both grounds. Sometimes the same event may give rise to more than one ground for termination, as a result the landlord may serve more than one Notice of Termination citing the same event as the reason for both of the Notices. For example, if the tenant damages the fire alarm system in the residential complex, the landlord may serve a Notice to Terminate alleging an illegal act and a second notice alleging an impairment of safety.

Although the landlord is permitted to give Notices of Termination with different termination dates, confusion to the tenant should be minimized. The Notices may be challenged on the basis that they are confusing and therefore defective. In the worst case, an application may be dismissed.

Date When Application May Be Filed

In a Notice of Termination for non-payment of rent, the landlord may specify any date of termination, so long as it is at least 14 days (7 days for a weekly tenancy) after the day the notice is given to the tenant (see section 59). The landlord must then wait to apply until at least the day after the termination date specified in the Notice (see subsection 74(1)).

An eviction application based on damages, interference with reasonable enjoyment or overcrowding (sections 62, 64 or 67) may not be brought until after the seven day period for the tenant to remedy the situation has passed without the tenant complying with that remedy. For example, if the tenant paid for the damages within the seven days following the Notice being

---

2   *Darraugh Construction and Investment Ltd. v. Cain* (1988), 30 OAC 1, in which the landlord's name was typed in by the landlord's solicitor.

3   *Re Bianci and Aguanno* (1983), 42 OR 76 (Div. Ct.).

4   *Dumi Construction Ltd. V. Greenspan* (1977), 15 OR (2d) 808 (Co. Ct.).

5   *Kuzyk v. SK Properties* (November 22, 2001), Toronto Docket No. 106/01, [2001] OJ No. 5260 (Div. Ct.) Re: TSL-18855.

6   *Ball v. Metro Capital Property and Lockhurst* (December 19, 2002), Toronto Docket No. 48/02 (Div. Ct.) Re: TNL-31297.

7   *Dumi*, supra note 4, and *Forrest Estates Home Sales Inc. v. Gwyn* (1987) Doc. No. 131-1987 (Ont. Dist. Co.).

given, no application could be made. Otherwise, the tenant doesn't void the Notice and the landlord could apply on or after the 8th day after giving the Notice to the tenant.

For all other types of eviction applications (e.g., personal use, safety, illegal act, tenant's notice to vacate, etc.), the application may be filed on or after the day the Notice is given.

Under subsection 69(2), an eviction application based on any ground other than unpaid rent must be filed within 30 days after the termination date set out in the Notice of Termination; otherwise, the application will be dismissed.[8]

Completeness of the Application

It is the landlord's responsibility to ensure that their application is correct and complete.

Staff of the Board will check applications for completeness in accordance with Rule 8; however, the Board Member who will make a decision on the application will ultimately determine whether or not it meets the requirements of the legislation. Where it does not, the application may be dismissed.

Other Claims That May Be Filed with an Eviction Application

An eviction application may be combined with an application for which no Notice of Termination is required. For example, a landlord may seek termination of the tenancy for an illegal act and can also apply for an order for rent arrears and/or compensation for damages caused by the tenant. In such a situation the landlord would have to give the tenant a Notice of Termination for the illegal act, but would not have to give a Notice of Termination for the rent arrears or compensation for damages. It is desirable that an application for damages be supported by estimates for the work alleged to be necessary, preferably from a reputable contractor or supplier, since a Member may refuse to issue an order for an unsupported amount. If the landlord is unsuccessful in proving the application for illegal act, but is successful in proving the rent arrears or damages, the Board will issue an order for the rent arrears or damages, but will not issue a termination of the tenancy.

In any Board order which terminates a tenancy for damages or rent arrears the Board will inquire whether the landlord is holding last month's rent from the tenant and credit the tenant with this amount.

Where a Notice of Termination Becomes Void

Subsection 59(3) provides that a Notice of Termination given for rent arrears is void if, before the day the landlord applies for eviction, the tenant pays the rent arrears and any additional rent that is be due under the tenancy agreement on the date the tenant makes the payment. The purpose of this provision is to create finality when the tenant pays the amount required to bring the rent up to date.

Thus, if the tenant pays the rent that was owed when the Notice was given, and does so before the end of the current

rental period, the Notice is void. If the tenant has voided the Notice of Termination, the landlord cannot file an application with the Board based on that Notice. However, if the tenant does not pay the arrears before the end of that rental period and another rental period begins, the rent for that rental period as well as the previous arrears must be paid before the landlord applies in order to void the Notice.

For example:

A landlord gives a Notice of Termination for Non-Payment of Rent on May 2nd, specifying that the tenant owes $800 for the rental period of May 1st to 31st, with a termination date of May16th. The earliest date that the landlord could apply to the Board is May 17th and the tenant could void the Notice by paying $800 on or before May 16th. However, if the landlord does not apply to the Board in the month of May the tenant could also void the Notice by paying $800 on or before May 31st.

In the same example, if the landlord waited to give the Notice of Termination until May 20th, specifying a termination date of June 3rd, the tenant could void the Notice by paying $800 on or before May 31st. However, if the payment was made on or after June 1st, the tenant would have to pay $1600 in order to void the Notice.

Where a Notice of Termination is given for damages, interference with reasonable enjoyment or overcrowding (sections 62, 64 or 67), and it is the first Notice within six months, the Notice is void where a tenant corrects the behaviour that led to the giving of the Notice within seven days of receiving it. If the tenant does not correct the behaviour within the seven days the landlord then has thirty days to file an application with the Board. However, if the tenant corrects the behaviour within the seven days of receiving the Notice, but within six months after the first Notice was given, once again contravenes the RTA as specified under section 68, then the landlord may give the tenant a second Notice and can apply to the Board based on the second Notice immediately after the second Notice is served.

Payment of Arrears After the Application Is Filed

If, before the hearing, the landlord receives payment from the tenant of the full arrears (see the Guideline entitled "Eviction for Failure to Pay Rent" regarding the amount required), any additional rent that is owing as of the date the tenant makes the payment, plus the application filing fee, the landlord should advise the Board so that the application may be treated as discontinued pursuant to subsection 74(2) and the hearing may be cancelled.

However, if only partial payment is made, the landlord need not advise the Board before the hearing, but should do so at the hearing.

If the landlord informs the Board of receipt of a partial payment after filing the application, any such amounts will be taken into account in issuing the order.

---

8   *Knapp v. Herauf* (June 25, 2004), Ottawa Docket No. 03-DV-947 (Div. Ct.) Re: EAL-36746.

Payment Made After the Order Becomes Enforceable

See Guideline 11—Eviction For Failure to Pay Rent

Multiple Landlords

If more than one landlord entered into the tenancy, and only one of them gives a Notice of Termination, they take a risk that the tenant will object to it at the hearing. The Notice may not be sufficient if any of the landlords' names are missing from the Notice, although it is sufficiently signed if any one of the landlords signs it.

The same may be true of the application. If there are multiple landlords, all should be named in the application, although one may sign it as agent for the others.

If the Notice was given by a different landlord than the applicant, this may be proper if the property has been sold and the new landlord is the applicant. However, both the purchaser and vendor should be named and sign the application if there is rent owing to each.

Multiple Tenants

If the landlord has entered into a tenancy agreement with more than one tenant, the Notice of Termination should name and be given to all tenants. This may be done in one Notice naming all the tenants. Although a Notice to a tenant may be served by giving it to any apparently adult person in the unit, if one of the tenants lives at another address, they must be served separately in accordance with the RTA and Rules of Practice.

Where there is a subtenant or assignee these persons should also be named in the Notice of Termination. However, other occupants, such as guests of the tenant, need not be named on the Notice of Termination for the landlord to obtain possession of the rental unit because the Board orders vacant possession of the rental unit, in orders terminating the tenancy.

Expiry of the Eviction Order

Under section 81 of the RTA, an order of the Board that evicts someone expires within 6 months of the date the order unless it is filed with the appropriate Court Enforcement Office before that time. This expiration provision applies notwithstanding any appeal proceeding that may be initiated in a court of competent jurisdiction. Once an eviction order expires, there is no authority to renew it, nor will the landlord be able to apply again for the same remedy for the same time period.

Release Date: January 31, 2007

INTERPRETATION GUIDELINE #11
EVICTION FOR FAILURE TO PAY RENT

Interpretation Guidelines are intended to assist the parties in understanding the Board's usual interpretation of the law, to provide guidance to Members and promote consistency in decision-making. However, a Member is not required to follow a Guideline and may make a different decision depending on the facts of the case.

This Guideline deals with applications based on a tenant's failure to pay rent. (See also Guideline 10 on "Procedural Issues regarding Eviction Applications.")

Method of Ordering Arrears[1]

If the landlord's application for termination based on arrears of rent is granted, the tenant will be ordered to pay: a) rent arrears up to the termination date in the notice of termination; and b) lump sum compensation for use of the rental unit from the termination date in the notice to the order date. The rent deposit and interest owing thereon will be deducted from the arrears and compensation in accordance with subsection 87(4) of *Residential Tenancies Act* ("the RTA"). Daily compensation will then be ordered from the order date until the tenant vacates.

If the landlord is attempting to enforce the order, the landlord has an obligation to inform the Court or the Court Enforcement Office of any rent payments the tenant made that are not reflected in the order.

If the tenant vacated the unit after the application was filed but before the date of the hearing, the tenant will be ordered to pay arrears plus compensation only up to the date they vacated, less the rent deposit and interest.

If the order does not evict the tenant but rent is found owing, the tenant may be ordered to pay arrears up to the end of the current month. The rent deposit will not be deducted from the arrears because the tenancy has not been terminated.

The determination of arrears is usually based on the principle that payments are applied to the earliest rent owing. For example, if the tenant did not pay the May rent, but paid in June, the payment for June will be applied to May leaving the June rent outstanding.

Ordering Arrears of Rent Where the Tenant Has Vacated the Rental Unit

At hearings about arrears of rent, the Member must decide if the tenant was "in possession of the rental unit" at the time the landlord filed the application with the Board.

If the tenant owes the landlord arrears of rent, the landlord can serve the tenant with a notice of termination. This notice states that the tenant must pay all of the arrears of rent by a date specified in the notice, known as a termination date. If the tenant moves out of the unit by the termination date, the tenancy will be considered terminated effective that date.[2] If the tenant terminated the tenancy by moving out of the rental unit by the termination date, the Board does not have the jurisdiction to consider an application for arrears of rent filed by the landlord, even if the tenant still owes rent to the landlord.

---

1   For simplicity, the descriptions in this Guideline assume monthly payment of rent. if the tenancy was on a weekly or other basis, it should be adjusted accordingly.

2   See RTA, s. 43(2)(a).

If the tenant does not move out by the termination date, but moves out of the rental unit before the landlord files an application with the Board requesting termination of the tenancy for non-payment of rent, the Board cannot issue such an order, even if the tenant owes arrears of rent to the landlord. Under subsection 87(1) of the RTA, the landlord may only apply to the Board for an order for the payment of rent if the tenant was "in possession of the rental unit" when the application was filed.

Whether or not the tenant is "in possession" of a rental unit depends, on whether the tenant exercises some "form of control over that unit as demonstrated by factors such as access to, use of, or occupation of the unit.[3] The landlord is expected to be able to provide evidence about efforts made to determine whether the tenant is still in possession of the unit. Such evidence may include:

- Whether the tenant returned keys to the landlord;
- Whether the tenant gave a notice to the landlord or it is otherwise clear that the tenant intends to move out;
- Whether utility service to the unit has been disconnected and the unit has been without gas or electricity for some time prior to the hearing;
- Whether the tenant has actually been observed moving out of the unit by the landlord or others;
- Whether the landlord has changed the locks and/or taken steps to re-rent the unit.

The existence of an unexpired lease, by itself, is not proof of "possession" under the RTA. There must be proof of actual use, control or occupancy of the rental unit by the tenant.

If evidence provided to the Member establishes that the tenant was in possession of the unit when the landlord filed the application, the Board has authority to consider the landlord's application. If the tenant is still in possession of the unit as of the hearing date, the tenant can be ordered to pay the landlord all arrears of rent and compensation owing up to that point.

In some cases, the evidence may establish that the tenant moved out of the rental unit after the application was filed, but before the hearing date. In that case, the Board's order will generally include a determination that the tenancy ended on the date the tenant moved out. Further, the order will generally: (1) end the tenancy effective the date the tenant moved out of the rental unit without ordering enforcement through the Sheriff's Office; and (2) require the tenant to pay arrears up to the date specified in the termination notice, and lump sum compensation for use of the unit from the termination date in the notice to the date the tenancy ended. Unlike orders for arrears and termination where the tenant is in possession of the unit on the hearing date, the order would not provide the tenant with an opportunity to continue the tenancy by paying all of the arrears by a specified date. Moreover, as there is a finding that the tenancy has ended, the tenant's rent deposit and interest

owing on it will be deducted from the arrears and compensation ordered to the landlord.

Arrears Less Than a Rent Deposit

A notice of termination is not invalid simply because the landlord holds a rent deposit that is greater than the rent owing. The rent deposit can only be applied to the last month of the tenancy. Therefore, the landlord should not apply the deposit to the rent arrears before applying to evict the tenant.

The amount that is owed to the landlord on the order date may be a negative amount, after the deposit and interest are deducted from the rent and compensation owing to the landlord. If so, the landlord would owe money to the tenant. In that case, the Board may order the landlord to pay the tenant the amount that will be owed as of the order date. The authority for this lies in section 205 of the RTA which states that the Board may order that "The landlord or the tenant shall pay to the other any sum of money that is owed as a result of this order."

Non-Sufficient Funds Charges

Under section 87 of the RTA, where a landlord applies for an order for the payment of arrears of rent, the application may include a claim for the amount of NSF charges paid to a financial institution in respect of cheques tendered to the landlord by the tenant, plus the landlord's administrative charges in respect of those cheques. The administrative charges are limited to a maximum of $20.00 per cheque per section 17 of Regulation 516/06.

These charges, if claimed, will normally be awarded and, if the order terminates the tenancy, the tenant will have to pay these amounts in addition to the other amounts payable in order to avoid eviction. See also the section below on Amount Payable to Prevent an Eviction.

Although a landlord may apply for NSF charges, they cannot be claimed in an N4 notice of termination. Under subsection 59(3) of the RTA, a notice of termination is void if the tenant pays the arrears and the additional rent that has become owing. There is no requirement for the tenant to pay NSF charges to void the notice. Therefore, including NSF charges on an N4 will likely invalidate the notice.

Similar Charges

Other amounts may be owed to the landlord for charges permitted under the RTA or regulations, such as the cost of installing a mobile home under section 166 of the RTA, or for transferring a tenant to another unit in a social housing complex under section 17 of Regulation 516/06. Although the RTA allows a landlord to levy these charges, the RTA does not provide for their recovery in an application to the Board. A landlord should therefore not include such charges in a notice of termination or application for non-payment of rent.

Certain charges are not permitted by the RTA, even if they are set out in the tenancy agreement. This includes non-refundable key deposits, most types of administrative charges, and late payment charges in excess of what is permitted. See section 17 of Regulation 516/06.

---

[3]   See the Ontario Court of Appeal's unanimous judgment in *1162994 Ontario Inc. v. Bakker, et al.*, [2004] OJ No. 2565 (Ont. CA) (hereinafter *"Bakker"*).

Utilities Charges

In all cases, the Member must review the tenancy agreement to determine if the tenant is required to pay their portion of the costs of utilities.

When a landlord and tenant are entering into a tenancy agreement, they may agree that utilities will be included in the rent. In this case, the landlord is responsible for paying all utility bills and the rent would remain unchanged despite any fluctuations in these costs.

Alternatively, the landlord and tenant may agree that utilities will not be included in the rent, and that the tenant will be responsible for paying all utility costs directly to the utility company. In this case it is clear that the payment of the utility costs is not rent, and even if the landlord pays the bill because the tenant fails to, they would not be able to claim the amount as rent arrears.

In the case of a building containing not more than six rental units where the landlord supplies a utility to each of the rental units in the building, the tenancy agreement may require the tenant to reimburse the landlord for a portion of the cost of the utility in accordance with the rules made under Ontario Regulation 394/10. In any such case, the utility is not considered a service that falls within the definition of "rent."

The landlord cannot include amounts for which the tenant fails to reimburse the landlord for the utility charge in an application for the payment of rent arrears or in an application for termination of the tenancy and eviction of the tenant based on the tenant's failure to pay the utility charge.

Therefore, any unpaid amounts for utilities will not be included in the calculation of arrears of rent, although they may be a debt owing to the landlord that may be recovered by the landlord in the courts.

Rent Deposits

A landlord may require a tenant to pay a rent deposit of no more than one month's rent, so long as the landlord does so on or before entering into the tenancy agreement in accordance with subsection 106(1) of the RTA. If the tenant does not provide a rent deposit, the Board cannot order the tenant to pay one. It follows that if the landlord claims a rent deposit on the notice of termination it will invalidate the notice.

The landlord may require the tenant to update the rent deposit when the rent increases so that the deposit is equal to the lawful rent for the last month: see subsection 106(3) of the RTA.

Tenant Issues

Under section 82 of the RTA, a tenant may raise any issue that could be the subject of a tenant application. If the Board determines that the tenant is entitled to money (e.g., a rent abatement or rebate), it will be deducted from any amount owing to the landlord.

May a Guarantor Be Ordered to Pay Rent Arrears

There are tenancies that the landlord only accepted on the basis that a person other than the tenants would guarantee that the rent would be paid, should the tenants not be able to pay. The question is whether the Board may order a guarantor to pay rent arrears if the landlord includes them with the tenants as respondents to the application.

In most cases, the guarantor has no express right of possession and, even if they do, no one expects them to ever occupy the rental unit.

The Board will not make an order against guarantors because they are not tenants. The RTA does not authorize the Board to deal with such claims, even if they are related to the issue of rent arrears. Landlords may seek enforcement of such obligations through the courts.

Relief from Eviction

Where the Board finds there is unpaid rent, the Board must consider whether to delay or refuse the eviction under section 83 of the RTA. In some cases, refusing or delaying the eviction is discretionary; in others, refusing the eviction is mandatory. Even if the eviction claim in the application is refused or delayed, the tenant will be ordered to pay any arrears to the landlord. A payment schedule for the arrears may be imposed upon the tenant under section 204 as a condition of giving relief under section 83. See also Guideline 7 on "Relief from Eviction" for further discussion of this point.

Amount Payable to Prevent an Eviction

Section 74 of the RTA provides that a tenant may avoid an eviction in three circumstances.

Before the order is issued

Subsection 74(2) provides that if the tenant pays the landlord the full arrears, the application fee and any additional rent that is owed as of the date of payment by the tenant, before the eviction order is issued, the landlord's application will be discontinued.

After the order is issued

Under subsection 74(3), an order must specify the amount of rent arrears, the daily compensation payable and any costs ordered by the Board. The order will also set out any amount payable for NSF and administration charges. The order must also inform the tenant and the landlord that the order will become void under subsection 74(4) if the tenant pays the landlord or the Board the amount specified in the order before it is enforceable. An order is enforceable on the date the order specifies that the Court Enforcement Office (Sheriff) may give possession to the landlord.

If the tenant pays the amount specified in the order to the Board, staff of the Board will issue a notice to the landlord and tenant acknowledging that the order is void. If the tenant pays the entire amount to the landlord or part to the landlord and part to the Board, the tenant may file a motion with the Board, without notice to the landlord, asking for a Member to issue an order determining that the tenant has paid the full amount due and confirming that the order is void. Such an order will be made without holding a hearing. However, within ten days after it is issued, a landlord may, on notice to the tenant, make a motion to set the order aside. A hearing will be held to determine the landlord's set aside motion.

After the order is enforceable

Under subsection 74(11), if the tenant pays to the landlord or to the Board the amount specified in the order and any additional rent owing after it becomes enforceable but before it is enforced by the sheriff, the tenant may file a motion with the Board, on notice to the landlord, to set aside the eviction order. The eviction order is stayed and cannot be enforced until the Board issues an order lifting the stay.

The Board will hold a hearing on the motion. If the tenant paid some or all of the amount owing to the landlord by non-certified cheque, and the landlord is concerned that the cheque may be returned NSF, the member holding the hearing can grant an adjournment or permit post-hearing submissions to allow time for the cheque to clear before making their final order.

If the Board determines that the tenant paid the arrears and any additional rent owed to the landlord as of the date of the motion hearing, any NSF and administration charges and the costs ordered by the Board, the Board will make an order declaring the eviction order to be void. However, under subsection 74(15), if the Board determines that the landlord has paid a non-refundable amount under the *Administration of Justice Act* for the purpose of enforcing the order (e.g. sheriff fees), the Board will specify that amount in the motion order and require the tenant to pay that amount into the Board by a specified date.

If the tenant pays the specified amount by the specified date, a Board employee will issue a notice to the tenant and the landlord acknowledging that the eviction order is void.

If the Board determines that the tenant did not pay the specified amount by the specified date, a Board employee will issue a notice stating that the stay of the order ceases to apply and the eviction order may be enforced.

A motion to void an order after it has become enforceable may be made only once during the period of the tenant's tenancy agreement with the landlord: see subsection 74(12).

Amended: January 4, 2011

INTERPRETATION GUIDELINE #12
EVICTION FOR PERSONAL USE

Interpretation Guidelines are intended to assist the parties in understanding the Board's usual interpretation of the law, to provide guidance to Members and promote consistency in decision-making. However, a Member is not required to follow a Guideline and may make a different decision depending on the facts of the case.

This Guideline deals with interpretation questions respecting eviction applications under the *Residential Tenancies Act, 2006* ("the RTA"), based on use of the rental unit by: the landlord; a family member of the landlord; or a person who provides or will provide care services to the landlord or a family member of the landlord where the person receiving the care services resides or will reside in the building. It also deals with eviction by the landlord for personal use of a unit by: a purchaser; a family member of the purchaser; or a person who provides or will provide care services to the purchaser or a family member of the purchaser if the person receiving the care services resides or will reside in the building.

A family member may be the landlord's (or purchaser's) spouse, or a child or parent of one of them. The term "spouse" includes opposite-sex couples and same-sex couples who are married or who live together in conjugal relationships outside of marriage.

For general information about eviction applications, see Guideline 10, entitled "Procedural Issues regarding Eviction Applications."

Personal Use by the Landlord or Landlord's Family

Section 48 of the RTA permits the landlord to give notice of termination to a tenant if the landlord, in good faith, requires the unit for residential occupation by: the landlord; the landlord's spouse; a child or a parent of either the landlord or the landlord's spouse; or a person who provides or will provide care services to the landlord or a family member of the landlord where the person receiving the care services resides or will reside in the building. The termination date in the landlord's notice of termination must be at least 60 days after the notice is given and must be the last day of a fixed term tenancy, or if there is no fixed term, on the last day of a rental period. For example, if the current month is January and the lease expires on June 30 of the same year, the termination date should be June 30. Another example may arise on a month to month lease where notice is provided to the tenant on January 20. In this scenario, the earliest the termination date on the notice can be is March 31 which is 60 days after the notice is given and on the last day of the monthly rental period.

The landlord may apply to the Board as soon as this notice has been given, but any order issued may not be effective before the termination date in the notice. During the notice period, the tenant may give the landlord ten days written notice to terminate the tenancy at an earlier date.

Requirement of Good Faith

The issue that arises in some cases is whether the landlord or a family member has a real intention to reside in the rental unit. Subsection 72(1) addresses this concern by requiring the landlord to file with the Board an affidavit sworn by the person who personally requires the rental unit certifying that the person in good faith requires the rental unit for his or her own personal use.

Personal Use by a Purchaser or Their Family

Section 49 of the RTA permits the landlord to give notice of termination to a tenant if:

(a) the landlord has entered into an agreement of purchase and sale to sell a residential complex containing no more than 3 units or a condominium unit, and

(b) the purchaser, in good faith, requires possession of the complex or the unit for residential occupation by the purchaser, his or her spouse, or a child or parent of one of them.

Agreement of Purchase and Sale

Before a landlord may give a notice under section 49, there must be an agreement of purchase and sale to sell the residential complex. The Board may refuse an application if it is not reasonably certain that a completed sale will result from the agreement. If a term or condition of the agreement makes it uncertain that the deal will be completed, it may be appropriate to delay the application until the sale becomes more certain.

The Board may also dismiss the application if the purchase is a sham created for the purpose of evicting the tenant. For example, a transfer to a family member should be examined. A sale for much less than market value may raise questions. Section 202 provides authority to look at the real nature of any transactions.

A landlord applying based on a notice under section 49 is well advised to file with the application a copy of the agreement, together with an explanation of the circumstances of the intended sale.

Requirement of Good Faith

The requirement is similar to that related to section 48 (see above). The requirement relates to the genuine intention of the purchaser and the person who declares they intend to occupy the unit (see subsections 49(1) and 72(1) of the RTA).

Personal Use by a Person Who Provides or Will Provide Care Services

Subsection 48(1)(d) and 49(1)(d) of the RTA permit a landlord to give notice of termination to a tenant if the landlord or purchaser, in good faith, requires the unit for residential occupation by a person who provides or will provide care services to the landlord or purchaser, or the landlord or purchaser's spouse, parent, child, or spouse's parent or child.

The person receiving the care must reside or be going to reside in the building, related group of buildings, mobile home park or land lease community in which the rental unit is located.

Under section 2 of the RTA, "care services" is defined as meaning "subject to the regulations, health care services, rehabilitative or therapeutic services or services that provide assistance with the activities of daily living."

The termination date in the notice of termination must be at least 60 days after the notice was given and must be the last day of a fixed term tenancy, or if there is no fixed term, on the last day of a rental period. The landlord may apply to the Board as soon as this notice has been given, but any order issued may not be effective before the termination date in the notice. During the notice period, the tenant may give ten days written notice to terminate the tenancy earlier.

Requirement of Good Faith

The requirement is similar to that related to section 48 (see above). The requirement relates to the genuine intention of the landlord and the person who declares they intend to occupy the unit (see subsections 48(1) and 72(1) of the RTA).

Requirement of Good Faith

The case law under the similarly worded provision of the *Tenant Protection Act* ("the TPA") indicates that the landlord must have a real or genuine desire to occupy the rented premises. Tenants may believe that the landlord's intention is not genuine or honest,[1] and seek to discredit it. The Ontario Divisional Court has said that the real issue is whether the landlord is genuine in their intention to occupy the rental unit.[2]

The Divisional Court has also held that the landlord does not have to prove their good faith beyond a reasonable doubt.[3] The correct test is whether the Member believes that good faith exists on a balance of probabilities. Thus the Member must decide whether it is more likely that there is good faith than not.

A tenant may wish to prove that the same landlord gave a notice of termination for personal use of another unit earlier, obtained possession and then rented it to another tenant. This is not determinative evidence that the landlord lacks good faith in the present case,[4] but it is a "similar fact" situation that may be considered, at least in weighing the landlord's evidence. Under clause 202(b) the Board shall ascertain the real substance of activities and have regard to the pattern of activities relating to the residential complex or the rental unit.

The evidence of the landlord should be reviewed to determine if it convinces the Member that the landlord or family member will move into the unit within a reasonable time after the unit becomes vacant. Evidence of previous problems between the current tenant and the landlord may be relevant to the genuineness of the landlord's intention to use the unit as stated in the notice. It may also be considered in reviewing requests for relief from eviction (see below).

Where a landlord provides notice to a tenant under sections 48 or 49 in bad faith and the tenant moves out of the unit as a result of the landlord notice or an application to or an order by the Board based on such a notice and no person specified under

---

[1] Good faith was defined in *Semeniuk v. White Oak Stables Ltd.* (1991),27 ACWS (3d) 505 (BCCA) as honestly, without fraud, collusion or participation in wrong doing.

[2] *Beljinac v. Salter* [2001] OJ No. 2792 (Div. Ct.) Re: TSL-21378. Also see Feeney v. Noble (1994), 19 OR (3d) 762 (Div. Ct.) in which the Court decided that this requirement does not imply a "complete bona fides (i.e., untainted by any element of bad faith and total probity)."

[3] *Kulusic v. Kennedy*, unreported Dec. 7, 1989 decision (file #51/89) (Div. Ct.).

[4] *Re Yarmuch and Jacobson* (1985), 34 ACWS (2d) 145 (Ont. Dist. Ct.).

the appropriate subsection has occupied the unit within a reasonable time after the former tenant vacated the rental unit, subsection 57 of the RTA provides that the Board may make:

- An order that the landlord pay a specified sum to the tenant for all or any portion of any increased rent that the former tenant has incurred or will incur for a one-year period after vacating the rental unit, and a reasonable out-of-pocket moving, storage and other like expenses that the former tenant has incurred or will incur;
- An order for abatement of rent;
- An order that the landlord pay to the Board an administrative fine not exceeding the greater of $25,000 and the monetary jurisdiction of the Small Claims Court; or,
- Any other order that the Board considers appropriate.

The Landlord Requires the Unit—Test to Be Applied
The Ontario Divisional Court found that the reasonableness of the landlord's intention to occupy the unit was not important because the real test was the genuine want and desire for the unit.[5] In the leading case of *Kennealy v. Dunne*,[6] the English Court of Appeal stated that:

A landlord need not establish that his requirement of possession was reasonable, only that he bona fide wanted and genuinely had the immediate intention to occupy the premises as a residence.

Some court cases have held that the word "requires" means wants, and not needs. Accordingly, the landlord has no obligation to prove that the unit is the only option or the best one for the person intending to occupy the unit. However, in other cases, the Court concluded from the lack of real need for the unit, and usually from other circumstances such as disputes with the tenant, that the landlord lacked good faith in their desire to evict the tenant.

The burden of proof is on the landlord. It is relevant to the good faith of the landlord's intention to occupy the unit to determine the likelihood that the intended person will move into it.

Corporate Landlords and Shareholders of a Corporation
Section 103 of the *Landlord and Tenant Act* ("the LTA") was similar in wording to section 51 of the TPA and section 48 of the RTA. Therefore, in interpreting seciton 48 of the RTA, it is appropiate to consider how courts have interpreted those provisions of the LTA and TPA.

A number of decisions denied corporations the right to use section 103 of the LTA, finding that only a human landlord

could personally occupy the premises.[7] In *D.E.S.K. Properties Ltd. v. Skene*,[8] the County Court found:

Although in some circumstances a corporation may be regarded as a facade, the fact that the premises here are owned by a corporation prevents an Order being made under s. [103]. I am satisfied that [Mr. H.] bona fide requires possession of the apartment, but it is the corporation whose shares he owns that is the landlord, not [Mr. H.] ... . A corporation and its shareholders (even where, as here, one person owns all the shares) are two separate entities.

The landlord appealed the decision to the Divisional Court, but the appeal was dismissed.[9]

In contrast, in other instances, courts have taken a more flexible approach to the interpretation of the legislation. Courts have found that the sole shareholder of a corporation may also be a "landlord," as defined by the LTA, and may thus be entitled to use this ground for eviction for their personal occupation or that of their family member.

For example, in *Megan Investments Ltd. v. Funston*,[10] Philp J. held that where a corporation owns premises, the sole shareholder and officer may qualify as a landlord if the evidence establishes that he or she is "the person giving or permitting occupation" of the premises. In *Duke's Trailer Court Limited v. Block*,[11] Platana J. followed and extended the reasoning of *Megan Investments* to allow a controlling shareholder of a family held corporation to claim that he acted separately from the landlord company and was another landlord with a right of occupation.

In *Melhuish and Walsh v. 580472 Ontario Ltd. and Strelchuk*,[12] the Court found that the TPA's requirements were sufficiently met where the individual who sought to rely on the TPA was the beneficial owner of the rental unit, even though a numbered company was shown as the owner of the rental unit in the records of the land register. In support of the application, an officer of the corporate landlord swore a statutory declaration stating that the corporation is solely a trustee and holds the title to the rental unit for and on behalf of the individual, the beneficial owner. The Court found that it was clear that the individual was the beneficial owner of the premises and a landlord.

The Board is required to ascertain the real substance of all transactions relating to a residential complex or a rental unit and

---

5 *Beljinac v. Salter*, [2001] OJ No. 2792 (Div. Ct.) Re: TSL-21378.

6 [1977] 2 All ER 16 (CA).

7 For example, see *629576 Ontario Ltd. v. Ogg*, (1986) 42 RPR 310 (Ont. Dist. Ct., Kileen DCJ).

8 (1982), 4 TLLR 101 (Co. Ct.).

9 See (1983), 4 TLLR 103 (Div. Ct.).

10 [1992] OJ No. 1290, (1992), 25 RPR (2d) 63 (Ont. Gen. Div.).

11 [1997] OJ No. 2415, (1997), 41 OTC 129, 10 RPR (3d) 194 (Ont. Gen. Div.).

12 [2002] OJ No. 4343 (Div. Ct.).

the good faith of the participants in making findings on an application. Where the residential complex or rental unit is owned by a corporation, the Board must examine the real substance of the facts in each case to try to determine whether the sole shareholder of a corporate landlord can seek to rely on sections 48 and 49. In *Melhuish*, the Court noted section 188 of the TPA, now section 202 of the RTA. Section 202 of the RTA provides:

> *In making findings on an application, the Board shall ascertain the real substance of all transactions and activities relating to a residential complex or a rental unit and the good faith of the participants and in doing so,*
>
> *(a) may disregard the outward form of a transaction or the separate corporate existence of participants; and*
>
> *(b) may have regard to the pattern of activities relating to the residential complex or the rental unit.*

Consistent with the approach of the Court in *Melhuish* and section 202 of the RTA, the Board must examine the real substance of the particular facts of a case to identify a landlord who can rely on section 48 of the RTA.

Restriction on "Co-ownerships"

Co-ownership involves a number of individuals owning a building through a corporation or as tenants-in-common. Subsection 72(2) applies when such a building has been marketed as single units. This method of offering a building for sale on a unit basis avoids the rules of the *Condominium Act*. The co-owner has no rights to the unit they are apparently buying, except by agreement with the other co-owners. Their rights respecting the unit may only be the net revenue from that unit, but may also include the right to occupy the unit.

Subsection 72(2) provides protection for tenants of units that have been sold in this way to co-owners. Even if the co-ownership agreement purports to give the "unit owner" the right to occupy the unit, they cannot do so unless they meet the test set out in either clause 72(2)(a) or 72(2)(b).

Subsection 72(2) restricts the right of such a landlord to apply for possession for landlord's or purchaser's own use. Specifically subsection 72(2) provides:

(2) The Board shall not make an order terminating a tenancy and evicting the tenant in an application under section 69 based on a notice of termination under section 48 or 49 *where the landlord's claim is based on a tenancy agreement or occupancy agreement that purports to entitle the landlord to reside in the rental unit* unless,

   (a) the application is brought in respect of premises situate in a building containing not more than four residential units; or

   (b) one or more of the following people has previously been a genuine occupant of the premises:

      (i) the landlord,

      (ii) the landlord's spouse,

      (iii) a child or parent of the landlord or the landlord's spouse, or

      (iv) a person who provided care services to the landlord, the landlord's spouse, or a child or parent of the landlord or the landlord's spouse.

This is not a general prohibition on landlords of complexes with more than four rental units. The [italicized] words most commonly refer to a co-ownership situation where specific co-owners claim rights to certain units.

Relief from Eviction

Even though the Board has found that the landlord or purchaser requires the unit in good faith, which would result in an eviction order, the Board must consider, having regard to all the circumstances, whether or not to refuse to grant the application or to postpone the eviction for a period of time. In some cases, refusing or delaying the eviction is discretionary; in others, refusing the eviction is mandatory. See Guideline 7, entitled "Relief from Eviction."

Amended: January 4, 2010

INTERPRETATION GUIDELINE #13
OTHER POWERS OF THE BOARD

Interpretation Guidelines are intended to assist the parties in understanding the Board's usual interpretation of the law, to provide guidance to Members and promote consistency in decision-making. However, a Member is not required to follow a Guideline and may make a different decision depending on the facts of the case.

Section 201 of the *Residential Tenancies Act, 2006* ("the RTA") states:

Other powers of Board

201(1) The Board may, before, during or after a hearing,

   (a) conduct any inquiry it considers necessary or authorize an employee of the Board to do so;

   (b) request a provincial inspector or an employee of the Board to conduct any inspection it considers necessary;

   (c) question any person, by telephone or otherwise, concerning the dispute or authorize an employee of the Board to do so;

   (d) permit or direct a party to file additional evidence with the Board which the Board considers necessary to make its decision;

   (e) view premises that are the subject of the hearing; or

   (f) on its own motion and on notice to the parties, amend an application if the Board considers it appropriate to do so and if amending the application would not be unfair to any party.

Same

(2) In making its determination, the Board may consider any relevant information obtained by the Board in addition to the evidence given at the hearing, provided that it first informs

the parties of the additional information and gives them an opportunity to explain or refute it.

Same

(3) If a party fails to comply with a direction under clause (1)(d), the Board may,

(a) refuse to consider the party's submissions and evidence respecting the matter regarding which there was a failure to comply; or

(b) if the party who has failed to comply is the applicant, dismiss all or part of the application.

Parties may view premises with Board

(4) If the Board intends to view premises under clause (1)(e), the Board shall give the parties an opportunity to view the premises with the Board.

This Guideline is intended to provide guidance on powers of the Board under section 201 of the RTA. The Board does not gather evidence for or on behalf of the parties. The parties are responsible for bringing all relevant evidence and witnesses they wish the Member to consider to the hearing. However, the Board may, on its own initiative or at the request of a party, decide to exercise its discretion under section 201 to conduct an inquiry, question a person, view premises, amend an application or permit or direct a party to file additional evidence. This discretion will generally be exercised where the information at issue is relevant and necessary to the application and there is no other way to obtain the information or no other evidence that may be utilized in its place. The discretion under section 201 should be considered in light of section 171 of the RTA which states "The Board shall adopt the most expeditious method of determining the questions arising in a proceeding that affords to all persons directly affected by the proceeding an adequate opportunity to know the issues and be heard on the matter."

Each subsection is reviewed in turn.

a. Conduct any inquiry it considers necessary or authorize an employee of the Board to do so.

- There may be certain limited circumstances where a Member determines that it is necessary to instruct an employee of the Board to make an inquiry before, during or after the hearing. Where possible, the purpose of such an inquiry should be limited to clarifying or obtaining necessary information.

- Where the inquiry is to be conducted by a Board employee, the Member will provide the employee with clear direction as to the nature and scope of the inquiry in writing. The Board employee will provide the results of their inquiry to the Member in writing.

- The results of the inquiry should be provided to the parties within the time and according to the method that the Member directs or orders. The parties should be given reasonable opportunity to review and respond to any information provided.

- Examples where a Member may request a Board employee to make an inquiry include: contacting a party prior to a hearing to ascertain a party's availability for a proposed hearing date; determining the status of a related Board application; or determining when a post-hearing submission will be filed.

b. Request a provincial inspector or an employee of the Board to conduct any inspection it considers necessary.

- In special circumstances, a Member may determine that it is necessary to request an inspection because it is not possible for the parties to bring forward the necessary evidence in any other form such as photographs, inspection reports, or witnesses. For example, an inspection may be requested of a unit to determine whether or not there are appliances in the unit or if the damage alleged has occurred.

- Where a Member determines an inspection is necessary, either a provincial inspector or a Board employee will be requested to carry out the inspection.

- The Member will provide the provincial inspector or Board employee a written direction setting out the details of the inspection (e.g. unit address, time to conduct the inspection, and the purpose of the inspection). The provincial inspector or Board employee will, in turn, provide the Member with a written response describing their observations or findings.

- The results of the inspection should be provided to the parties within the time and according to the method that the Member directs or orders. The parties should be given reasonable opportunity to review and respond to any information provided.

c. Question any person, by telephone or otherwise, concerning the dispute or authorize an employee of the Board to do so.

- A Member may have some questions relating to a dispute or wish to clarify information already received. For example, the Member may be unable to read one sentence in an affidavit due to poor penmanship.

- In these types of situations where a Member wishes to question a person by telephone or otherwise concerning the dispute, the Member will usually ask a Board employee to question that person. The Member will provide the Board employee a written request setting out the issues or questions they have regarding the matter. The Board employee will provide the Member with a response to these issues and questions in writing.

- Where the Member or the staff employee has received a response to their questions, that response will be provided to the parties within the time and according to the method that the Member directs or orders. The parties should be given reasonable opportunity to review and respond to any information provided.

d. Permit or direct a party to file additional evidence with the Board which the Board considers necessary to make its decision.

- See Rule 19. Rule 19 provides disclosure rules in situations where a Member may wish to clarify the contents of an application, dispute, motion or other document filed with the Board.
- Note that subsection 201(3) provides that if a party fails to comply with such a direction, the Board may:
  - ◆ refuse to consider the party's submissions and evidence respecting the matter regarding which there was a failure to comply; or
  - ◆ the party who has failed to comply is the applicant, dismiss all or part of the application.

e. View premises that are the subject of the hearing.

- Premises will normally be viewed in special circumstances only.
- Subsection 201(4) states that if the Member intends to view premises, the Member should give the parties an opportunity to view the premises with the Member.
- In order to provide parties adequate opportunity to view premises with the Member, parties should be provided with reasonable notice of the date and time of the viewing. Where possible, the parties should be canvassed for possible dates and times for the viewing.

f. On its own motion and on notice to the parties, amend an application if the Board considers it appropriate to do so and if amending the application would not be unfair to any party.

- The Board may on its own motion consider amending an application before, during or after a hearing. For example to add a party or to remove a party.
- A Member shall decide whether or not to amend an application before, during or after a hearing taking into consideration the following factors:
  - ◆ Any prejudice a party may experience as a result of the amendment
  - ◆ Whether the amendment is significant enough to warrant any delay that may be caused by the amendment
  - ◆ Whether the amendment is necessary
  - ◆ Any other relevant factors

Subsection 201(2) provides that in making its determination, the Board may consider any relevant information obtained by the Board in addition to the evidence given at the hearing, provided that it first informs the parties of the additional information and gives them an opportunity to explain or refute it.

- Parties should be informed of any additional information under consideration by the Member within the time and according to the method that the Member directs or orders. The Member must also file any such information with the Board.

- The parties should be given reasonable opportunity to review and respond to any information provided.

Release Date: January 31, 2007

INTERPRETATION GUIDELINE #14 APPLICATIONS FOR RENT INCREASES ABOVE THE GUIDELINE

Interpretation Guidelines are intended to assist the parties in understanding the Board's usual interpretation of the law, to provide guidance to Members and promote consistency in decision-making. However, a Member is not required to follow a Guideline and may make a different decision depending on the facts of the case.

All increases in rent are subject to the rules set out in the *Residential Tenancies Act, 2006* ("the RTA"). Subsection 126(1) of the RTA provides for applications to the Board by landlords for rent increases that are in addition to the yearly guideline increase a landlord may take. A landlord's application may include some or all of the rental units or a portion of the rental units in the residential complex.

Applications for above the guideline increases ("AGIs") in rent can be made in any or all of the following cases:

1. An extraordinary increase in the cost for municipal taxes and charges, an extraordinary increase in the cost of utilities or an extraordinary increase in the cost for both municipal taxes and utilities, for the residential complex or any building in which the rental units are located.
2. Eligible capital expenditures incurred respecting the residential complex or one or more of the rental units in it.
3. Operating costs related to security services provided in respect of the residential complex or any building in which the rental units are located by persons not employed by the landlord.

This guideline is intended to assist parties in understanding the law and procedures applicable to the various kinds of AGIs.

The Nature of the Application

Section 120 of the RTA requires the Minister to set the guideline for rent increases every year. The Board does not set the guideline and has no jurisdiction to increase or decrease the guideline.

The purpose of section 126 of the RTA is to allow landlords to apply for an increase in rent above the guideline in three specific circumstances where they have incurred expenses that are not taken into account in calculating the guideline.

Maintenance Issues

Despite the fact that an AGI application is filed by the landlord a tenant may raise issues concerning breaches of maintenance. However, the Board is limited to considering only *existing ser-*

ious breaches of the landlord's maintenance obligations as set out in subsection 126(12). Further the Board is limited to the remedies that it may order if it finds that there is a serious breach. Pursuant to subsection 126(13) of the RTA, if the Board finds a serious breach in maintenance it shall dismiss the AGI application with respect to the affected rental unit or make an order as provided for in paragraph (b) of subsection 126(13), that the rent not be increased for the rental unit until the landlord makes the appropriate motion with notice to the tenant and the Board permits the increase, where the landlord has not:

- completed items on work orders related to a serious breach of health, safety, housing or maintenance standards;
- completed work, repairs or replacements ordered by the Board under paragraph 4 of subsection 30(1) of the RTA and was found by the Board to be related to serious breaches of subsection 20(1) or section 161 of the RTA; or
- is in serious breach of subsection 20(1) or section 161 of the RTA.

The Board cannot award a rent abatement to a tenant on an AGI order.

If the tenant believes that the landlord has breached the maintenance obligations set out in the RTA, the tenant may file their own application about maintenance whether or not the maintenance issues are raised at the AGI hearing. For further information on tenant applications for breaches of maintenance obligation see Interpretation Guideline 5: Breach of Maintenance Obligations which discusses both the landlord's maintenance obligations and the types of remedies that may be awarded on the tenant's application.

3% limitation

Subsection 126(11) of the RTA provides that the maximum annual increase that may be allowed in an application based on capital expenditures or security services or both is 3% above the guideline. Where an application justifies more than 3%, the rent is increased by 3% in the first year and any remaining increase may be taken in subsequent years, to a maximum of two additional years at 3% per year, according to the prescribed rules in section 33 of O. Reg. 516/06.

The 3% limitation does not apply where the application is based on an increase in the cost of municipal taxes and charges, or utilities. Where an increase is justified by these categories, the landlord may take the entire increase in the first year.

Exception for Mobile Home Parks & Land Lease Communities

Section 167 of the RTA contains an exception to subsection 126(11) where a landlord incurs a capital expenditure with regard to a mobile home park or a land lease community for "infrastructure work" as defined in subsection 167(2) and section 51 of O. Reg. 516/06, required to be carried out by the Government of Canada or Ontario or a municipality, or an agency of any of them. In these circumstances, the Board has

the jurisdiction to set the number of years over which the justified rent increase may be taken.

Charging the Approved Rent Increase

Where a landlord has applied for an increase above the guideline, all rules regarding notices of rent increase still apply. Where a landlord has filed an AGI and gives a tenant a notice of rent increase before the Board orders such an increase, the tenant may choose to pay only the amount that the landlord could lawfully charge, without the order. If the tenant chooses to pay a higher amount and the application is unsuccessful, or the Board orders a lesser amount, the landlord owes that tenant any amount overpaid. If the AGI is successful and the tenant has not paid the amount required by the order, the tenant owes the landlord the difference between the amount paid and the amount required by the order, provided the landlord has served a proper notice of rent increase for that amount. If the Board makes the order for an above the guideline rent increase three months or more after the FED of a rent increase, s.205 of the RTA allows the Board to order that any money owing by the tenant as a result of the ordered rent increase can be paid by the tenant in monthly installments over a period of no more than 12 months.

Subsection 33(2) of O. Reg. 516/06 provides that where a landlord does not take an increase in the 12-month time period for which it is ordered, the landlord may not take the increase at a later date. The right to take that increase is therefore lost.

First Effective Date (FED) in an AGI Application

All AGI applications must be filed at least 90 days before the effective date of the first intended rent increase that is being claimed in the application.

Filing the Application

Because of the nature of an application to increase the rent above the guideline, much of the evidence to support the application is documentary. Section 22 of O. Reg. 516/06 provides for timely disclosure of supporting material by requiring that:

1. if the application is based on an extraordinary increase in the cost for municipal taxes and charges or utilities or both, the landlord must file with the application,
   i) Evidence of the costs claimed and proof of payment of the costs, and
   ii) Any information that effectively reduces the landlord's costs, including, but not limited to, grants, financial assistance, rebates and refunds. If the information is not available when the application is filed, the landlord continues to have an obligation to file the information, if it becomes available at any time before the hearing is completed; and
2. if the application is based on capital expenditures, the landlord must file with the application documentation,

i) on a Board approved form, details about each invoice and payment for each capital expenditure item, and

ii) on a Board approved form, details about the rents for all rental units in the residential complex that are affected by any of the capital expenditures,

iii) evidence of the costs claimed and proof of payment of the costs, including any information that effectively reduces the landlord's costs, including grants and assistance from any level of government and insurance, resale, salvage and trade-in proceeds, rebates and refunds. If that information is not available when the application is filed, the landlord continues to have an obligation to file the information, if it becomes available at any time before the hearing is completed;

iv) two additional photocopies of the application and the material that accompanies the application and, a compact disc containing the material that accompanies the application in portable document format (PDF). See following for exception:

Exception to iv): a landlord does not have to provide a compact disc where the residential complex contains six or fewer residential units and the residential complex is located in a rural or remote area and the landlord cannot reasonably provide the compact disc.

A Member may refuse to allow the landlord to rely on documents that were not filed in a timely manner. The result of such a refusal will often be that the landlord is unable to prove that the claimed expense was incurred.

Where an application only relates to operating costs, a landlord must also be prepared to comply with the disclosure requirements of Rule 19.2 of the Board's Rules of Practice. That rule provides that a landlord who files an AGI must be prepared to disclose at the hearing, the rent for each unit in the complex, the date the rent was established for a new tenant and the date the rent was last increased for existing tenants.

Also, subsection 126(4) of the RTA provides that where an application includes a claim for capital expenditures, the landlord must make information that accompanies the application available to the tenants of the residential complex in accordance with the prescribed rules. Section 23 of O. Reg. 516/06 sets out the following rules related to the material referred to under subsections 22(1) and (2):

1. On the request of a tenant subject to the application, the landlord shall provide the tenant with a compact disc containing the material provided to the Board in PDF for a charge of not more than five dollars;

2. Instead of option one, the landlord and the tenant may agree that the landlord will provide the tenant with

either a photocopy of the material for no more than the landlord's reasonable out-of-pocket costs for the photocopying or an email of the material in PDF, at no charge to the tenant;

3. Despite option one, if a landlord has not provided the Board with a compact disc, the landlord must, on the tenant's request, provide the tenant with a photocopy of the material provided for a charge of not more than five dollars;

4. If the landlord has an office in or close to the residential complex, the landlord must, during normal business hours and at no charge, make a photocopy of the material provided available for viewing by tenants subject to the application; and

5. The landlord must, in the application, inform every tenant subject to the application of the ways in which a tenant may obtain access under this section to the material.

Written or Oral Hearing

Pursuant to section 184 of the RTA, the Board generally schedules AGI applications for an oral hearing. However, section 5.1 of the *Statutory Powers Procedure Act* ("the SPPA") provides authority for tribunals to hold written hearings where the tribunal has made rules regarding written hearings. Rule 22 of the Board's Rules of Practice sets out the Board's procedure for written hearings.

Adjournments

Section 21 of the SPPA gives the Board the jurisdiction to adjourn hearings, where it is shown that an adjournment is required to permit an adequate hearing to be held. Further guidance with respect to adjournments is pertained in Guideline #1.

As with all other applications, it is expected that applicants will be ready to proceed with the hearing on the date that is set for the AGI hearing and that respondents, properly served, will also be prepared to proceed.

The most common reasons given by parties requesting adjournments in AGI applications are that the landlord requires additional time to file documents or that the tenants require additional time to prepare for the hearing. Since section 22 of O. Reg. 516/06 requires the applicant to file all documentary evidence with the application, a hearing will not normally be adjourned in order to allow these documents to be filed. Instead, the hearing will proceed but the landlord will not be permitted to rely on the documents that were not properly filed.

Similarly, since landlords are required by Rule 10.4 to serve the notice of hearing in an AGI application at least 30 days before the date of the hearing, it is expected that tenants will have ample time to prepare for the hearing and to retain a representative. Hearings will therefore not be adjourned where tenants have not made reasonable efforts to take advantage of the time that they have had.

The Board reserves a substantial amount of hearing time for AGI applications. This resource of the Board cannot be recovered if the hearing is adjourned. Often, AGI applications involve a large number of tenants who may be inconvenienced if required to attend more than once. These factors will be considered when parties request adjournments.

In addition, a landlord seeking to file documents that should have been filed with the application, must seek leave to extend the time requirement for filing. The Member will consider the factors set out in Rule 15.6 in making that decision. Leave will not be granted where the reason for failure to file on time is purely neglect on the part of the applicant.

Mediation and Consent Orders

As with all other applications, the Board encourages parties to AGI applications to settle the application with the assistance of one of the Board's mediators. The outcome of mediation can be 1) a mediated agreement, or 2) a consent order.

Where an AGI application is resolved by a mediated agreement and the application is with regard to a rental unit that is not a mobile home or a land lease home or a site for either, subsection 194(3) of the RTA limits the increase to an amount equal to the sum of the guideline plus 3% of the previous year's lawful rent.

It is clear that if all of the parties are in attendance and they negotiate a settlement that results in a consent order, in the absence of circumstances that render the agreement invalid, such as fraud, duress or misrepresentation, they are bound by the order. This applies even though the order is not the one that would have been made, had there been a hearing.[1]

Where all of the tenants are not in attendance at the hearing, the approach of the Board is to presume that the tenants not in attendance admit the facts supported in the application. Therefore, where the application is properly filed, the tenants in attendance at the hearing and the landlord may agree to a consent order for an increase that is not greater than the evidence filed with the application would support.

An order issued on consent permitting a rent increase must specify the percentage increase that is attributed to an extraordinary increase or a capital expenditure. In the case of a rent increase due to capital expenditures the Board order must also include a date on which the rent decrease will take effect if the tenant continues to occupy the rental unit. In the case of an extraordinary increase in the costs for utilities the order must set out the adjusted base year utilities costs pursuant to subsection 29(4) of O. Reg. 516/06. These requirements flow from

sections 128 and 129 of the RTA, which require that the landlord decrease the rent due to decreases in the costs of utilities and/or the elapse of the amortization period for capital expenditures, by the percentage increase allowed in the Board order.

Issues at the Hearing

(a) Taxes and Utilities

Paragraph 1 of subsection 126(1) of the RTA allows landlords to apply for an increase above the guideline if they experienced an extraordinary increase in the cost for municipal taxes and charges or utilities, or both, for the whole residential complex or any building in which the rental units are located.

Subsection 126(2) of the RTA provides that "extraordinary increase" means an extraordinary increase as defined by or determined in accordance with the regulations. Section 28 of O. Reg. 516/06 provides that an increase in the cost of municipal taxes and charges or utilities is extraordinary if it is greater than the guideline plus 50 per cent of the guideline. The Board will use the guideline for the calendar year in which the FED for the application falls. If the guideline is less than zero, any increase in the cost of municipal taxes and charges or utilities is deemed to be extraordinary.

A landlord may choose to apply for either municipal taxes and charges or utilities, or both. If the application is for only one category, the costs for the other category are not relevant. The allowance to be included in the total justified rent increase will be determined according to the rules set out in section 29 of O. Reg. 516/06.

Section 29 of O. Reg. 516/06 allows landlords to apply for an AGI based on an increase in municipal taxes and charges as a result of an appeal of a tax assessment.

Municipal taxes and charges are defined under section 2 of the RTA and section 41 of O. Reg. 516/06. Municipal taxes and charges include:

- taxes charged to a landlord by the municipality (which include education taxes levied under Division B of Part IX of the *Education Act*);
- charges levied on a landlord by the municipality; and
- taxes levied on a landlord's property in unorganized territory.

However, municipal taxes and charges do not include the following:

- charges for inspections done by a municipality related to an alleged breach of a health, safety, housing or maintenance standard;
- charges for emergency repairs carried out by a municipality;
- charges for work in the nature of a capital expenditure carried out by a municipality;
- charges for services, work or non-emergency repairs performed by a municipality related to the landlord's non-compliance with a by-law;
- penalties, interest, late payment fees and fines;

---

[1] See the decisions of the Divisional Court in *Torgis v. Brajovic* (January 14, 2002), Brampton Divisional Court File No. 01-BN-2696; *Carlson v. Kaneff Properties* (January 14, 2002), Toronto Divisional Court File No. 176/01, [2002] OJ No. 361; and *Berbatovci v. Crescent Village* (July 25, 2002), Toronto Divisional Court File No. 428/02.

- any amount spent by a municipality to arrange for vital service for a rental unit in accordance with a vital service by-law plus an administrative fee of 10 per cent of that amount; or
- any other prescribed charges under section 41 of O. Reg. 516/06.

Utilities are defined in section 1 of the RTA. They are heat, electricity and water. A landlord making a claim for an AGI based on an increase in the cost of utilities must provide the cost for each of these three utility sub-categories. As a result, a decrease in cost in one sub-category will offset an increase in another sub-category. Where the landlord fails to prove the costs in all categories, the application with regard to utilities will be dismissed.

It should be noted that clause 24(1)(a) of O.Reg. 516/06 states that when determining the amount of operating costs in an application filed on or after July 1, 2010, the Board cannot include any goods and services tax, harmonized sales tax or provincial sales tax paid by the landlord with respect to the utility.

Tenants have argued that, where a landlord experiences a temporary increase in the cost of utilities, and then there is a decrease in the following year, an order based on the increase should be denied because the result is a windfall to the landlord, since the increase, once granted, is never removed from the rent. It was argued that the Ontario Rental Housing Tribunal had the jurisdiction to take this approach based on the "real substance" of the transaction, as is required by section 188 of the *Tenant Protection Act, 1997*.

The Divisional Court addressed this position in its decision in *Scott Burton et al v. Leadway Apartments Ltd.*,[2] which they examined section 188 of the *Tenant Protection Act, 1997* that contained similar wording to section 202 of the RTA. The Court ruled that the Ontario Rental Housing Tribunal did not have the jurisdiction to depart from the regulations in deciding this issue. The Court of Appeal subsequently denied a motion for leave to appeal that Divisional Court decision.

However, the RTA addresses situations where the cost of a utility decreases in the years following the increase order under section 126. For information on rent decreases due to decreases in utility costs see section 128 and sections 35-37 of O. Reg. 516/06 which address rent reductions due to utility cost decreases. Such a decrease has sometimes been referred to as "costs no longer borne."

(b) Security Services

Paragraph 3 of subsection 126(1) of the RTA allows landlords to apply for an AGI based on operating costs related to security services provided in respect of the residential complex or any building in which the rental units are located. Eligible costs, however, only include services provided by persons who are not the landlord's employees. The allowance will be determined according to the rules set out in section 30 of O. Reg. 516/06.

For the application to be allowed the landlord must prove either an increase from the Reference Year to the Base Year (see subsection (c) below) or costs incurred in this category for a new service. The service must also have been provided by persons not employed by the landlord. For example, if the superintendent provides this service in addition to his/her regular duties and responsibilities, any increases in costs will not be allowed.

(c) Accounting Periods for AGI Applications Based on Utilities and Security Services

When landlords file AGI application based on operating costs for utilities or security services, they are required to provide the costs for the prescribed accounting periods. Section 19 of O. Reg. 516/06 sets out the accounting periods to be used for calculating an allowance for operating costs for utilities or security services. The accounting periods include a Base Year (BY) and a Reference Year (RY). The BY for operating costs for utilities or security services is the most recently completed 12-month period chosen by the landlord that ends 90 days before the effective date of the first intended rent increase (FED) applied for. The RY is the 12-month period immediately preceding the BY. If the landlord claims an extraordinary increase in the cost of utilities and security services, the accounting periods chosen for utilities must be the same as those chosen for operating costs for security services.

Where there is a prior RTA order that allowed an AGI due to an extraordinary increase in the cost of utilities or operating costs for security services, subsection 19(2) of O. Reg.516/06 requires that the BY for a subsequent AGI application start and end on the same days as the BY in the prior order. This rule applies even if a new landlord has purchased the residential complex, or the landlord has switched the FED in the subsequent application to a different month of the year.

(d) Capital Expenditures

Paragraph 2 of subsection 126(1) of the RTA allows landlords to apply for an AGI if they incurred eligible capital expenditures respecting the residential complex or one of the rental units in it. The amount of a capital expenditure item and the allowance will be determined according to the rules set out in sections 16 and 27 of O. Reg. 516/06.

What May Be Allowed as a Capital Expenditure in an AGI Application

In order for a capital expenditure to be allowed in an AGI application,

- it must be eligible,
- it must meet the definition set out in the regulations,
- it must have been incurred by the landlord at the time the application is filed, and
- it must have been completed within the prescribed time.

Non-Arms Length Transactions

If a landlord incurs costs that arise from a transaction that involves related persons this would be considered by the Board

---

[2] (August 26, 2002, Toronto Divisional Court File No. 86/02).

as a non-arm's length transaction. In such a situation, the Board will only consider that part of the landlord's cost that is less than or equal to the cost that would arise from a similar market transaction. Section 25 of O. Reg. 516/06 defines what constitutes non-arm's length transactions.

Definition of Capital Expenditure

Section 18 of O. Reg. 516/06 provides that capital expenditure means:

> an expenditure for an extraordinary or significant renovation, repair, replacement or new addition, the expected benefit of which extends for at least five years including,
>
> (a) an expenditure with respect to a leased asset if the lease qualifies, and
>
> (b) an expenditure that the landlord is required to pay on work undertaken by a municipality, local board or public utility, other than work undertaken because of the landlord's failure to do it
>
> but, does not include,
>
> (c) routine or ordinary work undertaken on a regular basis or undertaken to maintain a capital asset in its operating state, such as cleaning and janitorial services, elevator servicing, general building maintenance, grounds-keeping and appliance repairs, or
>
> (d) work that is substantially cosmetic in nature or is designed to enhance the level of prestige or luxury offered by a unit or residential complex

The Board will consider all of the circumstances, including the size of the complex, the nature of the work, its effect on and importance to the unit or complex, and the amount of the expenditure when determining if the expenditure is extraordinary or significant.

The period of the expected benefit is determined as of the time that the expenditure is incurred. Therefore, if a landlord incurs an expenditure on an item that is expected to last more than five years but the item does not, the landlord is not disqualified from recovery of the expenditure, for this reason alone.

Subsection 126(7) of the RTA provides that subject to subsection 126(8) and (9), a capital expenditure is an eligible capital expenditure for the purposes of this section if,

- it is necessary to protect or restore the physical integrity of the residential complex or part of it;

- it is necessary to comply with subsection 20(1) or clauses 161(a) to (e);
- it is necessary to maintain the provision of a plumbing, heating, mechanical, electrical, ventilation or air conditioning system;
- it provides access for persons with disabilities;
- it promotes energy or water conservation; or

- it maintains or improves the security of the residential complex or part of it.

These terms set out in subsection 126(7) of the RTA are not defined in the Act or the regulations, with the exception of "physical integrity." According to subsection 18(1) of O. Reg. 516/06, physical integrity means the integrity of all parts of a structure, including the foundation, that support loads or that provide a weather envelope and includes, without restricting the generality of the foregoing, the integrity of:

- the roof, exterior walls, exterior doors and exterior windows;
- elements adjacent to the structure that contribute to the weather envelope of the structure; and
- columns, walls and floors that support loads.

Subsection 126(8) provides that a capital expenditure to replace a system or thing is not an eligible capital expenditure for the purposes of this section if the system or thing that was replaced did not require major repair or replacement, unless the replacement of the system or thing promotes,

- access for persons with disabilities;
- energy or water conservation; or
- security of the residential complex or part of it.

Subsection 126(9) provides that a capital expenditure is not an eligible capital expenditure with respect to a rental unit for the purposes of this section if a new tenant entered into a new tenancy agreement in respect of the rental unit and the new tenancy agreement took effect after the capital expenditure was completed.

Work Undertaken by a Municipality, Local Board or Public Utility

According to paragraph (b) of subsection 18(1) of O. Reg. 516/06, if a landlord is obligated to pay for capital work undertaken by a municipality, local board or a public utility, the expenditure also qualifies as a capital expenditure (unless the work is undertaken because of the landlord's failure to do it).

For example, a municipality may upgrade the sewer system and require a landlord to pay for the service improvement by a special levy on the municipal tax bill. The landlord can claim the upgraded sewer system as a capital expenditure. The special levy charged by the municipality will be the costs incurred by the landlord.

If a municipality charges a landlord the costs for certain capital work because the landlord failed to do it, the work does not qualify as a capital expenditure. For example, a municipality issued a work order requiring a landlord to make repairs to the balconies of an apartment building because they were unsafe. The landlord failed to do the repairs. The municipality did them and charged the landlord the costs in the municipal tax bill. This work cannot be considered as a capital expenditure.

Had the landlord done the work as a result of a work order, the fact that a work order had been issued does not remove the work from the definition of a capital expenditure.

Leased Assets

According to subsection 18(2) of O. Reg. 516/06, an expenditure on an item that is leased also qualifies as a capital expenditure if substantially all the risks and benefits associated with the leased asset are passed to the lessee and, at the commencement of the lease, any one or more of the following four conditions are met:

1. The lease provides that the ownership of the asset will pass to the lessee at or before the expiry of the lease;
2. The lease provides that the lessee has an option to purchase the asset when the term expires, at a price that is less than what the market value of the asset will be at that time;
3. The term of the lease is at least 75% of the useful life of the asset as determined in accordance with section 27 of O. Reg. 516/06, but without regard to any part of section 27 that prevents the useful life from being determined to be less than 10 years; or
4. The net present value of the minimum lease payments is at least 90% of the asset's fair market value at the commencement of the lease.

According to paragraph 4 of subsection of section 18(2) of O. Reg. 516/06, the net present value is determined using the interest rate fixed by section 20 of O. Reg. 516/06. The rate is the chartered bank administered conventional five-year mortgage interest rate on the last Wednesday of the month before the month in which the application is filed, as reported by the Bank of Canada.

Capital Expenditures That Are "Incurred" and "Completed"

In addition to meeting the definition of capital expenditures, the items claimed must have been incurred by the landlord at the time the application is filed and they must have been completed during the specific time period required by the regulations.

Subsection 126(1), paragraph 2 of the RTA allows a landlord to apply for a capital expenditure that they (and/or the previous landlord) have incurred.

"Incurred" is defined in section 18 of O. Reg. 516/06. It means that payment in full of the amount of the capital expenditure, other than any hold back that is required under the *Construction Lien Act*, must have been made by the time the application is filed. If a capital expenditure relates to a lease, "incurred" means the assumption of the obligations under the lease. If an expenditure relates to work undertaken by a municipality, local board or public utility, "incurred" means that the work is completed.

In order for a capital expenditure item to be allowed, paragraph 2 of subsection 26 of O. Reg. 516/06 requires that the work must have been completed during the 18 month period that ends 90 days before the FED.

There are instances in which a project takes more than 18 months to complete. Since a landlord cannot apply before the project is completed and it would be unreasonable to conclude that the intention of the regulation was to exclude recovery for such projects, the Board will allow recovery, provided that the project was completed within the prescribed period. However, this approach does not allow a landlord who has undertaken several projects with regard to similar work, over an extended period, to recover for all of the projects in one application. For example, a landlord who repairs one part of a roof five years ago, does another repair three years ago and another within the last six months, will not be able to recover all that was spent in one application, on the theory that the work of repairing the roof was completed six months ago.

The Amount of a Capital Expenditure

If an item qualifies as a capital expenditure, the Member must determine the amount to be allowed when calculating the allowance. Subsection 26(5) of O. Reg. 516/06 specifies that the amount for a capital expenditure is calculated by totaling:

A. the purchase price, cost of leased assets, and the installation, renovation and construction costs, and
B. the value of the landlord's own labour,
less:
C. any grant or other assistance from a federal, provincial or municipal government or insurance, salvage, resale or trade-in proceeds.

Landlord's Own Labour

The value of the landlord's own labour in carrying out the work related to a capital expenditure may be recognized when determining the amount of the capital expenditure item. Subsection 26(3) of O. Reg. 516/06 provides that the value of the landlord's own labour should be calculated by multiplying the amount of time the landlord spent by a reasonable rate of pay based on their experience and skill in the type of work done.

If the amount of time they spent is more than what is reasonable based on their experience and skill, the Board will allow the reasonable amount of time. The Board will only allow the value of the landlord's own labour that does not exceed what a skilled tradesperson would charge. The value of the landlord's own labour does not include any amount relating to the management and administration of the capital work.

This type of cost will normally only be recovered by landlords who are individuals and not by corporations whose employees or agents do work at the complex.

Government Loans and Grants

If a landlord received financial assistance from the federal, provincial or municipal government, the appropriate amount of the grant or forgivable loan must be subtracted from the purchase price, installation, renovation and, construction costs of each affected capital expenditure item.

Revenue from Insurance, Salvage, Resale or Trade-in

In addition to government assistance, the landlord must also provide information regarding any revenue received from insurance, salvage, resale or trade-in proceeds. The amount of a capital expenditure must be reduced by the amount reported under these categories.

Useful Life

According to subsection 27(1) of O. Reg. 516/06, the useful life of a capital expenditure item is determined from the prescribed Schedule subject to the following rules:

1. where the useful life set out in Column 2 of the Schedule is less than 10 years, the useful life of work done or a thing purchased shall be deemed to be 10 years;

2. where a thing is purchased and has previously been used, the useful life of the thing shall be determined taking in to account the length of time of that previous use;

3. if the work done or thing purchased does not appear in the Schedule, the useful life of the work or thing shall be determined with reference to items with similar characteristics that do appear in the Schedule; and

4. despite paragraphs 2 and 3 above, for the purposes of making a finding under this section, the useful life of work done or a thing purchased shall not be determined to be less than 10 years.

Subsection 27(2) further states that if the useful life of work done or a thing purchased cannot be determined under subsection 27(1) because the work or thing does not appear in the Schedule and no item with similar characteristics appears in the Schedule, the useful life of the work or thing shall be what is generally accepted as the useful life of such work or thing but in no case shall the useful life be determined to be less than 10 years.

Section 129 of the RTA provides that if the tenant continues to occupy the rental unit, the landlord will reduce the rent on the date and by the percentage increase that is attributed to the capital expenditure in the Board order. Section 38 of O. Reg. 516/06 provides the rules for calculating the date for the time the rent decrease can take place. The landlord will reduce the rent on the date and by the percentage increase that is attributed to the capital expenditure in the Board order.

Allocation of Costs

If the amount of a capital expenditure or operating cost involves non-residential components or other residential complexes and/or the AGI application covers only some of the units in the complex, the Member will allocate the amount so that only the portion of the amount that is applicable to the units covered by the application is allowed.

Section 24 of O. Reg. 516/06 prescribes the rules for allocating operating costs and/or capital expenditures to the residential complex, if the costs also relate to non-residential components in the complex or other residential complexes. According to subsection 24(2) of O. Reg. 516/06, costs can be allocated based on one or more of these factors:

- the area (i.e. square footage) of the complex;
- the market value of the complex; or
- the revenue generated in the complex.

The usual approach is to allocate based on square footage. This is because, in the usual case, an expenditure will benefit all parts of a complex equally. If the allocation of costs would be unreasonable using any of these methods, the costs should be allocated in reasonable proportions according to how much of the costs and expenditures are attributable to the residential components in the complex or the residential complex. This is set out in subsection 24(3) of O. Reg. 516/06.

The decision on allocation is made with regard to each expenditure. It is therefore possible that different methods may be chosen when allocating different cost categories. Landlords are required to indicate in the application form which method(s) they have chosen to allocate the costs between residential and non-residential (or other residential) components. However, the Board may choose a different method found to be more reasonable.

A cost category may affect some or all of the units covered by the application. The Member will allocate the cost and allowance for a cost category if:

- the AGI application covers only some of the units in the complex; and
- the cost category affects units not covered by the application.

In this case, the Board must adjust the cost and allowance so that only the part of the cost and allowance that is applicable to the units covered by the application will be passed on to those units. Landlords are required to provide information in the application about which cost categories affect which units, and information about which units are covered by the application. However, the Board is not bound by this information and will allocate the cost based on a finding as to which units benefit from the expenditure.

The applicable costs and allowances are calculated by multiplying the total costs or allowances by an allocation factor. If an operating cost category affects units not covered by the application, the allocation factor is set out in subsection 21(1) of O. Reg. 516/06. The formula is:

$$\text{Allocation Factor} = \frac{\text{Total rents for rental units subject to the application \& affected by the operating cost category}}{\text{Total rents for rental units affected by the application}}$$

For the purpose of subsection 21(1) of O. Reg. 516/06, the rent for the rental unit that is vacant or not rented is deemed to be the average rent charged for the rental units in the residential complex.

The allowances for capital expenditure are calculated on a unit by unit basis. The method for calculating the allowance is determined under subsection 26(6) of O. Reg. 516/06 and the allowance for the unit for each capital expenditure takes into account the fact that the capital expenditure may not affect all rental units in the complex.

Release Date: July 1, 2010

INTERPRETATION GUIDELINE #15
AMENDING AN ORDER

Interpretation Guidelines are intended to assist the parties in understanding the Board's usual interpretation of the law, to provide guidance to Members and promote consistency in decision-making. However, a Member is not required to follow a Guideline and may make a different decision depending on the facts of the case.

The Board's authority to amend an order comes from section 21.1 of the *Statutory Powers Procedure Act*. It gives the Board authority to correct "a typographical error, error of calculation or similar error made in its order or decision." These are referred to as clerical errors.

The procedure for dealing with a request to amend an order can be found in Rule 28 of the Board's Rules of Practice.

What Is a Clerical Error?

A clerical error may be a Board error, or an error made by a party in documentation submitted to the Board that ends up being transcribed into an order or decision. A clerical error may include any of the following:

- An incorrect name or address. For example, if the name or address is incorrect on the order but correct on the application, the error is likely clerical. If the name or address is incorrect on the application but the respondent received it and had an opportunity to participate in the proceeding, the error is likely clerical.
- An incorrect date. The order sets a date for doing something that is impossible to comply with or is not what the Member intended.
- An incorrect amount. The Member made an arithmetic error or misplaced a decimal point.
- An omission. The member inadvertently failed to include an essential term or condition in the order.

An error is not clerical if, for example:
- The name or address on the application is incorrect and the respondent may not have received the application.
- The error is brought to light by new evidence, or by evidence that was presented at the hearing but overlooked.
- The member has changed his or her mind on an issue.
- The error is a serious error.

Determining Clerical Error

A party may request that an order be amended to correct a clerical error. The Member who issued the order will consider

the request to amend unless the Member is on an extended absence: Rule 28.5. If the Member is on an extended absence, the Vice Chair will consider the request to amend: Rule 28.6.

Considering the Request to Amend

The Member should review the request to amend and dispose of it in accordance with Rule 28.7. In considering the request to amend:

- If the Member determines there is no clerical error, the Member will send a letter to the party who made the request informing the party that the request has been denied.
- If the Member determines there is an obvious clerical error that should be corrected, and the amendment will not cause prejudice to the other party, the Member may decide to amend the order without seeking submissions.
- The Member can also make any consequential amendments without seeking submissions.
- Where a party may be prejudiced by the amendment, the Member should invite submissions or hold a hearing in accordance with Rule 28.7.

Seeking Submissions

Submissions may be requested by way of a direction letter to the parties. The direction letter should:

- inform the other party that a request to amend the order has been received, and enclose the request;
- direct the parties to make submissions to the Board within a prescribed time. Generally a period of 10 to 15 days will be sufficient.

Where submissions are received, the Member may make a decision based solely on the submissions and the request to amend and without holding a hearing. If the request to amend is denied without holding a hearing, a denial letter should be sent to the parties.

Holding a Hearing

The Member may hold a hearing to determine if the order contains a clerical error. If the request to amend is denied after holding a hearing, an order will be issued explaining why the request to amend has been denied. If the request to amend is granted, an amended order will be issued.

Amending the Order

If the Member determines that there is a clerical error in the order or decision and that it should be amended, an amended order will be issued that explains why the order is being changed and what the changes are, including any consequential amendments.

Other Considerations

Consequential Amendments

An amendment to one part of the order may require an amendment to another part. In some cases, it may also be necessary to "update" the order to reflect any amounts that have been paid or have become owing since the original order was issued.

Stays

A party may ask that the order be stayed until a decision is made. The request should explain the prejudice that a party will suffer if the order is not stayed until a decision is made.

A Member may decide to issue a stay of the original order, whether or not it was requested and without seeking submissions or holding a hearing.

A stay will not always be necessary. However, where the request to amend concerns an alleged error in an eviction order, and the Member determines that it may be necessary to seek submissions or hold a hearing, a stay will generally be issued. A stay may also be issued if the request to amend is received close to the effective date of the order, and the Member needs time to consider the request before making a decision.

The stay will be issued in the form of an interim order. If the request to amend is denied and the order is not amended, an order must be issued lifting the stay. If the request to amend is granted and order is amended, the stay must be lifted in the amended order.

Serious Errors

A member cannot amend an order to correct a serious error. A serious error can only be corrected by way of review under Rule 29 and Guideline 8.

If the Member determines that the order may contain a serious error, the Member may: a) deny the request to amend if the order does not contain a clerical error; or b) in exceptional cases, refer the matter to the Vice Chair who can initiate a review of the order.

Release Date: January 31, 2007

INTERPRETATION GUIDELINE #16
ADMINISTRATIVE FINE

Interpretation Guidelines are intended to assist the parties in understanding the Board's usual interpretation of the law, to provide guidance to Members and promote consistency in decision-making. However, a Member is not required to follow a Guideline and may make a different decision depending on the facts of the case.

Purpose of a Fine

An administrative fine is a remedy to be used by the Board to encourage compliance with the *Residential Tenancies Act, 2006* ("the RTA"), and to deter landlords from engaging in similar activity in the future. This remedy is not normally imposed unless a landlord has shown a blatant disregard for the RTA and other remedies will not provide adequate deterrence and compliance. Administrative fines and rent abatements serve different purposes. Unlike a fine, a rent abatement is intended to compensate a tenant for a contravention of a tenant's rights or a breach of the landlord's obligations.

An administrative fine should not be confused with costs. Administrative fines are payable to the Minister of Finance and not to a party. Costs may be ordered where a party's conduct in the proceeding before the Board was unreasonable and may be ordered payable to a party or to the Board. See Guideline 3, Costs, for details.

When Can a Fine Be Levied

A fine may be ordered in relation to the activities set out under:

- subsection 29(1), paragraphs 2 to 6 of the RTA relating to tenant applications alleging that the landlord, superintendent or agent of the landlord has:
  - withheld the reasonable supply of any vital service, care service or food that it is the landlord's obligation to supply under the tenancy agreement or deliberately interfered with the reasonable supply of any vital service, care service or food;
  - substantially interfered with the reasonable enjoyment of the rental unit or residential complex for all usual purposes by the tenant or a member of their household;
  - harassed, obstructed, coerced, threatened or interfered with the tenant during the tenant's occupancy of the rental unit;
  - altered the locking system on a door giving entry to the rental unit or the residential complex or caused the locking system to be altered during the tenant's occupancy of the rental unit without giving the tenant replacement keys; or
  - illegally entered the rental unit.
- subsection 41(2) and (3) where the landlord has breached an obligation:
  - to not sell, retain or otherwise dispose of the tenant's property before 72 hours have elapsed after the enforcement of the eviction order; or,
  - to make an evicted tenant's property available to be retrieved at a location close to the rental unit during the prescribed hours within the 72 hours after the enforcement of an eviction order.
- subsection 57(1), clause (a) to (c) relating to a former tenant's application alleging that:
  - The landlord gave a notice of termination for personal use in bad faith, the former tenant moved out as a result of the notice or as a result of an application to or order made by the Board based on the notice and no person referred to in clause 48(1)(a), (b), (c), or (d) occupied the rental unit within a reasonable time after the former tenant vacated the rental unit;
  - The landlord gave a notice of termination for personal use by the purchaser in bad faith, the former tenant moved out as a result of the notice or as a result of an application to or order made by the Board based on the notice and no person referred to in clause 49(1)(a), (b), (c), or (d) or

49(2)(a), (b), (c), or (d) occupied the rental unit within a reasonable time after the former tenant vacated the rental unit; or

♦ The landlord gave a notice of termination to demolish, convert, or to do extensive repairs or renovations in bad faith, the former tenant moved out as a result of the notice or as a result of an application to or order made by the Board based on the notice and the landlord did not demolish, convert, or repair or renovate the rental unit within a reasonable time after the former tenant vacated the rental unit.

• section 114 where the landlord has failed to give a new tenant written notice about the lawful rent for the rental unit where an order under paragraph 6, 7 or 8 of subsection 30(1) is in effect and the new tenant has made an application under subsection 115(1) to determine lawful rent or requiring the landlord to rebate rent paid in excess of any rent that may be lawfully charged.

The Board's authority to order an administrative fine in these circumstances is set out in the RTA under section 31(1)(d), 41(6), 57(3) paragraph 3, and 115(3) respectively.

Notice of Fine

Where a tenant requests a fine in an application, this will serve as notice to the landlord that a fine may be ordered. A Member may however, after hearing the evidence, consider ordering a fine even though it has not been requested. In either situation, the Member must give the parties an opportunity to make submissions on the issue.

Ordering a Fine

A Member may impose a conditional fine in an interim order to encourage compliance with the RTA. For example, a Member may order a fine for each day that the landlord fails to comply with a term or condition in the interim order, such as putting an illegally evicted tenant back into possession. The interim order should state precisely what the landlord is required to do and the consequences of failing to comply. The total amount of the fine, if any, should be set out in the final order based on the relevant circumstances as discussed at the hearing.

Where a landlord has committed several breaches, the Member need not order a separate fine for each breach. Rather, the Member may order one fine based on the overall pattern of activities alleged in the application.

In setting the amount of the fine, the Member may consider:

• the nature and severity of the breach
• the effect of the breach on the tenant
• any other relevant factors.

The amount of the fine should be commensurate with the breach.

Failure to Pay a Fine

Under section 196 of the RTA, where the Board receives information that an applicant owes money to the Board as a result of failing to pay any fine, fee or costs, the Board may, pursuant to its Rules:

• refuse to allow an application to be filed where such information is received on or before the day the application is submitted,
• stay or discontinue a proceeding where such information is received after the application has been filed but before a hearing is held,
• or delay issuing an order or discontinue the application where such information is received after a hearing of the application has begun.

See Rule 9, Refusing to Accept or Proceed with an Application, for details.

Amended: January 4, 2011

INTERPRETATION GUIDELINE #17: HUMAN RIGHTS

Interpretation Guidelines are intended to assist the parties in understanding the Board's usual interpretation of the law, to provide guidance to Members and promote consistency in decision-making. However, a Member is not required to follow a Guideline and may make a different decision depending on the facts of the case.

Introduction

The Ontario *Human Rights Code*[1] ("the Code") is the primary source for human rights law at tribunals such as the Landlord and Tenant Board (the Board). By reason of subsection 47(1) of the Code, the Code applies to the Board as a provider of services and facilities.

This means every person has the right to equal treatment, without discrimination, with respect to Board services and facilities, pursuant to section 1 of the Code. Although the Board's services and facilities are designed to be accessible, some persons may require additional accommodation from the Board in order to access its services and facilities.

The Board must interpret the *Residential Tenancies Act, 2006*[2] ("the RTA") in light of the Code. In *Walmer Developments v. Wolch*, the Divisional Court held that "... the Code is the law of Ontario and its provisions must inform any Ontario decision maker in its deliberations."[3] This means the Board must consider and apply the Code when, for instance, exercising its authority to delay or refuse an eviction, and determining, whether the landlord has accommodated the tenant to the point

---

[1] *Human Rights Code*, RSO 1990, c. H-19, as amended.

[2] *Residential Tenancies Act*, SO 2006, c. 17.

[3] 2003 CanLII 42163 (ONSCDC), para. 18.

of undue hardship. The Code may also apply to certain applications filed by tenants against landlords.

According to subsection 47(2) of the Code, the Code is paramount over all other provincial laws, including the RTA. This is consistent with subsection 3(4) of the RTA which states that if a provision of the RTA conflicts with a provision of another law, other than the Code, the provision of the RTA applies. The Supreme Court of Canada has confirmed that an administrative tribunal such as the Board has authority to find that a provision of an Act does not apply if it conflicts with the Code.[4]

This Guideline addresses the following types of Code issues that may arise in Board proceedings:

1. A person requires accommodation from the Board in order to access the Board's services and participate in the Board's proceedings;
2. A tenant asserts that the Member should grant relief from eviction because they are covered by one or more of the categories in subsection 2(1) of the Code, such as disability, and the landlord has not accommodated them to the point of undue hardship;
3. A tenant asserts in a tenant's application that the landlord has contravened the Code; and
4. A party asserts that a provision of the RTA conflicts with the Code.

Code Issues Not Considered by the Board

Some Code issues cannot be considered by the Board because the RTA does not apply to the situation. For instance, a person alleging that a landlord refused to provide them with a rental unit based on a Code ground of discrimination should contact the Human Rights Tribunal of Ontario. The Board has no jurisdiction to deal with such matters unless the person has paid a rent deposit and the landlord does not provide vacant possession of the rental unit, or return the rent deposit, in accordance with section 107 of the RTA.

1. Accommodation in a Board proceeding

According to section 1 of the Code, the Board is required to accommodate the needs of all persons who use the Board's services. Section 1 provides that every person has a right to equal treatment with respect to services without discrimination because of race, ancestry, place of origin, colour, ethnic origin, citizenship, creed (religion), sex (including pregnancy, gender identity), sexual orientation, age, marital status, family status or disability. Disability is defined by subsection 10(1) of the Code to include both physical conditions and mental disorders.

Section 183 of the RTA states that the Board shall adopt the most expeditious method of determining the questions arising in a proceeding that provides all persons directly affected an adequate opportunity to know the issues and be heard on the matter. Although the Board's services and hearings are designed

---

[4] *Tranchemontagne v. Ontario (Director, Disability Support Program)*, 2006 CanLII 14 (SCC).

to be accessible to as many people as possible, some persons covered under section 1 of the Code may require additional accommodation from the Board in order to have an adequate opportunity to know the issues and be heard on the matter.

a. Where a party requests accommodation

Parties seeking accommodation should make their needs known to Board staff as soon as possible, preferably in writing, so that the necessary arrangements can be made.

The party must participate in the accommodation process by working with the Board so that the appropriate accommodation can be implemented. Accommodation must be provided in a manner that respects dignity and allows the party to participate in the Board's process. More information about the Board's policy on accommodation, and how to request accommodation, can be found in the Board's Human Rights Policy [**policy currently under development**].

In many cases, the needs of parties covered by section 1 of the Code can be accommodated with relatively minor changes to the Board's standard hearing procedures. For example, a party, witness or representative:

- with a physical disability may have difficulty bringing their evidence forward to the Member and require the assistance of security personnel;
- with a speech or hearing impairment may need all parties to speak slowly and loudly, or have the chairs in the hearing room positioned to enable lip reading;
- with a visual impairment may require the use of assistive devices;
- with diabetes may be permitted to consume juice or food in the hearing room as needed;
- with cognitive impairments may require multiple breaks during the hearing, a longer than usual scheduled hearing, a late or early start time for the hearing, additional time to present their evidence, or adjournments;
- with a disability relating to mental illness may need a support person (such as a social worker or family member) to sit with them during the hearing;
- may request that a hearing not be scheduled on a particular day because it is a religious holy day for that individual; or
- may be provided with an opportunity to consult with on-site Tenant Duty Counsel where available before proceeding with the hearing (applies to tenants only).

If, on the day of the hearing, a party believes that they do not have an adequate opportunity to participate in the proceeding and require accommodation, they should bring their concerns to the attention of the presiding Member as soon as possible during the hearing. Depending upon the circumstances, the Member may require the party to provide sufficient evidence to establish that they are covered under section 1 of the Code and need accommodation. The Member must be respectful of the party's privacy interests and should not require the party to disclose more information than is needed to make the necessary determination respecting the issue of accommodation.

If the party requesting accommodation is disclosing intimate personal information, the Member may consider excluding the public from the hearing room under Rule 24 of the Board's Rules of Practice, "Restricting Public Access to the Hearing" and section 9 of the *Statutory Powers Procedure Act.* However, the other parties to the application are entitled to remain in the hearing room, examine all of the evidence submitted to the Board, conduct cross-examination and make submissions solely with regard to the issue of accommodation as it relates to the Board's hearing procedures.

The nature and extent of any accommodation is determined by the Member on a case-bycase basis upon consideration of the evidence and submissions made by all of the parties. However, even if one party objects to the requested accommodation, the Member is still obliged to provide the accommodation necessary to permit the party to participate in the hearing.

If the party cannot be adequately accommodated at the hearing, the Member will generally grant an adjournment and liaise with Board staff to ensure that the necessary accommodation will be in place for the next hearing date.

b. Accommodation issues arising during a hearing

Members must be attentive to indications which suggest a party may require accommodation in order to participate in the hearing, even if the party does not request any accommodation from the Board. Pursuant to section 201 of the RTA, the Member may on their own initiative ask questions and request submissions from both sides to determine if the party requires accommodation. As discussed above, the Member may consider different methods of accommodation to ensure a fair hearing with an opportunity for participation by all parties.

c. Where the capacity of a party is at issue

Members must also be attentive to indications which suggest a party may be unable to participate in a hearing due to a lack of mental capacity, even if the party does not bring this issue to the attention of the Board. Pursuant to section 201 of the RTA, the Member may need to ask questions and request submissions from both sides to determine if the party understands the nature or purpose of the hearing, appreciates the possible consequences of the hearing and can communicate with their legal representative, if they have one.

Where a party may lack capacity and is not represented at the hearing, the Member may consider different methods of accommodation to ensure a fair hearing with an opportunity for participation by all parties, even if no request for accommodation has been made. Examples include standing down the hearing to allow a tenant to consult with on-site Tenant Duty Counsel, where available, or adjourning the hearing to allow the party to obtain assistance from a family member, social worker or another person of the party's choosing.

Under Ontario law, all adults are assumed to be capable unless they have been found to be incapable by an assessor appointed under the *Substitute Decisions Act, 1992*[5] ("the SDA"). Such an assessment may result in someone else being appointed to look after that person's interests. The Board does not have the authority to find that a party to one of its proceedings is incapable within the meaning of the SDA or order that someone else represent that party in a Board hearing.

It should not be assumed that a person who is incapable of one thing is incapable of everything. A person who is incapable of making treatment decisions, or a person who is incapable of managing their money such that a guardian has been appointed, may still be capable of participating in a hearing and instructing their legal representative. Incapacity can be issue-specific.

d. Conduct during a Board hearing

Members have an obligation to ensure that all hearings are conducted in a manner that is respectful towards all of the participants. Members must also control the proceedings to ensure that the conduct of a party, witness, spectator or representative does not infringe upon another person's rights under the Code to equal treatment with respect to services. For example, a Member will not permit a hearing participant to make derogatory comments about a party's race, religion, or sexual orientation.

2. Landlord applications

Issues relating to any of the grounds set out in subsection 2(1) of the Code may be raised during Board hearings. Subsection 2(1) of the Code provides that everyone has the right to equal treatment with respect to housing, without discrimination because of race, ancestry, place of origin, colour, ethnic origin, citizenship, creed (religion), sex (including pregnancy, gender identity), sexual orientation, age, marital status, family status, disability, or the receipt of public assistance. "Disability" is defined by subsection 10(1) to include both physical conditions and mental disorders.

Code issues are most commonly raised when a landlord files an application to evict a tenant because of the tenant's conduct, and the tenant asserts that:

- the tenant has a disability;
- the landlord has discriminated against the tenant;
- the tenant's conduct is caused by the disability; and
- the landlord has not accommodated the tenant up to the point of undue hardship.

The Member must first determine, after hearing from all parties, whether the landlord has established that the tenant engaged in the alleged conduct. If the landlord does not meet this burden of proof, the application is dismissed. If the landlord meets the burden of proof, the Member will then consider the tenant's claim that the landlord has not met its obligations under the Code having regard to the following criteria:

---

5   *Substitute Decisions Act*, SO 1992, c. 30, as amended.

a. Is the tenant protected under subsection 2(1) of the Code

The tenant must provide sufficient information to establish that they are covered by one or more of the categories set out in subsection 2(1) the Code, such as disability. Sometimes this will not be difficult for the tenant to establish because the disability is not in dispute. In other cases, the tenant may need to submit evidence, such as a letter from a doctor or other medical forms, to establish that they have a disability as defined in the Code.

The Member must be respectful of the tenant's privacy interests and should not require the tenant to disclose more information than is needed to make the necessary determination. For example, a party with a disability may not need to disclose their specific diagnosis if sufficient medical evidence about the impact or effect of the disability is submitted to the Member. If the tenant is disclosing intimate personal information, the Member may consider excluding the public from the hearing room under Rule 24 of the Board's Rules of Practice, "Restricting Public Access to the Hearing" and section 9 of the *Statutory Powers Procedure Act*. However, the other parties to the application are entitled to remain in the hearing room, examine all of the evidence submitted to the Board and make submissions.

b. Has the tenant been discriminated against contrary to the Code

If the Member determines that the tenant falls within one or more of the categories contained in subsection 2(1) of the Code, the tenant must next establish that the landlord has discriminated against the tenant. In some cases, the discrimination may be clear. For example, the landlord is seeking to evict the tenant simply because the tenant practices a particular religion. In other cases, the discrimination may be indirect, such as a rule or standard applied by the landlord that appears neutral but has the effect of discriminating against the tenant because the tenant belongs to one or more of the categories contained in subsection 2(1) of the Code. For example, a requirement that all tenants remove their belongings from cupboards and drawers to enable the landlord to fumigate all of the rental units may discriminate against tenants who are unable to perform such tasks because of a physical disability. If the landlord is seeking to evict a disabled tenant for failing to comply with this requirement, the Member would take such discrimination into account in applying the Code.

The Divisional Court in *Connelly v. Mary Lambert Swale Non-Profit Homes*[6] suggested that where the landlord's application for eviction is based on the tenant's conduct, the Member must also consider whether the conduct has been directly caused by the tenant's disability.

If the grounds for eviction contained in the landlord's application are unrelated to the tenant's membership within one or more of the categories contained in subsection 2(1) of the Code, the Member cannot find that the tenant has been discriminated against by the landlord. For example, if the landlord has filed an application for termination of the tenancy based on arrears of rent, the fact that the tenant has a hearing impairment is likely not relevant to the Member's determination of the merits of the landlord's application. However, even if the Member finds that the landlord's application is unrelated to the tenant's membership within one or more of the categories contained in subsection 2(1) of the Code, the Member may still take all of the tenant's circumstances into account when considering relief from eviction pursuant to section 83 of the RTA. Both scenarios are discussed below.

c. Has the landlord accommodated the tenant to the point of undue hardship

Once the Member determines that the tenant is covered by one or more of the categories contained in subsection 2(1) of the Code and has been discriminated against by the landlord, the legal burden shifts to the landlord to show that it has accommodated the tenant to the point of undue hardship.

Section 11 of the Code provides that a right under the Code is infringed where a person identified by a Code ground is excluded because of neutral rules or requirements that are not "reasonable and bona fide in the circumstances." According to subsection 11(2) of the Code, this determination requires a consideration of whether the needs of the group to which the tenant belongs can be accommodated without undue hardship to the landlord. In other words, section 11 allows the landlord to demonstrate that the requirement, qualification or factor applied by the landlord is "reasonable and bona fide" by showing that the needs of the group to which the tenant belongs cannot be accommodated without undue hardship.

Subsection 17(1) of the Code contains a similar provision that specifically applies to disability. Subsection 17(1) states that a right is not infringed if the person with a disability is incapable of performing or fulfilling the essential duties or requirements attending the exercise of the right. In other words, there is no violation of the Code if the tenant is unable, because of a disability, to "... act as is reasonably required of a tenant."[7] However, according to subsection 17(2) of the Code, this defence is not available to the landlord unless it can be shown that the needs of the tenant cannot be accommodated without undue hardship.

In *Walmer Developments v. Wolch*[8] the Divisional Court stated that the limitation on the rights of a disabled person in section 17 must be read narrowly, as befits the purpose of the RTA, and the requirement for accommodation of the needs of the person is a keystone of the Code.

In determining whether the landlord has satisfied its duty to accommodate the tenant pursuant to either subsection 11(2) or 17(2) of the Code, the Member should consider the following criteria:

---

[6]   2007 CanLII 52787 (ONSCDC), para. 8.

[7]   *Walmer Developments v. Wolch*, 2003 CanLII 42163 (ONSCDC), para. 31.

[8]   Ibid., para. 34.

Landlord's knowledge of the tenant's circumstances

The Member must determine whether the landlord was aware, prior to filing the eviction application that the tenant is covered by one or more of the categories set out in subsection 2(1) the Code, such as disability. The duty to accommodate exists only for needs that are known to the landlord.[9] However, this does not mean that a tenant with a disability is obliged to provide the landlord with full details of their medical condition and history. In *Eagleson Co-Operative Homes, Inc. v. Théberge*,[10] the Court found that the landlord had received an uncontradicted medical opinion from the resident's doctor stating that she was unable to participate in any volunteer work due to medical reasons, and it was a violation of the Code to require a person with a mental disability to divulge private medical information as a condition of maintaining her accommodation.

Even if the tenant does not tell the landlord about the disability, the landlord cannot be willfully blind. If a disability is obvious, the landlord will be considered to have constructive knowledge of it and therefore should have attempted to address the issue with the tenant prior to taking steps to evict the tenant.

Tenant's role in the accommodation process

If a tenant wants accommodation under the Code, the tenant has a duty to provide the landlord with sufficient information about their needs so that the landlord can determine possible accommodation. The tenant also has a duty to cooperate with the landlord in the development and implementation of the accommodation. If the tenant refuses to cooperate, the landlord can argue it has fulfilled its duty to accommodate.

Has the landlord developed and implemented an appropriate accommodation plan

The landlord will be expected to provide evidence about the steps the landlord has taken to address the problem, if any, prior to applying to the Board for eviction.

In developing accommodation for the tenant, the landlord should have regard to three guiding principles identified by the Ontario Human Rights Commission:

1. accommodation must be provided in a manner that respects dignity;
2. accommodation must be individualized to meet the needs of the specific person; and
3. accommodation must provide for the inclusion of people protected under the Code.

Where the landlord is unable to immediately provide the ideal form of accommodation, other options such as phased-in, interim or alternative accommodation must be implemented by the landlord.

Will the accommodation cause undue hardship

A landlord must accommodate the tenant up to the point that any further accommodation would cause undue hardship. The Courts have considered this issue in several decisions.

In *Walmer Developments v. Wolch*[11] the Ontario Rental Housing Tribunal (now the Board) found that the tenant had interfered with the reasonable enjoyment of the landlord and other tenants by engaging in conduct such as screaming loudly and causing food to catch on fire on her stove. The Divisional Court found that the Tribunal had erred in evicting the tenant because the Member had failed to consider the tenant's disability pursuant to the Code. At paragraph 35, the Court stated that the Tribunal "... must consider whether any disruption in the enjoyment of other tenants may be sufficiently alleviated by a reasonable accommodation of the disabled tenant without undue hardship to the landlord." The Court rejected the argument that the tenant could not, because of her disability, act as is reasonably required of a tenant, so as not to disturb her neighbours and found that accommodation would be appropriate in this case. The Court ordered the parties to enter into an arrangement whereby the landlord informs the tenant's relatives at the first sign of trouble, so that they can intervene.

In *Canadian Mental Health Association v. Warren*[12] the Tribunal found that the tenant had created disturbances within the residential complex by shouting, screaming, slamming doors, verbally abusing and threatening other tenants, activating the smoke detectors, continually threw garbage out of her second storey window and that her unit was in such a state of hazardous disarray that it posed a real threat of fire. The Member determined that the tenant was disabled within the meaning of the Code. The Member accepted that the landlord's accommodation attempts included the negotiation and mediation of agreements which provided the tenant with relief from eviction, taking part in a "transition team" which had been formed to assist the tenant in resolving her problems, assigning caseworkers to deal with the tenant's needs, and installing less sensitive smoke detectors. The Member concluded that the landlord's accommodation met the requirements of section 17 of the Code and that the accommodation had now reached the point of undue hardship. The Divisional Court upheld the Tribunal's decision, finding that "there was overwhelming evidence of accommodation, to the point of undue hardship, on the facts before the Tribunal."

In *McKenzie v. Supportive Housing in Peel*[13] the Tribunal found that the tenant had seriously impaired the safety of the superintendent by stabbing the superintendent with a pen. The superintendent required medical attention and the tenant was convicted of assault. The tenant by her own testimony was disabled within the meaning of the Code. The member found that the landlord had done everything in its power to attempt

9   See *Bathurst-Vaughan Mall Limited v. Eini*, 2009 CanLII 3550 (ONSCDC).

10   2006 CanLII 29987 (ONSCDC).

11   2003 CanLII 42163 (ONSCDC).

12   2004 CanLII 16439 (ONSCDC).

13   2006 CanLII 7838 (ONSCDC).

to accommodate the tenant to the point of undue hardship, but that the tenant had refused to accept help. In upholding the Tribunal's decision, the Divisional Court quoted with approval the following passage from the ORHT decision:

> [3] … Therefore, I find that the Landlord has done everything in its power to attempt to accommodate the tenant to the point of undue hardship, and has thus satisfied its requirements under the Ontario Human Rights Code. Further, permitting the tenant to continue residing [in the] rental unit would constitute an undue hardship to the building Superintendent, in light of the safety concerns raised by the tenant's conduct.

In *Connelly v. Mary Lambert Swale Non-Profit Homes*,[14] the Tribunal found that the tenant was addicted to drugs and was operating a crack house in the complex. The Divisional Court found that the tenant's drug addiction must be considered a disability, but upheld the Tribunal's order evicting the tenant. The Court held that:

> [10] On the finding of the Tribunal, no accommodation is possible. The appellant denied he was dealing drugs from his apartment. He denied that his conduct created difficulties both for the respondent and its tenants.
>
> [11] The Tribunal found that the appellant's operation of a crack house substantially interfered with the rights of the other tenants.
>
> [12] We reject any suggestion there is an obligation on the respondent to permit the tenant to operate a crack house in order to accommodate his disability. We conclude that such an attempt at accommodation would be an undue hardship to the respondent by substantially interfering with the rights of the other tenants.

Subsection 17(2) of the Code also prescribes three considerations when assessing whether an accommodation would cause undue hardship. These are:

1. cost
2. outside sources of funding, if any
3. health and safety requirements, if any.

If issues relating to cost, outside sources of funding or health and safety requirements are relevant to the proceeding, it is the landlord's obligation to provide evidence respecting these three considerations if arguing that any or further accommodation would cause undue hardship.

Costs will amount to undue hardship if they are quantifiable, shown to be related to the accommodation, and are so substantial that they would alter the essential nature of the enterprise or so significant that they would substantially affect its viability.

For further guidance on undue hardship, see the Ontario Human Rights Commission's Policy and Guidelines on Disability and the Duty to Accommodate under "Policies" on the Commission's website at www.ohrc.on.ca.

Relief from eviction

In *Walmer Developments v. Wolch*[15] the Divisional Court held that the Ontario Rental Housing Tribunal (now the Board) must consider and apply the Code when exercising its authority to grant relief from eviction. A Member considers such relief pursuant to section 83 of the RTA. Section 83 states that the Member must have regard to all the circumstances to determine whether it would be unfair to refuse the landlord's eviction application or postpone the enforcement of the eviction order.

If the Member determines that the landlord has failed to accommodate a tenant covered by one or more of the categories contained in subsection 2(1) of the Code up to the point of undue hardship, the Member must consider relief from eviction in accordance with clause (a) of subsection 83(1) of the RTA. However, even if relief is granted, the Member may still consider whether other types of conditions and requirements should be ordered to address the conduct or problem at issue. The authority to make such orders comes from subsection 204(1) of the RTA.

In some cases a Member may find that there are no Code-related grounds for relief for eviction. For example, the Member may find that the reason for the landlord's application is unrelated to the fact that the tenant belongs to one or more of the categories contained in subsection 2(1) of the Code, or that the landlord has met the obligation to accommodate the tenant to the point of undue hardship. However, in these circumstances the Member must still consider granting relief from eviction having regard to all of the circumstances of the parties pursuant to section 83 of the RTA. For example, there may be no connection between a landlord's application for arrears of rent and the fact that the tenant uses a wheelchair. However, the Member could take into account the difficulty the tenant may experience in finding alternative wheelchair accessible accommodation, and thus delay enforcement of the eviction order pursuant to section 83.

3. Tenant applications

A tenant may allege in a tenant's application that the landlord has contravened the Code. Such allegations may relate to a number of different sections of the RTA and the Code.

For example, a tenant may allege that the landlord has substantially interfered with the tenant's reasonable enjoyment of the rental unit in contravention of section 22 of the RTA by failing to make changes to the unit that are necessary to accommodate the tenant's physical disability. The Member's consideration of such a claim will be similar to that described above with respect to Code issues raised pursuant to section 83 of the RTA. The Member must first determine whether the tenant falls

---

14 2007 CanLII 52787 (ONSCDC).

15 2003 CanLII 42163 (ONSCDC).

within one or more of the categories contained in subsection 2(1) of the Code and has been discriminated against by the landlord. The Member must then determine whether the landlord has accommodated the tenant to the point of undue hardship. If the tenant's claim is successful, the Member has the authority pursuant to clause (f) of subsection 31(1) of the RTA to order the landlord to make necessary changes to the rental unit or residential complex to accommodate the tenant's needs.

A tenant may also allege in a tenant's application that the landlord has harassed, obstructed, coerced, threatened or interfered with the tenant in contravention of section 25 of the RTA, and that the landlord acted in this way because the tenant is covered by one of the grounds set out in subsection 2(1) the Code. Such conduct may also contravene subsection 2(2) of the Code which provides that tenants have a right to freedom from harassment by the landlord or the landlord's agent. The Member will consider such claims in determining whether the landlord contravened the RTA, and if so, what the appropriate remedy should be.

4. Conflict between the RTA and the Code

Tribunals that can decide questions of law, such as the Board, have the jurisdiction to consider whether a legislative provision within its mandate is consistent with the Code. This does not mean that the Board has the authority to find that the legislative provision in question is invalid, as a Court may determine. However, if the Board finds that there is a conflict between a legislative provision and the Code, the Board has the authority to determine that the provision does not apply to the proceeding, pursuant to section 47 of the Code. Section 47 of the Code is applied when there is conflict between a legislative provision and the Code to ensure that the Code takes precedence.

Therefore, a party to a Board proceeding may argue that a particular section of the RTA should not be applied because it is in conflict with the Code's provisions.

Release Date: October 15, 2009

INTERPRETATION GUIDELINE #18
RESTRICTING PUBLIC ACCESS TO IN-PERSON AND ELECTRONIC HEARINGS

Interpretation Guidelines are intended to assist the parties in understanding the Board's usual interpretation of the law, to provide guidance to Members and promote consistency in decision-making. However, a Member is not required to follow a Guideline and may make a different decision depending on the facts of the case.

Rule 24 of the Board's Rules of Practice states that hearings will be open to the public unless the Member believes that there is sufficient reason to deny public access. Hearings closed to the public are called in camera hearings.

The right of the public to attend a hearing is based on the principle that the public is entitled to access to tribunals that decide disputes in a quasi-judicial proceeding. Parties and members of the public should be aware that Board hearings are open to the public, subject to the provisions for a closed hearing set out in section 9 of the *Statutory Powers Procedure Act* (SPPA). Section 9 provides that a hearing shall be open to the public except where:

> (a) matters involving public security may be disclosed; or
>
> (b) intimate financial or personal matters or other matters may be disclosed at the hearing of such a nature, having regard to the circumstances, that the desirability of avoiding disclosure thereof in the interests of any person affected or in the public interest outweighs the desirability of adhering to the principle that hearings be open to the public.

Factors that the Board may consider under the SPPA include:

- whether the request to close the hearing is based on something more than a mere desire for privacy;
- whether the disclosure of certain information would cause harm to public security or to the government, including consideration of the disclosure of confidential economic information, information concerning issues of national security or information concerning on-going police investigations;
- the potential harm a party may suffer if intimate details of their private life, including, financial and/or health information, were made public;
- the negative impact that access to the public may have to the ability of the parties to properly present their case;
- whether the case involves allegations of sexual assault, harassment, or child abuse and the potential identification of victims of sexual assault or child abuse;
- whether a timid witness' testimony would be compromised if not given in a closed setting;
- whether the case involves information about a young offender.

Electronic Hearings

In some cases, the Board will hold an electronic hearing, usually by telephone or video-conference. The SPPA requires that an electronic hearing be open to the public unless the Board is of the opinion that it is either not practical to hold a hearing that is open to the public, or one of the criteria for closing the hearing applies to the application.

There are a number of practical reasons why electronic hearings conducted by the Board may not be open to the public. For example, the hearing room may not be large enough to accommodate the public as well as the parties, their witnesses and the Member. Further information regarding electronic hearings can be found in Rule 21 of the Board's Rules of Practice.

Media Interests

Section 2(b) of the *Canadian Charter of Rights and Freedoms* ("the Charter") provides that freedom of expression, including freedom of the press, is a fundamental freedom. Having regard to the Charter, where the Board considers a request to hold the hearing in camera, members of the media who are present at the hearing should be given the opportunity to make submissions regarding whether the hearing should be closed. Where the media opposes a request to close the hearing, the Board may:

(i) decide to close the hearing;

(ii) keep the hearing open; or

(iii) hold an open hearing but issue a publication ban on evidence heard at the hearing.

When Will the Board Deal with a Request for an in Camera Hearing?

It is appropriate for a Member to hear a request for an in camera hearing as a preliminary motion. In deciding whether to restrict access to the hearing, the Member may hear evidence and submissions from the parties, their representatives and any other interested person (such as a member of the media) in a hearing room closed to the public. On the basis of the evidence and submissions, the Member will decide if the application itself will proceed as a hearing open to the public or in camera.

If the Member decides to hold the hearing in camera, access to the hearing will be limited to the parties and their representatives. Witnesses may be excluded in any hearing, whether open or in camera, by an order excluding a witness until the witness has given evidence. In some circumstances the hearing will be closed for only that portion in which the sensitive information is disclosed.

In order to avoid or reduce inconvenience to other parties and members of the public, a Board Member may deal with the request at of the end of the hearing block. Alternatively, a Member may proceed with a party's motion to close the hearing in the absence of the public, and, if the Member decides that the hearing itself should be closed, the Member may direct that hearing to be held down to the end of the hearing block, or, may adjourn it to another day.

Where a hearing is closed to the public, the Member will record the hearing separately from the other hearings in a hearing block.

Release Date: January 4, 2011

INTERPRETATION GUIDELINE #19
THE LANDLORD'S RIGHT OF ENTRY INTO
A RENTAL UNIT

Interpretation Guidelines are intended to assist the parties in understanding the Board's usual interpretation of the law, to provide guidance to Members and promote consistency in decision-making. However, a Member is not required to follow a Guideline and may make a different decision depending on the facts of the case.

A tenant has the right to possession and reasonable enjoyment of the rental unit. A landlord has the right to enter the rental unit in certain circumstances when the landlord follows the procedures set out in the *Residential Tenancies Act, 2006* ("the RTA").

Legislation

Sections 26 and 27 of the RTA describe the situations in which a landlord may enter the rental unit.

Entry Without Notice

Section 26 provides that a landlord may enter the rental unit without notice:

- in cases of emergency;
- If the tenant consents to the landlord entering the unit at the time the landlord enters;
- where the tenancy agreement requires the landlord to clean the rental unit at regular intervals, the landlord may enter at the times specified in the agreement, or, if no times are specified, between 8:00 a.m. and 8:00 p.m.; and
- if the landlord and the tenant have agreed the tenancy will be terminated or one of them has given notice of termination to the other, the landlord may enter the unit to show it to prospective tenants between 8 a.m. and 8 p.m. and, before entering, the landlord informs or makes a reasonable effort to inform the tenant of the landlord's intention to enter. A landlord must make reasonable efforts, depending upon the facts and circumstances of each case, to give the tenant advance notice in order to permit the tenant to be prepared for entry into the unit by the landlord to show the unit to prospective tenants.

A landlord may not enter the rental unit without notice to perform repairs even where the tenant has requested the repairs unless the landlord obtains the tenant's consent to enter the unit at the time the landlord goes to the unit to make the repairs.

Entry with Notice

Section 27 provides that a landlord may enter a rental unit in accordance with written notice given to the tenant at least 24 hours before the time of entry in the following circumstances:

- to carry out a repair or replacement or to do work in the unit;
- to allow a potential mortgagee or insurer of the residential complex to view the rental unit;
- to allow a person who holds a certificate of authorization within the meaning of the *Professional Engineers Act* or a certificate of practice within the meaning of the *Architects Act* or another qualified person to make a physical inspection of the rental unit to satisfy a requirement imposed under subsection 9(4) of the *Condominium Act, 1998;*

- to carry out an inspection of the rental unit, if,
  - (i) the inspection is for the purpose of determining whether or not or not the rental unit is in a good state of repair and fit for habitation and complies with health, safety, housing and maintenance standards, consistent with the landlord's obligations under subsection 20(1) or section 161 of the RTA; and
  - (ii) it is reasonable to carry out the inspection.
- for any other reasonable reason for entry set out in the tenancy agreement.

In addition, s. 27(2) of the RTA provides that the landlord, or, with the landlord's written authorization, a broker or salesperson registered under the *Real Estate and Business Brokers Act, 2002*, may enter a rental unit provided that they have given written notice to the tenant at least 24 hours before they enter to allow a potential purchaser to view the unit.

In any case where at least 24 hours written notice has been given to the tenant, the written notice must set out:

- the reason for entry;
- the date the landlord will enter; and
- the time of entry between 8:00 a.m. and 8:00 p.m.

Reason for Entry

The entry must be for one of the reasons set out in section 27, described above.

The notice should provide as many details as possible with respect to the proposed entry, including details with respect to the repair or replacement or with respect to an inspection of the rental unit. In considering whether or not the notice complies with the RTA, the Board may consider whether details about the entry have been provided to the tenant.

Who May Enter

The RTA gives a landlord the right to enter. A landlord's agent, for example, a superintendent or a person hired by the landlord, may also enter the rental unit on behalf of a landlord.

Where someone other than the landlord or the superintendent has been hired to do work in the unit, the landlord or the superintendent should attend with the hired person to permit entry into the unit by the person.

Specifying the Time of Entry

Where a specific time of entry is known, it should be stated in the notice. Where it is not possible to state a specific time of entry, the notice may provide a reasonable window of time for entry.

What is a reasonable window of time will depend upon the facts and circumstances in each case. Where the landlord exercises control over the work being done and who is doing the work, the notice should be reasonably specific with respect to the time for entry. Where the landlord does not exercise control over the work being done or the person who is doing the work, the notice should set out a reasonable window of time for entry.

For example, where the work is being done by a cable or telephone company and the company specifies a reasonable window of time when it will be at the rental unit, a landlord

may reasonably specify that same window. Where the same or similar work is being done in a number of units on the same day, a reasonable window of time may be specified. In determining whether the specified window of time is reasonable, consideration should be given to the type and complexity of repair, replacement or work being undertaken, the location of the work and the extent to which the entry affects the tenant's ability to use the rental unit.

The Divisional Court in *Wrona v. Toronto Community Housing Corporation* found that while a landlord is not required to specify the exact hour and minute of a required entry into a rental unit, a written notice providing for a nine hour period for entry to permit the landlord to carry out an annual inspection of smoke detector equipment does not comply with the requirements that the notice specify a time of entry between 8:00 a.m. and 8:00 p.m.

Frequency of Entry

In carrying out repairs, replacements and other work, the landlord should make reasonable efforts to limit the frequency of entries to those actually necessary to accomplish the work.

The landlord should also make reasonable efforts to limit the frequency of entries in other circumstances allowed under section 27 of the RTA such as carrying out inspections of the rental unit.

If the Board determines that the landlord has made unnecessary or unreasonable entries into the rental unit, the Board may find that the landlord has interfered with or harassed the tenant or that the landlord has substantially interfered with the tenant's reasonable enjoyment of the rental unit or the residential complex.

Methods of Service of the Notice

The written notice by the landlord for entry into the rental unit may be given to the tenant in one of the methods for giving notice set out in section 191 of the RTA. As permitted by Rule 5.1(d) of the Board's Rules of Practice, the written notice for entry may also be given by posting it on the door of the rental unit.

Tenants' Rights and Responsibilities

A tenant may remain in the rental unit while the landlord exercises their right of entry. However, the landlord's right of entry can be exercised if the tenant is not in the rental unit at the time of entry.

A tenant has the right to deny entry to the landlord if the landlord has not met the requirements under the RTA relating to entry. A tenant does not have the right to deny entry simply because the time of entry is not convenient to the tenant.

The tenant must:
  - (i) not interfere with the landlord's right of entry;
  - (ii) not interfere with the landlord and its agents; and
  - (iii) take whatever steps are necessary to provide access to rooms where the work is to occur, including safely restraining pets in the rental unit.

Statutory Guideline Rent Increases, 1975-2011

Guideline percentage	Time period	Statute
8	July 29, 1975 – October 26, 1977	RPRRA[1]
6	October 27, 1977 – July 31, 1985	RPRRA, RTA[2]
4	August 1, 1985 – December 31, 1986	RTA, RRRA[3]
5.2	January 1, 1987 – December 31, 1987	RRRA
4.7	January 1, 1988 – December 31, 1988	RRRA
4.6	January 1, 1989 – December 31, 1989	RRRA
4.6	January 1, 1990 – December 31, 1990	RRRA
5.4	January 1, 1991 – December 31, 1991	RRRA
6	January 1, 1992 – December 31, 1992	RRRA
4.9	January 1, 1993 – December 31, 1993	RCA[4]
3.2	January 1, 1994 – December 31, 1994	RCA
2.9	January 1, 1995 – December 31, 1995	RCA
2.8	January 1, 1996 – December 31, 1996	RCA
2.8	January 1, 1997 – December 31, 1997	RCA
3.0	January 1, 1998 – December 31, 1998	RCA
3.0	January 1, 1999 – December 31, 1999	TPA[5]
2.6	January 1, 2000 – December 31, 2000	TPA
2.9	January 1, 2001 – December 31, 2001	TPA
3.9	January 1, 2002 – December 31, 2002	TPA
2.9	January 1, 2003 – December 31, 2003	TPA
2.9	January 1, 2004 – December 31, 2004	TPA
1.5	January 1, 2005 – December 31, 2005	TPA
2.1	January 1, 2006 – December 31, 2006	TPA
2.6	January 1, 2007 – December 31, 2007	TPA
1.4	January 1, 2008 – December 31, 2008	RTA
1.8	January 1, 2009 – December 31, 2009	RTA
2.1	January 1, 2010 – December 31, 2010	RTA
0.7	January 1, 2011 – December 31, 2011	RTA

[1] *Residential Premises Rent Review Act.*

[2] *Residential Tenancies Act.*

[3] *Residential Rent Regulation Act.*

[4] *Rent Control Act, 1992.*

[5] *Tenant Protection Act, 1997.*

Table of Concordance

Residential Tenancies Act, 2006

s. 1	Purposes of Act
s. 2	Interpretation
s. 3	Application of Act
s. 4	Provisions conflicting with Act void
s. 5	Exemptions from Act
s. 6	Other exemptions
s. 7	Exemptions related to social, etc., housing
s. 8	Rent geared to income
s. 9	Application to determine issues
s. 10	Selecting prospective tenants
s. 11	Information to be provided by landlord
s. 12	Tenancy agreement
s. 13	Commencement of tenancy
s. 14	"No pet" provisions void
s. 15	Acceleration clause void
s. 16	Minimize losses
s. 17	Covenants interdependent
s. 18	Covenants running with land
s. 19	Frustrated contracts
s. 20	Landlord's responsibility to repair
s. 21	Landlord's responsibility re services
s. 22	Landlord not to interfere with reasonable enjoyment
s. 23	Landlord not to harass, etc.
s. 24	Changing locks
s. 25	Privacy
s. 26	Entry without notice
s. 27	Entry with notice
s. 28	Entry by canvassers
s. 29	Tenant applications
s. 30	Order, repair, comply with standards
s. 31	Other orders re s. 29
s. 32	Eviction with termination order
s. 33	Tenant's responsibility for cleanliness
s. 34	Tenant's responsibility for repair of damage
s. 35	Changing locks

Tenant Protection Act, 1997

	N/A
s. 1	Interpretation
s. 2	Application of Act
s. 16	Provisions conflicting with Act void
s. 3	Exemptions from Act
s. 4	Exemptions from rules relating to rent
s. 5	Exemptions related to social, etc., housing
s. 6	Rent geared to income
s. 7	Application to determine issues
s. 38	Selecting prospective tenants
	N/A
s. 8	Tenancy agreement
s. 9	Commencement of tenancy
s. 15	"No pet" provisions void
s. 14	Acceleration clause void
s. 13	Minimize Losses
s. 11	Covenants interdependent
s. 12	Covenants running with land
s. 10	Frustrated contracts
s. 24	Landlord's responsibility to repair
s. 25	Landlord's responsibility re services
s. 26	Landlord not to interfere with reasonable enjoyment
s. 27	Landlord not to harass, etc.
s. 23	Changing locks
s. 19	Privacy
s. 20	Entry without notice
s. 21	Entry with notice
s. 22	Entry by canvassers
s. 32	Tenant applications
s. 110(2)	Application for relief
s. 34	Order, repair, comply with standards
s. 110(2)	Application for relief
s. 35	Other orders re s. 32
	N/A
s. 29	Cleanliness
s. 30	Tenant's responsibility for damage
s. 23	Changing locks
s. 36	Locking systems, landlord application re alteration
s. 37	Locking systems, order

Residential Tenancies Act, 2006		Tenant Protection Act, 1997	
s. 36	Tenant not to harass, etc.	s. 28	Tenant not to harass, etc.
s. 37	Termination only in accordance with Act	s. 39	Tenancy terminated
s. 38	Deemed renewal where no notice	s. 40	Deemed renewal where no notice
s. 39	Restriction on recovery of possession	s. 41	Restriction on recovery of possession
s. 40	Distress abolished	s. 31	Distress abolished
s. 41	Disposal of abandoned property if unit vacated	s. 42	Disposal of abandoned property, unit vacated
s. 42	Disposal of property, unit abandoned	s. 79	Landlord may dispose of property, abandoned unit
s. 43	Notice of termination	s. 43	Notice of termination
s. 44	Period of notice	s. 47	Period of notice
s. 45	Effect of payment	s. 45	Effect of payment
s. 46	Where notice void	s. 44	Where notice void
s. 47	Tenant's notice to terminate, end of period or term	s. 46	Tenant's notice to terminate tenancy, end of period or term
s. 48	Notice, landlord personally, etc., requires unit	s. 51	Notice, landlord personally, etc., requires unit
s. 49	Notice, purchaser personally requires unit	s. 52	Where purchaser personally requires unit
s. 50	Notice, demolition, conversion or repairs	s. 53	Notice, demolition, conversion or repairs
s. 51	Conversion to condominium, security of tenure	s. 54	Conversion to condominium, security of tenure
s. 52	Compensation, demolition or conversion	s. 55	Compensation, demolition or conversion
s. 53	Tenant's right of first refusal, repair or renovation	s. 56	Tenant's right of first refusal, repair or renovation
s. 54	Tenant's right to compensation, repair or renovation	s. 57	Tenant's right to compensation, repair or renovation
s. 55	Tenant's right to compensation, severance	s. 58	Tenant's right to compensation, severance
s. 56	Security of tenure, severance, subdivision	s. 59	Security of tenure, severance, subdivision
s. 57	Former tenant's application where notice given in bad faith	s. 32(1)8–10	Tenant applications
s. 58	Notice at end of term or period, additional grounds	s. 60	Notice end of term, additional grounds
s. 59	Nonpayment of rent	s. 61	Nonpayment of rent
s. 60	Termination for cause, misrepresentation of income	s. 62	Termination for cause, illegal acts, misrepresentation
s. 61	Termination for cause, illegal act		
s. 62	Termination for cause, damage	s. 63	Termination for cause, damage
s. 63	Termination for cause, shorter notice period		N/A
s. 64	Termination for cause, reasonable enjoyment	s. 64	Termination for cause, reasonable enjoyment
s. 65	Termination for cause, reasonable enjoyment of landlord in small building		N/A
s. 66	Termination for cause, act impairs safety	s. 65	Termination for cause, act impairs safety
s. 67	Termination for cause, too many persons	s. 66	Termination for cause, too many persons
s. 68	Notice of termination, further contravention	s. 67	Notice of termination, further contravention
s. 69	Application by landlord	s. 69	Application by landlord
s. 70	No application during remedy period	s. 74	Notice gives seven days to correct
s. 71	Immediate application	s. 75	Immediate application
s. 72	Landlord or purchaser personally requires premises	s. 70	Landlord personally requires premises
s. 73	Demolition, conversion, repairs	s. 71	Demolition, conversion, repairs
s. 74	Nonpayment of rent	s. 72	Nonpayment of rent
s. 75	Illegal act	s. 73	Illegal act or misrepresentation of income
s. 76	Application based on animals	s. 74	Correction; animals

Residential Tenancies Act, 2006

s. 77	Agreement to terminate, tenant's notice
s. 78	Application based on previous order, mediated settlement
s. 79	Abandonment of rental unit
s. 80	Effective date of order
s. 81	Expiry date of order
s. 82	Tenant issues in application for nonpayment of rent
s. 83	Power of Board, eviction
s. 84	Expedited eviction order
s. 85	Effect of eviction order
s. 86	Compensation, unit not vacated
s. 87	Application
s. 88	Arrears of rent when tenant abandons or vacates without notice
s. 89	Compensation for damage
s. 90	Compensation, misrepresentation of income
s. 91	Death of Tenant
s. 92	Landlord may dispose of property
s. 93	Termination of tenancy [Superintendent's Premises]
s. 94	Application to Board
s. 95	Assignment of tenancy
s. 96	Tenant's notice to terminate, refusal of assignment
s. 97	Subletting rental unit
s. 98	Tenant application
s. 99	Tenant's notice, application re subtenant
s. 100	Unauthorized occupancy
s. 101	Overholding subtenant
s. 102	Compensation, overholding subtenant
s. 103	Compensation, unauthorized occupant
s. 104	Miscellaneous new tenancy agreements
s. 105	Security deposits, limitation
s. 106	Rent deposit may be required
s. 107	Rent deposit, prospective tenant
s. 108	Postdated cheques, etc.
s. 109	Receipt for payment
s. 110	Landlord's duty, rent increases
s. 111	Landlord not to charge more than lawful rent
s. 112	Lawful rent when this section comes into force
s. 113	Lawful rent for new tenant
s. 114	Notice to new tenant, order under par. 6, 7 or 8 of s. 30 (1) in effect
s. 115	Application by new tenant
s. 116	Notice of rent increase required
s. 117	Compliance by landlord, no notice required

Tenant Protection Act, 1997

s. 76	Agreement to terminate, tenant's notice
s. 77	Application based on previous order, mediated settlement
s. 78	Abandonment of rental unit
s. 83	Effective date of order
s. 83.1	Expiry date of order
	N/A
s. 84	Power of Tribunal, eviction
	N/A
s. 85	Effect of eviction order
s. 45	Compensation, unit not vacated
s. 86	Compensation/Arrears of rent
	N/A
s. 87	Compensation for damage
s. 88	Compensation, misrepresentation of income
s. 49	Death of tenant
s. 50	Landlord may dispose of property
s. 68	Superintendent's premises
s. 80	Superintendent's premises
s. 17	Assignment of tenancy
s. 48	Notice by tenant [assignment refused]
s. 18	Subletting rental unit
s. 32(1)1	Tenant applications
s. 32(2)	Tenant applications
s. 33	Order re assignment, sublet
s. 90	Tenant's notice, application re subtenant
s. 81	Unauthorized occupancy [application]
s. 86(2.1)	Compensation, unauthorized occupant
s. 82	Overholding subtenant
s. 89	Compensation, overholding subtenant
s. 45	Compensation, unit not vacated
s. 125	Miscellaneous new tenancy agreements
s. 117	Security deposits, limitation
s. 118	Rent deposit may be required
s. 118.1	Rent deposit, prospective tenant
s. 119	Postdated cheques
s. 120	Receipt for payment
s. 122	Landlord's duty, rent increases
s. 121	Landlord not to charge more than lawful rent
s. 123	Lawful rent when this Act comes into force
s. 124	New tenant
	N/A
	N/A
s. 127	Notice of rent increase required
	N/A

Residential Tenancies Act, 2006

s. 118	Deemed acceptance where no notice of termination
s. 119	12-month rule
s. 120	Guideline increase
s. 121	Agreement
s. 122	Tenant application
s. 123	Additional services, etc.
s. 124	Coerced agreement void
s. 125	Decrease in services, etc.
	N/A
s. 126	Application for above guideline increase
s. 127	Two ordered increases
s. 128	Utilities [Reductions of Rent]
s. 129	Capital expenditures [Reductions of Rent]
s. 130	Reduction in services
s. 131	Municipal taxes
s. 132	Application for variation
s. 133	Application, reduction in municipal taxes
s. 134	Additional charges prohibited
s. 135	Money collected illegally
s. 136	Rent deemed lawful
s. 137	Suite meters
s. 138	Apportionment of utility costs
s. 139	Agreement required
s. 140	Information to tenant
s. 141	Tenancy agreement: consultation, cancellation
s. 142	Entry to check condition of tenant
s. 143	Assignment, subletting in care homes
s. 144	Notice of termination
s. 145	Termination, care homes
s. 146	Notice of termination, demolition, conversion or repairs
s. 147	External care providers
s. 148	Transferring tenancy
s. 149	Rent in care home
s. 150	Notice of increased charges
s. 151	Certain charges permitted
s. 152	Application
s. 153	Interpretation
s. 154	Park rules
s. 155	Information about property assessment
s. 156	Tenant's right to sell, etc.
s. 157	Landlord's right of first refusal
s. 158	Advertising a sale
s. 159	Assignment
s. 160	Restraint of trade prohibited
s. 161	Responsibility of landlord
s. 162	Mobile home abandoned
s. 163	Death of mobile home owner
s. 164(1)	Termination under s. 50
s. 164(2)	Termination under s. 50

Tenant Protection Act, 1997

s. 128	Deemed acceptance where no notice of termination
s. 126	12-month rule
s. 129	Guideline increase
s. 130	Agreement
s. 131	Tenant application
s. 132	Additional services
s. 133	Coerced agreement void
s. 134	Decrease in services, etc
s. 135	Increase to maximum rent
s. 138	Increased operating costs, capital expenditures
s. 139	Two ordered increases
	N/A
	N/A
s. 142	Reduction in rent, reduction in services
s. 136	Municipal taxes reduced
s. 137	Application for variation
s. 143	Reduction in rent, reduction in taxes
s. 140	Additional charges prohibited
s. 144	Money collected illegally
s. 141	Rent deemed lawful
	N/A
	N/A
s. 91	Agreement required
s. 92	Information to tenant
s. 93	Tenancy agreement: consultation, cancellation
s. 94	Entry check condition of tenant
s. 95	Assignment, subletting in care homes
s. 96	Notice of termination
s. 97	Termination, care homes
s. 98	Notice of termination, demolition, conversion or repairs
	N/A
s. 99	Transferring tenancy
s. 100	Rent in care home
s. 101	Notice of increased charges
s. 102	Certain charges permitted
s. 103	Part applies to land lease communities
s. 104	Interpretation
	N/A
	N/A
s. 105	Tenant's right to sell, etc.
s. 106	Landlord's right of first refusal
s. 107	Advertising a sale
s. 108	Assignment
s. 109	Restraint of trade prohibited
s. 110	Responsibility of landlord
s. 111	Mobile home abandoned
s. 112	Death of mobile home owner
s. 113	Extended notice of termination, special cases
	N/A

Residential Tenancies Act, 2006

s. 165	Assignment of existing tenancy agreement
s. 166	Entrance and exit fees limited
s. 167	Increased capital expenditures
s. 168	Board
s. 169	Composition
s. 170	Chair and vicechair
s. 171	Quorum
s. 172	Conflict of interest
s. 173	Expiry of term
s. 174	Power to determine law and fact
s. 175	Members, mediators not compellable
s. 176	Rules and Guidelines Committee
s. 177	Information on rights and obligations
s. 178	Employees
s. 179	Professional assistance
s. 180	Reports
s. 181	Board may set, charge fees
s. 182	Fee refunded, review
s. 183	Expeditious procedures
s. 184	SPPA applies
s. 185	Form of application
s. 186	Combining applications
s. 187	Parties
s. 188	Service
s. 189	Notice by Board
s. 190	Board may extend, shorten time
	N/A
s. 191	How notice or document given
s. 192	How notice or document given to Board
s. 193	Time
s. 194	Board may mediate
s. 195	Money paid to Board
s. 196	Board may refuse to proceed if money owing
s. 197	Where Board may dismiss
s. 198	Joinder and severance of applications
s. 199	Application severed
s. 200	Amendment and withdrawal of applications
s. 201	Other powers of Board
s. 202	Findings of Board
	N/A
s. 203	Determinations related to housing assistance
s. 204	Conditions in order
s. 205	Order payment
s. 206	Agreement to settle matter
	N/A
s. 207	Monetary jurisdiction; deduction of rent; interest
s. 208	Notice of decision
s. 209	Order final, binding
s. 210	Appeal rights
s. 211	Board may appeal Court decision
s. 212	Substantial compliance sufficient

Tenant Protection Act, 1997

s. 114	New tenant
s. 115	Entrance and exit fees limited
s. 116	Increased capital expenditures
s. 157	Tribunal established
s. 158	Composition
s. 159	Chair and vicechair
s. 160	Quorum
s. 161	Conflict of interest
	N/A
s. 162	Power to determine law and fact
s. 163	Members, mediators not compellable
s. 164	Rules and Guidelines Committee
s. 165	Information on rights and obligations
s. 166	Employees
s. 167	Professional assistance
s. 168	Reports
s. 169	Tribunal may set, charge fees
s. 170	Fee refunded, review
s. 171	Expeditious procedures
s. 184	SPPA applies
s. 172	Form of application
s. 173	Combining applications
s. 174	Parties
s. 175	Service
	N/A
s. 176	Tribunal may extend, shorten time
s. 177	File dispute
s. 178	How notice or document given
s. 179	How notice or document given to Tribunal
s. 180	Time
s. 181	Tribunal may mediate
s. 182	Money paid to Tribunal
s. 182.1	Tribunal may refuse to proceed if money owing
s. 183	Where Tribunal may dismiss
s. 185	Joinder and severance of applications
s. 185.1	Application severed
s. 186	Amendment and withdrawal of applications
s. 187	Other powers of Tribunal
s. 188	Findings of Tribunal
s. 189	Correction of deemed rent
	N/A
s. 190	Conditions in order
s. 191	Order payment
	N/A
s. 192	Default orders
s. 193	Monetary jurisdiction; deduction of rent; interest
s. 194	Notice of decision
s. 195	Order final, binding
s. 196	Appeal rights
s. 197	Tribunal may appeal Court decision
s. 198	Substantial compliance sufficient

Residential Tenancies Act, 2006		Tenant Protection Act, 1997	
s. 213	Electronic documents	s. 198.1	Electronic documents
s. 214	Contingency fees, limitation	s. 199	Contingency fees, limitation
s. 215	Definition	s. 145	Definition
s. 216	Bylaws respecting vital services	s. 146	Bylaws respecting vital services
s. 217	Notice by supplier	s. 147	Notice by supplier
s. 218	Inspection	s. 148	Inspection
s. 219	Services by municipality	s. 149	Services by municipality
s. 220	Appeal	s. 150	Appeal
s. 221	Payments transferred	s. 151	Payments transferred
s. 222	Use of money	s. 152	Use of money
s. 223	Immunity	s. 153	Immunity
s. 224	Prescribed standards and complaints	s. 154	Prescribed standards and complaints
s. 225	Inspector's work order	s. 155	Inspector's work order
s. 226	Review of work order	s. 156	Review of work order
s. 227	Duties of Minister	s. 200	Duties of Minister
s. 228	Delegation	s. 201	Delegation
s. 229	Investigators and inspectors	s. 202	Investigators and inspectors
s. 230	Inspections	s. 203	Inspection and investigation
s. 231	Warrant	s. 204	Warrant
s. 232	Protection from personal liability	s. 205	Protection from personal liability
s. 233	Offences requiring knowledge	s. 206(1)	Offences
s. 234	Other offences	s. 206(2)	Other offences
s. 235	Harassment, interference with reasonable enjoyment	s. 206(3)	Harassment, interference with reasonable enjoyment
s. 236	Attempts	s. 206(4)	Attempts
s. 237	Directors and officers	s. 206(5)	Directors and officers
s. 238	Penalties	ss. 206(6), (7)	Penalties
s. 239	Limitations	ss. 206(8), (9)	Limitations
s. 240	Evidence	s. 207	Evidence
s. 241	Regulations	s. 208	Regulations
s. 242	Applications made under *Tenant Protection Act, 1997*	N/A	
s. 243	Proceedings before other bodies under earlier legislation	N/A	
s. 244	Orders, etc., under former Act	N/A	
s. 245	Information from former Rent Registry	N/A	
s. 246	Use of certain forms	N/A	
ss. 247 to 261	Amendments to other Acts	N/A	
ss. 262 to 263	Commencement date and short title	N/A	

Discussion of Rent Discounts

As noted in Chapter 16, Increasing the Rent, this appendix addresses how to calculate the lawful rent, especially if the landlord has not followed the discount rules. The reference to the effective rent in the examples below is not a legislative concept. Rather, it is a concept borrowed from commercial leasing, which enables the landlord (or the tenant) to consider the amount of rent that the face rent and discounts are equivalent to if the tenant were paying the same amount during the period of the tenancy.

Landlords can give a discount by providing a rent-free period or periods of up to three months. If a discount is provided at all, the most common discount is one month's rent. In particularly soft markets, discounts can sometimes reach two months' rent. However, as a practical matter, most landlords find that giving a two-month discount results in the new tenant moving out at the end of the lease period.

The discount rules are found in s. 111 of the *Residential Tenancies Act* (RTA), and in ss. 10 through 14 of O. Reg. 516/06.

To determine the lawful rent, add the rent actually paid to the eligible discount and divide that amount by the number of rental periods in the 12-month period: O. Reg. 516/06, s. 12(2). The other relevant sections and subsections of ss. 10 to 14 of O. Reg. 516/06 provide the details of eligible discounts and the interaction between a prompt payment discount and other discounts.

The best way to learn the discounting rules is by working through various examples. Review the following examples carefully and be sure that you understand why the discounts in examples G1, G2, G3, and G4 are valid and why the discounts in examples G5 and G6 do not accomplish what was intended.

Example G1   **Valid Discount (as per RTA s. 111(2)(a) and O. Reg. 516/06, s. 10)**

Face rent:	$1,000 per month, with the first month rent-free
Rent payments:	$0 for month 1, $1,000 per month for months 2 to 12
Total rent paid:	$11,000 per year
Lawful rent:	$1,000 per month, calculated as [($1,000 × 11) + $1,000] ÷ 12
Effective rent:	$916.67 per month, calculated as $11,000 ÷ 12

Example G2   **Valid Discount (as per RTA s. 111(2)(c) and O. Reg. 516/06, subparagraph 12(6)1.i)**

Face rent:	$1,000 per month, with a discount of one month's rent allowed over the first 8 months ($125 discount per month for 8 months)
Rent payments:	$875 per month for months 1 to 8, $1,000 per month for months 9 to 12
Total rent paid:	$11,000 per year
Lawful rent:	$1,000 per month, calculated as [($875 × 8) + ($1,000 × 4) + $1,000] ÷ 12
Effective rent:	$916.67 per month, calculated as $11,000 ÷ 12

Example G3   **Valid Discount (as per RTA s. 111(2)(c) and O. Reg. 516/06, subparagraph 12(6)1.i)**

Face rent:	$1,000 per month, discount of a half-month free in months 1 and 7
Rent payments:	$500 for month 1, $1,000 for months 2 to 6, $500 for month 7, and $1,000 for months 8 to 12
Total rent paid:	$11,000 per year
Lawful rent:	$1,000 per month, calculated as [($500 × 2) + ($1,000 × 10) + $1,000] ÷ 12
Effective rent:	$916.67 per month, calculated as $11,000 ÷ 12

Example G4   **Valid Discount (as per RTA s. 111(2)(a) and O. Reg. 516/06, s. 10)**

Face rent:	$1,000 per month, with the first 2 months free
Rent payments:	$0 for months 1 and 2, $1,000 for months 3 to 12
Total rent paid:	$10,000 per year
Lawful rent:	$1,000 per month, calculated as [($1,000 × 10) + $2,000] ÷ 12
Effective rent:	$833.33 per month, calculated as $10,000 ÷ 12

Example G5   **Invalid Discount**

Face rent:	$1,000 per month, one month free, spread over the whole term of the tenancy ($83.33 discount per month)
Rent payments:	$916.67 for months 1 to 12
Total rent paid:	$11,000 per year
Lawful rent:	$972.22 per month, calculated as [($916.67 × 12) + ($83.33 × 8)] ÷ 12
Effective rent:	$916.67 per month, calculated as $11,000 ÷ 12

Note: The lawful rent is calculated using the maximum eligible number of months—namely, 8. Even though the lawful rent is not as high as the face rent, the landlord here is not breaking the law in any way because the rent actually collected, $916.67, is lower than the lawful rent, $972.22, in each month. In the following year, the landlord would be charging an illegal rent increase, and an unlawful rent, if he or she applied a full guideline rent increase to the $1,000 face rent.

Example G6   Invalid Discount

Face rent: $1,000 per month, with the first 4 months free

Rent payments: $0 for months 1 to 4, $1,000 for months 5 to 12

Total rent paid: $8,000 per year

Lawful rent: $916.67 per month, calculated as [($1,000 × 8) + $3,000] ÷ 12

Effective rent: $666.67 per month, calculated as $8,000 ÷ 12

Note: The lawful rent is calculated using the maximum eligible discount of $3,000 ($1,000 × 3 rent-free months). Here it is arguable that the landlord is charging an unlawful rent because the discount pattern is not eligible and in some months the landlord is charging $1,000, whereas the lawful rent is $916.67.

DISCOUNTS IN ORAL TENANCY AGREEMENTS

Eligible discounts in oral tenancy agreements, other than prompt-payment discounts, are limited to the largest discount in one rental period. When rent is paid monthly, one rental period is one month.

Example G1 is valid for an oral tenancy agreement.

For an oral tenancy agreement, lawful rent in example G2 is $927.08, recalculated as follows:

[($875 × 8) + ($1,000 × 4) + $125] ÷ 12

For an oral tenancy agreement, lawful rent in example G3 is $958.33, recalculated as follows:

[($500 × 2) + ($1,000 × 10) + $500] ÷ 12

For an oral tenancy agreement, lawful rent in example G4 is $916.67, recalculated as follows:

[($0 × 2) + ($1,000 × 10) + $1,000] ÷ 12

For an oral tenancy agreement, lawful rent in example G5 is $923.61, recalculated as follows:

[($916.67 × 12) + $83.33] ÷ 12

For an oral tenancy agreement, lawful rent in example G6 is $750, recalculated as follows:

[($0 × 4) + ($1,000 × 8) + $1,000] ÷ 12

DISCOUNTS IN SUBSEQUENT YEARS

Discounts may be used in subsequent years, provided that they follow the same limits.

In example G7, below, it is assumed that the guideline for year 2 is 2 percent.

Example G7   (Example G1 Continued for Year 2)

Face rent:	$1,020 per month
Rent payments:	$0 for month 1, $1,020 per month for months 2 to 12
Total rent paid:	$11,220 per year
Lawful rent:	$1,020 per month, calculated as [($1,020 × 11) + $1,020] ÷ 12
Effective rent:	$935 per month (2% more than $916.67 per month)

A landlord can remove a discount, or switch discount patterns from year to year, as long as the landlord complies with the limits on amount and timing.

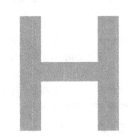

Human Rights Code: Excerpts Related to Rental Housing

RSO 1990, Chapter H.19

CONTENTS

. . .

PART I   FREEDOM FROM DISCRIMINATION

Services

1. Every person has a right to equal treatment with respect to services, goods and facilities, without discrimination because of race, ancestry, place of origin, colour, ethnic origin, citizenship, creed, sex, sexual orientation, age, marital status, family status or disability.

Accommodation

2(1) Every person has a right to equal treatment with respect to the occupancy of accommodation, without discrimination because of race, ancestry, place of origin, colour, ethnic origin, citizenship, creed, sex, sexual orientation, age, marital status, family status, disability or the receipt of public assistance.

Harassment in accommodation

(2) Every person who occupies accommodation has a right to freedom from harassment by the landlord or agent of the landlord or by an occupant of the same building because of race, ancestry, place of origin, colour, ethnic origin, citizenship, creed, age, marital status, family status, disability or the receipt of public assistance.

Contracts

3. Every person having legal capacity has a right to contract on equal terms without discrimination because of race, ancestry, place of origin, colour, ethnic origin, citizenship, creed, sex, sexual orientation, age, marital status, family status or disability.

Accommodation of person under eighteen

4(1) Every sixteen or seventeen year old person who has withdrawn from parental control has a right to equal treatment with respect to occupancy of and contracting for accommodation without discrimination because the person is less than eighteen years old.

Idem

(2) A contract for accommodation entered into by a sixteen or seventeen year old person who has withdrawn from parental control is enforceable against that person as if the person were eighteen years old.

Employment

5(1) Every person has a right to equal treatment with respect to employment without discrimination because of race, ancestry, place of origin, colour, ethnic origin, citizenship, creed, sex, sexual orientation, age, record of offences, marital status, family status or disability.

Harassment in employment

(2) Every person who is an employee has a right to freedom from harassment in the workplace by the employer or agent of the employer or by another employee because of race, ancestry, place of origin, colour, ethnic origin, citizenship, creed, age, record of offences, marital status, family status or disability.

Vocational associations

6. Every person has a right to equal treatment with respect to membership in any trade union, trade or occupational association or self-governing profession without discrimination because of race, ancestry, place of origin, colour, ethnic origin, citizenship, creed, sex, sexual orientation, age, marital status, family status or disability.

Sexual harassment
Harassment because of sex in accommodation

7(1) Every person who occupies accommodation has a right to freedom from harassment because of sex by the landlord or agent of the landlord or by an occupant of the same building.

Harassment because of sex in workplaces

(2) Every person who is an employee has a right to freedom from harassment in the workplace because of sex by his or her employer or agent of the employer or by another employee.

Sexual solicitation by a person in position to confer benefit, etc.

(3) Every person has a right to be free from,

(a) a sexual solicitation or advance made by a person in a position to confer, grant or deny a benefit or advancement to the person where the person making the solicitation or advance knows or ought reasonably to know that it is unwelcome; or

(b) a reprisal or a threat of reprisal for the rejection of a sexual solicitation or advance where the reprisal is made or threatened by a person in a position to confer, grant or deny a benefit or advancement to the person.

Reprisals

8. Every person has a right to claim and enforce his or her rights under this Act, to institute and participate in proceedings under this Act and to refuse to infringe a right of another person under this Act, without reprisal or threat of reprisal for so doing.

Infringement prohibited

9. No person shall infringe or do, directly or indirectly, anything that infringes a right under this Part.

PART II   INTERPRETATION AND APPLICATION
Definitions re: Parts I and II

10(1) In Part I and in this Part,

"age" means an age that is 18 years or more;

"disability" means,

(a) any degree of physical disability, infirmity, malformation or disfigurement that is caused by bodily injury, birth defect or illness and, without limiting the generality of the foregoing, includes diabetes mellitus, epilepsy, a brain injury, any degree of paralysis, amputation, lack of physical co-ordination, blindness or visual impediment, deafness or hearing impediment, muteness or speech impediment, or physical reliance on a guide dog or other animal or on a wheelchair or other remedial appliance or device,

(b) a condition of mental impairment or a developmental disability,

(c) a learning disability, or a dysfunction in one or more of the processes involved in understanding or using symbols or spoken language,

(d) a mental disorder, or

(e) an injury or disability for which benefits were claimed or received under the insurance plan established under the *Workplace Safety and Insurance Act, 1997*;

"equal" means subject to all requirements, qualifications and considerations that are not a prohibited ground of discrimination;

"family status" means the status of being in a parent and child relationship;

"group insurance" means insurance whereby the lives or well-being or the lives and well-being of a number of persons are insured severally under a single contract between an insurer and an association or an employer or other person;

"harassment" means engaging in a course of vexatious comment or conduct that is known or ought reasonably to be known to be unwelcome;

"marital status" means the status of being married, single, widowed, divorced or separated and includes the status of living with a person in a conjugal relationship outside marriage;

"record of offences" means a conviction for,

(a) an offence in respect of which a pardon has been granted under the *Criminal Records Act* (Canada) and has not been revoked, or

(b) an offence in respect of any provincial enactment;

"services" does not include a levy, fee, tax or periodic payment imposed by law;

"spouse" means the person to whom a person is married or with whom the person is living in a conjugal relationship outside marriage.

Pregnancy

(2) The right to equal treatment without discrimination because of sex includes the right to equal treatment without discrimination because a woman is or may become pregnant.

Past and presumed disabilities

(3) The right to equal treatment without discrimination because of disability includes the right to equal treatment without discrimination because a person has or has had a disability or is believed to have or to have had a disability.

Constructive discrimination

11(1) A right of a person under Part I is infringed where a requirement, qualification or factor exists that is not discrimination on a prohibited ground but that results in the exclusion, restriction or preference of a group of persons who are identified by a prohibited ground of discrimination and of whom the person is a member, except where,

   (a) the requirement, qualification or factor is reasonable and bona fide in the circumstances; or

   (b) it is declared in this Act, other than in section 17, that to discriminate because of such ground is not an infringement of a right.

Idem

(2) The Tribunal or a court shall not find that a requirement, qualification or factor is reasonable and bona fide in the circumstances unless it is satisfied that the needs of the group of which the person is a member cannot be accommodated without undue hardship on the person responsible for accommodating those needs, considering the cost, outside sources of funding, if any, and health and safety requirements, if any.

Idem

(3) The Tribunal or a court shall consider any standards prescribed by the regulations for assessing what is undue hardship.

Discrimination because of association

12. A right under Part I is infringed where the discrimination is because of relationship, association or dealings with a person or persons identified by a prohibited ground of discrimination..

Announced intention to discriminate

13(1) A right under Part I is infringed by a person who publishes or displays before the public or causes the publication or display before the public of any notice, sign, symbol, emblem, or other similar representation that indicates the intention of the person to infringe a right under Part I or that is intended by the person to incite the infringement of a right under Part I.

Opinion

(2) Subsection (1) shall not interfere with freedom of expression of opinion.

Special programs

14(1) A right under Part I is not infringed by the implementation of a special program designed to relieve hardship or economic disadvantage or to assist disadvantaged persons or groups to achieve or attempt to achieve equal opportunity or that is likely to contribute to the elimination of the infringement of rights under Part I.

Application to Commission

(2) A person may apply to the Commission for a designation of a program as a special program for the purposes of subsection (1).

Designation by Commission

(3) Upon receipt of an application, the Commission may,

   (a) designate the program as a special program if, in its opinion, the program meets the requirements of subsection (1); or

   (b) designate the program as a special program on the condition that the program make such modifications as are specified in the designation in order to meet the requirements of subsection (1).

Inquiries initiated by Commission

(4) The Commission may, on its own initiative, inquire into one or more programs to determine whether the programs are special programs for the purposes of subsection (1).

End of inquiry

(5) At the conclusion of an inquiry under subsection (4), the Commission may designate as a special program any of the programs under inquiry if, in its opinion, the programs meet the requirements of subsection (1).

Expiry of designation

(6) A designation under subsection (3) or (5) expires five years after the day it is issued or at such earlier time as may be specified by the Commission.

Renewal of designation

(7) If an application for renewal of a designation of a program as a special program is made to the Commission before its expiry under subsection (6), the Commission may,

   (a) renew the designation if, in its opinion, the program continues to meet the requirements of subsection (1); or

   (b) renew the designation on the condition that the program make such modifications as are specified in the designation in order to meet the requirements of subsection (1).

Effect of designation, etc.

(8) In a proceeding,

    (a) evidence that a program has been designated as a special program under this section is proof, in the absence of evidence to the contrary, that the program is a special program for the purposes of subsection (1); and

    (b) evidence that the Commission has considered and refused to designate a program as a special program under this section is proof, in the absence of evidence to the contrary, that the program is not a special program for the purposes of subsection (1).

Crown programs

(9) Subsections (2) to (8) do not apply to a program implemented by the Crown or an agency of the Crown.

Tribunal finding

(10) For the purposes of a proceeding before the Tribunal, the Tribunal may make a finding that a program meets the requirements of a special program under subsection (1), even though the program has not been designated as a special program by the Commission under this section, subject to clause (8)(b).

Age sixty-five or over

15. A right under Part I to non-discrimination because of age is not infringed where an age of sixty-five years or over is a requirement, qualification or consideration for preferential treatment.

Canadian Citizenship

16(1) A right under Part I to non-discrimination because of citizenship is not infringed where Canadian citizenship is a requirement, qualification or consideration imposed or authorized by law.

Idem

(2) A right under Part I to non-discrimination because of citizenship is not infringed where Canadian citizenship or lawful admission to Canada for permanent residence is a requirement, qualification or consideration adopted for the purpose of fostering and developing participation in cultural, educational, trade union or athletic activities by Canadian citizens or persons lawfully admitted to Canada for permanent residence.

Idem

(3) A right under Part I to non-discrimination because of citizenship is not infringed where Canadian citizenship or domicile in Canada with the intention to obtain Canadian citizenship is a requirement, qualification or consideration adopted by an organization or enterprise for the holder of chief or senior executive positions.

Disability

17(1) A right of a person under this Act is not infringed for the reason only that the person is incapable of performing or fulfilling the essential duties or requirements attending the exercise of the right because of disability.

Accommodation

(2) No tribunal or court shall find a person incapable unless it is satisfied that the needs of the person cannot be accommodated without undue hardship on the person responsible for accommodating those needs, considering the cost, outside sources of funding, if any, and health and safety requirements, if any.

Determining if undue hardship

(3) In determining for the purposes of subsection (2) whether there would be undue hardship, a tribunal or court shall consider any standards prescribed by the regulations.

Special interest organizations

18. The rights under Part I to equal treatment with respect to services and facilities, with or without accommodation, are not infringed where membership or participation in a religious, philanthropic, educational, fraternal or social institution or organization that is primarily engaged in serving the interests of persons identified by a prohibited ground of discrimination is restricted to persons who are similarly identified.

Solemnization of marriage by religious officials

18.1(1) The rights under Part I to equal treatment with respect to services and facilities are not infringed where a person registered under section 20 of the *Marriage Act* refuses to solemnize a marriage, to allow a sacred place to be used for solemnizing a marriage or for an event related to the solemnization of a marriage, or to otherwise assist in the solemnization of a marriage, if to solemnize the marriage, allow the sacred place to be used or otherwise assist would be contrary to,

    (a) the person's religious beliefs; or

    (b) the doctrines, rites, usages or customs of the religious body to which the person belongs.

Same

(2) Nothing in subsection (1) limits the application of section 18.

Definition

(3) In this section,

"sacred place" includes a place of worship and any ancillary or accessory facilities.

Separate school rights preserved

19(1) This Act shall not be construed to adversely affect any right or privilege respecting separate schools enjoyed by separate school boards or their supporters under the *Constitution Act, 1867* and the *Education Act*.

Duties of teachers

(2) This Act does not apply to affect the application of the *Education Act* with respect to the duties of teachers.

Restriction of facilities by sex

20(1) The right under section 1 to equal treatment with respect to services and facilities without discrimination because of sex is not infringed where the use of the services or facilities is restricted to persons of the same sex on the ground of public decency.

Minimum drinking age

(2) The right under section 1 to equal treatment with respect to services, goods and facilities without discrimination because of age is not infringed by the provisions of the *Liquor Licence Act* and the regulations under it relating to providing for and enforcing a minimum drinking age of nineteen years.

Recreational clubs

(3) The right under section 1 to equal treatment with respect to services and facilities is not infringed where a recreational club restricts or qualifies access to its services or facilities or gives preferences with respect to membership dues and other fees because of age, sex, marital status or family status.

Tobacco and young persons

(4) The right under section 1 to equal treatment with respect to goods without discrimination because of age is not infringed by the provisions of the *Smoke-Free Ontario Act* and the regulations under it relating to selling or supplying tobacco to persons who are, or who appear to be, under the age of 19 years or 25 years, as the case may be.

Residential accommodation
Shared accommodation

21(1) The right under section 2 to equal treatment with respect to the occupancy of residential accommodation without discrimination is not infringed by discrimination where the residential accommodation is in a dwelling in which the owner or his or her family reside if the occupant or occupants of the residential accommodation are required to share a bathroom or kitchen facility with the owner or family of the owner.

Restrictions on accommodation, sex

(2) The right under section 2 to equal treatment with respect to the occupancy of residential accommodation without discrimination because of sex is not infringed by discrimination on that ground where the occupancy of all the residential accommodation in the building, other than the accommodation, if any, of the owner or family of the owner, is restricted to persons who are of the same sex.

Prescribing business practices

(3) The right under section 2 to equal treatment with respect to the occupancy of residential accommodation without discrimination is not infringed if a landlord uses in the manner prescribed under this Act income information, credit checks, credit references, rental history, guarantees or other similar business practices which are prescribed in the regulations made under this Act in selecting prospective tenants.

. . .

PART V   GENERAL

Act binds Crown

47(1) This Act binds the Crown and every agency of the Crown.

Act has primacy over other Acts

(2) Where a provision in an Act or regulation purports to require or authorize conduct that is a contravention of Part I, this Act applies and prevails unless the Act or regulation specifically provides that it is to apply despite this Act.

Regulations

48(1) The Lieutenant Governor in Council may make regulations,

    (a) prescribing standards for assessing what is undue hardship for the purposes of section 11, 17 or 24;

    (a.1) prescribing the manner in which income information, credit checks, credit references, rental history, guarantees or other similar business practices may be used by a landlord in selecting prospective tenants without infringing section 2, and prescribing other similar business practices and the manner of their use, for the purposes of subsection 21 (3);

    (b) prescribing matters for the purposes of clause 43(3)(g);

    (c) respecting the Human Rights Legal Support Centre;

    (d) governing any matter that is necessary or advisable for the effective enforcement and administration of this Act.

Ontario Regulation 290/98

BUSINESS PRACTICES PERMISSIBLE TO LANDLORDS IN SELECTING PROSPECTIVE TENANTS FOR RESIDENTIAL ACCOMMODATION

1(1) A landlord may request credit references and rental history information, or either of them, from a prospective tenant and may request from a prospective tenant authorization to conduct credit checks on the prospective tenant.

(2) A landlord may consider credit references, rental history information and credit checks obtained pursuant to requests under subsection (1), alone or in any combination, in order to assess the prospective tenant and the landlord may select or refuse the prospective tenant accordingly.

(3) A landlord may request income information from a prospective tenant only if the landlord also requests information listed in subsection (1).

(4) A landlord may consider income information about a prospective tenant in order to assess the prospective tenant and the landlord may select or refuse the prospective tenant accordingly only if the landlord considers the income information together with all the other information that was obtained by the landlord pursuant to requests under subsection (1).

(5) If, after requesting the information listed in subsections (1) and (3), a landlord only obtains income information about a prospective tenant, the landlord may consider the income information alone in order to assess the prospective tenant and the landlord may select or refuse the prospective tenant accordingly.

2(1) A landlord may require a prospective tenant to obtain a guarantee for the rent.

(2) A landlord may require a prospective tenant to pay a security deposit in accordance with sections 117 and 118 of the *Tenant Protection Act, 1997*.

3. In selecting a prospective tenant, a landlord of a rental unit described in paragraph 1, 1.1, 2 or 3 of subsection 5(1) or subsection 6(1) of the *Tenant Protection Act, 1997* may request and use income information about a prospective tenant in order to determine a prospective tenant's eligibility for rent in an amount geared-to-income and, when requesting and using the income information for that purpose only, the landlord is not bound by subsections 1(3) and (4).

4. Nothing in this Regulation authorizes a landlord to refuse accommodation to any person because of race, ancestry, place of origin, colour, ethnic origin, citizenship, creed, sex, sexual orientation, age, marital status, family status, handicap or the receipt of public assistance.

Glossary

abatement   reduction in a rent because of deficiencies in a rental unit or building

above-guideline rent increase   a rent increase greater than the guideline

adjournment   postponement, usually of a hearing, and usually at the time that the hearing was to begin or after it has begun

administrator   a person who is appointed by the court to administer the property of a person who has died without naming an executor in a will

affidavit   a document in a board or court proceeding in which a person sets out facts, and signs before a public official while swearing that the facts are true

affirm   approve and leave in place

allegations   statements about facts that may or may not be true

appellant   the person who makes an appeal

arrears   payments that are past due

assignment of a tenancy   a tenant turning over the rights and obligations of a tenancy to a different tenant

bad faith   for improper purposes, in order to obtain an unfair advantage

bylaws   rules about public behaviour, usually enacted by a municipality

care home   building for people to receive care services such as health care or assistance with daily living

collateral   as part of

condominium   a type of ownership of individual units, generally in a multi-unit development or project

consideration   something of value given by both parties that induces each of them to enter into an agreement

co-operative   ownership of a building by several people together, where each person has the right to occupy one unit in the building, and exclude the other owners from that unit

co-owner   someone who owns property in common or jointly with one or more other persons

corporation   a legal entity distinct from its shareholders or members, with liability separate from its shareholders or members, vested with the capacity of continuous succession

debtor   a person who owes another person money

direction   a document telling someone to do something

disclosure   revealing information or giving copies of documents

discretion   independent decision-making power

Divisional Court   a branch of the Superior Court of Justice of Ontario in which judges hear appeals and applications for judicial review, including appeals of final orders from the Landlord and Tenant Board, Small Claims Court, and other administrative tribunals

eviction   removal of a tenant from a rented property, not by the tenant's choice

exclusive jurisdiction   being the only legal body that can rule on a particular matter

executor   a person who is appointed in a will to administer the property of the person who made the will after that person dies

forfeiture   losing a right because of failing to comply with one's obligations

good faith   honestly, for the stated purpose, not meaning to obtain an unfair advantage

grandfathered   a situation or action is said to be grandfathered when it is allowed to continue even though a new rule or set of rules would prohibit it, or would impose new conditions on the person doing it

guideline   a percentage fixed each year by which a landlord can increase the rent without the board's approval

hearing   a formal meeting at which a decision-maker hears evidence and argument in order to make a decision

jurisdiction   the limits on what the board can decide and how it must go about making its decisions

lawful rent   the rent that a landlord is permitted to charge a tenant

legal non-conforming right   the right of an owner to continue a pre-existing use of a property after a zoning bylaw comes into force that prohibits the use

licence   an agreement for the use of a property in which the owner does not give the user the full rights that a tenant would have

market rent   the rent that a landlord can expect to receive for a particular rental unit or type and size of rental units

negligent   failing to take proper care

non-profit housing co-operative   non-profit housing community where the residents are members of a co-op corporation, which typically owns the whole property, and are actively involved in the running of the community

notice of entry   notice that the landlord intends to enter the rental unit

Ontario Court of Appeal   Ontario's highest court, which considers appeals from decisions of the Superior Court of Justice and the Ontario Court of Justice, including the Divisional Court

overhold   a situation where the tenant remains in a rental unit after the tenancy has been terminated

prejudice   inability or reduced ability to deal with a situation because of an act or omission

process server   a person whose job is to deliver court documents and other important notices

public housing   rental housing provided by a government body, usually at reduced rent to people with low income

rent geared to income   a rent determined on the basis of the tenant's income, which in Ontario social housing is usually 30 percent of the tenant's income

res judicata   latin for "the thing has been decided"; once a claim is heard and decided by a court or tribunal, it cannot be heard again

rescheduling   postponement, usually of a hearing, before the hearing was scheduled to begin

rescind   cancel

respondent   the person who is on the other side of an appeal made by an appellant

right of first refusal (to rent)   a right to be allowed to rent before the renovated unit is offered to other prospective tenants

rules of natural justice   the legal principle that parties affected by a decision are entitled to be given a fair opportunity to present their case to an unbiased decision maker

security of tenure   the right of a residential tenant in Ontario to keep the tenancy unless the landlord has a specific reason to end the tenancy, as set out in the *Residential Tenancies Act*

seized   having begun to hear evidence in an application, the specific adjudicator must continue to hear the case until its resolution

serve   deliver a legal document to a person the document affects

services and facilities   things provided with a rental unit such as parking, appliances, common-area cleaning, lockers, laundry facilities, heating, and air conditioning

severance   a consent under the *Planning Act* to the division of land into two or more separate pieces of land

shareholder   someone who holds shares in a corporation

sheriff   officer who enforces orders of the courts or the board

smart meter   a meter that tracks how much electricity is being used and relays to the hydro provider the time of day in which that electricity is being used

social housing   housing provided by a city or provincial housing authority, or other agencies such as non-profit housing corporations, primarily to those with low incomes

Statutory Powers Procedure Act   the Ontario statute that sets out the basic procedural rules for all tribunals

sublet of a tenancy   a tenant turning over the rights and obligations of a tenancy to a different tenant for a limited period of time

summons   a document that the board will prepare or sign that requires a person to attend a hearing to give evidence

Superior Court of Justice   the highest trial court in Ontario in which individual judges decide important civil cases and serious crimes

tandem parking space   a parking space immediately in front of or behind another parking space

tenancy agreement   an agreement in which a property or part of a property is rented by a landlord to a tenant

utilities   heat, hydro, and water supplied to the rental unit

vital services   fuel oil, electricity, gas, hot water, cold water, and heat between Sept 1 and June 15

wilful   intentional or deliberate

writ of possession   an order of the court that directs the sheriff to evict a person and give possession of a property to a person named in the writ of possession

References

Assessment Act, RSO 1990, c. A.31.

Bankruptcy and Insolvency Act, RSC 1985, c. B-3.

Co-operative Corporations Act, RSO 1990, c. C.35.

Creditors' Relief Act, RSO 1990, c. C.45.

Criminal Code, RSC 1985, c. C-46.

Developmental Services Act, RSO 1990, c. D.11.

French Language Services Act, RSO 1990, c. F.32.

Homes for Special Care Act, RSO 1990, c. H.12.

Human Rights Code, RSO 1990, c. H.19.

Innkeepers Act, RSO 1990, c. I.7.

Landlord and Tenant Act, RSO 1990, c. L.7.

Mejia v. Cargini, [2007] OJ No. 437, 222 OAC 74, 2007 CarswellOnt 666 (Div. Ct.).

Personal Property Security Act, RSO 1990, c. P.10.

Peterson v. Charboneau (January 13, 1998), file no. 97-DV-12 (Ont. Div. Ct.)
    [unreported].

Planning Act, RSO 1990, c. P.13.

Price v. Turnbull's Grove Inc. (2007), 85 OR (3d) 641 (CA).

Provincial Offences Act, RSO 1990, c. P.33.

Re Metro Capital Management Group (*sub nom. Ball v. Metro*), 2002 CarswellOnt
    8691 (Div. Ct.).

Reference re: Act to Amend the Residential Tenancies Act (NS) (1996), 131 DLR (4th)
    609 (SCC).

Rent Control Act, 1992, SO 1992, c. 11.

Residential Premises Rent Review Act, 1975, SO 1975 (2nd sess.), c. 12.

Residential Rent Regulation Amendment Act, 1991, SO 1991, c. 4.

Residential Tenancies Act, 2006, SO 2006, c. 17.

Social Housing Reform Act, 2000, SO 2000, c. 27.

Statutory Powers Procedure Act, RSO 1990, c. S.22.

Tenant Protection Act, 1997, SO 1997, c. 24.

Index